PRINCIPLES OF FREE TRADE AGREEMENTS

FROM GATT 1947 THROUGH NAFTA RE-NEGOTIATED 2018

Ralph H. Folsom

Professor of Law
University of San Diego
A.B. Princeton University, J.D. Yale Law School
LLM London School of Economics

CONCISE HORNBOOK SERIES™

WEST
ACADEMIC
PUBLISHING

© 2019 LEG, Inc. d/b/a West Academic
    444 Cedar Street, Suite 700
    St. Paul, MN 55101
    1-877-888-1330

Printed in the United States of America

ISBN: 978-1-64020-130-9

Preface

Veteran users of my international trade books will note the expanded world-wide focus on free trade agreements in this Concise Hornbook. The reason for this volume is relatively simple. **Free trade agreements (FTAs) of many varieties have dominated global trade for over a decade.** This dominance is likely to continue for many years on every continent. Already, more than half of all international trade takes place under FTAs.

The origins of free trade agreements (FTAs) and customs unions (CUs) lie in Article 24 of the GATT 1947 agreement. Article 24 permits but attempts to regulate their creation, an effort that met failure early on in connection with the European Economic Community Treaty of 1957 (EEC) and various developing world agreements. A sleeping giant for decades, the significance of FTAs was re-awakened by the path-breaking Canada-U.S. FTA of 1989. In 1994, NAFTA triggered an onslaught of FTAs around the world, overwhelming the impact of the establishment of the World Trade Organization in 1995.

Perhaps surprisingly, the hostility of President Trump to multilateral trade agreements like TPP-12, the WTO, the EU and NAFTA 1994, has caused the number of FTAs to increase. America's traditional trade partners have rushed to secure free trade deals not involving the USA. TPP-11, the Japan-EU FTA, and the expanded Mexico-EU FTA provide excellent examples. Meanwhile, despite being characterized by President Trump as "the worst trade deal ever", the United States, Canada and Mexico completed re-negotiation of NAFTA in 2018. All this, and more, is covered in this book.

It has been a genuine pleasure to prepare *Principles of Free Trade Agreements, From GATT 1947 through NAFTA Re-Negotiated 2018.* I hope that students, lawyers, government officials and people in business will find it a useful and insightful presentation on a timely topic. In preparing this book, I have attempted to address the interests not only of Americans, but also persons located outside the USA who are concerned about the law and economics of free trade agreements.

Active links for the e-book and downloadable versions of this Concise Hornbook have been provided throughout. A consolidated, edited text of NAFTA Re-Negotiated 2018, the pending USMCA Agreement, is Appended.

Your comments and suggestions are most welcome.

Ralph H. Folsom
rfolsom@sandiego.edu

July, 2019

About the Author

Ralph H. Folsom has been a Professor at the University of San Diego School of Law since 1975. A graduate of Princeton University, Yale Law School and the London School of Economics (LLM), Professor Folsom teaches, writes and consults extensively in the field of international business law.

Folsom has been a Senior Fulbright resident scholar in Singapore and a Visiting Professor at the University of Hong Kong, University of Aix-Marseille, University of Brest, University of Paris, University of Toulouse, University of Puerto Rico, Monash University in Australia and Tecnológico de Monterrey in México.

Professor Folsom has authored a range of books with West Academic Publishing. These include a popular course book, now in its 13th edition, on *International Business Transactions* (co-author).

Professor Folsom has also written in the West Academic Concise Hornbook Series:

Principles of International Litigation and Arbitration,

Principles of International Trade Law,

Principles of International Business Transactions (co-author), and

Principles of European Union Law including BREXIT.

Acknowledgments

I wish to thank my brother, W. Davis Folsom, Emeritus Professor of Business Studies at University of South Carolina (Beaufort). Brother Davis extensively tutored me about the economics of free trade agreements and opened many doors to understanding. We initially collaborated with pleasure on *Understanding NAFTA and Its International Business Implications* (1996), an interdisciplinary publication written just after NAFTA 1994 came online, followed by a professional treatise titled *NAFTA Law and Business*.

Our latest joint effort is forthcoming: *NAFTA Re-Negotiated, USMCA 2018 and Its Business Implications* in a Nutshell.

I also wish to thank the numerous professors around the world who have supported my international business law writings for many years. For this volume, I am especially indebted to Professors David Gantz, Michael Gordon and Matthew Schaefer.

Lastly, I very much appreciate the support of West Academic Publishing. They authorized an allotment of pages that permitted reproduction of critical documents, including a consolidated version of the pending USMCA 2018 Agreement, the sequel to NAFTA 1994.

Linked Web Resources

NAFTA, CAFTA-DR, KORUS, USMCA and U.S. Free Trade Agreements:

www.ustr.gov/trade-agreements/free-trade-agreements

Free Trade Agreements in the Americas:

www.sice.oas.org/agreements_e.asp

Asia Pacific Trade and Investment Agreements:

www.unescap.org/content/aptiad

https://aric.adb.org/fta-country

Global Coverage of Free Trade Agreements:

www.bilaterals.org

www.wto.org/english/tratop_e/region_e/rta_participation_map_e.htm

https://en.wikipedia.org/wiki/List_of_free-trade_agreements

Summary of Contents

Table of Contents

PRINCIPLES OF FREE TRADE AGREEMENTS

FROM GATT 1947 THROUGH NAFTA RE-NEGOTIATED 2018

Chapter 1

THE ESSENTIALS OF INTERNATIONAL TRADE AND TRADE LAW

Analysis

NOTE: For more extensive international trade law and WTO coverage, see R. Folsom, *Principles of International Trade Law* (West Academic Publications). Selected provisions of the GATT 1947 and 1994, various WTO agreements, and the WTO Dispute Settlement Understanding (DSU) are appended in that Concise Hornbook.

---

§ 1.0   Trade Deficits, Patterns and Treaties

The United States is one of a few central players in the world of international trade. It has engaged in foreign trade from the moment of its independence over two centuries ago. Indeed, one of the reasons independence was sought was England's imposition of severe restrictions on trade between the colonies and foreign nations, intended to preserve the benefits of international trade for England.

Less than two centuries from achieving independence, the United States became a leading trade power in the world. For over a decade after World War II, the United States was in the envious and economically advantageous position of being the major center of production of finished goods for export. But with extraordinary economic growth in Japan and Europe, by the 1980s the United States no longer dominated world trade. It had to compete for sales abroad, and also in the domestic market within the United States. Traditional surpluses in the balance of trade with most nations in some cases began to be reversed. The United States has had to deal with increasingly large trade deficits with Japan, and more recently, the most challenging trade partner—China.

Trade Deficits

The trade surplus of earlier decades has become a trade deficit of disturbing proportions. The deficit status of U.S. international trade in the 1990s and into the new millennium caused trade to be a topic of common conversation. The U.S. trade deficit is often perceived as threatening jobs for American workers and the consequent diminishment of quality of life of the American people. This has generated annual Congressional proposals of an increasingly restrictive nature. U.S. exports have continued to grow, especially in the service and technology areas, but imports of goods have grown more rapidly. Even the periodic fall of the dollar, making U.S. exports cheaper, has not reversed the trade deficit, which has escalated under President Trump.

The importance of trade and its underlying economic relations should be apparent. But the huge capacity of the United States to consume foreign products is out of balance with its ability to find reciprocal consumption for its exports. That is due to many reasons, including problems of quality, real and perceived, problems of barriers to trade imposed by every nation, and problems of government leadership. Those who view the United States from abroad continually point to excessive consumption and inadequate savings, and to the budget deficit, as the principal reasons for the deteriorating U.S. trade position. Congress and the administration hear the complaints, but make few corrections. It is easier to blame other nations, a trait President Trump exemplifies. After all, the United States still generates a formidable share of world trade and will continue to do so for a while longer.

Even individual U.S. states have remarkable trade statistics. California alone generates billions of dollars of world trade, making its "gross state product" greater than the gross national products of all but a few nations of the world. In the last few years, however, the per capita standard of living of several other nations has reached and exceeded that in the United States.

Some developed nations are unusually dependent on international trade in goods and services. The Netherlands, for example, depends on exports for over 75% of their Gross Domestic Product (GDP). Roughly 50% of the GDPs of Sweden, Germany and Switzerland derive from exports. Canada, New Zealand, France and Britain come in at about 25%, China at 19%, with the United States at approximately 12%.

International trade law has a long and controversial history. Many nations, especially in their early stages of development, are fearful of trade across borders. International trade is a competitive force, one that typically shakes up domestic economic interests and results in trade specialization. It is a powerful engine of change, creating winners and losers in its comparative advantage path. It is now certain, for example, that China's admission to the WTO in 2001 contributed to a significant negative impact on U.S. manufacturing jobs and wages in the Midwest, but also shipment to China of 60% of all U.S. exports of soybeans. Simultaneously, WTO membership helped to lift hundreds of millions of Chinese out of poverty, but also caused the laying off of millions of Chinese state-owned enterprise employees.

Trade is a powerful competitive force increasing the selection of goods and services available in national economies and enhancing domestic market price competition. Wal-Mart's heavy importation of inexpensive Chinese goods, for example, notably reduced U.S. consumer costs, particularly for lower income and displaced Americans. That said, President Trump's America First election revealed deep resentment of the consequences of trade, especially the resulting massive U.S. trade deficit with China, and sizeable trade deficits with Japan, Mexico and Germany. The Trump Administration asserts that China's trade surplus is the product of unfair trade practices and production subsidies. Forgotten in the political dialogue are modest U.S. trade surpluses with Hong Kong, the United Kingdom, Canada, Brazil, Saudi Arabia and Singapore.

There is a need to "unpack" trade deficit data. For example, roughly 65% of the value of iPhones shipped from China originates in the U.S., yet their full value appears in U.S.-China trade data. Roughly 40% of the value all Mexican goods crossing into the United States is American in origin. Furthermore, U.S. trade deficit numbers tend to be portrayed in goods only (especially by the Trump Administration), omitting trade surpluses in services, and not considering foreign investment capital flows.

Many economists maintain that high overall trade deficit countries like the United States reflect substantial consumer and government spending along with low rates of savings. Low overall trade deficit or surplus countries like Germany and China reflect high savings rates and restrained spending patterns. In short, trade deficits and surpluses do not reflect a win/lose zero sum game. They are instead a reflection of internal, notably fiscal, strengths and weaknesses of various countries. Despite U.S.-initiated tariff wars (see Sections 1.17 and 1.18), U.S. trade deficits rose to record levels in the first two years of the Trump presidency. This outcome is clearly not what the President had in mind for one of his favorite measurements of international trade success.

World Trade Patterns

Trade traditionally has been measured by the exchange of tangible goods, both raw materials and finished products. This is sometimes referred to as "merchandise trade". The prominence of oil as a trading commodity, and the economic power exerted in the 1970s by the Organization of Petroleum Exporting Countries (OPEC), resulted in a considerable shift of wealth caused by remarkable changes in the price of a single commodity. The power of OPEC diminished in the 1980s and 1990s due to an oversupply of oil and conflict both within the oil industry and within OPEC. Since the millennium, OPEC power and oil prices first rose and then collapsed with the advent of "fracking" and horizontal drilling techniques that have generated substantial amounts of U.S. oil and gas production.

Energy remains the ultimately important global commodity. It played a critical role in the decision of the United States to commence the Gulf and Iraq Wars, and to become engaged in the war against ISIS in the Middle East. Extractable raw materials remain the principal source of wealth for many nations. Nations which produce many natural and agricultural resources, from tin to bananas, have attempted to create cartels resembling OPEC which will give them control of their economic destiny.

Services Trade

In recent years, attention on items of trade and therefore value has shifted from an exclusive focus on tangibles and technology, to an area of trade and economic relations far more difficult to define. That area is trade in services such as advertising, banking, insurance, accounting, consulting, entertainment, construction, tourism, education and the vast area of computer services. For the most part, trade in services is not subject to tariffs. Nontariff barriers (NTBs), often in the form of licenses or permits, predominate. Cross-border trade in legal services also makes a contribution, particularly by large multinational U.S. law firms. U.S. trade in these "invisibles" is measured in billions annually. Trade in tangibles is marred by an increasing deficit, but U.S. trade in services is marked by an increasing surplus.

Many other nations are eager to develop their own services, and to protect them from encroachment by the developed nations. The negotiations in the Uruguay Round that created the WTO on trade in services were an especially difficult part of the overall trade talks. The industrialized nations, led by the United States, for the most part successfully negotiated lowering trade barriers to services, over the objections of important developing nations such as India and Brazil. These nations fear dominance in ownership of services by the industrialized nations.

The final WTO agreement, the General Agreement on Trade in Services (the GATS), reflected many restrictions and reservations by developing nations determined to establish and maintain their own service sectors. The ability of the WTO to govern trade in services is critical to keeping service-oriented nations like the United States a supporter of this important multilateral trade regulating organization.

The Rise of Asia

Viewing the constantly changing world trade patterns as they have developed to this moment, the dominance of the United States which was prevalent decades ago has diminished substantially and is unlikely to reoccur. This trend is attributable to the prominence of Japan in manufacturing and designing products which meet current consumer demands, to the entry of China and re-entry of India in the world trade arena, to the cooperation of the European nations within the European Union, and to the movement through successive stages of development of many nations, especially the "Four Dragons" or "Four Tigers" of Asia—Hong Kong, South Korea, Singapore and Taiwan.

Increased "world market share" is the goal of every nation, and nations joust over international trade issues. Asian nations, like others, closely regulate foreign investment coming into the country, and create trade incentives to stimulate greater exports to other countries.

The spectacular success of Japan and China as exporters combined with a creativity to block imports has led to a sequence of protests and trade sanctions by the United States and the European Union, most notably by President Trump. See Sections 1.17 and 1.18. However accurately Japan or China may be accused of being unfair traders and of using a host of regulatory nontariff trade barriers (NTBs) to keep foreign goods and investment out, the United States often fails to consider that trade imbalances may be as much caused by domestic failures as by foreign intransigence.

Nontariff Trade Barriers

Japan and China are not alone in using nontariff regulatory barriers, such as environmental rules and product and health safety laws. NTBs have arisen to protect domestic industry as the earlier protection by high tariffs has diminished via GATT, WTO and free trade negotiations. Every nation has developed its own methods of keeping imports at bay.

The United States, for example, has employed agricultural quotas and environmental/conservation regulations in this manner. The French provoked a stream of protest by requiring that documentation for imported goods be written in French. France established a "consultative commission for international trade" charged to watch for "abnormal" and excessive imports and unfair export practices of other countries. Meaning, of course, an agency for domestic business to complain to when affected by imports, regardless of their own efficiency in production. In the United States, similar complaints are filed with the Office of the U.S. Trade Representative.

Other nations have responded in various ways to the impact of imports. Restricted by their agreements to specific tariff levels as members of the WTO, they have carried nontariff barriers to a new height of originality. These barriers may assume the form of health or safety standards, packing or labeling requirements, environmental regulations, and many other rules which may in theory seem justified, but in practice are structured or interpreted so as to eliminate or reduce imports and benefit domestic industries.

Lawyers retained to deal with these nontariff barriers, as well as subsidies, dumping or rules of origin, have become the major beneficiaries of these complex trade laws. They alone know how to work through the maze of details in lengthy definitions included in trade laws, treaties and multilateral agreements. For example, foreign targets of a U.S. dumping charge must expend enormous resources responding to such charges, thus making these actions themselves another costly form of nontariff barrier.

Not all nations participated in the GATT 1947 or are members of its replacement, the WTO. By the 1970s, nontariff trade barriers (NTBs) began to be addressed by the GATT, including agreements designed to lessen NTBs, including complex customs valuation procedures, import licensing systems, and product health, safety and environmental standards. But the GATT NTB agreements were optional, and most of the developing world membership opted out. By the 1990s international trade was at a crossroad.

Trade Incentives

Goods which are sold in one nation are not necessarily either goods produced domestically by locally owned manufacturers, or goods produced abroad by foreign owned manufacturers. They may be goods produced *domestically* by *foreign* owned manufacturers. Or they may be goods produced *abroad* by domestic manufacturers.

Investing abroad is an alternative to exporting goods abroad. Foreign investment shares some benefits of trade. The foreign manufacturer receives the profit, but the host nation of the foreign investment obtains jobs and technology. Raw materials or parts may be sent by the foreign manufacturer, to create what is little more than an assembly plant in the host nation, or raw materials and parts may be purchased in the host nation, adding to the benefits of permitting investment owned by foreign entities. See R. Folsom, *Foreign Investment Law including Investor-State Arbitrations* in a Nutshell.

While trying to hold imports to reasonable levels, every nation wants to be a major exporter. It is, after all, exports that provide the means to pay for imports. The urge to export leads to another scheme of laws. They are usually laws of encouragement in contrast to laws of discouragement which typify the import rules. They may be fashioned in the way of granting tax benefits, offering export financing or insurance, overlooking trade restraint elements of permitted export cartels, or tying permitted imports to the level of exports.

The United States, for example, in enacting the 1982 Export Trading Company Act (ETC), followed the practice of nations such as Japan in assisting exporters. The ETC Act was designed to permit small and medium U.S. firms to gain information about foreign trade opportunities and techniques, and to have easier access to financing for export activity. Strident debate over renewing U.S. Export-Import

(EXIM) Bank funding continues. Many EXIM export financings have benefited U.S. multinationals such as Boeing and GE.

The Legal Framework of Trade

Every nation engaged in international economic relations develops a legal framework defining its role. That framework will consist of domestic trade laws, including its acceptance of international laws regulating cross-border transactions, and participation in international organizations that establish trade rules. The United States has developed by legislative and executive action an extensive set of domestic rules governing international trade, many reflecting WTO rules. It has also been a major creator and participant in many organizations which influence or govern trade.

The World Trade Organization, successor to the GATT 1947, is by far the most important such organization. Its "package deal" of about 20 agreements are almost entirely mandatory for its 165 or so member countries and customs areas. Members must incorporate WTO rules into their legal system and obey WTO rules at the risk of authorized retaliation if they do not. Roughly 98% of all world trade is covered by the WTO agreements. The United Nations has played a disappointingly minor role in trade, although UNCITRAL, the United Nations Commission on International Trade Law, has become an important forum for the harmonization of rules affecting trade, such as the Convention on International Sale of Goods (CISG).

Regional economic relations have also increased trade among groups of nations. The European Union and NAFTA 1994 are the two most important areas which have reduced barriers to internal trade, although sometimes at the expense of increasing barriers to external trade. Free trade and customs union agreements have been proliferating. See Chapter 5. But however important may be participation in bilateral or multilateral trade agreements or organizations, the will of a single participant to abide by freer trade rules will be expressed in its domestic trade laws and policies. It is under such national laws that multinational enterprises operate.

International trade law has a long and controversial history. Many nations, especially in their early stages of development, are fearful of trade across borders. International trade is a competitive force, one that typically shakes up domestic economic interests. It is a powerful engine of change, creating winners and losers in its path. The law of international trade, for better or worse, shapes the scope and direction of this force.

The United States in its early years sheltered "infant" agricultural and industrial sectors behind protective tariffs and regulatory restraints. When the Great Depression of the 1930s arrived, the United States enacted highly protective tariffs under the Smoot-Hawley Tariff Act of 1930. These tariffs were intended to wall off the U.S. economy from foreign competition, in theory "saving American jobs for American citizens". Other nations around the world retreated from international trade through similarly protective laws. Fear of foreign trade (and foreigners) reached a zenith that most economists agree deepened and prolonged the Great Depression. World War II rescued the United States from the Depression, but did nothing to remove the Smoot-Hawley tariffs and encourage other nations to do likewise.

Here is a provocative excerpt from a 1930 letter signed by over 1000 economists opposing Smoot-Hawley:

> "We are convinced that increased protective duties would be a mistake. They would operate, in general, to increase the prices which domestic consumers would have to pay. By raising prices, they would encourage concerns with higher costs to undertake production, thus compelling the consumer to subsidize waste and inefficiency in industry. At the same time, they would force him to pay higher rates of profit to established firms which enjoyed lower production costs. A higher level of protection, such as is contemplated by both the House and Senate bills, would therefore raise the cost of living and injure the great majority of our citizens.
>
> Few people could hope to gain from such a change. Miners, construction, transportation and public utility workers, professional people and those employed in banks, hotels, newspaper offices, in the wholesale and retail trades, and scores of other occupations would clearly lose, since they produce no products which could be protected by tariff barriers.
>
> The vast majority of farmers, also, would lose. Their cotton, corn, lard, and wheat are export crops and are sold in the world market. They have no important competition in the home market. They cannot benefit, therefore, from any tariff which is imposed upon the basic commodities which they produce. They would lose through the increased duties on manufactured goods, however, and in a double fashion. First, as consumers they would have to pay still higher prices for the products, made of textiles, chemicals, iron, and steel, which they buy. Second, as producers, their ability to sell their products would be further restricted by the barriers placed in the way of foreigners who wished to sell manufactured goods to us.
>
> Our export trade, in general, would suffer. . . . There are already many evidences that such action would inevitably provoke other countries to pay us back in kind by levying retaliatory duties against our goods. There are few more ironical spectacles than that of the American Government as it seeks, on the one hand, to

promote exports through the activity of the Bureau of Foreign and Domestic Commerce, while, on the other hand, by increasing tariffs it makes exportation ever more difficult. President Hoover has well said, in his message to Congress on April 16, 1929, "It is obviously unwise protection which sacrifices a greater amount of employment in exports to gain a less amount of employment from imports."

Almost ninety years later, a letter from more than 1,100 economists revived this message in the face of President Trump's protectionist measures, outlined in Sections 1.16, 1.17 and 1.18.

Despite its economic power and leadership in the development of modern trade law, the United States retains some of its early fear and concerns about international commerce, notably under the Trump Administration. This is particularly apparent when U.S. free trade agreements are debated and undertaken, but also when the U.S. invokes import trade remedies and controls exports of goods and technology. Little wonder then that developing nations, many not much more than 50 years old and created out of colonial empires, hesitate to embrace the panoply of modern international trade law.

The need to balance the protection of local industries from harm by foreign competitors and the encouragement of trade across national borders is a recurrent theme in the law of international economic relations. There has been a shift in recent years toward freer international trade because of diminished restrictions on imported goods. However, trade problems associated with the movement of goods across national borders still arise because of restrictive trade devices which impede or distort trade. In most countries, "trade adjustment assistance" to adversely damaged workers has been inadequate.

Common protective devices include tariff barriers (*e.g.*, normal import and export duties, and special antidumping and subsidy countervailing duties), as well as nontariff trade barriers (NTBs) such as quotas, import and export licensing procedures, safety, environmental, health and other regulatory standards, complex customs procedures, and government procurement policies. For example, France once required that all video recorders entering France had to do so through a small customs post at Poitiers and carry documentation written in French. Product distribution practices have been an effective NTB in Japan. The United States has a host of NTB restraints, and the Trump Administration has suggested invocation of protective trade remedies and rules for six "core industries"—steel, aluminum, vehicles, aircraft, shipbuilding and semiconductors.

Commencing in 1932 under President Roosevelt, the United States began to unwind its Smoot-Hawley tariffs, particularly via reciprocal trade agreements, the first of which was with Canada. World War II ultimately rescued the United States from the Depression, but did little to significantly remove high tariffs in Europe, Asia, America and elsewhere. International trade law was at a crossroads.

Trade Treaties

Early efforts by countries to limit disruptive trade practices were traditionally found in bilateral treaties of Friendship, Commerce and Navigation (FCN), some of which remain in force, such as that between the United States and Japan. Such treaties opened the territory of each signatory to greater imports, at times controversially under "unequal treaty" terms favoring European nations and the United States in Asia, for example. Bilateral FCN treaty clauses were usually linked to other preferential trade agreements. Such linkage was most often accomplished through a reciprocal "most favored nation" (MFN) clause. In a MFN clause, both parties agree that more favorable trade arrangements are immediately *also* available to the other FCN signatory.

FCN treaties also focused on promoting foreign investment across borders, shipping and basic trade and investment principles of "national treatment"; the right to be taxed, regulated and generally treated in the same legal manner as domestic businesses.

At this point, the United States has moved beyond many of its FCN treaties to bilateral Trade and Investment Framework Agreements (TIFAs, below), Free Trade Agreements (FTAs, Chapters 4, 5 and 6)) and Bilateral Investment Treaties (BITs, Chapter 7). All three can be found at www.ustr.gov. FCN trade and investment law principles, notably MFN and national treatment, carry over into these agreements. TIFAs are centered on dialogue about trade and investment issues. They often precede the more advanced legal regimes of FTAs and BITs.

The United States has numerous TIFAs with individual countries and regional economic groups. The U.S. has TIFAs with Angola, Ghana, Liberia, Mauritius, Mozambique, Nigeria, Rwanda, South Africa and the Common Market for Eastern and Southern Africa (COMESA), the East African Community, the West African Economic and monetary Union (WAEMU) and the South African Customs Union (titled as a Trade, Investment and Development Agreement). The U.S. also has TIFAs with Algeria, Bahrain, the Caribbean Common Market (CARICOM), Egypt, the Gulf Cooperation Council, Georgia, Iceland, Iraq, Kuwait, Lebanon, Libya,

Oman, Qatar, Saudi Arabia, Switzerland, Tunisia, Turkey, Ukraine, the United Arab Emirates, Uruguay and Yemen. Additional TIFAs have been concluded with Afghanistan, collectively with five Central Asian nations, the Maldives, Nepal, Pakistan, Sri Lanka, the ASEAN group (Association of South East Asian Nations), Brunei, Cambodia, Indonesia, Malaysia, New Zealand, the Philippines, Thailand and Vietnam.

GATT 1947 and the World Trade Organization (1995)

The most dramatic and far reaching trade agreements in modern times originate from the General Agreement on Tariffs and Trade (GATT, 1947) and its successor, the World Trade Organization (WTO). Commencing in 1995, the WTO package of international trade agreements establishes a legal baseline for some 165 member states. A list of the WTO agreements, including GATT 1994, is reproduced below.

Normal Tariffs

The materials that follow move first to a review of the GATT 1947. The GATT was an international forum among Contracting States which regularly held multilateral trade negotiations (MTN) seeking ways of advancing international trade in goods (and only goods), most notably by diminishing Depression-era tariffs. These periodic negotiations cumulatively reduced tariff barriers by an average of up to eighty percent below those existing in the Great Depression. After the most recent multilateral negotiations completed in 1994, average tariff rates of developed countries on dutiable manufactured imports were cut from 6.3 percent to 3.9 percent. These are the tariffs each country is "bound to" after each negotiating round. They are often referred to as "normal" or MFN tariffs, appearing in the U.S. Harmonized Tariff Schedule (HTS) under Column One.

Additional AD and CVD Tariffs

The GATT/WTO system allows certain exceptions to MFN tariff levels. The two most important are "antidumping duties" (ADs) and "countervailing duties" (CVDs). Such duties are intended to "remedy" what the GATT/WTO has agreed are unfair international trade practices. Think of them as special tariffs which, in authorized circumstances, are additional to MFN tariffs.

Antidumping duties are a permissible trade response where an enterprise prices its goods for sale in the country of importation at a level that is less than that charged for comparable sales in the home country (i.e., at "less than fair value" (LTFV)). Hence AD generally counteract private sector discriminatory pricing. Countervailing duties are a permissible response to certain "subsidies" given in another country that favor its exports in the international marketplace. Hence CVD counteract governmental subsidies. AD and CVD cannot simultaneously be applied. *See* U.S.-AD and CVD Duties (China), WT/DS 379/AB/R (2011).

The WTO system recognizes and permits both antidumping duties and countervailing duties, providing of course the respective requirements are satisfied. Each "trade remedy" also is governed by a separate Agreement ("Code") that provides more detail on the circumstances under which member states may impose these exceptional duties. Because the AD and CVD Codes are mandatory in the WTO system, they provide the foundation for a reasonably uniform body of legal rules for trade remedies among WTO members.

Under the WTO Antidumping Agreement (AD Code) and the WTO Subsidies and Countervailing Measures Agreement (CVD Code), a country may impose a special duty on products of another WTO member state only if two requirements are met. First, the country must find sufficient evidence of an unfair trade practice, either dumping (sales at less than fair value) or prohibited or actionable subsidies. Second, the practice must cause a sufficiently significant injury to a domestic industry. In the case of dumping or subsidies, this requires proof that the practice has caused or threatens to cause "material injury" to a domestic industry, or that it has "materially retarded" the establishment of such an industry. Thus, the substantive grounds for the determination of the existence of "dumping" and of a "countervailable (actionable) subsidy" are different, but the domestic injury standard is essentially the same.

Neither of these trade remedies in favor of domestic producers is based on any notion of reciprocity. That is, neither arises because another country has restricted the importation of U.S. goods into its markets. Antidumping and countervailing duties instead address unfair selling prices of dutiable imported goods.

Trade Safeguards

Safeguard and market disruption proceedings are anticipated by Article XIX of the General Agreement on Tariffs and Trade (GATT). A WTO "Safeguards Agreement" emerged from the Uruguay Round of negotiations. In contrast to the statutory remedies against dumping and countervailable subsidies, safeguard proceedings are not targeted at unfair international trade practices. Rather, the goods are assumed to be fairly traded but imports are in such an unexpected volume that protection is appropriate to *temporarily* allow the domestic industry to adjust to the new competitive environment.

In the United States, businesses may seek protection from import competition by initiating what are known as "escape clause" (safeguard) proceedings under the Trade Act of 1974. Escape clause proceedings can involve imports from anywhere in the world, and are authorized by Section 201 of the Trade Act (19 U.S.C. 2251). Escape clause proceedings are also typically found in the free trade agreements of the United States.

In addition, "market disruption proceedings" can also provide temporary relief from import competition. Market disruption proceedings concern imports from communist nations and are authorized by Section 406 of the 1974 Trade Act (19 U.S.C. 2436). They are similar but not identical to escape clause proceedings. Either may result in the imposition of U.S. import restraints, or presidential negotiation of export restraints from the source country.

Import injury relief available under the Trade Act of 1974 is basically of two kinds: (1) Presidential relief designed to temporarily protect domestic producers of like or directly competitive products; and (2) governmental assistance to workers and firms economically displaced by import competition. This assistance is intended to enhance job opportunities and competitiveness. Protective relief tends to be awarded when the President believes that U.S. industry needs time to adjust. Governmental assistance is seen as a means to accommodate the injury caused by import competition. In either case, adjustment to import competition is the longer term goal, hopefully resulting in more competitive U.S. industries and markets.

The GATT allows, temporarily, "safeguard" or "escape clause" trade remedies for up to a maximum of four years. Such remedies may include additional tariffs, as President Trump elected to impose on imported solar panels and clothes washers in 2018. See Section 1.17. Safeguard tariffs apply to all the world, not just named exporting countries. Since safeguards do not target unfair practices, compensation (often reduced tariffs on the entry of goods into the safeguarding country) must be paid to exporting countries hit by safeguard remedies.

National Security Remedies

Chapter XXI of the GATT preserves the right of states to act in ways each member considers necessary for the protection of its "essential security interests" relating to fissionable materials, traffic in arms, or taken in time of war or an international relations emergency. President Trump in 2018 unilaterally placed highly controversial "national security" tariffs on U.S. steel and aluminum imports, triggering retaliatory "re-balancing tariffs" around the globe. See Section 1.17. The Trump administration asserts that these tariffs are not justiciable under Chapter XXI of GATT, treating that provision as an unchallengeable blank check. Most other WTO members disagree and have filed complaints with the WTO seeking review of Trump's national security tariffs. In April of 2019, a WTO panel ruled that "national security" issues are justiciable, affirming Russia's right to restrict the flow of Ukrainian goods in transit to Kazakhstan. The panel found there was an emergency in international relations that justified Russia's trade restraints.

For a much more detailed review of WTO and U.S. trade remedies, see Folsom, *Principles of International Trade Law*, Chapters 4, 5, and 6.

§ 1.1   The General Agreement on Tariffs and Trade (GATT 1947)

Core Principles

United States, British and other participants in the 1994 Bretton Woods, New Hampshire meetings recognized a post-War need to reduce trade obstacles in order to foster freer trade. They envisioned the creation of an International Trade Organization (ITO) to achieve the desired result. Fifty-three countries met in Havana in 1948 to complete drafting the Charter of an ITO that would be the international organizational umbrella underneath which negotiations could occur periodically to deal with tariff reductions and other trade law matters. A framework for such negotiations had already been staked out in Geneva in 1947, in what was expected to be only a transitional document, the General Agreement on Tariffs and Trade (GATT 1947) in goods.

Twenty-three nations participated in that first GATT session, India, Chile, Cuba and Brazil representing the developing world. China participated; Japan and West Germany did not. Stringent trading rules for goods (and only goods) were adopted only where there were no special interests of major participants to alter them. The developing nations objected to many of the strict rules, arguing for special treatment justified on development needs, but they achieved few successes in drafting GATT 1947. Some commenters believe GATT 1947 was in essence a deal struck between the United States and Europe, especially Britain.

The ITO Charter was never ratified. The United States Congress in the late 1940s was unwilling to join more new international organizations. Thus U.S. ratification of the ITO Charter could not be secured. Nonetheless, moving by way of the President Truman's power to issue executive orders, the United States did join twenty-one other countries, as Contracting Parties, in signing a Protocol of

Provisional Application of the General Agreement on Tariffs and Trade (61 Stat. Pts. 5, 6) (popularly called the "GATT 1947 Agreement").

One notable feature of this protocol was the exemption of existing trade restraints of the Contracting States. Because of the failure to create the ITO, the GATT 1947 Agreement evolved from its "provisional" status into the premier international trade body, GATT the organization based in Geneva. It was through this organization that tariffs were steadily reduced over decades by means of increased membership and GATT negotiating Rounds. Today, the GATT 1947 Agreement has been replaced by the substantially similar GATT 1994 Agreement, part of the World Trade Organization "package" of trade agreements that took effect in 1995. *See* Section 1.3. The United States, having denied the creation of the ITO in the late 1940s, had to wait more that forty years for a second bite at the apple. When that opportunity finally came, the U.S. was among the strongest proponents of the WTO.

Trade in Goods: MFN Treatment

One of the central features of GATT 1947 and 1994 is Article I, which makes a general commitment to the long standing practice of "most favored nation treatment" (MFN) by requiring each Contracting Party to accord unconditional MFN status to goods from all other Contracting Parties. Thus, any privilege or tariff granted by a Contracting Party to products imported from any other country (not necessarily a WTO member) must also be "immediately and unconditionally" granted to any "like product" imported from any Contracting Parties. Article 1 of the GATT (1947) and (1994) spells out the golden rules of MFN trading:

> "With respect to customs duties and charges of any kind imposed on or in connection with importation or exportation or imposed on the international transfer of payments for imports or exports, and with respect to the method of levying such duties and charges, and with respect to all rules and formalities in connection with importation and exportation, and with respect to all matters referred to in paragraphs 2 and 4 of Article III, <u>any advantage, favor, privilege or immunity granted by any contracting party to any product originating in or destined for any other country shall be accorded immediately and unconditionally to the like product originating in or destined for the territories of all other contracting parties</u>." (emphasis added).

MFN principles essentially ban de jure and de facto tariff and trade discrimination. For leading WTO Appellate Body decisions on the application of MFN rules, see EC-Bananas, WT/DS27/AB/R (1997), Canada-Autos, WT/DS139/AB/R (2000).

There are two major exceptions to the MFN obligation of Article I: Free trade areas and customs unions and differential and more favorable treatment of goods from developing countries (the 1979 Enabling Clause. See Chapter 2. General exceptions contained in GATT Articles XX and XXI, including national security, may also apply.

Trade in Goods: National Treatment

GATT Article III incorporates the practice of according "national treatment" to imported goods by providing, with enumerated exceptions, that they shall receive the same tax and regulatory treatment as domestic goods. In this context, national treatment requires that "like products" of the exporting GATT Contracting State be treated no less favorably than domestic products of the importing State under its laws and regulations concerning sale, internal resale, purchase, transportation and use. Physical properties, consumer perspectives and tariff classifications all contribute to evaluating the "likeness" of products. See EC-Asbestos, WT/DS 135/AB/R (2001).

In addition to film distribution quotas (Article IV), two major exceptions apply to Article III: Government procurement policies (see Section 1.10), and authorized subsidization of domestic industries.

The core text of Article III provides:

> "The contracting parties recognize that internal taxes and other internal charges, and laws, regulations and requirements affecting the internal sale, offering for sale, purchase, transportation, distribution or use of products, and internal quantitative regulations requiring the mixture, processing or use of products in specified amounts or proportions, should not be applied to imported or domestic products so as to afford protection to domestic production.
>
> The products of the territory of any contracting party imported into the territory of any other contracting party shall not be subject, directly or indirectly, to internal taxes or other internal charges of any kind in excess of those applied, directly or indirectly, to like domestic products. Moreover, no contracting party shall otherwise apply internal taxes or other internal charges to imported or domestic products in a manner contrary to the principles set forth in paragraph 1. * * *
>
> The products of the territory of any contracting party imported into the territory of any other contracting party shall be accorded treatment no less favorable than that accorded to like products of national origin in respect of all laws, regulations and requirements affecting their internal sale, offering for sale, purchase, transportation, distribution or use. The provisions of

this paragraph shall not prevent the application of differential internal transportation charges which are based exclusively on the economic operation of the means of transport and not on the nationality of the product."

Where GATT permits nondiscriminatory "duties, taxes and other charges," the powers of a Contracting Party are limited even as to these devices. First, GATT Article X requires that notice be given of any new or changed national regulations which affect international trade, by requiring the prompt publication of those "laws, regulations, judicial decisions and administrative rulings of general application." Second, the Contracting Parties commit themselves "from time to time" to a continuing series of multilateral tariff negotiations (MTN) to seek further reductions in tariff levels and other barriers to international trade. Such negotiations are to be "on a reciprocal and mutually advantageous basis." GATT negotiated tariff rates (called "concessions" or "bindings"), which are listed in the "Tariff Schedules", are deposited with GATT by each participating country. These concessions must be granted to imports from any Contracting Party, both because of the GATT requires MFN treatment, and also because Article II specifically requires use of the negotiated rates.

The 1947 GATT Agreement and its subsequent multinational negotiating rounds were quite successful in reducing tariff duty levels on trade in goods. *See* Section 1.2 below. This was its original purpose, and the mechanism was well-adapted to accomplishing that goal. However, its effectiveness was also limited to trade in goods, and primarily to reduction of tariffs in such trade. It was not designed to affect trade in services, trade-related intellectual property rights or trade-related investment measures. As tariff duty rates declined, the trade-distorting effects of these other issues became more important. They, along with NTBs, are all addressed in the 1995 package of WTO agreements.

Trade in Goods: General Exceptions

Even within "trade in goods," the 1947 GATT had limitations. It included a Protocol of Provisional Application which allowed numerous grandfathered exceptions to Members' obligations under the GATT Agreement. The Protocol exempted from GATT disciplines the national laws of Member States which were already enacted and in force at the time of adoption of the Protocol. This "grandfather clause" no longer applies under GATT 1994.

Framers of GATT 1947 were well aware that a commitment to freer trade could cause serious, adverse economic consequences from time to time within part or all of a country's domestic economy, particularly its labor sector. The GATT 1947 and 1994 contains at least seven safety valves (in nine clauses of the Agreement) to permit a country, in appropriate circumstances, to respond to domestic pressures while remaining a participant in GATT. Two safety valves deal with unfair trade practices: Antidumping tariff duties (AD) and countervailing duties (CVD) applied against select government subsidies. AD and CVD apply to specific countries in addition to normal WTO-negotiated tariffs. Another important safety valve concerns "safeguard procedures", a temporary time out from import surges, invoked in 2018 by President Trump to impose additional tariffs against solar panel and clothes washers from anywhere in the world. See Section 1.17.

General omnibus exceptions to the GATT are established in Chapter XX, notably for measures "necessary" to protect public morals, and human, animal and plant life or health. See U.S.-Shrimp, WT/DS 58/AB/R (1998) (protection of endangered sea turtles). Evaluating whether measures are "necessary" requires consideration of reasonably available alternative approaches to achieve public policy goals. See Brazil-Tyres, WT/DS332/AB/R (2007) (ban on imports of retreaded tires upheld) and EC-Asbestos, WT/DS/AB/R (2001) (ban on asbestos imports upheld). Another general exception concerns measures "relating to" the conservation of exhaustible natural resources. See China-Raw Materials, WT/DS 394, 395, 398 (Panel, 2011) (export quota on bauxite and export duty on fluorspar did not relate to conservation). Other general exceptions concern trade in gold and silver, prison labor, protection of national treasures, commodity agreements, government stabilization plans and products in general or local short supply.

All of these general exceptions are subject to the qualifying language of the Article XX "chapeau": They may not be applied in an arbitrary or unjustifiably discriminatory manner, or constitute a disguised restriction on international trade. See U.S.-Shrimp, 21.5, WT/DS58/AB/RW (2001) (unjustifiable and arbitrary discrimination found in U.S. shrimp import restraints intended to conserve endangered sea turtles). For additional examples of the application of these exceptions and its chapeau, see Section 1.7.

WTO members, in accordance with GATT Articles XII, XV and XVIII, may generally undertake trade and monetary exchange restraints necessary to deal with their balance of payments needs.

Chapter XXI of the GATT preserves the right of states to act in ways each member considers necessary for the protection of its "essential security interests" relating to fissionable materials, traffic in arms, or taken in time of war or an international relations emergency. President Trump in 2018 placed "national security" tariffs on U.S. steel and aluminum imports, triggering retaliatory "re-balancing tariffs" around the globe and a WTO dispute complaints. See Sections 1.1 and 1.17.

§ 1.2 The GATT 1947 Multinational Trade Negotiations (Rounds)

Under the auspices of GATT 1947 Article XXVIII, the Contracting Parties committed themselves to hold periodic multinational trade negotiations (MTN or "Rounds"). They completed eight such Rounds with the GATT membership steadily increasing:

Geneva (1947) with 21 countries

Annecy (1948) with 27 countries

Torquay (1950) with 33 countries

"Dillon Round" Geneva (1960–62) with 36 countries

"Kennedy Round" Geneva (1964–67) with 74 countries

"Tokyo Round" Geneva (1973–79) with 85 countries

"Uruguay Round" Geneva (1986–94) with 128 countries

The WTO Doha Round (2001–15) with 164 countries is dead

The largest exporters by volume of particular goods generally take the lead on tariff reduction negotiations. While the first five Rounds concentrated on item by item tariff reductions, the "Kennedy Round" (1964–1967) was noted for its achievement of across-the-board tariff reductions. In 1961, GATT began to consider how to approach the increasing trade disparity with the developing world. In 1964, GATT adopted Part IV, which introduced a principle of "diminished expectations of reciprocity". Reciprocity remained a goal, but developed nations would not expect concessions from developing nations which were inconsistent with developmental needs. For the developing nations, non-reciprocity meant freedom to protect domestic markets from import competition. Import substitution was a major focus of developmental theory in the 1960s, and developing nations saw keeping their markets closed as a way to save these domestic industries.

Part IV of GATT 1947 resulted in a substantial growth in developing nation Contracting Parties. Although they also sought preferential treatment of their exports, that was a demand which would remain unsatisfied for another decade and longer when GATT approved "generalized tariff preference" (GSP) schemes for developing members.

Nearly a dozen major agreements on nontariff barrier issues were produced in the Tokyo Round. Not all nations participated in the GATT 1947 or are members of its replacement, the WTO. The "Tokyo Round" (1973–1979) engendered agreements about several areas of nontariff barrier (NTB) trade restraints, including agreements designed to lessen NTBs such as complex customs valuation procedures, import licensing systems, and product health, safety and environmental standards. But the Tokyo NTB agreements were optional, and most of the developing world membership opted out. By the 1990s international trade was once again at a crossroad.

In 1986, the "Uruguay Round" of multilateral trade negotiations began at a Special Session of the GATT Contracting States. This Uruguay Round included separate negotiations on trade in goods and on trade in services, with separate groups of negotiators dealing with each topic. Subtopics for negotiation by subgroups included nontariff barriers, agriculture, subsidies and countervailing duties, intellectual property rights and counterfeit goods, safeguards, tropical products, textiles, investment policies, and dispute resolution. The negotiating sessions were extraordinarily complex, but were able to achieve a successful conclusion at the end of 1993, giving birth to the World Trade Organization (WTO) in 1995.

WTO Negotiating Rounds

In 1999 an attempt at launching a "Seattle Round" led by President Clinton failed with violence in the streets. Two years later, the "Doha Round" was successfully launched in Qatar covering all existing WTO fields as well as E-commerce, trade and the environment, debt and finance, and special and differential treatment and assistance for developing countries. Developed WTO countries pushed foreign investment, competition policy, transparency in procurement, and trade facilitation topics. At Cancun in 2003, the WTO developing nations rejected these topics, focusing on agricultural trade barriers to their exports.

Scheduled for completion in 2005, the Doha Round of WTO negotiations collapsed in July 2008 after marathon sessions. India and China, in particular, insisted upon Special Safeguard Mechanisms against surges in agricultural imports, provisions the U.S. and EU did not accept. The members were in agreement on nearly all other areas of the Doha Round negotiations. WTO trade initiatives since Doha have been limited to *optional* trade facilitation, information technology and agricultural export subsidy agreements.

The Doha Round formally died in 2015. This caused many nations to accelerate their participation in bilateral and regional free trade agreements.

§ 1.3   The World Trade Organization (WTO 1995)

Directory of Agreements

Creating the rules-based World Trade Organization, despite the leading role of the United States, was not easy. Eight years in negotiation, the major issue was trade in agricultural goods, with the EU maintaining a strongly protective position and the Cairns Group led by the USA seeking to reduce agricultural trade barriers and subsidies. In the end, a modest compromise was achieved in the WTO Agreement on Agriculture, discussed below.

What drove that compromise? In this author's opinion, the United States played two critical cards: First, it aggressively undertook unilateral, totally unauthorized trade actions against "foreign country practices" under Section 301 of the Trade Act of 1974, revitalized by President Trump against China in 2018. See Section 1.18. Under considerable pressure, these actions primarily opened up foreign markets to U.S. exports. Second, the United States played the NAFTA card, commencing negotiations and reaching an extensive free trade and foreign investment agreement with Mexico and Canada. NAFTA 1994 negotiations ran more or less one year ahead of the Uruguay Round, influencing the content of and pushing forward the creation of the WTO and its package of agreements.

That said, significant differences between the WTO Agreements and NAFTA 1994 exist. A chart comparing NAFTA and WTO coverage is presented below. For example, NAFTA covers business visas, state trading, competition policy, and has an entire chapter dedicated to energy, all of which are absent from the WTO package. The WTO Agreements cover customs valuation and pre-shipment inspection, which NAFTA 1994 does not. Nothing in the WTO package of agreements touches on labor or the environment, NAFTA's two side agreements.

On market access, procurement, investment and most services, NAFTA 1994 went further and faster than the Uruguay Round WTO agreements. There is significant overlap on intellectual property where NAFTA's leading edge was particularly influential. The WTO Agreement on Agriculture, on the other hand, exceeded by a good measure NAFTA's trade opening initiatives. The WTO package also addressed basic telecommunications, which was mostly omitted from NAFTA 1994. The WTO has (since 1997) fostered an information technology tariff reduction agreement, but Mexico does not participate.

These differences may help explain why the basic rule of NAFTA 1994 dispute settlement is that the complaining country normally has the prerogative of choosing as between NAFTA 1994 (or the pending USMCA 2018) and WTO procedures. For details and examples, see R. Folsom, *Principles of International Litigation and Arbitration 2d,* Chapter 10 (West Academic Publishing).

The WTO Package Deal

The WTO is the product of the Uruguay Round of GATT negotiations, which was successfully completed in 1994. The Uruguay Round produced a package of agreements, the Agreement Establishing the World Trade Organization and its Annexes, which include the General Agreement on Tariffs and Trade 1994 (GATT 1994) and a series of Multilateral Trade Agreements (the Covered Agreements).[1] These agreements extend way beyond trade in goods to trade in services, trade-related intellectual property rights, trade-related investment measures, and a binding system of dispute settlement. All of the Covered Agreements are non-negotiable; they are mandatory. Four Plurilateral Trade Agreements are optional, though two of these Agreements (Dairy and Bovine Meat) have been rescinded. In addition to the WTO package, new members typically make specific additional trade and trade law commitments in their "Accession Agreements".

GATT 1947 and GATT 1994 are two distinct agreements. GATT 1994 incorporates the provisions of GATT 1947, except for the Protocol of Provisional Application, which is expressly excluded. Thus, the problems created by exempting the existing national laws at the time of the adoption of the Protocol have been avoided by this exclusion. Otherwise, in cases involving a conflict between GATT 1947 and GATT 1994, GATT 1947 controls. The WTO will be guided by the decisions, procedures and customary practices under GATT. The WTO package of agreements are routinely construed in light of the Vienna Convention on the Interpretation of Treaties. *See, e.g.,* EC-Chicken, WT/DS269/AB/R (2005).

Annexed to the WTO Agreement are several Multilateral Trade Agreements. As to trade in goods, they include Agreements on Agriculture, Textiles, Antidumping, Subsidies and Countervailing Measures, Safeguards, Technical Barriers to Trade, Sanitary and Phytosanitary Measures, Pre-shipment Inspection, Rules of Origin, and Import License Procedures. In addition to trade in goods, they include a General Agreement on Trade in Services and Agreements on Trade-Related Aspects of Intellectual Property Rights and Trade-Related Investment Measures.

Affecting all of these agreements is the Understanding on Rules and Procedures Governing the Settlement of Disputes (DSU). All of the Multilateral Trade Agreements are generally binding on all

---

[1]   *See* 33 Int. Legal Mat. 1130 (1994).

members of the World Trade Organization. Moreover, should a conflict arise between GATT 1994 and one of these Agreements, the latter prevails. Hence in WTO dispute proceedings where a conflict may exist, panels are required to first examine the specific Multilateral Agreement before taking up the GATT 1994 issue. *See* EC-Sardines, WTO/DS231/AB/R (2002) and U.S.-Internet Gambling, WT/DS 285/AB/R (2005).

Existing WTO members may declare "non-application" of all these Agreements vis-a-vis new members, thus opting out of their application to them. The United States, for example, declared non-application of the WTO Agreements to Armenia, Moldova, Georgia, Mongolia and the Kyrgyz Republic when those nations joined the WTO, although these declarations were subsequently revoked for all but Moldova. The U.S. still has not accepted application of the WTO to Kazakstan, a WTO member.

In addition to the Multilateral Trade Agreements, there are also Plurilateral Trade Agreements, which are annexed to the WTO Agreement. These agreements, however, are not binding on all WTO members, and states can choose to adhere to them or not. They include Agreements on Government Procurement, Trade in Civil Aircraft, International Dairy (rescinded), and an Arrangement Regarding Bovine Meat (rescinded). Member states which do not join the plurilateral trade agreements do not receive reciprocal benefits under them. Participating members agree to utilize the DSU to settle Plurilateral Trade Agreement disputes.

WORLD TRADE ORGANIZATION AGREEMENTS

AGREEMENT ESTABLISHING THE WORLD TRADE ORGANIZATION

ANNEX 1A: AGREEMENTS ON TRADE IN GOODS

1 General Agreement on Tariffs and Trade 1994

  (a) Understanding on the Interpretation of Article II:1(b) (tariff concessions)

  (b) Understanding on the Interpretation of Article XVII (state trading enterprises)

  (c) Understanding on Balance-of-Payments Provisions

  (d) Understanding on the Interpretation of Article XXIV (free trade areas and customs unions) **See Chapter 2.**

  (e) Understanding on the Interpretation of Article XXV (waivers)

(f)   Understanding on the Interpretation of Article XXVIII (modification of tariff schedules)

(g)   Understanding on the Interpretation of Article XXXV (non-application of GATT)

2   GATT 1994 **(See Section 1.3)**

3   Agreement on Agriculture **(See Section 1.8)**

4   Agreement on Sanitary and Phytosanitary Measures **(See Section 1.7)**

5   Agreement on Textiles and Clothing **(See Section 1.6)**

6   Agreement on Technical Barriers to Trade **(See Section 1.7)**

7   Agreement on Trade-Related Investment Measures **(See Section 1.12)**

8   Agreement on Implementation of Article VI (antidumping and countervailing duties)

9   Agreement on Implementation of Article VII (customs valuation)

10   Agreement on Pre-Shipment Inspection

11   Agreement on Rules of Origin **(See Section 1.10)**

12   Agreement on Import Licensing Procedures **(See Section 1.6)**

13   Agreement on Subsidies and Countervailing Measures

14   Agreement on Safeguards

ANNEX 1B: General Agreement on Trade in Services and Annexes **(See Section 1.9)**

ANNEX 1C: Agreement on Trade-Related Aspects of Intellectual Property Rights, Including Trade in Counterfeit Goods **(See Section 1.11)**

ANNEX 2:   Understanding on Rules and Procedures Governing the Settlement of Disputes **(See Sections 1.14 and 1.15)**

ANNEX 3:   Trade Policy Review Mechanism **(See Section 1.4)**

ANNEX 4:   Plurilateral Trade Agreements

ANNEX 4(a) Agreement on Trade in Civil Aircraft

ANNEX   4(b) Agreement   on   Government
Procurement **(See Section 1.13)**

ANNEX   4(c) International   Dairy   Arrangement
(rescinded)

ANNEX 4(d) Arrangement Regarding Bovine Meat
(rescinded)

Accession Agreements undertaken by new members may add to
or subtract from the WTO package of mandatory multilateral
agreements. China, for example, agreed to the application of special
"safeguard" rules against its exports for a limited period of time after
its WTO admission in 2001 and to specific restraints on export taxes.

The duties of the World Trade Organization are to facilitate the
implementation, administer the operations and further the objectives
of all these agreements. Its duties also include the resolution of
disputes under the agreements, reviews of trade policy and
cooperation with the International Monetary Fund (IMF) and the
World Bank. To achieve these goals, the WTO Agreement provides a
charter for the new organization, but for only minimalist
institutional and procedural capabilities, and no substantive
competence. Thus, there is a unified administration of pre-existing
and new obligations under all agreements concerning trade in goods,
including the Uruguay Round Agreements. In addition, the
administration of the new obligations on trade in services,
intellectual property and foreign investment were brought under the
same roof.

The WTO as an institution has no power to bring actions on its
own initiative. Under the provisions of the WTO Agreement, only the
members of WTO can initiate actions under the Dispute Settlement
Understanding. Enforcement of WTO obligations is primarily
through permitting members to retaliate or cross retaliate against
other members, rather than by execution of WTO institutional
orders. See Section 1.6. As Article 3.2 of the DSU suggests, many
panel and Appellate Body decisions utilize the Vienna Convention on
Interpretation of Treaties to clarify the meaning of the WTO package
of agreements.

Admission to and Exit from the WTO

The existing 130 or so members of GATT 1947 became the
WTO's founding member states. Admission to the World Trade
Organization is in common practice by "consensus." In theory, this
gives each member a veto over applicant countries, though a formal
two-thirds affirmative vote could be employed. In reality, no nation
wishing to join has ever formally been vetoed, though many have

been long delayed. Iran's desire to join has basically been frustrated by U.S. refusal to negotiate on WTO entry. It took, for example, well over a decade to negotiate acceptable terms of entry for the People's Republic of China in 2001, Vietnam in 2007 and Russia in 2012.

Such negotiations are handled individually by member states, not by the WTO as an organization. United States negotiations with China were particularly lengthy and difficult, one principal issue being whether China should be admitted as a developing or developed nation, which is normally a self-selected choice. The issue was fudged, with China treated differently within the WTO mandatory package of agreements. The issue remains controversial. See Section 1.16. China's admission also brought in Chinese Taipei (Taiwan). Hong Kong, admitted under British rule, remains a separate WTO member.

Essentially, applicant counties make an offer of trade liberalization commitments and compliance with the mandatory Covered Agreements to join the WTO. This offer is renegotiated with interested member states, some 40 nations regarding China, including the European Union which negotiates as a unit (NAFTA does not). Regarding China, the last member to reach agreement on WTO admission was Mexico, which extracted stiff promises against the dumping of Chinese goods. The various trade commitments made by the applicant in these bilateral negotiations are consolidated into a final accession protocol, which is then approved by "consensus." At this writing there are approximately 165 WTO member states.

Any member may withdraw with six months' notice. Although this has never happened, there is speculation that the Trump Administration might consider doing so.

§ 1.4   WTO Decision-Making

The World Trade Organization is structured in three tiers. One tier is the Ministerial Conference, which meets biennially and is composed of representatives of all WTO members. Each member state has an equal voting weight. This is unlike the representation in the IMF and World Bank where there is weighted voting, and financially powerful states have more power over the decision-making process. The Ministerial Conference is responsible for all WTO functions, and is able to make any decisions necessary. It has the power to authorize new multilateral negotiations and to adopt the results of such negotiations. The Ministerial Conference, by a three-fourths vote, is authorized to grant waivers of obligations to members in exceptional circumstances. It also has the power to adopt interpretations of Covered Agreements. When the Ministerial

Conference is in recess, its functions are performed by the General Council.

The second tier is the General Council which has executive authority over the day to day operations and functions of the WTO. It is composed of representatives of all WTO Members, and each member has an equal voting weight. It meets whenever it is appropriate. The General Council also has the power to adopt interpretations of Covered Agreements.

The third tier comprises the councils, bodies and committees which are accountable to the Ministerial Conference or General Council. Ministerial Conference committees include Committees on Trade and Development, Balance of Payment Restrictions, Budget, Finance and Administration. General Council bodies include the Dispute Settlement Body, the Trade Policy Review Body, and Councils for Trade in Goods, Trade in Services and Trade-Related Intellectual Property Rights. The Councils are all created by the WTO Agreement and are open to representatives of all member states. The Councils also have the authority to create subordinate organizations. Other committees, such as the Committee on Subsidies and Countervailing Measures are created by specific individual agreements.

Trade Policy Review Mechanism

Of the General Council bodies, the two which are most important are the Dispute Settlement Body (DSB) and the Trade Policy Review Body (TPRB). The DSB is a special meeting of the General Council, and therefore includes all WTO members. It has responsibility for resolution of disputes under all the Covered Agreements, discussed in more detail in Section 1.14 under Dispute Resolution.

The purpose of the Trade Policy Review Mechanism (TPRM) is to improve adherence to the WTO agreements and obligations, and to obtain greater transparency. In that regard, the TPRM supplements the general trade law transparency requirements of Chapter X of the GATT. Individual Members of WTO each prepare a "Country Report" on their trade policies and perceived adherence to the WTO Covered Agreements. The WTO Secretariat also prepares a report on each Member, but from the perspective of the Secretariat.

The Trade Policy Review Body (TPRB) then reviews the trade policies of each member based on these two reports. At the end of the review, the TPRB issues its own report concerning the adherence of the member's trade policy to the WTO Covered Agreements. The TPRB has no enforcement capability, but the report is sent to the next meeting of the WTO Ministerial Conference. It is then up to the

Ministerial Conference to evaluate the trade practices and policies of the member.

Consensus Rules

The process of decision-making in the WTO Ministerial Conference and General Council relies upon "consensus" as the norm, just as it did for decision-making under GATT 1947. "Consensus", in this context means that no member formally objects to a proposed decision. Thus, consensus is not obtained if any one member formally objects, and has often been very difficult to obtain, which proved to be a weakness in the operation of GATT. However, there are many exceptions to the consensus formula under WTO, and some new concepts (such as "inverted consensus") which are designed to ease the process of decision-making under WTO.

Article IX(1) of the WTO Agreement first provides that "the practice of decision-making by consensus" followed under GATT shall be continued. The next sentence of that provision, however, states that "where a decision cannot be arrived at by consensus, the matter at issue shall be decided by voting", except where otherwise provided. The ultimate resolution of the conflict between these two sentences is not completely clear.

There are a number of exceptions to the requirement for consensus that are expressly created under the WTO Agreement. One such exception is decisions by the Dispute Settlement Body, which has its own rules (see Section 1.14). Another set of exceptions concerns decisions on waivers, interpretations and amendments of the Covered Agreements. Waivers of obligations may be granted and amendments adopted to Covered Agreements only by the Ministerial Conference. Amendments of Multilateral Trade Agreements usually require a consensus, but where a decision on a proposed amendment cannot obtain consensus, the decision on that amendment is to be made in certain circumstances by a two-thirds majority vote. In "exceptional circumstances", the Ministerial Conference is authorized to grant waivers of obligations under a Covered Agreement by a three-fourths vote. Another exception to the consensus requirement allows procedural rules in both the Ministerial Conference and the General Council to be decided by a majority vote of the members, unless otherwise provided.

Operationally speaking, the WTO membership rarely meets in its entirety. Alliances and groups within the membership meet to undertake WTO decisions. For example, the "Cairns Group" of 18 member-states has focused on agricultural trade issues and endured as a group for some time. Groups and alliances often shift depending upon the subject matter.

§ 1.5   WTO Agreements and U.S. Law

The WTO Covered Agreements concern not only trade in goods, but also trade in services (GATs), trade-related aspects of intellectual property (TRIPs) and trade-related investment measures (TRIMs). The basic MFN and national treatment concepts that GATT 1947 applied to trade in goods (see Section 1.1) are now applied to these areas through GATS and TRIPs. The basic concepts of GATT 1947 and its associated agreements are elaborated and clarified through interpretive "understandings". In addition, there is an attempt to transform all protectionist measures relating to agriculture (such as import bans and quotas, etc.) into only tariff barriers, which can then be lowered in subsequent MTN Rounds (a process known as "tariffication"). Some of the WTO provisions, particularly those concerning trade in goods, are discussed in more detail below in relation to United States trade law.

GATT 1947, GATT 1994, the WTO Agreement and the other Covered Agreements have not been ratified as treaties. They therefore comprise international obligations of the United States only to the extent that they are incorporated in United States' implementing legislation. GATT 1947 was not considered controlling by the courts of the United States, which have always held themselves bound only to the U.S. legislation actually enacted. The WTO Covered Agreements standing on their own will be considered to have a non-self-executed status, and therefore are likely to be regarded in the same manner as GATT 1947.

Fast Track

The United States enacted legislation to implement WTO and the Covered Agreements on December 3, 1994. The implementing legislation was submitted to Congress under the "fast track" procedures of 19 U.S.C.A. § 2112. The statutory authority for "fast track" procedures also required that the President give 90 days' notice of his intention to enter into such an agreement. Fast track required that the WTO Agreements be considered by Congress as negotiated by the President, with no Congressional amendments via the implementing legislation. Nevertheless, the Uruguay Round Agreements Act of 1994 was adopted with relatively little controversy. Similar fast track procedures were in place for the Doha Round of WTO negotiations under the Trade Promotion Authority Act of 2002, but expired in July of 2007.

Fast track was renewed in 2014 under President Obama and presently is in effect until July 2021. See Section 4.0.

§ 1.6   Import/Export Quotas and Licensing, Textiles and Clothing

In addition to requiring MFN and national treatment, GATT 1947 and 1994 prohibits use of certain kinds of quantitative restrictions. Subject to exceptions such as balance of payment crises, Article XI prohibits "prohibitions or restrictions" on imports and it specifically prohibits the use of "quotas, import or export licenses or other measures" to restrict imports from a Contracting Party. Quotas include voluntary export restrain agreements. See Japan-Semiconductors, GATT Panel Report (1988). If utilized, Article XIII requires non-discrimination in quantitative trade restrictions, by barring an importing Contracting State from applying any prohibition or restriction to the products of another Contracting State, "unless the importation of the like product of *all* third countries. . . is similarly prohibited or restricted." (emphasis added).

The WTO has significantly reduced the number of trade quotas. By 2005, the Agreement on Textiles eliminated quotas long maintained under the Multi-Fiber Arrangement. *See* Section 1.7. Voluntary export restraints (quotas) are severely limited by the Safeguards Agreement. In addition, the WTO removes trade quotas by advancing "tariffication," replacing quotas with tariffs— sometimes even at extraordinarily high tariff rates. Tariffication is the approach adopted in the WTO Agricultural Agreement.

Quantity restrictions, such as numerical quotas on the importation or exportation of goods continue to exist, despite GATT Article XI which calls for their elimination, subject to a number of broadly worded exceptions to relieve critical shortages, to ensure domestic price controls, and to remediate short supply conditions. "Tariff-rate quotas" admit a specified quantity of goods at a preferential rate of duty. Once imports reach that quantity, tariffs are normally increased. WTO disputes concerning quotas have resulted in a number of panel and Appellate Body decisions that largely treat import rules that can create de facto quantitative restraint effects as prohibited by Article XI. For example, in *India-Autos* (WTO/DS16/AB/R (2002) "trade balancing" rules requiring producers to export in order to import were held to breach Article XI.

The Agreement on Textiles eliminated in 2005 the quotas long maintained under the Multi-Fibre Arrangement. The demise of MFA textile quotas in 2005, as widely expected, accelerated Chinese and other Asian textile exports to the United States. Responding to domestic pressures, the United States repeatedly invoked special safeguard protections against textile and clothing imports during the ten-year phase-out period that ended in 2005. Since then the average

U.S. bound and applied tariff on textile products has been around 8 percent.

Import (but not export) licensing schemes are allowed when quotas are permitted. On export licensing, see Section 1.6. International concern about delays which result from cumbersome import licensing procedures was manifested in the 1979 Tokyo Round MTN Import Licensing Code (which most developing countries refused to sign). The United States adhered to this Code, as did a reasonable number of other developed nations. The Uruguay Round made the Agreement on Import Licensing Procedures (1994) binding on all World Trade Organization members. The Agreement's objectives include facilitating the simplification and harmonization of import licensing and licensing renewal procedures, ensuring adequate publication of rules governing licensing procedures, and reducing the practice of refusing importation because of minor variations in quantity, value or weight of the import item under license.

§ 1.7   GATT/WTO Nontariff Trade Barrier Codes

TBT and SPS Codes

There are numerous nontariff trade barriers applicable to imports. Many of these barriers arise out of safety and health regulations. Others concern the environment, consumer protection, product standards and government procurement. Many of the relevant rules were created for legitimate consumer and public protection reasons. They were often created without extensive consideration of their international impact as potential nontariff trade barriers. Nevertheless, the practical impact of legislation of this type is to ban the importation of nonconforming products. Thus, unlike tariffs which can always be paid, and unlike quotas which permit a certain amount of goods to enter the market, nontariff trade barriers have the potential to totally exclude foreign exports.

Multilateral GATT negotiations since the end of World War II have led to a significant decline in world tariff levels, particularly on trade with developed nations. As steadily as tariff barriers have disappeared, nontariff trade barriers (NTBs) have emerged. Health and safety regulations, environmental laws, rules regulating products standards, procurement legislation and customs procedures are often said to present NTB problems.

Negotiations over nontariff trade barriers dominated the Tokyo Round of the GATT negotiations during the late 1970s. A number of optional NTB "codes" (sometimes called "side agreements") emerged from the Tokyo Round. These concerned subsidies, dumping, government procurement, technical barriers (products standards), customs valuation and import licensing. In addition, specific agreements regarding trade in bovine meats, dairy products and civil aircraft, as well as government procurement, were also reached. The United States accepted all of these NTB codes and agreements except the one on dairy products. Most of the necessary implementation of these agreements was accomplished in the Trade Agreements Act of 1979. Nearly all of the developing members of GATT opted out of these NTB codes.

Additional NTB codes were agreed upon under the Uruguay Round ending in late 1994 and became part of the WTO legal regime. All of the NTB areas covered by the Tokyo Round Codes were revisited, and new codes created for sanitary and phytosanitary measures (SPS), trade-related investment measures (TRIMs), pre-shipment inspection, rules of origin, escape clause safeguards and trade-related intellectual property rights (TRIPs). Unlike the Tokyo Round Codes, the WTO nontariff barrier codes (save a few plurilateral codes) are **mandatory** for all members. The United States Congress approved and implemented these Codes, along with the optional WTO Procurement Code, in December of 1994 under the Uruguay Round Agreements Act.

One problem with nontariff trade barriers is that they are so numerous. Intergovernmental negotiation intended to reduce their trade restricting impact is both tedious and difficult. There are continuing attempts through the World Trade Organization to come to grips with additional specific NTB problems. Furthermore, various trade agreements of the United States have been undertaken in this field. For example, the Canada-United States Free Trade Area Agreement and the NAFTA built upon the existing GATT agreements in attempting to further reduce NTB problems between the United States, Canada and Mexico.

SPS Code

The SPS Code strongly encourages the use of international SPS standards, such as the Codex Alimentarius Commission. But member states may proceed to enact their own nondiscriminatory SPS rules, subject to the Code's mandates, notably that they be based upon risk assessments and scientific evidence. There is some suggestion in the decisions of the WTO Appellate Body that SPS measures must be "proportional" to the risks involved. See *Japan-Apples*, WT/DS245/AB/R (2003).

Some of the difficulties of these NTBs are illustrated in the *EU Beef Hormones* case (WT/DS 26/AB/R (1998). The Sanitary and Phytosanitary Code (SPS Code) basically requires adherence to international food standards, or a scientific basis for regulatory rules governing food products. The EU, adhering to "precautionary principles," banned imports of growth-enhancing hormone-treated beef from the U.S. and Canada as a health hazard. The Appellate Body ruled in 1997 under the SPS Code that, since the ban was stricter than international standards, the EU needed scientific evidence to back it up. The Appellate Body noted the EU had failed to undertake a scientific risk assessment, and the EU's scientific reports did not provide any rational basis to uphold the ban. In fact, the primary EU study had found no evidence of harm to humans from the growth-enhancing-hormones. If the "relevant scientific evidence is insufficient", there is limited recognition of precautionary principles in Article 5.7 of the SPS Code.

The Appellate Body concluded that the ban violated the EU's SPS obligations, and required the EU to produce scientific evidence to justify the ban within a reasonable time, or to revoke the ban. Arbitrators later determined that 15 months was a reasonable time. But the EU failed to produce such evidence and the U.S. retaliated (as authorized) by imposing substantial tariffs on EU imports. Late in 2004, the EU commenced WTO proceedings asserting that new scientific studies and precaution justified its ban and required removal of U.S. retaliation. This WTO proceeding also went against the EU, again in the absence of adequate proof of scientific basis. *See* U.S.-Continued Suspension in EC-Hormones, WT/320/AB/R (2008). Finally, in 2009, a phased four-year settlement of the *Beef Hormones* dispute was reached. The U.S. got a higher quota to export hormone-free beef to the EU in return for phasing out its retaliatory tariffs on EU goods.

TBT Code

Widespread use of "standards" requirements as NTB import restraints resulted in 1979 in the GATT Agreement on Technical Barriers to Trade (called the "Standards Code"). This Code was made operative in the United States by the Trade Agreements Act of 1979, and was followed by a reasonable number of other developed nations.

Its successor is the WTO Agreement on Technical Barriers to Trade (1994) (TBT Code). By explicit provision in Article 1.5 of the TBT Code, the SPS Code takes precedence over the TBT Code. The Appellate Body has held that both Codes take precedence over GATT 1994 issues. The TBT Code is binding on all WTO members. It strongly favors conforming use of international product standards, such as those of the International Standards Organization. See EC-Sardines, WT/DS231/AB/R (2002) (EC marketing rule not based on Codex Alimentarius standard). In general, the TBT Code deals with the problem of manipulation of product standards and labels, product testing procedures, and product certifications in order to slow or stop imported goods. To this end, the TBT Code requires NTBs to be not more trade restrictive than necessary to effectuate legitimate governmental objectives.

The TBT Code provides, in part and subject to some exceptions, that imported products shall be accorded treatment (including testing treatment and certification) no less favorable than that accorded to like products of national origin or those originating in any other country. It also requires that WTO members establish a central office for standards inquiries, publish advance and reasonable notice of requirements that are applicable to imported goods, and provide an opportunity for commentary by those who may be affected adversely. The TBT Code establishes an international committee to deal with alleged instances of noncompliance. Various United States TBT, notably dolphin-safe and imported meat origin labels as well as flavored cigarette standards, have been challenged in WTO dispute settlement proceedings.

§ 1.8   The WTO Agreement on Agriculture

Agricultural issues played a central role in the Uruguay Round negotiations and are critical to the Doha Round as well. More than any other issue, they delayed completion of the Uruguay Round from 1990 to 1993. The agreement reached in December of 1993 is a trade liberalizing, market-oriented effort. Each country has made a number of commitments on market access, reduced domestic agricultural support levels and export subsidies. The United States Congress approved these commitments in December of 1994 by adopting the Uruguay Round Agreements Act.

Broadly speaking nontariff barriers (NTBs) to international agricultural trade are replaced by tariffs that provide substantially the same level of protection. This is known as "tariffication." It applies to virtually all NTBs, including variable levies, import bans, voluntary export restraints and import quotas. *See* Chile-Price Band System, WT/DS207/AB/R (2002). Tariffication applies specifically to U.S. agricultural quotas adopted under Section 22 of the Agricultural Adjustment Act. All agricultural tariffs, including those converted from NTBs, are to be reduced by 36 and 24 percent by developed and developing countries, respectively, over 6 and 10 year periods. Certain minimum access tariff quotas apply when imports amount to less than 3 to 5 percent of domestic consumption. An escape clause exists for tariffed imports at low prices or upon a surge of importation depending upon the existing degree of import penetration.

Regarding domestic support for agriculture, some programs with minimal impact on trade are exempt from change. These programs are known as "green box policies." They include governmental support for agricultural research, disease control, infrastructure and food security. Green box policies were also exempt from GATT/WTO challenge or countervailing duties for 9 years. Direct payments to producers that are not linked to production are also generally exempt. This will include income support, adjustment assistance, and environmental and regional assistance payments. Furthermore, direct payments to support crop reductions and *de minimis* payments are exempted in most cases.

After removing all of the exempted domestic agricultural support programs, the agreement on agriculture arrives at a calculation known as the Total Aggregate Measurement of Support (Total AMS). This measure is the basis for agricultural support reductions under the agreement. Developed nations reduced their Total AMS by 20 percent over 6 years, developing nations by 13.3 percent over 10 years. United States reductions undertaken in 1985 and 1990 meant that little or no U.S. action was required to meet this obligation. Agricultural export subsidies of developed nations were reduced by 36 percent below 1986–1990 levels over 6 years and the quantity of subsidized agricultural exports by 21 percent. Developing nations had corresponding 24 and 14 percent reductions over 10 years.

All conforming tariffications, reductions in domestic support for agriculture and export subsidy alterations were essentially exempt from challenge for 9 years within the GATT/WTO on grounds such as serious prejudice in export markets or nullification and impairment of agreement benefits. However, countervailing duties could be levied against all unlawfully subsidized exports of agricultural goods except for subsidies derived from so-called national "green box policies". In *U.S.—Upland Cotton* (WTO/DS267/AB/R (2005), the Appellate Body affirmed that member states must not only conform to the Agreement on Agriculture, but also the SCM Agreement. In that decision, U.S. compliance with the Agriculture Agreement was acknowledged, but its "Step-2" payments to cotton users favoring domestic over imported cotton (local content subsidies) were held to violate the SCM Agreement.

§ 1.9   The General Agreement on Trade in Services (GATS)

Because protectionist barriers to international trade in services were stifling, the United States and other developed countries insisted that there should be a General Agreement on Trade in Services (GATS). In the United States, services account for over two-thirds of the Nation's GDP and provide jobs for nearly two-thirds of the work force. Services account for almost one-third of U.S. exports in sectors such as tourism, education, construction, telecommunications, transport and health. In contrast, most developing nations are minimal exporters of services, save by means of exporting their people, but migration was not included as a subject under the GATS.

Market access for services is a major focus of the General Agreement on Trade in Services (GATS), a product of the Uruguay Round of Negotiations. The GATS defines the supply of services broadly to include providing services across borders or inside member states with or without a commercial presence therein. Apart from ensuring transparency of national regulatory controls over services, the core GATS Article XVII commitment is to afford most-favored-nation treatment to service providers, subject to country-specific, preferential trade agreement or labor market integration agreement exemptions, such as audio-visual services in the EU.

In addition, each WTO member state made under GATS XVI specific schedule of commitments (concessions) on opening up their markets in services' sectors negotiated using the WTO Services Sectoral Classification List. They further agreed under Article XVI to provide national treatment to their services' commitment schedule. For example, to what degree may foreign banks or foreign economic consultants provide services, and are they entitled to national treatment? The answers to those questions will be found in the GATS specific commitments of each member. Much to its consternation, the United States was found to have failed to exclude Internet gambling services under its GATS commitments' schedule. This caused Antigua-Barbuda to prevail in a dispute that alleged U.S. gambling laws discriminatorily prohibited its right to export such services to the U.S. market. *See* U.S.—Gambling, WT/DS285/AB/R (2007). The United States also lost the argument that its Internet gambling services' restraints were justifiable on public morals' grounds. This argument failed as discriminatory under the "chapeau" of the GATS Article XIV general exceptions (similar to GATT Article XX general exceptions discussed in Section 1.1).

Special "GATS Rules" govern use of safeguards against surges of services' imports, subsidies applicable to services' exports, and government procurement of services. General GATS exceptions apply (for example, government supplied services), as do national security GATS exceptions.

National laws that restrict the number of firms in a market, that are dependent upon local "needs tests", or that mandate local incorporation are regulated by the GATS. Various "transparency" rules require disclosure of all relevant laws and regulations, and these must be administered reasonably, objectively and impartially. Specific service market access and national treatment commitments are made by various governments in schedules attached to the agreement. These commitments may be modified or withdrawn after 3 years, subject to a right of compensation that can be arbitrated. Certain mutual recognition of education and training for service-sector licensing occurs. State monopolies or exclusive service providers may continue, but must not abuse their positions. Detailed rules are created in annexes to the GATS on financial, telecommunications and air transport services. Under the Telecommunications Reference Paper (TRP), for example, the United States successfully argued that Telmex had abused its monopoly position in Mexico by charging discriminatory, non-cost-oriented connection fees for foreign calls. *See* Mexico—Telecoms, WT/DS204/AB/R (2004).

The U.S. Congress approved and implemented the GATS agreement in December of 1994 under the Uruguay Round Agreements Act. Subsequently, early in 1995, the United States refused to extend most-favored-nation treatment to financial services. The European Union, Japan and other GATS nations then entered into an interim 2-year agreement which operated on MFN principles. Financial services were revisited in 1996–97 with further negotiations aimed at bringing the United States into the fold. These negotiations bore fruit late in 1997 with 70 nations (including the United States) joining in an agreement that covers 95 percent of trade in banking, insurance, securities and financial information. This agreement took effect March 1, 1999.

The GATS has reduced unilateral U.S. action under Section 301 to gain access to foreign markets for U.S. service providers. This reduction flows from U.S. adherence to the Dispute Settlement Understanding (DSU) that accompanies the WTO accords. The DSU obligates its signatories to follow streamlined dispute settlement procedures under which unilateral retaliation is restrained until the offending nation has failed to conform to a World Trade Organization ruling.

GATS Disputes

GATS, and the 1996 Protocol on Telecommunications and 1997 Protocol on Financial Services, have generated only a handful of WTO disputes. Here is a sampling of them:

1. EC—Regime for the Importation, Sale and Distribution of Bananas, WT/DS27/AB/R (1997) (traders of goods may also be traders of services, such as wholesaling or retailing,

GATS Articles II and XVII apply to de jure and de facto discrimination).

2. Canada—Certain Measures Concerning Periodicals, WT/DS31/AB/R (1997) (GATT and GATS co-exist, no override).

3. Canada—Certain Measures Affecting the Automotive Industry, WT/DS139,142/R (2000) (coverage under GATS must be determined before assessment of consistency with GATS obligations).

4. Mexico—Measures Affecting Telecommunication Services WT/DS204/R(2004)(Mexican cross-border interconnection rates not cost-oriented and unreasonable in breach of Telecoms Annex, failure to allow access to private leased-circuits also violated commitments) (settled with rate reductions and increased access).

5. United States—Measures Affecting The Cross-Border Supply of Gambling and Betting Services, WT/DS 285/AB/R (2005) (gambling included in U.S. recreational services' commitments, U.S. import ban amounted to "zero quota" in breach of GATS Article XVI, necessary to protect public morals under Article XIV defense but discriminatory enforcement regarding Interstate Horseracing Act fails to meet "chapeau" requirements) (U.S. pays compensation to all GATS signatories except Antigua and Barbuda, the complaining party. . . . $21 million retaliation authorized in 2008).

6. China—Certain Measures Affecting Electronic payment Systems, WT/DS413/R (2012) (discriminatory restraints on foreign electronics payment services' suppliers violate GATS commitments).

§ 1.10   The WTO and Rules of Origin

The Uruguay Round accord on rules of origin is, in reality, an agreement to agree. A negotiations schedule was established along with a WTO Committee to work with the Customs Cooperation Council on harmonized rules of origin. Certain broad guiding principles for the negotiations are given and considered binding until agreement is reached. These principles are:

• Rules of origin applied to foreign trade must not be more stringent than applied to domestic goods.

• Rules of origin must be administered consistently, uniformly, impartially and reasonably.

- Origin assessments must be issued within 150 days of a request and remain valid for three years.

- New or modified rules or origin may not be applied retroactively.

- Strict confidentiality rules apply to information submitted confidentially for rule of origin determinations.

To date, no WTO agreement on rules of origin has been reached. As a result, diverse national, free trade and customs union rules of origin predominate. For NAFTA 1994 rules of origin, see Chapter 4. For USMCA 2018 rules of origin, see Chapter 6.

§ 1.11 The Trade-Related Aspects of Intellectual Property Rights Agreement (TRIPs)

The Uruguay Round accords of late 1993 include an agreement on trade-related intellectual property rights (TRIPs). This agreement is binding upon the roughly 165 nations that are members of the World Trade Organization. In the United States, the TRIPs agreement has been ratified and implemented by Congress under the Uruguay Round Agreements Act. There is a general requirement of national and most-favored-nation treatment among the parties.

Many developed nations had been trying unsuccessfully to promote expanded intellectual property rights through the U.N.-created World Intellectual Property Rights Organization (WIPO). WIPO agreements are not mandatory, and much of the developing world had declined to opt into their terms. Much to the benefit of private parties in the developed world, the TRIPs Code covers the gamut of intellectual property. It has de facto become a near-global IP Code.

On copyrights, there is protection for computer programs and databases, rental authorization controls for owners of computer software and sound recordings, a 50-year motion picture and sound recording copyright term, and a general obligation to comply with the Berne Convention (1971 version) (except for its provisions on moral rights).

On patents, the Paris Convention (1967 version) prevails, 20-year product and process patents are available "in all fields of technology", including pharmaceuticals and agricultural chemicals. However, patents can be denied when necessary to protect public morals or order, to protect human, animal or plant life or health, and to avoid serious environmental prejudice. The TRIPs provisions did not stop the Indian Supreme Court in 2013 from denying Novartis a patent on its cancer drug, Gleevac. The court took the view that Novartis was engaged in "evergreening", i.e., making small, inconsequential changes to existing patents and that Indian law could require proof of "improved therapeutic efficacy" before a patent grant.

Article 31 of the TRIPs permits compulsory licensing of patents in national emergencies or other circumstances of extreme urgency, subject to a duty to reasonably compensate the patent owner. Thailand has issued compulsory licenses on a range of cancer, heart disease and AIDS drugs. There is considerable controversy over pharmaceutical patents based on traditional medicines of indigenous peoples, which some see as bio-piracy. Proposals have been made to amend TRIPs to require disclosure of the origins of bio-patents, obtain informed consent from the indigenous communities involved, and share the benefits of such patents.

Note that by incorporating the Berne and Paris conventions, TRIPs and the WTO DSU become an enforcement mechanism for those longstanding treaties. For trademarks, the Paris Convention also rules, service marks become registrable, internationally prominent marks receive enhanced protection, the linking of local marks with foreign trademarks is prohibited, and compulsory licensing is banned. But gray market trading and related IP issues are explicitly not covered by TRIPs, allowing each WTO member state to differ on such law.

In addition, trade secret protection is assisted by TRIPs rules enabling owners to prevent unauthorized use or disclosure. These rules closely parallel those of NAFTA. Integrated circuits are covered by rules intended to improve upon the Washington Treaty. Lastly, protection of industrial designs and geographic indicators of product origin (*e.g.*, Canadian Whiskey) are also part of the TRIPs regime.

Mandatory IP infringement and anti-counterfeiting remedies are included in the TRIPs, for both domestic and international trade protection. There are specific provisions governing injunctions, damages, judicial and customs seizures, and discovery of evidence. Willful trademark counterfeiting and copyright piracy on a commercial scale must be criminalized. Counterfeit goods may not be re-exported by customs authorities in an unaltered state.

The Medicines Agreement

Late in 2001, the Doha Round of WTO negotiations were launched. These negotiations have reconsidered the TRIPs agreement, particularly as it applies to developing nations. Their compliance deadline for the TRIPs rules on patents for pharmaceuticals was extended to 2016, thereby allowing a continuation of cheaper, local generics. In addition, a Declaration on the TRIPs Agreement and Public Health was issued at the Qatar

Ministerial Conference. This 2001 Declaration includes the following statement:

> "We agree that the TRIPs Agreement does not prevent Members from taking measures to protect public health. Accordingly, while reiterating our commitment to the TRIPs Agreement, we affirm that the Agreement can and should be interpreted and implemented in a manner supportive of WTO Members' right to protect public health and, in particular, to promote access to medicines for all."

A "Medicines Agreement" waiver (2003) and amendment to TRIPs (2005) implement this Declaration. Compulsory licensing and/ or importation of generic copies of patented medicines needed to address developing nation public health problems are authorized. Such activities may not pursue industrial or commercial policy objectives, and different packaging and labeling must be used in an effort at minimizing the risk of diversion of the generics to developed country markets. Under pressure from the United States, a number of more advanced developing nations (such as Mexico, Singapore and Qatar) agreed not to employ compulsory licensing except in situations of national emergency or extreme urgency. Canada, China, the EU, India, South Korea and other members, on the other hand, have licensed production of drugs for nations incapable of pharmaceutical production.

Special 301—Prioritization of U.S. Intellectual Property Rights Disputes

The Special 301 procedures established by the 1988 Omnibus Trade and Competitiveness Act are permanent features of United States trade legislation. These procedures are located in Section 182 of the Trade Act of 1974. Under these procedures the United States Trade Representative is required to identify foreign countries that deny adequate and effective protection of intellectual property rights, or deny fair and equitable access to United States persons that rely upon intellectual property protection. The USTR is given discretion to determine whether to designate certain of these countries to be "priority countries."

If so designated, a mandatory Section 301 investigation must follow in the absence of a determination that this would be detrimental to U.S. economic interests or a negotiated settlement of the intellectual property dispute. Once designated, Special 301 investigations and retaliations against priority countries must ordinarily be decided within 6 months by the USTR. Whether to retaliate or not is discretionary with the USTR, but retaliation is not authorized if the country in question enters into good faith negotiations or makes "significant progress" in bilateral or multilateral negotiations towards increased protection for intellectual property rights.

Many commentators have observed that unilateral use of Section 301 prior to creation of the WTO helped push the U.S. agenda in the TRIPs negotiations. Since 1994, if the dispute is covered by the WTO TRIPs agreement, the United States should avoid using unilateral Section 301 trade sanctions and pursue WTO dispute settlement. President Trump has seemingly ignored this obligation in applying Section 301 tariffs on Chinese goods. See Chapter 6.

In identifying priority foreign countries in the intellectual property field, Section 182 indicates that the USTR is to prioritize only those countries that have the most "onerous or egregious" practices, whose practices have the greatest adverse impact on United States products, and are not entering into good faith negotiations bilaterally or multilaterally to provide adequate and effective protection of intellectual property rights. For these purposes, the term "persons that rely on intellectual protection" covers those involved in copyrighted works of authorship or those involved in the manufacture of products that are patented or subject to process patents. Interestingly, this definition does not include those who rely on United States trademarks.

However, the relevant definitions include trademarks in connection with the denial by foreign countries of adequate and effective protection of intellectual property rights. The definition of practices that deny fair and equitable market access in connection with intellectual property rights appear to be limited to copyrights and patents. This denial must constitute a violation of provisions of international law or international agreements to which both the United States and that country are parties or otherwise constitute a discriminatory nontariff trade barrier.

Regular reports to Congress are required of the USTR by Section 182. The USTR has chiefly placed foreign country intellectual property practices on watch lists rather than formally designating priority countries. These watch lists are divided as between "priority watch lists" and "secondary watch lists." Many nations have been listed by the USTR since 1989 in this fashion. This has the practical effect of placing pressure on those nations to enter negotiations with the United States that will improve their protection of intellectual property rights.

The use of these lists gives the USTR more room to negotiate settlements with the countries concerned. For example, the USTR formally named China, India and Thailand as the first "priority countries" for Special 301 purposes. The formal process of negotiation backed up by a mandatory Section 301 investigation and potential sanctions was begun. Thailand was cited for its failure to enforce copyrights and for the absence of patent protection for pharmaceuticals. India was named because its patent laws are deficient from the U.S. perspective, particularly on compulsory licensing and the absence of pharmaceutical protection. Extensive book, video, sound recording and computer software piracy in India was also cited.

United States Special 301 investigations and watch lists, now including "Out-of-Cycle Reviews of Notorious Markets", have continued relentlessly in spite of the WTO TRIPs agreement. The USTR has filed numerous TRIPs complaints with the WTO. Filings have been made, for example, against Denmark, Sweden, Ireland, Ecuador, Greece, Portugal, India, Russia, Pakistan, Turkey and, not surprisingly, China. See Section 1.17.

TRIPs Disputes

Dozens of TRIPs complaints have been initiated under WTO dispute settlement procedures. Most have been settled, but a few have resulted in WTO Panel and Appellate Body Reports. Here is a sampling of those disputes:

1. India—Patent Protection for Pharmaceutical and Agricultural Chemical Products, WT/DS50/AB/R (1998)("mailbox rule" patent applications for subjects not patentable in India until 2005 inadequate, denial of exclusive marketing rights in breach of TRIPs Article 70.9).

2. Canada—Term of Patent Protection, WT/DS170/AB/R (2000) (pre-TRIPs Canadian patents must receive 20 year term).

3. U.S.—Section 110 (5) Copyright Act, WT/DS160/R (2000) (copyright exemption for "homestyle" dramatic musical works consistent with Berne Convention, "business use" exemption inconsistent with Berne and therefore in breach of TRIPs) (settled by payment).

4. Canada—Pharmaceutical Patents, WT/DS114/R (2000) (Canadian generic pharmaceutical regulatory review and stockpiling patent rights' exceptions not sufficiently "limited").

5. U.S.—Section 211 Appropriations Act, WT/DS176/AB/R (2002) (prohibition against registering marks confiscated by Cuban government, e.g. HAVANA CLUB rum, without original owner's consent violates Paris Convention and TRIPs, trade names covered by TRIPs).

6. EC—Trademarks and Geographical Indications WT/DS 174,290/R (2005) (EC regulation violates national treatment and most-favored treatment obligations to non-EC nationals, procedural violations also found).

7. China—Measures Affecting The Protection and Enforcement of Intellectual Property Rights, WT/DS362/R (2009) (China's implementation of TRIPs upheld as to criminal law thresholds and disposal of confiscated, infringing goods by customs authorities, rejected as to denial of copyright protection for works not authorized for release in China).

8. China—Measures Affecting Trading Rights and Distribution Services for Certain Publications and Audiovisuals Entertainment Products, WT/DS363/AB/R (2009) (China's ADV restrictions limited to state-owned or approved channels violate WTO Accession Protocol, GATT 1994 and GATS; Restraints not necessary to protect public morals).

9. European Communities—Information Technology Tariffs, WT/DS375–377 (2010) (EU tariffs on cable converter boxes with Net capacity, flat panel computer screens and printers that also scan, fax or copy violated 1996 Information Technology Agreement zero tariff rules).

§ 1.12 The Trade-Related Investment Measures Agreement (TRIMs)

The WTO package of mandatory agreements includes TRIMs, Trade-Related Investment Measures. This is the only WTO agreement concerning foreign investment law, an area which is almost devoid of common international rules. The WTO is a trade law organization, hence its coverage of foreign investment is only "trade-related". In practice, this means that TRIMs is almost exclusively concerned with "performance requirements", i.e. national rules requiring designated performances by foreign investors. There are 14 performance requirements enumerated in and broadly prohibited by TRIMs. They fall into three general categories: (1) Local content rules; (2) Trade balancing rules; and (3) Export requirements.

Regarding performance requirements, TRIMs tracks the GATT Article III rule of "national treatment" and Article XI proscription against quotas. But member states may "deviate temporarily" from these principles, thus undermining their impact. Trade-related investment practices which are deemed inconsistent with TRIMs are listed illustratively in an Annex. These include minimum domestic content rules (say 50% of the value of the foreign investor's products must be sourced locally), limitations on imports used in production, the linkage of allowable imports to export requirements, export quotas or percentage of production requirements, and restrictions on foreign exchange designed to limit imports.

Perhaps because of their limited scope and soft prohibition, there have been very few TRIMs disputes. The United States and others did succeed in challenging Indonesia's local content requirements for autos. See Indonesia—Certain Measures Affecting the Automobile Industry, WT/DS/AB/R 54, 55, 59 & 64 (1998).

§ 1.13 The Optional WTO Public Procurement Code

Where public procurement is involved, and the taxpayer's money is at issue, virtually every nation has some form of legislation or tradition that favors buying from domestic suppliers. The Tokyo Round GATT Procurement Code was not particularly successful at opening up government purchasing. Relatively few GATT members and the United States adhered to that Procurement Code. This was also partly the result of the 1979 Code's many exceptions. For example, the Code did not apply to contracts below its threshold amount of $150,000 SDR (about $171,000 since 1988), service contracts, and procurement by entities on each country's reserve list (including most national defense items). Because procurement in the European Union and Japan is often decentralized, many contracts fell below the SDR threshold and were therefore GATT exempt. By dividing up procurement into smaller contracts national preferences were retained. United States government procurement tends to be more centralized and thus more likely to be covered by the GATT Code. This pattern may help explain why Congress restrictively amended the Buy American Act in 1988.

The Uruguay Round WTO Procurement Code took effect in 1995 and replaced the 1979 Tokyo Round GATT Procurement Code. The WTO Code expanded the coverage of the prior GATT Code to include procurement of services, construction, government-owned utilities, and some state and local (sub-central) contracts. The U.S. and the European Union applied the new Code's provisions on government-owned utilities and sub-central contracts as early as April 15, 1994. Other participants include Armenia, Aruba, Chinese Taipei (Taiwan), Iceland, Japan, Korea, Israel, Lichtenstein, Norway, Singapore and Switzerland. Nearly all developing nations have opted out of the WTO Procurement Code, though China has expressed interest in it.

Various improvements to the procedural rules surrounding procurement practices and dispute settlement under the WTO Code attempt to reduce tensions in this difficult area. For example, an elaborate system for bid protests is established. Bidders who believe the Code's procedural rules have been abused will be able to lodge, litigate and appeal their protests. The WTO Procurement Code became part of U.S. law in December of 1994 under the Uruguay Round Agreements Act. The United States has made, with few exceptions, all procurement by executive agencies subject to the Federal Acquisition Regulations under the Code's coverage (i.e., to suspend application of the normal Buy American preferences to such procurement). Thirteen U.S. states have not ratified the WTO Procurement Code. The economic stimulus and auto bail-out legislation of the Obama administration raised questions of U.S. compliance with the Code.

Chapter 13 of the North American Free Trade Area Agreement opened government procurement to U.S., Canadian and Mexican suppliers on contracts as small as $25,000. However, the goods supplied must have at least 50 percent North American content. These special procurement rules effectively created an exception to the GATT Procurement Code which otherwise applied. The thresholds are $50,000 for goods and services provided to federal agencies and $250,000 for government-owned enterprises (notably PEMEX and CFE). These regulations are particularly important because Mexico, unlike Canada, has not traditionally joined in GATT/WTO procurement codes. In December 2011 Canada-U.S. procurement provisions were incorporated in a long awaited agreement to expand the WTO Procurement Code. This expansion selectively brought more types of procurement contracts, notably service contracts, and more sub-central government entities within the Code's coverage. Contract value thresholds were also selectively lowered.

Under the USMCA 2018 agreement, Canada and the United States will fall back exclusively on the WTO Procurement Code, while Mexico and the U.S. will utilize bilateral procurement USMCA rules. See Chapter 6.

§ 1.14 WTO Dispute Settlement

GATT 1947 did not have an institutional charter, and was not intended to become an international organization on trade. It did later develop institutional structures and acquired quasi-organizational status, but there was always a lack of structure. This lack was most often perceived in the somewhat over-stated inability of GATT to resolve disputes which were brought to it. Indeed, GATT

1947 members could block the formation of a panel to hear a dispute. Moreover, GATT panel decisions could be blocked by the losing state! Hence most GATT 1947 dispute settlement panel reports were un-adopted, and as such "the GATT acquis" is said to merely provide guidance in the context of WTO dispute settlement. *See* Japan-Alcoholic Beverages II, WTO/DS/R 8, 10, 11 (1996).

The WTO provides a unified, mandatory, and exclusive intergovernmental system for settling trade disputes governed by WTO law through the Dispute Settlement Understanding (DSU) using the Dispute Settlement Body (DSB). There are no private remedies, though private sector interests are often motivating elements. In the United States, private parties and their attorneys can attempt to trigger WTO dispute settlement proceedings by filing complaints with the U.S. Trade Representative (USTR), a presidential appointee. Whether to pursue WTO trade law complaints is entirely discretionary for the USTR. Under the terms of the DSU, the USTR can pursue complaints of breach of WTO agreement obligations, or nullification or impairment of benefits accruing under WTO agreements.

The DSB is a special assembly of the WTO General Council, and includes all WTO members. There are six stages in the resolution of disputes under WTO:

1)   Consultation;

2)   Panel establishment, investigation and report;

3)   Appellate review of the WTO panel report;

4)   Adoption of the panel or Appellate Body decision;

5)   Implementation of the decision adopted; and

6)   Compensation or authorized retaliation.

There is also a parallel process for binding arbitration, if both parties agree to submit this dispute to arbitration, rather than to a DSB panel. In addition, the party subject to an adverse decision may seek arbitration as a matter of right on issues of compliance and authorized retaliation.

Although the DSU offers a unified dispute resolution system that is applicable across all sectors and all WTO Covered Agreements, there are many specialized rules for disputes which arise under them. Such specialized rules appear in the Agreements on Textiles, Antidumping, Subsidies and Countervailing Measures, Technical Barriers to Trade, Sanitary and Phytosanitary Measures, Customs Valuation, General Agreement on Trade in Services, Financial Services and Air Transport Services. The special provisions in these individual Covered Agreements govern, where applicable, and prevail in any conflict with the general provisions of the DSU.

Under WTO, unlike under GATT 1947, the DSU practically assures that panels will be established upon request by a member state. Further, under WTO, unlike GATT 1947, the DSU virtually ensures the adoption of unmodified panel and appellate body decisions. It accomplishes this by requiring the DSB to adopt panel reports and appellate body decisions automatically and without amendment unless they are rejected by a consensus of all members. This "inverted consensus" requires that all members of the DSB, including the state that prevailed in the dispute, decide to reject the dispute resolution decision. Not surprisingly, this has never happened because if any member formally favors that decision (the winner in the dispute for example), it becomes binding. This inverted consensus requirement is imposed on both the adoption of panel reports or appellate body decisions and also on the decision to establish a panel.

The potential resolutions of a dispute under DSU range from a "mutually satisfactory solution" agreed to by the parties under the first, or consultation phase, to authorized retaliation under the last, or implementation phase. The preferred solution is always any resolution that is mutually satisfactory to the parties. After a panel decision, there are three types of remedies available to the prevailing party, if a mutually satisfactory solution cannot be obtained. One is for the respondent to bring the measure found to violate a Covered Agreement into conformity with the Agreement. A second is for the prevailing Member to receive monetary or tariff concession compensation from the respondent which both parties agree is sufficient to compensate for any injury caused by the measure found to violate a Covered Agreement.

Finally, if no such agreement can be reached, a prevailing party can be authorized to suspend some of its concessions under the Covered Agreements to the respondent. These suspended concessions, called "retaliation," can be authorized within the same trade sector and agreement; or, if that will not create sufficient compensation, can be authorized across trade sectors and agreements.

The entire WTO dispute resolution process, from filing a complaint to authorized retaliation, can take roughly three years. One perspective on WTO dispute settlement seeks a rule-oriented use of the "rule of law". The other seeks a power-oriented use of diplomacy. The United States and less developed countries have traditionally sought to develop a rule-oriented approach to international trade disputes. The European Union and Japan have traditionally sought to use the GATT/WTO primarily as a forum for diplomatic negotiations, although the EU now ranks second in number of WTO dispute proceedings.

These different views created part of the conflict at the December 1999 Seattle WTO meeting (which failed to launch the Millennium Round) and subsequent failure of the Doha Round. If the DSB is a court, its proceedings should be open and "transparent." However, if it is just another form of government-to-government diplomacy, that has always been held in secret.

Phase 1, Consultation

Any WTO Member who believes that the Measures of another Member are not in conformity with the Covered Agreements may call for consultations on those measures. The respondent has ten days to reply and must agree to enter into consultation within 30 days. If the respondent does not enter into consultations within the 30-day period, the party seeking consultations can immediately request the establishment of a panel under DSU, which puts the dispute into Phase 2.

Once consultations begin, the parties have 60 days to achieve a settlement. The goal is to seek a positive solution to the dispute, and the preferred resolution is to reach whatever solution is mutually satisfactory to the parties. If such a settlement cannot be obtained after 60 days, the party seeking consultations may request the establishment of a panel under DSU, which moves the dispute into Phase 2.

WTO member third parties with an interest in the subject-matter of the consultations may seek to be included in them. If such inclusion is rejected, they may seek their own consultations with the other member state. Alternatives to consultations may be provided through the use of conciliation, mediation or good offices, where all parties agree to use the alternative process. Any party can terminate the use of conciliation, mediation or good offices and then seek the establishment of a panel under DSU, which also will move the dispute into Phase 2.

Phase 2, Panel Establishment, Investigation and Report

If consultations between the parties fail, the party seeking the consultations (the complainant) may request the DSB to establish a panel to investigate, report and resolve the dispute. The DSB must establish such a panel upon request, unless the DSB expressly decides by consensus not to establish the panel. Since an "inverted consensus" is required to reject the establishment of the panel and the complainant member must be part of that consensus, it is almost guaranteed that a panel will be established. Roughly 100 panels were established in the first five years of operation of the DSU, and many more since then.

Almost any WTO member state may intervene in the dispute. No specific legal or trade interest in the dispute is required since every WTO member has a legal interest in seeing that WTO rules are observed. Hence, for example, the United States intervened in the *Bananas* dispute between Latin American exporters and the European Union. One measure of the significance of the dispute is how many and which WTO members join either side of the dispute, resulting in say seven states against ten.

The WTO Secretariat maintains a list of well-qualified persons who are available to serve as panelists, mainly international trade law specialists drawn from the world of law practice, the academe and government service. The panels are usually composed of three individuals from that list who are not citizens of either party. If the parties agree, a panel can be composed of five such individuals. The parties can also agree to appoint citizens of a party to a panel. Panelists may be either nongovernmental individuals or governmental officials, but they are to be selected so as to ensure their independence. Thus, there is a bias towards independent individuals who are not citizens of any party. If a citizen of a party is appointed, his government may not instruct that citizen how to vote, for the panelist must be independent. By the same reasoning, a governmental official of a non-party member state who is subject to instructions from his or her government would not seem to fit the profile of an independent panelist.

The WTO Secretariat proposes nominations of the panelists. Parties may not normally oppose the nominations, except for "compelling reasons." The parties are given twenty days to agree on the panelists and the composition of the panel. If such agreement is not forthcoming, the WTO Director-General is authorized to appoint the panelists, in consultation with other persons in the Secretariat.

Complaints brought to DSB panels can involve either violations of Covered Agreements, or non-violation nullification and impairment of benefits under the Covered Agreements. A prima facie case of nullification impairment arises when one member infringes upon the "obligations assumed under a Covered Agreement." Such infringement creates a presumption against the infringing member, but the presumption can be rebutted by a showing that the complaining member state has suffered no adverse effect from the infringement. A classic nullification and impairment complaint concerns use of government subsidies after tariff reductions cause increased imports. See the *Australian Subsidy* case, 2 GATT Panel B.I.S.D. 188 (1950).

The panels receive pleadings and rebuttals and hear oral arguments. Panels can also engage in fact development from sources outside those presented by the parties. Thus, the procedure has aspects familiar to civil law courts. A panel can, on its own initiative, request information, including from experts selected by the panel. It can also obtain confidential information in some circumstances from an administrative body which is part of the government of a member state, without any prior consent from that state. A panel can establish its own group of experts to provide reports on factual or scientific issues. In a series of rulings commencing with the *Shrimp-Turtles* decision in 1998, the WTO Appellate Body has affirmed the right of panels and itself to elect to receive unsolicited informational and argumentative briefs or letters from non-governmental organizations (NGOs), business groups and law firms representing persons interested in the dispute.

A panel is obligated to produce two objectively assessed written reports—an interim and a final report. These reports are normally drafted by the WTO Secretariat, subject to review by the panelists. A panel is supposed to submit a final written report to the DSB within six months of its establishment. The report will contain its findings of fact, findings of law, a decision and the rationale for its decision. Before the final report is issued, the panel is supposed to provide an interim report to the parties. The purpose of this interim report is to apprize the parties of the panel's current analysis of the issues and to permit the parties to comment on that analysis. The final report of the panel need not change any of the findings or conclusions in its interim report, unless the panel is persuaded to do so by a party's comments. However, if it is not so persuaded, it is obligated to explain in its final report why not. At this writing, well over 200 WTO panel reports have been issued.

The decisions in panel reports are final as to issues of fact. The decisions in panel reports are not necessarily final as to issues of law. Panel decisions on issues of law are subject to review by the Appellate Body, which is Phase 3, and explained below. Any party can appeal a panel report, and appeals are usually taken.

Phase 3, Appellate Review of the Panel Report

Appellate review of panel reports is available at the request of any party, unless the DSB rejects that request by an "inverted consensus." There is no threshold requirement for an appellant to present a substantial substantive legal issue. Thus, most panel decisions are appealed as a matter of course. However, the Appellate Body can only review the panel reports on questions of law or legal interpretation.

The Appellate Body (AB) is a unique institution in the international trade organization and its process. GATT 1947 had nothing comparable to it. The Appellate Body is composed of seven members (or judges) who are appointed by the DSB acting by consensus to four-year terms. Each judge may be reappointed, but only once, to a second four-year term. Each judge is to be a recognized authority on international trade law and the Covered Agreements. To date, Appellate Body members have been drawn mostly from the academe and retired justices. They have come from Germany, Japan, Egypt, India, New Zealand, the Philippines, Argentina, China, the United States and other WTO member nations.

The review of any panel decision must be performed by three judges out of the seven. At this writing, the Trump Administration has been vetoed three appointments to the Appellate Body. Should this trend continue there will be only two AB members by late 2019 and it will not be able to function. Many consider this to be a "stealth war" by the United States against the rules-based multilateral WTO system and a way to avoid WTO review of highly debatable Trump tariffs. See Sections 1.17–1.19.

The parties do not have any influence over which judges are selected to review a particular panel report. There is a schedule, created by the Appellate Body, for the rotation for sitting of each of the judges. Thus, a party might try to appear before a favored judge by timing the start of the dispute settlement process to arrive at the Appellate Body at the right moment on the rotation schedule, but this limited approach has major difficulties.

The Appellate Body receives written submissions from the parties and has 60, or in some cases 90, days in which to render its decision. The Appellate Body review is limited to issues of law and legal interpretation. The panel decision may be upheld, modified, or reversed by the Appellate Body decision. Appellate Body decisions are anonymous, and ex parte communications are not permitted. Appellate Body decisions do not represent binding precedent. That said, many have observed a desire on the part of the Appellate Body to achieve consistency and a willingness to discuss its prior rulings when rendering decisions.

Phase 4, Adoption of the Panel or Appellate Body Decision

Appellate Body determinations are submitted to the DSB. Panel decisions which are not appealed are also submitted to the DSB. Once either type of decision is submitted, the DSB must automatically adopt them without modification or amendment at its next meeting unless the decision is rejected by all members of the DSB acting by "inverted consensus", which has never happened.

An alternative to Phases 2 through 4 is arbitration, if both parties agree. The arbitration must be binding on the parties, and there is no appeal from the arbitral tribunal's decision to the DSB or Appellate Body.

Phase 5, Implementation of the WTO Decision

Once a panel or Appellate Body decision is adopted by the DSB, implementation is a three-step process. In the first step, the member found to have a measure which violates its WTO obligations has "a reasonable time" (usually 15 months) to bring those measures into conformity with its WTO obligations. That remedy is the preferred one, and this form of implementation is the principal goal of the WTO dispute settlement system. To date, most disputes have resulted in compliance in this manner.

If the adequacy of compliance is disputed, such disputes typically return to the WTO panel that rendered decision on the merits. The panel then determines, acting as an arbitrator, the amount (if any) of authorized retaliation. The retaliation process is discussed below.

Phase 6, Compensation or Authorized Retaliation

Both "compensation" and "retaliation" provide only for indirect enforcement of DSB decisions. There is no mechanism for direct enforcement by the WTO of its decisions through WTO orders to suspend trade obligations.

Compensation

If the violating measures are not brought into WTO conformity within a reasonable time, the parties proceed to attempt to negotiate an agreement on monetary or tariff compensation granted by the party in violation to the injured party. Such compensation could comprise tariff concessions over and above those already available under the WTO Covered Agreements. See Section 1.0. The nature, scope, amount and duration of these additional tariff concessions is at the negotiating parties' discretion, but each side must agree that the final compensation package is fair and is properly related to the injury caused by the violating measures.

Arguably, tariff concessions might need to be extended under MFN principles to all WTO members. That is perhaps why few such compensation agreements have ever been achieved. By making cash payments, the United States compensated most of the WTO membership after losing a dispute to Antigua about whether it had "reserved" (excepted) Internet gambling from coverage under the GATS. *See* Section 1.9. The United States also financially compensated the EU in a copyright dispute involving small business use of music, and Brazil after losing a significant subsidies dispute concerning cotton. *See* Section 1.15.

Authorized Retaliation

If the parties cannot agree on an appropriate amount of compensation within twenty days, the party injured by the violating measures typically seeks authority from the DSB to retaliate against the party whose measures violated its WTO obligations. In other words, complainant seeks authority to suspend some of its WTO obligations in regard to the respondent. The retaliation must ordinarily be within the same sector and agreement as the violating measure. "Sector" is sometimes broadly defined, as all trade in goods, and sometimes narrowly defined, as in individual services in the Services Sectoral Classification List. "Agreement" is also broadly defined. All the agreements listed in Annex IA to the WTO Agreement are considered a single agreement.

If retaliation within the sector and agreement of the violating measure is considered insufficient compensation, the complainant may seek suspension of its obligations across sectors and agreements. This is known as "cross-sector retaliation, arguably the "nuclear option" in WTO dispute settlement (see below).

The DSB must grant the complainant's request to retaliate within 30 days unless all WTO members reject it through an "inverted consensus." (Article 22.6, D.S.U.) However, the respondent may object to the level or scope of the retaliation. The issues raised by the objection will be examined by either the Appellate Body or by an arbitrator. The respondent has a right, even if arbitration was not used in Phases 2 through 4, to have an arbitrator review in Phase 5 the appropriateness of the complainant's proposed level and scope of retaliation. The arbitrator will also examine whether the proper procedures and criteria to establish retaliation have been followed. The Phase 5 arbitration is final and binding, and the arbitrator's decision is not subject to DSB review.

In addition to objecting to the level of authorized retaliation, the responding WTO member may simultaneously challenge the assertion of noncompliance (Article 21.5, D.S.U.). This challenge will ordinarily be heard by the original panel and must be resolved within 90 days. Thus the request for authorized retaliation and objections thereto could conceivably be accomplished before noncompliance is formally determined. In practice, WTO dispute settlement has melded these conflicting procedures such that compliance and retaliation issues are decided together, typically by the original panel.

Retaliation in Action

Retaliation has rarely been authorized and even less rarely imposed. The amount of a U.S. retaliation permitted against the EU after the WTO *Bananas* and *Beef Hormones* decisions were not implemented by the EU was contested. The arbitration tribunals for this issue were the original WTO panels, which did not allow the entire amount of the almost $700 million in retaliatory tariffs proposed by the United States. The U.S. was authorized and levied retaliatory tariffs amounting to about $300 million against European goods because of the EU failure to implement those WTO decisions.

Since 2000, Congress has authorized rotating WTO retaliatory tariffs in "carousel" fashion upon different goods. The threat of carousel retaliation contributed to an April 2001 settlement of the *Bananas* dispute. In 2009, a four-year settlement of the *Beef Hormones* dispute was reached. The U.S. gets a higher quota to export hormone-free beef to the EU in return for phasing out its retaliatory tariffs on EU goods. The U.S. threat of carousel sanctions was again instrumental to this settlement.

Perhaps the most dramatic use of retaliation occurred in a tax subsidy dispute. The amount of EU retaliation permissible after the U.S. lost (for the second time) under WTO subsidy rules concerning Internal Revenue Code extraterritorial export tax preferences (FISCs) was disputed. A WTO panel, serving as an arbitrator, authorized approximately $4 *billion* in EU retaliation against U.S. exports. This retaliation commenced in March of 2004 and escalated monthly until the U.S. capitulated by amending the I.R.C. late in 2004.

Cross-Sector Retaliation

In a landmark ruling, a WTO panel acting as an arbitrator authorized Ecuador to remove protection of intellectual property rights regarding geographical indicators, copyrights and industrial designs on European Union goods for sale in Ecuador. This authorization was part of Ecuador's $200 million compensation in the *Bananas* dispute. The WTO panel acknowledged that Ecuador imports mostly capital goods and raw materials from the European Union and that imposing retaliatory tariffs on them would adversely harm its manufacturing industries. This risk supported "cross-retaliation" under Article 22.3 of the DSU outside the sector of the EU trade violation.

Allowance of cross-sector IP retaliation was probably the most critical driver behind the 2001 settlement of the *Bananas* dispute. Cross-sector retaliation was also authorized against the U.S. after losing a GATS dispute to Antigua on Internet gambling restraints.

The United States settled this dispute with nearly all WTO members save Antigua via compensation. At this writing, Antigua is still debating whether and how to retaliate.

§ 1.15   U.S. Involvement in WTO Disputes

The WTO dispute resolution process has been invoked more frequently than many expected. The United States has been a complainant or a respondent in hundreds of disputes since 1995. It has won about 86% of the disputes when filing complaints, and has lost about 75% when responding to WTO complaints. The U.S. track record on compliance with WTO decisions is generally good, though not always with alacrity despite repeated losses (notably regarding zeroing in antidumping proceedings, see Folsom, *Principles of International Trade Law*). The U.S. has on occasion only complied after authorized retaliation by the complaining party. Sometimes the U.S. has avoided compliance via compensation.

The U.S. and the EU have been involved as the complainant or respondent in roughly 80% of all WTO disputes since it became operational in 1995, with China disputes on the rise since 2001.

The United States has settled a number of disputes prior to WTO panel decisions, and remains in consultation on other disputes that may be decided by a WTO panel. For the latest summary of all WTO disputes, including many not involving the United States, see www.wto.org.

The sampling of disputes summarized below illustrates the WTO dispute settlement process in action.

United States WTO Disputes

The United States lost a dispute initiated by Venezuela and Brazil concerning U.S. standards for reformulated and conventional gasoline. The offending U.S. law was amended to conform to the WTO ruling. It won on a complaint initiated jointly with Canada and the European Union regarding Japanese taxes on alcoholic beverages. Japan subsequently changed its law. When Costa Rica complained about U.S. restraints on imports of underwear, the U.S. let the restraints expire prior to any formal DSB ruling at the WTO. Similar results were reached when India complained of U.S. restraints on wool shirts and blouses. The United States won a major dispute with Canada concerning trade and subsidies for periodicals This celebrated *Sports Illustrated* dispute proved that WTO remedies could be used to avoid Canada's cultural industries exclusion under NAFTA 1994. See Section 4.1.

In the longstanding *Bananas* dispute noted above, the United States joined Ecuador, Guatemala, Honduras and Mexico in successfully challenging EU import restraints against so-called "dollar bananas." The EU failed to comply with the Appellate Body's ruling. Retaliatory measures were authorized and imposed on EU goods by the United States, along with cross-sector IP retaliation by Ecuador and others. In April 2001, the *Bananas* dispute was settled on terms that generally converted EU quotas to tariffs by 2006, though limited preferential quotas for ACP exporters were retained. A patent law complaint by the U.S. against India prevailed in the DSB and ultimately brought changes in Indian law regarding pharmaceuticals and agricultural chemicals.

In *Beef Hormones,* also noted above, the European Union lost twice before the Appellate Body for want of proof of a "scientific basis" for its ban on hormone beef. It refused to alter its import restraints and absorbed $200 million in retaliatory tariffs on selected exports to Canada and the United States. In 2009, an arguably pro-European settlement was reached. The U.S. effectively got a higher quota to export hormone-free beef to the EU, in return for phasing out over four years its retaliatory tariffs on EU goods. The U.S. threat of carousel sanctions, i.e. rotating goods subject to retaliation, was instrumental to this settlement. Meanwhile, because the U.S. beef industry failed to timely ask for a continuation of the retaliatory tariffs, the Federal Circuit ruled in 2010 that they expired in 2007. Refunds were given to importers of EU products who paid those tariffs.

The United States prevailed against Argentina regarding tariffs and taxes on footwear, textiles and apparel. It lost a challenge (strongly supported by Kodak) to Japan's distribution rules regarding photo film and paper. In this dispute the U.S. elected *not* to appeal the adverse WTO panel ruling to the Appellate Body. In contrast, the European Union took an appeal which reversed an adverse panel ruling on its customs classification of computer equipment. The U.S. had commenced this proceeding. Opponents in many disputes, Japan, the United States and the European Union united to complain that Indonesia's National Car Program was discriminatory and in breach of several WTO agreements. They prevailed and Indonesia altered its program.

India, Malaysia, Pakistan and Thailand teamed up to challenge U.S. shrimp import restraints enacted to protect endangered sea turtles. The WTO Appellate Body generally upheld their complaint and the U.S. has moved to comply. The adequacy of U.S. compliance is being challenged by Malaysia. The European Union and the United States jointly opposed Korea's discriminatory taxes on alcoholic beverages. This challenge was successful and Korea now imposes flat non-discriminatory taxes. The United States also complained of

Japan's quarantine, testing and other agricultural import rules. The U.S. won at the WTO and Japan has changed its procedures.

In a semiconductor dumping dispute, Korea successfully argued that the U.S. was not in compliance with the WTO Antidumping Agreement. The United States amended its law, but Korea has instituted further proceedings alleging that these amendments are inadequate. The United States did likewise after Australia lost a subsidies dispute relating to auto leather. The reconvened WTO panel ruled that Australia had indeed failed to conform to the original adverse DSB decision. A U.S. challenge concerning India's quotas on imports of agricultural, textile and industrial products was upheld. India and the United States subsequently reached agreement on a timeline for removal of these restraints.

Closer to home, New Zealand and the United States complained of Canada's import/export rules regarding milk. Losing at the WTO, Canada agreed to a phased removal of the offending measures. The United States also won against Mexico in an antidumping dispute involving corn syrup, but lost a "big one" when the Appellate Body determined that export tax preferences granted to "Foreign Sales Corporations" of U.S. companies were illegal.

Another "big one" went in favor of the United States. The European Union challenged the validity under the DSU of unilateral retaliation under Section 301 of the Trade Act of 1974. Section 301 has been something of a bete noire in U.S. trade law, but the WTO panel affirmed its legality in light of Presidential undertakings to administer it in accordance with U.S. obligations to adhere to multilateral WTO dispute settlement. To be sure, this ruling will be cited in WTO challenges by China against President Trump's Section 301 tariffs. See Section 1.18.

U.S. involvement in WTO dispute settlement continues to be extensive. The Appellate Body ruled that U.S. countervailing duties against British steel based upon pre-privatization subsidies were unlawful. The European Union prevailed before a WTO panel in its challenge of the U.S. Antidumping Act of 1916, since repealed. U.S. complaints against Korean beef import restraints and procurement practices were upheld. Canada's patent protection term was also invalidated by the WTO under a U.S. complaint. European Union complaints concerning U.S. wheat gluten quotas and the royalty free small business provisions of the Fairness in Music Licensing Act of 1998 have been sustained. The *Wheat Gluten* dispute questions the legality of U.S. "causation" rules in escape clause proceedings under Section 201 of the Trade Act of 1974.

A WTO Panel ruled that the Byrd Amendment violated the WTO antidumping and subsidy codes. The Byrd Amendment (Continued Dumping and Subsidy Act of 2000) authorizes the Customs Service to forward AD and CVD duties to affected domestic producers for qualified expenses. Eleven WTO members including the EU, Canada and Mexico challenged the Amendment. This ruling was affirmed by the WTO Appellate Body and retaliation was authorized. Late in 2005, the U.S. repealed the Byrd Amendment, subject to a contested two-year phase out. The Appellate Body also ruled against Section 211 of the Omnibus Appropriations Act of 1998 denying trademark protection in connection with confiscated assets (the "HAVANA CLUB" dispute). U.S. compliance with these rulings has been slow in forthcoming. The United States and other complainants prevailed in a WTO proceeding against Indian local content and trade balancing requirements for foreign auto manufacturers. These requirements violated the TRIMs agreement.

The European Union commenced raising tariffs against U.S. goods under the WTO retaliation authorized out of the FSC/export tax subsidy dispute. Monthly increments were planned until either the U.S. complied or the EU reached the maximum of roughly $4 billion annually it was authorized to retaliate. In the Fall of 2004, the United States repealed the extraterritorial income exclusion and the EU subsequently removed its retaliatory tariffs. Antigua-Barbuda won a WTO panel ruling under the GATS against certain U.S. Internet gambling restraints. Retaliation was authorized, and the U.S. settled with nearly all members by offering compensation. The U.S. won a panel decision against Mexico's exorbitant telecom interconnection rates, but lost a 2004 cotton subsidy challenge by Brazil. Retaliation by Brazil was authorized.

The United States also lost a second dispute with the EU about pre-privatization countervailable subsidies, in particular the legality of the U.S. "same person" methodology. The U.S. won a SPS dispute against Japanese quarantine of U.S. apples, while losing an important softwood lumber "zeroing" methodology complaint brought by Canada. The U.S. repeatedly lost on zeroing disputes brought by other WTO members before grudgingly amending its antidumping rules. The Mexico-United States "sugar war" came to a head before the Appellate Body. Mexico's 20% soft drink tax on beverages not using cane sugar, its 20% distribution tax on those beverages, and related bookkeeping requirements were found to violate GATT Article III and not exempt under Article XX(d).

Subsequently, the two countries settled their dispute by agreeing, effective in 2008, to free trade in sugar and high fructose corn syrup. Sugar remains one of the most highly protected sectors of the U.S. economy sheltered behind quotas dating back to the 1930s. Commonly triple the world commodity price of sugar, U.S. sugar quotas drove Hershey Chocolates among others to move its factories abroad. The CIA reports that sugar producers in Jamaica switched to marijuana as a consequence of U.S. sugar import quotas.

The U.S. failed to persuade the Appellate Body to require the European Union under GATT Article X (3) to undertake a major overhaul of its customs law system targeting inconsistencies therein among the 28 member states. The United States lost a cotton subsidy challenge by Brazil. The United States agreed to pay $147 million annually to provide technical assistance to Brazilian cotton farmers. In return, Brazil has suspended retaliatory tariffs and cross-sector IP sanctions authorized by the WTO because of U.S. cotton subsidy violations. In 2009, a WTO panel ruled that Airbus had received $20 billion in illegal EU "launch" subsidies. By 2010, that same panel found Boeing the recipient of $5 billion in federal research contract subsidies that violated the WTO Subsidies Code. These longstanding disputes remain ongoing and are frequently cited by Trump administration critics of the WTO dispute settlement process.

§ 1.16   China Involvement in WTO Disputes

China, a member since 2001, is involved in a growing number of WTO disputes. Here is a sampling of those disputes.

Canada, the European Union and the United States complained against Chinese duties on imported auto parts (10 percent) that rose to those on complete autos (25 percent) if the imported parts exceeded a fixed percentage of the final vehicle content or price, or if specific combinations of imported auto parts were used in the final vehicle. In addition, extensive record keeping, reporting and verification requirements were imposed when Chinese auto companies used imported parts. In July of 2008, a WTO panel ruled that these "internal charges" violated Articles III (2) and III (4) of the GATT and China's accession commitments. The core Panel ruling, affirmed by the Appellate Body, found China's auto parts measures discriminatory in favor of domestic producers, a violation of the national treatment standard for taxes and regulations. This ruling marked the first time since China's admission in 2001 that it was held in breach of its WTO commitments and obligations.

Less than one month after losing this dispute, China enacted a clever "green tax" on gas-guzzling autos, most of which just happen to be imported. The sales tax on cars with engine capacities over 4.1 litres has been doubled to 40%. Autos with engines between 3 and 4.1 litres are taxed at 25%, up from 15%. Most Chinese-made cars have engines with 2.5 litres or less. Autos with engines between 1 and 3 litres remain taxed at 8% and 10%. The smallest cars with engines below 1 litre have their sales tax reduced from 3 to 1 percent. This green tax seemingly was intended to achieve protective results similar to China's Auto Parts tariff structure.

Other disputes challenging China's compliance with WTO law have been undertaken. They concern China's auto export subsidies and CVDs on auto imports, protection and enforcement of intellectual property rights (2009 WTO panel ruled against China), trade and distribution of publications and audiovisual entertainment products and services (2009 Appellate Body ruled against China), commodity export tariffs and restrictions (2012 WTO Appellate Body ruled against China), application of Chinese AD to U.S. grain-oriented flat rolled steel (GOES) (2012 WTO Appellate Body ruled against China) and discriminatory treatment of foreign electronic payment services (2012 WTO panel ruled against China). China's record of compliance with these WTO rulings resembles that of the U.S., somewhat spotty and not always prompt.

China, in turn, has challenged U.S. safeguard measures applied to Chinese steel exports (2010 WTO Panel rejected challenge) and tires (2011 WTO Panel rejected challenge). It has challenged U.S. antidumping and countervailing duties on paper products from China (2011 WTO Panel ruled against U.S. dual assessment of AD and CVD duties), as well as U.S. AD on Chinese solar panels. China has also applied AD duties to U.S. exports, *e.g.* chicken.

In a major dispute, China challenged in 2017 continued U.S. and EU application of nonmarket economy rules in antidumping disputes. China has also challenged President Trump's solar panel and clothes washers safeguard tariffs, as well as Trump's "national security" steel and aluminum tariffs. See Sections 1.17 and 1.18. Numerous U.S. CVDs against a range of Chinese goods were successfully challenged in 2018 on procedural grounds by China before a WTO panel. Meanwhile, the United States is challenging Chinese export restrictions on raw materials and alleged unlawful subsidization of aluminum, rice, wheat and corn.

The Trump Administration notably filed in 2018 a WTO complaint, joined by Japan and the European Union, against alleged patent violations of Articles 3 and 28 of TRIPs. These allegations assert that foreign patent holders are unable to stop Chinese licensees from continuing to use patented technology after licenses expire. They also assert Chinese discrimination against and less favorable mandatory adverse contract terms for imported foreign technology. The U.S. specifically cites four Chinese laws as the source of these TRIPs violations: The PRC Foreign Trade Law, Contract Law, Chinese-Foreign Equity Joint Venture Law, and the PRC

Regulations on the Administration of the Import and Export of Technologies.

§ 1.17 America First and Trump Tariffs

Trump Tariffs

President Trump has imposed a range of new tariffs, that is to say taxes, on U.S. imports since taking office. For details and issues concerning the U.S. and WTO trade law referenced below that underlie these tariffs, see Folsom, *Principles of International Trade Law*.

Softwood Lumber and Paper

Picking up a decades-long dispute, the Trump Administration quickly levied 20% NAFTA and WTO enabled countervailing duty (CVD) tariffs against Canadian softwood lumber. U.S. timber companies are smiling while U.S. home builders face rising costs, mostly passed on to home buyers. Canada covered the losses to its lumber companies, and expects to win as it has in the past on NAFTA and WTO appeals.

A 22% antidumping tariff (AD) on Canadian magazine paper was levied by the Trump Administration in 2018, then withdrawn by request of the complaining firm, Ohio's Verso Corp. after it settled with Canadian exporters for a $42 million share of the AD tariffs that will be refunded by U.S. Customs to them.

Clothes Washers

In 2018, President Trump dusted off a little-used WTO-approved Safeguard remedy allowing temporary trade restraints when imports surge causing serious damage or its threat. A three year 20 to 50% Safeguard tariff has been imposed since 2018 on clothes washers from any source except Canada, plus up to a 50% tariff on washer parts, an anti-screwdriver assembly plant tactic. Developing countries eligible for U.S. GSP tariff treatment representing less than 3% of U.S. washer imports are also exempt, a provision not benefiting Thailand at over 3% for example.

"Country hopping" in Asia by Korea's LG and Samsung companies, the main culprits in this scenario, had previously avoided country-specific U.S. AD tariffs. Whirlpool USA, the complainant, is increasing production, while the two Korean companies, after raising their prices in the U.S., built plants in the USA.

When utilizing Safeguard tariffs, the U.S. must consider "compensating" the exporting countries and the EU, all of which are seeking such relief. Those same parties have filed WTO challenges asserting the illegality of this Trump Administration Safeguard tariff, and enacted comparable Safeguard tariffs to protect their markets from diversionary sales from other exporting countries hit by the Trump tariffs.

Solar Panels

The Trump Administration has imposed a four year 30%, declining to 15%, Safeguard tariff on solar panels from any source (except over 3% GSP developing nations). These tariffs mostly target China's large volume, subsidized low price exports that have helped create a large number of solar panel installation jobs in the USA, along with plenty of renewable energy. Korea, Malaysia, Thailand and Vietnam also notably export solar panels to the U.S., some of their production a result of country hopping Chinese investments. Compensation claims and illegality challenges by exporting nations are again pending at the WTO.

The solar complaint was filed by two bankrupt U.S. producers, one Chinese owned, the other German owned, after a rash of U.S. solar panel companies left the market. The solar panel Safeguard tariffs will generally increase solar panel costs and reduce installation jobs. That said, JinkoSolar of Shanghai announced plans in 2018 to build solar panels in a new Jacksonville Florida plant to supply Florida Power and Light with some seven million panels over four years, provided Asian made solar cells are admitted to the USA. Other investors, mindful of Trump's tariffs and immediate tax write-offs, have also announced plans to expand solar panel operations in America. The big winner has been First Solar with plants in Vietnam and Malaysia. First Solar is exempt from the U.S. solar tariffs because of its different technology.

Steel and Aluminum National Security Tariffs

Unilaterally invoking in 2018 what many call a "nuclear" trade remedy option, the Trump Administration adopted a 25% "national security" tariff on steel imports for an indefinite duration. On aluminum imports there is a 10% national security tariff. The Department of Commerce Reports on invocation of these tariffs cite the "welfare" of these U.S. industries as "critical" to "minimum operations of the economy and government". Seeking to ensure that 80% of U.S. capacity is being used, both tariffs were proclaimed under a long dormant provision of Section 232 of the Trade Expansion Act of 1962, upheld as constitutional in *American Institute for Intl Steel v. U.S.* (Ct. Intl. Trade 3/25/19). Other countries, fearing diversion of steel and aluminum no longer gaining entry to the U.S., are scrambled to impose their own trade restrictions on these metals.

U.S. officials also assert that China exports steel to Vietnam, Korea, Malaysia and other Asian countries where minimal galvanizing, re-rolling and color-coating of rolled steel are said to constitute a "substantial transformations". Such products are then labeled as originating from those Asian nations, thus escaping U.S. tariffs and import controls. In addition, outright customs fraud by brazen freight forwarders is alleged as Asian countries repack, relabel and transship Chinese goods destined for the USA.

Contrary to other Trump Administration officials, U.S. Defense Department Secretary Mattis maintained that these import tariffs actually "impair" national security, and warned of a "negative impact" on key allies. The Economist magazine, noting that the vast majority of U.S. steel and aluminum imports are for civilian purposes, scathingly referred to the Trump administration claim of acting in the name national security as "spurious".

Canada at about 17% is the number one source of U.S. steel imports, followed by Brazil, Korea, Mexico, Russia, Turkey, Japan, Germany, Taiwan and in tenth place, China. Canada supplies nearly 50% of all U.S. imports of aluminum, followed by Russia and the United Arab Emirates. China, already under AD and CVD steel and aluminum U.S. tariffs, is a minor exporter of steel and aluminum goods to the USA, though critics maintain its overcapacities drive down market prices.

The many United States manufacturers using steel and aluminum in their goods, from cars to high-tech components to aluminum cans, have argued these tariffs will raise costs and consumer prices, and result in large job losses. For example, layoffs arrived swiftly at the American Keg Company, the only U.S. producer of stainless steel beer kegs and Caterpillar maintains the tariffs cost it over $100 million in 2018. That said, a few new and previously closed U.S. steel mills have announced plans to advance production with small increases in jobs. Bottom line: Many more U.S. jobs are at stake among fabricators of goods using imported steel and aluminum than among U.S. producers of those metals.

Steel import tariffs have been imposed by every U.S. President since Ronald Reagan, including Barack Obama. Steel exports almost always increase from exempt countries, frequently for example Mexico and Canada. One study estimates that when President George W. Bush imposed 30% steel Safeguard tariffs in 2002, overall about 200,000 steel-related jobs were lost, a decidedly America Last outcome.

Canada and Mexico were initially exempted from the steel and aluminum tariffs, which took effect March 23, 2018, pending the outcome of NAFTA's re-negotiation. Korea, the EU, Brazil, Argentina, and Australia got temporary "exemptions" to May 1, 2018 from the Treasury Department. Japan, under continuing pressure to negotiate a bilateral FTA with the U.S., did not. Korea's exemption became permanent under KORUS II (see Chapter 6), subject to export quotas of dubious WTO legality. The remaining May 1st exemptions were extended to June 1, 2018. Take it or leave it agreements with Australia, Brazil and Argentina followed the KORUS II pattern, though Brazil's steel makers chose export quotas while its aluminum sector agreed to a 10 % U.S. tariff.

The problem with quota systems is that traders and speculators can game them by stockpiling goods, subsequently flooding markets when quota periods open. This produces shortages and even higher profits as the quota time limit arrives, only to start the process all over again. Quotas may also shift exporters to high-value products such as luxury autos versus economy cars, thus upgrading import competition. Broadly speaking, the use of quotas is significantly restricted by WTO law. See Section 1.6.

Canada, Mexico and the EU all promised to retaliate if U.S. steel and aluminum tariffs ultimately applied to its exports. June 1st arrived and the Trump Administration announced steel and aluminum "national security" tariffs against these longtime trade, military and political allies. They in turn responded with WTO complaints and announced equivalent value "rebalancing tariffs" on U.S. exports to take effect by July 1, 2018. Trump's steel and aluminum tariffs continue to apply to Mexico and Canada even after the signing of the USMCA 2018 re-negotiation of NAFTA 1994.

Steel and aluminum prices in the United States have risen significantly behind the Trump tariff wall. Specific high-need steel and aluminum imports may be permitted by Department of Commerce, and thousands of petitions have been filed by U.S. importers. These petitions can be opposed, often successfully by the four major U.S. steel producers (Nucor, U.S. Steel, AK Steel and Timken Steel), arguing they can provide the goods in question. A limited number of such petitions have been granted. Thus the micro-management of U.S. steel imports has opened up anti-competitive forces.

Responses to Trump's Steel and Aluminum Tariffs, Are Autos Next?

Retaliatory "rebalancing" tariffs against the U.S. steel and aluminum tariffs are underway or expected, with U.S. agricultural exports a prime target. India, Japan, Russia, Turkey, and others are retaliating in addition to the EU, Mexico, Canada and China (below). The EU vocally created a 10-page target $3.4 billion rebalancing list that included politically precise retaliation targets: U.S. made jeans (California), Harley Davidsons (Wisconsin), boats (South Carolina), orange juice (Florida), peanut butter (Georgia), bourbon whiskey (Kentucky), cranberries (Wisconsin and Massachusetts) and corn (Iowa).

Mexico's list of retaliatory U.S. exports includes steel, cheese, Tennessee Whiskey, pork, apples, grapes, cranberries, lamps and potatoes. Mexico, by the way, is the biggest U.S. apple export market. Canada's $12.8 billion list covers U.S. steel, aluminum, sailboats, beer kegs, yogurt, chocolate (hello Hershey), orange juice and other products. Insulted at the idea that it is a national security risk to the USA, the Trump team might wish to recall that Canada buys even more U.S. farm goods than China. Canada has also been planning new pipelines to ship its oil and gas to Asia.

With less noise volume, citing U.S. "wanton destruction" of the WTO trading system, China undertook a review of its huge U.S. sorghum, soybean and hog imports, creating near-panic conditions in the U.S. farm belt. U.S. colleges and universities, increasingly dependent on high-paying Chinese students to make ends meet, are shaking their heads in concern. Boeing, the number one consumer of aluminum in America, is worried about potential lost sales if China retaliates, and so is Boeing's extensive workforce. Farm and earth moving machinery makers John Deere and Caterpillar joined the crowd of U.S., industry opponents. These fears carried over to the pending China-specific Section 301 tariffs.

Fortunately, China's retaliation to the U.S. steel and aluminum tariffs was measured: $3 billion new 15% to 25% rebalancing tariffs on roughly 128 commodities including U.S. fruit, nuts, pork, ginseng, ethanol, wine, scrap aluminum and steel pipe exports, approximately matching the $3 billion in U.S. Safeguard tariffs applicable to Chinese exports of steel and aluminum. The pork tariffs at 25% hit Trump country states like Iowa, North Carolina and Indiana especially hard. As the steel and aluminum tariffs have cascaded through U.S. metal manufacturers' supply chains, costs and prices have risen. Some firms are moving production out of the USA to lower cost centers abroad. So too are Chinese firms caught up in the U.S.-PRC tariff war (below), moving particularly to Southeast Asia and even Mexico.

In turn, President Trump in June of 2018 ordered a Section 232 report on the national security implications of U.S. imports of automobiles, trucks and auto parts. About a quarter of all the cars sold in the USA are imported, with Mazda, Subaru, Jaguar, VW and BMW high on the list of companies with minimal or no U.S. production. The President has threatened market bending and inflationary 25% auto tariffs. By country, Japanese, European Union, Chinese, Canadian and Mexican auto exports are at greatest risk.

The latter two have protection via exemption quotas under the USMCA 2018. See Chapter 6.

Japan and the EU, lacking such protections, have commenced serious negotiations on trade with the United States. The threat of auto tariffs clearly brought them to the table. See Chapters 5 and 3. The Report on autos and U.S. national security was completed in late February 2019. It was not released. President Trump has until late May 2019 to decide whether to take action on national security grounds against auto imports into the USA.

U.S. invocation of the national security nuclear option, largely (but arguably not entirely) a self-judging blank check under GATT/ WTO (see Section 1.1) and nearly all free trade agreement rules, provoked a poignant reaction from Mario Draghi, head of the EU Central Bank: "If you put tariffs against your allies, one wonders who the enemies are."

Murmurs of "trade wars", described by President Trump as "good, and easy to win", emerged everywhere after the U.S. steel and aluminum Section 232 tariffs. Indeed, just when trade experts believe the United States, Japan, Korea, Canada and the EU should be uniting their strength to counter China as a trade and technology superpower, President Trump has been making that extremely difficult. Why is an excellent question?

§ 1.18   A Tech-Driven U.S.-China Tariff War

Trump and China

Few countries took more abuse than China in the U.S. Presidential election race of 2016, particularly for its massive trade surplus in goods and services with the United States, $337 billion in 2017. Roughly 20% of all U.S. imports come from China, and several studies affirm China's adverse impact since joining the WTO in 2001 on U.S. manufacturing jobs.

Upon taking office, President Trump proceeded to question U.S. adherence to the "One China" policy which suggests that Taiwan is not independent from the PRC. It was only after President Trump reaffirmed this Policy that President Xi Xinping visited him in Florida for what seemed to be an amicable meeting. Subsequently, President Trump withdrew, contrary to numerous prior tweets and pronouncements, assertions that China was a currency manipulator. Perhaps he realized that China had in recent years spent about $1 trillion from its reserves keeping the Yuan up in the market.

President Trump then waited for China's support against North Korea, which had been mostly limited to U.N.-derived trade sanctions. Relatively minor foreign trade and investment law changes were made by China, and its control and militarized "development" of the South China Sea advanced.

The U.S. Section 301 Report on China

After a lengthy study by the USTR of China's trade and technology acquisition practices, generally treated as not falling within WTO jurisdiction, President Trump invoked another dormant U.S. **unilateral** trade remedy, Section 301 of the Trade Act of 1974. Section 301 focuses on "unreasonable", "unjustifiable" and "discriminatory" trade practices of foreign countries. The President has broad powers to respond with tariffs and trade restraints against "actionable" Section 301 conduct. In addition, expanded restrictions on Chinese tech and other investments and acquisitions in the USA were recommended in the USTR's report.

Apart from outright IP, trade secret and confidential business information theft, often via state-sponsored hacking, the USTR report zeroed in on forced or pressured technology transfers (TT) inside China. One such technique is associated with China's mandatory joint venture rules (autos, insurance, cloud computing, telecommunications) as a condition of access to China's vast market.

Forced disclosure of software source codes and data localization rules under China's recent Cybersecurity Law were noted in the USTR report. So was mandatory R & D in China, technology R & D and acquisition inside the USA, Europe and elsewhere, the Made in China 2025 ultra-high-tech program (see Folsom, et al., *International Business Transactions: A Problem-Oriented Course Book* (2019), Problem 9.4), and Chinese control of licensing and improvement technology. The report also cited technology transfers undertaken "voluntarily" by Microsoft, Qualcomm, Apple and others.

A Tech-Driven Tariff War

Round One. Citing the USTR tech transfer report and the massive U.S. trade deficit with China, trade relations took a stormy tumble in March of 2018. The Trump Administration announced its intention to impose approximately $50 to $60 billion unilateral Section 301 tariffs of 25% on some 1300 Chinese exports, file a patent practices complaint against China at the WTO, and implement stringently restrictive policies against Chinese investments in the United States, especially in the tech field. That tariff amount roughly corresponds to what the Trump Administration claims Chinese "cheaters" have gained through technology theft and forced technology transfer practices.

The list of China imports targeted for these tariffs includes aircraft engines, vessels, heavy machinery, industrial robots, lithium-ion batteries, semiconductor production equipment, flat screen televisions, printers, household appliances, midsize cars, electric vehicles, printing equipment, base metals, medicines (insulin), medical equipment (defibrillators, pacemakers, replacement joints), machine tools, electrical equipment, chemicals, and select information and communication technology items. About 47% of all the TVs sold in the USA are imported from China, 83% of PC monitors, 34% of lithium batteries and substantial printer ink and cartridges. Prices on these and other listed items will rise noticeably. All totaled the U.S. list comprises about 10% of the roughly $500 billion Chinese exports in 2017 to the USA.

China's dependency on exports have dropped dramatically over the past decade from 35% to 19% of its GDP. This diminishes the impact and force of Trump's China tariffs. Less obviously, Asian (notably Japanese and Korean) suppliers of components that are incorporated into Chinese exports to the U.S. will also be collaterally hit if these tariffs materialize.

These Section 301 China tariffs were careful to try to reduce their punishing impact on retailers and consumers, especially shoppers in lower/middle end markets like Walmart and Target. China supplies roughly 42% of the clothing and 72% of the footwear sold in the United States. These items were not on the initial Section 301 China tariff list. Other items not on the initial list include: furniture, personal computers, laptops, and travel gear.

Round Two. Within 24 hours of the announcement of the list of President Trump's Section 301 China tariffs, the PRC released a 25% retaliatory tariff list on 106 U.S. exports valued at $50 to $60 billion, including: Soybeans, corn, wheat, beef, orange juice, chemicals, smaller aircraft (think Boeing), larger passenger vehicles and SUVs (think U.S.-made BMWs and Mercedes Benz), electric vehicles (think Tesla), auto parts, propane and cotton. All totaled the list comprises about 38% of U.S. exports in 2017 to the PRC. American farmers and ranchers let it be known they are not at all happy with their potential losses. Nearly 60% of U.S. exports of soybeans go to China, which immediately commenced restricting U.S. soybean shipments.

Simultaneously, China, having dramatically accelerated its antidumping/anti-subsidy investigation, announced 178.5% tariffs targeting roughly $1 billion annual sorghum exports from the USA. A "shot over the bow" you could say.

Round Three. Within 24 hours of publication of China's proposed retaliatory list and sorghum announcement, President Trump ordered the USTR to come up with a second list for an additional $100 to $200 billion U.S. tariffs on Chinese goods. China vowed absolutely, "no options ruled out", to retaliate again if and when this happened. $150 billion in Chinese tariffs on U.S. exports would exceed the entire value of the $137 billion U.S. exports of goods to China in 2017.

Round Four. China's response to Round Three was initially conciliatory. In a 2018 public lecture, stressing a "new phase of opening up", President Xi Xinping indicated that China's 25% tariff on auto imports would be reduced (it is now 15%). He also suggested that maximum foreign shareholdings in Chinese enterprises and mandatory joint ventures would be relaxed (notably for autos, below), protection of intellectual property would be increased (there is a new national IP Appeals Court), and that greater foreign access to China's financial sector would be (and was) undertaken. Shortly thereafter, all foreign auto companies were allowed to wholly own their operations starting in 2022, and for electrified car plants as of 2019.

President Trump was not conciliatory. In late September of 2018, $200 billion in additional 10% U.S. tariffs were made applicable to thousands of Chinese exports. These tariffs were set to rise to 25% by the end of the year. As a result, roughly half of all U.S. imports from China became subject to Trump tariffs. China responded the following day with $60 billion in 5% to 10% tariffs on thousands of U.S. exports. Trump in turn threatened to adopt $267 billion more tariffs on Chinese goods, essentially covering all the PRC's exports to the United States.

Unable to fully go tit-for-tat on tariffs, China is likely to consider other retaliatory measures. For example, the controlled value of the Chinese Yuan has drifted downwards almost 10%, roughly covering the initial 10% Round Three Trump tariffs of September 2018. Other options might include more reduced purchases of goods and services originating in the USA, and/or "geo-political" sanctions regarding the South China Sea, North Korea and elsewhere. It could commence a government encouraged "people's boycott" of travel to the USA and a general boycott of American goods, including Made in China U.S. brands (Apple, Ford, Chevrolet, KFC, Starbucks, Nike, P & G cosmetics). China has a history of "people's wars" against Japan in 2012 over a territorial dispute, the Philippines in 2016 after losing a South China Sea arbitration, and South Korea in 2017 when U.S. missiles were installed.

Or, in many opaque ways, the PRC could just simply make life difficult for U.S. firms operating in and outside the Middle Kingdom. Already, as the USTR's report noted, the PRC has restrained the use of VPNs (virtual private networks) by foreign businesses seeking to avoid government monitors and blocked website access via its Great Firewall. Chinese review of U.S. multinational mergers and acquisitions has stiffened. See R. Folsom, *Foreign Investment Law including Investor-State Arbitrations* in a Nutshell. China's ultimate trade war weapon is the $1.2 trillion in U.S. Treasuries it owns. Even a small reduction or threatened diminishment in those holdings would drive up U.S. interest rates and rock Wall Street. This would presumably also undermine China's U.S. Treasury Bond portfolio.

Round Four Truce. Starting December 1, 2018, China and the United States agreed to a 90-day truce (subsequently extended) in pursuit of reduced trade tensions. This truce postponed the raise in U.S. Round Four tariffs to 25% and China's Round Four retaliatory tariffs (above). China quickly reduced its tariffs on U.S. autos to from 40% to 15%, announced enhanced punishments and penalties for IP theft, noticeably downplayed its Made in China 2025 program, authorized new GMO imports, and re-commenced purchase of U.S. soybeans and natural gas. Relatively little progress was made early on concerning core U.S. issues, PRC subsidies and forced technology transfers.

Meanwhile the United States poured fuel on the flames of dispute. The United States announced a wave of cyber-theft allegations, including notably from Navy contractors, universities and the NIH. It also issued trade secret theft indictments, most prominently against China's global telecom giant, Huawei. On the day the truce was announced, U.S. authorities sought extradition from Canada of the Chief Financial Officer and daughter of Huawei's founder, asserting deliberate violations of U.S. export controls against Iran. China quickly took several Canadians in the PRC into custody.

China-U.S. Trade War Overview

Trump and Trade may represent a "tipping point" in global relations. Trump tariffs against the goods of steadfast allies and free trade partners lack strategic thinking in a world where the PRC will soon have the globe's biggest economy. U.S. farmers and others worry that export markets lost in this war may never return. To quote Nebraska Senator Ben Sasse: "This is dumb".

Playing a long game, China seems to perceive that its one-party, authoritarian state can endure more trade war punishment than the U.S. democracy.

§ 1.19 Trump and the World Trade Organization

The Trump tariffs noted above, imposed as countervailing, safeguard and national security duties, fall within the scope of WTO authorized trade remedy rules and are being challenged within its dispute settlement system. Note, however, that the Trump administration claims national security tariffs are not WTO justiciable. See Section 1.14. Trump Section 301 tariffs against China fail to follow the U.S. commitment to take trade disputes to the WTO, but the Administration argues that the tech issues with China fall outside the scope of the WTO package of agreements and therefore can be unilaterally imposed. On balance, Trump tariffs undermine the WTO as a trade organization, which seems to be exactly what the president and his staff intend.

The Trump Administration launched an extensive review and report on U.S. participation in the World Trade Organization (WTO), the ultimate rules-based multilateral agreement embraced by approximately 165 countries and customs territories. Special attention was given to WTO "most-favored-nation" trade principles, trade remedies and dispute resolution. That report was also highly critical of WTO procedures, specific trade remedy decisions, and especially "activism" and "overreach" on the part of the WTO Appellate Body.

President Obama blocked the reappointment of an Appellate Body member accused of "judicial overreach". In what amounts to a hostile act, the United States under President Trump has refused to allow any renewal or new appointments to the WTO Appellate Body (AB), shrinking its membership from seven to four. What was normally a 90-day process is taking many months. By the Fall of 2018, there were only three AB members, the minimum quorum necessary for it to conduct proceedings. See Section 1.14.

Late in 2019, unless the United States permits new AB members, the Appellate Body will cease to function with only one member. Work-around alternatives that would result in voluntary arbitrations by disputing members as an alternative to Appellate Body are under study, with the U.S. of course not expected to volunteer.

It is not at all clear why the U.S. is engaged in this hostile act, particularly given its numerous successes in WTO dispute settlement proceedings (see Section 1.15). Perhaps the Trump administration is fearful of WTO review of the legality of its "national security" tariffs (see Section 1.16) and its Section 301 tariffs against China (see Section 1.17). At the same time, the Trump Administration seems to be trying to benefit from WTO dispute settlement. In 2018 it filed a complaint with the WTO alleging patent violations of TRIPs by China (see Section 1.16).

Chapter 2

REGULATING FREE TRADE AGREEMENTS

Analysis

§ 2.0   One-Way Free Trade: GSP, CBI, AGOA and More

Some goods may enter the United States at less than most-favored-nation tariff levels or duty free. This occurs because of special tariff preferences incorporated into United States law (outlined below). It is important to realize that these preferences create valuable trading opportunities for U.S. importers and exporters located in qualified nations. These people are the clients for whom lawyers work to secure duty free entry into the United States market. Duty free entry is, of course, the ultimate goal of all exporters and importers involved in United States trade. Various free trade and customs union agreements (including NAFTA and other FTAs of the United States) achieving duty free outcomes are discussed below.

The widest and most significant of the U.S. duty free programs is known as the Generalized System of Preferences (GSP) adopted through the GATT. The European Union (see Chapter 3) and Japan have their own versions of GSP. The U.S. GSP is a complex system of duty free tariff preferences benefiting selected goods originating in developing nations and intended to foster their economic improvement. Irregularly and often retroactively renewed, the U.S. GSP is now operative through 2020. Its major beneficiaries are India, Thailand and Brazil, but take note that President Trump intends to "graduate" India (and Turkey) from the GSP program, and Brazil has suggested it may voluntarily give up "developing country" WTO status.

Another U.S. program is the Caribbean Basin Economic Recovery Act of 1983 (also known as the Caribbean Basin Initiative, CBI), which permits certain goods to enter the United States market duty free. To a significant degree, the CBI duty free program was duplicated in the Andean Trade Preference Act of 1991 initially benefiting Colombian, Ecuadorian, Bolivian and Peruvian goods. In 2010, the Africa Growth and Opportunity Act (AGOA) granted duty and quota free entry to the U.S. market for apparel made from U.S. fabric and yarn. AGOA, expanded in scope and applicable until 2025, covers much of sub-Saharan Africa. It is now the second most significant source of one-way duty free entry of goods into to the USA. Exports from Nigeria, Angola and South Africa top the list of source countries.

In addition, an important "duty free" category allows fabricated U.S.-made components shipped abroad for assembly to return to the U.S. without tariffs on the value of the components. Authorization for this importation is found in Section 9802.00.80 of the Harmonized Tariff Schedule. Goods of this type are subject to a United States Customs duty limited in amount to the value added by foreign assembly operations. This provision is perhaps best known in connection with Latin American maquiladoras.

The least restrictive rules of origin for duty free entry of goods into the United States apply to its insular possessions. These include American Samoa, Guam, Johnson Island, Kingman Reef, Midway Islands, Puerto Rico, the U.S. Virgin Islands and Wake Island. Generally speaking, goods from such possessions may contain up to 70 percent foreign value and still be admitted duty free.

Some of these duty free programs overlap and effectively compete with each other. It might be helpful to think of them in terms of concentric geographic circles. The widest circle is Section 9802.00.80 which applies to the entire globe. The next circle represents the GSP system and most developing nations. Inside that circle is the Caribbean Basin Initiative, the Andean Initiative, and U.S. insular possessions followed by NAFTA 1994 and other U.S. free trade agreements. A manufacturer based in the Caribbean may seek duty free entry into the United States market under Section

9802.00.80, the GSP program or the CBI, but not U.S. free trade agreements, save the Dominican Republic. To most developing nations, these are selectively discriminatory duty free programs that undermine their GSP benefits.

Unusual trade opportunities can arise by linking U.S. duty free entry programs with those of the European Union (EU). For example, the Union has its own complicated and different GSP program, its equivalent of Section 9802.00.80, and two selective duty free programs for developing nations. The latter are known as its Mediterranean Policy and Cotonou Conventions. See Chapter 3. A producer in Israel can quite possibly gain duty free access to the EU (under its Mediterranean Policy) and to the United States (under the Israeli-U.S. FTA). A producer in Jamaica might achieve similar results under the Cotonou Conventions, the CBI and/or the GSP programs of the EU and the United States.

For more extensive coverage of global one-way free trade opportunities, see R. Folsom, *Principles of International Trade Law* and *Principles of European Union Law including BREXIT*.

§ 2.1   The Diverse Content of Free Trade Agreements

A word about nomenclature: Not all "free trade agreements" (FTAs) are titled as such. In Asia, for example, many FTAs are called "Cooperation Agreements" or "Economic Cooperation Agreements". See Chapter 5. Canada likes to title its FTAs "Comprehensive" and/or "Progressive". The re-negotiated version of NAFTA has a number of titles, some of which do not even use the word "Trade". See Chapter 6.

Hereafter, this book will stick with FTAs as a generic title, noting that the **CONTENT** of these agreements differs widely around the globe. See *Free Trade Choices* below.

There is a massive movement towards free trade agreements (FTAs) and customs unions (CUs) throughout the world, though not often of the consequence of that occurring in Europe and North America. Some of these developments are a competitive by-product of European and North American integration. Others simply reflect the desire (but not always the political will) to capture the economic gains and international negotiating strength that such economic relations can bring. This is particularly true of attempts at free trade and customs unions in the developing world.

The explosion of such agreements creates systemic risks for the World Trade Organization (WTO), which reports that all of its members are partners in one or more regional or bilateral trade agreements. Several studies indicate that the EU and the USA have offered less trade liberalization in WTO talks in product areas they had previously granted preferential tariffs in their FTAs. Here is a sampling of FTA agreements around the globe: Hong Kong-China, Japan-Singapore, Russia-CIS states, New Zealand-China, Mexico-Israel, Canada-Peru, EU-South Africa, Chile-South Korea, the South Asian Free Trade Area (India, Pakistan, Bangladesh, Nepal, Bhutan, Sri Lanka), and the list goes on. See Section 2.2 and the Lists of Operational Multilateral and Bilateral Free Trade Agreements in Sections 2.10 and 2.11.

Prof. Bhagwati of Columbia University cleverly calls this the "spaghetti bowl". As Prof. Bhala of the University of Kansas has observed, whether this amounts to competitive trade liberalization or competitive trade imperialism is a provocative question.

The Spaghetti Bowl

A variety of factors help explain why FTAs have become the leading edge of international trade law and policy. Difficulties encountered in the GATT/WTO Uruguay, "Seattle" and Doha Rounds of multilateral trade negotiations are certainly crucial. GATT/WTO regulatory failures regarding free trade agreements have also fueled this reality (see below).

Yet these "negatives" do not fully explain the free trade feeding frenzy. A range of attractions are also at work. For example, free trade agreements often extend to subject matters beyond WTO competence. Foreign investment law is a prime example, and many FTAs and CUs serve as investment magnets. Government procurement, optional at the WTO level, is also often included. Competition policy and labor and environmental matters absent from the WTO are sometimes covered. In addition, free trade agreements can reach beyond the scope of existing WTO agreements. Services is one "WTO-plus" area where this is clearly true. Intellectual property rights are also being "WTO-plussed" in free trade agreements.

FTAs and CUs are politically and economically selective. In other words, they avoid not only global most-favored-nation principles, but also domestically "sensitive" national politics and economics. For example, Singapore's absence of farm exports helped make it an ideal U.S., EU and Japanese free trade partner. The micro-sized economy of Chile contributed to its attraction as a free trade partner with Mexico, China, the European Union, the United States and others. U.S. free trade deals with Jordan, Bahrain and Oman fit economically in a similar fashion, not to mention national security objectives.

Like it or not, the "spaghetti-bowl" maze of FTAs and CUs is driven by powerful negative and positive forces. It is not only the preferred trade medium of today, but also the future. President Trump is driving other countries into FTAs faster than he is withdrawing the United States from them. See Chapters 5 and 6.

Already more than half of world trade is conducted under FTAs and CUs. While international trade lawyers may celebrate full employment, it bears remembering that FTAs and CUs are discriminatory. They could render MFN the least favored status in world trade. Such an outcome would be especially harmful to the world's poorest nations, those with whom few partners seek a preferential trade agreement. See the multilateral and bilateral Lists of operational FTAs in Sections 2.10 and 2.11.

Free Trade Choices

There is a continuum of sorts, a range of options to be considered when nations contemplate economic integration. In **"free trade areas"** (FTAs), tariffs, quotas, and other barriers to trade among participating states are reduced or removed while individual national trade barriers vis-à-vis third party states are retained. Each FTA partner retains its own external tariff and customs controls, including the right to negotiate FTA with other nations. This is true of NAFTA since 1994 and the hundreds of FTAs now prevalent around the globe.

But there are many varieties of FTAs. Some are limited to trade in goods, which tends to be the case in Asia. See ASEAN in Chapter 5. Others cover only industrial goods, removing the always touchy area of agricultural trade. See EFTA in Chapter 3. Many retain the use internally of countervailing, antidumping, safeguard or national security tariffs under appropriate circumstances and are thus do not always constitute "free trade". See, for example, the Trump tariffs discussed in Section 1.16.

Some move beyond mere removal of tariff barriers, taking on much more difficult nontariff regulatory barriers (NTBs) governing health, safety, environmental and other rules. One reason to do this is that the WTO package does not cover the environment. Another is to achieve a depth not found in the WTO TBT and SPS agreements. See Section 1.7. For WTO-plus NTB approaches, see EU legislation in Section 3.4. Compare the WTO-minus coverage of NTBs under NAFTA 1994 presented in Section 4.3.

FTAs may also cover trade in services, especially those of major traders, for example NAFTA 1994 and USMCA 2018 (Chapters 4 and 6), CETA 2017 (Chapter 3), TPP-12 and TPP-11 (Chapter 5), and the Japan-EU Economic Partnership Agreement of 2018 (Chapter 5).

Once again, FTA coverage of services frequently exceeds that of the GATS agreement. In addition, intellectual property and technology transfers are sometimes included in FTAs in ways that go well beyond the 1995 WTO TRIPs agreement discussed in Section 1.11. See the TPP-12 and USMCA agreements in Chapters 5 and 6.

United States FTAs almost always extensively cover foreign investment and related dispute settlement. See Chapters 4 and 6. This topic is largely absent from the WTO package, which focuses only on performance requirements under the TRIMs agreement. See Section 1.12. Foreign investment is also frequently absent from Pacific Rim FTAs. See Chapter 5.

An increasingly wide range of labor (notably ILO) and environmental rules (covering fishing, timbering, climate change, marine debris, sea life, flora and fauna, ozone layer, endangered and invasive species, and more) have been included in post-NAFTA FTAs. Furthermore, gender, rule of law, human rights, indigenous peoples, cultural industries, anti-corruption, currency manipulation, state-owned enterprises, procurement (optional in the WTO package), maritime transport, business visas, competition (antitrust) law, data localization and privacy, corporate social responsibility and governance, fraud, biologics, digital trade, e-commerce, and other areas of law not at all found in the mandatory WTO package of agreements have been incorporated into more recent FTAs. See Chapters 5 and 6.

Note that the absence of coverage under WTO rules removes the possibility of invoking WTO remedies, an option for example under NAFTA 1994 and USMCA 2018. See Chapters 4 and 6. For such areas, the only remedies available will be those found in bilateral or multilateral FTAs.

Customs Unions and Beyond

Economic integration under FTAs is sometimes surpassed in customs union, common market, economic community or economic union agreements. All such agreements are built around internal free trade rules.

"Customs unions" (CUs) remove internal trade barriers among participating states and also create common trade barriers as regards third-party states. Customs unions have a common external tariff and common customs code. Only the union, not its member states, may negotiate trade agreements with other nations, including FTAs and customs union agreements. The EU customs union is preeminent, see Chapter 3. Another notable CU is that of MERCOSUR, see Section 2.5.

"Common markets" go further than customs unions by providing for the free movement of factors of production (goods, services, capital, people) among participating states. In the European Union, this body of law is known as the fundamental "Four Freedoms". NAFTA 1994 and USMCA 2018 notably omit general free movement of people rights, limiting movement to business and professional persons under special visas. See Sections 4.10 and 6.8.

"Economic communities" build on common markets by introducing some harmonization of basic national policies related to the economy of the community, *e.g.* transport, taxation, securities, insurance, the environment, employment law and regional growth. The EU started as the European Economic Community (EEC) in 1957.

Finally, *"economic unions"* may embrace a more or less complete harmonization of national policies related to the economy of the union, *e.g.* company laws, E-commerce, consumer protection, intellectual property and technology, currencies, and government subsidies and procurement. The difference between an economic community and an economic union relates only to the number and importance of harmonized national policies. Such unions may also integrate politically, and on foreign affairs, security, defense and human rights.

The United States, moving from the Articles of Confederation to the U.S. Constitution of 1789, arguably was the first economic union of note. The USA has a common external tariff, enjoys widespread internal free trade under the Commerce Clause, and has numerous federal common market and economic community policies, along with unity in foreign affairs.

The EEC of 1957 evolved first into the European Community, dropping the word Economic from its title in 1993. By 2009, it re-named itself the European Union.

Trade Creation and Trade Diversion

All economic integration agreements are inherently discriminatory in their international trade impact. As non-universalized trade preferences, they tend to simultaneously *create trade* among participating states and *divert trade* between those states and the rest of the world. Thus, while trade creation may represent an improvement in the allocation of scarce world resources, trade diversion may generate an opposite result.

With free trade agreements, diversionary trade effects are usually not distinct because of the absence of a common trade wall against outsiders. Trade diversion nonetheless occurs. "Rules of origin" in free trade area agreements keep third-party imports from seeking the lowest tariff or highest quota state and then exploiting the trade advantages within a free trade area. Under rules of origin, free trade areas are "free" only for goods substantially originating therein. This causes member state goods to be preferred over goods from other states. Rules of origin under a free trade agreement can be as trade diversionary as common external tariffs in customs unions. For different rules of origin approaches, see CUSFTA 1989 and NAFTA 1994 in Chapter 4, and the USMCA 2018 rules of origin in Chapter 6.

§ 2.2   GATT Article 24 FTAs and CUs for Goods

Article 24 of the General Agreement on Tariffs and Trade (GATT) (1947 and 1994) attempts to manage the internal trade-creating and external trade-diverting effects of FTAs, Customs Unions and similar arrangements. Proposals for free trade areas and custom unions must be submitted to a formal GATT/WTO review procedure during which "binding" recommendations are possible to bring the proposals into conformity. Such recommendations might deal with Article 24 requirements for the elimination of internal tariffs and other restrictive regulations of commerce on "substantially all" products originating in a customs union or free trade area. Or they might deal with Article 24 requirements that common external tariffs not be "on the whole higher or more restrictive" in effect than the general incidence of prior existing national tariffs. The broad purpose of Article 24, acknowledged therein, is to facilitate trade among the GATT/WTO contracting parties and not to raise trade barriers.

Most free trade and customs union agreements have passed through this review mechanism *without* substantial modification. The GATT, not economic agreements, most often has given way. For example, during GATT review of the 1957 Treaty of Rome creating what is now the European Union, many "violations" of the letter and spirit of Article 24 were cited. The derivation of the common external tariff by arithmetically averaging existing national tariffs was challenged as more restrictive of trade than previous arrangements. Such averaging on a given product fails to take account of differing national import volumes. If a product was faced originally with a lower than average national tariff and a larger than average national demand, the new average tariff is clearly more "restrictive" of imports than before. Averaging in high tariffs of countries of low demand quite plausibly created more restrictions on third-party trade. If so, the letter and spirit of Article 24 were breached.

Despite these and other arguments, the Treaty of Rome passed through GATT study and review committees without final resolution of its legal status under Article 24. Postponement of these issues became permanent. GATT attempts—through the lawyer-like conditions of Article 24 to maximize trade creation and minimize trade diversion—must be seen as generally inadequate. Treaty terms became negotiable demands that were not accepted. Decades later, the ineffectiveness of GATT/WTO supervision of free trade and customs union agreements continues. At best Article 24 exerts a marginal influence over their contents. Whether the extraordinary proliferation of preferential agreements undermines or supports WTO trade policies is hotly debated.

GATT Regulatory Reform Attempts

The Uruguay Round, which created the World Trade Organization, presented an opportunity to come to grips with the regulatory failure of Article 24. Agreement was reached in 1994 on an "Understanding on the Interpretation of Article 24," which presently binds the roughly 165 member nations of the WTO. This Interpretation reaffirms that free trade area and customs union agreements *must* satisfy the provisions of Article 24, clarifies the manner in which before and after evaluations of common external tariffs are to be undertaken, limits in most cases interim agreements to 10 years, and details Article 24 notification, report and recommendation duties and processes.

Most importantly, the 1994 Understanding on Interpretation expressly permits invocation of standard WTO dispute settlement procedures (DSU) regarding any Article 24 matters. All that said, the 1994 Understanding did not come to grips with the systemic ambiguities that led to Article 24's early and ongoing regulatory failure.

The failure to launch a new round of WTO negotiations in Seattle (1999), followed by delays and failure of the Doha Round that commenced in 2001, has contributed to the feeding frenzy of CU and FTA agreements. Supported by provisional application of a 2006 Doha Round WTO Transparency Mechanism, hundreds of agreements have been notified to the WTO. A large additional number are believed *not* to have been notified. In general, most of the notified agreements are bilateral, not regional in character.

Meanwhile, the WTO Regional Trade Agreements Committee, working by consensus, has been unable since 1995 to complete even one assessment of a FTA or CU agreement's conformity to GATT Article 24 or GATS Article 5 (see Section 2.3). The same is true for WTO Committee on Trade and Development "review" of Enabling Clause arrangements (see Section 2.4).

It has been suggested that this record can be explained by the ambiguous relationship between Committee reports and WTO dispute settlement proceedings. For example, can such reports be used in evidence in WTO dispute proceedings? Can fact-finding by WTO Secretariat and information gathered for WTO regulatory purposes be similarly used? This "dispute settlement awareness" makes WTO members reluctant to provide information or agree on conclusions that could later be used or interpreted in DSU proceedings.

Decades later, the ineffectiveness of GATT/WTO supervision of free trade and customs union agreements continues. At best Article 24 exerts a marginal influence over their contents. The extraordinary proliferation of preferential agreements undermines WTO trade policies (see Chapter 1).

Thus, FTAs and CUs, intended under GATT to be exceptions to nondiscriminatory MFN trade principles, represent an exception that has become the rule.

§ 2.3   GATS Integrated Services Agreements

Since 1995, "economic integration agreements" (EIAs) covering services are permitted under Article 5 of the General Agreement on Trade in Services (GATS). Such agreements, which can be staged, must have "substantial sectoral coverage," eliminate "substantially" all discrimination in sectors subject to multilateral commitments, and not raise the "overall" level of barriers to trade in GATS services compared to before the EIA. EIAs involving developing nations are to be accorded "flexibility." Like GATT Article 24 customs unions, there is an Article 5 duty to compensate EIA nonparticipants.

Review of GATS Article 5 notifications is undertaken, when requested by the WTO Council for Trade in Services, by the Committee on Regional Trade Agreements (CRTA). Thus, whereas CRTA examinations of GATT Article 24 agreements are required, such examinations are optional under GATS. Nevertheless, numerous Article 5 examinations have been conducted, including notably the services components of the North American Free Trade Agreement (NAFTA 1994), the EEC Treaty (1957) and EU Enlargement (2004), Japan's FTAs with Singapore, Mexico and Malaysia, China's FTAs with Hong Kong and Macau, and various U.S. free trade agreements.

None of these examinations has resulted in a final report on consistency with GATS Article 5. This pattern continues the GATT/WTO record of regulatory failure regarding economic integration agreements.

§ 2.4   Developing World Free Trade, the Enabling Clause (1979)

Developing nations in Africa, the Caribbean, Central America, South America and Southeast Asia (among others) began adopting free trade and customs union agreements as early as the 1960s. In 1979, under what is commonly called the Enabling Clause, the GATT parties decided to permit developing nations to enter into differential and more favorable bilateral, regional or global arrangements among themselves to reduce or eliminate tariffs and nontariff barriers applicable to trade in goods.

Like Article 24 of GATT, noted above, the Enabling Clause constitutes an exception to most-favored nation trade principles. It has generally been construed to authorize developing world free trade area and customs union agreements. Whether the Enabling Clause was intended to take such agreements out of Article 24 and its requirements, or be construed in conjunction therewith, is unclear. However, the creation of alternative notification and review procedures for Enabling Clause arrangements suggests Article 24 is inapplicable.

Notification to GATT of Enabling Clause arrangements is mandatory. Since 1995, the WTO Committee on Trade and Development (CTD) is the forum where such notifications are reviewed, but in practice not examined in depth. Enabling Clause arrangements should be designed to promote the trade of developing countries and not raise external trade barriers or undue trade difficulties. Consultations with individual GATT members experiencing such difficulties must be undertaken, and these consultations may be expanded to all GATT members if requested.

Unlike GATT Article 24 and GATS Article 5, neither compensation to nonparticipants nor formal reporting on the consistency with the Enabling Clause of developing nation arrangements is anticipated. The ASEAN-China (2004), India-Sri Lanka (2002), and "revived" Economic Community of West African States (ECOWAS 2005) agreements illustrate notified but unexamined preferential arrangements sheltered by the Enabling Clause.

§ 2.5   African, Islamic World, Caribbean, Latin American, and Southeast Asian FTAs

Several groups, sometimes overlapping and often poorly implemented, have been formed in Africa, a continent with little internal trade. In 1966 the central African countries of Cameroon, Central African Republic, Chad, Congo (Brazzaville) and Gabon formed the Economic and Customs Union of Central Africa (Union Douaniere et Économique de l'Afrique Centrale: UDEAC) to establish a common customs and tariff approach toward the rest of the world and to formulate a common foreign investment code.

In 1967 Kenya, Tanzania and Uganda created the East African Community (EAC) in an attempt to harmonize customs and tariff practices among themselves and in relation to other countries. The practical effect of that Community has frequently been negated by political strife, but of late it has enjoyed a comeback and, combined with Rwanda, Burundi and South Sudan, has developed a customs union.

In 1974 six French-speaking West African nations formed the West African Economic Community (known by its French initials CEAO), which expanded to become the Economic Community of West African States (ECOWAS), now encompassing 15 nations. ECOWAS was initially created by treaty in 1975 to coordinate economic development and cooperation, with a revised treaty signed in 1993. Some progress on liberalized industrial trade has been made and a Cooperation, Compensation and Development Fund established. ECOWAS is also involved in peacekeeping missions in West Africa, and has established an active court, the ECOWAS Community Court of Justice. A subset of French-speaking ECOWAS countries formed the West African Economic and Monetary Union (WAEMU or UEMOA) in 1994 as a customs and monetary union, with Portuguese-speaking Guinea-Bissau joining later.

In 1991, the Organization of African Unity (OAU) member states agreed to a Treaty Establishing the African Economic Community. This wide-ranging Treaty embraces 51 African nations, and includes a regional Court of Justice, although its practical prospects remain uncertain. In 1995, 12 southern African countries, with post-apartheid South Africa participating for the first time, targeted free trade under the Southern African Development Community. A more limited grouping of South Africa, Botswana, Namibia, Lesotho and Swaziland comprise the Southern African Customs Union (SACU), created in 2002 and focused primarily of trade in goods. SACU was created after the South Africa-EU FTA of 1999, which remains in force.

A 20-member Common Market for Eastern and Southern Africa (COMESA) has also been created. In 2015, COMESA, SADC and the EAC agreed to work toward a 26-member free trade area. In 2018, 44 African nations signed the African Continental Free Trade Area agreement, with South Africa and Nigeria, the two largest African economies abstaining.

Islamic World

Bahrain, Kuwait, Oman, Qatar, Saudi Arabia, and United Arab Emirates formed the Gulf Cooperation Council (GCC) in 1981 with objectives to establish freedom of movement, a regional armaments industry, common banking and financial systems, a unified currency policy, a customs union, a common foreign aid program, and a joint, international investment company, the Gulf Investment Corporation. The Council has implemented trade and investment rules concerning tariffs on regional and imported goods, government contracts, communications, transportation, real estate investment, and freedom of movement of professionals. Progress has been made on a Uniform Commercial Code and a Commission for Commercial Arbitration of the Gulf States.

The GCC also has a major 1990 trade and cooperation agreement with the EU. The GCC has a number of FTAs with Middle East and North African (MENA) countries, and notably with Singapore since 2013. In 2003, the non-Arab states of Iran, Pakistan, Turkey, Afghanistan and six Central Asian nations signed an Economic Cooperation Organization Trade Agreement (ECOTA). In 2004, Jordan, Egypt, Tunisia and Morocco signed the Agadir free trade agreement. There is also a Greater Arab Free Trade Area, now encompassing 18 Arab nations.

In 2017, a broad economic boycott led by Saudi Arabia of "progressive" Qatar, home to Al Jezeera media, emerged in the Gulf. Qatar, hosting a major U.S. military base, seems to have taken the boycott in stride. Nevertheless, the Qatar boycott clearly undermines GCC goals.

Caribbean

Established in 1973, the Caribbean Community (CARICOM) now includes 15 Caribbean states. The 1989 Grand Anse Declaration commits CARICOM to establishment of its own common market. Nine CARICOM members are also members of the Organisation of Eastern Caribbean States (OECS), including a 2010 agreement on economic union. Some 37 nations signed the Association of Caribbean States agreement in 1994 with long-term economic integration goals.

The longstanding United States economic boycott of Cuba under Fidel Castro has isolated that nation. U.S. policy has not stopped Canada and Mexico from actively trading and investing (tourism especially) in Cuba. And it certainly propelled post-Soviet Cuba into a close relationship with Venezuela under Chavez and Maduro, including a well-known "doctors for oil" agreement. Cuba's larger problem is its regime's isolationist tendencies, fear of "capitalist pollution" and dogmatic ideology. But the winds of change are blowing in Havana, and a dollarized-economy is emerging from the underground. In 2015, the U.S. and Cuba commenced "normalization" of their relations, but a softer embargo remains in place, tightened under President Trump.

Latin America

Numerous countries in Latin America were members of the Latin American Free Trade Association (LAFTA) (1961) which had small success in reducing tariffs and developing the region through cooperative industrial sector programs. These programs allocated industrial production among the participating states. The Latin American Integration Association (LAIA) (1981), the eleven-member successor to LAFTA, is continuing arrangements for intra-community tariff concessions. They agreed to a 50 percent tariff cut on LAIA goods.

Latin America became a central focus in the 1990s of economic integration. Mexico not only signed a free trade agreement with the United States and Canada, it also agreed to free trade with Colombia, Venezuela, Chile, Bolivia, Costa Rica, Nicaragua, Guatemala, Honduras, El Salvador, Peru and Uruguay. Furthermore, Mexico has negotiated free trade agreements with Japan, the European Union, EFTA (European Free Trade Assn) and entered in 2013 into The Pacific Alliance with Peru, Chile and Colombia.

Argentina, Brazil, Paraguay and Uruguay signed a treaty establishing the MERCOSUR (Southern Cone) common market in 1991 and Chile and Bolivia joined them as Associates in 1996. MERCOSUR is a moderately well-functioning customs union, not a free trade agreement. Venezuela under Chavez created the Peoples' Trade Treaty in 2007 aligned with Cuba, Bolivia, Nicaragua, Ecuador and others. Venezuela finally obtained membership in MERCOSUR in 2012, only to be evicted on human rights grounds a few years later.

ANCOM ("The Cartagena Agreement") was founded by Bolivia, Chile, Colombia, Ecuador, and Peru in 1969 primarily to counter the economic power of Argentina, Brazil and Mexico and to reduce dependency upon foreign capital and technology. Its Decision No. 24 regulating foreign investment and technology transfers was widely copied during the 1970s. A major boost came in 1973 with the addition of Venezuela, but some of the fragile dynamics of the regional grouping are illustrated by Chile's withdrawal in 1977, Bolivia's withdrawal in 1981 and resumption of membership barely four months later, and Peru's economic (but not political) withdrawal in 1991 and return in 1996.

In 1958 Costa Rica, El Salvador, Guatemala, Honduras and Nicaragua formed the Central American Common Market (CACM), another victim of political strife, but still functioning in a limited way, primarily as a result of the 2005 Central American Free Trade Agreement (CAFTA-DR) with the United States. CAFTA-DR also incorporates the Dominican Republic from the Caribbean.

All of this activity occurred against the background of the Free Trade Area of the Americas (FTAA) initiative of the United States (below). In 2003 the ANCOM and MERCOSUR groups nominally agreed upon free trade, at least partly to counterbalance United States power in the FTAA negotiations. The United States, pursuing in turn a divide and conquer strategy, has attempted bilateral free trade agreements with all ANCOM members save Venezuela. The U.S. now has FTAs with Chile, Peru, and Colombia.

The Free Trade Area of the Americas (FTAA)

The U.S. "Enterprise for the Americas Initiative" (EAI) under elder President Bush raised hopes of economic integration throughout the Americas against a background of competitive regionalism in trade relations, especially between the European Union and North America. At the Americas Summit in Miami, President Clinton and 33 Latin American heads of state (only Fidel Castro was absent) renewed this hope by agreeing to commence negotiations on a Free Trade Area of the Americas (FTAA). The year 2005 was targeted at the Summit for creation of the FTAA.

Preparatory working groups have met since 1995 to discuss the following topics: (1) Market Access; (2) Customs Procedures and Rules of Origin; (3) Investment; (4) Standards and Technical Barriers to Trade; (5) Sanitary and Phytosanitary Measures; (6) Subsidies, Antidumping and Countervailing Duties; (7) Smaller Economies; (8) Government Procurement; (9) Intellectual Property Rights; (10) Services; (11) Competition Policy; and (12) Dispute Settlement. It is expected that each of these areas would be covered in any FTAA agreement. Formal FTAA negotiations were delayed several times, particularly because of differences between Brazil-led MERCOSUR and U.S.-led NAFTA 1994.

Divisions were particularly evident during the November 2003 FTAA ministerial meeting in Miami. Lowered expectations, known as FTAA-Lite, reflect U.S. refusal to budge on agricultural protection and trade remedies, and Brazilian refusal to fully embrace investment, intellectual property, services and procurement "free trade." Absent successful resolution of these issues in the WTO Doha Round negotiations, an unlikely prospect at this writing, FTAA-Lite, even with different levels of country commitments, seems unlikely.

The absence of U.S. fast track authority and the general perception that political support for free trade in the United States is weak has clearly slowed FTAA developments. MERCOSUR and Brazil in particular seized the opportunity to move towards South American free trade. At this point, MERCOSUR's trade associates include every South American nation. This puts it in a much better position to negotiate terms and conditions with the NAFTA/CAFTA bloc than individual countries or sub-groups within South America.

Southeast Asian Free Trade

Some interesting moves toward developing world free trade and rule-making have been taken by the Association of Southeast Asian Nations (ASEAN). Its problems, failures and successes are representative of developing world attempts at legal and economic integration. ASEAN has its genesis in the 1967 Bangkok Declaration, with common trade rules in various states of growth, implementation and retrenchment. ASEAN has internal tariff preferences, industrial development projects, "complementation schemes," and regional joint ventures.

An important juncture in the integration process is the point in time at which member countries of a regional group accept a supranational mechanism for enforcing the regime's law irrespective of national feelings and domestic law within a member country. The ASEAN Secretary-General once remarked that ASEAN's Secretariat was "a postman collecting and distributing letters." The surrender of national sovereignty to ASEAN institutions has been a painfully slow process.

ASEAN was formed in 1967 by Indonesia, Malaysia, the Philippines, Singapore and Thailand. Brunei joined in 1984, Vietnam in 1995. Laos and Myanmar (Burma) joined in 1997, and Cambodia in 1999. Rarely have such culturally, linguistically and geographically diverse nations attempted integration. The Bangkok Declaration establishing ASEAN as a cooperative association is a broadly worded document. Later proposals were made for a formal ASEAN treaty or convention, but were rejected as unnecessary. The Bangkok Declaration sets forth numerous regional, economic, cultural and social goals, including acceleration of economic growth, trade expansion and industrial collaboration.

The Bangkok Declaration establishes several mechanisms, but little supranational legal machinery, to implement its stated goals. An annual ASEAN Meeting of Foreign Ministers is scheduled on a rotational basis among the Member States. Special meetings are held "as required." The Declaration provides for a Standing Committee composed of the Foreign Minister of the state in which the next annual Ministerial Meeting is to be held, and includes the ambassadors of other ASEAN States accredited to that state. The

Declaration also provides for "Ad Hoc Committees and Permanent Committees of specialists and officials on specific subjects." Each member state is charged to set up a National Secretariat to administer ASEAN affairs within that Member State and to work with the Ministerial Meeting and the Standing Committee.

There have been relatively infrequent meetings of the ASEAN heads of government. This contrasts with the semiannual European "summits" that have kept that group moving forward along the path of integration. The third ASEAN summit was held in Manila in 1987. This summit produced an agreement for the promotion and protection of investments by ASEAN investors (national and most-favored-nation treatment rights are created), made revisions to the basic ASEAN joint venture agreement, and continued the gradual extension of regional tariff and nontariff trade preferences. Goods already covered by the ASEAN tariff scheme were given a 50 percent margin of preference. New items received a 25 percent preferential margin. The nontariff preferences generally co-opt GATT rules, *e.g.* regarding technical standards and customs valuation.

The fourth ASEAN summit in 1992 committed the parties to the creation of a free trade area within 15 years. Five years were cut from this schedule by agreement in 1994, but operational reality has eluded ASEAN free trade (AFTA). In 2003, a "watershed" date for complete integration in an ASEAN Economic Community targeted 2020. In 2007, this target date was changed to 2015, a reflection of the fear that ASEAN risks being overwhelmed by the powerhouse economies of China, India, Korea and Japan. In 2016, the ASEAN common market was officially launched. Despite the fanfare, its prospects seem limited.

All that said, ASEAN as a group has limited free trade in goods agreements with China, Japan, Korea and India. It is not at all clear to what degree ASEAN exports have increased under these agreements other than by becoming more active suppliers of natural resources and components to these major-economy partners.

For more on Pacific Rim FTAs, see Chapter 5 and the Asia Regional Integration Center List of FTAs in Section 2.9.

§ 2.6   Text of GATT 1947/1994 Article 24

Article XXIV: Territorial Application—Frontier Traffic—Customs Unions and Free-trade Areas

1.   The provisions of this Agreement shall apply to the metropolitan customs territories of the contracting parties and to any other customs territories in respect of which this Agreement has been accepted under Article XXVI or is being applied under Article XXXIII or pursuant to the Protocol of Provisional Application. Each such customs territory shall,

exclusively for the purposes of the territorial application of this Agreement, be treated as though it were a contracting party; *Provided* that the provisions of this paragraph shall not be construed to create any rights or obligations as between two or more customs territories in respect of which this Agreement has been accepted under Article XXVI or is being applied under Article XXXIII or pursuant to the Protocol of Provisional Application by a single contracting party.

2.   For the purposes of this Agreement a customs territory shall be understood to mean any territory with respect to which separate tariffs or other regulations of commerce are maintained for a substantial part of the trade of such territory with other territories.

3.   The provisions of this Agreement shall not be construed to prevent:

(*a*)   Advantages accorded by any contracting party to adjacent countries in order to facilitate frontier traffic;

(*b*)   Advantages accorded to the trade with the Free Territory of Trieste by countries contiguous to that territory, provided that such advantages are not in conflict with the Treaties of Peace arising out of the Second World War.

4.   The contracting parties recognize the desirability of increasing freedom of trade by the development, through voluntary agreements, of closer integration between the economies of the countries parties to such agreements. They also recognize that the purpose of a customs union or of a free-trade area should be to facilitate trade between the constituent territories and not to raise barriers to the trade of other contracting parties with such territories.

5.   Accordingly, the provisions of this Agreement shall not prevent, as between the territories of contracting parties, the formation of a customs union or of a free-trade area or the adoption of an interim agreement necessary for the formation of a customs union or of a free-trade area; *Provided* that:

(*a*)   with respect to a customs union, or an interim agreement leading to a formation of a customs union, the duties and other regulations of commerce imposed at the institution of any such union or interim agreement in respect of trade with contracting parties not parties to such union or agreement shall not on the whole be higher or more restrictive than the general incidence of the duties and regulations of commerce applicable in the constituent territories prior to the formation of such union or the adoption of such interim agreement, as the case may be;

(*b*)   with respect to a free-trade area, or an interim agreement leading to the formation of a free trade area, the duties and other regulations of commerce maintained in each of the constituent territories and applicable at the formation of such free-trade area or the adoption of such interim agreement to the trade of contracting parties not included in such area or not parties to such agreement shall not be higher or more restrictive than the corresponding duties and other regulations of commerce existing in the same constituent territories prior to the formation of the free-trade area, or interim agreement as the case may be; and

(c)   any interim agreement referred to in subparagraphs (a) and (b) shall include a plan and schedule for the formation of such a customs union or of such a free-trade area within a reasonable length of time.

6.   If, in fulfilling the requirements of subparagraph 5 (a), a contracting party proposes to increase any rate of duty inconsistently with the provisions of Article II, the procedure set forth in Article XXVIII shall apply. In providing for compensatory adjustment, due account shall be taken of the compensation already afforded by the reduction brought about in the corresponding duty of the other constituents of the union.

7. (a)Any contracting party deciding to enter into a customs union or free-trade area, or an interim agreement leading to the formation of such a union or area, shall promptly notify the CONTRACTING PARTIES and shall make available to them such information regarding the proposed union or area as will enable them to make such reports and recommendations to contracting parties as they may deem appropriate.

(b)   If, after having studied the plan and schedule included in an interim agreement referred to in paragraph 5 in consultation with the parties to that agreement and taking due account of the information made available in accordance with the provisions of subparagraph (a), the CONTRACTING PARTIES find that such agreement is not likely to result in the formation of a customs union or of a free-trade area within the period contemplated by the parties to the agreement or that such period is not a reasonable one, the CONTRACTING PARTIES shall make recommendations to the parties to the agreement. The parties shall not maintain or put into force, as the case may be, such agreement if they are not prepared to modify it in accordance with these recommendations.

(c)   Any substantial change in the plan or schedule referred to in paragraph 5 (c) shall be communicated to the CONTRACTING PARTIES, which may request the contracting parties concerned to consult with them if the change seems likely to jeopardize or delay unduly the formation of the customs union or of the free-trade area.

8.   For the purposes of this Agreement:

(a)   A customs union shall be understood to mean the substitution of a single customs territory for two or more customs territories, so that

(i)   duties and other restrictive regulations of commerce (except, where necessary, those permitted under Articles XI, XII, XIII, XIV, XV and XX) are eliminated with respect to substantially all the trade between the constituent territories of the union or at least with respect to substantially all the trade in products originating in such territories, and,

(ii)   subject to the provisions of paragraph 9, substantially the same duties and other regulations of commerce are applied by each of the members of the union to the trade of territories not included in the union;

(b)   A free-trade area shall be understood to mean a group of two or more customs territories in which the duties and other restrictive regulations of commerce (except, where necessary, those permitted under Articles XI, XII,

XIII, XIV, XV and XX) are eliminated on substantially all the trade between the constituent territories in products originating in such territories.

9.   The preferences referred to in paragraph 2 of Article I shall not be affected by the formation of a customs union or of a free-trade area but may be eliminated or adjusted by means of negotiations with contracting parties affected.* This procedure of negotiations with affected contracting parties shall, in particular, apply to the elimination of preferences required to conform with the provisions of paragraph 8 (a)(i) and paragraph 8 (b).

Ad Article XXIV: Paragraph 9

It is understood that the provisions of Article I would require that, when a product which has been imported into the territory of a member of a customs union or free-trade area at a preferential rate of duty is re-exported to the territory of another member of such union or area, the latter member should collect a duty equal to the difference between the duty already paid and any higher duty that would be payable if the product were being imported directly into its territory.

10.   The CONTRACTING PARTIES may by a two-thirds majority approve proposals which do not fully comply with the requirements of paragraphs 5 to 9 inclusive, provided that such proposals lead to the formation of a customs union or a free-trade area in the sense of this Article.

11.   Taking into account the exceptional circumstances arising out of the establishment of India and Pakistan as independent States and recognizing the fact that they have long constituted an economic unit, the contracting parties agree that the provisions of this Agreement shall not prevent the two countries from entering into special arrangements with respect to the trade between them, pending the establishment of their mutual trade relations on a definitive basis.

Ad Paragraph 11: Measures adopted by India and Pakistan in order to carry out definitive trade arrangements between them, once they have been agreed upon, might depart from particular provisions of this Agreement, but these measures would in general be consistent with the objectives of the Agreement.

12.   Each contracting party shall take such reasonable measures as may be available to it to ensure observance of the provisions of this Agreement by the regional and local governments and authorities within its territories.

§ 2.7   Text of the 1994 Uruguay Round Understanding on the Interpretation of GATT 1994 Article 24

Members,

Having regard to the provisions of Article XXIV of GATT 1994;

Recognizing that customs unions and free trade areas have greatly increased in number and importance since the establishment of GATT 1947 and today cover a significant proportion of world trade;

Recognizing the contribution to the expansion of world trade that may be made by closer integration between the economies of the parties to such agreements;

Recognizing also that such contribution is increased if the elimination between the constituent territories of duties and other restrictive regulations of commerce extends to all trade, and diminished if any major sector of trade is excluded;

Reaffirming that the purpose of such agreements should be to facilitate trade between the constituent territories and not to raise barriers to the trade of other Members with such territories; and that in their formation or enlargement the parties to them should to the greatest possible extent avoid creating adverse effects on the trade of other Members;

Convinced also of the need to reinforce the effectiveness of the role of the Council for Trade in Goods in reviewing agreements notified under Article XXIV, by clarifying the criteria and procedures for the assessment of new or enlarged agreements, and improving the transparency of all Article XXIV agreements;

Recognizing the need for a common understanding of the obligations of Members under paragraph 12 of Article XXIV;

Hereby *agree* as follows:

1.   Customs unions, free-trade areas, and interim agreements leading to the formation of a customs union or free-trade area, to be consistent with Article XXIV, must satisfy, *inter alia*, the provisions of paragraphs 5, 6, 7 and 8 of that Article.

Article XXIV:5

2.   The evaluation under paragraph 5(a) of Article XXIV of the general incidence of the duties and other regulations of commerce applicable before and after the formation of a customs union shall in respect of duties and charges be based upon an overall assessment of weighted average tariff rates and of customs duties collected. This assessment shall be based on import statistics for a previous representative period to be supplied by the customs union, on a tariff-line basis and in values and quantities, broken down by WTO country of origin. The Secretariat shall compute the weighted average tariff rates and customs duties collected in accordance with the methodology used in the assessment of tariff offers in the Uruguay Round of Multilateral Trade Negotiations. For this purpose, the duties and charges to be taken into consideration shall be the applied rates of duty. It is recognized that for the purpose of the overall assessment of the incidence of other regulations of commerce for which quantification and aggregation are difficult, the examination of individual measures, regulations, products covered and trade flows affected may be required.

3.   The "reasonable length of time" referred to in paragraph 5(c) of Article XXIV should exceed 10 years only in exceptional cases. In cases where Members parties to an interim agreement believe that 10 years would be insufficient they shall provide a full explanation to the Council for Trade in Goods of the need for a longer period.

Article XXIV:6

4.   Paragraph 6 of Article XXIV establishes the procedure to be followed when a Member forming a customs union proposes to increase a bound rate of duty. In this regard Members reaffirm that the procedure set forth in Article XXVIII, as elaborated in the guidelines adopted on 10 November 1980 (BISD 27S/26–28) and in the Understanding on the Interpretation of Article XXVIII of GATT 1994, must be commenced before tariff concessions are modified or withdrawn upon the formation of a customs union or an interim agreement leading to the formation of a customs union.

5.   These negotiations will be entered into in good faith with a view to achieving mutually satisfactory compensatory adjustment. In such negotiations, as required by paragraph 6 of Article XXIV, due account shall be taken of reductions of duties on the same tariff line made by other constituents of the customs union upon its formation. Should such reductions not be sufficient to provide the necessary compensatory adjustment, the customs union would offer compensation, which may take the form of reductions of duties on other tariff lines. Such an offer shall be taken into consideration by the Members having negotiating rights in the binding being modified or withdrawn. Should the compensatory adjustment remain unacceptable, negotiations should be continued. Where, despite such efforts, agreement in negotiations on compensatory adjustment under Article XXVIII as elaborated by the Understanding on the Interpretation of Article XXVIII of GATT 1994 cannot be reached within a reasonable period from the initiation of negotiations, the customs union shall, nevertheless, be free to modify or withdraw the concessions; affected Members shall then be free to withdraw substantially equivalent concessions in accordance with Article XXVIII.

6.   GATT 1994 imposes no obligation on Members benefiting from a reduction of duties consequent upon the formation of a customs union, or an interim agreement leading to the formation of a customs union, to provide compensatory adjustment to its constituents.

Review of Customs Unions and Free-Trade Areas

7.   All notifications made under paragraph 7(a) of Article XXIV shall be examined by a working party in the light of the relevant provisions of GATT 1994 and of paragraph 1 of this Understanding. The working party shall submit a report to the Council for Trade in Goods on its findings in this regard. The Council for Trade in Goods may make such recommendations to Members as it deems appropriate.

8.   In regard to interim agreements, the working party may in its report make appropriate recommendations on the proposed time-frame and on measures required to complete the formation of the customs union or free-trade area. It may if necessary provide for further review of the agreement.

9.   Members parties to an interim agreement shall notify substantial changes in the plan and schedule included in that agreement to the Council for Trade in Goods and, if so requested, the Council shall examine the changes.

10.   Should an interim agreement notified under paragraph 7(a) of Article XXIV not include a plan and schedule, contrary to paragraph 5(c) of Article XXIV, the working party shall in its report recommend such a plan and schedule. The parties shall not maintain or put into force, as the case may be, such agreement if they are not prepared to modify it in accordance with these recommendations. Provision shall be made for subsequent review of the implementation of the recommendations.

11.   Customs unions and constituents of free-trade areas shall report periodically to the Council for Trade in Goods, as envisaged by the CONTRACTING PARTIES to GATT 1947 in their instruction to the GATT 1947 Council concerning reports on regional agreements (BISD 18S/38), on the operation of the relevant agreement. Any significant changes and/or developments in the agreements should be reported as they occur.

Dispute Settlement

12.   The provisions of Articles XXII and XXIII of GATT 1994 as elaborated and applied by the Dispute Settlement Understanding may be invoked with respect to any matters arising from the application of those provisions of Article XXIV relating to customs unions, free-trade areas or interim agreements leading to the formation of a customs union or free-trade area.

Article XXIV:12

13.   Each Member is fully responsible under GATT 1994 for the observance of all provisions of GATT 1994, and shall take such reasonable measures as may be available to it to ensure such observance by regional and local governments and authorities within its territory.

14.   The provisions of Articles XXII and XXIII of GATT 1994 as elaborated and applied by the Dispute Settlement Understanding may be invoked in respect of measures affecting its observance taken by regional or local governments or authorities within the territory of a Member. When the Dispute Settlement Body has ruled that a provision of GATT 1994 has not been observed, the responsible Member shall take such reasonable measures as may be available to it to ensure its observance. The provisions relating to compensation and suspension of concessions or other obligations apply in cases where it has not been possible to secure such observance.

15.   Each Member undertakes to accord sympathetic consideration to and afford adequate opportunity for consultation regarding any representations made by another Member concerning measures affecting the operation of GATT 1994 taken within the territory of the former.

§ 2.8   Text of WTO Transparency Mechanism for Regional Trade Agreements

(Provisionally Adopted Dec. 14, 2006)

The General Council,

Having regard to paragraph 1 of Article IX of the Marrakesh Agreement Establishing the World Trade Organization ("WTO Agreement"); Conducting the functions of the Ministerial Conference in the interval between meetings pursuant to paragraph 2 of Article IV of the WTO Agreement; Noting that trade agreements of a mutually preferential nature ("regional trade agreements" or "RTAs") have greatly increased in number and have become an important element in Members' trade policies and developmental strategies; Convinced that enhancing transparency in, and understanding of, RTAs and their effects is of systemic interest and will be of benefit to all Members; Having regard also to the transparency provisions of Article XXIV of GATT 1994, the Understanding on the Interpretation of Article XXIV of GATT 1994 ("GATT Understanding"), Article V of GATS and the 1979 Decision on Differential and More Favorable Treatment, Reciprocity and Fuller Participation of Developing Countries ("Enabling Clause"); Recognizing the resource and technical constraints of developing country Members; Recalling that in the negotiations pursued under the terms of the Doha Ministerial Declaration1, in accordance with paragraph 47 of that Declaration, agreements reached at an early stage may be implemented on a provisional basis;

Decides:

A.   Early Announcement

1.   Without prejudging the substance and the timing of the notification required under Article XXIV of the GATT 1994, Article V of the GATS or the Enabling Clause, nor affecting Members' rights and obligations under the WTO agreements in any way: (a) Members participating in new negotiations aimed at the conclusion of an RTA shall endeavor to so inform the WTO. (b) Members parties to a newly signed RTA shall convey to the WTO, in so far as and when it is publicly available, information on the RTA, including its official name, scope and date of signature, any foreseen timetable for its entry into force or provisional application, relevant contact points and/or website addresses, and any other relevant unrestricted information.

2.   The information referred to in paragraph 1 above is to be forwarded to the WTO Secretariat, which will post it on the WTO website and will periodically provide Members with a synopsis of the communications received.

B.   Notification

3.   The required notification of an RTA by Members that are party to it shall take place as early as possible. As a rule, it will occur no later than directly following the parties' ratification of the RTA or any party's decision on application of the relevant parts of an agreement, and before the application of preferential treatment between the parties.

4.   In notifying their RTA, the parties shall specify under which provision(s) of the WTO agreements it is notified. They will also provide the full text of the RTA (or those parts they have decided to apply) and any related schedules, annexes and protocols, in one of the WTO official languages; if available, these shall also be submitted in an electronically exploitable format. Reference to related official Internet links shall also be supplied.

C.   Procedures to Enhance Transparency

5.   Upon notification, and without affecting Members' rights and obligations under the WTO agreements under which it has been notified, the RTA shall be considered by Members under the procedures established in paragraphs 6 to 13 below.

6.   The consideration by Members of a notified RTA shall be normally concluded in a period not exceeding one year after the date of notification. A precise timetable for the consideration of the RTA shall be drawn by the WTO Secretariat in consultation with the parties at the time of the notification.

7.   To assist Members in their consideration of a notified RTA: (a) the parties shall make available to the WTO Secretariat data as specified in the Annex, if possible in an electronically exploitable format; and (b) the WTO Secretariat, on its own responsibility and in full consultation with the parties, shall prepare a factual presentation of the RTA.

8.   The data referred to in paragraph 7(a) shall be made available as soon as possible. Normally, the timing of the data submission shall not exceed ten weeks—or 20 weeks in the case of RTAs involving only developing countries—after the date of notification of the agreement.

9.   The factual presentation provided for in paragraph 7(b) shall be primarily based on the information provided by the parties; if necessary, the WTO Secretariat may also use data available from other sources, taking into account the views of the parties in furtherance of factual accuracy. In preparing the factual presentation, the WTO Secretariat shall refrain from any value judgement.

10.   The WTO Secretariat's factual presentation shall not be used as a basis for dispute settlement procedures or to create new rights and obligations for Members.

11.   As a rule, a single formal meeting will be devoted to consider each notified RTA; any additional exchange of information should take place in written form.

12.   The WTO Secretariat's factual presentation, as well as any additional information submitted by the parties, shall be circulated in all WTO official languages not less than eight weeks in advance of the meeting devoted to the consideration of the RTA. Members' written questions or comments on the RTA under consideration shall be transmitted to the parties through the WTO Secretariat at least four weeks before the corresponding meeting; they shall be distributed, together with replies, to all Members at least three working days before the corresponding meeting.

13.   All written material submitted, as well as the minutes of the meeting devoted to the consideration of a notified agreement will be promptly circulated in all WTO official languages and made available on the WTO website.

D.   Subsequent Notification and Reporting

14.   The required notification of changes affecting the implementation of an RTA, or the operation of an already implemented RTA, shall take place as

soon as possible after the changes occur. Changes to be notified include, inter alia, modifications to the preferential treatment between the parties and to the RTA's disciplines. The parties shall provide a summary of the changes made, as well as any related texts, schedules, annexes and protocols, in one of the WTO official languages and, if available, in electronically exploitable format.

15.   At the end of the RTA's implementation period, the parties shall submit to the WTO a short written report on the realization of the liberalization commitments in the RTA as originally notified.

16.   Upon request, the relevant WTO body shall provide an adequate opportunity for an exchange of views on the communications submitted under paragraphs 14 and 15.

17.   The communications submitted under paragraphs 14 and 15 will be promptly made available on the WTO website and a synopsis will be periodically circulated by the WTO Secretariat to Members.

E.   Bodies Entrusted with the Implementation of the Mechanism

18.   The Committee on Regional Trade Agreements ("CRTA") and the Committee on Trade and Development ("CTD") are instructed to implement this Transparency Mechanism.3 The CRTA shall do so for RTAs falling under Article XXIV of GATT 1994 and Article V of GATS, while the CTD shall do so for RTAs falling under paragraph 2(c) of the Enabling Clause. For purposes of performing the functions established under this Mechanism, the CTD shall convene in dedicated session.

F.   Technical Support for Developing Countries

19.   Upon request, the WTO Secretariat shall provide technical support to developing country Members, and especially least-developed countries, in the implementation of this Transparency Mechanism, in particular—but not limited to—with respect to the preparation of RTA-related data and other information to be submitted to the WTO Secretariat. In their notification, Members may refer to official Internet links related to the agreement where the relevant information can be consulted in full, in one of the WTO official languages. The Director-General is invited to ensure consistency in the preparation of the WTO Secretariat factual presentations for the different types of RTAs, taking into account the variations in data provided by different Members.

G.   Other Provisions

20.   Any Member may, at any time, bring to the attention of the relevant WTO body information on any RTA that it considers ought to have been submitted to Members in the framework of this Transparency Mechanism.

21.   The WTO Secretariat shall establish and maintain an updated electronic database on individual RTAs. This database shall include relevant tariff and trade-related information, and give access to all written material related to announced or notified RTAs available at the WTO. The RTA database should be structured so as to be easily accessible to the public.

H.   Provisional Application of the Transparency Mechanism 22.

This Decision shall apply, on a provisional basis, to all RTAs. With respect to RTAs already notified under the relevant WTO transparency provisions and in force, this Decision shall apply as follows: (a) RTAs for which a working party report has been adopted by the GATT Council and those RTAs notified to the GATT under the Enabling Clause will be subject to the procedures under Sections D to G above. (b) RTAs for which the CRTA has concluded the "factual examination" prior to the adoption of this Decision and those for which the "factual examination" will have been concluded by 31 December 2006, and RTAs notified to the WTO under the Enabling Clause will be subject to the procedures under Sections D to G above. In addition, for each of these RTAs, the WTO Secretariat shall prepare a factual abstract presenting the features of the agreement. (c) Any RTA notified prior to the adoption of this Decision and not referred to in subparagraphs (a) or (b) will be subject to the procedures under Sections C to G above.

I.   Reappraisal of the Mechanism

23. Members will review, and if necessary modify, this Decision, in light of the experience gained from its provisional operation, and replace it by a permanent mechanism adopted as part of the overall results of the Round, in accordance with paragraph 47 of the Doha Declaration. Members will also review the legal relationship between this Mechanism and relevant WTO provisions related to RTAs.

ANNEX: Submission of Data by RTA Parties

1.   RTA parties shall not be expected to make available the information required below if the corresponding data has already been submitted to the Integrated Data Base (IDB), or has otherwise been provided to the Secretariat in an adequate format.

2.   For the goods aspects in RTAs, the parties shall submit the following data, at the tariff-line level: (a) Tariff concessions under the agreement: (i) a full listing of each party's preferential duties applied in the year of entry into force of the agreement; and (ii) when the agreement is to be implemented by stages, a full listing of each party's preferential duties to be applied over the transition period. (b) MFN duty rates: (i) a full tariff listing of each RTA party's MFN duties applied on the year of entry into force of the agreement; and (ii) a full tariff listing of each RTA party's MFN duties applied on the year preceding the entry into force of the agreement. (c) Where applicable, other data (e.g., preferential margins, tariff-rate quotas, seasonal restrictions, special safeguards and, if available, ad valorem equivalents for non-ad valorem duties). (d) Product-specific preferential rules of origin as defined in the agreement.

(e)   Import statistics, for the most recent three years preceding the notification for which they are available: (i) each party's imports from each of the other parties, in value; and (ii) each party's imports from the rest of the world, broken down by country of origin, in value. Trade and tariff data submissions in the context of an RTA notification can subsequently be included in the IDB, provided that their key features are appropriate. In this respect, see document G/MA/IDB/W/6 (dated 15 June 2000) for the Guidelines for Supplying PC IDB Submissions and documents G/MA/115 (dated 17 June 2002) and G/MA/115/Add.5 (dated 13 January 2005) for WTO Policy regarding the dissemination of IDB data. Data submissions can be furnished in PC database formats, spreadsheet formats, or text-delimited formats; the use of word-processing formats should be avoided, if possible. References to "tariff-line level" shall be understood to mean the detailed breakdown of the national customs nomenclature (HS codes with, for example, 8, 10 or more digits). It is crucial that all data elements supplied use the same national customs nomenclature or are associated with corresponding conversion tables. In the case of a customs union, the MFN applied common external tariff.

3.   For the services aspects in RTAs, the parties shall submit the following data, if available, for the three most recent years preceding the notification: trade or balance of payments statistics (by services sector/subsector and partner), gross domestic product data or production statistics (by services sector/subsector), and relevant statistics on foreign direct investment and on movement of natural persons (by country and, if possible, by services sector/subsector).

4.   For RTAs involving only developing countries, in particular when these comprise least developed countries, the data requirements specified above will take into account the technical constraints of the parties to the agreement.

§ 2.9   Text of GATS Article V: Economic Integration Agreements (1994)

1.   This Agreement shall not prevent any of its Members from being a party to or entering into an agreement liberalizing trade in services between or among the parties to such an agreement, provided that such an agreement:

(a)   has substantial sectoral coverage;

(b)   provides for the absence or elimination of substantially all discrimination, in the sense of Article XVII, between or among the parties, in the sectors covered under subparagraph (a), through:

(i)   elimination of existing discriminatory measures, and/or

(ii)   prohibition of new or more discriminatory measures, either at the entry into force of that agreement or on the basis of a reasonable time-frame, except for measures permitted under Articles XI, XII, XIV and XIV bis.

2.   In evaluating whether the conditions under paragraph 1(b) are met, consideration may be given to the relationship of the agreement to a wider process of economic integration or trade liberalization among the countries concerned.

3. (a) Where developing countries are parties to an agreement of the type referred to in paragraph 1, flexibility shall be provided for regarding the

conditions set out in paragraph 1, particularly with reference to subparagraph (b) thereof, in accordance with the level of development of the countries concerned, both overall and in individual sectors and subsectors.

(b) Notwithstanding paragraph 6, in the case of an agreement of the type referred to in paragraph 1 involving only developing countries, more favorable treatment may be granted to juridical persons owned or controlled by natural persons of the parties to such an agreement.

4. Any agreement referred to in paragraph 1 shall be designed to facilitate trade between the parties to the agreement and shall not in respect of any Member outside the agreement raise the overall level of barriers to trade in services within the respective sectors or subsectors compared to the level applicable prior to such an agreement.

5. If, in the conclusion, enlargement or any significant modification of any agreement under paragraph 1, a Member intends to withdraw or modify a specific commitment inconsistently with the terms and conditions set out in its Schedule, it shall provide at least 90-days advance notice of such modification or withdrawal and the procedure set forth in paragraphs 2, 3 and 4 of Article XXI shall apply.

6. A service supplier of any other Member that is a juridical person constituted under the laws of a party to an agreement referred to in paragraph 1 shall be entitled to treatment granted under such agreement, provided that it engages in substantive business operations in the territory of the parties to such agreement.

7. (a)Members which are parties to any agreement referred to in paragraph 1 shall promptly notify any such agreement and any enlargement or any significant modification of that agreement to the Council for Trade in Services. They shall also make available to the Council such relevant information as may be requested by it. The Council may establish a working party to examine such an agreement or enlargement or modification of that agreement and to report to the Council on its consistency with this Article.

(b) Members which are parties to any agreement referred to in paragraph 1 which is implemented on the basis of a time-frame shall report periodically to the Council for Trade in Services on its implementation. The Council may establish a working party to examine such reports if it deems such a working party necessary.

(c) Based on the reports of the working parties referred to in subparagraphs (a) and (b), the Council may make recommendations to the parties as it deems appropriate.

8. A Member which is a party to any agreement referred to in paragraph 1 may not seek compensation for trade benefits that may accrue to any other Member from such agreement.

§ 2.10   List of Operational Multilateral Free Trade Agreements (2019)

- Andean Community—1969
- ASEAN Free Trade Area (AFTA)—1992
- ASEAN-Australia-New Zealand Free Trade Area (AANZFTA)—2010
- Asia-Pacific Trade Agreement (APTA)—1975
- Central American Integration System (SICA)—1993
- Central European Free Trade Agreement (CEFTA)—1992
- Commonwealth of Independent States Free Trade Area (CISFTA)—2011
- Common Market for Eastern and Southern Africa (COMESA)—1994
- G-3 Free Trade Agreement (G-3)—1995
- Greater Arab Free Trade Area (GAFTA)—1997
- Dominican Republic-Central America Free Trade Agreement (DR-CAFTA)—2004
- East African Community (EAC)—2005
- Eurasian Economic Union (EAEU)—2015
- European Economic Area (EEA; European Union-Norway-Iceland-Liechtenstein)—1994
- European Union Customs Union (EUCU; European Union-Turkey-Monaco-San Marino-Andorra)—1958
- European Free Trade Association (EFTA)—1960
- Gulf Cooperation Council (GCC)—1981
- International Grains Agreement—1995 Comprising a Grains Trade Convention (GTC) and a Food Aid Convention (FAC)
- North American Free Trade Agreement (NAFTA) **(Pending replacement by USMCA)**—1994
- Pacific Alliance Free Trade Area (PAFTA)—2012
- South Asian Free Trade Area (SAFTA)—2004
- Southern African Development Community Free Trade Area (SADCFTA)—1980

- Southern Common Market (MERCOSUR)—1991
- Comprehensive and Progressive Agreement for Trans-Pacific Partnership (CPTPP)—2018

Source: Wikipedia 2019.

§ 2.11   List of Operational Bilateral Free Trade Agreements (2019)

Armenia has bilateral agreements with the following countries and blocs:

- Commonwealth of Independent States
  - Belarus
  - Kazakhstan
  - Kyrgyzstan
  - Moldova
  - Russia
  - Turkmenistan
  - Tajikistan
  - Uzbekistan
- Eurasian Economic Union
  - Eurasian Customs Union members
  - Vietnam free trade agreement
- European Union Armenia qualifies to export its products under the EU's Generalized System of Preferences (GSP)
- Georgia
- Ukraine
- United States Armenia qualifies to export its products under the U.S. Generalized System of Preferences (GSP) program

ASEAN has bilateral agreements with the following countries and blocs:

- ASEAN-China Free Trade Area (ACFTA), in effect as of 1 January 2010
- ASEAN-India Free Trade Area (AIFTA), in effect as of 1 January 2010

- ASEAN-Japan Comprehensive Economic Partnership (AJCEP), in effect as of 1 December 2008

- ASEAN-Korea Free Trade Area (AKFTA), in effect as of 1 January 2010

- ASEAN-Australia-New Zealand Free Trade Area (AANZFTA), in effect as of 1 January 2010

Caribbean Community (CARICOM) has bilateral agreements with the following countries:

- Costa Rica

- Dominican Republic

- Chile

- Australia

- Bolivia

- Canada

- Central America (Costa Rica, El Salvador, Honduras. Guatemala and Nicaragua)

- China

- Colombia

- Cuba

- Ecuador

- EFTA (Iceland, Liechtenstein, Norway and Switzerland)

- European Union

- Hong Kong SAR

- India

- Japan

- Malaysia

- MERCOSUR (Argentina, Brazil, Paraguay, Uruguay and Venezuela)

- Mexico

- Panama

- Peru

- Trans-Pacific Strategic Economic Partnership (Brunei, Chile, New Zealand and Singapore)

- Turkey

- South Korea
- United States
- Vietnam

The **People's Republic of China** has bilateral agreements with the following blocs, countries, and its two special administrative regions:

- ASEAN, China-ASEAN Free Trade Area (2010)
- Australia, China-Australia Free Trade Agreement (2015)
- Chile, China-Chile Free Trade Agreement (2006)
- Costa Rica, China-Costa Rica Free Trade Agreement (2011)
- Georgia, China-Georgia Free Trade Agreement (2017)
- Hong Kong, Mainland and Hong Kong Closer Economic Partnership Arrangement (CEPA) (2003)
- Iceland, China-Iceland Free Trade Agreement (2014)
- Macau, Mainland and Macau Closer Economic Partnership Arrangement (CEPA) (2003)
- Maldives, China-Maldives Free Trade Agreement (2017)
- New Zealand, China-New Zealand Free Trade Agreement (2008)[10]
- Pakistan, China-Pakistan Free Trade Agreement (2006)
- Peru, China-Peru Free Trade Agreement (2010)
- Republic of China (Taiwan), Economic Cooperation Framework Agreement (2010)
- Singapore, China-Singapore Free Trade Agreement (2009)
- South Korea, China-South Korea Free Trade Agreement (2015)
- Switzerland, China-Switzerland free trade agreement (2014)
- Eurasian Economic Union (2019)—Russia, Belarus, Kazakhstan, Armenia and Kyrgyzstan

Costa Rica has bilateral agreements with the following countries and blocs (date it took effect):

- Canada (1 November 2002)
- Chile (15 February 2002)
- People's Republic of China (1 August 2011)
- Caribbean Community (CARICOM) (15 November 2005)
  - Trinidad & Tobago (15 November 2005)
  - Guyana (30 April 2006)
  - Barbados (1 August 2006)
  - Belize (10 March 2011)
  - Jamaica (1 June 2015)
  - Still awaiting approval from:
  - Suriname
  - Antigua and Barbuda
  - Dominica
  - Grenada
  - Saint Kitts and Nevis
  - Saint Lucia
  - Saint Vincent and the Grenadines
- Colombia (1 August 2016).
- Dominican Republic (7 March 2002)
- EFTA (2 May 2014).
  - Norway (20 August 2014)
  - Switzerland (29 August 2014)
  - Liechtenstein (29 August 2014)
  - Iceland (5 September 2014)
- El Salvador Customs union, (1963, re-launched on 29 October 1993)
- European Union (October 1, 2013).
- Guatemala Customs union, (1963, re-launched on 29 October 1993)
- Honduras Customs union, (1963, re-launched on 29 October 1993)

- Mexico (January 1, 1995)
- Nicaragua Customs union, (1963, re-launched on 29 October 1993)
- Panama (31 July 1973, renegotiated and expanded for (1 January 2009)
- Peru (1 June 2013)
- Singapore (16 May 2013).
- United States (1 January 2009)

The **Eurasian Economic Union** consisting of Russia, Belarus, Kazakhstan, Armenia and Kyrgyzstan has following free trade agreements, see further here.

- Moldova (2013)
- Uzbekistan (2014)
- Egypt (2015)
- Tajikistan (2016)
- Vietnam (2016)
- China (2019)
- Iran (2021)

EFTA has bilateral agreements with the following countries—including dependent territories—and blocs:

- Albania
- Canada: Canada-European Free Trade Association Free Trade Agreement
- Chile
- Colombia
- Gulf Cooperation Council (GCC)
- Faroe Islands (autonomous entity of Denmark)
- Egypt
- Hong Kong
- Israel
- Jordan
- Lebanon
- Macedonia
- Mexico

- Morocco
- Palestinian Authority
- Serbia
- Singapore
- Southern African Customs Union
- Tunisia
- Singapore
- South Korea
- Turkey
- Ukraine

The **European Union** has bilateral agreements with the following countries and blocs:

- Albania SAA (2009)
- Algeria AA (2005)
- Andorra CU (1991)
- Bosnia and Herzegovina SAA (signed 2008, entry into force pending)
- Canada: Comprehensive Economic and Trade Agreement (provisionally applied)
- Chile AA (2003)
- Egypt AA (2004)
- Faroe Islands, autonomous entity of Denmark (1997)
- Israel AA (2000)
- Jordan AA (2002)
- Lebanon AA (2006)
- Macedonia SAA (2004)
- Mexico AA (2000)
- Montenegro SAA (2010)
- Monaco CU (1958, Franco-Monegasque Treaties)
- Morocco AA (2000)
- Palestinian Authority interim AA (1997)
- San Marino CU (2002)
- Serbia SAA (signed 2008, entry into force pending)

- South Africa AA (2000)
- South Korea: European Union-South Korea Free Trade Agreement (entered in to force on 13 December 2015)
- Switzerland FTA (1973)
- Tunisia AA (1998)
- Turkey CU (1996)
- EU Overseas Countries and Territories
- EU-Japan Economic Partnership Agreement (2018)

The **Faroe Islands** have bilateral agreements with the following countries and blocs:

- Switzerland
- Norway
- Iceland (The Hoyvík Agreement)
- The European Union

Georgia has bilateral agreements with the following countries and organizations:

- Turkey
- Ukraine
- European Union
- European Free Trade Association (Switzerland, Norway, Iceland, and Liechtenstein)
- Commonwealth of Independent States
  - Armenia
  - Azerbaijan
  - Kazakhstan
  - Kyrgyzstan
  - Moldova
  - Turkmenistan
  - Tajikistan
  - Uzbekistan
- People's Republic of China
- Hong Kong SAR

The **Gulf Cooperation Council (GCC)** has bilateral agreements with the following countries:

- EFTA (Entry into force: 1 July 2014)

India has bilateral agreements with the following countries and blocs:

- ASEAN (ASEAN-India Free Trade Area)
- SAFTA (South Asian Free Trade Area)
- European Union (negotiations stalled) & European Free Trade Association (EFTA) (negotiations stalled)
- Sri Lanka
- Singapore
- Thailand (separate from FTA agreement with ASEAN)
- Malaysia (separate from FTA agreement with ASEAN)

Japan has bilateral agreements with the following countries and blocs:

- Australia
- ASEAN (signed in 2008)
- Brunei (signed in 2007)
- Chile (signed in 2006)
- India (signed in 2011)
- Indonesia
- Malaysia (Japan-Malaysia Economic Partnership Agreement signed in 2005)
- Mexico (took effect in 2005)
- Mongolia
- Peru
- Philippines (signed in 2006)
- Singapore (signed in 2002)
- Switzerland (signed in 2009)
- Thailand (Japan-Thailand Economic Partnership Agreement signed in 2007)
- Vietnam (signed in 2008)
- EU-Japan Economic Partnership Agreement (signed in 2018)

Jordan has bilateral agreements with the following countries and blocs:

- Canada
- Algeria
- Libya
- Syria
- Kuwait
- Bahrain
- Peru
- United States (United States-Jordan Free Trade Agreement)
- The European Free Trade Association
- The European Union

The **Kyrgyz Republic** has bilateral agreements with the following countries:

- Kazakhstan (Entry into force: 11 November 1995)
- Moldova (Entry into force: 21 November 1996)
- Russian Federation (Entry into force: 24 April 1993)
- Ukraine (Entry into force: 19 January 1998)
- Uzbekistan (Entry into force: 20 March 1998)

Lebanon has bilateral agreements with the following countries and blocs:

- Gulf Cooperation Council (GCC)
- Iraq
- The European Union

Malaysia has bilateral agreements with the following countries:

- India
- Australia

Maldives has bilateral agreements with the following countries:

- China, China-Maldives Free Trade Agreement (2017)

MERCOSUR

- Israel
- Egypt

- Lebanon
- Palestine

Mexico has bilateral agreements with the following countries and blocs:

- o   Chile-Mexico Free Trade Agreement
- o   Colombia-Mexico Free Trade Agreement
- o   Costa Rica-Mexico Free Trade Agreement
- o   EFTA-Mexico Free Trade Agreement (Iceland, Liechtenstein, Norway, Switzerland)
- o   European Union-Mexico Economic Partnership
- o   Israel-Mexico Free Trade Agreement
- o   Japan-Mexico Economic Association Agreement
- o   Nicaragua-Mexico Free Trade Agreement
- o   Northern Triangle (El Salvador, Honduras and Guatemala)
- o   Panama
- o   Uruguay-Mexico Free Trade Agreement
- Framework agreements
  - o   MERCOSUR-Mexico Economic Association (Argentina, Brazil, Paraguay, Uruguay, Venezuela)
- Preferential trade agreements
  - o   Argentina
  - o   Brazil
  - o   Ecuador
  - o   Paraguay
  - o   Panama
  - o   Peru

Morocco has bilateral agreements with the following countries and blocs:

- The European Union
- The European Free Trade Association
- Jordan
- Egypt

- Tunisia
- State of Palestine
- United Arab Emirates
- Turkey
- United States

New Zealand free trade agreements:

- Australia (as Closer Economic Relations)
- Malaysia
- Singapore
- Thailand
- Chile
- People's Republic of China (see China-New Zealand Free Trade Agreement)
- Brunei (see Trans-Pacific Strategic Economic Partnership)
- Hong Kong (see Hong Kong-New Zealand Closer Economic Partnership Agreement)
- Republic of China (Taiwan)

Panama has bilateral agreements with the following countries:

- Chile
- Costa Rica
- El Salvador
- Guatemala
- Honduras
- Mexico
- Nicaragua
- Republic of China (Taiwan)
- Singapore
- United States

Republic of China (Taiwan) has bilateral agreements with the following countries:

- People's Republic of China, Economic Cooperation Framework Agreement
- El Salvador

- Guatemala
- Honduras
- Nicaragua
- New Zealand
- Singapore
- Panama

Peru has bilateral agreements with the following countries:

- Canada
- EFTA
- People's Republic of China
- Japan
- Mexico
- Singapore
- Thailand
- United States
- EU

Serbia has bilateral agreements with the following countries and blocs:

- EU (SAA)
- EFTA
- CEFTA
- Russia
- Belarus
- Turkey
- Kazakhstan
- United States (GSP)

Singapore has bilateral agreements with the following countries and blocs:

- Australia
- Brunei
- Chile
- Republic of China (Taiwan)
- European Free Trade Association

- Gulf Cooperation Council (GCC)
- India
- Japan
- Jordan
- New Zealand (separate from the Trans-Pacific Strategic Economic Partnership (see above) and is still in force)
- Panama
- Peru
- South Korea
- Sri Lanka
- People's Republic of China
- United States

South Korea has bilateral agreements with the following countries and blocs:

- ASEAN
- Australia Korea-Australia Free Trade Agreement KAFTA (2014)
- Canada (Canada-South Korea Free Trade Agreement)
- China
- Chile
- Colombia
- EFTA
- European Union (European Union-South Korea Free Trade Agreement) (entered in to force on 13 December 2015)
- India (Comprehensive Economic Partnership Agreement)
- New Zealand
- Peru
- Singapore
- Turkey
- United States (US)
- Vietnam

Switzerland (which has a customs union with Liechtenstein, sometimes included in agreements [*citation needed*]) has bilateral agreements with the following countries and blocs:

- Albania (Signed: 17.12.2009: Entry into force: 01.11.2010)
- Canada (Entry into force 01.07.2009)
- Chile (Entry into force: 01.12.2004)
- People's Republic of China (Entry into force: July 1, 2014)
- Colombia (Signed: 25.11.2008. Entry into force: 01.07.2011)
- Egypt (Entry into force: 01.09.2008)
- European Union (Entry into force: 01.01.1973; bilateral CH-EU)
- Faeroe Islands (Entry into force: 01.03.1995; bilateral CH-Faeroe)
- Israel (Entry into force: 01.07.1993)
- Japan (Entry into force: 01.09.2009. Bilateral CH-Japan)
- Jordan (Entry into force: 01.09.2002)
- Republic of Korea (Entry into force: 01.09.2006)
- Lebanon (Entry into force: 01.01.2007)
- Macedonia (Entry into force: 01.05.2002)
- Mexico (Entry into force: 01.07.2001)
- Morocco (Entry into force: 01.12.1999)
- Palestinian Authority (Entry into force: 01.07.1999)
- Peru (Signed: 24.06.2010 (EFTA) and 14.07.2010 (Peru). Entry into force on 01.07.2011)
- Serbia (Signed: 17.12.2009: Entry into force: 01.10.2010)
- Singapore (Entry into force: 01.01.2003)
- SACU (Entry into force: 01.05.2008)
- Tunisia (Entry into force: 01.06.2006)
- Turkey (Entry into force: 01.04.1992)

- Ukraine (Signed 24.06.2010. Entry into force 01.06.2012)

Thailand has bilateral agreements with the following countries:

- Australia
- India
- Japan (Japan-Thailand Economic Partnership Agreement signed in 2007)
- New Zealand
- Peru
- Chile

Tunisia has bilateral agreements with the following countries and blocs:

- Morocco
- The European Free Trade Association
- Jordan
- Senegal
- Egypt
- Algeria
- Libya
- Mauritania
- Turkey
- The European Union

United States has bilateral agreements with the following countries and blocs:

- Australia
- Bahrain
- Chile
- Colombia
- Costa Rica
- the Dominican Republic
- Dominican Republic-Central America Free Trade Agreement
- El Salvador
- Guatemala

- Honduras
- Israel
- Jordan
- Korea
- Nicaragua
- Oman
- Panama
- Peru
- Morocco
- Singapore

Source: Wikipedia 2019

Chapter 3

EUROPEAN CUSTOMS UNION AND FREE TRADE AGREEMENTS

Analysis

NOTE: What follows is an extremely abbreviated summary of the creation and evolution of the European Union (EU), its legal system, customs union, and free trade agreements and policies affecting international trade. For much more extensive coverage, and copies of governing EU treaties referenced below, see R. Folsom, *Principles of European Union Law including BREXIT* (West Academic Publications).

---

§ 3.1   The European Economic Community (EEC 1957)

In 1957, the European Economic Community was created under the Treaty of Rome by Italy, France, West Germany, Luxembourg,

Belgium and the Netherlands. Over time, additional members were added: Britain, Eire and Denmark in 1973, Greece in 1981, Spain and Portugal in 1986, Austria, Sweden and Finland in 1995, Poland, Hungary, The Czech Republic, Slovakia, Estonia, Lithuania, Latvia, Slovenia, Malta, and Cyprus in 2004, and Romania and Bulgaria in 2007. In 2007 the Reform Treaty (Treaty of Lisbon) was signed, eventually going into effect on December 1, 2009 among 27 nations. Under the latter treaty, the amended Treaty of Rome became the Treaty on the Functioning of the European Union (TFEU).

With Croatia joining in 2013, the EU now has 28 member states, although in June 2016 voters in the United Kingdom approved a referendum calling for that country to leave the EU, which is scheduled to happen in March 29, 2019. Apart from the United Kingdom, the only major nonmember nations in Western and Central Europe are Switzerland, Norway and Iceland.

§ 3.2 The European Free Trade Area (EFTA 1959)

The EEC Treaty as drafted in 1957 was much less "dirigiste" than its predecessor, the 1951 European Coal and Steel Treaty. Nevertheless, Britain once again abstained from membership because of the nature and extent of the European controls over the economy. Britain, too, was still preoccupied with its empire-based trade relations. Europe was important, but it had not yet become critical to British trading interests.

The fragmentation of Europe's economy during the 1950s became even more accentuated by the emergence of another competing organization. Led by Britain, many of the fringe or traditionally neutral nations of Western Europe organized themselves into the European Free Trade Association (EFTA) in 1959. Austria, Denmark, Iceland, Norway, Portugal, Sweden and Switzerland joined this undertaking. With eight nations, essentially surrounding the core six nations who created the EEC in 1957, Britain felt that it had contained French influence and ideas in the economic sphere.

True to British philosophy, the EFTA Treaty was very limited in scope. It applied only to free trade in industrial goods, omitting coverage of agriculture, transport, labor, capital, technology and services to mention only a few areas fully incorporated into the EEC Treaty. Moreover, the British view on the nature of the governmental institutions required to achieve industrial free trade prevailed. A single institution, the EFTA Council, was created. Since it normally followed a unanimous voting principle, each of the member states retained a veto over new policy developments within the EFTA group. The surrender of national sovereignties to EFTA was minimized, a theme that was to return decades later with BREXIT.

Thus, by 1960, Europe was economically allied in three major trade groups. France and an increasingly powerful West Germany led Italy and the Benelux states in the European Coal and Steel and Economic Communities. Britain and its partners were loosely integrated through the European Free Trade Association. And the whole of Eastern Europe came under the sway of Soviet dominance through COMECON. In addition, Finland became associated with EFTA and Greece and Turkey were associated with the EEC. Only Spain under Franco remained an economic outcast. More than a decade passed before major shifts in these alliances occurred.

EFTA and the EEC Reconciled

During the 1960s, Britain began to come to grips with the loss of its empire. Although special trading relations were often preserved with former colonies through the Commonwealth network, it became increasingly apparent that Britain's economic future lay more in Europe than Africa, Asia or the Caribbean. Moreover, the EEC had helped to spur a phenomenal economic recovery on the Continent at a time when many were questioning the competitiveness of British industry.

For these reasons, and others, Britain began to seek membership as early as 1961 (only two years after the formation of EFTA). France under the leadership of Charles De Gaulle would have none of it. Since the Treaty of Rome provided (as the Treaty on European Union still does) that all new memberships require a unanimous Council vote, France was effectively able to veto the British application. It was not until the resignation of De Gaulle in 1969 that the British were able in due course to secure membership in the EEC. New Members (1973) Agreement on the terms of British accession (including withdrawal from EFTA and the elimination of trade preferences with major Commonwealth nations) was reached in 1971, with an effective date of January, 1973.

The switch from EFTA to the EEC by Britain under Conservative Party leadership was undertaken with an ambivalence that continues to be evident. It was only with reluctance that the British accepted the surrenders of sovereignty inherent in the EEC Treaty. From 1973 onwards, more and more of the economic life of the United Kingdom would be governed by the four institutions of the European Community (now Union). British reluctance to join the Common Market was replayed in a 1975 national referendum under a Labor Party government. Approximately 60 percent of the populace voted to remain a member of the Community.

Denmark also switched sides in 1973. Norway was scheduled to become a member of the EEC at that time, and the terms of its membership had been negotiated, but the people of Norway rejected the Community in a national referendum. Ireland also joined the EEC in 1973.

In addition to the expansion of the EEC to nine members, 1973 brought an even greater degree of European economic integration. Although EFTA remained intact, each of the remaining EFTA nations signed bilateral trade treaties with the expanded Community. These treaties governed trade relations between all EFTA nations and the Community until 1994. They essentially provide for industrial free trade. Thus the 1973 enlargement of the European Economic Community was the catalyst for a widescale and comprehensive effort at Western European integration, a reconciliation of the EFTA and EEC trading alliances. This was an historic watershed in European economic integration.

European Economic Area (1994)

Relations between the Union and the EFTA states—with the exception of Switzerland—were put on a new footing with the entry into force of the Agreement on the European Economic Area (EEA) in 1994. The EEA establishes a free trade area larger than NAFTA and, in addition, provides that the four fundamental freedoms of the internal market of the Union (free movement of goods, persons, services and capital) as well as the competition rules and certain horizontal policies (social policy, consumer protection, environment, statistics and company law) are applied throughout the EEA area. The EFTA states had to adopt the "acquis communautaire", i.e. the established EU law in all these areas.

A special EFTA Surveillance Authority was set up with powers similar to those of the Commission, and also an EFTA Court, resembling the European Court of Justice. However, the EEA Agreement did not create a customs union, thus there is no common external customs tariff nor application of EU free trade agreements. Excluded are also such sensitive subjects like agriculture, fisheries and economic and monetary policy. The lasting importance of the EEA Agreement is difficult to assess since several EFTA countries joined the EU in 1995, and *it now applies only to Norway, Iceland and Lichtenstein. These countries make contributions to the EU budget.*

§ 3.3   The EU Legal System

The Europeans have been creating law at dazzling though sometimes irregular speed. Without an understanding of these areas, it is almost impossible to function as a lawyer on EU matters.

The two founding treaties of the European Union, the Treaty on the Functioning of the European Union (TFEU) and the Maastricht Treaty on European Union (TEU), are the "primary" sources of regional law. They are "quasi-constitutional." The treaties have a common set of core institutions, as described below. These are the Council, the Commission, the Parliament and the Court of Justice. These institutions, supplemented by the European Council, European Central Bank and other EU bodies, and by national legislatures, courts and tribunals, have been busy generating a remarkably vast and complex body of "secondary" law.

Some law is adopted directly at the regional level, but much of it is enacted by national governments under regional "direction." Similarly, some (and the most important) of the case law is created by decisions in the European Court of Justice and its companion General Court (see below), but much development also occurs in the national courts, acting in many instances with "advisory rulings" from the Court of Justice. European secondary law also includes international obligations, sometimes undertaken through "mixed" regional and national negotiations and ratifications.

There are two main types of legislative acts, directives and regulations (see below). These acts should be distinguished from declarations, resolutions, guidelines, notices, policy statements, recommendations, opinions and individual decisions, all of which rarely involve legislative acts and are sometimes referred to as "soft law."

The Reform Treaty of 2009, in new TFEU provisions, enumerates categories and areas of exclusive, shared and supportive EU competences or powers. These enumerations determine when and to what degree the EU and/or the member states may legislate. Exclusive EU competences include the customs union, internal market competition rules, marine conservation, and the Common Commercial Policy (external trade and investment relations). The Union also has exclusive competence over international agreements provided for in EU legislative acts, necessary to enable the exercise of its internal powers, or those agreements whose conclusion may affect common rules or alter their scope. In all these areas, member states may legislate only if empowered by the Union to do so, or to implement EU acts.

When the TFEU enumerates a shared competence, the Union may legislate. Member states may legislate only to the extent the EU has not done so or ceased to exercise a shared competence. Shared competences include the internal market, social policy, cohesion, agriculture and fisheries, the environment, consumer protection, transport, trans-European networks, energy, the area of freedom, security and justice, and common public health safety concerns. Special more-permissive rules allow member states greater latitude in the areas of research, technology development, space, third world development and humanitarian aid.

Lastly, the Union is authorized to legislate in support of, to coordinate with, or to supplement (but not supersede) member state competence in areas designated in Article 6 of the TFEU. These include human health, industry, culture, tourism, education and training, youth, sport, civil protection and administrative cooperation. EU acts in these areas may not entail harmonization of member state laws or regulations.

EU Legislation

Article 288 of the TFEU clarifies the powers of the Council and the Commission to make regulations and issue directives. EU regulations are similar in form to administrative regulations commonly found in North America. EU directives, on the other hand, have no obvious parallel. A directive establishes regional policy. It is then left to the member states to implement the directive in whatever way is appropriate to their national legal system. This may require a new statute, a Presidential decree, an administrative act or even a constitutional amendment. Sometimes it may require no action at all. As Article 288 indicates, a directive is "binding as to the result to be achieved" but "leave[s] to the national authorities the choice of form and methods." The vast majority of the legislative acts of the 1980s single market campaign were directives. Regulations have since become more common. All directives contain time limits for national implementation. The more controversial the policy, the longer the likely allotment of time. The Reform Treaty of 2009 makes it clear member states must adopt all measures necessary to implement legally binding Union acts.

The Commission initiates the process of legislation by drafting proposals, which the Council (comprised of ministers from the governments of the member states) has the power to adopt into law. Although the Council and Parliament may request the Commission to submit legislative proposals, neither can force the Commission to do so except through litigation before the Court of Justice. Only the Commission can draft legislative proposals. This makes the Commission the focal point of lobbying activities, a point not lost on U.S. companies with stakes in EU legislative outcomes, such as the banking, bio-tech and software directives.

The Commission's legislative proposals are always influenced by what it believes the Council and Parliament will accept. The Council, however, has the right to amend legislative proposals by unanimous vote. Parliament's role was traditionally consultative. Over time, it became and remains the source of *proposed* amendments. Note that Parliament does not have the power to enact law! This absence of legislative power is so fundamental that many observers decry a "democratic deficit" in Europe. This deficit has been partially "remedied" by conveying "co-decision" powers to Parliament. These powers amount to a Parliamentary right, in the absence of conciliation with the Council, to veto selected legislative proposals.

EU Council

The foregoing analysis of legislative process illustrates the dominant role of the Council in regional affairs. The Council, also known since 1993 as the Council of the European Union (EU Council), consists of representatives of the governments of the member states. Thus there are presently 28 Council members since the accession of Croatia in 2013. However, the people who comprise the Council change according to the topic at hand. The national ministers of foreign affairs, agriculture, economy and finance (ecofin), social affairs, environment, etc. are sent to Brussels to confer and vote on matters within their competence. Some refer to the Ecofin Council, the Environment Council, the Agriculture Council and so forth in order to differentiate the various Councils. Several different Council meetings can take place at once.

Most of the voting in the Council now takes place on a qualified majority basis. The rules that define this procedure are given in Article 238 of the TFEU. Since November 1, 2014, a qualified majority is defined as at least 55% of the members of the Council (with a minimum number of 15) who represent member states comprising 65% of the population of the Union. Any blocking minority must include at least 4 Council members. Thus a relatively simplified "double majority" voting system was undertaken in 2014.

EU Commission

The pivotal role of the European Commission in the law-making process should be evident. Apart from administrative cooperation on criminal and police matters, where a quarter of the member states can initiate EU acts, the Commission alone drafts legislative proposals. The Commission can also prosecute when proper legislative procedures are not followed. Furthermore, in certain areas, notably agricultural and competition law, the Council has delegated to the Commission the authority to issue implementing regulations and decisions that establish law. These acts detail administrative rules rather than create new or broad policies. Thus the Council establishes the "target prices" for agriculture, but the

Commission issues thousands of regulations aimed at actually realizing these goals.

The Commission has also promulgated an important series of "group exemption" regulations for business competition law. These cover franchising, technology transfers, distribution and a variety of other business agreements. Lastly, the Commission is authorized by Article 106 of the TFEU to issue (on its own initiative) *directives* addressed to member states regarding public enterprises. This authority avoids the usual legislative process. The Reform Treaty of 2009 added a citizen's initiative procedure. One million EU citizens from a significant number of member states may "invite" the Commission to submit proposals in areas of regional concern.

The Commission performs a number of functions in addition to those concerning law-making. The most important of these include its prosecutorial powers against individuals and enterprises for breach of selected laws, and against member states for failure to adhere to their treaty obligations. The Commission negotiates international trade and other agreements. It also administers the EU budget and publishes a general and a series of specific annual reports (*e.g.*, on competition policy), all of which are a good way to survey regional affairs.

Unlike the ministers of the Council, Commissioners are not supposed to function as representatives of their nations. Commissioners are appointed by a qualified majority of the Council subject to Parliament's approval for five-year renewable terms. The President of the Commission is similarly appointed by the European Council and Parliament. Great pains are taken to ensure the independence of Commissioners from their home governments. Article 245 of the TFEU stipulates that Commissioners must be chosen on the basis of competence and their independence must be "beyond doubt." Any breach of this trust by Commissioners could lead to compulsory retirement or dismissal by the President of the Commission.

Court of Justice of the European Union

The EU is unique among regional economic organizations in having a powerful and active court to enforce its laws and treaties. The Court of Justice of the European Union (CJEU) rules on disputes involving EU laws and treaties. Its decisions are binding on EU institutions and the member nations' governments.

The CJEU consists of three courts, the Court of Justice (informally called the European Court of Justice (ECJ)), the General Court, and the Civil Service Tribunal. The Court of Justice hears referrals from national courts regarding the proper interpretation of

EU law, claims brought by the Commission against member states for failure to comply with EU obligations, claims brought by member states against EU institutions, and appeals from decisions of the General Court. The General Court hears claims by individuals and corporations (and in some cases by member states) against EU institutions. The Civil Service Tribunal hears disputes between EU institutions and their staff.

Article 267 TFEU vests jurisdiction in the European Court to give "preliminary rulings" (sometimes called "advisory rulings") on the interpretation of the Treaty, the validity and interpretation of acts by the Union's institutions and other matters. These rulings occur when national courts or tribunals (faced with an issue of Union law) request them. Article 267 requests or "references" are discretionary with the judges of the lower-level courts and tribunals of the member states. They cannot be initiated as a matter of right by litigants, nor by arbitrators designated by contract to resolve a dispute when those arbitrators are not functioning as a court or tribunal of a member state. This is a particularly notable decision because ever increasing numbers of business and trade disputes are being taken to binding arbitration.

Whenever a national court considers a reference necessary to enable judgment, it may seek the advice of the European Court by posing questions to it. It may do so even when the European Court or a higher national court has already ruled on the question of EU law at hand. In other words, the common law doctrine of binding precedent does not remove the discretion of lower courts to invoke Article 267. Similarly, the fact that appeals are mandatory under national law does not block utilization of Article 267 references to the ECJ if the lower court believes such a reference is necessary to enable it to give judgment.

In practice, lower courts refer EU law issues to the ECJ quite regularly. Assuming the request comes from a proper national court or tribunal, the European Court of Justice cannot refuse the reference, even when it has already ruled on the EU legal issue. Once underway, the Commission almost always files a written brief expressing its opinion in Article 267 proceedings. The government of the member state whose court or tribunal is the source of the reference typically does so as well. Private parties "interested" in the questions being referred may not intervene. After a preliminary ruling of the European Court is secured, the national court is obliged to implement that ruling in its final judgment. The ruling is also binding on appeal of that judgment, and (at a minimum) persuasive in courts of other nations.

Decisions of the EU courts are binding on EU institutions, member states, and perhaps most importantly, the national courts of the member states. Over time, the EU courts have issued key decisions on a wide range of issues affecting trade and investment, including tariff policies, nontariff trade barriers, competition law and intellectual property.

§ 3.4   The EU Customs Union and Common Market

The free movement of goods within Europe is based upon the creation of a customs union. Under this union, the member states have eliminated customs duties among themselves, *including* antidumping and countervailing duties. They have established a common customs tariff and customs code for their trade with the rest of the world. *The EU, not individual member states, also has exclusive authority to negotiate trade agreements and treaties, including EU free trade and customs union agreements.*

Quantitative restrictions (quotas) on trade between member states are also prohibited, except in emergency and other limited situations. The right of free movement applies to goods that originate in the Common Market and to those that have lawfully entered it and are said to be in "free circulation." Thus U.S. exports to the EU, having cleared customs into its Common Market, can be moved across internal EU borders at will.

The establishment of the customs union has been a major accomplishment, though not without difficulties. The member states committed themselves not only to the elimination of tariffs and quotas on internal trade, but also to the elimination of "measures of equivalent effect." The elastic legal concept of measures of equivalent effect has been interpreted broadly by the European Court of Justice and the European Commission to prohibit a wide range of trade restraints, such as administrative fees charged at borders which are the equivalent of import or export tariffs. Charges of equivalent effect to a tariff must be distinguished from internal taxes that are applicable to imported and domestic goods. The latter must be levied in a nondiscriminatory and non-protective manner, while the former are prohibited entirely, there has been a considerable amount of litigation over this distinction.

Nontariff Trade Barriers

Nontariff trade barriers (NTBs) were the principal focus of the 1980s Europe without Internal Frontiers campaign for a fully integrated Common "Single Market". Many legislative acts were adopted which target NTBs. When possible, a common European standard is adopted. For example, legislation on auto pollution requirements adopts this methodology. Products meeting these standards may be freely traded in the Common Market. Traditionally, this approach (called "harmonization") has required the formation of a consensus as to the appropriate level of protection.

Once adopted, harmonized standards must be followed. This approach can be deceptive, however. Some harmonization directives contain a list of options from which member states may choose when implementing those directives. In practice, this leads to differentiated national laws on the same so-called harmonized subject. Furthermore, in certain areas (notably the environment and occupational health and safety), the TFEU expressly indicates that member states may adopt laws that are more demanding. The result is, again, less than complete harmonization.

Many efforts at the harmonization of European environmental, health and safety, standards and certification, and related law have been undertaken. Nearly all of these are supposed to be based upon "high levels of protection." Some have criticized what they see as the "least common denominator" results of harmonization of national laws under the campaign for a Europe without internal frontiers. One example involves the safety of toys. Directive 88/378 permits toys to be sold throughout the Common Market if they satisfy "essential requirements." These requirements are broadly worded in terms of flammability, toxicity, etc. There are two ways to meet these requirements: (1) produce a toy in accordance with CEN standards (drawn up by experts); or (2) produce a toy that otherwise meets the essential safety requirements. Local language labeling requirements necessary for purchaser comprehension have generally, though not always, been upheld.

The least common denominator criticism may be even more appropriate to the second legislative methodology utilized in the internal market campaign. The second approach is based on the *Cassis* principle of mutual reciprocity. Under this "new" minimalist approach, EU legislation requires member states to recognize the laws of other member states and deem them acceptable for purposes of the operation of the Common Market. For example, major legislation has been adopted in the area of professional services. By mutual recognition of higher education diplomas based upon at least three years of courses, virtually all professionals have now obtained legal rights to move freely within the Union in pursuit of their careers. This is a remarkable achievement.

Article 36 TFEU

The provisions of the EEC Treaty of Rome (now TFEU) dealing with the establishment of the customs union do not adequately address the problem of nontariff trade barriers (NTBs). As in NAFTA and the world community, the major trade barrier within the European Union has become NTBs. To some extent, in the absence of a harmonizing directive completely occupying the field, this is authorized. Article 36 TFEU permits national restraints on imports and exports justified on the grounds of:

(1)   Public morality, public policy ("ordre public") or public security;

(2)   The protection of health and life of humans, animals or plants;

(3)   The protection of national treasures possessing artistic, historical or archeological value; and

(4)   The protection of industrial or commercial property.

Article 36 amounts, within certain limits, to an authorization of nontariff trade barriers among the EU nations. This "public interest" authorization exists in addition to, but somewhat overlaps with, the Rule of Reason exception formulated under Article 34 in *Cassis* above. However, in a sentence much construed by the European Court of Justice, Article 36 continues with the following language: "Such prohibitions or restrictions shall not, however, constitute a means of arbitrary discrimination or a disguised restriction on trade between member states."

In a wide range of decisions, the Court of Justice has interpreted Article 36 in a manner which generally limits the ability of member states to impose NTB barriers to internal Union trade. Britain, for example, may use its criminal law under the public morality exception to seize pornographic goods made in Holland that it outlaws, but not inflatable sex dolls from Germany which could be lawfully produced in the United Kingdom. Germany cannot stop the importation of beer (*e.g.*, Heineken's from Holland) which fails to meet its purity standards. This case makes wonderful reading as the Germans, seeking to invoke the public health exception of Article 30, argue all manner of ills that may befall their populace if free trade in beer is allowed. See *Commission v. Germany* (1987) Eur. Comm. Rep. 1227. Equally interesting are the unsuccessful Italian health protection arguments against free trade in pasta made from common (not durum) wheat, the failure of French standards' arguments against free trade in foie gras, and the rejection of Spain's "chocolate substitutes" labeling rule for chocolate containing vegetable fats.

But a state may obtain whatever information it requires from importers to evaluate public health risks associated with food products containing additives that are freely traded elsewhere in the Common Market. This does not mean that an importer of muesli bars to which vitamins have been added must prove the product healthful, rather that the member state seeking to bar the imports must have an objective reason for keeping them out of its market. Assuming such a reason exists, the trade restraint may not be disproportionate to the public health goal. A notable ECJ opinion invalidated a French public health ban on U.K. beef imports maintained after a Commission decision to return to free trade following the "mad cow" outbreak. See *National Farmers Union v. Secretariat General* (2002) Eur. Comm. Rep. I-9079.

Public security measures adopted under Article 36 can include external as well as internal security. In one case, the validity of national CoCom restrictions on the export of strategic goods to the U.S.S.R. was noted. An unusual case under the public security exception contained in Article 36 involved Irish petroleum products' restraints. The Irish argued that oil is an exceptional product always triggering national security interests. Less expansively, the Court acknowledged that maintaining minimum oil supplies did fall within the ambit of Article 36. The public policy exception under Article 36 has been construed along French lines (ordre public). Only genuine threats to fundamental societal interests are covered. Consumer protection (though a legitimate rationale for trade restraints under *Cassis*), does not fall within the public policy exception of Article 36. Permitting environmental protesters to block the Brenner Pass for 30 hours was acceptable public policy in support of fundamental assembly and expression rights.

Intellectual Property Rights as Trade Barriers

A truly remarkable body of case law has developed around the authority granted national governments in Article 36 TFEU to protect industrial or commercial property ("intellectual property") by restraining imports and exports. These cases run the full gamut from protection of trademarks and copyrights to protection of patents and know-how. There is a close link between this body of case law and that developed under Article 101 TFEU concerning restraints on competition. Trade restraints involving intellectual property arise out of the fact that such rights are nationally granted. Owners of intellectual property rights within the Union are free under most traditional law to block the unauthorized importation of goods into national markets. There is a strong tendency for national infringement lawsuits to serve as vehicles for the division of the Common Market.

Considerable energy has been spent by the Commission on developing Common Market rights that would provide an alternative to national intellectual property rights. Late in 1993, the Council reached agreement on an EU trademark regime and the Council adopted Directive 89/104, which harmonizes member state laws governing trademarks. As a result, for example, the United Kingdom enacted the Trade Marks Act of 1994. The Court of Justice has ruled that goods bearing trademarks registered somewhere in the EU may be freely circulated marked with an "R" in a circle after the trademark. National law on unfair competition cannot be used to impede trade in such goods on the grounds that the mark in question is not registered in the country of sale. In the copyright field, several directives have harmonized European law, perhaps most importantly mandating copyrights for computer software.

A long-proposed EU Patent Convention finally came into force in 2014 as the EU Unitary Patent (UP) regime. It is applicable in all EU member states save Spain and Italy, miffed by the omission of their languages as "official". The UP regime operates in French, German or English through its headquarters in Paris. It can issue or revoke a Common Market patent valid in any contracting state. Transfers and licenses for part of the Union are possible. The cost saving UP is an alternative to (but not a replacement for) national patent and European Patent Convention rights. However, the UP requires its signatories to harmonize national patent laws to conform to Unitary Patent rules on infringement, litigation procedures, exhaustion of rights and other issues. New Unified Patent Courts of First Instance and Appeal have been created in Luxembourg. By 2021 their centralized jurisdiction will govern infringement and validity disputes concerning national patents, European patents and Unified patents.

The European Court of Justice has addressed IP trade barrier problems and generally resolved against the exercise of national intellectual property rights in ways which inhibit free trade *inside* the Union. In many of these decisions, the Court acknowledges the existence of the right to block trade in infringing goods, but holds that the exercise of that right is subordinate to the TFEU. The Court has also fashioned a doctrine which treats national intellectual property rights as having been exhausted once the goods to which they apply are freely sold on the market. One of the few exceptions to this doctrine is broadcast performing rights which the Court considers incapable of exhaustion. Records, CDs and cassettes embodying such rights are, however, subject to the exhaustion doctrine once released into the market.

Such goods often end up in the hands of third parties who then ship them into another member state. The practical effect of many of the rulings of the Court of Justice is to remove the ability of the owners of the relevant intellectual property rights from successfully pursuing infringement actions in national courts. When intellectual property rights have a single proprietor and have been placed on goods by consent, as when a licensor authorizes their use in other EU countries, then infringement actions to protect against parallel imports of the goods to which the rights apply are usually denied. This may not be the case, however, when voluntary trademark assignments that are not anticompetitive are involved. In such cases, the ECJ has demonstrated some concern for consumer confusion when trade in parallel goods occurs.

It is only when intellectual property rights do not have a single proprietor (thus sharing a "common origin") or the requisite consent is absent that they stand a chance of being upheld so as to stop trade in infringing products. Compulsory licensing of patents, for example, does not involve consensual marketing of products. Patent rights may therefore be used to block trade in goods produced under such a license. But careful repackaging and resale of goods subject to a common or even different trademark may occur against the objections of the owner of the mark. And compulsory licensing cannot be conditioned upon import bans applicable to the beneficiary licensee. Such bans offend the free movement of goods law of the EU and unfairly create investment incentives.

Centrafarm Case, Exhaustion Doctrine

An excellent example of the application of the exhaustion doctrine developed by the Court of Justice in the intellectual property field, as applied to a U.S. company, can be found in the *Centrafarm* case. 1974 Eur. Comm. Rep. 1147. The United States pharmaceutical company, Sterling Drug, owned the British and Dutch patents and trademarks relating to "Negram." Subsidiaries of Sterling Drug in Britain and Holland had been respectively assigned the British and Dutch trademark rights to Negram. Owing in part to price controls in the UK, a substantial difference in cost for Negram emerged as between the two countries. Centrafarm was an independent Dutch importer of Negram from the UK and Germany.

Sterling Drug and its subsidiaries brought infringement actions in the Dutch courts under their national patent and trademark rights seeking an injunction against Centrafarm's importation of Negram into The Netherlands. The Court of Justice held that the intellectual property rights of Sterling Drug and its subsidiaries could not be exercised in a way which blocked EU trade in "parallel goods." In the Court's view, the exception established in Article 36 for the protection of industrial and commercial property covers only those rights that were specifically intended to be conveyed by the grant of national patents and trademarks.

Blocking trade in parallel goods after they have been put on the market with the consent of a common owner, exhausting the IP rights in question, was not intended to be part of the package of IP benefits conveyed. If Sterling Drug succeeded, an arbitrary discrimination or disguised restriction on Union trade would be achieved. Thus the European Court of Justice ruled in favor of the free movement of goods within the Common Market even when that negates clearly existing national legal remedies.

While the goal of creation of the Common Market can override national intellectual property rights when internal trade is concerned, these rights apply fully to the importation of goods from *outside* the European Union. North American exporters of goods allegedly subject to rights owned by Europeans may therefore find entry into the EU challenged by infringement actions in national courts. But, in reverse, U.S. owners of EU intellectual property rights may do likewise. This is notably true regarding trade in gray market goods. Levi Strauss, citing its British trademarks, successfully kept low-price (made in the USA) Levi's out of the EU. Monsanto, on the other hand, was unable to invoke its European GMO patent rights to block importation of Argentinian bioengineered soybeans.

EU Agricultural Policy and International Trade Barriers

Here are the basic principles governing what is perhaps the most controversial of all Union policies, the Common Agricultural Program (CAP). The inclusion of agricultural trade was a critical element to the politics of the Union and remains largely without precedent in other regional economic treaties throughout the world. For many reasons, including the desire for self-sufficiency in food and the protection of farmers, free trade in agricultural products is an extremely sensitive issue.

When the Common Market was established in 1957, France and Italy had substantial farming communities, many of which were family based and politically powerful. Both countries envisioned that free trade in agricultural products could threaten the livelihoods of these people. The solution, as outlined in the Treaty, was to set up a "common organization of agricultural markets." The objectives of the CAP include the increase of productivity, the maintenance of a fair standard of living for the agricultural community, the stabilization of markets, and the provision of consumer goods at reasonable prices. It has not proved possible to accommodate all of these objectives.

Consumer interests have generally lost out to farmers' incomes and trading company profits.

Target prices for some commodities (*e.g.*, sugar, dairy products and grain) are established and supported through Union market purchases at "intervention levels". "Variable import levies" (tariffs) are periodically changed to ensure that cheaper imports do not disrupt CAP prices. External protection of this type is also extended to meat and eggs. Fruit, vegetables and wine are subject to quality controls which limit their flow into the market. Wine and agricultural products are subject to regulated designations of origin, Rioja wine from Spain and Feta cheese from Greece, for examples. Such regulations do not extend to generic food names, such as edam, jenerver (gin) and emmenthal, which can be freely traded with proper labels indicating variations in product qualities.

In recent years, perhaps the most controversial "common organization" has been for bananas. The Europeans import bananas under a complex quota system adopted in 1993 that favors former colonies and dependencies. Internally and externally those affected have gone bananas over this regulation. Several challenges originating from Germany failed before the European Court of Justice, but in the end the United States, Mexico, Ecuador, Guatemala and Honduras prevailed in the World Trade Organization. After suffering "authorized retaliation" in the form of tariffs on EU exports, the Europeans adjusted their "common organization" for bananas by replacing its quotas with non-preferential tariffs.

The European Agricultural Guidance and Guarantee Fund (better known by its French initials as FEOGA) channels the Union agricultural budget into export refunds, intervention purchases, storage, and structural adjustment. Agricultural policy regulations cannot discriminate against like or substitute products. But the bias towards producers, not consumers, in the CAP has been consistently upheld by the Court of Justice. Agricultural goods, like industrial products, can trigger free movement litigation.

In one case, for example, the Court of Justice suggested that British animal health regulations were a disguised restraint on Union trade in poultry and eggs. As with industrial goods, if the real aim is to block imports, such regulations are unlawful measures of equivalent effect to a quota. On the other hand, the United Kingdom could establish a Pear and Apple Development Council for purposes of technical advice, promotional campaigns (not intended to discourage competitive imports), and common quality standards for its members. But it could not impose a mandatory fee to finance such activities.

Apart from variable tariff protection, CAP quality control regulations can serve to keep foreign agricultural products from entering the European Union market. For example, the ban on beef hormones adopted by qualified majority vote in the late 1980s stirred opposition internally. In the United States, the beef hormones legislation was vehemently opposed by the White House, but accepted by the renegade Texas Department of Agriculture which offered as much hormone-free beef to the Union as it would buy. The Texas offer delighted the EU Commissioner on Agriculture who rarely has a U.S. ally and is said to have wired: "I accept."

A veritable maze of legislation and case law governs the CAP. For many years, special agricultural "monetary compensation amounts" (MCAs) have been collected at national borders, greatly contributing to the failure to achieve a Europe without internal trade frontiers. It was not until 1987 that firm arrangements were realized to dismantle the MCA system. In most years, the net effect of the CAP is to raise food prices in the EU substantially above world price levels. The CAP has meant that agriculture is heavily subsidized. Indeed, it continues to consume a major share of the Union budget and at times seems like a spending policy that is out of control.

The Common Agricultural Policy does include a variety of "structural" programs intended to reduce the size of the farm population, increase the efficiency of its production, and hold down prices. These programs have involved retirement incentives, land reallocations, and training for other occupations. There has been a gradual reduction in the number of EU farmers over the years. In 1988, the Council adopted rules designed ultimately to reduce agricultural expenditures by linking total expenditures to the Union's rate of economic growth, establishing automatic price cuts when production ceilings are reached, and creating land set-aside and environmental protection incentives for farmers.

France and Italy, in the early years of the EU, became major beneficiaries of CAP subsidies. West Germany, with a minimal agricultural sector, was the primary payor under the program. It, in turn, principally benefitted from the custom union provisions establishing free trade in industrial goods. Hence a basic tradeoff was established in 1957 by the Treaty of Rome. France and Italy would receive substantial agricultural subsidies out of the regional budget while West Germany gained access for its industrial goods to their markets. Germany now holds a 25 percent share of internal EU trade. Britain, like Germany, saw itself as a net payor under the CAP. It has repeatedly been able to negotiate special compensatory adjustments as a consequence.

Greece, Spain, Portugal and Ireland, on the other hand, looked forward eagerly to membership as a means to CAP subsidies. These countries, along with unified Germany, Austria, Sweden and Finland (whose agricultural subsidies were actually reduced upon joining the CAP), are often the least efficient producers of agricultural products. As such, they stand to lose the most if the CAP is substantially replaced by market forces.

Each enlargement of the Union plugs more farmers into the extraordinary CAP subsidy system and the ten new members admitted in 2004 will gain full payments by 2013. Thus the really big cost for CAP followed enlargement of the European Union to include Hungary and Poland, among others. The Amsterdam and Nice Treaties notably failed to resolve ongoing disputes over agricultural reform. A last minute deal in 2002 capped costs at their 2006 level plus 1 percent a year starting in 2007. In theory this will force a gradual winding down of CAP subsidies. Significant efforts are being made to de-couple CAP subsidies from production levels, notably for cotton, tobacco and olive oil. Production quotas for milk were dismantled in 2015, and for beet(sugar) in 2017. Meanwhile, one wonders just how much longer European taxpayers will continue to pay for the CAP.

In the main like the United States, the European Union seems unable to stabilize the level of its agricultural subsidies. This results in overproduction ("butter mountains" and "wine lakes") and frequent commodity trade wars. A significant amount of fraud to obtain CAP subsidy payments has occurred. In 1989, the House of Lords Select Committee on the European Community released a scathing report on subsidy abuses entitled "Fraud against the Community." Others legitimately farm marginal land with lots of fertilizer. The excess produce is stored, used in social welfare programs and frequently "dumped" in cheap sales abroad. Despite its incredible cost, the CAP remains one of the political and economic cornerstones of the Union.

External protests from North America notwithstanding, the CAP is unlikely to disappear. The provocative question much debated in the Uruguay Round of GATT negotiations is whether a mutually satisfactory reduction in the level of North American and European Union subsidies to agriculture can actually be achieved. In 1992 the Council of Agricultural Ministers agreed as an internal matter to cuts in support prices of 29 percent for cereals, 15 percent for beef and 5 percent for butter. Farmers received direct payments representing the income lost from the price cuts. Further price cuts and direct payments were agreed in 1999. It was hoped that these reductions would reduce EU export subsidies on agricultural goods and international trade tensions.

They also supported the argument that the extraordinary level of European subsidization of agriculture was simply not sustainable in cost or EU politics. European Union agricultural trade restraints are of enormous consequence to North American exporters. Equally significant are EU "export refunds" on agricultural commodities, refunds that affect the opportunities of North American exporters in other parts of the world. The United States has consistently argued (at times successfully) that these refunds violate the GATT rules on subsidies, while at the same time increasing its own export subsidies on agricultural goods. The result has been an agricultural "trade war" between the U.S. and the EU.

Each side has sought to outspend the other on agricultural export subsidies in a market that has been wonderful to buyers. Major attempts at a resolution or at least diminishment of the agricultural trade war were undertaken in the Uruguay Round of GATT negotiations during the late 1980s and early 1990s. Late in 1992, both sides announced the resolution of a number of longstanding subsidies' disputes (notably on oilseeds) and a compromise on the contested Uruguay Round agricultural trade issues. Agreement was reached on 20 percent mutual reduction in internal farm supports and a 21 percent mutual reduction on export subsidies measured on a volume basis over 6 years using a 1986–90 base period.

After a year of French protests and further negotiations, this agreement was formally incorporated into the WTO accords. Under it, the Union has been gradually switching from production and export subsidies to direct income support for farmers and rural businesses. This decoupling of agricultural subsidies from output has steadily progressed and is crucial to the long-term viability of the CAP. Tensions between Europe and the United States on agricultural trade have of late diminished (though hardly disappeared), but repeated U.S. Farm Bills threaten to reignite them.

The EURO

The EURO is the common currency of 19 of the 28 EU members (collectively called the "Eurozone"). It was initially adopted by 11 nations in 1999, with coins and currency introduced in 2002 and national currencies phased out and eliminated. Of the 15 EU nations in 1999, Britain, Denmark and Sweden refused to adopt the EURO, and Greece initially did not meet the fiscal qualifications (Greece joined in 2001). Since 2001, an additional 7 nations from eastern and southern Europe have adopted the EURO. In addition, a few small countries use the EURO even though they are not part of the agreements creating the monetary union, and several countries have their national currencies fixed to the Euro. Nine countries are currently members of the EU but not the Eurozone (Britain, Denmark, Sweden, Poland, Czech Republic, Hungary, Bulgaria, Romania and Croatia).

The arrival of the EURO has important implications for the United States and the dollar. For decades, the dollar has been the world's leading currency, although its dominance has been declining since the early 1980s. Use of the Deutsche Mark and Yen in commercial and financial transactions, and in savings and reserves, had been steadily rising. The EURO is likely to continue the dollar's decline in all of these markets. It is certainly the hope of many Europeans that they have successfully created a rival to the dollar. NAFTA, in contrast, does not even hint at a common North American currency.

As part of the creation of the EURO, the member nations established the European Central Bank (ECB) and the European System of Central Banks (ECSB). The ECB and ECSB are governed by an executive board of six persons appointed by the member states and the governors of the national central banks. The ECB and the ECSB are independent of any other European institution and in theory free from member state influence. Their primary responsibility is to maintain price stability, specifically keeping price inflation below two percent per year. The main functions of the ECB and ECSB are: (1) defining and implementing regional monetary policy; (2) conducting foreign exchange operations; (3) holding and managing the official foreign reserves of the member states; and (4) supervising the payments systems. The ECB has the exclusive right to authorize the issue of bank notes within the Common Market and must set interest rates to principally achieve price stability.

Regrettably, the fiscal enforcement system established when the EURO was created did not work. Since 1999, many EURO states have been under threat of sanction for failure to comply with the maximum 3 percent budget deficit rule. Yet no Eurozone member state was ever sanctioned, suggesting this system for controlling national deficits was toothless. In a death knell, sanctions for failure to comply with 3 percent rule were held unenforceable by the European Court of Justice. See *Commission v. Council* (2004) Eur. Comm. Rep. I-6649 (Case C-27/04). The initial enforcement system was replaced by the 2012 Treaty on Stability, Coordination and Governance discussed below.

The global financial crisis of 2008, high debt and continuing sluggish economic performance have put intense pressure on the weaker Eurozone economies, notably Greece, Cyprus, Spain, Portugal, Ireland and Italy. Financial rescue packages ("bailouts") of debt-ridden Eurozone members have sometimes been necessary, including three successive bailouts of Greece subject to austerity conditions. In March 2012, with market pressures and threats of a Greek default or exit from the Eurozone escalating, 25 of the then-27 EU members (minus Britain and the Czech Republic) adopted a Treaty on Stability, Coordination and Governance (TSCG) intended to provide a "permanent" solution to the EURO crisis, including a permanent 900 billion Euro loan fund, a Fiscal Compact, and ECB purchases of national government debt ("quantitative easing").

The EURO Crisis Continues

The EURO was conceived as a unifier for Europe. It has become instead a divisive wedge among creditors and austerity weary debtor nations. That said, by 2014 Ireland and Portugal had refinanced and exited their bailouts without credit line safety nets, taken to be "success" stories. Cyprus did likewise in 2016. But Greece, Italy and Spain remain troubled, and the Eurozone crisis is anything but over.

With deflation and economic stagnation apparent, the ECB undertook starting in 2015 a massive, unprecedented and controversial "quantitative easing (QE)" program buying up national government debt. This program resembled that which the U.S. Federal Reserve had been pursuing for some time. In 2016, the ECB extended its bond buying program to selected corporate debt and reduced bank loans to zero interest for up to four years. These QE policies reduced European government borrowing costs, tended to reinforce European equity prices, and weakened the EURO (thus enhancing exports). But they appear to have had diminishing returns, pushing ECB bank deposit interest rates into negative territory for example. The ECB terminated its QE program in 2019.

Greece elected a government strongly opposed to the austerity conditions attached to its bailouts, lowering the Grexit threshold. There is cause for opposition to the austerity loan conditions. Over the first six years, Greece received over 240 billion Euros in bailout funds, plus the private sector debt restructuring, yet its economy has shrunk by at least 25%, and its debt to GDP ratio has risen dramatically to over 175%. In short, the bailouts and their conditions have proven self-destructive, making it less (not more) likely that Greece can ever repay its debts.

Greek society pays a very heavy price: Unemployment is widespread, poverty is growing, young people and bank deposits are fleeing, property values are speedily descending, and disillusionment is pervasive. Corruption and tax evasion remain entrenched.

Amidst another Greek crisis in 2015, the EURO initially plunged in value, but rallied somewhat by mid-2015, just in time for a third bailout of Greece by the Troika comprised of the ECB, EU Commission and IMF. This bailout, like its predecessors and over IMF objections, did not reduce the amount of Greek national debt. One year later in 2016, it was déjà vu all over again. Greece needed more financial support to avoid default, and the IMF, after a somewhat scathing internal review of its participation in the second Greek bailout, pushed hard for debt reductions. Germany and the EU limited their support to extending Greek debt maturities, along with interest rate and debt repayment caps. This support was notably contingent upon pension and tax collection reforms in Greece.

By 2019, little had had changed: The IMF was still unwilling to participate in the third bailout, Germany unwilling to write off Greek debt, and the Greek government and its people suffering from austerity fatigue.

An essential question is whether a Greek default can be absorbed without taking down other Eurozone states and the EURO itself? In other words, whether a Greek default would prove contagious is the key systemic question. Portugal and Ireland, the bailout "success" stories, remain deeply indebted. Spain and Italy have survived on cash infusions that make the debt of Greece look miniscule, and major Italian banks appear insolvent. Nativist French politician Marine Le Pen ran on a Frexit platform promising to withdraw from the EURO in the 2017 French elections, and Italian anti-EURO parties now control that government.

The 2012 ESM mechanism has yet to be invoked, and Commission review of Fiscal Compact compliance has been "flexible". Hence the "permanent" solution to the EURO crisis created in 2012 is in doubt. Even some of the world's best financial market wizards say there is no clear-cut answer to the question of what happens in Europe or globally if Greece defaults or a EURO member withdraws from the Zone.

§ 3.5   EU Trade Relations with the United States, Japan and China

United States-EU Trade

Trade between the United States and the European Union is voluminous, roughly in balance and increasingly fractious. A focal point in recent years has been agricultural trade, especially the problem of export subsidies and nontariff trade barriers (notably Europe's banana quotas, beef hormone bans and freeze on GMO approvals) there are many contentious issues. For example, Airbus subsidies have been said to threaten Boeing and vice-versa, disputes that are pending at the WTO. The single market legislative campaign led to fears concerning the erection of a "Fortress Europe" in banking, insurance, broadcasting and other areas. There is a general concern in North America that Europe is turning inward and protective, a concern that is reciprocated by the Europeans since President Trump took office.

A particularly contentious issue has been the field of public procurement, notably the provision of the Utilities Directive which provides for a preference of tenders for supplies which contain less than 50 percent materials originating outside the Union. The dispute between the United States and the European Union was settled in negotiations which led to the conclusion of two agreements.

The Union, for its part, has begun imitating the United States' practice of issuing annual reports voicing its objections to U.S. trade barriers and unfair practices. Extraterritorial U.S. jurisdiction has been a constant complaint, including the Helms-Burton Cuban LIBERTAD and Iran-Libya Sanctions Act. These reports have also targeted Section 301 of the Trade Act of 1974. The U.S. invoked Section 301 in trade disputes with the EU over the use of animal hormones and EU regulation of oil seeds. The European Union perceives Section 301 to be a unilateral retaliatory mechanism that runs counter to multilateral resolution of trade disputes through the GATT/WTO.

This perception has not stopped the Union from partially duplicating this mechanism in EU law protections against "illicit commercial practices."90 Nevertheless, since the United States has been taking the bulk of its trade disputes to the WTO under its Dispute Settlement Understanding, the Europeans have less to complain about on this score. An EU challenge to Section 301 before the WTO was rejected in recognition of the U.S. commitment not to employ Section 301 when WTO remedies can be pursued.

Another issue that has been prominently and regularly mentioned is the problem (from the EU perspective) of the diversity of state and local regulation of procurement, product standards, the environment, financial services and taxation. U.S. critics of Europe's legislative diversity could not have said it better. Recent reports by the EU on U.S. trade practices identified major areas of complaint: unilateral U.S. trade legislation; extraterritorial trade law; national security restraints; Buy American policies; import fees, quotas and paperwork; agricultural export subsidies; tax rules on transfer pricing, autos and unitary income taxation; selectively high tariffs; the multiplicity of product standards; services; intellectual property rights; and investment. Perhaps both sides are headed for stronger central government regulation of trade-impacting measures.

Each has a lot at stake in trade with the other. The tough question is whether the World Trade Organization dispute resolution procedures can be made to work so as to preserve mutually beneficial trade relations between the Union and the United States. Trade relations between the EU and the U.S. have improved in limited ways under the Transatlantic Economic Partnership Program (1995). Starting in 2009 there is agreement on use of International Financial Reporting Standards, replacing U.S. Generally Accepted Accounting Principles. Common standards for electric cars have been developed.

Deep underlying conflicts remain, especially regarding cultural goods (TV shows, films), agriculture, GMOs, airplane subsidies, and procurement. It is this author's view that NAFTA and the EU have been competing with good reason for possession of the world's largest market. Larger markets bring greater leverage in intergovernmental trade negotiations, economies of scale, improved "terms of trade" (pay less for imports, receive more for exports), and enhanced abilities to exercise global economic leadership. And so the struggle for market power is likely to continue.

Trump and Europe

At over $1 trillion a year, the trading relationship between the United States and the European Union is the largest in the world, accounting for over one-third of global trade. Europe had a trade in goods surplus in 2016 of approximately $270 billion, while the U.S. had a trade in services surplus of $55 billion. Viewed individually for 2017, net U.S. goods and services trade with Britain generated a slight surplus, a slight deficit with France, a small deficit with Italy and a notable deficit of $68 billion with Germany. EU job and technology creating investment in the U.S. amounted in 2016 to about $200 billion, with each side having over $5 trillion invested in the other.

The U.S.-EU negotiations for a Transatlantic Trade and Investment Partnership (TTIP) initiated by President Obama have disappeared. After considerable delay, Canada and the EU implemented their Comprehensive Economic and Trade Partnership (CETA) in 2017, and Mexico substantially re-negotiated its year 2000 EU free trade deal in 2018. The EU also implemented a major FTA with Japan in 2019. See Chapters 3 and 5 for commentary and links to these agreements.

The EU free trade initiatives with Canada and Mexico were in part driven by the prospect of a NAFTA re-negotiation failure. These agreements allow duty free trade in autos, avoiding an EU tariff of

10%, Canadian tariff of 6.1%, and Mexican tariff of about 7%. U.S. car exporters, including U.S.-based European and Asian firms, may have to pay these tariffs to their competitive disadvantage.

Subjecting the European Union to U.S. national security tariffs on steel and aluminum (see Section 1.17) has generated equivalent EU retaliation. President Trump's threat to impose 25% national security tariffs on all U.S. auto imports sparked increased dialogue in 2018–19 between the EU and the United States aimed, a bit unrealistically, at negotiation of a "no subsidies, no nontariff trade barriers, and no tariffs outside industrial goods" agreement. Limited progress has been made toward such an outcome. Should the U.S. auto tariffs happen, the EU has promised to retaliate with 25% "rebalancing tariffs" on U.S. goods.

For decades, though not without disputes taken to the WTO, the United States and Europe have maintained a critically important strategic and economic partnership. NATO, for example, counts 22 of the 28 EU states as members. President Trump's rejection of the Paris accord on climate change, the Iran nuclear agreement, the short range missile treaty with Russia, and his G7 plus Russia goals also signal the potential for a dramatic shift in European-U.S. relations. All this suggests that America First policies and tariffs of the Trump administration place much at risk.

Japan and China-EU Trade

The European Union's trade relations with Japan and China are less voluminous, less in balance and (at least superficially) less fractious than with the United States. Japan and China run an annual surplus in its trade with the EU, but the amount is much smaller than the huge surplus they accumulate in trading with the States. Many Europeans speak quietly and with determination about their intent to avoid the "United States example" in their trade relations with Japan and China. Less quietly, some national governments imposed rigorous quotas on the importation of Japanese autos and instituted demanding local content requirements for Japanese cars assembled in Europe.

The Union, for its part, has frequently invoked antidumping proceedings against Japanese and especially Chinese goods. It has demonstrated a willingness to create arcane rules of origin that promote its interests at the expense of Japan and China. At the GATT/WTO level, however, Japan and the EU share common concerns about retaining their agricultural support systems. These concerns place them in opposition to the U.S. and others who seek to liberalize world trade in agricultural products.

The meteoric economic rise of China, combined with U.S. withdrawal from the Trans-Pacific Partnership (TPP) under President Trump, pushed Japan and the European Union into an historic free trade agreement in 2018. Each is expected to get greater (but not 100%) access to the other's markets, notably Japanese autos to Europe and EU agricultural goods to Japan. For more coverage and a link to the agreement, see Sections 5.5 and 5.9.

§ 3.6   EU International Trade Governance

Article 218 TFEU establishes the procedures used in the negotiation of most trade agreements with the European Union. Basically, the Commission proposes and then receives authorization from the Council to open negotiations with third countries or within an international organization. When the Commission reaches tentative agreement, conclusion or ratification must take place in the Council. If the Commission alone concludes an agreement, the European Court of Justice will declare void the act whereby the Commission sought to conclude the agreement. The Council votes by qualified majority on Common Commercial Policy agreements.93 These include most GATT/WTO agreements.

The Council votes unanimously on association agreements and on international agreements undertaken via Article 352 (*e.g.*, environmental conventions prior to 1987). The 1993 Treaty on European Union amended Article 218 to provide that the Council must also vote unanimously on international agreements covering areas where a unanimous vote is required to adopt internal EU rules. Parliament's role in international agreements was expanded by the TEU and the Reform Treaty of 2009. Its assent must now be obtained for virtually all EU trade and foreign investment agreements. The Council is also authorized to take emergency measures to cut off or reduce trading with other nations for common foreign or security policy reasons.

An opinion of the European Court as to the compatibility with the TFEU of the proposed agreement and the procedures used to reach it may be obtained in advance at the request of the Commission, Council or a member state. There are no public proceedings when such opinions are sought. Use of this advance ruling procedure may forestall judicial review at a later date of the compatibility of Union agreements with the Treaty. This lesson was vividly made when the Court of Justice rejected the final draft of the 1991 European Economic Area Agreement between the EU and EFTA because it considered the provisions on judicial control incompatible with the authority of the Union's legal order.98 This rejection sent the Agreement back for renegotiation and a new set of dispute settlement procedures which subsequently met with ECJ approval.

Trade agreements and other international treaties of the European Union are subject to judicial review by the Court of Justice as "acts" of its institutions. Moreover, such agreements are binding on the member states which must ensure their full implementation. When the European Court holds international agreements of the Union to be "directly effective" EU law, individuals may rely upon them in national litigation. The direct effects doctrine has led to cases where citizens end up enforcing the trade agreements of the EU despite contrary law of their own or other member state governments.

ERTA and WTO Agreements Cases

Article 220 TFEU gives the Commission the power to represent the Union within the General Agreement on Tariffs and Trade (GATT)/WTO. This representation affords EU nations much more bargaining power over tariffs and other trade issues with Canada, the United States, and Japan than they ever had individually. The exact extent and delimitation of the Union competences and the competences of the member states were disputed. With regard to the many Uruguay Round agreements, therefore, the European Commission requested the European Court of Justice to render an opinion to determine whether the Union was competent to conclude the Agreement establishing the World Trade Organization (WTO), in particular as regards the Agreement on Trade in Services (GATS), the Agreement on Trade-Related Aspects of Intellectual Property Rights, including trade in counterfeit goods (TRIPS), and with respect to products and/or services falling within the ECSC and EURATOM Treaties. This WTO Agreements opinion is discussed below.

Article 207 TFEU conveys the power to enter into international commitments to the European Union. This is the case by implication even when there is no express Treaty authorization to enter into international agreements necessary to achieve internal Common Market objectives. A prominent *ERTA* decision of the European Court holds the scope of the Union's trade agreements power to be coextensive with all *effective* surrenders of national sovereignty accomplished under the Treaty. *Commission v. Council*, 1971 Eur Comm. Rep 263 Thus, if an internal economic policy matter is governed by existing EU law, the external aspects of that policy are (either expressly or *by implication*) exclusively within the Union's competence.

More recently, the Court of Justice revisited the ERTA doctrine in an opinion reviewing the Uruguay Round trade agreements. The European Community had long represented the member states in the GATT and exclusively negotiated these agreements. But the General Agreement on Trade in Services (GATS) and the Agreement on Trade-Related Aspects of Intellectual Property (TRIPS) raised special concerns since the Treaty and ERTA were ambiguous as to whether the Union or the member states or both had the power to conclude these agreements.

The Court of Justice, in the complex *WTO Agreements* Opinion 1/94, 1994 Eur. Comm. Rep. I-5267, ruled that the Union had exclusive power regarding trade in goods agreements (including agriculture) based on Article 207 authorizing the Common Commercial Policy. While the cross-frontier supply of services not involving movement of persons also fell under Article 207, all other aspects of the GATS did not. Regarding TRIPS, only the provisions dealing with counterfeit goods came under the Community's exclusive Article 207 authority. Noting that the effective surrender of national sovereignty over intellectual property is not (yet) total and that internal trade in services is not "inextricably linked" to external relations, the Court ruled the competence to conclude GATS and TRIPs was jointly shared by the Community and the member states. Likewise, they share a duty to cooperate within the WTO in the administration of these agreements and disputes relating to them.

Subsequently, under the Lisbon Treaty of 2009, trade in services, trade-related intellectual property rights, and notably foreign direct investment became exclusive EU competences.107 Court of Justice Opinion No. 2/15 issued May 16, 2017 regarding the first of the EU's "new generation" free trade agreements between Singapore and the EU affirmed this exclusivity, excepting portfolio investment and foreign investor-state dispute settlement. The Court also held that air and maritime services, certain government procurement, non-commercial aspects of IP rights, renewable energy, and sustainable development labor and environmental standards fell within the EU's exclusive competence. Since the EU-Singapore agreement goes beyond the EU's exclusive competences, it must be ratified by all 40 national and regional parliaments of the member states. This results in a prolonged and problematic process as Canada (below) has learned.

Member State Involvement

Article 351 TFEU indicates that most treaties the member states reached prior to joining the EU continue to be valid even if they impact on areas now governed by Union law. Many bilateral treaties of Friendship, Commerce and Navigation fall within this category despite their impact on immigration, employment and investment opportunities. For example, such a dispute between Germany and the Commission concerned the compatibility of the preference-provision in the Utilities Directive for supply contracts with the German-American Treaty of Friendship and Commerce of 1953. Member states are required to take all appropriate steps (*e.g.*, upon renewal) to eliminate any incompatibilities between national trade and investment agreements and the Treaty. Whether prior treaties can be invoked so as to negate or fail to fulfill Treaty obligations is unclear.

As a rule, member states may not negotiate trade treaties in EU-occupied fields. They may do so on a transitional basis in areas where the Union lacks authority or (less clearly) has not effectively implemented its authority. For example, in the early 1970s the EU had not developed an effective overall energy policy, although it clearly had competence in the coal and nuclear fields. Thus, the International Energy Agreement achieved through the Organization for Economic Cooperation and Development (OECD) in 1975 after the first oil shocks is not an EU agreement. In contrast, the Union clearly had competence in the field of export credits. OECD arrangements in this area are exclusively the province of the Union with no residual or parallel authority in the member states.

Likewise, in 2002 the ECJ ruled that bilateral "open skies" aviation agreement between eight individual member states and the United States were illegal incursions into an exclusively EU domain. A United States-European Union open skies agreement followed in 2008.

The *ERTA* and to a lesser degree the *WTO* decisions of the European Court, combined with the expanding competence of the Union, leaves less and less room for national governments to enter into trade agreements. Several ECJ decisions suggest that the Union's external authority parallels its internal powers even if it has not effectively implemented those powers. However, recognizing the sensitivities involved, "mixed agreements" negotiated by the Commission (acting on a Council mandate) and representatives of the member states are frequently used. Both the Union and the member states are signatories to such accords. This has been done with the "association agreements" authorized by Article 217 TFEU, certain of the WTO Codes, the Ozone Layer Convention and the Law of the Sea Convention.

The Court of Justice has upheld the validity of mixed international agreements and procedures, but suggested that absent special circumstances their use should not occur when the Union's exclusive jurisdiction is fully involved. In other words, mixed procedures should be followed only when the competence to enter into and implement international agreements is in fact shared between the Union and its member states. The Treaty of Nice (2003) makes it clear that trade agreements relating to cultural and audiovisual services, educational services, and social and human health services are shared competences. The Reform Treaty (2009) contains a lengthy list of shared competences that are found at Article 4(2) TFEU.

New Generation EU Trade Treaty Governance

The Reform Treaty of 2009 also clarified that trade in goods and services, trade-related intellectual property rights, and foreign investment matters are an exclusive EU competence, as are the customs union, business competition rules, EURO zone monetary policy, and marine biology conservation policies. Article 3 TFEU further indicates that the Union has exclusive competence to conclude international agreements provided for by EU legislative act, necessary to enable the EU to exercise its internal powers, or where concluding an international agreement may affect common rules or alter their scope. In all of these areas, therefore, trade agreements can only be concluded by the European Union and need only be approved by the European Parliament. Some have referred to this outcome as a "fast track" compared to mixed agreement ratifications by all national and regional parliaments.

The European Court of Justice ruled in Opinion 2/15 concerning the EU-Singapore FTA that ratifications by all national and regional parliaments are not needed if there is no coverage of portfolio investments or investor-state dispute settlement in the FTA. Since these matters were part of that FTA, 28 national and 10 regional approvals were necessary. The same holds true for the investment provisions of CETA, otherwise operational in 2017. Opinion 2/15 suggests that separating EU FTA and investment agreements might make for smoother governance, which is exactly what took place in 2018 as Japan and the EU signed a free trade agreement with no investment coverage. These two agreements are linked in Sections 3.14 and 3.15 below.

§ 3.7   EU Free Trade and Other Trade Agreements

Free Trade Agreements

Mexico and the European Union reached a free trade agreement in 2000 that was expansively re-negotiated in principle in 2018. See Section 3.13 for a link to this agreement. Mexico, with its NAFTA membership, thus remains a production center with duty free access to the world's two largest consumer markets. The same is true for Israel.

The Union has been aggressively pursuing other free trade agreements. South Africa, Madagascar, Ukraine, Serbia, Bosnia, Moldova, Montenegro, Armenia, Lebanon, Syria, Jordan, Egypt, Morocco, Tunisia, Algeria, Peru, Colombia, Central America (6 nations), Chile, Singapore, Vietnam, Guyana, Albania, Macedonia, Palestinian Authority, and South Korea have signed on. In total, the EU has 40 free trade agreements covering over 70 non-European countries.

Turkey has a goods customs union agreement with the EU. Canada and the EU inked an historic Comprehensive Economic and Trade Agreement (CETA) in 2013 that finally reached fruition in 2017. A major Japan-EU FTA took effect early in 2019. For more these EU FTAs, see Chapter 5 and the links in Sections 3.14 and 3.15 below.

Agreements with India, ASEAN, MERCOSUR and the Gulf Council may follow. One notable feature of EU free trade agreements is the inclusion of a Human Rights and Democracy Clause backed up by potential trade sanctions.

For coverage of EU foreign investment law and treaties, see Chapter 7.

Duty Free Access to the EU Common Market

The end-game so far as exporters to the European Union are concerned is unlimited duty free access. Except for raw materials, few North American exports will qualify for such treatment. However, subsidiaries based in developing nations, free trade or customs union partners or EFTA countries may achieve this goal. This is possible because of the Union's adherence to the GSP program, its Mediterranean basin trade agreements, the Lomé/ Cotonou Conventions, and the EEA Agreement with certain EFTA countries, all noted below. There are, of course, exceptions and controls (quotas, NTBs) that may apply under these programs. Nevertheless, the Common Market is so lucrative that careful study of its external trade rules is warranted.

Such studies can realize unusually advantageous trade situations. For example, many developing nations are Lomé Convention participants or GSP beneficiaries. The goods of some of these nations are also entitled to duty free access to the United States market under the U.S. version of the GSP program, the Caribbean Basin Economic Recovery Act (1983), the Andean Trade Preference Act (1991) or various U.S. free trade agreements. See Chapter 2. A producer strategically located in such a nation (*e.g.*, Jamaica) can have the best of both worlds, duty free access to the European Union and the United States. The same applies for Israel which not only has a free trade agreement with the Union but also with the United States.

Since 2000, this ideal outcome has been most importantly available via Mexico, which is a member of NAFTA and has a free trade agreement with the European Union. In 2017, the EU and Canada implemented a free trade deal that creates duty free access to the EU, and in 2019 a Japan-EU FTA took effect.

EU Generalized Tariff Preferences (GSP)

The European Union participates in the generalized system of tariff preferences (GSP) initiated within the GATT to give one-way duty free access to industrial markets for selected goods coming from the developing world. This policy is implemented in the common customs tariff regulations. The Central European countries were added to the Union's GSP list for the interim period between the collapse of the Communist regimes and the entry into force of the free trade and economic association agreements concluded with the EU. The countries of the former USSR are GSP beneficiaries until any free-trade agreement with them comes into force, and provided they undertake to open their markets to developing-country exports.

Approximately 150 non-European developing nations now benefit from the GSP trade preferences of the EU, including China. Burma was suspended from the EU program in 1997 for human rights concerns, but has since re-qualified. Since 1998, goods from South Korea, Hong Kong and Singapore no longer qualify. Similarly, the Four Dragons were "graduated" (i.e., no longer treated as developing nations) out of the United States' GSP program in 1989. Brazil, Argentina and Uruguay have also been graduated.

A revised GSP regime entered into force in 1995. A solidarity mechanism was introduced and applicable in exceptional circumstances: Beneficiary countries whose exports of products covered by the GSP in a given sector exceed 25 percent of all beneficiaries' exports of those products in that sector will be excluded from GSP entitlement for that sector irrespective of their level of development. In addition sector/country graduation was introduced on the basis of relative specialization (ratio of a beneficiary country's share of total Union imports in a given sector), coupled with a development weighing (development index, combining a country's per capita income and the level of its exports as compared with those of the Union). Both mechanisms were phased in gradually to keep within the framework of overall neutrality.

In 2001, the EU began phasing in complete duty free access for the world's poorest 49 countries, a program known as "Everything But Arms". Special duty free preferences have been granted to developing countries that combat illegal drug production. Pakistan received this status, over strenuous objections by India before the World Trade Organization. The WTO Appellate Body rejected the EU scheme in 2004 as discriminatory, and in breach of the Enabling Clause.

Subsequent EU amendments continued special duty free tariff status for countries implementing 27 international conventions related to human and labor rights, the environment and good governance (including drug trafficking). Pakistan remains ineligible for special treatment. The WTO Appellate Body upheld the EU scheme in 2004.

The European Union system of generalized tariff preferences is selectively applied when about 130 "sensitive products" are involved. In other words, there are limitations (quotas and tariff ceilings) on duty free access to the Common Market if the goods compete with Union manufacturers. However, these GSP limitations do not apply to products already receiving duty free access under the Cotonou Convention or the Union's Mediterranean Policy. Thus, nations that are covered by the latter trade rules still obtain some margin of preference over other third world GSP beneficiaries.

Association Agreements

Article 217 TFEU authorizes the Union to conclude association agreements with other nations, regional groups and international organizations. The Council must act unanimously in adopting association agreements. Since the Single European Act of 1987, association agreements also require Parliamentary assent (which it threatened to withhold from renewal of the Israeli-EU association agreement unless better treatment of Palestinian exports to the Union is achieved). The network of trade relations established by association agreements covers much of the globe. Those who are "associated" with the EU usually receive trade and aid preferences which, as a practical matter, discriminate against non-associates. Arguments about the illegality of such discrimination within the GATT/WTO and elsewhere have typically not prevailed.

Article 217 indicates that association agreements involve "reciprocal rights and obligations, common action and special procedures" (emphasis added). The reciprocity requirement mirrors GATT law on non-preferential trading and free trade area agreements. European Union association agreements usually establish wide-ranging but hardly reciprocal trade and economic links. Greece for many years prior to membership was an EU associate. Turkey has been an associate since 1963. These two agreements illustrate the use of association agreements to convey high levels of financial, technical and commercial aid as a preliminary to membership. Turkey now has a customs union with Europe. Another type of association agreement links the remaining EFTA nations with the European Union. These agreements originally provided for industrial free trade and symbolize an historic reconciliation of the EU (then EEC) and EFTA trading alliances in 1973.

Mediterranean Policy

Still another type of association agreement involves pursuit of what the EU refers to as its "Mediterranean Policy." This policy acknowledges the geographic proximity and importance of Mediterranean basin nations to the Union. The Mediterranean is viewed as a European sphere of influence. Most of these association agreements grant trade preferences (including substantial duty free EU entry) and economic aid to Mediterranean nations without requiring reciprocal, preferential access for Union goods. Agreements of this type have been concluded with Algeria, Morocco, Tunisia, Egypt, Jordan, Lebanon, Syria, Israel, the former Yugoslavia, Malta and Cyprus.

These agreements are not at all uniform. They may be asymmetrical free trade agreements with the final goal of a customs union (Malta, Cyprus), or without such goal (Israel, Maghreb countries) or simple cooperation agreements (*e.g.* Egypt). In 1995, Europe and these partners agreed to create a Mediterranean industrial free trade zone. Since then, EU trade agreements in the Mediterranean basin have moved significantly towards reciprocal trade preferences.

Central and Eastern Europe

Because the former Soviet Union and its European satellites refused for many years to even recognize the European Community (now Union), some bilateral trade and cooperation agreements between those nations and the member states continue in place. It was not until 1988 that official relations between the Union and COMECON were initiated. As more democracy has taken hold, first generation trade and aid ("Partnership and Cooperation") agreements were concluded by the EU with Hungary, Poland, the Czech and Slovak Federal Republic, Bulgaria and nearly every other Central European nation. Similar agreements were concluded with the Baltic states, Slovenia, Albania, Russia, Ukraine and other former Soviet nations.

The Union advanced to second generation "association agreements" with some of these countries. These are known as "Europe Agreements." They anticipate substantial adoption of EU law on product standards, the environment, competition, telecommunications, financial services, broadcasting, and a host of other areas. Free movement of workers is not provided. Free trading will emerge over a ten-year period with special protocols on sensitive products like steel, textiles and agricultural goods. More fundamentally, these agreements are clearly focused on the eventual incorporation of these countries into the Union, as many did in 2005 along with Romania and Bulgaria in 2007.

With respect to the former USSR, the basis of the relationship between the EU and the Commonwealth of Independent States initially was the Trade and Cooperation Agreement of 1989 concluded with the Soviet Union. This agreement has been replaced by bilateral Partnership and Cooperation Agreements. The negotiations with Ukraine were concluded in March 1994, with Kazakhstan and Kyrgyzstan in May 1994, with Russia in June 1994, and with Moldova in July 1994.

These new agreements laid down the framework for future commercial and economic cooperation and created a new legal basis for the development of trade and investment links. For example, the agreement with Russia on trade and trade-related issues removed all quotas and other quantitative restrictions on Russian exports to the European Union, with the exception of certain textile and steel products. In 2004, responding to the admission of 10 new EU member states, Russia and the European Union concluded a Partnership agreement. Customs duties on cargo shipments between Russia its Kaliningrad enclave on the Baltic Sea are dropped, tariffs generally lowered, Russian steel quotas increased and EU antidumping duties relaxed. The European Union has also promised to guarantee language rights for the Russian-speaking minorities in Estonia and Latvia.

Russia has become increasingly concerned with the eastern drift of EU memberships. It is organizing its own Eurasian Economic Union to counterbalance EU expansion. Belarus, Kazakhstan and Armenia have signed on. Ukraine, Moldova and Georgia, on the other hand, are expected to become EU associates and eventually members.

Other International Agreements

In addition, the European Union has a host of other trading and cooperation agreements. These include agreements with Sri Lanka, Pakistan, Bangladesh, India, China the ASEAN group (Thailand,

Malaysia, The Philippines, Cambodia, Laos, Myanmar, Brunei, and Indonesia), the Andean Pact (Bolivia, Colombia, Ecuador, Peru), Argentina, Uruguay, and Brazil.

In 1990, a Cooperation Agreement was signed with the countries of the Gulf Cooperation Council (GCC): Kuwait, Saudi Arabia, Bahrain, Qatar and the United Arab Emirates. Following the establishment of the MERCOSUR common market by Brazil, Paraguay, Uruguay and Argentina, the Union has begun discussions with MERCOSUR concerning a free trade agreement.

The Lomé/Cotonou Conventions, Economic Partnership Agreements

The 1957 Treaty of Rome, in a section entitled the "association of overseas territories and countries," was intended to preserve the special trading and development preferences that came with "colonial" status. France, Belgium, Italy and The Netherlands still had a substantial number of these relationships. Article 200 TFEU completely abolished (after a transitional period) tariffs on goods coming from associated overseas territories and countries. There is no duty on the part of these regions to reciprocate with duty free access to their markets for EU goods. Although some territories continue to exist (*e.g.*, French territories like Polynesia, New Caledonia, Guadeloupe, Martinique, etc.), most of the once associated overseas colonies are now independent nations. This is true as well for most of the former colonies of Britain, Denmark, Portugal and Spain.

As independence arrived throughout Asia, Africa and elsewhere, new conventions of association were employed by the EU as a form of developmental assistance. The first of these were the Yaoundé Conventions (1964 and 1971) with newly independent French speaking African states. These conventions were in theory free trade agreements, but the African states could block almost any EU export and the Union in turn could protect itself from agricultural imports that threatened its Common Agricultural Policy. A healthy amount of financial and technical aid from the Union was thrown into the bargain.

When Britain joined in 1973, it naturally wished to preserve as many of the Commonwealth trade preferences as it could. The Yaoundé Conventions were already in place favoring former French colonies south of the Sahara. The compromise was the creation of a new convention, the first Lomé Convention (1975), to expand the Yaoundé principles to developing Caribbean and Pacific as well as English-speaking African nations. The fourth Lomé Convention

(1990) governed trade and aid between the EU and a large number of African, Caribbean and Pacific (ACP) states.

Lomé IV was replaced in 2000 by the Cotonou Agreement, which will operate for 20 years. The Cotonou nations presently include: Angola, Antigua & Barbuda, Bahamas, Barbados, Belize, Benin, Botswana, Burkina Faso, Burundi, Cameroon, Cape Verde, Central African Republic, Chad, Comoros, Congo, Djibouti, Dominica, Dominican Republic, Equatorial Guinea, Eritrea, Ethiopia, Fiji, Gabon, Gambia, Ghana, Grenada, Guinea, Guinea Bissau, Guyana, Haiti, Ivory Coast, Jamaica, Kenya, Kiribati, Lesotho, Liberia, Madagascar, Malawi, Mali, Mauritania, Mauritius, Mozambique, Namibia, Niger, Nigeria, Niue, Palau, Papua New Guinea, Rwanda, St. Christopher & Nevis, St. Lucia, St. Vincent & The Grenadines, Samoa, Sao Tomé & Principe, Senegal, Seychelles, Sierra Leone, Solomon Islands, Somalia, South Africa, Sudan, Suriname, Swaziland, Tanzania, Togo, Tonga, Trinidad & Tobago, Tuvalu, Uganda, Vanuatu, Zambia and Zimbabwe.

Perhaps the most important feature of this lengthy listing is the developing nations that are not Cotonou Convention participants. Unless they fall within the Union's Mediterranean Policy, they are apt to perceive the Lomé/Cotonou Conventions as highly discriminatory against their exports and economic interests.

Unlike the Yaoundé Conventions, the Lomé Conventions did not create (even in theory) reciprocal free trading relationships. While the Lomé states retained substantial duty free access to the Common Market, the Union obtained no comparable benefit. The Lomé nations did promise not to discriminate in trading among EU countries and to grant each most-favored-nation benefits. This meant, in practice, that they were free to block imports from the EU whenever desired. This one-sided relationship was continued temporarily under the Cotonou Agreement through 2008.

Thereafter six regionally organized economic partnership agreements mutually embracing free trade were established, to be fully implemented by 2020. It is hoped that each region will internally adopt free trade principles. A variety of "development" preferences are also granted by the Union in the Cotonou Convention. These include expensive purchasing obligations on sugar, for example. There is no free movement of persons as between the ACP states and the Union. However, whenever such persons are lawfully resident and working in the other's territories, they must be given national treatment rights.

Most significantly, the Cotonou nations now participate in two innovative EU mechanisms designed to stabilize their agricultural and mineral commodity export earnings. These programs are known as STABEX and MINEX (also known as SYSMIN). STABEX covers (inter alia) ground nuts, cocoa, coffee, cotton, coconut, palm, rawhides, leather and wood products, and tea. MINEX deals with copper, phosphates, bauxite, alumina, manganese, iron ore, and tin. These programs are an acknowledgement of the economic dependence of many Lomé nations on commodity exports for very large portions of their hard currency earnings.

Some have argued vigorously that STABEX and MINEX perpetuate rather than relieve this dependence. Both programs provide loans and grants in aid to Lomé nations who have experienced significant declines in export earnings because of falling commodity prices, crop failures and the like. The greater the dependency and decline, the larger the EU financial transfers. These sums are not, for the most part, tied to reinvestment in the commodity sectors causing their payment, nor to the purchase of Union products or technology. In a world where most development aid is tied (i.e., must usually be spent on the donor's products or projects), STABEX and MINEX represent a different approach. Many Latin American nations have lobbied the United States to create similar mechanisms for their commodities.

The Lomé IV Convention (1990) added several new features carried over under the Cotonou Agreement (2000). The European Union now financially supports structural adjustments in ACP states, including remedies for balance of payments difficulties, debt burdens, budget deficits, and public enterprises. Cultural and social cooperation, trade in services, and environmental issues are also addressed. For example, an agreement not to ship toxic and radioactive waste was reached. The Convention builds upon earlier provisions by specifying protected human rights such as equal treatment, civil and political liberty, and economic, social and cultural rights. Financial support from the EU is given to ACP nations that promote human rights and has been withheld after military coups.

The one-way nature of ACP trade benefits is inconsistent with WTO obligations. The EU has therefore undertaken to negotiate two-way "Economic Partnership Agreements (EPA)" with six groupings of ACP states. The first such EPA was finalized in 2008 with 13 Caribbean nations. Duties on nearly all European exports will be phased out by 2033, trade in services is eased, and procurement as well as investment rules are established. The second EPA was completed in 2016 with southern Africa, with other EPAs with west Africa and east Africa in the works.

§ 3.8   BREXIT

This section concerns BREXIT, the pending withdrawal of the United Kingdom from the European Union. Many provocative issues with substantial impact on EU and U.K. investment, discussed below, have been on the negotiating table.

Since 2009, Article 50 of the Treaty on European Union (TEU) permits member states to commence withdrawal negotiations from the European Union. Prime Minister Cameron, wanting badly to be re-elected in 2015 and seeking to appease the hard-core Euroskeptic wing of his Conservative Party, promised in his campaign to re-negotiate Britain's position in the EU and hold a referendum on remaining an EU member state. He won re-election, and after negotiating modest changes in U.K.-EU relations, put the Remain or Leave issue to a public vote.

In a hotly contested campaign, with free movement of people within the EU a prominent issue, Leave supporters made statements that were simply untrue, for example that Britain would save not pay money by leaving and that the National Health Service would directly benefit from these savings. At no point did the leaders of the Leave movement present a clear plan for or picture of its consequences.

After approval by 52% of its voters in a high turnout June 2016 national referendum and strong approval by the House of Commons, Britain commenced two-year withdrawal negotiations on March 29, 2017, nearly the same date as the 60th anniversary of the EU. London, Scotland and Northern Ireland voted heavily to remain, but the rest of England provided the Leave campaign with victory. Theresa May, a Minister in David Cameron's Cabinet and a quiet Remain supporter, became Prime Minister shortly after the referendum in the wake of Cameron's resignation. For a considerable period, she simply said "BREXIT means BREXIT".

Seeking to raise her bargaining power with the EU under a clear mandate from the British people and undermine her Party's Euroskeptic wing, Prime Minister May held a snap election in June of 2017. Much to her surprise and that of the pollsters, the Conservative Party actually lost majority control of the U.K. Parliament. Many factors were in play during the snap election, but it appears that at least some British voters had second thoughts about the wisdom of BREXIT.

The Conservatives were consequently forced to govern in coalition with a small Protestant-dominated Northern Ireland party, the DUP. This coalition is fragile. The DUP wants agricultural subsidies post-BREXIT, continued access to EU development funds for poorer regions, and a "frictionless" border with Ireland. Basically the DUP leans toward remaining in the EU.

Any BREXIT deal will need qualified majority approval by the EU Council, which for these purposes means 20 out of 27 member states constituting at least 65% of the EU population must affirm the deal, plus some regional parliaments (those of Belgium for example). The consent of the European Parliament as well as the U.K. Parliament will also be needed. All these consents mandated a rapid timetable within the two year negotiating period.

If no exit deal is reached and no additional time for negotiation unanimously agreed, Britain was to cease to be a member of the EU March 29, 2019 (subsequently extended).

Many in the EU feel Britain should "pay a price" to leave. Put another way, to paraphrase one EU leader: "It cannot be the case that Britain ends up better off outside the EU than inside". Overall, the adverse trade consequences of BREXIT for the Britain appear more significant than for the EU. The U.K., for example, sends nearly 50% of its exports to the EU, while less than 10% of EU exports end up in Britain. That said, Britain is the largest market for EU exports and the fifth biggest economy in the world, considerations which play in the U.K.'s favor.

BREXIT Issues

Residency Rights. Students, retirees, workers and their families enjoy residency rights throughout the Union. What happens to the nearly 1 million Poles, 270,000 French citizens, and the other 2 million or so EU nationals working in Britain? What happens to the 1.2 million British retirees and others on the continent? One could argue that Britain has obtained a younger, more skilled taxpaying workforce under the EU free movement of people regime. The EU in turn has received a goodly number of higher cost British seniors.

The House of Lords voted in 2017 to allow all EU nationals to remain in the U.K., with no guarantee of reciprocity, a position backed by a detailed plan of the Prime Minister issued after the 2017 snap election. The European Parliament immediately called the Prime Minister's plan "second class" treatment. What about EU professionals and restaurant owners who have exercised their EU "right of establishment" to set up shop in the U.K., and vice-versa? What about local health care rights that normally come with cross-border residency?

Fearing the worst, a number of British citizens began efforts to obtain other EU passports as a means to preserving free movement and other EU rights. Dual nationality in Ireland, Sweden and Germany rank high on this list. Despite all these issues, both sides have committed to amicably working out the details of cross-border residency and healthcare.

Business Passport Rights. Much of the EU services sector operates on "passport" principles under EU law. Bankers, securities firms, insurance companies and the like need only obtain a license in one EU state, which then basically qualifies them to do business in the other member states. Britain, London and The City comprise the financial center of Europe, using British licenses to springboard throughout the EU. Continuation of cross-border trade in services after BREXIT will hinge on whether EU and U.K. regulatory rules are deemed "equivalent", the same issue that presently applies to the United States service providers in the EU.

Without passport rights, British, U.S. and global finance and service companies licensed in the UK created plans for and began a slow-moving but steady BREXIT-driven exodus. This has benefited Frankfurt, Paris, Dublin and even New York. There was little discussion of the passport rights of EU companies doing business in the UK.

Investment. Many foreign, especially Asian and North American, investors have set up manufacturing and service centers in Britain. For example, Japanese car companies are notably invested in the United Kingdom. Japan was sufficiently worried about BREXIT that its government delivered a detailed memo of concern to the U.K. soon after the vote to leave.

British and foreign manufacturers based in the U.K. are especially nervous about going from zero tariff entry into the EU to paying tariffs to gain entry to what will remain the world's largest common market. Autos, for example, are subject to 10% EU import tariffs, agricultural goods subject to 30–40% tariffs. In addition, nontariff regulatory barriers will emerge if British health, safety and environmental standards differ from those of the EU.

British and foreign investors essentially put a hold on investment or expansion of existing operations in the U.K. after the BREXIT vote while negotiations proceeded. Just before the scheduled BREXIT deadline of March 29, 2019, Honda announced it would exit production in the U.K. in favor of USA and Japanese plants, and Nissan announced it would do likewise in transferring production to Japan. Jaguar Land Rover is cutting U.K. employment by thousands of jobs. Dyson, of vacuum cleaner fame, is moving its headquarters to Singapore prior to inaugurating an electric vehicle. It seems fair to say, that many investors perceive that BREXIT in any form (see below) represents a clear and present danger.

Trade Relations. Prior to BREXIT, Britain derives its tariff and trade relations with the world predominantly via the EU. Absent a post-BREXIT agreement with the EU, Britain could revert to World Trade Organization rules, a complex negotiation in its own right with important implications for the U.K., the EU and WTO partners like the United States. For example, 25% of all American exports to the EU go to Britain.

Britain after BREXIT is hoping for lots of free trade agreements (FTAs) and foreign investment deals. The United States, Canada, Japan, Australia, New Zealand, South Africa, India, China and others are on this wish list and initial dialogues have commenced, but is that hope realistic? During the anticipated BREXIT transition period up to Jan 2021, assuming there will not be a No-Deal exit, the U.K. remains subject to and the beneficiary of EU customs union law and the roughly 40 EU free trade agreements with 70 FTA partners. Assuming the Withdrawal Agreement (see below) is put into effect, Britain could negotiate but not sign FTAs with other parties during the transition period, a less than likely prospect in the absence of knowing the future of U.K.-EU relations. It took, for example, many years for the EU-Canada bilateral agreement (CETA) to finally come to fruition. The EU negotiators repeatedly signaled that a CETA-plus deal was the best Britain could hope for post-BREXIT.

Some BREXIT supporters suggested pursuing "soft exit" Norwegian or Swiss models for relations with the EU post-exit. But these complicated models for the most part involve acceptance of free movement of people, the EU customs union, cash contributions to the EU budget, and deference to EU/EFTA Court decisions. Would a soft exit" really be an exit?

EU negotiators absolutely insisted that "sufficient progress" be made on the U.K.'s balance due (see Money Matters below), the rights of EU and British residents in the other's territory (above), and Northern Ireland (below) before any discussion of subsequent relations could take place. With little bargaining power, Prime Minister May acquiesced to this approach.

Northern Ireland, Scotland and Gibraltar. Every political district in Scotland voted in 2016 to remain in the EU, but the Conservatives won 12 districts in the June 2017 snap election. The Scotch voted against leaving the U.K. several years prior. A second referendum could achieve Scottish independence in search of EU membership.

Most districts in Northern Ireland voted to remain. Peace and border-free transit has been directly linked under the Good Friday Accords to Irish and U.K. membership in the EU. After BREXIT, the

Ireland/Northern Ireland border will be the only land crossing between Britain and the EU. This issue turned out to be the most difficult of all to resolve, and was basically fudged during the transition period agreement and could generate a No-Deal BREXIT.

Ireland, a low-tax manufacturing center for many U.S. multinationals, ships substantial goods to the EU using Britain as an inexpensive land-bridge. This will be a rat's nest of customs law after BREXIT. In addition, Ireland's food imports and exports from and to the U.K. are significant. Thus Ireland has a big stake in BREXIT.

Spain, which could veto any BREXIT deal, insists on an agreement that clarifies the future of Gibraltar, that very British and strategic enclave located where the Med and the Atlantic Ocean meet. Ideally, Spain wants Gibraltar back. It is also worried about Scotland joining the EU, perhaps setting a dangerous precedent for Catalonian independence.

Money Matters. The EU presented Britain with an expensive "bill" for what it perceives the U.K. will owe the Union upon departure in 2019. The demand for cash included Britain's liabilities under the generous, entirely unfunded EU pension scheme. It also covered pre-BREXIT and post-BREXIT EU projects under the current British-approved EU budget running from 2013 through 2020.

The "Bill" was subject to intense bargaining. By March of 2018, Britain had doubled its original estimate of what it was willing to pay to approximately 45 billion Euros. That amount stunned many Leave backers, who were led to believe BREXIT would result in a net savings not loss. In addition, Britain will lose two well-staffed and well-paid EU agencies, one on Medicines (EMA), the other on banking (EBA), along with civil nuclear power benefits associated with EURATOM. The EU, on the other hand, will lose a sizeable net payor into its annual budget.

And the List of Issues Goes on. What about immigration, an issue central to the BREXIT vote. Since Britain maintains its own border controls, relatively little impact may occur. But France has taken steps to reduce its willingness to cooperate on immigrants waiting in Calais to enter the U.K.

What about the areas where there has arguably been a positive impact by Britain on the EU: Foreign and defense affairs, governance, spending, security, and market-driven solutions. What about the common agricultural, aviation and fisheries markets created by the EU? Retention of the Fisheries regime has been especially contentious.

What about the EU's voluminous "acquis communautaire", its vast body of legislation, regulations, and case law? Prime Minister May secured a misnamed "Great Repeal Bill" that incorporated all EU rules (some 19000 in number) into British law. Upon exit, with EU law no longer supreme, Parliament is expected to selectively remove, alter or retain the Great Repeal Bill rules. An intense battle between pro- and anti-BREXIT Parliamentarians, including within the Conservative Party, is sure to follow.

Many European Union rules seem inescapable since all goods exported from Britain will need to conform to EU law, and extensive cross-border supply chains compel compliance. For example, all auto imports must under the EU End of Life Vehicles Directive be 95% reusable or recyclable.

The Prime Minister has been outspoken against remaining subject to the jurisdiction of the European Court of Justice (ECJ) (above). If the U.K. retains EU rules, do not interpretations of those rules by the ECJ come along with them?

What about the future of the EU? If Britain can exit, whatever the price, why not others? In 2017–18, anti-EU political parties made themselves felt in Dutch, French, German, Austrian, and Italian elections. Marine Le Pen, leader of the National Front Party in France, openly ran on a platform promising a national referendum on leaving the EU (FREXIT). She was resoundingly defeated by Emmanuel Macron, a strong pro-EU candidate, now President of France, but anti-EU sentiment remains strong in Europe.

BREXIT Withdrawal Agreement

Prime Minister May often said "better no deal, than a bad deal," suggesting she was open to a No-Deal exit on March 29, 2019. In the summer of 2018, some two years after taking office, the Prime Minister finally released an official "Chequers Plan" resembling a "soft" BREXIT exit. This plan centered on free trade in goods under EU rules and EU free trade agreements, reduced service sector integration (think loss of passport rights), and submission indirectly to the jurisdiction of the European Court of Justice. An uproar in her Conservative Party ensued, several hard core Brexiteer Cabinet members resigning. Negotiations with the EU resumed, ultimately leading to rejection of the Chequers Plan by the EU in October 2018.

Intense negotiations continued. Both sides, governmentally and in the private sector, began stockpiling essential products, spare parts, food and medicine in case a chaotic No-Deal emerges in March of 2019. Virtually all major businesses in the EU and U.K. re-examined their BREXIT contingency plans. And, with younger Brits in the forefront, there is a campaign for a so-called People's Vote on the terms of Britain's exit, in other words a second referendum on Remaining or Leaving.

By mid-November 2018 a 585-page Draft Withdrawal Agreement was agreed by the EU and the May administration. The Prime Minister presented it as the only possible negotiated exit agreement. The Prime Ministers Cabinet quickly "approved" the draft without an internal vote, two members of the Cabinet resigning the next day. Thus the draft deal was kicked to the British Parliament, where opposition was immediately fierce, and vote on approval or disapproval was expected mid-December 2018.

Here is a very brief summary of the Withdrawal Agreement:

1.   The United Kingdom will pay a divorce bill of approximately $50 billion to the European Union.

2.   Each side will protect the legal rights and status of each other's citizens currently living in the other's jurisdiction.

3.   During a 21-month transition period from March 2019 thru December 2020, there will be a complete standstill with relations unchanged, including free movement of persons. All EU decisions undertaken during the transition period are binding on the U.K. This period can be extended once for two years by mutual agreement.

4.   The primary goal of the transition period is to reach an EU-U.K. free trade and future relations agreement without triggering "hard" customs and immigration border checks between Ireland and Northern Ireland, preferably by as yet unknown technological means. This agreement will not continue the right of free movement of citizens between the Britain and the EU. (Author's Note: It took nine years to negotiate the Canada-EU free trade agreement known as CETA, and twelve years to negotiate the EU-Swiss bilateral trade deals. Is 21 months feasible to agree on a U.K.-EU free trade and cooperation agreement?)

5.   Absent such an agreement, Britain will remain temporarily in the EU customs union (which includes related EU Free Trade and WTO commitments, but not the EU Fisheries agreement). Whilst a member of the EU customs union, the U.K. also promises to abide by most EU Single Market regulations, as well as EU rules on state aids, the environment, labor and taxation. In contrast, Northern Ireland would continue to participate fully in the EU Single Market for services, goods, capital, and people, subject to all related EU rules.

6.   Absent a free trade and future relations deal, the U.K. would need agreement of the EU to leave the customs union, which is thought to be a "backstop" guarantee against a hard Ireland/Northern Ireland border. Arbitrators will decide if and when the

backstop is no longer needed. Thus Britain would largely abide by EU customs and Single Market rules it could no longer influence as a member state. Critics refer to this possible rule-taker status as "vassalage", and note that it could last indefinitely.

7. Should a dispute arise, it will be reviewed by a joint committee and an arbitration panel. On matters of EU law, the arbitrators must refer questions to the European Court of Justice for a binding ruling.

In addition to the Withdrawal Agreement, the EU and U.K. struggled to agree on a short, nonbinding Political Declaration regarding their future relations, sometimes referred to as a Blind BREXIT. Notably, Spain pushed for direct negotiations with the U.K. on the future of Gibraltar, and several EU members sought greater access to U.K. fisheries, which will be the subject of a new, undoubtedly contentious agreement. The Political Declaration also calls for the establishment of a comprehensive security partnership.

Britain and BREXIT

On November 25, the leaders of the 27 EU states met and endorsed the Withdrawal Agreement and the Political Declaration. The U.K. Parliament was expected to address both items in December of 2018, but after contempt proceedings and faced with a large negative vote in Parliament, Prime Minister May delayed consideration of the Withdrawal Agreement until January 2019. Shortly thereafter she survived a No Confidence vote (200 to 117) within the Conservative Party. The Prime Minister subsequently attempted with little success to gain assurances from the EU that British participation in the EU customs union, and the Northern Ireland backstop, would truly be "temporary." The official U.K. legal opinion on the Agreement, revealed only by force of contempt proceedings successfully initiated in Parliament, suggested that the Agreement could result in a "stalemate." Parliament also passed a rule indicating it might dictate the path of BREXIT negotiations if the Agreement was defeated.

Meanwhile, the day before the scheduled December vote in the U.K. Parliament, the European Court of Justice opined that Britain could withdraw its Exit petition, thus remaining an EU member state. Should the Withdrawal Agreement be approved by the British Parliament, review and approval by the European Parliament would be required. The EU, assuming BREXIT would occur with no deal on March 29, 2019, announced in December 2018 a list of short-term emergency measures it is willing to put in place, provided Britain reciprocates. These concern: Airline flights, financial services, customs, road transport, climate policy, treatment of U.K. citizens residing in the 27 EU states, livestock and animal products and personal data.

On Jan. 15, 2019, the House of Commons overwhelmingly rejected the Withdrawal Agreement by a vote of 432 to 202, a "thumping" (as the British say) drawing 118 votes from the Conservative Party and 10 votes from their DUP ally. The next day, Prime Minister May survived a no confidence vote triggered by the Labor Party. Under a specific Parliamentary mandate adopted just prior to the vote on Withdrawal, she became obliged to indicate how her government intended to proceed by January 21.

That date arrived and the Prime Minister announced she was opposed to a second referendum as "damaging to social cohesion by undermining faith in our democracy". She ruled out seeking an extension of the March 29 deadline from the EU, and kept the no-deal exit "on the table". The Prime Minister did indicate that fees associated with EU nationals seeking settlement of their post-BREXIT status would be waived. Her bottom line Plan B differed little from the Withdrawal Agreement that had been thumped by Parliament the week before.

Shortly thereafter, the House of Commons voted against extending BREXIT negotiations, against a no-deal exit March 29th, and instructed Prime Minister May to seek to re-negotiate the Withdrawal Agreement with emphasis on changing the "backstop" provisions regarding Northern Ireland and continued U.K. participation in the EU customs union. The European Union quickly reaffirmed that no alteration of the terms of the Withdrawal Deal was possible. The EU repeated its desire to finalize an agreement on future relations as soon as possible.

On March 12, the Withdrawal Agreement was once again "thumped" by a 391 to 242 negative vote in the U.K. Parliament which also reaffirmed its opposition to a no-deal exit, then just days away. Parliament voted in favor of requesting an extension of the March 29 deadline, but did not specify the reasons for or the length of any extension, which had to be approved by all 27 other EU states. A third attempt by the Prime Minister to obtain approval of the Withdrawal Agreement was blocked as repetitious by the Speaker of the House of Commons. A week before March 29, the EU Council of leaders unilaterally gave Britain two, alternative extensions:

April 12 if the Agreement failed to be approved by the U.K. Parliament prior to March 29. April 12 is the deadline for Britain to decide to take part in the May 23, 2019 European Parliament elections; or

May 22 (the day before European Parliament elections) if the Withdrawal Agreement was approved by March 29.

Prime Minister May announced that if the Withdrawal Agreement was approved, she would step down to allow new leadership to undertake negotiations on the future of EU-U.K. relations. Nevertheless, on March 29th, the U.K. Parliament for the third time thumped the Withdrawal Agreement by a vote of 344 to 286. Working against the April 12 deadline, various "indicative" votes in Parliament followed, indicating no consensus on an alternative way forward. The Prime Minister subsequently commenced negotiations on a compromise BREXIT agreement with the Labour Party in hopes of obtaining a majority vote in Parliament. Labour primarily seeks an agreement to permanently remain in the EU customs union, and a vote of the people on such an exit from the EU.

The Prime Minister petitioned the EU for an extension to June 30. After much debate and internal compromise the EU agreed to extend the BREXIT deadline to October 31, 2019, indicating again that the Withdrawal Agreement would not be changed, but the non-binding Political Declaration could be altered.

As the clock runs down, six BREXIT outcomes seem plausible:

1.   A No-Deal Exit October 31, 2019

2.   Rejection or affirmation of BREXIT after a People's Vote second referendum,

3.   Withdrawal of the BREXIT petition, leaving the U.K. fully inside the EU,

4.   Approval of the Withdrawal Agreement by the U.K. and EU Parliaments,

5.   A different withdrawal agreement acceptable to the U.K. and EU, or

6.   Another extension of the BREXIT deadline.

§ 3.9   A Timeline of European Integration

1949—COMECON Treaty (Eastern Europe, Soviet Union)

1950—European Convention on Human Rights

1951—European Coal and Steel Community (ECSC) ("Treaty of Paris")

1957—European Economic Community Treaty (EEC) ("Treaty of Rome"), European Atomic Energy Community Treaty (EURATOM)

1959—European Free Trade Area Treaty (EFTA)

1968—EEC Customs Union fully operative

1973—Britain and Denmark switch from EFTA to EEC; Ireland joins EEC; Norway rejects membership; remaining EFTA states sign industrial free trade treaties with EEC

1979—Direct elections to European Parliament

1981—Greece joins EEC

1983—Greenland "withdraws" from EEC

1986—Spain and Portugal join EEC; Portugal leaves EFTA

1987—Single European Act amends EEC Treaty to initiate campaign for a Community without internal frontiers by 1993; qualified majority legislative votes commence

1990—East Germany merged into Community via reunification process

1991—COMECON defunct; trade relations with Central Europe develop rapidly

1993—Maastricht Treaty on European Union (TEU); EEC Treaty renamed EC Treaty

1995—Austria, Finland, and Sweden join EU; Norway votes no again

1999—Amsterdam Treaty

1999—Common currency (EURO) managed by European Central Bank commences with 11 members

2002—ECSC Treaty expires; coverage added to EC Treaty

2003—Treaty of Nice; EU Charter of Fundamental Rights "declared"; draft Constitution for Europe released

2004—Cyprus, Estonia, Slovenia, Poland, Hungary, the Czech Republic, Slovakia, Latvia, Lithuania, Malta join EU

2005—Constitution for Europe overwhelmingly defeated in France and Netherlands

2007—Accession of Bulgaria and Romania; Reform Treaty of Lisbon proposed

2008—Irish voters reject Reform Treaty

2009—Reform Treaty approved in Ireland . . . takes effect Dec. 1; EU Charter of Fundamental Rights becomes binding law; EC Treaty renamed Treaty on the Functioning of the European Union (TFEU)

2010—Greece and Ireland bailed out; 1 trillion EURO financial crisis safety net created

2011—Portugal bailed out; EURO in crisis

2012—Spanish and Italian banks bailed out, Greece bailed out again; EURO in extreme crisis; Treaty on Stability, Coordination and Governance (TSCG) adopted by 25 member states creating a permanent European Stability Mechanism crisis loan fund and a Fiscal Compact with balanced budget rules; ECB agrees to buy unlimited short-term national bonds

2013—Croatia joins EU, Cyprus bailed out

2014—Scotland votes to remain in the UK

2015—Greece bailed out for third time; mass migration to Europe; terrorism inside EU increases

2016—UK votes to leave EU (BREXIT); migrant and terrorist waves escalate

2017—BREXIT negotiations commence

2019—BREXIT negotiations scheduled to end

§ 3.10   Major Amendments of the 1957 EEC Treaty

1987—Single European Act

1993—Maastricht Treaty

1999—Amsterdam Treaty

2002—ECSC Treaty folded into EC Treaty

2003—Treaty of Nice

2005—Defeat of Treaty establishing Constitution for Europe

2009—Reform Treaty of Lisbon

§ 3.11   Chronology of European Union Member Countries (28)

1957—France, Germany, Italy, Belgium, Netherlands, and Luxembourg create EEC (6)

1973—United Kingdom, Eire and Denmark (9)

1981—Greece (10)

1986—Spain and Portugal (12)

1995—Austria, Finland, and Sweden (15)

2005—Cyprus, Estonia, Slovenia, Poland, Hungary, Czech Republic, Slovakia, Latvia, Lithuania, and Malta (25)

2007—Bulgaria and Romania (27)

2013—Croatia (28)

2019—BREXIT (27?)

§ 3.12   Chronology of Euro Zone Participants (19)

1999: Germany, France, Ireland, Spain, Portugal, Austria, Italy, Netherlands, Luxembourg, Belgium, Finland

2001—Greece

2007—Slovenia

2008—Cyprus, Malta

2009—Slovakia

2011—Estonia

2014—Latvia

2015—Lithuania

§ 3.13   The European Union as a Trade Policy Model

The European Union has served as a model for economic integration elsewhere in world. For example, the Andean Community (ANCOM) modeled itself on the EEC (as the EU was then called), as did the Southern African Customs Union (SACU), and the Central American Common Market (CACM), all noted in Section 2.5. These regional economic groups have suffered internal discord, economic stress and limited success. *See especially* D. Gantz, *Regional Trade Agreements: Law, Policy and Practice* (2009). Yet, for the most part, they still aspire to become as comprehensive and effective as the European Union. MERCOSUR, established in 1991 by Brazil, Argentina, Paraguay and Uruguay, probably comes closest to reproducing the EU model.

The EU trade policy model contrasts with the ASEAN (Association of Southeast Asian Nations) and LAFTA (now ALADI, the Latin American Integration Association) groups. See Section 2.5. These groups have targeted more limited goals as free trade areas. Neither rises to the significance or depth of NAFTA 1994 or its 2005 sequel, CAFTA-DR (the Central American Free Trade Agreement between the United States, Costa Rica, Guatemala, Nicaragua, El Salvador, Honduras and the Dominican Republic). Hundreds of bilateral free trade agreements have been negotiated since NAFTA, including some by the European Union, notably with Canada (CETA 2017) and Japan (2018). See Chapter 5.

At this writing, the European Union and NAFTA 1994 (and USMCA 2018) present competing trade policy models that have each drawn adherents in the developing world. Apart from their core economic differences (customs union v. free trade area), the EU model embraces a remarkable legal superstructure to achieve economic integration, notably the regional legislative and litigation systems of the Union. In contrast, the NAFTA/CAFTA model is minimalist, legally speaking. Multiple varieties of arbitration are generally used to resolve disputes, and there are no regional legislative or litigation systems.

Which model offers the best way forward? The Transatlantic Trade and Investment Partnership (TTIP) negotiations commenced in 2013 by the United States and the European Union moved along a track that resembled NAFTA 1994 and CETA 2017. That said, with BREXIT, the apparent collapse of the Doha Round of World Trade Organization (WTO) negotiations, along with U.S. withdrawal by President Trump from the Obama Administration's hard won Trans-Pacific Partnership (TPP), analysis of this question has taken on added meaning, particularly since the emergence of the TPP-11 and Trump administration's re-negotiation of NAFTA.

§ 3.14   Link to 2018 EU-Mexico Agreement in Principle Modernizing Their 2000 FTA

(http://trade.ec.europa.eu/doclib/docs/2018/april/tradoc_1567 91.pdf)

§ 3.15   Link to EU-Japan Economic Partnership Agreement (2018)

(http://trade.ec.europa.eu/doclib/docs/2018/august/tradoc_157 228.pdf)

§ 3.16   Link to EU-Canada Comprehensive Economic Partnership (CETA 2017)

(http://trade.ec.europa.eu/doclib/docs/2014/september/tradoc _152806.pdf)

Chapter 4

CUSFTA 1989 AND NAFTA 1994

Analysis

For more extensive treatment of CUSFTA 1989 and NAFTA 1994, see R. Folsom and W.D. Folsom, *NAFTA Re-Negotiated, USMCA 2018 and Its Business Implications* in a Nutshell (forthcoming).

§ 4.0   U.S. Fast Track Procedures and Free Trade Agreements

Fast Track

Some recent U.S. efforts to reduce trade restrictions have been multilateral or regional efforts (*e.g.*, the WTO, NAFTA 1994 and CAFTA-DR). Others have been bilateral, such as the U.S. free trade agreements. In both situations, Congress intermittently since 1974 has given quite broad authority to the President, or the President's representative, to reduce or eliminate U.S. tariffs on a reciprocal "fast track" basis. For U.S. free trade partners, fast track generally means that once they reach a deal Congress can vote it up or down but cannot alter it, though in recent years Congress has effectively tacked on additional requirements, notably regarding labor and the environment.

Fast track originated as a compromise after Congress refused to ratify two major components of the Kennedy Round of GATT negotiations. The first such authorization lasted from 1991 to 1996, and made possible U.S. implementation of NAFTA in 1993 and the WTO package of agreements in 1995. From 1996 onward, Congress refused to grant fast track authority to President Clinton.

The Trade Act of 2002 authorized President George W. Bush to negotiate international trade agreements on a fast track basis, a procedure that requires Congress to vote within 90 legislative days up or down, without amendments, on U.S. trade agreements. In return, Congress receives substantial notice and opportunity to influence U.S. trade negotiations conducted by the U.S. Trade Representative (USTR). President Bush and the USTR quickly completed and Congress approved free trade agreements with Chile and Singapore, and thereafter with Morocco, Australia, Central America/Dominican Republic (CAFTA-DR), Peru, Jordan, Oman, and Bahrain. The President's fast track authority expired in July 2007 after agreements with Colombia, Panama and South Korea had been signed. Approval of these FTAs by Congress under fast track was delayed several years into the Obama administration.

Congress granted fast track trade promotion authority to President Obama in the summer of 2015, lasting beyond his Presidency through June 2018. With all three NAFTA nations participating in the Trans-Pacific Partnership (TPP) agreement. NAFTA 1994 could have been effectively updated by the TPP. President Trump, however, withdrew the U.S. from the TPP agreement almost immediately upon taking office in 2017. The remaining 11 TPP states subsequently signed on to a modified TPP-11 agreement minus the United States in 2018. The TPP and TPP-11 agreements are discussed in Chapters 5 and 6.

In 2018, President Trump requested and obtained, in the absence of Congressional disapproval, a three-year extension of fast track authority running to July 2021.

U.S. Free Trade Agreements

The United States has entered into a growing number of major free trade agreements listed in Section 5.2. The second was with Canada, and this agreement was adopted through the United States-Canada Free Trade Area Agreement Implementation Act of 1988.

The Canada-U.S. Agreement (CUSFTA) was fully implemented by January 1, 1998 and is discussed below.

The United States negotiated along with Canada and Mexico a three-way North American Free Trade Area Agreement (NAFTA). NAFTA took effect January 1, 1994 with full implementation in nearly all areas by the year 2003. NAFTA 1994 was incorporated into United States law by the North American Free Trade Agreement Implementation Act of 1993.

Late in 2001, Jordan and the United States agreed on free trade. In 2003, the United States reached free trade agreements with Chile and Singapore, notably incorporating coverage of E-Commerce and digital products. Early in 2004, free trade between the United States and five Central American states (CAFTA) plus the Dominican Republic, and with Australia and Morocco, was agreed. More bilateral free trade deals were struck with Bahrain, Oman and Peru, and additional agreements with Panama, Colombia and South Korea took effect in 2012.

These trade agreements provide new duty free import opportunities into the U.S. market. Unlike the one-way U.S. free trade programs (see Section 2.0), these agreements are reciprocal. That is to say they open up foreign markets to United States exports on a duty free basis. In addition, they establish detailed rules targeting nontariff trade barriers (NTBs) among the parties.

President Donald Trump repeatedly renewed his intention to renegotiate or withdraw from NAFTA 1994. Any NAFTA nation can withdraw from the NAFTA agreement upon six months' notice. Coverage of NAFTA's re-negotiation and its outcome is presented in Chapter 6.

§ 4.1   Canada-U.S. Free Trade (CUSFTA, 1989)

North American economic integration began in earnest when Canada and the United States concluded a broad free trade and foreign investment agreement in 1989. Without intending to do so, the Canada-United States Free Trade Agreement (CUSFTA) laid the foundations for NAFTA 1994. In the United States, CUSFTA was almost a non-event. In Canada, the agreement was much contested. Special Parliamentary elections focused on CUSFTA kept the Mulroney government in power, which was critical to Canadian ratification of the agreement.

NAFTA 1994 did not repeal the Canada-United States Free Trade Agreement. The CUSFTA agreement continued and still continues to govern selected areas of trade (as specified in NAFTA 1994 and the USMCA). Officially, the United States and Canada "suspended" their 1989 agreement. **If NAFTA 1994 failed or either Canada or the United States withdrew from it, CUSFTA would come out of suspended animation and continue to bind the two countries.** There is no comparable arrangement for the United States and Mexico.

Understanding the CUSFTA agreement is important because it served as the model upon which NAFTA 1994 was built. In some areas, the terms of NAFTA were identical or nearly so. In others, minor or major changes were made which are best understood as attempts at improving upon the early experience of free trade and expanded foreign investment. NAFTA 1994 and NAFTA Re-Negotiated 2018 insights can still be drawn from CUSFTA even as it lies in suspended animation.

The Canada-United States Free Trade Agreement was limited in its scope and purposes. Nevertheless, the CUSFTA agreement is lengthy and relatively complex. It is comprised of eight Parts that are divided into a total of twenty-one Chapters. Each chapter is comprised of various Articles and accompanying Annexes. Above all CUSFTA was a pragmatic agreement.

Core Commitments—Federalism, Supremacy and Nondiscrimination

Chapter One of the Agreement contains a listing of CUSFTA objectives. Internal trade barriers on goods *and* services are to be eliminated, fair competition facilitated and investment opportunities liberalized. Effective procedures to administer CUSFTA, to resolve disputes, and cooperation to expand and enhance the benefits of the agreement were also listed as objectives.

In realizing these objectives, Canada and the U.S. promised to "ensure that all necessary measures are taken in order to give effect to [CUSFTA's] provisions, including their observance by state, provincial and local governments" (Article 103). This obligation was a major commitment, particularly for Canada since it has a relatively weak federal system with the provinces retaining considerable power. Binding the two federal governments to free trade was relatively simple. Binding their political subdivisions has proven more difficult.

Canada and the United States affirmed their existing 1989 bilateral and multilateral trade agreements. They self-servingly declared their agreement consistent with Article 24 of the original (pre-Uruguay Round) General Agreement on Tariffs and Trade (GATT 1947). Article 24 governs the establishment of free trade areas by GATT signatories (see Chapter 2), and CUSFTA did indeed ultimately pass examination by a GATT working party.

If there are inconsistencies between CUSFTA and then existing trade agreements, CUSFTA is supreme (Article 104). Under this supremacy rule, for example, conflicts with the GATT 1947 agreement would apparently result in regional rules prevailing. This potential was somewhat minimized via incorporating by reference into CUSFTA various GATT provisions, including the 1979 Procurement Code and Articles III, XI and XX of the GATT 1947.

There are a number of specific exceptions to CUSFTA supremacy, some limited in scope, if conflicts arise with any of the following agreements: (1) The GATT rules on antidumping and countervailing duties; (2) the GATT rules on balance of payments problems; (3) the OECD Code of Liberalization of Capital Movements; (4) the Income Tax Convention between Canada and the U.S.; and (5) the International Monetary Fund Agreement. In addition, it is generally specified that CUSFTA is *not* supreme on agriculture, emergency trade relief, wine and spirits, trade in goods, energy, tariff waivers and investment matters. These exceptions had less impact than their numbers imply.

Canada and the United States broadly promised to grant "national treatment" on investment and trade matters. Each side thus agreed to treat the other's investors and traders in the same manner as their own, a general promise not to discriminate on the grounds of nationality. In addition, Article III of the GATT 1947 agreement, along with its interpretative notes, was specifically incorporated into CUSFTA. Article III stipulates national treatment for goods on taxation, fees and charges, distribution or sale requirements, transport rules, and domestic sourcing (among other matters). *Id.* Furthermore, the existing GATT interpretations of Article III were to be applied under CUSFTA. Several Article III disputes subsequently went to binding arbitration under Chapter 18 of CUSFTA (below).

A state or provincial treatment rule was also created. Regarding like, directly competitive or substitutable goods, treatment that is no less favorable than the most favorable treatment that the state or province grants to any goods is required. Hence, unlike at the federal level, this rule was not one of identical treatment, but a variation on most-favored-nation (MFN) treatment. The states and provinces were obliged to treat goods from the other country in the best manner they treated goods coming from anywhere, including their own state or province. Arguably, this duty provided greater protection from nondiscrimination than simply national treatment.

Trade in Goods

Part Two of the 1989 Canada-United States Free Trade Agreement, covered in Chapters 3 through 12, governs free trade in goods. This central goal must be measured against a history of substantial free trade in goods prior to 1989. Canada, for example, had been exporting more than 75 percent of its goods to the U.S. on a duty-free basis prior to the CUSFTA agreement. Most goods were entering the United States at an average 5 percent tariff. Hence, tariffs were not really a significant trade relationship.

Both countries were much more concerned with nontariff trade barriers (NTBs), such as health, safety, environmental and technical product regulations. NTBs sometimes excluded goods totally from either market and each country sometimes applied international trade remedies to limit the cross-border flow of goods. With its commanding dependency on access to the U.S. market, this Part of the CUSFTA agreement was critical to Canada. Conversely, the United States was ready to make concessions on trade in goods in order to obtain benefits on trade in services, technology and cross-border investment.

Tariffs and Quotas

Canada and the United States agreed to a phased elimination of the tariffs applicable to their trade in goods. Article 401 created a schedule for import tariff removals starting in 1989 and ending in 1998. This schedule was not subsequently altered by NAFTA. Schedule A goods immediately became duty free on January 1, 1989. Schedule B goods became duty free after 5 years of 20 percent annual reductions on January 1, 1993. Schedule C goods became duty free on January 1, 1998 after 10 years of 10 percent annual reductions. Schedule C goods included the most tariff-sensitive, such as agricultural products, textiles and clothing. Thus, at this writing, President Trump notwithstanding, trade between Canada and the United States is largely free of tariffs.

Export taxes (tariffs) were prohibited at the outset of the CUSFTA agreement. Canada and the U.S. also agreed not to employ "customs user fees" which function like tariffs. The United States phased out its existing fees as applied to Canadian goods. In addition, private sector requests for accelerated tariff reductions ahead of the timelines in the CUSFTA Schedules were allowed. Companies and industries filed a surprising number of petitions for acceleration with their governments. Canadian and United States officials then met and decided which tariffs to reduce on an accelerated basis. Considerable acceleration in tariff removals were achieved under CUSFTA and this innovative process continued under NAFTA 1994.

The CUSFTA agreement, unlike the customs unions of Europe and MERCOSUR, did not embrace the creation of a common external tariff. In other words, the United States and Canada retained their own tariffs on goods entering their markets. Goods from the rest of the world are still, even after NAFTA 1994 and USMCA 2018, subject to United States or Canadian (not CUSFTA, NAFTA or USMCA) tariffs.

Nevertheless, certain external tariff tensions were addressed in CUSFTA. These primarily concerned foreign goods that entered Canada or the United States and were subsequently shipped to the other country. The widespread practice of "drawback" under customs law was the main issue. The refunding of tariffs that manufacturers pay on imported goods after they are exported, or incorporated or consumed in the production of goods subsequently exported, is the essence of drawback. Drawback can take the form of waivers or reductions in such duties. Either way, manufacturers have lower costs because of the customs refund. Supporters of drawback argue that the imported goods have really not come to rest, merely passed through, and therefore should be beneficially tariffed.

Canada and the United States recognized that drawbacks created problems for their free trade agreement. Manufacturers obtaining them could sell at lower costs than competitors not benefiting from drawback. To solve this problem, Canada and the United States agreed to all but eliminate drawbacks on goods they trade, and were scheduled have done so by 1996. However, this commitment was notably altered by the NAFTA agreement of 1994.

Another external tariff tension that CUSFTA remedied was waivers of tariffs triggered by "performance requirements." Such requirements were primarily found in Canadian law. Often, a Canadian manufacturer had to incorporate a minimum amount of Canadian content, purchase or substitute Canadian goods, and maintain minimum export percentages. Manufacturers meeting Canadian performance requirements were recipients of drawback or tariff waivers as an investment incentive. This resulted in an unfair advantage for Canadian manufacturers competing under CUSFTA with United States companies that did not obtain comparable benefits. Article 405 of CUSFTA prohibited new or expanded tariff waivers based upon performance requirements (i.e., a "standstill" was stipulated). For all but Auto Pact goods, tariff waivers were eliminated in 1998.

Regarding trade quotas and their equivalents, Canada and the United States agreed to apply Article XI of the GATT 1947. Thus most quotas were banned, excepting notably agricultural, fishery or marketing quotas. Several Article XI disputes were arbitrated under Chapter 18 of CUSFTA (below).

The Origin of Goods

Free trade agreements like CUSFTA, NAFTA 1994 and USMCA have a critical problem. Since Canada and the United States did not establish a common external tariff, other nations in theory could ship their goods into the country with the lowest tariff and then benefit from free trade. If so, third party goods could "free ride" on CUSFTA. To prevent this, Canada and the United States crafted rules to decide which goods came from their countries and allowed only those goods to be freely traded. All other goods are subject to national tariffs and trade restraints as they cross the border.

The CUSFTA "rules of origin" became one of the most complex and controversial of the agreement's provisions. Canada and the United States, with different legal traditions in this area, undertook a path-breaking set of rules of origin. To start, they agreed that all goods "wholly obtained or produced" within either or both of their nations could be freely traded. Since this rule applies mainly to minerals, agricultural goods and fish, it was not difficult to fulfill.

Manufactured goods, not so clearly Canadian or United States in origin, were another story. In the global economy, with multinationals producing goods and parts in many nations, it is hard to ascertain which products come from where. In the United States, the origin of goods has typically been decided under the doctrine of "substantial transformation." See *Anheuser-Busch Brewing Assn v. United States,* 207 U.S. 556 (1908). If in the process of manufacture, a material or part was "substantially transformed" into a new product, then its foreign origin was lost. The material or part so transformed originates as a matter of U.S. law in the country of transformation.

Unfortunately, the doctrine of substantial transformation in U.S. customs law has many imprecisions. Canada and the United States, having adopted the Harmonized Tariff System (HTS) of classification of goods, moved in a different direction. Under Article 301 of CUSFTA, they agreed as a general rule that whenever items of third party origin were transformed to a degree that their tariff classification under the HTS changed, then those items originated in Canada or the United States. But packaging, combining or diluting goods of third party origin was insufficient. The core CUSFTA rule of origin was therefore linked to changes in HTS tariff classifications. This approach embodied the idea but provided more precision than the doctrine of substantial transformation. For more on the HTS system, see R. Folsom, *Principles of International Trade Law.*

Canadian legal traditions and priorities were the primary source of additional CUSFTA "content" rules of origin. The CUSFTA content rules of origin applied only to trade in selected (but quite a large number) goods. These rules generally had to be satisfied *in addition to* the basic rule of change in tariff classification. In a few instances, the content origin of the goods sufficed for free trade.

Canada and the United States agreed, in most circumstances, on a 50 percent CUSFTA content rule. The value of materials originating in Canada or the United States plus the direct cost of processing performed in either or both countries had to exceed 50 percent of the value of the goods crossing the border. Only if this content rule was satisfied could many goods be freely traded under CUSFTA. Thus companies whose economic contribution to the region was less significant could not participate in free CUSFTA trade.

The 50 percent CUSFTA content rule of origin proved difficult to apply. In one noted case, it became especially controversial regarding Honda automobiles. *See* Cantin and Lowenfeld, 87 *Amer.J.Int'l Law* 375 (1993). The dispute centered on how to treat third party content that was "rolled up." Honda-U.S. exported auto engines with 10 percent third party content to Honda-Canada. Since the value of the engines was 90 percent United States in origin, when Honda-Canada installed the engines in its automobiles, it "rolled up" (treated as American) the 10 percent third party content when it subsequently shipped the autos to the United States.

Canada took the position that the engines were 100 percent American in origin. But U.S. Customs ruled that the 10 percent third-party engine value could not be rolled up in this manner, which meant that overall the autos did not meet the 50 percent CUSFTA content rule. They therefore could not be freely traded and were subject to United States tariffs. The *Honda* case reverberated in the NAFTA 1994 negotiations. Important changes were later made in the North American rules of origin for automobiles. *See* below.

Special rules of origin for textiles and clothing were created under CUSFTA and then tightened under NAFTA 1994. Demanding "fabric-forward" production requirements were stipulated so as to exclude third party textile goods from CUSFTA free trade. Certain fabrics (like silk) were exempt from these special CUSFTA origin requirements.

Product Standards

Canada and the United States focused on technical product standards as nontariff trade barriers in Chapter 6 of their agreement. Unusually, and importantly, Chapter 6 did not apply to state, provincial or local governments. The GATT Code on Technical

Barriers to Trade of 1979 was affirmed by the two countries. This Code provided that technical standards and product certification systems could not be used to create obstacles to trade, and foreign goods had to be treated no less favorably on standards than domestic goods. Coverage of process and production methods (PPMs) was omitted from the 1979 Code.

Under CUSFTA, "standards-related measures" (SRM) (including production processes) and "product approval procedures" were subject to free trade goals (Article 603). If the demonstrable purpose of standards was to achieve legitimate domestic objectives without excluding goods fulfilling those objectives, then CUSFTA's terms were met. Otherwise, a disguised obstacle to Canada-United States trade might occur and breach the treaty. Regarding each other's standards and certification systems, Canada and the United States generally granted mutual recognition. This approach meant that most goods certified as meeting technical standards by Canada or the United States could be freely traded.

A separate and detailed Chapter 7 was created for agricultural, food and beverage products. For these goods, a unification or harmonization approach was adopted for both standards and inspection procedures. In further contrast, CUSFTA's harmonized "sanitary and phytosanitary" (SPS) rules were made binding on state, provincial and local governments.

Free Trade Exceptions

Article 1201 of CUSFTA incorporated Article XX of the GATT 1947 agreement. Article XX creates general exceptions to the free movement of goods. These exceptions, however, may not be used in ways constituting "a means of arbitrary or unjustifiable discrimination" or "a disguised restriction on international trade."

The exceptions to international free trade in goods found in Article XX of the GATT include restraints of trade justified on grounds of public morals, protection of human, animal or plant life or health, compliance with laws and regulations which are compatible with the GATT, prison labor, and protection of national historic or artistic treasures. Article XX also exempts international restraints of trade undertaken to conserve natural resources (jointly undertaken with restraints on the domestic sector), to adhere to intergovernmental commodity agreements or domestic price stabilization programs, and in response to supply shortages.

Canada attempted to invoke Article XX to conserve Pacific salmon and herring as exhaustible natural resources by means of "landing" requirements. A CUSFTA dispute settlement panel ruled against Canada, finding that these requirements were enacted to restrain trade as well as conserve the species (CDA–89–1807–01). The panel doubted that the alleged conservation benefits were sufficiently large to justify the commercial inconvenience of landing *all* salmon and herring caught in Canada's Pacific waters. Despite this ruling, and CUSFTA Commission efforts at compromise, Canada has continued to impose limited landing requirements as Canadian fisherman assert excessive catches by U.S. boats.

A second group of CUSFTA general exceptions to free trade, borrowed from GATT 1947, deal with "national security." Article 2003 of CUSFTA was essentially lifted from Article XXI of the GATT 1947 agreement. Under it, restrictions on the flow of security-related information, actions to protect national security interests (such as non-proliferation of nuclear weapons), and United Nations peace and security obligations were recognized exceptions to CUSFTA free trade.

However, there was a special agreement regarding energy goods. Such goods could not be restricted except as necessary to: (1) Supply the Canadian or United States military when facing domestic armed conflicts; (2) fulfill critical defense contracts; (3) implement nuclear non-proliferation agreements; or (4) respond to direct threats of disruption in the supply of nuclear defense materials. This proviso reinforced the general CUSFTA commitments made to free trade in energy discussed below.

Canadian Cultural Industries Exclusion

Canada has a long history of supporting cultural industries through investment, financial, tax and other governmental acts. The 1989 free trade and foreign investment agreement between Canada and the United States excluded "cultural industries" from its scope. **This exclusion has been retained under NAFTA 1994 *and* the pending USMCA 2018.** The Canadian cultural industry exclusion covers the entire gamut of the NAFTA 1994 and NAFTA Re-Negotiated agreements. It applies to goods, services, investment, intellectual property, and dispute settlement.

The argument for this exclusion is not to keep American culture out of the market, but instead to assure a Canadian presence as well. Indeed, Canada maintains that it has neither attempted nor succeeded in keeping out American cultural products and services. That certainly seems right. Over 90 percent of Canada's movie screens and more than 80 percent of its news and TV broadcasts are U.S. controlled. Books of U.S. origin occupy 60 percent of all Canadian shelf space and U.S. magazines take 80 percent of the English-language market.

Cultural industries are defined those engaged in publishing, distributing or selling:

- Books, periodicals and newspapers (except their printing or typesetting);

- Films or videos; audio or video music recordings; or printed or machine readable music;

- Public radio communications;

- Radio, television and cable TV broadcasting; and

- Satellite programming and broadcasting network services (Article 2012).

One practical effect of securing the cultural industries exclusion has been to insulate Canada's broadcasting regulations from regional scrutiny. In Canada, content requirements and airtime rules are an important means by which the Canadian Radio-Television and Telecommunications Commission (CRTC) restricts the amount of foreign broadcast material. Current broadcasting regulations employ a quota system mandating Canadian content for a minimum of 60 percent of all programming and 50 percent of prime time. Comparable quotas apply to films, broadcast TV, cable TV and satellite transmissions. "Canadian content" is calculated under a points system traditionally requiring that the producer be Canadian and that at least 6 of 10 key creative positions be filled by Canadians. In addition, most production and distribution expenses must be paid to Canadians.

The requirements for radio are similar and focus on the nationality of the composer and performer, and the location and performance of the selection. The government also provides subsidies and tax incentives for national broadcasting enterprises which have financial difficulty in complying with content quotas. Furthermore, investment regulations effectively limit U.S. ownership or control of Canadian cultural enterprises. For example, Canada refused to permit Borders to open a super-bookstore in Toronto even after securing a Canadian partner as a majority owner. Ironically, although these economically driven rules ensure a national presence in broadcasting, they do not guarantee Canadian cultural content.

All that said, technology has greatly diminished the effectiveness of Canada's audio-visual content rules. Satellite transmission and Internet streaming have made particular inroads. There is a thriving gray market for dishes aimed at U.S. satellites receiving services paid via a U.S. billing address. More broadly, the Internet has undermined Canada's cultural industry trade restraints in ways that mostly avoid even the most determined regulator.

Canadian limits on access to Netflix titles, for example, have been widely circumvented by obtaining U.S. Internet addresses via virtual private networks (VNP) installed on Canadian computers and other devices.

In contrast, there is no cultural industry exclusion under NAFTA 1994 or USMCA 2018 applicable to Mexico-United States trade and foreign investment. Integration of U.S.-Mexican cultural industries is occurring. In 1996, for example, the United States and Mexico reached agreement allowing companies in either country to compete for provision of satellite services, including direct-to-home and direct broadcast services. Each country retains the right to impose "reasonable" ownership, content and advertising regulations, but Mexico (unlike Canada) will not impose local content requirements.

There are exceptions and qualifications to the general exclusion of Canadian cultural industries from CUSFTA, NAFTA and NAFTA Re-Negotiated free trade. Tariff reductions were specified under CUSFTA for film, cassettes, records, cameras, musical instruments and the like. Additional tariff reductions were agreed to in NAFTA 1994. Responding to a United States complaint about Canadian cable TV "pirates," copyright royalties must be paid when U.S.-sourced free transmissions are retransmitted to the Canadian public by cable. In addition, no alteration or non-simultaneous retransmission of such broadcasts is permitted without the permission of the copyright holder. Likewise, no retransmission of cable or pay TV can occur without such authorization.

Occasionally, United States investors may acquire a Canadian cultural industry company by merger or acquisition. If ordered to divest, the U.S. investor must be paid open market value by Canada. Canada, for example, forced Simon & Shuster to divest a Canadian textbook publisher to a Canadian company, which subsequently went bankrupt. No other parties being interested, the Canadian government was obliged to buy the textbook publisher, and sold it back to Simon & Shuster.

Canadian Cultural Industries Exclusion— The Sports Illustrated Dispute

Canada's cultural industry exception comes with a price. The United States can unilaterally implement retaliation for cultural industry protection. The U.S. can undertake "measures of equivalent commercial effect" against acts that would have been "inconsistent" with CUSFTA but for the cultural industries exclusion (Article 2005.2). There is no need to utilize CUSFTA's dispute settlement procedures prior to retaliation, which can be anything except a violation of the free trade agreement. The United States could, for example, pursue "Section 301" investigations and unilateral retaliation under the Trade Act of 1974. *See* R. Folsom, *Principles of International Trade Law.* Each year the United States Trade Representative must identify new Canadian acts, policies and practices affecting cultural industries.

Both Canada and the United States have sought to minimize the potential for cultural industry disputes through negotiations. The "successful" resolution of the Country Music Television (CMT) dispute in 1995 is often cited as an example. CMT of Nashville had, in the absence of a Canadian competitor, been licensed as a Canadian cable TV distributor. When a competitor emerged, CMT's license was revoked by the CRTC. CMT then petitioned the USTR for Section 301 relief, and an investigation was commenced. Intergovernmental negotiations resulted in the creation of a partnership of the two competitors, which was then licensed by the CRTC.

Cultural industry disputes have also been diverted from CUSFTA by using the World Trade Organization as an alternative forum. In March of 1997, a WTO Dispute Settlement Panel ruled that Canada's taxes, import regulations and postal subsidies concerning magazines (and advertising) violated the GATT 1994 agreement (WT/DS31/AB/R (1997). This longstanding dispute centered on *Sports Illustrated.* Canada was seeking to protect and ensure "Canadian issues" of periodicals and prevent the export of its advertising revenues. The United States overcame culturally-based Canadian policies by electing to pursue WTO remedies, although Canada's compliance was disputed. In May of 1999, a settlement was reached. United States publishers may now wholly-own Canadian magazines. In addition, Canada will permit U.S. split-run editions without Canadian editorial content. Such editions may contain Canadian advertisements not in excess of 12 percent by lineage (rising to 18 percent).

Professor Oliver Goodenough has thoughtfully analyzed Canada's preoccupation with culture. *See* 15 *Ariz. J. Int'l & Comp. Law* 203 (1998). He believes that the cultural industry exclusion reflects a weak national identity and that a principal purpose is to rally Canadians around their flag in a "recurring pageant of threat and defense." Professor Goodenough notes that the "war" against Hollywood is primarily protective of Anglophone Canada. Francophone Canada, with a healthy cultural identity, has already demonstrated resilience to U.S. and Anglophonic Canadian influences.

Reaching into the literature on "culture transmission theory," Professor Goodenough finds that most foreign influences will "bounce off" healthy cultures without government intervention or, at the very least, compartmentalize such influences in ways which separate them from hearth and home. He concludes that Canada is "defending the imaginary to death" and if it continues to press its cultural protection policies: "[I]t will indeed be to the death, a death brought about not by 'invasion' from the south, but by the incomparably better claims to culturally-based nationhood possessed by Francophone Quebec and by the First Nation Peoples. Rather than acting as a rallying cry for national preservation, cultural protection provides the intellectual basis for a break-up of Canada."

Procurement

The GATT Procurement Code of 1979, along with past (1986) and future (1995) amendments, was incorporated by reference into CUSFTA. The agreement, however, surpassed the Code as it existed in 1989 in several important ways. The number of goods eligible for free procurement trade was increased, the value of eligible contracts decreased to $25,000 U.S. and its equivalent in Canadian dollars, and a general rule of most-favored-treatment for goods with at least 50 percent cost-based CUSFTA origin was established. Canada and the United States also agreed to create opportunities to challenge procurement awards before administrative authorities, a remedy followed in NAFTA 1994, the 1995 WTO Procurement Code and USMCA 2018 for Mexico and the United States. See Chapter 6.

Temporary Safeguard Import Restraints

In a step well ahead of the rest of the world, Canada and the United States agreed to dramatically reduce their rights to take unilateral, temporary action against import surges. When such surges cause or threaten serious injury to domestic producers of similar or competing products, Article XIX (the "escape or safeguards clause") of the GATT permits taking relief in the form of tariffs, quotas, voluntary trade restraints or other protection measures. Nations impacted by such relief can retaliate equivalently. Canada and the United States significantly limited each other's right to pursue *bilateral* escape clause relief. After 1997, CUSFTA totally eliminated bilateral escape clause relief except with the other's unlikely consent. This ban continued in effect under NAFTA 1994, but was softened under USMCA 2018. See Chapter 6.

A different type of escape clause relief (known as "global actions") could be undertaken when the trade involves third parties. If global actions were taken under the GATT, neither Canada nor the United States may restrict imports from the other unless they are "substantial" and "contributing importantly" to injury or its threat (Article 1102). However, several WTO Appellate Body rulings cast doubt on the legality of excluding or favoring Canada or Mexico in global escape clause proceedings. See *U.S.-Lamb Meat from New Zealand*, WT/DS 177/AB/R (May 16, 2001).

While the huge amount of trade between Canada and the United States is not always harmonious, CUSFTA virtually took Canada-United States trade out of escape clause proceedings. In contrast, NAFTA 1994 established a number of escape clauses to insure against the possibility of import surges from Mexico. Temporary import restraints were even subject to a special "understanding" supplementing NAFTA 1994.

Wine, Beer and Spirits

The barriers to trade in alcoholic beverages between the United States and Canada presented a complex regulatory maze. Beer was so difficult that little agreement was reached and existing restraints were retained on both sides of the border. Wine and spirits were dissected under Chapter 8 of CUSFTA and these rules remained in force under NAFTA 1994.

Nondiscriminatory national treatment and most-favored sub-national treatment on licensing the sale of wine and spirits was required. Wine and spirits licensing had to be undertaken using normal commercial considerations without causing disguised barriers to trade. Prompt, fair and objective appeals from administrative boards were to be made available to applicants from either side of the border. Furthermore, pricing decisions by public distributors had to be nondiscriminatory, but could reflect actual cost-of-service differentials between handling domestic and imported wines or spirits. Canadian price mark-ups above those levels were removed between 1989 and 1995.

Regulations governing the distribution of wine and spirits are also subject to general national and most-favored treatment rules. Certain traditional exceptions continue in force. For example, Ontario and British Columbia oblige private sellers to favor wines originating in their provinces. And Quebec requires food stores to sell wine bottled in that province. Canada did eliminate longstanding blending requirements on U.S. bulk distilled spirits, and the exclusive right to sell products labeled Bourbon Whiskey and Canadian Whiskey was recognized. Under NAFTA 1994, exclusivity was also extended to Tennessee Whiskey and Mexican Tequila and Mezcal.

The extensive CUSFTA 1989 dismantling of restrictive trade regulations governing wine and spirits contrasts with the coverage of beer. Restrictive and discriminatory beer practices in effect on October 4, 1987 were retained. Only new restraints had to conform to the national and most-favored treatment obligations. Notably, Canada and the United States reserved their GATT 1947 rights and obligations for wine, spirits *and* beer. The GATT subsequently provided a venue to challenge some of the trade restraints on beer preserved by CUSFTA. *See* GATT Doc. DS17/R (Oct. 16, 1991); BISD395/206 (June 19, 1991). Ontario, for example, maintained "warehouse charges" and "environmental" taxes that mostly hit U.S. beer. The United States at one point slapped a 50 percent tariff on Ontario beer. By filing GATT complaints and engaging in negotiations, both countries largely succeeded in removing restraints of trade on beer. Hopefully this will at last resolve the Canadian-U.S. "beer wars."

Energy

Canada exports large amounts of oil, gas, coal, electricity and uranium to the United States. This helps meet the energy-hungry needs of the United States. Thus the CUSFTA 1989 provisions on trade in energy goods contained in Chapter 9 were unusually significant. Similar provisions were retained under NAFTA 1994, but there was a dispute about their meaning if an energy crisis occurs.

The Canadian National Energy Board (NEB) regulates trade in energy goods by licensing surplus exports. The NEB has the power to regulate the prices of Canadian energy imports and exports, determining whether prices are "just and reasonable." The United States perceived this price regulation as constituting minimum export price controls. Article 902(2) of the CUSFTA agreement bans such price controls. CUSFTA also disallows charging higher than domestic prices for energy exports. Furthermore, since Canada taxes the export of energy goods, Article 903 prohibits discriminatory taxation. Export taxes and fees are permissible only if they are imposed domestically, and Canada adjusted export taxes on energy as a consequence.

Perhaps most importantly for the national security of the United States, Canadian law authorizes the NEB to restrain energy exports in times of crisis, as Canada did during the world oil shocks of the 1970s. Article 904(a) of CUSFTA is less than a model of clarity but seems to remove this authorization as it might apply to exports to the United States. Canada appeared instead obliged in a crisis to maintain the prior proportion of exports to domestic production. The standard proportions among the various energy exports to the United States had apparently also to be maintained. The only exception to these duties was if sharing under the International Energy Program is imposed. NAFTA Re-Negotiated 2018 dropped these controversial provisions.

Motor Vehicles

Under their bilateral Auto Pact of 1965, Canada and the United States substantially embraced free trade in new automobiles and OEM parts. The Auto Pact was retained under CUSFTA (and NAFTA 1994) subject to some changes. Tariffs on auto parts traded between Canada and the United States were extinguished. Canada's historic blockage of the importation of used vehicles from the United States was also eliminated. The United States adopted the more rigorous 50 percent regional content test of origin found in CUSFTA, but permitted manufacturers to average their value content over 12 months.

On the Canadian side, the Auto Pact was limited under CUSFTA to the Big Three and by special exception CAMI (a General Motors-Suzuki joint venture). No other manufacturers (including various Japanese companies) could acquire preferential Auto Pact status. They and other manufacturers had to meet the general CUSFTA rule of origin content requirements. Canada further agreed to abolish tariff refunds and waivers for non-Auto Pact producers. But Canada retained its sales to production performance ratio obligations and various "Canadian value-added" content rules for Auto Pact companies.

By 1998 the United States and Canada had removed virtually all tariffs on automotive goods.

Services

The United States, with many highly competitive service providers, sought a general commitment to free trade in services from Canada. Chapters 14 and 17 of CUSFTA make it clear that the U.S. failed to obtain free trade in services as a general rule. Substantial free trade in "covered" services was all that could be agreed upon. Annex 1408 of the CUSFTA agreement lists the services subject to its free provision rules. This list included some glaring omissions, such as transportation, that were not remedied until NAFTA 1994.

Service providers and service seekers acquired benefits under CUSFTA. The "provision" of covered services included the right to be located in one country and service clients in the other. Provision embraced production, distribution, sale, purchase, marketing, delivery and use of covered services. Provision also included access to and use of domestic distribution systems. Beneficiaries could establish a "commercial presence" to facilitate covered services, such as establishing a sales agency or branch office in the other country. The right to invest in order to provide covered services was also protected. Indeed, virtually *any* activity associated with the provision of covered services was allowed, including the organization, control, operation, maintenance and disposition of companies, branches, agencies, offices or other facilities to conduct business as well as borrowing money and handling property.

Who could provide services was clarified in Article 201 of the CUSFTA agreement. Canadian and United States nationals *and* enterprises principally carrying on business in either country were the main beneficiaries. Such businesses had to be incorporated or otherwise constituted under Canadian or United States laws. The Agreement's focus on principal place of business meant that Canadian or U.S. businesses owned or controlled by individuals or companies from other nations benefited from free trade in CUSFTA-covered services. Denial of these third party benefits was possible only if the service was provided "indirectly." This exception functioned like a rule of origin. It ensured that only service providers with substantial businesses in Canada or the United States could partake of free trade.

Cross-border CUSFTA service providers and seekers received "no less favorable" treatment than nationals and enterprises under Canadian and United States laws. For each federal government, national treatment was the general rule. Each state, province or local government was obliged to grant most-favored treatment to service providers and seekers. Ironically, while California could give less than most-favored treatment to New York service providers, it could not do so to Canadians. Since CUSFTA's beneficiaries included enterprises principally carrying on business in Canada or the United States, third party subsidiaries qualified for national and most-favored services treatment.

There were significant exceptions to the CUSFTA standards for service providers. Canada and the United States indefinitely retained (in their 1989 form) inconsistent statutes and regulations. Furthermore, Article 1402.3 allowed for deviations in treatment for prudential, fiduciary, health and safety or consumer protection reasons. Any such different treatment had to be "equivalent in effect" to that applied domestically for the same reasons. No deviation could require the establishment of a commercial presence in order to provide services in the other country. And, borrowing from GATT 1947 language relating to goods, no deviation (including tax laws), could serve as a means to "arbitrary or unjustifiable discrimination" or a "disguised restriction" on CUSFTA trade in services.

Canada and the United States retained their own licensing and certification systems for services. They agreed that these systems should "relate principally to competence or the ability to provide" covered services. (Article 1403) Licensing and certification could not discriminatorily impair or restrain access. Existing inconsistent statutes and regulations were indefinitely retained, but no new licensing or certification statute or regulation could require a commercial presence, arbitrarily discriminate, or disguise a trade restraint.

Financial Services

The provisions of Chapter 17 of CUSFTA reflect the complexity and sensitivity of the financial services sector. For purposes of Chapter 17, "financial services" were defined so as to exclude securities underwriting and sales of insurance policies. Insurance services were generally a covered service under Chapter 14 of CUSFTA.

Each country made commitments to alter specific statutes and regulations to benefit the other's financial sector. These commitments were retained under NAFTA 1994. Canada made commitments on financial services in three key sectors:

(1)   Greater U.S. ownership of Canadian banks;

(2)   Deregulation   of   U.S.-controlled   foreign   bank subsidiaries; and

(3)   Reduced application of Canada's foreign investment control laws.

The United States also made three major commitments on financial services:

(1)   Permission for U.S. banks to underwrite Canadian debt;

(2)   Extension of future U.S. Glass-Steagall Act (48 Stat. 162) amendments to Canadian-controlled financial institutions; and

(3)   A promise not to restrict interstate branching rules.

The Canadian commitments allow United States residents and U.S. companies controlled by such persons to acquire Canadian banks and federally regulated trust, loan and life insurance companies. However, no one person could own more than 10 percent of a Schedule A bank class of securities. Limits on the total domestic assets of banking subsidiaries controlled by U.S. citizens or permanent residents were removed, as were restraints on the transfer of loans from subsidiaries to their parent companies. Moreover, new branches of U.S.-controlled banking subsidiaries could be opened without getting the approval the Minister of Finance. More broadly, Canada agreed not to apply its investment review powers over U.S. financial institutions in a manner that would be inconsistent with the "aims" of Chapter 17.

The United States commitments permit federally regulated U.S. banks to underwrite and market the debt of Canada, its political subdivisions, and the debt of Canadian agencies backed by full faith and credit. This authority is an exception to the general prohibition against U.S. banks dealing in securities contained in the Glass-Steagall Act of 1933. Canadian public debt has been more readily sold in the United States as a consequence. If the U.S. amends the Glass-Steagall Act or its regulations at any future time (which it has now done), Canadian-controlled financial institutions must be given equal treatment. For these limited purposes, a financial institution controlled directly or indirectly by persons who ordinarily reside in Canada suffices. In the event of federal regulation of interstate branches, the United States agreed not to adopt or apply any laws that would be more restrictive on Canadian banks than those in force at the state level on October 4, 1987.

These commitments notwithstanding, Canada and the United States publicly expressed mutual dissatisfaction with treatment of financial institutions in the other's country. Both promised no reduction in existing rights and privileges, except if the benefits from future deregulation of financial markets are not extended to each other absent "normal regulatory and prudential considerations." Canada and the United States now give each other notice and an opportunity to comment on proposed financial regulations. Consultation between the Canadian Department of Finance and the U.S. Treasury Department is frequent. Such consultations generally displace regional dispute settlement procedures.

Foreign Investment

Chapter 16 of CUSFTA 1989 governed laws, regulations and policies generally affecting cross-border investment by Canadian or United States investors. However, financial services, cultural industries, transportation services, government procurement and services not covered by CUSFTA did not benefit from Chapter 16. CUSFTA created a rule of national treatment at the federal level and most-favored treatment at lower levels of government. Such rules covered establishing new businesses, acquiring or selling existing ones, and conducting business operations.

The foreign investment rules of CUSFTA applied *only* to United States and Canadian nationals, governments and enterprises they controlled. This differed from CUSFTA free trade in services which benefited third party providers established or principally doing business in Canada or the United States. Nevertheless, it was forbidden to require that shareholders include nationals of either country. Nor could investors be forced due to nationality to divest a qualified investment.

Perhaps most importantly, Canada undertook to amend its 1985 Investment Canada Act (ICA). The ICA normally applied to foreign acquisitions of Canadian businesses worth more than 5 million Canadian dollars. CUSFTA did not suspend the ICA's application to U.S. acquisitions of existing Canadian businesses, but it did alter the thresholds triggering Canadian review. Only direct acquisitions or sales of Canadian firms subject to CUSFTA that exceed $150 million Canadian dollars could be reviewed by Canada's investment authorities. Indirect acquisitions of Canadian businesses were not reviewable unless they fell in the economic sectors excluded from CUSFTA. These commitments were continued under NAFTA 1994.

The United States could not trigger dispute settlement about any Canadian decision under the ICA regarding an acquisition by a U.S. investor. Significantly from the point of view of existing U.S. investors in Canada, the $150 million threshold also triggers a "right of exit." Canadian investments below that amount can be sold to non-Canadians without ICA review.

Performance requirements were a central focus of CUSFTA's investment rules. They could not be imposed as a condition to allowing or operating an investment. Article 1603 prohibited (for CUSFTA investors) performance requirements on exports, obligations to substitute or purchase local goods or services, and domestic content minimums. Even so, certain types of performance requirements (notably employment, technology transfer, or research and development obligations) were permissible for CUSFTA investors. With third party investors, any performance requirement could be used, provided this did not have a "significant impact" on trade between Canada and the United States.

Direct or indirect nationalization or expropriation of investments held by each other's investors was banned by CUSFTA 1989. The only exception was for nondiscriminatory public purposes in accordance with due process of law and upon payment of prompt, adequate and effective compensation at fair market value. Cross-border CUSFTA investors were free to transfer their profits, dividends, royalties, fees, interest and other earnings or proceeds from the sale or liquidation of their investments. Canada or the United States could prevent such transfers (acting equitably, without discrimination and in good faith) under their bankruptcy, insolvency, creditors' rights, securities, criminal, currency transfer reporting, tax withholding or court judgment enforcement laws. New tax or subsidy rules were allowed provided they did not arbitrarily or unjustifiably discriminate between Canadian or U.S. investors, or function as a disguised restriction on the CUSFTA benefits of those investors.

Note that there were no provisions allowing foreign investors to file claims against governments for damages as a result of alleged violations of rights created under CUSFTA 1989. Such remedies became a controversial focus of dispute settlement under NAFTA 1994. See Section 4.7.

Temporary Visas for Business Persons

Chapter 15 of CUSFTA 1989 governed *temporary* entry for business persons engaged in trading goods or services, or cross-border investors. Similar provisions can be found under NAFTA 1994. Four groups of persons were granted preferential treatment: (1) Business visitors; (2) professionals; (3) traders and (substantial) investors; and (4) intra-company transferees. In the event of disputes concerning the entry of business persons, all available appeals in Canada or the United States had to be first pursued. Only if there was a pattern of restrictive practices was dispute settlement under Chapter 18 of CUSFTA an option.

All four categories were exempted from labor certification or employment validation tests demonstrating in advance that a local person could not fulfill the needs that these business persons temporarily met. On the other hand, all such business persons had to meet the standard national security, public health and safety requirements for entry. Except for business visitors, employment authorization prior to entering the other country was required. Tens of thousands of Canadian professionals took advantage of CUSFTA 1989 to head south for employment in the United States.

CUSFTA Dispute Settlement

Dispute settlement under NAFTA 1994 replaced comparable procedures first established under CUSFTA. Chapter 18 of CUSFTA employed consultations and if necessary arbitration to settle most kinds of disputes. Chapter 19 of CUSFTA utilized special binational panels to resolve antidumping and countervailing duty disputes. All of the CUSFTA dispute settlement decisions, including those cited in this chapter, can be obtained at www.nafta-sec-alena.org.

None of CUSFTA's dispute settlement procedures were mandatory. For example, disputes that could be resolved under CUSFTA, the GATT 1947 agreement, or the GATT Tokyo Round Codes could be pursued in either forum. Practically speaking, forum shopping as between Chapters 18 and 19 and the GATT (now WTO) was perfectly acceptable. However, once an avenue of relief was chosen by the complaining party, the dispute had to be resolved there exclusively.

One reason behind this legitimization of forum shopping was the sorry state of GATT 1947 and GATT Code dispute settlement procedures in 1989. "Working-groups" or panels composed of experts who were not from the nations in dispute issued a "report." This report made findings of fact, rendered conclusions of law, and made remedial recommendations which were forwarded to the GATT Council. Lengthy, cumbersome and subject to a consensus vote in the GATT Council, GATT dispute settlement in 1989 was not really binding as each nation could negate the panel's ruling. Even if the process worked, compliance was essentially voluntary.

The GATT (now WTO) does offer political advantages as a dispute settlement forum. Its membership of about 165 nations frequently means that others will join in the dispute, thus raising visibility and pressure. This was true for CUSFTA in 1989 and remained true under NAFTA 1994. However, NAFTA 1994 complicated the forum selection process (see below). USMCA 2018 also provides complainants with a WTO dispute settlement option. See Chapter 6.

Intergovernmental CUSFTA Dispute Settlement

Dispute settlement under Chapter 18 of the CUSFTA agreement applied in most instances, but notably not concerning financial services. The Canada-United States Trade Commission (TC) was the center of the Chapter 18 dispute settlement process. International trade representatives of Canada and the United States or their designees constituted the CUSFTA Trade Commission, which was aided by Secretariats in Ottawa and Washington, D.C. There were three stages to Chapter 18 dispute settlement: (1) Bilateral Consultations; (2) Trade Commission Review; and (3) Binding Arbitration.

The CUSFTA Trade Commission was after 1994 largely supplanted by the NAFTA Trade Commission. The CUSFTA Commission provided a forum to discuss CUSFTA disputes. Consultations always preceded Commission deliberations. Questions of implementation, interpretation, application, allegedly inconsistent action, or "nullification and impairment" of benefits expected under the CUSFTA agreement fell within its jurisdiction. The CUSFTA Commission had the power to delegate its responsibilities to ad hoc committees and working-groups. It could also obtain the advice of nongovernmental individuals or groups. The Commission promulgated its own rules and procedures and functioned by cooperative consensus.

Notice as far in advance as possible was required of any proposed law with the potential to materially affect the operation of CUSFTA. With or without notice, Canada and the United States undertook to consult in good faith and "make every attempt" at a mutually satisfactory resolution. A meeting of the CUSFTA Trade Commission became mandatory only if no resolution was had within 30 days. The Commission then sought to resolve the dispute promptly, relying at its discretion on mediators acceptable to both sides.

For most disputes the CUSFTA Commission could refer the matter to binding arbitration only by mutual agreement. If no consensus was reached to refer the dispute to arbitration, the fallback was to appoint a panel of experts. Only in disputes concerning emergency escape clause proceedings was binding arbitration mandatory. The Commission could set the terms for arbitration of CUSFTA disputes, but unless it directed otherwise an arbitration panel was established following the provisions of Article 1807. Under Article 1807, two panelists were chosen by each side with the fifth member (absent agreement) chosen by lot. A list of qualified panelists was established by the Commission. The confidential arbitration panel set its own procedural rules, including a hearing and the right of reply.

An innovative provision of CUSFTA 1989 authorized the submission of memoranda by the governments of Canada and the United States acting jointly if possible, or singly if not, to courts or administrative tribunals in either country. Such submissions could only concern issues of interpretation, but they could be requested by a national court or tribunal entertaining CUSFTA issues in litigation. This little used request authority resembled somewhat the advisory ruling procedure followed in Europe as between national courts and the European Court of Justice. Memoranda on interpretative issues could be submitted whenever the governments of Canada or the United States considered it meritorious.

A related authority can be found in Chapter 20 of the NAFTA 1994 agreement. Article 2020 authorizes the NAFTA Commission to forward "agreed interpretations" to national judicial and administrative bodies. If no agreed interpretation can be reached, individual member state opinions can be submitted. All such submissions are *not* binding upon the national court or tribunal considering how to interpret NAFTA 1994.

Arbitration Decisions under CUSFTA Chapter 18

Chapter 18 of CUSFTA resulted in five binding arbitrations. Other trade disputes were taken to the GATT, and some contentious issues resolved during the NAFTA and Uruguay Round negotiations.

In the first Chapter 18 arbitration panel, the United States complained against Canadian landing requirements for fish (mostly salmon) caught in their waters. A prior GATT panel ruling against Canadian fish export controls had led to the landing requirements.

The CUSFTA arbitration panel ruled with one dissent in favor of the United States argument that the requirements unfairly increased the burden of exporting Canadian fish in violation of GATT Article XI and were not exceptions under GATT Article XX, discussed above (CDA–89–1807–01). Canada accepted the panel's findings. A mutually satisfactory settlement was then reached, but salmon fishing in the Northwest remains a remarkably divisive issue to this day.

The second arbitration panel under Chapter 18 upheld United States limits on the sale of undersized lobsters. By a split vote, argued under GATT Articles III and XI which were incorporated by reference into the CUSFTA agreement, the panel decided that since both Canadian and United States lobsters were affected there was no unlawful trade restraint (USA–89–1807–01). The third CUSFTA panel upheld, contrary to a U.S. Customs Service ruling, Canada's practice of including certain interest payments in the costs of production of automobiles (USA–92–1807–01). This issue arose when Canada determined CUSFTA content in ascertaining origin under Article 304. The panel followed the Vienna Convention of the Law of Treaties in interpreting CUSFTA even though the United States is not a party to that Convention.

The fourth arbitration panel generally agreed with Canada's interpretation of Article 701.3 of the CUSFTA agreement (CDA–92–1807–01). Minimum pricing of durum wheat for sale to the United States was at issue. This dispute was surrounded by U.S. perceptions of unfair subsidization of Canadian wheat exports. Once again, the Vienna Convention was invoked to interpret CUSFTA. Canadian wheat exports have remained the center of considerable controversy, trade complaints and intergovernmental memoranda of understanding imposing tariff rate quotas.

The fifth and final CUSFTA arbitration panel concerned Puerto Rico's refusal to allow entry of "improperly certified" long-life milk from Quebec (USA–93–1807–01). Articles III and XI of the GATT were at issue. This panel generally supported the U.S. position that it was entitled to enforce its standards against Canadian goods. The panel suggested that if both countries were essentially using the same inspection standards then entry should have been allowed as a matter of good faith so as to avoid nullification and impairment of CUSFTA trade benefits. Ongoing equivalency discussions between the two trade partners were recommenced.

Dumping and Subsidy Dispute Settlement

Dispute settlement under CUSFTA Chapter 19 was limited to two types of international trade law actions: antidumping and countervailing duty proceedings. Both are GATT-authorized and regulated. *See* Chapter 1.

Such proceedings are typically commenced at the request of industries that face import competition and can ultimately result in the imposition of special tariffs on imported goods. Antidumping duties apply to imported goods or services sold at below home country prices (price discrimination) that injure or threaten domestic industries. Countervailing duties apply to imported goods that have benefited from export or specific domestic governmental subsidies and have injured or threaten national industries.

Thus antidumping actions challenge private sector activities while countervailing duty actions question governmental acts. The amount of tariff duties possible is the margin of the dump or the level of subsidy determined to exist. Many antidumping duty proceedings (the most prevalent) are "settled" when the exporter agrees to raise its prices. Countervailing duty disputes may also be settled by intergovernmental accords. *See* the *Softwood Lumber Agreement* (below).

Antidumping and countervailing duty actions had been frequently used by the United States to impede entry of Canadian goods. Chapter 19 thus attempted to respond to critical Canadian concerns.

Canada and the United States had long acknowledged through the GATT the unfairness of dumping and subsidy practices. Unlike the European Union, they were unwilling to eliminate internal utilization of these trade remedies. GATT Codes on antidumping and countervailing duties provided the basic ground rules, but GATT dispute settlement was inadequate in the 1980s. Most importantly, Canada was distrustful of lengthy judicial reviews and law in U.S. courts of administrative antidumping and countervailing duty determinations. Prime Minister Mulroney actually walked away from the CUSFTA negotiating table to emphasize their concerns. **The end result was a unique form of dispute settlement under Chapter 19 of CUSFTA that was largely replicated in NAFTA 1994 and the pending USMCA 2018, procedures which exist nowhere else in the world.**

Under Chapter 19, binational panels of mutually approved experts (mostly international trade lawyers and law professors) ultimately decided antidumping and countervailing duty disputes. Prior to CUSFTA, the final resolution of such disputes had been in the national courts. Each country selected two panelists with an additional panelist chosen by mutual agreement. Each side had four opportunities to reject the other side's proposed panelists. No cause for rejection was required. A majority of the panelists had to be lawyers in good standing.

The administrative proceedings of Canada and the United States determining the existence of dumping or a countervailable subsidy remained in place. These decisions are made by the International Trade Administration (Commerce Dept.) in the United States and by the Deputy Minister of National Revenue for Customs and Excise in Canada. Likewise, the domestic proceedings used to decide if there has been material injury (or its threat) to a domestic industry were also retained. These decisions are made by the U.S. International Trade Commission and the Canadian Import Tribunal.

All Chapter 19 proceedings were pursued under the laws of Canada and the United States, neither of which was substantively changed by CUSFTA 1989. The critical change was the remarkable surrender of judicial sovereignty accomplished by Chapter 19. After CUSFTA, all final national administrative determinations in antidumping or countervailing duty proceedings were only "appealable" by all interested parties to a quasi-judicial binational CUSFTA panel.

When an antidumping or subsidy proceeding came before a CUSFTA panel, the legal principles that would have been used by a court in the importing country controlled. For binational panels reviewing final U.S. determinations this meant that U.S. Supreme Court and Federal Circuit Court of Appeal (but not Court of International Trade) decisions were binding precedent. By its terms, CUSFTA provided that previous panel decisions were not to be treated as precedent. NAFTA 1994 and NAFTA Re-Negotiated 2018 also retain these rules.

There were no new CUSFTA standards for review. With much controversy, each panel proceeded to apply the different standards of judicial review traditionally found in the law of Canada and the United States. For example, Canada's standards of review under the Federal Court Act § 28(1) are failure to observe principles of natural justice, jurisdictional abuse, errors in law, and pervasive, capricious or insupportable erroneous findings of fact. The standards of the U.S. Tariff Act of 1930 §§ 516A(b)(1)(A) and (B) are findings or conclusions unsupported by substantial evidence in the record or otherwise not in accordance with law.

There were over fifty CUSFTA Chapter 19 panel decisions, with more than two-thirds of them reviewing U.S. antidumping and countervailing duty determinations. Not surprisingly, trade in steel products garnered first place in the pursuit of market protection. The U.S. steel industry, in particular, has a long history of resorting to antidumping and countervailing duties to obtain shelter from import competition. Many observers have noted that the mere filing of AD and CVD complaints can produce some breathing room for domestic industries.

Most Chapter 19 panel decisions under CUSFTA were rendered in less than a year. Technically, these decisions either affirmed the final determination under review or, reversing, referred the determination back to the relevant administrative tribunal. It was up to that tribunal to take appropriate action. If it did not, and a second panel review took place, the agency was typically instructed to act in a not inconsistent manner by the second or (infrequently) third panel. The only further review, a final appeal by Canada or the United States (not the interested parties) of a panel decision, could come before an "Extraordinary Challenge Committee" (ECC). Such Committees were composed of three mutually acceptable judges.

ECC review of binational Chapter 19 panel decisions was intended to be truly extraordinary. In fact, there were only three such reviews (see below) between 1989 and 1994. All of them were raised by the United States. Many believe these challenges were politically motivated, in part to persuade Congress to extend fast track trade agreements authority to the President and in part to assuage key private sector interests. Challenges to CUSFTA (and NAFTA 1994) panel decisions were allowed only in limited circumstances such as if a panel member engaged in gross misconduct, was biased, or had a serious conflict of interest. Challenges could also be raised if the panel departed seriously from a fundamental rule of procedure or it manifestly exceeded its powers, authority or jurisdiction. The challenger has the duty to prove that the error alleged materially influenced the panel's decision and threatened the integrity of the review process.

Binational Panel and Extraordinary Challenge Committee Decisions under Chapter 19

Chapter 19 dispute settlement under CUSFTA 1989 in the five years prior to NAFTA 1994 was voluminous. With a few exceptions, most analyses of these decisions suggest an objective and not terribly politicized process. But the ability of binational panels to expertly rule under Canadian and United States law has been hotly contested. A prominent U.S. judge involved in the infamous *Softwood Lumber* dispute wrote a blistering dissent. *See* ECC–94–1904–01–USA (Wilkey, J.). Some administrative determinations had to be repeatedly reviewed by CUSFTA panels before compliance was achieved. One must wonder whether Chapter 19, which was intended to reduce trade tensions and suspicions, did not instead intensify Canada-U.S. antidumping and countervailing duty disputes.

Appeals to CUSFTA Extraordinary Challenge Committees demonstrated limited opportunities for relief. For example, the first Extraordinary Challenge Committee decision concerned U.S. countervailing duties on Canadian exports of pork (ECC–91–1904–01–USA). The initial binational panel decision questioned the substantiality of the evidence supporting the International Trade Commission's domestic injury determination. Upon reconsideration, the ITC found a threat of material injury to the U.S. domestic pork industry for a second time. A second binational panel decision ruled that the ITC had exceeded its notice for the proceedings, and issued specific evidentiary instructions to the ITC.

The ITC's next decision bitterly denounced the second binational panel's ruling. The ITC asserted that the panel's decision violated fundamental principles of CUSFTA and contained egregious errors of U.S. law. Nevertheless, the ITC acquiesced. It determined no threat of material injury expressly (and only) because of the binding nature of the CUSFTA panel's decision. The United States Trade Representative alleged gross error and sought review by Extraordinary Challenge Committee of the panel's *Pork* rulings. The Committee unanimously held that there was no gross error even if some of the panel determinations might not have followed U.S. rules of evidence. The Committee did caution panels not to rely on evidence not appearing in the record of the national proceedings.

The second extraordinary challenge concerned exports of live swine from Canada (EEC–93–1904–01–USA). Once again the Committee unanimously ruled against the challenge, although it did acknowledge that the panel may have made errors of law.

Softwood Lumber Dispute

The bitterly disputed binational panel decisions on U.S. countervailing duty actions against Canadian exports of softwood lumber did not conclude with the third Extraordinary Challenge Committee proceeding in 1994 from which Judge Wilkey so vigorously dissented. Trade tensions and negotiations continued. Canada, the victor before the Challenge Committee, appeared to realize that it might lose the next time around if changes in U.S. countervailing duty law were recognized. Indeed, these changes were undertaken specifically for that purpose. In 1996, a "settlement" was reached.

The 1996 Softwood Lumber Agreement applied to Alberta, British Columbia, Ontario and Quebec. It committed Quebec, for example, to raising its "stumpage" (timbering) fees. British Columbia (the largest exporter) promised to impose taxes on shipments of lumber to the U.S. above designated levels starting at 9 billion board feet. In addition, the Canadian federal government promised to impose taxes if exports exceed 14.7 billion board feet. The U.S. government and forest industry, in turn, pledged not to commence a countervailing duty action for 5 years so long as the agreement was followed.

In 2001, the 1996 Agreement lapsed and U.S. countervailing duties on Canadian lumber were renewed, followed by Canadian challenges under NAFTA 1994 and within the WTO. Billions of dollars in U.S. antidumping and countervailing duties on Canadian lumber were collected. In 2006, a second Softwood Lumber Agreement was achieved. Canada, then with about 34 percent of the U.S. softwood lumber market, agreed to impose rising export taxes if prices fall below specified trigger levels. About 80 percent of the duties previously collected were returned to Canadian producers. The Second Agreement was to be "dispute-free" for a minimum of three years. Nevertheless, the U.S. commenced arbitration proceedings before the London Court of Arbitration (LCIA) in 2007 and 2009 challenging the adequacy of Canadian implementation of the Agreement. Several LCIA rulings subsequently found Canada in breach of the 2006 Agreement. The 2006 Agreement was extended to October 2015.

To this day, softwood lumber disputes continue. Indeed, the Trump Administration levied countervailing duties on Canadian lumber in 2017 prior to commencing re-negotiation of NAFTA. See Section 1.17. Canada promised compensation to its exporters, and filed yet another dispute under NAFTA 1994 and before the WTO.

The legal and political controversy surrounding Chapter 19 panel decisions under CUSFTA sometimes blurs their practical consequences for tariffs and trade between the two countries. A careful reconstruction of that impact has been undertaken by a leading international trade attorney. *See* Mercury, 15 *N.W. J. Int'l Law & Bus.* 525 (1995). This study demonstrates that Canadian exporters were disproportionate beneficiaries in terms of CUSFTA Chapter 19 outcomes.

§ 4.2   Getting to NAFTA 1994

NAFTA 1994 did not repeal the Canada-United States Free Trade Agreement. The United States and Canada have "suspended" their 1989 agreement. If NAFTA fails to be re-negotiated or either Canada or the United States withdraws from it, CUSFTA will come out of suspended animation and continue to bind the two countries.

The U.S. free trade agreement with Canada in 1989 was nothing less than path breaking; the most sophisticated free trade agreement in the world. For most Canadians and Americans, revising the design to include Mexico required considerably more effort and discomfort. The discomfort came from years of observing protectionist Mexican trade policies, uncontrolled national debt, corruption, and the sense, somehow, that Mexico just did not "fit." In the end, these perspectives were overcome.

Mexico under Presidents de la Madrid, Salinas, Zedillo, and Fox had been unobtrusively breaking down its trade barriers and reducing the role of government in its economy. More than half of the enterprises owned by the Mexican government a decade ago have been sold to private investors, and more are on the auction block. Tariffs have been slashed to a maximum of 20 percent and import licensing requirements widely removed. Export promotion, not import substitution, became the highest priority. Like the U.S. and Canada, Mexico (since 1986) participates in the General Agreement on Tariffs and Trade (GATT) and World Trade Organization (WTO). See Chapter 1. This brought it into the mainstream of the world trading community on a wide range of fronts, including participation in nearly the full range of the Uruguay Round WTO agreements.

Mexican debt, hopefully, promises to become a manageable problem, although the collapse of the peso in 1994 and its slide in 2008/09 cast doubt on this. One party rule has ended nationally and in several states, with signs of an ever more pluralistic democracy on the horizon. Admittedly, political and economic corruption still runs deep within Mexico, but the winds of change are blowing. Major prosecutions of leading police, union and business leaders are underway. Perhaps most significantly, the rapid privatization of the state-owned sector of the economy combined with increasing tolerance of international competition has reduced not only the need for government subsidies but also the opportunity for personal enrichment by public officials.

Presidents Bush and Salinas, and Prime Minister Mulroney, pushed hard in 1991 to open "fast track" negotiations for a free trade agreement. In 1992, these efforts reached fruition when a NAFTA agreement was signed by Canada, the United States and Mexico with a scheduled effective date of Jan. 1, 1994. President Bush submitted the agreement to Congress in December 1992.

President Clinton supported NAFTA generally, but initiated negotiations upon taking office for supplemental agreements on the environment and labor. This delayed consideration of the NAFTA agreement in Congress until the Fall of 1993. Ratification was considered under fast track procedures which essentially gave Congress 90 session days to either ratify or reject NAFTA without amendments. After a bruising national debate that fractured both Democrats and Republicans with each party doing its best to avoid

Ross Perot's strident anti-NAFTA attacks, ratification was achieved in mid-November, just weeks before NAFTA's effective date. During this same period, Canada's Conservative Party suffered a devastating defeat at the polls. This defeat was partly a rejection by the Canadian people of the earlier ratification of NAFTA under Prime Minister Mulroney.

The United States is Mexico's largest trading partner, accounting in 1994 for nearly 70 percent of all Mexican trade and more than 60 percent of its foreign direct investment. In contrast, trade with Mexico in 1994 totaled only 7 percent of all U.S. international trade. Those facts help explain why Mexico has been the major beneficiary of the NAFTA 1994 accord.

§ 4.3   NAFTA 1994—Goods, Rules of Origin

Although each partner affirmed its rights and obligations under the General Agreement on Tariffs and Trade (GATT), NAFTA 1994 generally took priority over other international agreements in the event of conflict. The NAFTA, for example, prevailed over the former Multi-Fiber Arrangement on trade in textiles. Certain exceptions to this general rule of supremacy apply; the trade provisions of the international agreements on endangered species, ozone-depletion and hazardous wastes notably take precedence over the NAFTA (subject to a duty to minimize conflicts). Unlike the GATT/WTO, the NAFTA makes a general duty of national treatment for goods binding on all states, provinces and local governments of the three countries.

Prior to NAFTA 1994, Mexican tariffs on U.S. goods averaged about 10 percent; U.S. tariffs on Mexican imports averaged about 5 percent. Under NAFTA, Mexican tariffs were eliminated on all U.S. exports within ten years except for corn and beans which were subject to a fifteen-year transition. United States tariffs on peanuts, sugar and orange juice from Mexico also lasted 15 years. Immediate Mexican tariff removals under the "A" list covered about half the industrial products exported from the United States. Further tariff eliminations were made for the "B" list after 5 years, and will occur for the "C" list when the treaty matures in ten years. Accelerated tariff reduction may occur by bilateral accord. The existing Canada-U.S. tariff reduction schedule remained in place.

Escape clause rules and procedures are generally applicable to United States-Mexico trade under the NAFTA. These permit temporary trade relief against import surges subject to a right of compensation in the exporting nation. During the 10-year transition period, escape clause relief could be undertaken as a result of NAFTA tariff reductions only once per product for a maximum in most cases of 3 years. The relief was the "snap-back" to pre-NAFTA tariffs. After the transition period, escape clause measures may only be undertaken by mutual consent. If a global escape clause proceeding is pursued by one NAFTA partner, the others must be excluded unless their exports account for a substantial share of the imports in question (top five suppliers) and contribute importantly to the serious injury or threat thereof (rate of growth of NAFTA imports must not be appreciably lower than total imports).

Rules of Origin

Mexico has the highest average tariffs on imported goods, the U.S. has the lowest, and Canada falls in the middle. Since free trade in goods only applies to goods that originate in North America, non-originating goods are subject to the normal tariffs of Canada, Mexico and the United States. Origin determinations are thus critical to NAFTA traders. There are Uniform NAFTA Regulations governing rules of origin and customs procedures, including a common Certificate of Origin.

Article 401 of the NAFTA 1994 agreement starts with the primary rule that all goods wholly obtained or produced entirely inside NAFTA originate there. Canadian lumber, U.S. apples and Mexican oil provide examples. Such goods fall under NAFTA Preference Criterion A. Article 415 authorizes free trade in goods made from materials that "originate" exclusively within NAFTA, Preference Criterion C. Agricultural, timber and mining products almost always qualify as such. A laptop computer whose components all come from Mexico, Canada or the United States would qualify under Criterion C.

Article 401 adopts the change of tariff classification rule initiated in CUSFTA. *See* Chapter 2. Subject to various exceptions, goods produced in one or more of the three countries with non-originating materials may be freely traded when all such materials (excepting a *de minimis* amount) undergo a change in tariff classification based upon the Harmonized Tariff System (HTS). Ordinarily this requires a change at the HTS product classification level and is known as Preference Criterion B. This Criterion is the most commonly used of all NAFTA's rules of origin for goods. *See* Example 1 below and *Cummins v. United States*, 454 F.3d 1361 (Fed. Cir. 2006) (crankshafts from Brazil not Mexico, no change in tariff classification).

Meeting the change in tariff classification rule of origin is sometimes insufficient to allow free trading. Some goods must *also* contain a minimum "regional value content" (discussed below) to qualify under Preference Criterion B. For example, footwear, chemicals and automobiles fall in this category. There are fewer such content requirements under NAFTA than under CUSFTA. Electronics and machinery are generally exempt. See Example 2 below.

Article 401 also permits certain assembly goods that do not undergo a change in tariff classification to be freely traded if their regional value content is sufficient. This is NAFTA Preference Criterion D. For goods with very small non-originating content, NAFTA creates a *"de minimis"* rule of origin. Article 405 generally permits free trade in goods whose non-originating value is 7 percent or less. Such goods, in other words, are treated as originating in North America and may be freely traded.

Here are two U.S. Customs Service examples of goods that qualify for free trade under NAFTA 1994 Criterion B:

Example 1

Frozen pork meat (HTS heading 0203) is imported into the U.S. from Hungary and combined with spices imported from the Caribbean (HTS subheadings 0907–0910). Then, the spiced meat is mixed with cereals grown and produced in the U.S. to make fresh pork sausage (HTS heading 1601).

The Annex 401 rule of origin for HTS heading 1601 states:

"A change to heading 1601 through 1605 from any other chapter."

Since the frozen meat is classified in Chapter 2 and the spices are classified in Chapter 9, these non-NAFTA-originating materials meet the tariff shift requirement. Note that one does not need to consider whether the cereal meets the applicable tariff shift requirement, as the cereal is itself NAFTA-originating.

In conclusion, the fresh pork sausage is originating under NAFTA.

Example 2

A manufacturer purchases inexpensive textile watch straps made in Taiwan (HTS heading 9113), to be assembled with originating mechanical watch movements (HTS heading 9108) and originating cases (HTS heading 9112). The value of the straps is less than seven percent (7%) of the total cost of the final watch (HTS heading 9102).

The rule of origin under Annex 402 for HTS heading 9102 states:

"A change to heading 9101 through 9107 from any other chapter;
A change to heading 9101 through 9107 from 9114, whether or not

there is also a change from any other chapter, provided there is a regional value content of not less than:

a)   60 percent where the transaction value method is used, or

b)   50 percent where the net cost method is used."

Remember that only non-originating materials need to meet the required tariff shift requirement, and, in this case, the textile straps are the only non-originating component. As the value of the straps is less than seven percent (7%) of the total cost of the finished watch, the *de minimis* rule applies, and the finished watch is originating under NAFTA.

NAFTA 1994 Regional Value Content

Article 402 established NAFTA's "top down" regional content valuation methods. These methods represent a change from CUSFTA's "bottom up" measurement of value for purposes of determining the origin of goods. There were two NAFTA 1994 regional content valuation methods: transaction value and net cost value.

In most instances, the importer seeking to qualify goods for duty free treatment under NAFTA could elect between the transaction value or net cost methods. The net cost method is generally thought to be the more difficult rule of origin. For most transactions among related parties, the net cost method must be used. Manipulation of prices in transfers among corporate affiliates might otherwise take advantage of NAFTA's transaction value method. The net cost method must also be followed if Customs rules the transaction value method "unacceptable."

The NAFTA 1994 transaction value method followed the GATT Customs Valuation Code of 1979 to which Canada, Mexico and the United States adhere. This method starts with an analysis of the F.O.B. price paid, including generally commissions, transport costs to the point of direct shipment, royalties on the goods, and manufacturing proceeds upon resale. Profits are included in the transaction value method of establishing the origin of goods as part of the price paid. The value of non-originating materials is then subtracted to arrive at the regional value content of the goods expressed in percentage terms. Normally, this percentage must be at least 60 percent in order to free trade the goods under NAFTA.

The NAFTA 1994 net cost method starts with a product's net cost to determine its regional value content. The value of non-originating materials is then subtracted. For NAFTA purposes, net cost is defined as total cost less expenses of sales promotion, marketing, after-sales service, royalties, shipping and packing, non-allowable interest charges and other "excluded costs." There are three authorized methods of allocating costs in calculating net cost (Article 402.8). The producer gets to elect among these methods (provided the allocation of all costs is consistent with the Uniform NAFTA Regulations on Rules of Origin and Customs Procedures).

A regional content of 50 percent or more calculated on a net cost basis qualified most goods for free trade under NAFTA. For light duty motor vehicles and their parts, a regional value content rising to 62.5 percent since 2002 is required. Other automotive goods must possess to 60 percent regional content since 2002. Automotive goods must be valued on a net cost basis.

The value of non-originating materials (VNM) is excluded under both methods when determining the NAFTA origin of goods. This value is usually based on transaction values. If necessary, alternative values as determined under the GATT Customs Valuation Code of 1979 are used. "Intermediate materials" fabricated by producers are generally treated as originating, a rule which benefits vertically integrated producers.

NAFTA 1994 embraced an "all or nothing" roll up approach to non-originating materials that resolves some of the disputes that emerged under CUSFTA. In sum, the value of non-originating materials in components used to produce a good that is North American in origin is excluded from the VNM calculation in assessing regional content. This means that for both the transaction value and net cost methods, these materials are excluded in the determination of non-originating value. However, a tracing requirement for automobiles is added. The value of non-originating automotive materials must be traced back through suppliers. In the United States, cumulation provisions allow free trade partners to use inputs from other countries with which the U.S. free trades and still qualify for preferential treatment.

Components that did not originate in NAFTA but possess some originating materials, on the other hand, are rolled down on the same all or nothing basis. In other words, these originating materials are included in the determination of non-originating value. However, a nonintegrated producer may "accumulate" such originating material when calculating the regional value content of finished goods.

A diagram of the transaction (TV) and net cost (NC) methods of calculating regional value content percentages is provided in Article 402 of the agreement. For these purposes VMC equals the value of non-originating material.

Regional Value Content	=	TV-VNM
TV	×	100
Regional Value Content	=	NC-VNM
NC	×	100

Rules of Origin, Textiles and Apparel

Like automobiles, textiles and apparel had unique NAFTA 1994 rules of origin. Special production requirements were created that protect North American manufacturers. There is a "yarn forward" rule. This requires: (1) use of North American spun yarns; (2) to make North American fabrics; (3) that are cut and sewn into clothing in North America. Similarly, cotton and man-made fiber yarns have to be "fiber forwarded" for North American free trade.

These "triple transformation" rules of origin had a substantial impact. Initially, Mexican imports (heavily comprised of U.S. content) displaced East Asian apparel, though less so after 2001 when China joined the World Trade Organization. Furthermore, Mexico raised its tariffs on non-NAFTA textiles in the wake of its 1995 financial crisis, while continuing NAFTA tariff reductions. The margin of preferential access to Mexico for Canadian and United States textiles was thus magnified. Exports of U.S. textile components to Mexico have also been enhanced by greater allowance under NAFTA of maquiladora apparel sales inside Mexico. However, since 2005 when international textile and apparel quotas were eliminated by WTO agreement, Mexico has lost substantial market share to China and East Asia.

Silk, linen and other fabrics that are scarce in North America are exceptions from NAFTA's triple transformation rules, but must still be cut and sewn in North America. Textile products with less than 7 percent non-originating material measured by weight can also be freely traded. This amount is treated as *de minimis*. Some non-qualifying textiles and clothing may be preferentially traded under quotas within NAFTA. U.S. manufacturers have complained about Canadian exports of wool suits under preferential quotas.

Rules of Origin, Electronics

NAFTA 1994 created some unique rules of origin for consumer electronics products. These rules are based on changes in tariff classifications that contain particular components. For example, in order to qualify for free trade, traditional color television sets with screens over fourteen inches must contain a North American-made color picture tube. Since 1999, color television sets must also contain, among other things, North American amplifiers, tuners and power suppliers.

For a video cassette recorder to qualify for preferential treatment under NAFTA, it must contain a North American circuit board. For a microwave oven, all the major parts, except the magnetron, must be made in the North American countries. Computers must contain a North American motherboard. Traditional computer monitors, like color television sets, had to contain a North American color picture tube to be considered NAFTA originating.

The initial impact of NAFTA on the electronics and computer industries has been significant. United States, Japanese and Korean investment in electronics production facilities in Mexico grew, especially in the manufacture of those components that convey NAFTA origin. Mexican purchases of U.S. electronic components and finished goods produced in maquiladoras went up substantially. However, since 2001, as with textiles, there has been some disinvestment from Mexico as firms move their electronics plants to China and other low cost Asian manufacturing centers. More significantly, almost all production of flat screen TVs and monitors is done in Asia, not Mexico. The NAFTA free trade incentives just simply did not overcome Asia's lower production costs.

§ 4.4   NAFTA 1994—Energy

Canada and Mexico are important sources of United States energy imports. With oil embargoes in mind, energy security was a major goal for the United States in negotiating NAFTA 1994. Nevertheless, the United States was unable to obtain the same degree of energy security from Mexico that it secured from Canada. Under CUSFTA, Canada arguably promised in an energy crisis to maintain energy exports to the USA consistent with prior export levels. However, Canada unilaterally issued in 1993 a declaration interpreting CUSFTA as *not* requiring Canadian energy crisis exports at any given level or proportion.

Like cultural industries for Canada, energy was non-negotiable for Mexico. Chapter 6 of NAFTA 1994 deals with trade in energy and basic petrochemical goods. It opens with a most unusual sentence: "The Parties confirm their full respect for their Constitutions." This is an oblique reference to the revolutionary Mexican Constitution of 1917 that reserved ownership and development of natural resources to the state. Today this constitutional clause is most evident in PEMEX, the state oil, gas and basic petrochemical monopoly. CFE, the state electricity monopoly, also embodies revolutionary state ownership principles. Both of these monopolies are currently undergoing internal Mexican reforms. In 1992, prior to NAFTA, the private sector was allowed to invest in electrical generation facilities provided the energy produced was self-consumed or sold to CFE.

NAFTA 1994 Annex 602.3 demonstrates what "full respect" for the Mexican Constitution means. In it, Mexico reserves to its state a lengthy list of strategic activities: Exploration, exploitation, and refining of crude oil and natural gas; production of artificial gas and basic petrochemicals; pipelines; foreign trade in and transport, storage and distribution of the same; virtually the entire supply of electricity to the public in Mexico; and nuclear energy.

No private Canadian, Mexican or United States investment was permitted in these areas. However, it should be noted that basic petrochemicals include ethane, propane, butanes, pentanes, hexanes, heptanes, carbon black feedstocks and napthas. Compared to past Mexican law, this is a narrow definition. NAFTA investors may participate in all secondary and non-reserved basic petrochemicals, but there has been a slowdown in privatization of such opportunities. Transportation, distribution and storage of natural gas were opened to private investors (including foreigners) in 1995 and several U.S. companies have successfully bid on such opportunities. In 1999, Mexico proposed major structural reforms of its electricity sector, including privatization of power companies. Amendments to Mexico's constitutional law will be required. At this writing, reform of Mexico's electricity sector is still pending.

Cross-border trade in energy services was possible only by permit of the Mexican government. Cross-border trade in natural gas and basic petrochemicals is similarly allowed with PEMEX through regulated supply contracts. In some cases, Mexico will permit performance clauses in energy service contracts. Mexico's traditional opposition to sharing oil and gas ownership rights in PEMEX drilling contracts continues.

Mexico allowed 100 percent foreign ownership of new coal mines. Existing joint ventures can now become wholly-owned by NAFTA investors. Mexican tariffs on coal were completely removed at the outset. NAFTA nationals may own or operate electricity companies when the production is for the owner's use. Excess electricity must be sold to CFE at rates agreed upon by contract. Co-generation is another possibility when electricity is generated by industrial production. Once again, excess supplies go to CFE at agreed rates. Independent power production plants located in Mexico can be owned and operated by NAFTA nationals, but CFE gets the electricity. This has been done by leasing foreign-owned plants to CFE. In the border region, CFE may contract to sell electricity to United States utilities.

NAFTA 1994 incorporated by reference the GATT 1947 provisions relating to quotas and other restraints on trade in energy and petrochemical goods. Presumably, this applies to GATT Articles XI, XX and XXI. As in other areas, this incorporation permits utilization of NAFTA dispute settlement.

In addition, other rights and obligations relating to energy goods are established by NAFTA 1994. There is an express prohibition of import or export price controls that applies to all parties. In times of energy crises, Canadian (but not Mexican) restraints must be proportionate to past export/domestic utilization ratios. Crisis restraints may not push export prices higher than those charged domestically. And the normal channels of supply must be maintained. Mexico is also exempted from the NAFTA rules on restraining trade in energy goods for reasons of national security, but is required to adhere to the general NAFTA rules on national security trade restraints.

Energy export licensing was permissible under NAFTA 1994. Export taxes and other charges can be used only if they apply to energy goods consumed domestically. The regulation of energy was subject to NAFTA's general national and most-favored treatment duties. The more specific rules of Chapter 6 on trade restraints and export taxes also applied. NAFTA nations must also "seek" to ensure that energy regulation does not disrupt contractual relationships "to the maximum extent practicable." They must provide for "orderly and equitable" implementation of regulatory measures.

§ 4.5   NAFTA 1994—Services

Cross-border NAFTA 1994 trade in services was subject to national treatment, including no less favorable treatment than that most favorably given at federal, state or local levels. No member state may require that a service provider establish or maintain a residence, local office or branch in its country as a condition to cross-border provision of services. However, a general standstill on existing discriminatory or limiting laws affecting cross-border services was adopted. Mutual recognition of professional licenses is encouraged (notably for legal consultants and engineers), but not made automatic. All citizenship or permanent residency requirements for professional licensing were eliminated.

Additionally, a NAFTA 1994 country may deny the benefits of the rules on cross-border provision of services if their source is in reality a third country without substantial business activities within the free trade area. For transport services, these benefits may be denied if the services are provided with equipment that is not registered within a NAFTA nation. Most air, maritime, basic telecommunications and social services are not covered by these rules, nor are those that are subject to special treatment elsewhere in the NAFTA 1994 (*e.g.* procurement, financing and energy). Even so, the NAFTA considerably broadened the types of services covered by free trade principles: accounting, advertising, architecture, broadcasting, commercial education, construction, consulting, enhanced telecommunications, engineering, environmental science, health care, land transport, legal, publishing and tourism.

Whereas the CUSFTA allowed free trade in services only for those sectors that were positively listed in the agreement, the NAFTA 1994 adopted a broader "negative listing" approach. All services sectors were subject to free trade principles unless NAFTA 1994 specified otherwise.

Foreign Legal Consultants

Mexico has a unified national licensing system for attorneys (Abogados). Canada licenses its attorneys (Barristers and Solicitors) on a provincial basis. The 50 states of the United States and the District of Columbia do likewise. While the traditional perception that business lawyers are not fungible is open to challenge in a regional economy, it is reasonable to conclude that the services of Canadian, Mexican and United States lawyers cannot generally be substituted. Professor James Smith has argued that United States and Mexican legal traditions, constitutions and political systems are so "markedly different" that legal training and law practice in one country is more likely to "hinder rather than aid" in understanding each other's legal systems. *See* 1 U.S.-Mexico L.J. 85 (1993). Certainly the different Civil and Common Law legal traditions and ethical rules found in Quebec, the rest of Canada (ROC), Mexico, and among the states of the United States support this conclusion. On balance the broad exclusion of legal services from NAFTA 1994 seems justified, though less so for international business attorneys.

Against this background, NAFTA 1994 sought an alternative to mutual licensing of lawyers based on their national certifications. This alternative, the licensing of "foreign legal consultants," proved agreeable. A number of U.S. states had already authorized licensing foreign legal consultants primarily in order to retain opportunities for U.S. lawyers practicing abroad, especially in France. New York, California, Florida, Texas, Alaska, Connecticut, the District of Columbia, Georgia, Hawaii, Illinois, Michigan, New Jersey, Ohio, Oregon and Washington had done so prior to NAFTA. British Columbia, Ontario and Saskatchewan also licensed foreign legal consultants. Mexico had no experience with such licensure, but promised to do so under NAFTA for jurisdictions granting reciprocal rights to Mexican attorneys.

In Section B of Annex 1210.5, the NAFTA 1994 partners agreed to promote the licensing of foreign legal consultants. This, of course, is ultimately a decision for the states and provinces of the U.S. and Canada. It was also agreed that such consultants would be permitted to practice or give advice on the laws of their home jurisdiction. It is unclear whether this includes the right to practice "international law" as a foreign legal consultant. One could argue that since the law of NAFTA is by ratification or implementation part of the law of Canada, Mexico and the United States that foreign legal consultants should at a minimum be able to counsel on it.

The issue of just what law a foreign legal consultant can practice has split U.S. states. Alaska, California, Connecticut, Florida, Georgia and Texas only permit foreign legal consultants to advise on the law of their home jurisdictions. Nearly all the other participating states follow the Model Rule of the American Bar Association which permits practice of law except that of the licensing state and the United States.

The Trucking Dispute

Unlike CUSFTA, the NAFTA 1994 created a timetable for the removal of barriers to cross-border land transport services and the establishment of compatible technical, environmental and safety standards. This extends to bus, trucking, port and rail services. It should eliminate the historic need to switch trailers to Mexican transporters at the border. Cross-border truck deliveries in the border states were supposed to come on line late in 1995, but U.S. concerns about the standards of Mexican carriers and (one suspects) Teamsters Union influence have delayed this result. After 6 years, truckers were supposed to be able to move freely anywhere within NAFTA. In 2001, Mexico unanimously prevailed in a NAFTA arbitration panel on truck access to the United States.

President George W. Bush commenced a pilot cross-border trucking program, but funds for it were eliminated in the Obama economic stimulus bill (H.R. 1105). Mexico undertook, as permitted, retaliatory tariffs on selected U.S. goods. Finally, a settlement was reached in 2010 allowing certified Mexican trucks to role on U.S. highways. Mexico removed its retaliatory tariffs.

However, the pending USMCA 2018 Agreement would reverse this outcome and block long-distance Mexican trucking in the USA and Canada. See Section 6.8.

Telecommunications

Public telecommunications networks and services must be opened on reasonable and nondiscriminatory terms for firms and individuals who need the networks to conduct business, such as intra-corporate communications or so-called enhanced telecommunications and information services. This means that cellular phone, data transmission, earth stations, fax, electronic mail, overlay networks and paging systems are open to Canadian and American investors. Many of them have tried to enter the Mexican market, but have been largely stymied by Telmex and Carlos Slim.

Each NAFTA 1994 country must ensure reasonable access and use of leased private lines, terminal equipment attachments, private circuit interconnects, switching, signaling and processing functions and user-choice of operating protocols. Conditions on access and use may only be imposed to safeguard the public responsibilities of network operators or to protect technical network integrity.

Rates for public telecommunications transport services should reflect economic costs and flat-rate pricing is required for leased circuits. However, cross-subsidization between public transport services is not prohibited, nor are monopoly providers of public networks or services. Such monopolies may not engage in anticompetitive conduct outside their monopoly areas with adverse effects on NAFTA nationals. Various rights of access to information on public networks and services are established, and NAFTA 1994 limited the types of technical standards that can be imposed on the attachment of equipment to public networks.

Financial Services

Financial services provided by banking, insurance, securities and other firms are separately covered under the NAFTA 1994. Trade in such services is generally subject to specific liberalization commitments and transition periods. Financial service providers, including non-NAFTA providers operating through subsidiaries in a NAFTA country, are entitled to establish themselves anywhere within NAFTA and service customers there (the right of "commercial presence"). Existing cross-border restraints on the provision of financial services were frozen and no new restraints may be imposed (subject to designated exceptions).

Providers of financial services in each NAFTA nation received both national and most favored nation treatment. This includes equality of competitive opportunity, which is defined as avoidance of measures that disadvantage foreign providers relative to domestic providers. Various procedural transparency rules are established to facilitate the entry and equal opportunity of NAFTA providers of financial services. The host nation may legislate reasonable prudential requirements for such companies and, under limited circumstances, protect their balance of payments in ways which restrain financial providers.

The following are some of the more notable country-specific commitments on financial service made under NAFTA 1994:

United States—A grace period allowed Mexican banks already operating a securities firm in the U.S. to continue to do so until July of 1997.

Canada—The exemption granted U.S. companies under the Canada-U.S. FTA to hold more than 25 percent of the shares of a federally regulated Canadian financial institution was extended to Mexican firms, as was the suspension of Canada's 12 percent asset ceiling rules. Multiple branches may be opened in Canada without Ministry of Finance approval.

Mexico—Banking, securities and insurance companies from the U.S. and Canada are able to enter the Mexican market through subsidiaries and joint ventures (but not branches) subject to market share limits during a transition period that ended in the year 2000 (insurance) or 2004 (banking and securities). Finance companies are able to establish separate subsidiaries in Mexico to provide consumer, commercial, mortgage lending or credit card services, subject to a 3 percent aggregate asset limitation (which does not apply to lending by affiliates of automotive companies). Existing U.S. and Canadian insurers could expand their ownership rights to 100 percent in 1996. No equity or market share requirements apply for warehousing and bonding, foreign exchange and mutual fund management enterprises.

§ 4.6   NAFTA 1994—Foreign Investment

NAFTA's foreign investment law is extremely controversial and investor-state arbitrations were aggressively pursued. This generally remains a "hot area" of free trade law.

Investing in Mexico

The cross-border investment rules established in 1989 by Canada and the United States were reviewed in Chapter 3. NAFTA 1994 placed special emphasis on relaxation of Mexico's foreign investment controls. These controls find their roots in the revolutionary 1917 Mexican Constitution and the nationalization of foreign oil and gas interests in 1937 as well as the widespread adoption of foreign investment control commissions throughout Latin America during the 1970s. Under Mexican regulation of foreign investment since the 1940s, some industries were reserved for state ownership while others could only be owned by Mexicans. Foreigners were ordinarily allowed to invest in less sensitive industries, but often subject to mandatory joint venture requirements with majority Mexican ownership and "Calvo clause" rules limiting foreign investor dispute remedies to those available under Mexican law.

In 1973, Mexico promulgated an Investment Law that mandated more use of joint ventures if approved by the National Foreign Investment Commission. This Law was the most restrictive of its kind in Mexican history. By the 1980s, after years of mismanagement and corruption while awash in petroleum dollars, Mexico had a massive national debt problem. Foreign investment regulations issued by Presidential decree in 1989 shifted significantly towards allowance of wholly-owned subsidiaries. However, these regulations conflicted with the 1973 Investment Law. These uncertainties were finally resolved in 1993 as a direct consequence of NAFTA when Mexico adopted a new Law on Foreign Investment.

The 1993 Law is much more permissive of foreign investment without prior approval of by the Mexican Investment Commission. Although adopted on the eve of NAFTA, the 1993 Law opens many of the same doors to all investors, not just those from NAFTA. Investment opportunities based upon the NAFTA agreement that are not generally available include the suspension of many performance requirements, the phased removal of market share caps on financial services, and reduced thresholds triggering Investment Commission review. In addition, NAFTA investors are not subject to Mexico's mandatory joint venture rule, nor its "Calvo clause." Removal of these restrictions represents a major concession on the part of Mexico.

Acquisitions or sales of existing Mexican companies are generally subject to Commission review if exceeding $25 million U.S. This threshold increased to $150 million U.S. for NAFTA investors in 2003. For NAFTA investors, no permission from the National Commission is required to invest on a wholly-owned basis or acquire or sell Mexican companies whose values fall below this threshold.

NAFTA 1994 Investment Rights

In an unusual provision, Article 1112 subordinates all of Chapter 11 on investment to the rest of the NAFTA 1994 agreement. In other words, if there are inconsistencies between Chapter 11 and other parts of the NAFTA agreement, those other parts are supreme. That said, NAFTA 1994 provided investors and their investments with a number of important rights.

Canadian, Mexican and United States citizens, permanently resident aliens, and other designated persons are eligible to benefit from NAFTA's investment rules. In addition, most private and public, profit and nonprofit businesses "constituted or organized" under Canadian, Mexican or United States law also qualify. This coverage specifically includes businesses operating as corporations, partnerships, trusts, sole proprietorships, joint ventures and business associations.

Furthermore, in a notable change from CUSFTA, it is not necessary for such businesses to be owned or controlled by Canadian, Mexican or U.S. nationals or enterprises. As with services, this means that businesses owned by anyone which are "constituted or organized" inside NAFTA benefit from the agreement *provided* they carry on substantial business activities in North America. **Thus Asians, Europeans and Latin Americans (for example) could invest in North America and benefit from NAFTA 1994 investment rights and remedies.** See *Corn Syrup Sweeteners* below. Exceptions were made for NAFTA businesses owned or controlled by third parties from countries lacking diplomatic relations with or economically embargoed by Canada, Mexico or the United States.

Beneficiaries of NAFTA 1994 rights enjoyed a broad definition of "investment." This definition includes most stocks, bonds, loans, and income, profit or asset interests. Real estate, tangible or intangible (intellectual) business property, turnkey or construction contracts, concessions, and licensing and franchising contracts are also generally included (Article 1139). However, under Annex III, each member state reserves certain economic activities to its state or domestic investors. Mexico has done so under its 1993 Foreign Investment Law. For purposes of Chapter 11, investment is defined so as to exclude claims to money arising solely from commercial contracts for the sale of goods or services, or trade financing, and claims for money that do not involve the interests noted above.

Treatment of Foreign Investors and Investments

The NAFTA 1994 agreement established a so-called *"minimum standard of treatment"* for NAFTA investors and investments which is "treatment in accordance with international law," including "fair and equitable treatment and full protection and security" (Article 1105.) For example, if losses occur due to armed conflict or civil strife, NAFTA investors and investments must be accorded nondiscriminatory treatment in response. An official NAFTA interpretative ruling indicates that Article 1105 embraces treatment in accordance with "customary" international law, a ruling intended to limit the scope of protection afforded to foreign investors. In addition, limiting definitions of "fair and equitable treatment" and "full protection and security" have been established in subsequent U.S. free trade agreements.

Beyond this minimum, NAFTA 1994 investors and their investments are entitled to the better of national or most-favored-nation treatment from federal governments. Such treatment rights extend to establishing, acquiring, expanding, managing, conducting, operating, and selling or disposing of investments. From state or provincial governments, NAFTA investors and their investments are entitled to receive the most-favored treatment those governments grant their own investors and investments. Along these lines, United Parcel Service found Mexico lacking when it was initially limited to using smaller vans than Mexican competitors. UPS persuaded the United States to lodge a complaint under Chapter 20 (below) which led to intergovernmental consultations followed by NAFTA Commission mediation. These efforts lasted many months but eventually UPS got permission to use larger vans.

Article 1102 of NAFTA 1994 prohibits requiring minimum levels of equity holdings by nationals of the host government. Hence the historic bias in Mexican law towards mandatory joint ventures is overcome by NAFTA. No investor can be forced on grounds of nationality to sell or dispose of a qualified investment. Mandatory appointment of senior managers on the basis of nationality is also contrary to NAFTA. However, it is permissible to require boards of directors and corporate committees with majorities from one nationality or residence, provided this does not materially impair the investor's ability to exercise control. Canadian law often makes such stipulations. Residency requirements are generally authorized if there is no impairment of the treaty rights of NAFTA investors.

Article 1106 of NAFTA 1994 prohibits various investment performance obligations, including tax-related measures, in a scope that surpasses the WTO Agreement on Trade-Related Investment Measures (TRIMs 1995, see Section 1.12). Requirements relating to exports, domestic content, domestic purchases, trade balancing of foreign exchange inflows or earnings, import/export ratios, technology transfers, and regional or global sales exclusivity ("product mandates") are broadly prohibited. All other types of investment-related performance requirements, such as employment and research and development obligations, are not prohibited and therefore presumably lawful.

Article 1106.3 of NAFTA 1994 further prohibits conditioning the receipt or continued receipt of "an advantage" (e.g., a government subsidy or tax benefit) on compliance with requirements relating to domestic content, domestic purchases, domestic sales restraints or trade balancing. But "advantages" can be given when the requirements concern production location, provision of services, training or employing workers, constructing or expanding facilities, or carrying out research and development locally. By way of exception, domestic content or purchase requirements *and* advantages can be linked to investor compliance with: (1) Laws and regulations that are consistent with NAFTA; (2) laws necessary to protect human, animal or plant life or health; or (3) laws needed to conserve living or non-living exhaustible natural resources. However, such requirements cannot be applied arbitrarily or unjustifiably, and may not constitute a disguised restraint on trade or investment.

All monetary transfers relating to NAFTA investments are to be allowed "freely and without delay." (Article 1109) Such transfers must be possible in a "freely usable currency" at the market rate of exchange prevailing in spot transactions on the transfer date. For these purposes, monetary transfers specifically include profits, dividends, interest, capital gains, royalties, management, technical assistance and other fees, returns in kind, and funds derived from the investment. Sale or liquidation proceeds, contract payments, compensatory payments for expropriation and NAFTA dispute settlement payments are also encompassed.

Requiring investment-related monetary transfers or penalizing them is prohibited. However, such transfers can be controlled in an equitable, nondiscriminatory and good faith application of bankruptcy, insolvency, creditors' rights, securities, criminal, currency reporting and satisfaction of judgment laws. Whereas tax withholding was a justifiable basis for restricting monetary transfers under CUSFTA, this is not the case under NAFTA 1994. Special restraints may arise in connection with balance of payments problems and taxation laws.

Expropriation

Article 1110 of NAFTA 1994 generally prohibited direct or indirect nationalization or expropriation of NAFTA investments. Measures "tantamount to" nationalization or expropriation, such as creeping expropriation or confiscatory taxation, are also prohibited. Expropriation, nationalization or tantamount measures may occur for public purposes on a nondiscriminatory basis in accordance with due process of law and NAFTA's "minimum level of treatment" (above). Post-NAFTA U.S. free trade agreements have expressly limited the possibility of succeeding with "indirect" regulatory taking expropriation claims. See Section 5.2.

Any authorized expropriation must result in payment of compensation without delay. The amount of payment must be equivalent to the fair market value of the investment immediately prior to expropriation. In valuing the investment, going concern value, asset value (including declared tax values of tangible property) and other appropriate factors must be considered. Payment must be made in a manner that is fully realizable, such as in a "G7" currency (U.S. dollars, Canadian dollars, EUROs, British pounds sterling, Japanese yen). Interest at a commercially reasonable rate must also be included. If payment is made in Mexican pesos, this amount must be calculated as of the expropriation date in a G7 currency plus interest.

Certain governmental acts are not treated as expropriations. For example, NAFTA specifies that nondiscriminatory measures of general application that impose costs on defaulting debtors are not tantamount to expropriation of a bond or loan *solely* for that reason. Compulsory licensing of intellectual property rights is not an expropriation. Revocation, limitation or creation of such rights as allowed by Chapter 17 of NAFTA 1994 is also deemed not an expropriation.

These provisions embody an historic change in Mexico's position on expropriation law. Without explicitly saying so, Mexico has essentially embraced the U.S. position that under "international law" expropriation of foreign investments requires "prompt, adequate and effective" compensation. Mexico had specifically rejected this standard in negotiating a settlement of its oil and gas (and land) expropriations in the 1930s. Down through the years Mexico adamantly clung to its view that compensation would only be paid according to Mexican law. For investors protected under NAFTA 1994 (which are not just Canadian and U.S. investors), Chapter 11 represented the dawn of a new era.

Exceptions and Reservations, The Environment

Annexes I–IV of the NAFTA 1994 agreement reveal a host of investment-related reservations and exceptions. Many pre-existing, non-conforming regulations were grandfathered though most (not including basic telecommunications, social services and maritime services) are subject to a standstill agreement intended to avoid relapses into greater protection. In contrast, regulations promoting investment "sensitive to environmental concerns" are expressly authorized. Mexico's tradition of assessing the environmental impact of foreign investments will therefore continue. There is also a formal recognition that creating exceptions to environmental laws to encourage NAFTA investors to establish, acquire, expand or retain their investments is inappropriate. However, NAFTA's Chapter 20 dispute settlement mechanism cannot be invoked concerning this "commitment." Only intergovernmental consultations are mandatory.

Other investment-related exceptions concern government procurement, subsidies, export promotion, foreign aid and preferential trade arrangements. These exceptions apply mostly to the rules on nondiscriminatory treatment and performance requirements. Most general exceptions to NAFTA 1994, such as for Canadian cultural industries (above), also apply to its investment rules. The general "national security" exception, for example, allowed the United States to block the acquisition of U.S. companies by foreigners (including Canadians and Mexicans) under FINSA/FIRRMA national security regulations (50 U.S.C. App. § 2170). See Section 1.1. For more extensive coverage, R. Folsom, *Foreign Investment Law including Investor-State Arbitrations* in a Nutshell.

§ 4.7   NAFTA 1994—Arbitration of Investment Disputes

NAFTA 1994 created a highly innovative and increasingly controversial investment dispute settlement system. This system provides a way for foreign investors to challenge governmental and state enterprise acts and recover damages for violation of rights established in Chapter 11. Remarkably, investors may not only assert claims as individuals, but also on behalf of NAFTA enterprises they own or control directly or indirectly (Article 1117). This authorization avoids one of international law's most famous problems . . . "standing to sue" when the investor's only loss or damage is injury to its investment abroad. See *Belgium v. Spain (the "Barcelona Traction Case")*, 1970 Int'l Court of Justice 3 (preliminary objections).

Chapter 20 NAFTA 1994 dispute settlement does not apply to "investor-state disputes." Such disputes are instead subject to binding arbitration, another major concession on the part of Mexico which has always adhered to the "Calvo Doctrine." That doctrine (widely followed in Latin America) requires foreign investors to forego protection by their home governments, be treated as Mexican nationals, and pursue legal remedies exclusively in Mexico. *See* Article 27 of the Mexican Constitution.

Individual investors claiming that a government has breached NAFTA 1994 investment or state enterprise obligations, or that one of its monopolies has done so, commence the dispute resolution process. All claims are filed against the federal government even when it is state, provincial or local government action that is being challenged. This can place Canada, Mexico and the United States in the awkward position of defending sub-central governmental acts. See the *Metalclad* and *Loewen* arbitrations in Section 4.8.

The investor must allege that the breach of NAFTA 1994 caused loss or damage. Such claims must be asserted no later than three years after the date when knowledge of the alleged breach and knowledge of the loss or damage was first acquired or should have been first acquired. However, decisions by the Canadian or Mexican foreign investment control commissions, national security actions, and Canadian cultural industry reservations cannot be the basis for such a claim. Moreover, a host of reservations and exceptions contained in Chapter 11B deny access to NAFTA's investor-state arbitration remedy. Even so, as outlined below, the number of claims being filed is rising, some claims are producing unexpected results, and the process itself is under dispute.

Before submitting a claim to arbitration, individual investors must give 90 days' advance notice to the host country. Such notice must include an explanation of the issues, their factual basis and remedies sought. Claimants must also consent in writing to arbitrate under the procedures established in the NAFTA agreement. They *must waive* in writing their rights to initiate or continue any other damages proceedings. See *Commerce Group Corp. v. El Salvador* (ICSID, 2011) (CAFTA-DR tribunal dismisses complaint due to pending litigation). Individual investors need not, however, waive their rights to injunctive, declaratory or other extraordinary relief (not involving damages). These remedies may not be awarded through NAFTA arbitration of investor-state disputes.

Investment Dispute Arbitration Procedures, Appeals and Remedies

The NAFTA nations consented unconditionally in advance to the submission of investor claims to arbitration under NAFTA 1994 procedures. Furthermore, they agreed not to assert insurance payments or other investor indemnification rights as a defense, counterclaim, right of setoff or otherwise. **Arbitration of investor-state disputes continues in a more limited way as between Mexico and the United States under the pending USMCA 2018 Agreement. It is completely eliminated as between the United States and Canada. See Chapters 6 and 7.**

The investor submitting a claim to arbitration against a NAFTA state ordinarily can elect between the following arbitration rules:

(1) The ICSID Convention* if both member states adhere. (This is impossible at present since only the United States has ratified ICSID);

---

*   The Convention on the Settlement of Investment Disputes between States and Nationals of Other States (1966). The Convention is administered through the World Bank in Washington, D.C. and has been ratified by over 150 nations.

(2) The Additional Facility Rules of ICSID provided one-member state (i.e., the United States or more recently Canada) adheres to the ICSID Convention; or

(3) The U.N.-derived UNCITRAL Arbitration Rules.

NAFTA 1994 investor-state tribunals have three panelists. The investor and the state each choose one arbitrator. If possible, the third presiding panelist is chosen by agreement. The ICSID Secretary-General selects the presiding arbitrator if agreement is not reached within 90 days. That person is chosen from a consensus roster of acceptable names, but may not be a national from either side of the dispute.

Investor-state tribunals must decide the dispute in accordance with the NAFTA 1994 agreement and "applicable rules of international law." The responding state may raise defenses based upon reservations or exceptions contained in Annexes I–IV to the NAFTA agreement. In such instances, the NAFTA Commission (not the arbitration panel) will generally issue a binding ruling on the validity of such a defense. Defenses based upon permissible regulation of monetary transfers by financial institutions are generally decided by the NAFTA Financial Services Committee.

By agreement of the parties, the investor-state arbitration tribunal can obtain expert reports on factual issues concerning environmental, health, safety or other scientific matters. The tribunal may also order temporary relief measures to preserve rights or the full effectiveness of its jurisdiction. It may, for example, order the preservation of evidence. The tribunal cannot, however, order attachment or enjoin governmental regulations that are being challenged.

NAFTA 1994 investor-state tribunals were authorized to award investors or NAFTA enterprises actual *damages* and interest, or restitution of property, or both. At this writing, damages have been awarded against and paid by Canada and Mexico, but not the United States. See *Metalclad* and *S.D. Myers* arbitrations in Section 4.8. If the award is to an enterprise, any person may *also* pursue relief under "applicable domestic law." If restitution is ordered, the responsible member state may provide monetary damages and interest instead. NAFTA tribunals can apportion legal fees between the parties at their discretion. Such fees routinely run into hundreds of thousands, if not millions, of dollars. The costs of administering Chapter 11 tribunals, including generous fees for the arbitrators, often exceed $500,000. The losing party is typically required to pay these costs.

The award of the tribunal is binding on the parties, but subject to revision or annulment in the courts of the arbitration's situs. See *Metalclad* and *S.D. Myers*. Absent agreement, the arbitrators determine situs. Professor Brower and others have argued that a standing appellate body not unlike that of the WTO would provide greater legitimacy and uniformity to Chapter 11 arbitrations. See 36 *Vanderbilt J. Transnational Law* 37 (2003).

Awards are specifically not "precedent" in future NAFTA 1994 arbitrations (Article 1136), yet routinely cited and argued in Chapter 11 proceedings and decisions. NAFTA investor-state arbitration awards are supposed to be honored. Should this not occur, the investor may seek enforcement of the award. NAFTA nations agreed to provide the means for such enforcement. The NAFTA investor-state dispute settlement system meets the various requirements of the ICSID Convention, its Additional Facility Rules, the New York Convention on Recognition and Enforcement of Foreign Arbitral Awards (1958), and the Inter-American Convention on International Commercial Arbitration (1975).

Should it become necessary to judicially enforce an investor-state arbitration award, the New York Convention provides a likely recourse as all three nations adhere to it. However, U.S. courts have held the grounds for denying enforcement of NAFTA awards under the New York Convention limited strictly to its provisions. Thus, the longstanding U.S. doctrine of denying enforcement when arbitrators "manifestly disregard the law", a doctrine not incorporated in the New York Convention, was not applied in a NAFTA 1994 award enforcement proceeding. See *In re Arbitration between International Thunderbird Gaming Corp. v. United Mexican States,* 473 F.Supp.2d 80 (D.C.2007).

If there is no compliance with the award and enforcement proceedings fail, the investor's government may as a last recourse commence intergovernmental dispute settlement under Chapter 20 of NAFTA 1994. This panel rules on whether noncompliance inconsistent with the NAFTA agreement has occurred and can recommend compliance. If compliance still does not follow, benefits granted under NAFTA to the noncomplying nation may be suspended.

§ 4.8   Investor-State Arbitrations Under NAFTA 1994

Arbitrated Investor Claims against Host States

Investors did not hesitate to invoke the innovative investor-state arbitration procedures authorized under Section B of Chapter 11 of

NAFTA 1994. Since 2001, in an official Interpretation, Chapter 11 has been construed as not imposing a general duty of confidentiality. The NAFTA governments have therefore released all documents submitted to or issued by Chapter 11 arbitration tribunals. A particularly good collection of these materials can be found at www.naftaclaims.com. Moreover, since late 2003 open Chapter 11 hearings have become the rule, as have permissive procedures for non-party submissions (amicus curiae).

Many investors alleged state action that is "tantamount to expropriation." This is a claim that Article 1110 authorizes and one which could be construed to fit many fact patterns. National treatment and the NAFTA minimum standard of treatment (see above) were also commonly disputed. Some examples of these disputes follow.

Metalclad v. Mexico. A prominent dispute involved Metalclad Corp. of California, which had acquired a hazardous waste site operated by a Mexican company in Guadalcazar, San Luis Potosi subject to various federal approvals, all of which were obtained. State and local opposition to opening the site after an expensive clean-up resulted in the denial of a building permit in a newly created "ecological zone." Metalclad claimed these acts were tantamount to expropriation, and denial of national and the NAFTA minimum standards of treatment. It sought $90 million in damages from the Mexican federal government, which despite having supported the Metalclad contract was obliged to defend the hostile local and state actions. Metalclad received an award of $16 million under NAFTA Chapter 11 in 2000. The arbitration was conducted under the ICSID Additional Facility rules.

Mexico instituted judicial proceedings to set aside the award in British Columbia, the arbitration's legal *situs*. Canada intervened in support of Mexico. The arbitrators had found the Mexican regulatory action a breach of NAFTA's minimum standard based on a lack of "transparency," and tantamount to expropriation without adequate compensation.

The British Columbia Supreme Court, ruling under the B.C. International Arbitration Act, agreed that the expropriation decision fell within the scope of the dispute submitted and was therefore valid. It rejected, however, the transparency decision as beyond the scope of the submission. The court found no transparency obligations in Chapter 11, and none as a matter of *customary* international law (which traditionally bars only "egregious," "outrageous" or "shocking" conduct). Mexico subsequently paid Metalclad approximately $16 million U.S., the first payment by a state to an investor under Chapter 11.

Ethyl v. Canada and Methanex v. United States. A second prominent dispute involved Ethyl Corp. of the USA, which claimed $250 million U.S. damages against the Canadian government as a consequence of 1997 federal legislation banning importation or interprovincial trade of the gasoline additive, MMT. Canada was the first country to ban MMT as a pollution and health hazard, although California has also done so. MMT is a manganese-based octane enhancer alleged to interfere with the proper functioning of catalytic converters. Ethyl Corp. is the sole producer of MMT in North America. Ethyl claimed that the new law was tantamount to expropriation, violated NAFTA's national treatment standards and constituted an unlawful Canadian-content performance requirement (because the ban would favor Canadian ethanol as a substitute for MMT).

A dispute resolution panel under Canada's Agreement on Internal Trade struck down the interprovincial trade ban. In 1998, Canada withdrew its ban on MMT and paid $13 million to Ethyl Corp. Ethyl then withdrew its $250 million arbitration claim. Canada noted the current lack of scientific evidence documenting MMT harm, an apparent abandonment of the "precautionary principle." Environmentalists decried evidence of NAFTA's negative impact, and Europeans cited *Ethyl* as good reason to reject multilateral investment guarantee agreements in the OECD (Organization for Economic Cooperation and Development). Both groups believe Chapter 11 has created a privileged class of "super-citizens" who are a threat to state sovereignty.

Methanex Corp. of Canada submitted a claim that was in some ways the reverse of *Ethyl*. Methanex claimed that California's ban of the MTBE gasoline additive (for which it makes feedstock) amounted to an expropriation of its business interests and violated its minimum treatment rights. It sought $970 million in damages and simultaneously filed a petition under the North American Environmental Cooperation Agreement asserting that California failed to enforce its gasoline storage regulations, which Methanex saw as the source of MTBE water pollution. In 2002, the *Methanex* panel working under the UNCITRAL Rules largely rejected the complaint on jurisdictional grounds, allowing a limited re-filing on the question of intentional injury. The *Methanex* panel notably ruled that it would accept NGO amicus briefs, in this instance from the International Institute for Sustainable Development. This position was subsequently ratified for all Chapter 11 arbitrations by the NAFTA Free Trade Commission in 2003.

Loewen v. United States. The Loewen Group of Canada was held liable by a jury in 1995 to $500 million in a Mississippi breach of a funeral home contract suit. The case was settled for $150 million after the Mississippi Supreme Court required posting a $625 million bond prior to appealing the jury's verdict, a sum in excess of Loewen's net worth. In 1998, Loewen filed a claim under NAFTA alleging discrimination, denial of the minimum NAFTA standard of treatment, and uncompensated expropriation. This claim, like that of Ethyl Corp., was destined for controversy. Among other things, it challenged the discretion of American juries in awarding punitive damages. Note that it does so in a forum that does not give the American Trial Lawyers Association an opportunity to respond.

In 2003, the *Loewen* panel, calling the Mississippi decision "a disgrace," nevertheless ruled heavily against the bankrupt funeral home giant because its status as a Canadian (versus U.S.) company entitled to NAFTA investor rights was in doubt. Watch for a re-run challenging American punitive damages in the future.

Pope & Talbot v. Canada. Pope & Talbot, Inc. of Portland, Oregon claimed that the 1996 Softwood Lumber Agreement (see Chapter 2) violated the national treatment, most-favored-nation treatment, minimum treatment and performance requirements rules of NAFTA. The claim asserted that the company's British Columbia subsidiary was the victim of discrimination in that the Canadian export restraints required under that Agreement applied only to four Canadian provinces. Pope & Talbot sought $20 million in compensation from the Canadian government. Rejecting most of the claims, the *Pope and Talbot* panel found Canada did violate the NAFTA minimum standard of treatment in denying export authorization to the company's B.C. subsidiary.

Although the award was only about $460,000 U.S., the panel's reasoning set off fireworks. In its view, Article 1105 demanded something more than the level of treatment commanded by customary international law. "Fair and equitable treatment" and "full protection and security" were seen as "additive;" new and expansive norms created by NAFTA's novel investor protection regime.

The additive reading of *Pope & Talbot* was subsequently rejected by the British Columbia Supreme Court in *Metalclad* (above), and collectively negated by a binding interpretation of Article 1105 issued by the three NAFTA parties in 2001. This controversial, defensive interpretation "clarifies" that Article 1105 corresponds to and thus does not expand the *customary* international law standard of minimum treatment (see *Metalclad* above), and that a breach of a NAFTA obligation does not ipso facto constitute a breach of that Article.

S.D. Myers v. Canada. S.D. Myers is an Ohio company specializing in hazardous waste management of PCBs. Its Canadian affiliate imported PCBs from Ontario, to the consternation of the only Canadian PCB remediation company, Chem-Security of Alberta. In 1995, Canada banned PCB exports, intentionally giving Chem-Security a monopoly. S.D. Myers asserted this export ban violated the national treatment, performance requirements, expropriation and fair and equitable treatment provisions of Chapter 11. The arbitrators found in favor of S.D. Myers on the national treatment and fair and equitable treatment claims, awarding over $6,000,000 CDN in damages. Canada appealed to the courts of Ontario, the situs of the arbitration, and lost. In Ontario, at least, considerable deference is given to arbitral decisions. Compare British Columbia in *Metalclad* below. Subsequently, S. D. Myers and Canada settled the dispute.

Mondev v. United States. Mondev is a Canadian company engaged in commercial real estate development. It pursued various claims against the City of Boston and the Boston Redevelopment Authority in the Massachusetts courts, which were denied on sovereign immunity grounds. Mondev then filed a Chapter 11 claim arguing primarily unfair and inequitable treatment in the Massachusetts courts.

In its complaint, Mondev directly challenged the 2001 Interpretation of Article 1105, arguing it was de facto an amendment of the NAFTA agreement. Mondev also argued that customary international law should be construed in light of conclusions reached under hundreds of bilateral investment treaties and modern judgments. The tribunal recognized that fair and equitable treatment had evolved by 1994 (NAFTA's effective date) beyond what is "egregious" or "outrageous," and that bad faith on the part of states need not be shown. It then ruled against Mondev's denial of justice claims.

Glamis v. United States. Glamis, a Canadian mining company, alleged that government regulations limiting the impact of open-pit mining and protecting indigenous peoples' religious sites made its *proposed* California gold mine unprofitable. Under Chapter 11, it asserted violations of the NAFTA rules against government acts tantamount to expropriation, and denial of fair and equitable treatment. In June of 2009, a Chapter 11 tribunal accepted, in principle, that "regulatory taking" measures could amount to "creeping expropriation." That said, the tribunal undertook a detailed accounting of Glamis' alleged losses and found the mine project still had a net positive value of $20 million U.S. Hence it concluded Glamis was not impacted sufficiently to support a NAFTA expropriation claim.

While the outcome once again allowed the United States to avoid paying Chapter 11 damages, the willingness of the tribunal to entertain a regulatory taking claim was controversial (to put it mildly) and once again raised concerns that foreign investors may have greater rights under NAFTA than U.S. investors possess under United States law.

Corn Syrup Sweeteners v. Mexico. Late in 2009, a third Chapter 11 tribunal ruled against Mexico concerning its 20% tax from 2002 to 2007 on the production and sale of soft drinks using High Fructose Corn Syrup (HFCS). This tax was imposed in the context of a trade dispute between the U.S. and Mexico over HFCS exports south of the border and Mexican sugar exports headed north. U.S. agribusiness giants Cargill, Corn Products International and Archer Daniels Midlands, along with British Tate and Lyle's U.S. subsidiary, successfully argued that the tax constituted a "performance requirement" in violation of NAFTA Article 1106. The Mexican government was ordered to pay a total of $170 million plus interest.

AbitibiBowater v. Canada. In August 2010, the Canadian federal government agreed to pay $130 million CDN to settle a Chapter 11 claim by a U.S. pulp and paper multinational, AbitibiBowater (AB). In 2008, AB closed a longstanding mill in Newfoundland via bankruptcy, terminating 800 workers without severance. Newfoundland passed a law returning, without compensation, the company's water and timber rights to the crown, and expropriating with compensation AB lands, buildings and dams in the province. AB asserted NAFTA expropriation violations. This settlement, along with the *Glamis* decision (above), has raised concerns that resource-related NAFTA investor claims may increase. For example, a Brazilian company with a U.S. subsidiary received a $15 million settlement form Canada after alleging permit delays for rock quarrying.

Apotex v. Unites States. Apotex is a Canadian manufacturer of generic pharmaceuticals. It filed at least three Chapter 11 claims against the United States. These filings challenged U.S. federal court decisions denying its efforts to obtain "patent certainty" for drugs (in order to allow its generic versions to proceed), FDA denial of approval for another Apotex generic drug, and FDA import inspection practices for drugs. All of these complaints were rejected by a Chapter 11 arbitration panel in 2014.

Exxon/Mobil v. Canada. Exxon/Mobil developed off shore oil fields in Canadian waters. It first challenged Canadian Petroleum

Board rules mandating fees to support R & D in Newfoundland and Labrador in the Canadian courts and lost at trial and on appeal. Exxon subsequently filed a Chapter 11 claim which a panel affirmed in 2012, holding these fees amounted to NAFTA-prohibited "performance requirements." The damages awarded amounted to nearly $15 million.

Bilcon v. Canada. Bilcon of Delaware sought to develop a quarry and marine terminal in Nova Scotia, subject to environmental review. A joint federal/province review denied approval based upon "incompatibility with community core values". Bilcon alleged NAFTA Chapter 11 violations of the national and minimum treatment standards (the latter claim focused on fair and equitable treatment). By agreement, the UNCITRAL Rules controlled before the Permanent Court of Arbitration.

In a split 2015 decision, the arbitrators held in favor of Bilcon, noting particularly an absence of fair notice and treatment in the environmental review process, and a fundamental departure from the "likely significant adverse effects after mitigation" standard of evaluation required by Canadian law.

Eli Lilly v. Canada. Eli Lilly filed a claim for damages under Chapter 11 after Canadian courts invalidated patents on two of its blockbuster drugs on grounds that their utility was not shown. Eli Lilly argued unfair, inequitable and discriminatory treatment. A 2017 arbitration panel rejected these arguments, noting that the "promise of utility" doctrine developed by Canadian courts was well established, putting Eli Lilly on notice prior to its patent claims.

This dispute was unusual because it asserted violation of NAFTA Chapter 11 by Canadian *courts*, not by Canadian legislation or regulation. Subsequently, in June of 2017, the Canadian Supreme Court overturned the "promise doctrine" under its patent law.

Windstream Energy v. Canada and Mesa Power Group v. Canada. Windstream Energy of the USA sought to participate in Ontario's green energy program, and obtained a contract to build an offshore wind farm. Subsequently, Ontario imposed a moratorium on offshore wind projects pending further scientific study. This had the effect of suspending but not terminating the Windstream contract. Other participants in the program were offered alternative opportunities to join the green energy program, but Windstream was not.

Windstream filed a Chapter 11 complaint before the Permanent Court of Arbitration arguing discrimination, indirect expropriation and unfair and inequitable treatment. A 2017 arbitration panel rejected all but the unfair and inequitable treatment claim, recognizing that Ontario had not within a reasonable time clarified the relevant science or the status of the contract, leaving Windstream in legal limbo. It assessed 21 million Euros damages, minus certain adjustments, based upon the value of comparable transactions in Europe.

Mesa Power challenged Ontario's award of power purchase contracts under its green energy program as discriminatory and unfair under Chapter 11 before the Permanent Court of Arbitration in The Hague. In a split decision, the arbitrators rejected Mesa' claims of unfair bidding rules and procedures for power contracts.

Other Foreign Investor Claims of Note. Several U.S. companies commenced Chapter 11 proceedings against Canada asserting damages based on Quebec's moratorium on "fracking", the use of water and chemicals to release sub-surface oil and gas reserves.

After President Obama's rejection in 2015 of the Keystone Pipeline from Alberta's tar sands to Texas, Trans Canada has filed a Chapter 11 claim against the United States alleging discriminatory (non-national) treatment, breach of the duty of most-favored-nation treatment, U.S. governmental acts tantamount to expropriation, and unfair and inequitable treatment. Trans Canada sought in excess of $15 billion in damages, but withdrew its claim after President Trump approved the pipeline.

Summary. These examples of investor-state claims under NAFTA 1994 represent only a partial summary of the impact of Chapter 11. Lawyers learned that U.S. FTAs and BITs can be used to challenge or threaten to challenge all sorts of existing or proposed government actions, particularly regulatory decisions. There is leverage in these broad investor rights, and in its mandatory arbitral procedures. That said, **the United States has never lost an investment arbitration nor paid damages under NAFTA 1994.**

Mutations on the law of investor-state claims subsequently appeared in the U.S.-Chile, U.S.-CAFTA and U.S.-Panama/Peru/ Colombia free trade agreements. See Chapter 5. These mutations are in part a response to Congressional concerns expressed in the Trade Promotion Authority (fast-track) Act of 2002 that Chapter 11 of NAFTA 1994 accorded "greater substantive rights" to foreigners with respect to investment protection than enjoyed by U.S. investors in the United States.

§ 4.9   NAFTA 1994—Intellectual Property

NAFTA 1994 mandated adequate and effective intellectual property rights in all countries, including national treatment and effective internal and external enforcement rights. Specific commitments are made for virtually all types of intellectual property, including patents, copyrights, trademarks, plant breeds, industrial designs, trade secrets, semiconductor chips (directly and in goods incorporating them) and geographical indicators. NAFTA 1994 was the first international agreement to address trade secrets, and many of its IP provisions influenced the content of the WTO TRIPs agreement.

General IP Obligations

Specific commitments on patents, copyrights, trademarks, trade secrets and other intellectual property rights were made in the NAFTA 1994 agreement. These are discussed individually below. NAFTA 1994 also contains some general intellectual property rights obligations. Many of these obligations have counterparts under the TRIPs agreement. For example, except for secondary use of sound recordings, there is a general rule of national treatment.

There is also a general duty to protect intellectual property adequately and effectively, as long as barriers to legitimate trade are not created. At a minimum, this duty necessitates adherence to NAFTA Chapter 17. This general duty also embraces adherence to the substantive provisions of: The Geneva Convention of Phonograms (1971); the Berne Convention for the Protection of Literary and Artistic Works (1971); the Paris Convention for the Protection of Industrial Property (1967); and the 1978 or 1991 versions of the International Convention for the Protection of New Varieties of Plants. Protecting intellectual property rights more extensively than these Conventions is expressly authorized.

The process of intellectual property rights enforcement is covered in detail under NAFTA 1994. Speaking generally, these provisions require fair, equitable, and not unnecessarily complicated, costly or time-consuming enforcement procedures. Written notice, independent legal counsel, the opportunity to substantiate claims and present evidence, and protection of confidential information are stipulated for civil enforcement proceedings. Overly burdensome mandatory personal appearances cannot be imposed. Remedies to enjoin infringement (new to Mexico), prevent importation of infringing goods, and order payment for damages and litigation costs must exist. However, proof of knowing infringement or reasonable grounds for such knowledge is an acceptable criterion. Recovery of profits or liquidated damages must be available when copyright or sound recording infringement is involved. Disposition of infringing or counterfeit goods outside the ordinary channels of commerce or even by destruction is anticipated by NAFTA 1994. All administrative intellectual property rights decisions must be reviewable by a court of law.

Counterfeiting

Criminal penalties are required under NAFTA 1994 for willful trademark counterfeiting or copyright piracy undertaken on a commercial scale. For United States law on point, see the Trademark Counterfeiting Act of 1984 (18 U.S.C. § 2320 et seq.). When the counterfeit or pirated goods come from outside the region, those affected must be given the opportunity to bar importation and possibly obtain their destruction or other satisfactory disposal.

Despite strong provisions in NAFTA 1994 to fight counterfeiting and promote protection of intellectual property, Mexico is seen by some as still not measuring up. Annual submissions by the International Intellectual Property Alliance to the USTR under Special 301 procedures (19 U.S.C. § 2242) document the ineffectiveness of Mexico's anti-piracy law enforcement. Hundreds of millions of dollars of fake CDs, DVDs, software and the like can be found in Mexican marketplaces and the amount is increasing. Prosecutions to combat counterfeiting have been limited. For example, some 2500 Mexican government raids in 1998 netted just 35 convictions with no fines in excess of $1,000.

Mexico's Customs Law of 1996 placed border controls in the hands of the Mexican Institute of Industrial Property (IMPI) for the first time. This Institute was created in 1993 specifically for the task of enforcing Mexican intellectual property rights. Unlike the U.S. Patent and Trademark Office, IMPI has the power to enforce patent owners' rights against actual and potential infringers. It can prevent any commercialization of an infringing product, including removal from the stream of commerce. Mexico also has had, since 1993, a multi-departmental Anti-Piracy Commission. In 1998, the U.S. and Mexico reached agreement on new measures to combat counterfeiting in Mexico. These include a national anti-piracy campaign, tax crimes against counterfeiters, expeditious search and seizure and arrest warrants, and increased administrative enforcement resources. These measures in a limited way have helped to stem counterfeit goods in Mexico.

Gray Market Trading

NAFTA 1994 left each member state free to adopt its own rules on gray market trading. The question that gray market trading poses for NAFTA is the same as has been debated for decades in Europe. Should national intellectual property rights be allowed to function as trade barriers inside the region? Europe, especially the European Court of Justice, has by and large said no. *See* Section 17.13. In the European Union, free trade interests usually trump national intellectual property rights. Under NAFTA 1994, there is no clear answer. Chapter 17 takes pains to expand and protect national intellectual property rights, and specifically addresses the issue of counterfeiting, but not gray market trading. The relevant law of each NAFTA nation remains intact.

Patents

Article 1709 of NAFTA 1994 assured the availability of patents "in all fields of technology." New products and processes resulting from an inventive step that are capable of industrial application are patentable. Patents for pharmaceuticals, computer software, microorganisms and microbiological processes, plant varieties and agricultural chemicals were specifically included under NAFTA and caused changes in Mexican law. In addition, protection for layout designs of semiconductor integrated circuits was provided by Article 1710. All patent rights must be granted without discrimination as to field of technology, country of origin, and importation or local production of the relevant products.

NAFTA 1994 specifically reserved the right to deny patents for diagnostic, therapeutic and surgical methods, transgenic plants and animals, and for essentially biological processes that produce plants or animals. If commercial exploitation might endanger public morality or "ordre public" (state security) no patents need be granted. Patent denials to protect human, animal or plant life or health, or to avoid serious injury to nature or the environment, are also justifiable under NAFTA.

It was agreed that patents in NAFTA nations would run either for 20 years from the date of the filing of the patent application, or 17 years from the grant of patent rights (the traditional U.S. approach). However, the subsequent TRIPs agreement stipulates a 20-year patent term from the date of filing. Canadian, Mexican and United States patent laws now follow this rule. For pharmaceutical patents, effectively speaking, an additional five years of protection from generic competition is often achieved because NAFTA 1994 required five-year exclusivity for product approval test data. Under NAFTA, patent owners generally possess the right to prevent others from making, using or selling the invention without their consent. No mention is made of the right to block infringing or unauthorized imports. If the patent covers a process, this includes the right to prevent others from using, selling or *importing* products obtained directly from that process. Assignment or transfer of patents, and licensing contracts for their use and exploitation, are also expressly protected.

On the touchy subject of compulsory licensing, not authorized under U.S. law, governments may allow limited nonexclusive usage without the owner's authorization if the invention has not been used or exploited locally through production or importation. This is generally permissible only after reasonable attempts at securing a license. However, under emergency, competition law or public noncommercial circumstances, no prior attempt at securing a license is required. In all cases of compulsory licensing, there is a duty to adequately remunerate the patent owner. Significant changes in Canadian compulsory licensing of pharmaceuticals were made in 1993. These changes caused some pharmaceutical prices to rise in Canada.

Apart from compulsory licensing, NAFTA 1994 authorized "limited exceptions" to exclusive patents rights. Such exceptions may not "unreasonably conflict" with the normal exploitation of the patent. Nor may they "unreasonably prejudice" the owner's "legitimate interests." It is not clear how this broad authorization will be construed or applied.

Copyrights

The NAFTA 1994 provisions on copyrights promoted uniformity in North America. Canada, Mexico and the United States promised extensive protection of copyrights, sound recordings, program-carrying satellite signals and industrial designs. Copyrights are available on all works of original expression. These include books, articles, choreography, photographs, paintings, sculpture, films, videos, records, tapes, CDs and other traditionally copyrighted materials. In most instances, copyrights must be granted for at least 50 years. The United States grants 70-year copyrights, which are now required for Mexico and Canada under USMCA 2018. Computer programs and data compilations which constitute intellectual creations are subject to copyrights. Article 1707 requires criminal sanctions for makers and sellers of unauthorized decoding devices, and civil sanctions for unauthorized receivers of satellite signals.

Copyright holders also receive the rights enumerated in the Berne Convention for the Protection of Literary and Artistic Works (1971). However, translation and reproduction licenses permitted by the Berne Convention were not allowed under NAFTA 1994 if these needs could be fulfilled voluntarily by the copyright holder but for national laws. In addition, Article 1704.2 specifically conveys to copyright holders:

(1) Control over importation of unauthorized copies;

(2) First public distribution rights over the work (whether by sale, rental or otherwise);

(3) Control over communication of the work to the public; and

(4)   Control over commercial rental of computer programs.

If the original or a copy of a computer program is put on the market, this does not exhaust rental rights. Despite the specific reference to control over unauthorized imports in Article 1704.2, it is doubtful whether NAFTA 1994 can be construed so as to block free trade in copyrighted goods after their first sale in the United States, Canada or Mexico. The "first sale doctrine" limits an owner's rights to control copyrighted goods to their first sale or transfer. Thereafter, the goods can be freely exchanged.

Licensing and conveyance of copyrights, royalties and the like are freely transferable under NAFTA 1994. Assignment of works of creation to employers by employees is also protected. However, Article 1705.5 somewhat vaguely allows limits or exceptions in "special cases" that do not conflict with "normal exploitation" of the work. Presumably, "fair use" of copyrighted material falls within this provision. These exceptions may not unreasonably prejudice the owner's legitimate interests.

Trademarks

Trademarks are found on most products, and service and other marks are commonly used. The pervasiveness of marks arguably makes them the most important of NAFTA's intellectual property provisions. Such marks help make markets work by signaling attributes, qualities, price levels and other relevant information. The NAFTA 1994 provisions on marks fostered uniform law. They stop short, however, from establishing a regional trademark as the Europeans have done.

Canada, Mexico and the United States agreed to register trademarks, service marks, collective organizational marks and certification marks. All of these marks must be capable of distinguishing goods or services. Internationally "well-known" marks are given special protections against pirates. Whether a mark is "well-known" depends upon knowledge of it in the sector of the public normally dealing with the goods or services, including knowledge in the NAFTA country resulting from promotion of the mark there. A reasonable opportunity to petition to cancel trademark registrations must be granted. In contrast, a reasonable opportunity to oppose registration applications is not mandatory under NAFTA 1994. The nature of the goods or services *per se* cannot justify a refusal to register.

To apply for protection, there is no requirement of prior usage on goods or services. However, if actual usage does not occur within 3 years, Chapter 17 provided that registration may be denied. Immoral, deceptive, scandalous and disparaging marks, and those that falsely suggest a connection with or contempt of persons, institutions, beliefs or national symbols can be denied registration. No registration of words in English, French or Spanish that generically designate goods or services is permitted. Registration of marks indicating geographic origin can be rejected if "deceptively misdescriptive". Trademark registrations must be valid for at least 10 years. They can be renewed indefinitely provided use is continuous. If circumstances beyond the owner's control justify non-use, registrations can be continued. For all these purposes, the NAFTA nations agreed that use is continued when undertaken by franchisees or licensees.

NAFTA trademark owners can prevent persons from using identical or "similar" signs on identical or similar goods or services if this would cause a "likelihood of confusion." However, the "fair use" of descriptive terms may be allowed. Mandatory use of a second "local" trademark (as Mexico once required) is banned. Mandatory use that reduces the function of trademarks as source indicators is also prohibited. Furthermore, compulsory licensing of trademarks is contrary to NAFTA, but contractual licensing and assignment of trademarks can be conditioned.

Trade Secrets

NAFTA 1994 was the first international agreement on trade secret protection. Its primary impact has been on Mexican law. At a minimum, each nation must ensure legal means to prevent trade secrets from being disclosed, acquired or used without consent "in a manner contrary to honest commercial practices" (Article 1711). Breach of contract, breach of confidence, and inducement to breach of contract are specifically listed as examples of dishonest commercial practices. Moreover, persons who acquire trade secrets knowing them to be the product of such practices, or who were grossly negligent in failing to know this, also engage in dishonest commercial practices. This is true even if they do not use the secrets in question. NAFTA does not mention, however, the practice of "reverse engineering". This practice is thought to be common and has been authoritatively endorsed by the U.S. Supreme Court. See *Kewanee Oil Co. v. Bicron Corp.*, 416 U.S. 470 (1974).

For NAFTA purposes, information is "secret" if it is not generally known or readily accessible to persons who normally deal with it, has commercial value because of its secrecy, and reasonable steps have been taken to keep it secret. This definition ought to cover, for example, the secret formula for making Coca-Cola. Nevertheless, trade secret holders may be required to produce evidence documenting the existence of the secret in order to secure protection.

Release of such information to government authorities obviously involves risks that will need to be considered.

No NAFTA government may discourage or impede the voluntary licensing of trade secrets (often referred to as "know-how licensing"). Imposing excessive or discriminatory conditions on know-how licenses is prohibited. More specifically, in testing and licensing the sale of pharmaceutical and agricultural chemical products, there is a general duty to protect against disclosure of proprietary data.

In 1996, independently of NAFTA, the United States enacted the Economic Espionage Act, 18 U.S.C. § 1831 et seq. This Act creates criminal penalties for misappropriation of trade secrets. For these purposes, a "trade secret" is defined as "financial, business, scientific, technical, economic or engineering information" that the owner has taken reasonable measures to keep secret and whose "independent economic value derives from being closely held". All proceeds from the theft of trade secrets and all property used or intended for use in the misappropriation can be seized and forfeited.

The U.S. Defend Trade Secrets Act of 2016 creates a federal private right of action seeking an ex parte order to seize, in extraordinary circumstances, property necessary to prevent the propagation or dissemination of a trade secret. Injunctive and damages relief for actual losses and unjust enrichment may follow. However, the Act does not permit restricting an employee's movement to a competitor merely on the basis of what he or she knows unless an employer has grounds to believe the employee intends to misappropriate a trade secret. Criminal fines of the greater of $5,000,000 or three times the value of the stolen trade secret, including research, design and avoided reproduction costs, are established. The 2016 Act creates an alternative to state actions under the Uniform Trade Secrets Act, which in some states has been construed to permit barring employee movement if trade secret disclosure is "inevitable" in the performance of their new job.

§ 4.10 NAFTA 1994—Other Provisions

The provisions on temporary entry visas for business persons found in the CUSFTA were extended under the NAFTA 1994. These entry rights cover business persons, traders, investors, intra-company transferees and 63 designated professionals. Installers, after-sales repair and maintenance staff and managers performing services under a warranty or other service contract incidental to the sale of equipment or machinery are included, as are sales representatives, buyers, market researchers and financial service providers. White collar business persons only need proof of citizenship and documentation of business purpose to work in another NAFTA country for up to 5 years. Canadian professionals have flooded into the United States under NAFTA visas. Apart from these provisions, no common market for the free movement of labor is undertaken.

NAFTA 1994 embraced a competition policy principally aimed at state enterprises and governmentally sanctioned monopolies, mostly found in Mexico. State owned or controlled businesses, at all levels of government, are required to act consistently with the NAFTA when exercising regulatory, administrative or governmental authority (*e.g.* when granting licenses). Governmentally-owned and privately-owned state-designated monopolies are obliged to follow commercial considerations in their transactions and avoid discrimination against goods or services of other NAFTA nations. Furthermore, each country must ensure that such monopolies do not use their positions to engage in anticompetitive practices in non-monopoly markets. Since each NAFTA nation must adopt laws against anticompetitive business practices and cooperate in their enforcement, Mexico has revived its historically weak "antitrust" laws. A consultative Trade and Competition Committee reviews competition policy issues under the NAFTA 1994.

Other notable provisions in the NAFTA 1994 included a general duty of legal transparency, fairness and due process regarding all laws affecting traders and investors with independent administrative or judicial review of government action. Generalized exceptions to the agreement cover action to protect national security and national interests such as public morals, health, national treasures, natural resources, or to enforce laws against deceptive or anticompetitive practices, short of arbitrary discriminations or disguised restraints on trade. Balance of payments trade restraints are governed by the rules of the International Monetary Fund.

Taxation issues are subject to bilateral double taxation treaties, including a new one between Mexico and the United States. The "cultural industry" reservations secured by the CUSFTA now cover Canada and Mexico, but are not extended to Mexican-U.S. trade. A right of compensatory retaliation through measures of equivalent commercial effect is granted when invocation of these reservations would have violated the Canada-U.S. FTA but for the cultural industries proviso.

NAFTA 1994 is not forever. Any country may withdraw on 6 months' notice, something President Trump has repeatedly threatened. See Chapter 6. Other countries or groups of countries may be admitted to the NAFTA if Canada, Mexico and the United States agree and domestic ratification follows. In December of 1994, Chile was invited to become the next member of the NAFTA 1994.

Negotiations stalled for want of U.S. Congressional fast track negotiating authority, and subsequent bilateral free trade agreements between Chile and each of the three NAFTA nations.

§ 4.11   Dispute Settlement Under NAFTA 1994

The institutional dispute settlement arrangements accompanying NAFTA 1994 were minimal. A trilateral Trade Commission (with Secretariat) comprised of ministerial or cabinet-level officials met at least annually to ensure effective joint management of NAFTA is established. The various intergovernmental committees established for specific areas of coverage of the NAFTA 1994 (*e.g.* competition policy) to oversee much of the work of making the free trade area function. These committees operate on the basis of consensus, referring contentious issues to the Trade Commission.

Intergovernmental Disputes

Investment, dumping and subsidy, financial services, environmental, labor and standards disputes were subject to special dispute resolution procedures. A general intergovernmental NAFTA 1994 dispute settlement procedure was also established (Chapter 20). A right of consultation exists when one country's rights are thought to be affected. If consultations do not resolve the issue within 45 days, the complainant may convene a meeting of the Trade Commission. The Commission must seek to promptly settle the dispute and may use its good offices, mediation, conciliation or any other alternative means.

Absent resolution, and assuming the dispute falls under WTO jurisdiction, the complaining country or countries ordinarily *commence proceedings under the GATT/WTO or the NAFTA.* Once selected, the chosen forum becomes exclusive. However, if the dispute concerns environmental, safety, health or conservation standards, or arises under specific environmental agreements, the responding nation may elect to have the dispute heard by a NAFTA panel. In the tuna labeling dispute, however, the United States was unable to get Mexico to withdraw its WTO complaint. For more on WTO dispute settlement procedures, see Section 1.14.

NAFTA 1994 Chapters and WTO Agreements

The right of NAFTA governments to elect as between NAFTA and WTO remedies is limited by the substantive content of the NAFTA 1994 and WTO agreements. The NAFTA 1994 Chapters chart below indicates the closest parallel WTO agreements.

NAFTA 1994	WTO AGREEMENTS
Chapter 3, Trade in Goods	General Agreement on Tariffs and Trade 1994, Agreement on Textiles and Clothing
Chapter 4, Rules of Origin	Agreement on Rules of Origin
Chapter 5, Customs Procedures	No parallel
Chapter 6, Energy and Basic Petrochemicals	No parallel
Chapter 7, Agriculture and SPS Measures	Agreement on Agriculture, Agreement on SPS Measures
Chapter 8, Emergency Action	Agreement on Safeguards
Chapter 9, Product and Service Standards	Agreement on Technical Barriers to Trade
Chapter 10, Procurement	Agreement on Government Procurement (optional)
Chapter 11, Investment	Agreement on Trade-Related Investment Measures (TRIMs)
Chapter 12, Cross-Border Trade in Services	General Agreement on Trade in Services (GATS)
Chapter 13, Enhanced Telecommunications	See GATS, Basic Telecommunications Covered
Chapter 14, Financial Services	See GATS
Chapter 15, Competition Policy, Monopolies and State Enterprises	No parallel, but see Understanding on Interpretation of GATT Article XVII
Chapter 16, Temporary Entry for Business Persons	No parallel
Chapter 17, Intellectual Property	Agreement on Trade-Related Aspects of Intellectual Property Rights (TRIPs)
Chapter 18, Administrative Provisions	Not applicable
Chapter 19, Antidumping and Countervailing Duty Dispute Settlement	No parallel, but see DSU and Agreement on Implementation of GATT Article VI
Chapter 20, Dispute Settlement	Understanding on Rules and Procedures Governing the Settlement of Disputes (DSU)

Chapter 21, Exceptions	See GATT Articles XX, XXI and Understanding on GATT Balance of Payments Provisions
Agreement on Environmental Cooperation	No parallel
Agreement on Labor Cooperation	No parallel

Chapter 20 Dispute Settlement Procedures

Dispute settlement procedures under NAFTA 1994 Chapter 20 involve nonbinding arbitration by five persons chosen in most cases from a trilaterally agreed roster of experts (not limited to NAFTA citizens), with a special roster established for disputes about financial services. A "reverse selection" process is used. The chair of the panel is first chosen by agreement or, failing agreement, by designation of one side selected by lot. The chair cannot be a citizen of the selecting side but must be a NAFTA national. Each side then selects two additional arbitrators who are citizens of the country or countries on the *other* side.

The Commission has approved rules of procedure including the opportunity for written submissions, rebuttals and at least one oral hearing. Expert advice on environmental and scientific matters may be given by special procedures accessing science boards. Strict time limits are created so as to keep the panel on track to a prompt resolution. Within 90 days an initial confidential report must be circulated, followed by 14 days for comment by the parties and 16 days for the final panel report to the Commission. There is no "appeal" in Chapter 20 disputes from the arbitrators' decision. The WTO has its Appellate Body. See Chapter 1.

Early NAFTA Chapter 20 arbitrations concerned Canadian tariffication of agricultural quotas (upheld), U.S. escape clause relief from Mexican corn broom exports (rejected) and a successful Mexican challenge of the U.S. failure to implement cross-border trucking. Once the Trade Commission receives a final arbitration panel report, NAFTA required the disputing nations to agree within 30 days on a resolution (normally by conforming to the panel's recommendations). If a mutually agreed resolution does not occur at this stage, the complaining country may retaliate by suspending the application of equivalent benefits under the NAFTA 1994, which Mexico did during the trucking dispute. Any NAFTA country may invoke the arbitration panel process if it perceives that this retaliation is excessive.

When NAFTA 1994 interpretational issues are disputed before domestic tribunals or courts, the Trade Commission (if it can agree) can submit an interpretation to that body. In the absence of agreement within the Commission, any NAFTA country may intervene and submit its views as to the proper interpretation or application of the NAFTA to the national court or tribunal.

Dumping and Subsidy Disputes

The independent binational review panel mechanism established in the CUSFTA for dumping and subsidy duties was carried over at vigorous Canadian insistence into NAFTA 1994 and the pending **USMCA 2018,** along with the extraordinary challenge procedure to deal with allegations about the integrity of the panel review process. Chapter 19 panels are substituted for traditional judicial review at the national level of administrative dumping and countervailing duty orders. NAFTA 1994 did, however, seek to "professionalize" the process by adding judges and retired judges to the roster of acceptable Chapter 19 panelists. The panelists under CUSFTA were more often lawyers, economists or academicians.

Each party to the dispute chooses two panelists (invariably from their home country). Each party may peremptorily reject without cause four panelist selections. The fifth panelist is chosen by agreement if that is possible, or by lot if not. The panel then selects its chair (who must be a lawyer) by majority vote or failing that by lot. This panel selection procedure differs significantly from the "reverse selection" process used in Chapter 20 disputes (above).

Mexico has undertaken major developments to its law in this area. The procedures and rules for such panels generally follow those found in the CUSFTA. They are limited to issues of the consistency of the national decisions with domestic law, and once again have been numerous. United States administrative AD and CVD determinations (mostly annual reviews of prior proceedings) have been reviewed by NAFTA Chapter 19 panels more often than Canadian or Mexican determinations. Goods from Mexico have been involved in the U.S. determinations more than twice as frequently as Canadian goods.

Leather apparel, porcelain-on-steel cookware, cement, oil country tubular goods and fresh cut flowers provide examples of U.S. imports from Mexico that have been the subject of Chapter 19 panel decisions. Live swine, concrete, color picture tubes and carbon steel imports from Canada have also been decided under Chapter 19. Nearly all of these decisions have concerned the imposition of U.S. antidumping duties. U.S. exports of synthetic baler twine, steel sheet, malt beverages and refined sugar to Canada, and flat coated steel, steel plate and polystyrene to Mexico, provide examples of Chapter 19 panel decisions reviewing Canadian and Mexican AD and CVD determinations.

The never ending CUSFTA and NAFTA *Softwood Lumber* dispute involving repeated U.S. CVD tariffs on Canadian exports allegedly subsidized by unfair "stumpage fees" continues. The second Softwood Lumber Settlement Agreement between the two countries expired in 2015. The U.S. took several disputes under this settlement, as agreed, to the London Court of Arbitration. See Section 4.1. The dispute remains ongoing under the Trump administration. See Section 1.17.

Only three U.S.-requested extraordinary challenges to NAFTA Chapter 19 panel decisions were raised. These challenges concerned Cement from Mexico (ECC–2000–1904–01), Magnesium from Canada (ECC–2003–1904–01) and Softwood Lumber from Canada (ECC–2004–1904–01). All of them were rejected by the Extraordinary Challenge Committees, and none were as provocative as the ECC under CUSFTA.

AD and CVD disputes may also be taken to the WTO by NAFTA governments. In other words, binational panels are not exclusive. The *Softwood Lumber* dispute, for example, resulted in conflicting WTO and NAFTA panel rulings on domestic injury. While most NAFTA trade remedy disputes are resolved by binational panels, some have been settled with controversy. The "tomatoes dispute" provides a ready example.

Tomatoes Dumping Dispute

This dispute concerned Mexican exports of tomatoes at prices that were rapidly taking market share from U.S. growers. After failing to persuade the U.S. International Trade Commission to pursue escape clause relief, Florida growers alleged dumping by Mexican tomato producers early in 1996. This politically high profile petition eventually led to a "suspension agreement" between the U.S. Commerce Department and Mexican growers. The Department promised to suspend its antidumping probe (dumping at a 17.56 percent margin had been found) in return for a commitment by Mexican growers not to sell at less than a specified "reference price." This price was based on the lowest average import price in a recent period not involving dumping. It amounted in 1996 to 20.68 cents per pound. At that price, there was no limit on the volume of Mexican tomatoes that could be shipped to the U.S. market.

Critics from states like Arizona alleged "political blackmail" as the settlement came just days before the 1996 Presidential election vote. President Clinton carried Florida in 1996, something he had failed to do in 1992. In 2013, bowing to pressure from Florida growers, a revised, more restrictive suspension agreement was reached by the Obama administration shortly after his re-election to office. Thus a suspension agreement remains in force, raising prices and managing trade in a most remarkable manner. It has not, however, significantly slowed Mexico's market penetration. Prior to NAFTA 1994, Mexican tomatoes held about 30 percent of the U.S. market. At this point, Mexican tomatoes enjoy at least a 65 percent U.S. market share.

§ 4.12   The 1994 Side Agreements on Labor and the Environment

The NAFTA 1994 side agreements on labor (NAALC) and the environment (NAAEC) did not create additional substantive regional rules. Rather the side agreements basically create law enforcement mechanisms. The side agreements commit each country to creation of environmental and labor bodies that monitor compliance with the adequacy and the enforcement of *domestic* law. The Commission for Environmental Cooperation (CEC) (Montreal) and three National Administrative Offices (NAO) concerning labor matters are empowered to receive complaints. Negotiations to resolve complaints first ensue.

NAAEC Proceedings

In the absence of a negotiated solution, the NAAEC establishes five environmental dispute settlement mechanisms. *First*, the CEC Secretariat may report on almost any environmental matter. *Second*, the Secretariat may develop a factual record in trade-related law enforcement disputes. *Third*, the CEC Council can release that record to the public. *Fourth*, if there is a persistent pattern of failure to enforce environmental law, the Council will mediate and conciliate. *Fifth*, if such efforts fail, the Council can send the matter to arbitration and awards can be enforced by monetary penalties. No NAAEC dispute has ever gotten beyond Stage Three, release of a Factual record.

The Commission for Environmental Cooperation (CEC)

A trilateral Commission for Environmental Cooperation (CEC) was established under the NAAEC side agreement. **This Commission has been retained under the pending USMCA 2018 Agreement.** See Chapter 6. The Commission's Environmental Council of Ministers is comprised of cabinet-level officers from each member state. The Council can discuss, recommend and settle environmental disputes publicly by consensus. The Commission's Secretariat (located in Montreal) investigates, reviews and reports with recommendations to the Council on environmental matters. The Executive Director of the Secretariat rotates every three years among the NAAEC countries. He or she chooses the staff of the Secretariat on the basis of "competence and integrity." However, "due regard" must be given to recruiting "equitable proportions" from each country (Article 11). The CEC Council of Ministers and Secretariat are advised, especially on technical and scientific matters, by a 15-person Joint Public Advisory Committee.

Under the NAAEC, each member state agreed to maintain "high" levels of environmental protection, but this commitment is not enforceable through NAAEC dispute settlement. Rather, NAAEC focuses on enforcement of the individual environmental protection standards of each nation. This focus, politically speaking, targeted Mexico. There was a widespread perception in the United States that Mexican enforcement of its environmental laws states was inadequate. It is perhaps ironic therefore that many of the complaints lodged under NAAEC to date have challenged Canadian and U.S. environmental law enforcement.

CEC Article 13 Reports

Article 13 authorizes the CEC Secretariat to issue reports on virtually any environmental matter not involving law enforcement. Notice of intent to issue such a report must first be given to the CEC Council of Ministers. If the Council objects by a two-thirds vote, no report can be undertaken. Nongovernmental organizations (NGOs) and others can and have petitioned for Article 13 reports by the Secretariat. For example, the two first Article 13 reports concerned long range transport of air pollutants and the death of 40,000 migratory birds at the Silva Reservoir in Guanajuato. The latter report determined that avian botulism was the cause of the deaths and fostered a clean-up and cooperative information exchanges.

A 2004 report on the effects of transgenic maize in Mexico was noticeably high profile. Other reports have concerned continental pollutant pathways, electricity and the environment, green building in North America, and sustainable freight transport. An Article 13 report concerned water use in the Fort Huachuca, Arizona region. It was undertaken at the initiative of the CEC Secretariat after an Article 14 complaint (below) concerning riparian areas for migratory birds as dismissed. (The Secretariat determined that preparation of a factual record was not warranted.) Thus Article 13 reports can serve as an alternative to direct challenges raised under Article 14.

Article 14 Citizen and NGO Submissions

The NAAEC, under Article 14, contains its own submission, response and dispute resolution process. "Whistleblower" complaints can be filed with the CEC Secretariat by any person or nongovernmental organization (NGO) concerning workplaces, enterprises or sectors that produce NAAEC—traded or NAAEC—competitive goods or services. Article 14 submissions must allege that a NAAEC nation is not "effectively enforcing" *its* environmental law. See SEM–97–005 (submission challenging Canada's ratification [but not implementation by statute] of Biodiversity Convention did not concern effective enforcement of *Canadian* law). SEM stands for Submissions on Enforcement Matters. Guidelines for such submissions have been issued by the CEC Secretariat. They can be found at the Secretariat's excellent web site, www.cec.org.

The Secretariat can dismiss Article 14 submissions on a variety of grounds. For example, the NAAEC agreement stipulates that no ineffective enforcement of environmental law exists when the action or inaction reflects a reasonable exercise of official discretion in investigatory, prosecutorial, regulatory or compliance matters. Furthermore, since "environmental law" is defined in NAAEC as excluding occupational safety and health laws, and laws that primarily manage the harvest or exploitation of natural resources, such complaints can also be dismissed. *See* SEM–98–002 (submission concerning Mexican commercial forestry dispute dismissed). The submission must "appear to be aimed at promoting enforcement rather than harassing industry." (Article 14(1)(d)). It must also be filed in a timely manner. *See* SEM–97–004 (submission filed three years after Canadian environmental decision not timely).

The CEC Secretariat determines if the submission merits a response from the nation whose environmental law enforcement practices are being challenged. Private remedies available under national law must have been pursued and pending administrative or judicial proceedings will keep the CEC from moving forward on the complaint. See *Canadian Wetlands* and *Canadian Fisheries Act* (CEC rejects citizen and NGO submissions) SEM–96–002 and 003. Since the NAAEC requires extensive private access to environmental remedies, including the ability to file complaints with administrative authorities, access to administrative, quasi-judicial and judicial proceedings, and the right to sue for damages, mitigating relief and injunctions, exhausting national remedies first is a major prerequisite. In evaluating whether a submission merits a response, the Secretariat is also to be "guided" by whether the submission alleges "harm" to the complaining party. Proof of such harm is not mandatory, merely a relevant issue. Several of the Secretariat's early decisions suggest that it takes a liberal view of this "standing" question. See *Cozumel Pier*, SEM–96–001 (discussed below).

In addition, as the rejection by the Secretariat of the first two Article 14 submissions made clear, legislative actions that diminish environmental law enforcement cannot be challenged SEM–95–001 and 002. Thus complaints by various NGOs against the suspension of enforcement of the U.S. Endangered Species Act listing provisions and elimination of private remedies for U.S. timber salvage sales (both alleged to have been accomplished in appropriations bills) failed to proceed under Article 14.

CEC Factual Records

With or without a response from the member state alleged to be inadequately enforcing its law, the Secretariat must decide whether development of a factual record is warranted and inform the Council of its reasons. The Council must approve development of a factual record by a two-thirds vote. If there are past, pending, or possible national administrative or judicial proceedings, the Secretariat or Council are unlikely to allow this to occur. NAAEC governments are obliged to submit relevant information throughout the factual record process, but the Secretariat cannot enforce this obligation.

The third submission under Article 14 was made by Mexican NGOs alleging that the Mexican government had failed to conduct an environmental impact review before authorizing a cruise ship pier at Cozumel Island, SEM–96–001. The CEC Secretariat ruled that this complaint passed muster under Article 14 and compiled the first factual record under NAAEC, Factual Record No. 1 (1997). After summarizing the submission and Mexican response, the CEC "presented" facts with respect to the "matters raised in the submissions." In this record, the CEC adopts the role of a neutral finder of facts.

The second Factual Record concerned a submission that alleged that the Canadian government failed to enforce the Fisheries Act to ensure protection of fish and fish habitat in connection with hydroelectric dams in British Columbia, SEM–97–001. Subsequent Article 14 Factual Records have concerned Canadian enforcement of the Fisheries Act in the Arctic (Oldman River, SEM–97–006), logging rules in British Columbia (SEM–00–004), and mining in British Columbia (SEM–98–004).

Other Factual Records have covered U.S. law enforcement regarding migratory birds (SEM–99–002), Mexican enforcement of hazardous waste law in Tijuana (SEM–98–007), and Mexico City (SEM–03–004), shrimp farming regulations in Nayarit (SEM–98–006), wastewater river pollution in Sonora (SEM–97–002), pulp and paper mill pollution in Canada (SEM–02–003), Canadian migratory bird protection from logging (SEM–02–001), (SEM–04–006), access to environmental justice by Mexican Indigenous communities (Tarahumara, SEM–00–006), copper smelting pollution in Sonora, Mexico (Molymex II, SEM–00–005) pollution of Lake Chapala in Mexico (SEM–03–003), auto pollution in Quebec (SEM–04–007) and toxic pollutants in Montreal (SEM–03–005). All of these Records are available at www.cec.org.

NAALC Proceedings

The NAALC labor law enforcement system is a calibrated four-tier series of dispute resolution mechanisms. *First*, the NAOs may review and report on eleven designated labor law enforcement matters that correspond to the NAALC Labor Principles. *Second*, ministerial consultations may follow when recommended by the NAO. *Third*, an Evaluation Committee of Experts can report on trade-related mutually recognized labor law enforcement patterns of practice concerning eight of the NAALC Labor Principles (excluding strikes, union organizing and collective bargaining). *Fourth*, persistent patterns of failure to enforce occupational health and safety, child labor or minimum wage laws can be arbitrated and awards enforced by monetary penalties. No NAALC dispute has ever gotten beyond Stage Two, ministerial consultations. **The NAALC labor law system, including NAOs, is not repeated in the pending USMCA 2018.** See Chapter 6.

Labor Law Enforcement Submissions—Union Organizing

Early U.S. organized labor submissions to the United States NAO alleged the firing by U.S. and Japanese maquiladora subsidiaries of Mexican workers due to union organizing activities, U.S. NAO Submission Nos. 940001, 2 and 3. Public hearings were held at which Mexican workers, their attorneys and U.S. union supporters gave testimony. Honeywell, General Electric and SONY boycotted these hearings. The NAO Report in the Honeywell and GE cases was generally uncertain as to the legality of the firings under Mexican law, particularly because some of the dismissed workers accepted severance pay which indemnified the employers. No ministerial consultations were recommended, but some employees were reinstated and both Honeywell and GE made it clear to their managers that they did not want a reoccurrence of these events.

With SONY, the NAO Report cited "serious questions" about the legality of the firings and recommended ministerial consultations. These consultations resulted in a series of workshops, conferences, studies and meetings (including SONY representatives) on union registration and certification (especially of independent unions) in Mexico. In due course, the U.S. Secretary of Labor requested a follow-up NAO report. This report put a positive spin on developments in

Mexico concerning union organizing, a topic that NAALC does not allow to proceed to the next dispute settlement tier (an Evaluation Committee of Experts).

On the other side of the border, the Telephone Workers Union of Mexico (collaborating with the Communications Workers of America) (CWA) filed a submission with the Mexican NAO about worker dismissals and a plant closing at Sprint's La Conexion Familiar in San Francisco, OAN Mex. Submission No. 9501. Again, the allegation involved denial of labor's right to organize. The NLRB eventually ruled against Sprint and ordered rehiring of the workers. *See* 322 NLRB 774 (1996). On appeal, the D.C. Circuit found that the claim that plant was closed because of union organizing activities was not substantiated. *LCF, Inc. v. NLRB*, 129 F.3d 1276 (1997). The Mexican NAO has accepted submissions challenging U.S. labor law enforcement concerning workers in a solar panel plant in California, the Washington State apple industry, a Maine egg farm, migrant workers in New York, H-2B Visa workers, and the North Carolina ban on public sector collective bargaining, OAN Mex. Nos. 9801, 9802, 9803, 2001–01, 2003–1, 2005–01.

In the *Sprint* submission the Mexican NAO found "possible problems" in enforcement of U.S. labor law and recommended ministerial consultations. These consultations resulted in a public forum, a special report by the NAALC Commission on *Plant Closings and Labor Rights* (1997) in all three NAFTA nations, and monitoring of the pending NLRB proceeding based upon Sprint's actions. The report highlights widespread use of anti-union plant closing tactics in the United States (but not Canada or Mexico):

"U.S. labor law authorities actively prosecute unfair labor practice cases involving plant closings and threats of plant closing. They demonstrate a high level of success in litigation before the NLRB and the courts. However, despite this effective enforcement, the incidence of anti-union plant closings and threats of plant closing continues with some frequency. There appears to be significant variation in the types of statements employers are permitted to make about plant closings in connection with a union organizing effort.

The Secretariat examined all 89 federal appeals court decisions in cases involving plant closings and threats of plant closing published between 1986 and 1993. Of the cases, 70 arose in the context of a new union organizing campaign. Closings or partial closings prompted 32 cases, and 57 cases involved threats of closing. Courts of appeals upheld NLRB determinations that employers unlawfully closed or threatened to close plants in 84 of the 89 cases.

The Secretariat studied 319 decisions of the NLRB between 1990 and 1995 involving plant closings and the threats of closing. Of the total, 109 cases involved closings or partial closings, and 210 involved threats of closing. New union organizing campaigns in non-union workplaces were involved in 275 of these cases, while 44 involved existing unions. The NLRB found a violation by the employer in 283 of the 319 cases.

The Secretariat also looked at case files in two regional offices of the NLRB to determine the volume and disposition of cases that do not reach the level of a published determination by an adjudicator. Findings suggest that for every case that reaches a published decision, 10 cases are initiated at the regional office level. More than half of these are withdrawn or dismissed.

In more than 40 percent of cases where the regional office found merit in the charge, the NLRB General Counsel took the case to trial before an ALJ. This is 10 times the rate of enforcement in other cases of meritorious unfair labor practice charges against employers. These findings indicate that the NLRB takes plant closing cases very seriously and actively pursues them to a litigated conclusion. The General Counsel prevails in nearly 90 percent of such cases.

In the United States, resources were readily available to conduct survey research for information that could not be gleaned from administrative and judicial records. Union representatives surveyed reported what they believed to be plant closing threats occurring in half of the sampled union organizing campaigns during the 3-year period studied, with a higher incidence in industries more susceptible to closing such as manufacturing, trucking, and warehousing. Perceived plant closing threats were the largest single factor identified by respondents who decided to withdraw an election petition they had earlier filed, thus discontinuing the organizing campaign. When unions proceeded to an election, the overall union win rate where plant closing threats were reported to have occurred was 33 percent, compared with 47 percent in elections where no threats were reported to have taken place."

The fourth submission to the U.S. NAO was made by labor and human rights groups and a Mexican lawyers association. They claimed that an independent public sector Mexican union lost its representation rights to a rival union when the government merged the Fisheries Ministry into a larger Ministry of the Environment, Natural Resources and Fisheries, U.S. NAO Submission No. 9610 ("Pesca Union"). After a public hearing at which many testified, the NAO Report recommended ministerial consultations on the effect of International Labor Organization (ILO) Conventions (No. 87 was cited) on Mexican labor law, particularly the prohibition against more than one union in a governmental entity. The independent union subsequently had its registration restored by Mexican court order.

Another union organizing case came to the U.S. NAO in 1996, Submission No. 9602. The Communications Workers of America and its Mexican ally (the STRM) alleged that Taiwan-owned Maxi-Switch had a "protection contract" with a CTM union that was not employee approved. CTM is closely allied with the ruling PRI party. After scheduling public testimony, the complaint was withdrawn when registration was granted to a STRM-affiliated "independent" union in the Maxi-Switch maquiladora plant.

Other submissions accepted by the U.S. NAO concerning union organizing in Mexico have involved the Itapsa export processing plant in Ciudad de los Reyes (also filed with the Canadian NAO), and TAESA flight attendants, U.S. Submissions 9801 and 9901. A rare Canadian-oriented submission challenged Quebec law enforcement on union organizing at a McDonald's restaurant in St. Hubert, U.S. Submission 9803.

Perhaps the most bitter of all the union organizing complaints was that filed against Han Young, a Hyundai Corporation maquiladora making truck chassis in Tijuana, Mexico, U.S. NAO Submission No. 9702. Unions and labor groups from all three NAFTA nations alleged a brutal and blatant pattern of employer-CTM opposition to an independent union organizing effort. The U.S. NAO report documents threats, bribes, harassment, intimidation and dismissals. Moreover, the independent union's election victory was inexplicably nullified by the local Mexican labor Conciliation and Arbitration Board (CAB). At this point, with outrage and embarrassment evident in the NAO investigation, the Mexican federal and state governments intervened and negotiated a settlement allowing a second supervised election which the independents also won. The local CAB then delayed notifying the election results to Han Young which in turn refused to collectively bargain. Indeed, Han Young hired a large number of new workers just in time for the CTM to petition for a third union representation election.

NAO Submission Strategies

One pattern that emerged in NAALC dispute settlement is the cross-border alliance of U.S. organized labor with Mexican labor groups, particularly those that are part of the "forista" movement for independent unions. Another factor of note is the absence of any need to exhaust national administrative remedies, which is required under the NAAEC. Indeed, there are essentially no "standing to complain" requirements under NAALC. The NAOs can investigate and report at their discretion.

One example of creative use of the NAALC involves double barrel submissions. In at least two instances, organized labor and NGOs have filed complaints with both available NAOs. In one case, the U.S. NAO and the Canada NAO received essentially the same submission concerning union organizing and occupational safety at an auto parts plant in Ciudad de los Reyes, Mexico, U.S. Submission No. 9703 and Canada Submission No. 98–1. Each NAO then proceeded to review and report on inadequate Mexican labor law enforcement. Both NAOs recommended Ministerial Consultations.

Likewise, in the Fall of 1998, a coalition of NGOs headed by a Yale Law School group filed submissions with the Canadian and Mexican NAOs alleging ineffective enforcement of U.S. minimum wage and overtime pay laws against employers of foreign nationals, Submission Nos. Canada 98–2 and Mexico 9804. These complaints challenged U.S. Labor Department reporting of suspected immigration violations to the U.S. Immigration and Naturalization Service. They alleged that such practices deter immigrant workers from filing wage and hour complaints under U.S. law. On the same day that the Mexican NAO accepted the submission (Nov. 23, 1998), the U.S. government announced that a Memorandum of Understanding had been signed with the intent of dealing with these issues.

After a flurry of NAO submissions during the first decade of NAALC, the numbers have dropped significantly. It appears that NAALC as a labor law enforcement "remedy" is increasingly perceived to be not worth pursuing.

Pregnancy Discrimination in Mexico

As the number, scope and creativity of the submissions and reports continue to grow, NAALC appears to be more than the toothless tiger many have alleged it to be. For example, the U.S. NAO investigated allegations of widespread state-tolerated sex discrimination against pregnant women in maquiladora plants, Submission No. 9701. This complaint could have resulted (but did not) in a report by an Evaluation Committee of Experts (discussed above).

Human Rights Watch/Americas, the International Labor Rights Fund and the Association Nacional de Abogados Democraticos (the same complainants in the *Pesca Union* case above) filed this submission. They maintained that employers regularly used pregnancy tests to avoid the six weeks paid maternity leave required under Mexican law. The Mexican NAO challenged these complaints as beyond the scope of the NAALC, asserted that Mexican law adequately protects women from gender discrimination, and argued that there is no Mexican law against pre-employment pregnancy screening. The U.S. NAO hired an expert on Mexican labor law and gender issues and held public hearings in Brownsville, Texas at which workers and expert witnesses testified.

The NAO, in its report, reviewed Mexican constitutional and labor law, their enforcement bodies, the Alliance for Equality (the Mexican National Program for Women, 1995–2000), the Mexican Human Rights Commission and relevant international conventions. Post-employment pregnancy discrimination is clearly illegal in Mexico. On pre-employment law, one decision of note that emerged from the investigation was that of the Human Rights Commission for the Federal District which found pre-employment pregnancy screening a violation of Articles 4 and 5 of the Mexican Constitution. Here is the U.S. NAO analysis on point. Note especially its implications concerning the credibility of the Mexican NAO submissions in response to the complaint:

"[T]he Human Rights Commission for the Federal District offers a markedly different interpretation to that of the Mexican NAO on the legality of pre-employment pregnancy screening. The Commission found (1) that the federal agencies it investigated did, in fact, conduct pregnancy screening and, (2) this practice violated Mexico's Constitution.

The Mexican NAO has asserted that the recommendations of the Commission are not binding and do not establish jurisprudence. The enacting legislation for the Commission, however, imposes an obligation on the responding agencies to comply with the recommendations once they accept the findings of the report. Additionally, the Commission was created pursuant to the Mexican Constitution and implemented by Federal law. It is composed of prominent jurists, appointed by the President and confirmed by the legislature, and their recommendation, in this case, was complied with by Federal Government agencies. Further, though the case involved public sector agencies, in its recommendation the Commission made no distinction on the application of the appropriate constitutional guarantees between the public and private sectors.

The position of the Human Rights Commission on the legality of pregnancy screening is markedly different from that expressed by the Mexican NAO. Moreover, the *Alliance for Equality* recognized pregnancy screening as a problem and outlined a plan of action to address such discriminatory practices. That pregnancy screening occurs and is of concern is supported by information from companies conducting business in Mexico, women workers, and the submitters. It also appears that the intrusive nature of the questioning described in the submission goes beyond what is necessary to determine if an applicant for employment is pregnant.

An additional question is raised with regard to the lack of any legal procedure by which to bring cases of pre-employment gender discrimination. The Mexican NAO asserted that the FLL [Federal Labor Law] does not provide for the adjudication of cases involving pre-employment discrimination. CAB officials interviewed by HRW [Human Rights Watch] also indicated that the CABs had no jurisdiction over these cases as they involved issues that occurred prior to the establishment of the employment relationship. The Mexican NAO's position appears to go beyond the question of pre-employment pregnancy screening to also include the lack of a legal procedure for bringing any pre-employment discrimination issue. Since Mexican law clearly prohibits employers from discriminating in hiring for a variety of reasons, the Mexican NAO's response creates a question as to what process exists for bringing such pre-employment discrimination claims."

The NAO report issued in Submission No. 9701 recommended ministerial consultations. These resulted in a U.S.-Mexican agreement on an improved "action plan" to combat pregnancy discrimination in the workplace, though pregnancy discrimination at hiring is said to continue.

§ 4.13   Expanding NAFTA 1994

When Canada and the United States agreed to free trade in 1989, there was no expectation of extension of that agreement to Mexico or any other country. The NAFTA 1994 agreement, on the other hand, specifically anticipated growth by accession. Article 2204 invites applications to join NAFTA by countries or groups of countries without regard to their geographic location or cultural background. This is unlike the European Union which only allows "European" nations to join. The NAFTA Free Trade Commission is authorized to negotiate the terms and conditions of any new memberships. The resulting accession agreement must be approved and ratified by each NAFTA nation. Practically speaking, as in the European Union, this means that current members can veto NAFTA applicants.

In December 1994, at the "Summit of the Americas" in Miami, Canada and Mexico joined the United States formally invited Chile to apply for NAFTA membership. This invitation went nowhere because Congress repeatedly refused to authorize "fast track" negotiations by President Clinton. Fast track negotiations provide assurance to all concerned that Congress would not be able to alter the terms and conditions of Chile's accession. Under fast track, Congress would have to approve or disapprove the agreement by majority vote. Apart from partisan politics, one thorny issue was whether there would be side agreements with Chile on labor and the environment.

Absent U.S. fast track authority, Chile, Canada and Mexico steered different courses. Mexico and Chile renegotiated and expanded their pre-NAFTA free trade agreement. Canada and Chile reached agreement in 1997 on free trade along with side agreements that are similar to NAAEC and NAALC. Chile in 1996 became a free trade associate of MERCOSUR, the Southern Cone common market of Brazil, Argentina, Paraguay and Uruguay. All these free trade commitments flowed partly from want of U.S. fast track authority. They had an impact on trade and investment patterns. Some U.S. companies with Canadian subsidiaries, for example, shifted production and exports to Canada in order to take advantage of Canada-Chile free trade. When fast track authority was finally renewed in 2002, a U.S.-Chile FTA was the first to be signed.

§ 4.14   Quebec and NAFTA

In 1987, the "Meech Lake Accord" was reached. This agreement recognized Quebec as a "distinct society" in Canada. What the practical consequences of this recognition would have been will never be known. Quebec's adherence to the Meech Lake Accord was nullified when Manitoba, New Brunswick and ultimately Newfoundland failed to ratify the Accord. A second set of negotiations led in 1992 to the Charlottetown Accord which also acknowledged Quebec as a distinct society with its French language, unique culture and Civil Law tradition. This time a national referendum was held and its defeat was overwhelming. Quebec, five English-speaking Canadian provinces, and the Yukon territory voted against the Charlottetown Accord.

The Canadian Constitution of 1982 was adopted by an Act of the British Parliament. As such, the Act and the Constitution are thought to bind all Canadian provinces including Quebec. That province, however, has never formally ratified the Constitution of Canada. Since 1982 a series of negotiations have attempted to secure Quebec's ratification, and all have failed miserably.

The failure of these Accords moved Quebec towards separation from Canada. In 1994 and again in 2012, the Parti Quebecois came to power. It held a provincial referendum on separation in 1995. By the narrowest of margins, the people of Quebec rejected separation from Canada. Just exactly what "separation" would have meant was never entirely clear during the debate, perhaps deliberately so.

In 1998, Canada's Supreme Court ruled that Quebec could not "under the Constitution" withdraw unilaterally. To secede, Quebec would need to negotiate a constitutional amendment with the rest of Canada. The rest of Canada would, likewise, be obliged to enter into such negotiations if a "clear majority" of Quebec's voters approved a "clear question" on secession in a referendum. Subsequently, the Canadian Parliament legislated rules which will make it difficult for Quebec to separate, should it ever wish to do so. That prospect now seems more remote, particularly because the Parti Quebecois lost power in 2003, resumed power then lost control again.

If Quebec ever separates from Canada, this will raise fundamental issues about Quebec and NAFTA 1994 or the pending USMCA 2018 Agreement. Would Quebec be forced to negotiate for membership? If so, would English-speaking Canada veto its application? Might Quebec's relationship to Canada continue in some limited manner (such as for defense and international trade purposes) such that NAFTA/USMCA is not an issue at all?

Might Quebec automatically "succeed" to the NAFTA 1994 or USMCA 2018 treaty, thus becoming a member without application? Customary international practice maintains existing treaties when nations sub-divide. This practice was applied to the Czech Republic, Slovakia, and various states of the former Yugoslavia. Thus custom suggests that fears in Quebec about losing NAFTA 1994 or USMCA 2018 benefits are exaggerated.

§ 4.15   Link to Text of CUSFTA 1989

(http://www.worldtradelaw.net/nafta/Cusfta.pdf.download)

§ 4.16   Link to Text of NAFTA 1994

(https://ustr.gov/trade-agreements/free-trade-agreements/
north-american-free-trade-agreement-nafta)

Chapter 5

THE PROLIFERATION OF FREE TRADE AGREEMENTS

Analysis

For more extensive treatment of this material, see R. Folsom, *Principles of International Trade Law.*

§ 5.1   Free Trade Agreements (FTAs) After NAFTA 1994

NAFTA 1994 was a watershed event. In its wake, hundreds of free trade agreements have proliferated around the world, including for example the European Union and South Africa, Canada and Costa Rica, China and Chile, Japan and Singapore. Mexico has dozens of bilateral free trade agreements. The worldwide array of FTAs includes agreements between developed countries (such as between the United States and Australia), agreements between developed and developing countries (such as between Japan and Vietnam) and agreements between developing nations (such as between India and Sri Lanka). Leading nations have gathered together networks of free trade agreements:

(1) **Japan** has "Economic Partnership Agreements" (effectively free trade agreements) with Mexico, Chile, Thailand, the Philippines, Malaysia, Vietnam, Switzerland, India, Indonesia, Brunei, Singapore, Peru, Mongolia and the Association of Southeast Asian Nations (ASEAN), and an extensive FTA with the European Union and is a leader in the TPP-11.

(2) **China** has free trade agreements with its own Hong Kong and Macau Special Administrative Regions, Chile, Pakistan, Costa Rica, Peru, Singapore, New Zealand, Australia, South Korea, Iceland, Maldives and ASEAN.

(3) The **European Union** has numerous free trade agreements, including with Algeria, Chile, Egypt, Iceland, Israel, Jordan, Lebanon, Mexico, Morocco, Norway, Serbia, South Africa, Vietnam, Singapore, Japan, Canada, Tunisia and a customs union agreement with Turkey. See Chapter 3.

(4) The **United States** has 12 bilateral free trade agreements, with Australia (2004), Bahrain (2006), Chile (2004), Colombia (2012), Israel (1985), Jordan (2001), South Korea (KORUS 2012 and 2018), Morocco (2006), Oman (2006), Panama (2012), Peru (2007) and Singapore (2004), plus the NAFTA 1994 and pending USMCA 2018 agreement with Canada and Mexico and the Dominican Republic-Central America Free Trade Agreement (DR-CAFTA 2015) with the Dominican Republic, Guatemala, Honduras, El Salvador, Nicaragua and Costa Rica.

(5) **India** has free trade agreements with ASEAN, Sri Lanka, Malaysia, the Gulf Cooperation Council (GCC), Singapore, Korea, Japan, Afghanistan, Chile, MERCOSUR and leads the 7-nation South Asian FTA.

(6) **South Korea** has free trade agreements with ASEAN, India, Australia, Canada, the United States (KORUS I and II, see Chapter 6), China, Chile, Colombia, EFTA, the European Union (KOREU), Turkey, Vietnam, Peru, and Singapore.

(7) **Canada** has free trade agreements with Korea, the EU (CETA 2017), Chile, Peru, Colombia, Costa Rica, Israel, EFTA, Jordan, Panama, Honduras, and Ukraine, and is a leader in the TPP-11 (below).

(8) **Mexico** has free trade agreements with Chile, Colombia, Venezuela (dormant), Costa Rica, Bolivia,

Nicaragua, Guatemala, Honduras, El Salvador, Peru, Uruguay, the European Union, Japan and Israel. It also has an enhanced Pacific Alliance with Chile, Peru, and Colombia, and participates in the TPP-11 (below).

§ 5.2   U.S. FTAs from NAFTA to President Trump

The United States negotiated a number of free trade agreements post-NAFTA 1994 prior to the presidency of Donald Trump. These included FTAs with Australia, Bahrain, Chile, Colombia, Jordan, South Korea (KORUS), Morocco, Oman, Panama, Peru and Singapore, plus the Dominican Republic-Central America Free Trade Agreement (DR-CAFTA) with the Dominican Republic, Guatemala, Honduras, El Salvador, Nicaragua and Costa Rica.

United States free trade agreements after NAFTA 1994 evolved substantively. Coverage of labor and environmental law enforcement was folded into the trade agreement (compare NAFTA's side agreements) and all remedies are intergovernmental (compare private and NGO "remedies" in the side agreements reviewed in Chapter 4). Coverage of labor law was narrowed to core ILO principles: The rights of association, organization and collective bargaining; acceptable work conditions regarding minimum wages, hours and occupational health and safety; minimum wages for employment of children and elimination of the worst forms of child labor; and a ban on forced or compulsory labor.

Other NAFTA-plus provisions emerged. These are most evident regarding foreign investment and intellectual property. Regarding investor-state claims, for example, post-NAFTA U.S. free trade agreements insert the word "customary" before international law in defining the minimum standard of treatment to which foreign investors are entitled. This insertion tracks the official Interpretation issued in that regard under NAFTA 1994. Further, the contested terms "fair and equitable treatment" and "full protection and security" do not require treatment in addition to or beyond that customary standard, and do not create additional substantive rights. This language was defined for the first time:

> "fair and equitable treatment" includes the obligation not to deny justice in criminal, civil, or administrative adjudicatory proceedings in accordance with the principle of due process embodied in the principal legal systems of the world; and

> "full protection and security" requires each Party to provide the level of police protection required under customary international law.

More significantly perhaps, starting with the U.S.-Chile FTA, these agreements contain an Annex restricting the scope of "indirect expropriation" claims:

> Except in rare circumstances, nondiscriminatory regulatory actions by a Party that are designed and applied to protect legitimate public welfare objectives, such as public health, safety and the environment, do not constitute indirect expropriations.

Hence the potential for succeeding with "regulatory takings" investor-state claims has been reduced. The CAFTA-DR agreement anticipates creating an appellate body of some sort for investor-state arbitration decisions.

Regarding intellectual property, post-NAFTA FTAs moved into the Internet age. Protection of domain names, and adherence to the WIPO Internet treaties, were stipulated. E-commerce and free trade in digital products were embraced, copyrights extended to rights-management (encryption) and anti-circumvention (hacking) technology, protection against web music file sharing enhanced, and potential liability of Internet Service Providers detailed.

Less visibly, pharmaceutical patent owners obtained extensions of their patents to compensate for delays in the approval process, and greater control over their test data, making it harder for generic competition to emerge. They also gained "linkage," meaning local drug regulators must make sure generics are not patent-infringing before their release. In addition, adherence to the Patent Law Treaty (2000) and the Trademark Law Treaty (1994) was agreed. Anti-counterfeiting laws were tightened, particularly regarding destruction of counterfeit goods.

Other changes pushed further along the path of free trade in services and comprehensive customs law administration rules. Antidumping and countervailing duty laws remain applicable, but appeals from administrative determinations are taken in national courts, not binational panels. Except for limited provisions in the Chile-U.S. agreement, business visas drop completely out of U.S. free trade agreements, a NAFTA-minus development.

In sum, the United States generally used its leverage with smaller trade partners in the Americas, the Middle East and Pacific Rim to obtain more preferential treatment and expanded protection for its goods, services, technology and investors. Save for the 2012 KORUS agreement (see Chapter 6), the U.S. gave up relatively little in return, for example a modest increase in agricultural market openings.

§ 5.3   The Trans-Pacific Partnership (TPP-12, 2016) and TPP-11 (2018)

TPP-12

Negotiation of the TPP was led by the United States under President Obama's "pivot to Asia" and a desire to create a "next generation" FTA model. Late in 2015, a Trans-Pacific Partnership (TPP) agreement was reached among the three NAFTA nations plus Peru, Chile, Brunei, Singapore, Malaysia, Vietnam, Japan, Australia and New Zealand (but notably not China). These Pacific Rim partners comprise roughly 40% of world trade. The TPP contained notable developments on freer agricultural and food trade, trade in automobiles and auto parts, bio-similar pharmaceuticals, protection of foreign investment, a self-judging essential security exception, a bar on forced technology transfers as an investor performance requirement, and a procedural tune up of investor-state arbitrations resembling those of CETA 2017 (see Section 5.4).

Coverage of minimum wages and working hours, independent unions, technology protections including a prohibition of data localization requirements, anti-corruption obligations in the public and private sectors, due process and private action rights in competition (antitrust) proceedings, service sector openings, e-commerce, criminal sanctions for counterfeiting and trade secret theft, environmental protection and restraints on subsidies for state-owned enterprises (SOEs) were included in TPP-12. It also contained minimal currency manipulation rules, a much debated topic. South Korea, Taiwan and Indonesia expressed interest in joining the TPP, which clearly resembled a containment strategy relative to China's rising economic power.

As signed by President Obama, TPP ratification in the United States would have been under the fast track procedures, discussed in Section 4.0. President Trump's quick withdrawal from the TPP mooted this possibility. This decision has had broad consequences in the world of international trade. See Chapter 6. Perhaps most significantly, China, Japan, the EU, Canada and others have moved away from U.S. trade policy leadership and pursued other free trade partners.

The TPP-12 agreement in full is linked in Section 5.6. Its Contents, Annexes and Related Instruments are reproduced with links in Section 6.3.

TPP-11

The remaining TPP partners, led by Japan and Canada, signed an altered TPP-11 free trade agreement in 2018 covering roughly

15% of global trade. TPP-11 has been re-named the *Comprehensive and Progressive Trans Pacific Partnership (CPTPP)*. It incorporates most TPP provisions, subject to suspensions and side letters altering TPP-12.

Complete duty free trade in seafood, wine, sheep meat, cotton wool and most manufactured are anticipated under TPP-11. Autos will be subject to a 45% net cost TPP-11 content rule of origin, an advantage expected to favor Japanese exports. Significant intellectual property provisions secured under U.S. pressure, notably eight-year protection for biologic drugs, 70 year copyrights, five-year patent extensions after unreasonable delays in obtaining patents, and eight-year protection of pharmaceutical test data before generic approvals, were dropped.

Canada obtained a cultural industries exclusion, not unlike that of NAFTA 1994. Innovative TPP-12 rules on SOEs were largely retained, including principles of nondiscrimination, adherence to commercial considerations, and limitations on noncommercial governmental assists causing adverse effects and material injury. These rules were diminished for Malaysia in TPP-11. E-commerce trade coverage and protection for digital products drawn from TPP-12 are in TPP-11, but Vietnam has a five-year exception allowing greater control over and taxation of electronic payments along with a national office requirement.

Australia, New Zealand and Canada now have reduced trade barriers on agricultural exports to Japan, which may prove harmful to USA exports of wheat, dairy products, rice and beef. Transparency and anticorruption provisions follow APEC Codes and the UN Convention, with no tax deductions for corrupt payments to public officials. Trader/investor/professional visas resembling those of NAFTA 1994 are created, but in a change from TPP-12 migration of skilled labor is subject to local market need tests.

Labor and the environment are also part of TPP-11, potentially subject to trade sanctions. On labor, International Labor Organization principles dominate much as under TPP-12, though independent labor union rights have been delayed for Vietnam. Vietnam's labor costs are now roughly half those of China, incentivizing investment out of the PRC in the age of Trump tariffs. See Section 1.18. Australia now has reduced trade barriers on agricultural exports to Japan, which may prove adverse to US. exports of wheat, rice and beef. Transparency and anticorruption provisions follow APEC Codes and the UN Convention, with no tax deductions for corrupt payments to public officials.

Trader/investor/professional visas resembling those of NAFTA 1994 are created, but in a change from TPP-12 migration of skilled labor is subject to local market need tests. On the environment, separate agreements concern the Ozone, Ship Pollution, Biodiversity, Emissions, Invasive Species, Endangered Species, and Capture Fisheries. There is a public submission procedure that can trigger review of environmental issues.

Creation of state-to-state dispute settlement (SSDS) procedures is anticipated. Investor-state dispute settlement (ISDS) by arbitration and payment of damages is provided for but, as under TPP-12, use of domestic courts is first required. The right of member states to regulate in the public interest is made clear. But, in a deviation from TPP-12, ISDS arbitrations do not apply to investment contracts requiring government approval and contracts between companies and governments. Australia, which refused ISDS under the U.S.-Australian bilateral FTA, joined in TPP-11 ISDS. However, compulsory ISDS between New Zealand and five other TPP-11 nations is not mandatory.

No TPP-11 ISDS arbitrations may concern tobacco regulation, a ban originating in TPP-12 after R.J Reynolds abused ISDS remedies by purchasing a Hong Kong distributor in order to challenge Australia's plain packaging cigarette laws under a Hong Kong-Australia bilateral investment treaty (BIT) dating from the British era. This maneuver is a good example of foreign investment "treaty shopping". See Section 7.1.

The TPP-11 agreement is linked in Section 5.7. It took effect Feb. 1, 2019 with ratification still pending in Brunei, Malaysia, Chile and Peru. Malaysia has indicated its focus is presently on the RCEP negotiations led by China and ASEAN. See Section 5.5.

§ 5.4   The Canada-EU Comprehensive Economic and Trade Agreement (CETA 2017)

Given the withdrawal of the United States from the TPP, the uncertain future of TTIP negotiations between the U.S. and the EU, and the onslaught of FTAs Britain is expected to seek after BREXIT, one free trade agreement that now stands out as a trade policy model in the developed world is CETA, the Comprehensive Economic and Trade Agreement between Canada and the EU, provisionally operational since 2017.

Upon ratification, 98% of the tariffs on trade between the parties were eliminated, with tariffs on autos phasing out over seven years, subject to 50 to 55% Canadian content rules of origin except for a generous 20% content rule applicable to the first 100,000 Canadian auto exports. Considerable agreement on product standards and testing in the country of export was reached, and Canadian firms get to bid on EU contracts on the same footing as EU companies. Free trade in services is based on a "negative list", a first for the EU, and will rachet up if either party grants broader entry in any other subsequent free trade agreement. Mobility for service providers and business people is extensive, and mutual recognition of professional diplomas and licensing is anticipated.

Both parties have a history of protecting their agricultural and fish/seafood markets. After various transition periods, CETA renders nearly 95% of these markets duty free. There are exceptions for meat quotas on both sides and EU cheese export quotas. The EU obtained greater protection for geographic origin of products (Feta cheese, Parma ham), and increased pharmaceutical patent protection. Healthcare and education, along with cultural industries, are excluded under CETA, and Canada continues to control development of its natural resources.

Foreign investor rights and arbitral protections cover the entire EU, another first. Investor-state dispute settlement procedures, similar to those of NAFTA 1994, have been tuned up in response to numerous criticisms. Third party amicus briefs are allowed, frivolous complaints may be dismissed, biased arbitrators challenged, and there is considerably more transparency. After much debate and controversy, an Investment Dispute Court comprised of EU and Canadian members, will be created to decide investor-state disputes. Canada still gets to apply its Investment Act to EU nationals, subject to the "net benefit" to Canada test, but EU investments under $1.5 billion CDN escape review.

CETA is linked in Section 5.8.

§ 5.5   Pacific Rim Free Trade: ASEAN, RCEP, China, Japan, Russia, South Korea and India

The Pacific Rim has not developed a broad regional free trade agreement, though the China-led RCEP and ASEAN have taken steps in that direction. Other Pacific Rim free trade agreements are noted below.

Southeast Asian Free Trade

Some interesting moves toward developing world free trade and rule-making have been taken by the Association of Southeast Asian Nations (ASEAN). Its problems, failures and successes are representative of developing world attempts at legal and economic integration. ASEAN has its genesis in the 1967 Bangkok Declaration, with common trade rules in various states of growth, implementation and retrenchment. ASEAN has internal tariff preferences, industrial development projects, "complementation schemes," and regional joint ventures.

An important juncture in the integration process is the point in time at which member countries of a regional group accept a supranational mechanism for enforcing the regime's law irrespective of national feelings and domestic law within a member country. In contrast, the ASEAN Secretary-General once remarked that ASEAN's Secretariat was "a postman collecting and distributing letters." The surrender of national sovereignty to ASEAN institutions has been a painfully slow process.

ASEAN was formed in 1967 by Indonesia, Malaysia, the Philippines, Singapore and Thailand. Brunei joined in 1984, Vietnam in 1995. Laos and Myanmar (Burma) joined in 1997, and Cambodia in 1999. Rarely have such culturally, linguistically and geographically diverse nations attempted integration. The Bangkok Declaration establishing ASEAN as a cooperative association is a broadly worded document. Later proposals were made for a formal ASEAN treaty or convention, but were rejected as unnecessary. The Bangkok Declaration sets forth numerous regional, economic, cultural and social goals, including acceleration of economic growth, trade expansion and industrial collaboration.

The Bangkok Declaration establishes several mechanisms, but little supranational legal machinery, to implement its stated goals. An annual ASEAN Meeting of Foreign Ministers is scheduled on a rotational basis among the Member States. Special meetings are held "as required." The Declaration provides for a Standing Committee composed of the Foreign Minister of the state in which the next annual Ministerial Meeting is to be held, and includes the ambassadors of other ASEAN States accredited to that state. The Declaration also provides for "Ad Hoc Committees and Permanent Committees of specialists and officials on specific subjects." Each member state is charged to set up a National Secretariat to administer ASEAN affairs within that Member State and to work with the Ministerial Meeting and the Standing Committee.

There have been relatively infrequent meetings of the ASEAN heads of government. This contrasts with the semiannual European "summits" that have kept that group moving forward along the path of integration. The third ASEAN summit was held in Manila in 1987. This summit produced an agreement for the promotion and protection of investments by ASEAN investors (national and most-favored-nation treatment rights are created), made revisions to the basic ASEAN joint venture agreement, and continued the gradual extension of regional tariff and nontariff trade preferences. Goods already covered by the ASEAN tariff scheme were given a 50 percent margin of preference. New items received a 25 percent preferential margin. The nontariff preferences generally co-opt GATT rules, *e.g.* regarding technical standards and customs valuation.

The fourth ASEAN summit in 1992 committed the parties to the creation of a free trade area within 15 years. Five years were cut from this schedule by agreement in 1994, but operational reality has eluded ASEAN free trade (AFTA). In 2003, a "watershed" date for complete integration in an ASEAN Economic Community targeted 2020. In 2007, this target date was changed to 2015, a reflection of the fear that ASEAN risks being overwhelmed by the powerhouse economies of China, India, Korea and Japan. In 2016, the ASEAN common market was officially launched. Despite the fanfare, its prospects seem limited.

All that said, ASEAN as a group has limited free trade in goods agreements with China, Japan, Korea and India. It is not at all clear to what degree ASEAN exports have increased under these agreements other than by becoming more active suppliers of natural resources and components to these major-economy partners.

APEC

The Asia-Pacific Economic Cooperation (APEC) group has somewhat begun to address the Pacific Rim as a whole. The APEC group is comprised of 21 Asia-Pacific nations including the United States, but excluding India. Late in 1994 the APEC nations targeted free trade and investment for industrial countries by 2010 and developing countries by 2020. Nine industries were selected for initial trade liberalization efforts, which are moving at a snail's pace.

RCEP

As a counterbalance to the U.S.-led APEC and TPP, China has been promoting a Regional Comprehensive Economic Partnership (RCEP) with 16 nations including the 10 ASEAN nations, Australia, India, Japan, New Zealand and South Korea, but not the United States. RCEP was conceived by ASEAN as a way to unify its individual trade treaties with China, India, Japan, South Korea, Australia and New Zealand. Unlike the wide-ranging TPP and TPP-11, RCEP focuses primarily upon tariff reductions on trade in goods and select service sector openings.

Early signs after President Trump withdrew from the TPP-12 suggest China may seek to utilize RCEP to integrate much of the Pacific Basin, minus the United States, with its economy. RCEP is moving forward on a foreign investment pact.

China

China and Japan are clearly rivals for economic leadership of the region. By 2019, China had free trade agreements with its own Hong Kong and Macau Special Administrative Regions, Chile, Pakistan, Costa Rica, Peru, Singapore, New Zealand, Australia, South Korea, Iceland and ASEAN.

The role of China in Pacific Rim integration is critical. China is pushing for dominant influence in the Pacific Rim economic sphere. Hong Kong's return in 1997 and Macau in 1999 moved in this direction. China has cultivated trade and investment relations with Taiwan, South Korea and, to a lesser extent, Japan. China also has free trade deals that overlap with those of Japan (below), notably so with ASEAN and Australia.

Some commentators foresee, as a practical matter, the emergence of a powerful Southern China coastal economic zone embracing Hong Kong, Shenzhen SEZ, Macau, Zhuhai SEZ, and the Chinese province of Guangdong. The Pearl River delta area already serves as the world's leading electronics center. China's massive Belt and Road Initiative (BRI), while not a free trade agreement, is promoting Chinese alliances and economic interests across Eurasia and in Africa.

Japan

One provocative trade question is the future of Japan. It is not in the interest of any nation that Japan should feel economically isolated or threatened. To some degree, trade in East Asia is growing along lines that follow Japanese investment and economic aid decisions. By 2019, Japan had "Economic Partnership Agreements" (effectively free trade in goods agreements) with Mexico, Chile, Thailand, the Philippines, Malaysia, Vietnam, Switzerland, India, Indonesia, Brunei, Singapore, Peru, Mongolia and the Association of Southeast Asian Nations (ASEAN). These agreements essentially encircle China.

After refusing to negotiate a bilateral free trade agreement with President Trump, Japan in 2018 signed a major economic partnership agreement with the EU summarized immediately below. Japan also led the creation of TPP-11 (see Section 5.3).

Japan-EU Economic Partnership Agreement (2018)

Like CETA (above), the Japan-EU Economic Partnership Agreement of 2018 is a major example of free trade alternatives to America First trade policy. The agreement anticipates nearly full tariff removals on goods, notably reducing the 10% EU auto tariff to zero over 7 years. Honda, which has a large plant in the UK, announced in 2019 will close production in favor exporting from Japan under its new free trade agreement with the EU. The EU expects to export more agricultural, textile, chemicals, wood products and leather goods to Japan. Tariff rate quota limitations will protect Japan from EU wheat, dairy, pork, sugar, soft cheese and beef. Free trade will not apply to rice, Japan's "sacred" food sector, which is protected by a 777% tariff.

Many Japanese nontariff trade barriers (NTBs) will be clarified and relaxed, including those related motor vehicles, medical devices, textile labeling, and beer. In general, technical barriers to trade will be governed by international standards.

Trade in services is expanded beyond WTO commitments, notably in the following fields: Postal and courier services, telecommunications, finance, and international maritime transport. Temporary business and professional visas going beyond anything the EU had previously agreed to are adopted.

State-owned enterprises of either country will receive national treatment when buying or selling on commercial markets. Mutual procurement opportunities are expanded, especially in allowing EU firms to bid on tenders of 54 "core cities" in Japan.

There are obligations to recognize of the eight "fundamental" ILO Conventions, duty free electronic transmissions, and a bar on forced disclosure of source codes. Each side has acknowledged the "adequacy" of the other's data privacy regimes, a priority for the EU operating under its 2018 General Data Protection Regulation. Geographical indicators from Kobe beef to Feta cheese are protected.

In a first for a FTA, the parties reaffirmed their commitment to the Paris Accord on Climate Change. Various provisions promote sustainable development and corporate social responsibility. There is a specific chapter on corporate governance derived from G20/OECD Principles. The EU ban on imports of whale products is retained in the face of continued Japanese whaling practices. General state-to-state dispute settlement procedures are established.

Foreign investment rules and related dispute settlement are being negotiated separately. These are particularly sensitive to Japan, which has never had to defend itself in investor-state arbitration proceedings.

The Japan-EU Economic Partnership Agreement of 2018 took effect in 2019 and is linked in Section 5.9.

Trump and Japan

Japan has run a major trade surplus with the United States for decades, lowered somewhat by a U.S. trade surplus in services to a net deficit of $56 billion in 2017. Needless to say, this deficit collides with President Trump's America First trade policies. The Japanese, post President Trump's withdrawal from the TPP, rapidly undertook an extensive FTA with the European Union and led the way to the TPP-11 agreement. See Section 5.3. They also completed a major FTA with the EU which took effect early in 2019 (above).

Since the arrival of President Trump, Japan has generally declined or stalled negotiations on a bilateral FTA with the United States. This refusal helps explain why Japan did not receive a temporary exemption from the Trump national security steel and aluminum tariffs (see Section 1.17). That said, the threat of U.S. national security tariffs on autos generated greater trade discussions in 2019.

Russia

By 2019, Russia had an FTA with eight formerly Soviet satellite countries under the Commonwealth of Independent States (CISFTA). The CISFTA members are Russia, Ukraine, Moldova, Tajikistan, Armenia, Kazakhstan, Kyrgyzstan and Uzbekistan, with Ukraine suspended after Russian annexation of Crimea and occupation of parts of eastern Ukraine. Since 2015, Russia, Kazakhstan, Belarus, Armenia and Kyrgyzstan have joined together in the Eurasian Economic Union (EAEU), strategically linking China's BRI land bridge program with Europe. The EAEU has a FTA with Vietnam and is exploring others.

Russia, with considerable Siberian energy development finance from China, is busy developing a Northern Sea Route to exploit reduced artic ice. This strategic, cost-saving initiative connects China/Japan/Korea with Europe.

India

By 2019, India had free trade agreements with ASEAN, Sri Lanka, Malaysia, the Gulf Cooperation Council (GCC), Singapore, Korea, Japan, Afghanistan, Chile, and led the seven-nation South Asian FTA. India's major trade concern is being surrounded by China, notably via China's BRI links with Bangladesh, Nepal, Pakistan, the Maldives and Sri Lanka.

South Korea

By 2019, hustling Korea had free trade agreements with ASEAN, India, Australia, Canada, the United States (KORUS I and II), China, Chile, Colombia, EFTA, the European Union (KOREU), Turkey, Vietnam, Peru, and Singapore. At President Trump's insistence, the KORUS agreement was re-negotiated via a Protocol in 2018. See Section 6.6.

Summary Perspective

As America retreats from free trade, witness the FTAA, TPP-12, TTIP and NAFTA 1994, the world is not standing by. Leading Pacific Rim countries have stepped forward into the gap.

§ 5.6   Link to Trans Pacific Partnership (TPP-12 2016)

(https://ustr.gov/trade-agreements/free-trade-agreements/ trans-pacific-partnership/tpp-full-text)

§ 5.7   Link to Comprehensive and Progressive Trans-Pacific Partnership (TPP-11 2018)

(https://international.gc.ca/trade-commerce/trade- agreements-accords-commerciaux/agr-acc/cptpp-ptpgp/text- texte/cptpp-ptpgp.aspx?lang=eng)

§ 5.8   Link to Canada-EU Comprehensive Economic and Trade Agreement (CETA 2017)

(https://www.international.gc.ca/trade-commerce/trade- agreements-accords-commerciaux/agr-acc/ceta-aecg/text- texte/toc-tdm.aspx?lang=eng)

§ 5.9   Link to Japan-EU Economic Partnership Agreement (2018)

(http://trade.ec.europa.eu/doclib/docs/2018/august/tradoc_157 228.pdf)

Chapter 6

TRUMP AND FREE TRADE

Analysis

A consolidated, edited Text of the pending USMCA 2018 Agreement is Appended to this book.

§ 6.1   America First Trade Policy

For the first time in many years, international trade was a major issue in a U.S. Presidential election. In 2016, Donald J. Trump made it so. He campaigned and tweeted against trade deficits, currency manipulation, NAFTA 1994 as "the worst trade deal ever", and the signed but not ratified twelve-nation (minus China) Trans-Pacific Partnership (TPP). Rallying the oft-forgotten losers under U.S. trade policy, he swept into office in 2017 as the world took a deep breath and wondered what might come.

Major Trump administration trade initiatives have been undertaken in areas governed by WTO agreements. These include CVD tariffs against Canadian lumber, global safeguard tariffs on solar panels and clothes washers, and national security tariffs on steel and aluminum. See Section 1.17. Completely unilateral U.S. Section 301 tariffs have been applied to Chinese goods amidst a tech-driven trade war. See Section 1.18. All have been pursued under an America First mantra that undermines the WTO and has encouraged traditional U.S. trade partners to pursue free trade alternatives not involving the USA. See Section 1.19 and Chapter 5.

President Trump criticized and forced a limited renegotiation by Protocol of KORUS I, the U.S.-Korea 2012 bilateral Free Trade Agreement (see Section 6.6). With lots of bluster, the Trump administration spent over a year re-negotiating NAFTA 1994 with Canada and Mexico, two countries highly dependent on U.S. trade relations. The pending USMCA Agreement of 2018, reviewed in Section 6.8, is no doubt a model the President would like to utilize with Japan and the EU, two less dependent trade partners.

Withdrawal from the Trans-Pacific Partnership (TPP-12)

Negotiation of the Trans-Pacific Partnership (TPP) was led by the United States under President Obama's "pivot to Asia" and a desire to create a "next generation" FTA model. Late in 2015, a Trans-Pacific Partnership (TPP-12) agreement was reached among the three NAFTA nations plus Peru, Chile, Brunei, Singapore, Malaysia, Vietnam, Japan, Australia and New Zealand (but notably not China). These Pacific Rim partners comprise roughly 40% of world trade. South Korea, Taiwan and Indonesia expressed interest in joining the TPP, which clearly resembled a containment strategy relative to China's rising economic power.

As its Table of Contents (see Section 6.3) reveals, TPP-12 contained notable developments on freer agricultural and food trade, trade in automobiles and auto parts, bio-similar pharmaceuticals, protection of foreign investment, a self-judging essential security exception, a bar on forced technology transfers as an investor performance requirement, and a procedural tune up of investor-state arbitrations.

Coverage of minimum wages and working hours, independent unions, technology protections including a prohibition of data localization requirements, anti-corruption obligations in the public and private sectors, due process and private action rights in competition (antitrust) proceedings, service sector openings, e-commerce, criminal sanctions for counterfeiting and trade secret theft, environmental protection and restraints on subsidies for state-owned enterprises (SOEs) were included in TPP-12. It also contained minimal currency manipulation rules, a much debated topic.

For more on the content of TPP-12, see Section 5.3.

Trump and TPP-12

President Trump quickly withdrew from the multilateral Trans Pacific Partnership (TPP), essentially making a gift of trade leadership in Asia to China. President Xi Xinping at Davos accepted this gift, noting ongoing negotiations for its competing trade alliance: The Regional Cooperation and Economic Partnership (RCEP) comprised of the ASEAN states, South Korea, Japan, China and India, but not the United States. See Section 5.5.

As signed by President Obama, TPP ratification in the United States would have been under the fast track procedures, discussed in Chapter 4. President Trump's quick withdrawal from the TPP mooted this possibility. Note, however, that the U.S. already had bilateral FTAs, clearly a Trump preference in order to maximize bargaining power, with four of the 12 TPP partners (Chile, Peru, Singapore and Australia), plus free trade relations with Mexico and Canada under NAFTA 1994. The Trump Administration's dislike of multilateral trade agreements is reflected in the insightful words of Secretary of Commerce Wilbur Ross:

> "Say you're negotiating with 12 different countries. You go to the first one and you want some concession from them. They say, "Yes, we'll give you that concession, but we want something back." So that takes a little nick out of us. Then you go to the next country and you negotiate with them, they take a little nick. You keep doing that 12 times, you get a lot of nicks, and what happens is the other countries get the benefit of things they didn't even ask for because you had to give them to someone else. So I think that's a fundamental concern."

U. S. withdrawal from TPP has had broad consequences in the world of international trade. Perhaps most significantly, China, Japan, the EU, Canada and others have moved away from U.S. trade policy leadership and have pursued free trade partners elsewhere around the globe. See Chapters 3 and 5.

The full TPP-12 agreement is linked in Section 6.4 and its Contents, Annexes and Related Instruments are linked in Section 6.3.

Trump and TPP-11

The remaining TPP partners, led notably by Japan and Canada, signed an altered TPP-11 free trade agreement in 2018 covering roughly 15% of global trade. TPP-11 has been re-named the Comprehensive and Progressive Trans Pacific Partnership (CPTPP). This agreement borrows substantially from TPP-12, minus provisions closely associated with the United States, and subject to a variety of country-specific alterations. See Section 5.3 for TPP-11 details.

The TPP-11 took effect Feb. 1, 2019 with ratification still pending in Chile, Peru, Brunei and Malaysia. Its full text is linked in

Section 6.5. South Korea, Taiwan, Thailand, Colombia and even the United Kingdom have expressed interest in joining TPP-11.

§ 6.2 Linked Contents, Annexes and Related Instruments of TPP-12 (2016)

Preamble

1. **Initial Provisions and General definitions** | Chapter Summary

2. **National Treatment and Market Access** | Chapter Summary

   o Annex 2-D: Tariff Commitments

   - Australia General Notes to Tariff Schedule
   - Australia Tariff Elimination Schedule
   - Brunei General Notes to Tariff Schedule
   - Brunei Tariff Elimination Schedule
   - Canada General Notes to Tariff Schedule
   - Canada Tariff Elimination Schedule
   - Canada Appendix A Tariff Rate Quotas
   - Canada Appendix D Appendix between Japan and the United States on Motor Vehicle Trade
   - Chile General Notes to Tariff Schedule
   - Chile Tariff Elimination Schedule
   - Japan General Notes to Tariff Schedule
   - Japan Tariff Elimination Schedule
   - Japan Appendix A Tariff Rate Quotas
   - Japan Appendix B-1 Agricultural Safeguard Measures
   - Japan Appendix B-2 Forest Good Safeguard Measure
   - Japan Appendix C Tariff-Differentials
   - Japan Appendix D-1 Appendix between Japan and the United States on Motor Vehicle Trade
   - Japan Appendix D-2 Appendix between Japan and Canada on Motor Vehicle Trade

- Malaysia General Notes to Tariff-Schedule
- Malaysia Tariff Elimination-Schedule
- Malaysia Appendix A Tariff Rate Quotas
- Mexico General Notes to Tariff Schedule
- Mexico Tariff Elimination Schedule
- Mexico Appendix A-1 Tariff Rate Quotas and Appendix A-2 Country Specific Allocation for Sugar of Mexico
- Mexico Appendix C Tariff Differentials
- New Zealand General Notes to Tariff Schedule
- New Zealand Tariff Elimination Schedule
- Peru General Notes to Tariff-Schedule
- Peru Tariff Elimination Schedule
- Singapore General Notes to Tariff Schedule
- Singapore Tariff Elimination Schedule
- US General Notes to Tariff Schedule
- US Tariff Elimination-Schedule
- US Appendix A Tariff Rate Quotas
- US Appendix B Agricultural Safeguard Measures
- US Appendix C Tariff Differentials
- US Appendix D Appendix between Japan and the United States on Motor Vehicle Trade
- US Appendix E Earned Import Allowance Program
- Viet-Nam General Notes to Tariff Schedule
- Viet-Nam Tariff Elimination Schedule
- Viet-Nam Appendix A Tariff Rate Quotas

3. **Rules of Origin and Origin Procedures** | Chapter Summary
   o   Annex 3-D: Product Specific Rules
   o   Annex 3-D: Appendix 1—Automotive

4. **Textiles and Apparel** | Chapter Summary
   o   Annex 4-A: Textiles Product Specific Rule

      o   Annex 4-A Appendix 1: Short Supply List

5. **Customs Administration and Trade Facilitation** | Chapter Summary

6. **Trade Remedies** | Chapter Summary

7. **Sanitary and Phytosanitary Measures** | Chapter Summary

8. **Technical Barriers to Trade** | Chapter Summary

9. **Investment** | Chapter Summary

10. **Cross Border Trade in Services** | Chapter Summary

11. **Financial Services** | Chapter Summary

12. **Temporary Entry for Business Persons** | Chapter Summary

      o   Annex 12-A: Temporary Entry for Business Persons

- Australia
- Brunei
- Canada
- Chile
- Japan
- Malaysia
- Mexico
- New Zealand
- Peru
- Singapore
- Viet Nam

13. **Telecommunications** | Chapter Summary

14. **Electronic Commerce** | Chapter Summary

15. **Government Procurement** | Chapter Summary

      o   Annex 15-A: Government Procurement

- Australia
- Brunei
- Canada
- Chile
- Japan

- Malaysia
- Mexico
- New Zealand
- Peru
- Singapore
- United States
- Viet Nam

16. **Competition** | Chapter Summary

17. **State-Owned Enterprises** | Chapter Summary

18. **Intellectual Property** | Chapter Summary

19. **Labour** | Chapter Summary
    o US-BN Labour Consistency Plan
    o US-MY Labour Consistency Plan
    o US-VN Plan for Enhancement of Trade and Labour Relations

20. **Environment** | Chapter Summary

21. **Cooperation and Capacity Building** | Chapter Summary

22. **Competitiveness and Business Facilitation** | Chapter Summary

23. **Development** | Chapter Summary

24. **Small and Medium-Sized Enterprises** | Chapter Summary

25. **Regulatory Coherence** | Chapter Summary

26. **Transparency and Anti-Corruption** | Chapter Summary

27. **Administrative and Institutional Provisions** | Chapter Summary

28. **Dispute Settlement** | Chapter Summary

29. **Exceptions** | Chapter Summary

30. **Final Provisions** | Chapter Summary

Annexes

- Annex I: Non-Conforming Measures
  o Consolidated Formatting Note
  o Australia
  o Brunei

- o   Canada
- o   Chile
- o   Japan
- o   Malaysia
- o   Mexico
- o   New Zealand
- o   Peru
- o   Singapore
- o   United States
- o   Viet Nam
- •   Annex II: Non-Conforming Measures
- o   Consolidated Formatting Note
- o   Australia
- o   Brunei
- o   Canada
- o   Chile
- o   Japan
- o   Malaysia
- o   Mexico
- o   New Zealand
- o   Peru
- o   Singapore
- o   United States
- o   Viet Nam
- •   Annex III: Financial Services
- o   Consolidated Formatting Note
- o   Australia
- o   Brunei
- o   Canada
- o   Chile
- o   Japan
- o   Malaysia

- o   Mexico
- o   New Zealand
- o   Peru
- o   Singapore
- o   United States
- o   Viet Nam
- • Annex IV: State-Owned Enterprise
- o   Australia
- o   Brunei
- o   Canada
- o   Chile
- o   Malaysia
- o   Mexico
- o   New Zealand
- o   Peru
- o   United States
- o   Viet Nam

Related Instruments

- • **Market Access Related**
- o   US-AU Letter Exchange re Recognition of FTA TRQs in TPP
- o   US-AU Letter Exchange on Sugar Review
- o   US-CA Letter Exchange on Agricultural Transparency
- o   US-CL Letter Exchange on Distinctive Products
- o   US-CL Letter Exchange regarding Recognition of FTA TRQs in TPP
- o   US-JP Letter Exchange on Distinctive Products
- o   JP to US Letter on Safety Regulations for Motor Vehicles
- o   US-JP Letter Exchange on Operation of SBS Mechanism
- o   US-JP Letter Exchange on Operation of Whey Protein Concentrate Safeguard

- o   US-JP Letter Exchange regarding Standards of Fill

- o   US-JP Letters related to the PHP

- o   US-MY Letter Exchange on Auto Imports

- o   US-MY Letter Exchange on Distinctive Products

- o   US-NZ Letter Exchange on Distinctive Products

- o   US-PE Letter Exchange on Distinctive Products

- o   US-PE Letter Exchange on TRQs and Safeguards

- o   US-VN Letter Exchange on Distinctive Products of US

- o   US-VN Letter Exchange on Distinctive Products of VN

- **Textiles and Apparel Related**

  - o   US-BN Letter Exchange on Textiles and Apparel

  - o   US-MY Letter Exchange on Registered Textile and Apparel Enterprises

  - o   US-SG Exchange on Letters on Textiles and US-SG FTA

  - o   US-VN Letter Exchange on Registered Textile and Apparel Enterprises

- **Sanitary and Phytosanitary Related**

  - o   US-CL SPS Letter Exchange regarding Salmonid Eggs

  - o   US-CA Letter Exchange on Milk Equivalence

  - o   US-VN Letter Exchange on Catfish

  - o   US-VN Letter Exchange on Offals

- **Intellectual Property Related**

  - o   US-AU Letter Exchange on Selected IP Provisions

  - o   US-AU Letter Exchange on Article 17.9.7(b) of AUSFTA

  - o   US-CA Letter Exchange on IP Border Enforcement

  - o   US-CL Letter Exchange re Geographical Indications

- o US-CL Letter Exchange re Article 17.10.2 of US Chile FTA

- o US-JP Letter Exchange re Copyright Term

- o US-MY Letter Exchange re Articles 18.41 .50 and .52

- o US-MY Letter Exchange re Geographical Indications

- o US-MX Letter Exchange re Geographical Indications

- o US-MX Letter Exchange re Tequila and Mezcal

- o US-PE Letter Exchange re Article 16.14.3 of US-Peru TPA

- o US-VN Letter Exchange on Biologics

- o US-VN Letter Exchange re Geographical Indications

- **Services/Financial Services/E-Commerce**

  - o US-CL Letter Exchange regarding Express Delivery Services

  - o US-VN Letter Exchange on Pharmaceutical Distribution

  - o US-VN Letter Exchange regarding Electronic Payment Services

  - o US-AU Letter Exchange on Privacy

- **Temporary Entry**

  - o US-JP Letter Exchange re Temporary Entry

- **Government Procurement**

  - o US-AU Letter Exchange on AUSFTA GP Thresholds

  - o US-CA Letter Exchange re GP Thresholds

  - o Letter Exchange US-CA-MX re GP Procedures

- **SOEs**

  - o US-SG Letter Exchange on SOE Transparency

- **Environment**

  - o US-CL Understanding regarding Fisheries Subsidies and Natural Disasters

- o US-MY Exchange of Letters on Committee to Coordinate Implementation of Environment Chapters

- o US-PE Understanding regarding Biodiversity and Traditional Knowledge

- o US-PE Understanding regarding Conservation and Trade

- **Annex on Transparency and Procedural Fairness for Pharmaceutical Products and Medical Devices**

  - o US-AU Letter Exchange on Transparency and Procedural Fairness for Pharmaceuticals and Medical Devices

  - o US-JP Transparency and Procedural Fairness for Pharmaceuticals and Medical Devices

  - o US-PE Understanding re Transparency and Procedural Fairness for Pharmaceuticals and Medical Devices

US-Japan Bilateral Outcomes

- **US-Japan Motor Vehicle Trade Non-Tariff Measures** | Summary

  - o US-JP Letter Exchange on Certain Auto NTMs

  - o JP to US Letter on Motor Vehicle Distribution Survey

- **Japan Parallel Negotiations on Non-Tariff Measures** | Summary

  - o US-JP Letter Exchange on Non-Tariff Measures

§ 6.3 Link to Trans Pacific Partnership (TPP-12) 2016

(https://ustr.gov/trade-agreements/free-trade-agreements/ trans-pacific-partnership/tpp-full-text)

§ 6.4 Link to Comprehensive and Progressive Trans-Pacific Partnership (TPP-11) 2018

(https://international.gc.ca/trade-commerce/trade- agreements-accords-commerciaux/agr-acc/cptpp-ptpgp/text- texte/cptpp-ptpgp.aspx?lang=eng)

§ 6.5   KORUS Re-Negotiated (2018)

Trump and KORUS I and II

In August of 2017, the Trump Administration commenced re-negotiation of the 2012 U.S.-South Korea free trade agreement (KORUS I), expressing concerns about the modest U.S. trade deficit in goods with Korea, while ignoring a sizeable trade surplus in services for a net deficit in 2017 of about $10 billion. Several major Korean firms announced plans to invest in the United States, and Korea pulled its WTO Appellate Body member back home to negotiate with the Trump Administration. These negotiations were notably NOT undertaken under U.S. fast track trade promotion procedures (see Section 4.0). They were held instead via the Joint Committee process under KORUS I, thereby avoiding Congressional review and approval.

Then North Korea shot a missile over Japan and exploded a thermonuclear bomb. The United States, at a hefty price, promised South Korea major defense armaments and reduced but did not remove pressure to re-negotiate the KORUS I agreement.

The arrival of U.S. defensive radar and missile systems in South Korea, and the promise of more to come, caused China to organize a painful boycott of South Korean goods and tourism. South Korea and China have a free trade in goods agreement, and a number of prominent Korean companies (Lotte supermarkets, KIA cars) have production and distribution centers in the PRC. Hyundai sales in China dropped 34%. In 2018, having made its point, China lifted the boycott, but its impact lingers.

KORUS I re-negotiations were ongoing at U.S. forceful insistence, but moving slowly in early 2018. The main issues were Korean auto exports to the USA under a 55% KORUS I origin rule, resulting in roughly a $15 billion auto trade surplus. Korea's exports were in no way matched by U.S. auto exports, despite a generous Korean 25,000 entry waiver of its strict car safety and pollution rules. U.S. exports of agricultural, meat and food products to Korea were also contentious on both sides. The Trump Administration's unilateral 25% steel tariffs of 2018 threatened to hurt sizeable Korean exports, and were hard to explain to such a steadfast U.S. ally.

In the afterglow of the 2018 Winter Olympics held in South Korea, President Trump and North Korea's Kim Jong Un agreed to meet. KORUS I re-negotiations accelerated. Late in March the two sides announced a deal. The U.S. got a meaningless doubling to 50,000 cars of its quota per automaker to enter Korea without meeting local safety and environmental standards. The U.S., which had promised to lift in 2021 its 25% tariff on Korean pick-up trucks and cargo vans, none ever having been shipped to the USA, obtained an extension to 2041.

Korea got a permanent exemption from the 25% Trump steel tariffs (below), subject to a quota limit of 70% of the average Korean steel exports to the USA in 2015–2017. Korea is expected to easily make up for these lost exports in other markets, but pay attention to trade diversion restraints by other "collateral damage" countries like the EU, and WTO challenges to this bilateral voluntary export restraint (VER). The Korean steel industry parcels out the quotas among 54 categories of producers, some of which maxed out almost immediately in 2018.

Both sides agreed not to revise existing, contentious KORUS I agricultural trade rules. Increased transparency revisions on Korean customs procedures, and relaxed Korean pharmaceutical access and pricing rules, were also agreed.

All in all, a largely cosmetic, mutually face-saving revision of KORUS I was achieved. Call it KORUS II, but President Trump held back signing this "strong card" pending talks with North Korea. Furthermore, the President's threat to globally impose 25% "national security" tariffs on autos and auto parts places Korea's duty free access to the U.S. market at risk. See Section 6.1.

KORUS 2012 and the 2018 U.S.-Korea Protocol amending it are linked in Section 6.7. The Protocol took effect Jan. 1, 2019.

§ 6.6   Links to KORUS I and II

(https://ustr.gov/trade-agreements/free-trade-agreements/ korus-fta) amended by a U.S. Korea 2018 Protocol

(https://ustr.gov/trade-agreements/free-trade-agreements/ korus-fta/september-2018-korus-amendment-and- modification)

§ 6.7   NAFTA Re-Negotiated: The 2018 USMCA Agreement

The Negotiations

Early in 2017, the Trump administration notified Congress of its intent to re-negotiate NAFTA 1994 with Canada and Mexico under "fast track" as authorized in the Trade Promotion Authority Act of 2015. President Trump's prior tweets called NAFTA 1994 the "worst trade deal ever". He threatened to withdraw from NAFTA or impose high tariffs on Mexican goods in light of that country's sizeable trade surplus ($69 billion in 2017) in goods and services with the United

States. The U.S. states most involved in NAFTA 1994 trade were Texas, North Dakota, Michigan, Indiana, Kentucky and Vermont. They let their views be known vociferously in the re-negotiations.

Including merchandise and services, the U.S. actually had a small trade surplus with Canada in 2017, but President Trump continued to deny that reality, focusing only on a small goods deficit. This approach is about 100 years out of date: Some 150 million U.S. private sector jobs are in the services/technology sector, with tourism and intellectual property rights payments heading the list, followed by finance, insurance, telecommunications, information technology and professional services. U.S. jobs in manufacturing are dwarfed by comparison.

On balance, the initial Trump Administration NAFTA 1994 re-negotiation notice was remarkably moderate, as were the subsequently released U.S. negotiating objectives, which partly borrowed from the Trans-Pacific Partnership (TPP) agreement. NAFTA 1994 it seemed at first blush would only undergo a tune-up.

Many attribute this outcome to lobbying by major U.S. exporters to Mexico, especially farm products. Under NAFTA 1994, Mexico has become the largest foreign market for U.S. corn, dairy products, poultry and wheat. Manufacturers, fearing disruption and added costs, were quick to point out the high degree of supply chain integration among the NAFTA countries. Some components cross NAFTA borders repeatedly before a final product is finished.

When negotiations commenced in August 2017, the fundamental relationships between the three NAFTA partners had changed from 1994. Mexico and Canada were still heavily dependent on the U.S. market for their exports, and for technology and foreign investment capital. The United States, however, had become noticeably less dependent on foreign oil imports, but hardly self-sufficient. Mexico, contrary to its strong reservation of oil and gas rights in NAFTA 1994, at its own initiative had amended its Constitution and significantly opened oil and gas exploration to foreign investors. Meanwhile, Canada was still having trouble accepting the reality that satellite and Internet broadcasts, and WTO remedies, had rendered its cultural industries exclusion almost meaningless. See Section 4.1.

By 2017, principally as a result of WTO negotiations, Mexico's average MFN tariff on manufactured goods had fallen to approximately 8%, Canada to 4% and the U.S. to 3.5%. All three countries maintained generally higher tariffs on agricultural goods, and selectively higher tariffs on particular manufactured goods such as the 25% U.S. tariff on pick-up trucks, a legacy from a 1960s "chicken war" with Europe.

These national tariffs were, of course, not applicable to "North American goods", those goods meeting the NAFTA 1994 rules of origin. See Section 4.3. But tightening up the existing 62.5% auto rules of origin quickly became a focus in the U.S. approach to re-negotiation. The U.S. sought an 85% North American auto content rule, *plus* a 50% U.S. content rule. Tighter auto rules of origin, however, could cause manufacturers to move elsewhere, then pay U.S. tariffs (2.5% for passenger autos) upon entry. The U.S. also wished to re-think the rules on NAFTA trade remedies, such as safeguards, that could result in tariffs on Mexican and Canadian goods. Removal of the waiver for Buy American preferences enjoyed by Canada and Mexico under NAFTA also surfaced as a goal, along with a "balancing" of procurement opportunities as between the U.S. and Mexico and Canada combined. Stronger labor and environmental provisions than offered through the NAFTA side agreements were also on the negotiating table, with relatively little conflict.

So too, the U.S. sought to open up its neighbors' duty free rules for cross-border online sales, think Amazon. Canada started with an unbelievably low online tariff exemption of only $20 CDN (compared to $200 per day CDN for shopping in the USA and returning to Canada with the goods). Mexico had $50 US online limit, while United States buyers could import online up to $800 in duty free goods from either Canada or Mexico.

Other items on the U.S. agenda included improved protection of intellectual property rights, facilitation of cross-border data flows and a ban on forced localization of computer data on servers, opposition to Canadian dairy "supply management" restraints, better customs clearance procedures, tariffs on seasonal agricultural goods (berries for example), expanded coverage of state-owned enterprises, vague references to policing currency manipulation, and dispute settlement.

The U.S. focused particularly on elimination of NAFTA 1994 binational panel arbitration of dumping and subsidy disputes, which would return appeals to national courts. Arguing that it promoted outsourcing, the United States also wanted to make NAFTA 1994's controversial investor-state arbitration of disputes optional, forcing such disputes back into national courts or state-to-state negotiations.

Mexico and Canada also came to the table seeking change. Mexico, for example, emphasized its desire for coverage of security, narcotics and migration issues. Little attention was given to investor/trader/professional visas created under NAFTA 1994, but many talented Canadians and Mexicans working lawfully in the United States put their immigration lawyers on speed dial.

Canada reiterated that continued binational panel arbitration of trade remedy disputes could again be a deal-breaker, noting it had been involved in over 70 such proceedings since 1994, and that a previous Prime Minister had walked out of negotiations with the United States in order to obtain this unique appeal system. Canada also indicated it would like to see reduced application of Buy American procurement rules and a more "progressive" trade deal like that it achieved in TPP-11. See Chapter 5.

The NAFTA re-negotiations that commenced in August of 2017 were pushed by critical deadlines: The elections for the U.S. House of Representatives (November 2018) and the election of a new President of Mexico (July 2018). Nevertheless, negotiations proceeded at a slow pace, and deadlines for their conclusion were repeatedly extended. In the end the United States employed a divide and conquer strategy by first agreeing to a deal with Mexico, then inviting Canada to join in, which it did.

After a thorough "legal scrub", the leaders of Canada, Mexico and the United States signed a finalized NAFTA re-negotiated agreement (USMCA) on November 30, 2018, one day before Andres Manuel Lopez Obrador took office as President of Mexico. He had won in a landslide, mostly keeping quiet about his views on the agreement re-negotiated by his predecessor, President Pena Nieto.

The 2018 USMCA Agreement

The first issue was what to call the new trilateral agreement. The Trump administration, wishing to disassociate from the NAFTA title, prefers the name "United States-Mexico-Canada" (USMCA) Agreement. Canada prefers New NAFTA and/or CUSMA in English or ACEUM in French. Mexico calls it T-MEC in Spanish. For purposes of this book, I primarily call the NAFTA Re-Negotiated trilateral agreement USMCA 2018.

The 2018 agreement incorporates a mixture of provisions from CUSTA 1989, NAFTA 1994, the 2016 Trans-Pacific Partnership (TPP-12) agreement signed by President Obama but denied ratification by President Trump, and entirely new or revised NAFTA provisions. Nothing in USMCA alters the Trump administration's prior "national security" tariffs on U.S. steel and aluminum imports from Canada and Mexico. Both countries retaliated with "rebalancing tariffs" against a range of U.S. exports roughly approximating their trade losses on steel and aluminum. See Section 1.17. The Trump administration, following its KORUS II formula, is pushing Mexico and Canada to agree to export quotas on steel and aluminum.

Linked USMCA Contents, Annexes and Side Letters are reproduced in Section 6.9 and a consolidated, edited version of the pending USMCA 2018 Agreement is reproduced as an Appendix to this book.

USMCA Provisions with Little Change from NAFTA 1994

Intergovernmental Dispute Settlement. The Chapter 20 government dispute settlement provisions of NAFTA 1994, including the option to take most disputes to the WTO, was largely replicated in USMCA Chapter 31. As under NAFTA 1994, each side can block use of the Chapter 31 process by refusing to name panelists, which is not possible in WTO dispute settlement. Chapter 31 is particularly critical to the 2018 USMCA labor and environment provisions, along with other topics not covered by the WTO package of agreements. See Chapter 1.

Trade Remedy (AD and CVD) Dispute Settlement. Replacement of national court review of AD and CVD determinations with binational panels was retained in USMCA Chapter 10 at the strident insistence of Canada. No relief was provided for existing U.S. "national security" tariffs on steel and aluminum, and possibly in the future autos. Canada is notably the largest source of U.S. steel and aluminum imports. U.S. and WTO challenges to these tariffs are pending.

Safeguards (Escape Clause Proceedings). Despite considerable controversy and pressure, little change was made in 2018 to the NAFTA 1994 provisions on this trade remedy. The exclusion of NAFTA partners from global safeguard actions was retained.

Temporary Business Visas. Minor changes to NAFTA 1994 coverage are contained in USMCA Chapter 16.

Textiles. Small changes in USMCA Chapter 6 tighten up required North American sources.

Canada's Cultural Industry Exclusion. Fully retained under USMCA Chapter 32. See Section 4.1.

New or Notably Revised USMCA Provisions
Common to All Partners

National Security. The NAFTA 1994 "essential security interests" exception (Article 2102), resembling that of the GATT/WTO (see Section 1.1), references actions member nations consider necessary relating to: (1) Information disclosures; (2) traffic in arms and the supply of foreign militaries or security establishments; (3)

war time or international relations' emergencies; (4) nuclear weapons proliferation; or breaches of UN Charter peace and security obligations. USMCA Article 32.2 provides a more ironclad "national security" exception than found in the GATT/WTO and NAFTA 1994 rules:

> "Essential Security 1. Nothing in this Agreement shall be construed to: (a) require a Party to furnish or allow access to information the disclosure of which it determines to be contrary to its essential security interests; or (b) preclude a Party from applying measures that it considers necessary for the fulfilment of its obligations with respect to the maintenance or restoration of international peace or security, or the protection of its own essential security interests ".

Thus USMCA Article 32.2 is more readily construed to support the existing Trump administration "national security" tariffs on steel and aluminum, which continue to apply to Mexico and Canada. See Section 1.17. In addition, the Trump administration has threatened to apply global national security tariffs to U.S. auto imports. The USMCA anticipates just such action by creating quotas to shelter Mexican and Canadian autos from such tariffs if they should emerge.

Autos and Parts. Arguably, the most notable and contentious changes to NAFTA 1994 undertaken in USMCA 2018, concern the rules of origin for vehicles and their parts. To be free traded, passenger vehicles and light trucks after a three-year phase-in must contain 75% regional value content, up from 62.5%, both measured using the net cost method. In addition, 70% of the steel and aluminum content of such vehicles must originate in North America. The automotive tracing and "deemed originating" rules of CUSFTA and NAFTA 1994 were terminated in favor of regional content rules for key vehicle components such as engines and transmissions.

Furthermore, 40% of the value of autos and 45% for trucks must be produced by workers earning an average of $16 or more per hour (not including benefits and not indexed for inflation), well above prevailing Mexican wages. This "labor value content" rule favors U.S. and Canadian sourced parts and components, and eliminates the possibility of free trading entirely Mexican sourced vehicles. Note that it requires two calculations: Production line wages and labor value content percentages.

The complex rules governing these calculations are detailed in the USMCA and explained by Professor Matthew Schaefer in the 2019 edition of Folsom, Van Alstine, Ramsey and Schaefer, *International Business Transactions 13th,* a problem-oriented course book as follows:

"[T]he value from workers making $16/hour [must] "consist of at least 25 percentage points of high wage material and manufacturing expenditures, no more than 10 percentage points of technology expenditures, and no more than 5 percentage points of assembly expenditures." USMCA, Article 4–B.7(1)(d). The technology expenditures can include software (i.e. may "include expenditures on software development, technology integration, vehicle communications, and information technology support operations"). With autos becoming "smart" vehicles and more and more autonomous, software inputs are rapidly increasing and Canada believes this will help its producers meet the new labor wage content rules in auto rules of origin. * * * The USMCA provides that "the production wage rate is the average hourly base wage rate, not including benefits, of employees directly involved in the production of the part or component used to calculate the LVC, and does not include salaries of management, R&D, engineering, or other workers who are not involved in the direct production of the parts or in the operation of production lines." USMCA, Ch. 4, fn. 104. These new rules will essentially be phased in over three or more years."

All of these provisions were driven by the Trump administration's goal of bringing vehicle and parts production back home. As a practical matter it is estimated they will generate compliance costs estimated at between 3 to 5%.

An alternative to compliance with the new automobile rules of origin is to pay the U.S. passenger auto import tariff of 2.5%, assuming no new U.S. national security tariffs are applied to autos. The 2.5% alternative is not an option for manufacturers of pick-up trucks, vans and SUVs, all of which face a 25% U.S. tariff. Thus such producers are more likely to engage in production in the USA.

Side letters to USMCA 2018 anticipate that the United States may, as threatened, impose "national security" tariffs on autos from anywhere in the world, including its North American partners. Quotas in the side letters exempt 2.6 million Mexican passenger vehicles and light trucks and $108 billion in Mexican auto parts from any such future tariffs. Canada has an exemption for 2.6 million vehicles and $32.3 billion in auto parts. The quotas are currently well above 2018 Canadian export levels, noticeably less so for Mexican exports to the USA.

These quotas are not indexed for inflation, and hence in time are likely to be reached. In a backhanded way, they support the threat of U.S. national security tariffs on autos from Japan, the EU, China and Korea.

Currency Manipulation. Limited transparency and notification obligations regarding currency manipulation have been added to

USMCA 2018. None of the NAFTA partners have in the past been considered currency manipulators. Thus this provision was included as a model for future U.S. FTAs where currency manipulation may be an issue. Disputes regarding currency manipulation which are not associated with any of the North American partners are not subject to USMCA dispute settlement.

Non-Market Economies. Under USMCA Chapter 32 any party may terminate the agreement if a partner enters into a free trade agreement with a non-market economy (NME). This provision is clearly targeted at Canadian and Mexican relations with China, which the United States continues to treat as a NME for trade law matters, treatment that China is contesting before the WTO. See Section 1.18. It could also apply to Cuba and North Korea, but not Vietnam as a pre-existing partner with Canada and Mexico in the TPP-11 agreement that took effect in 2019.

Labor. Unlike the labor and environment "side agreements" to NAFTA 1994 (see Section 4.12), USMCA 2018 incorporates both areas into the core 2018 agreement and are "enforceable" thereunder. This follows the pattern of the G. W. Bush administration U.S. free trade agreements with Korea, Peru, Colombia and Panama, as well as TPP-12. An "Annex on Worker Representation in Collective Bargaining in Mexico" explicitly requires labor law amendments to better protect union organizing rights in Mexico, which did not notably improve under the 1994 side agreement. See Section 4.12.

All Parties agreed to adopt and maintain in law and in enforcement practice labor rights recognized in the International Labor Organization's Fundamental Principles. Imports of goods from forced labor are banned. Protections for migrant workers are included. Critics, notably the post-election New Democrat Coalition, have argued that enforcement of labor and environment commitments under USMCA 2018 is inadequate.

Environment. On the environment, USMCA 2018 borrows and expands upon TPP-12 with coverage banning subsidization of illegal, unreported and unregulated (IUU) fishing and shark finning. New provisions concern invasive alien species, whales and sea turtles, wild flora and fauna, forest management, ozone depletion, environmental impact assessments, as well as cooperation on air quality and marine debris. A side agreement preserves the Commission for Environmental Cooperation (CEC) created under NAFTA 1994. See Section 4.12.

Unlike the Japan-EU FTA of 2018, no mention of climate change is made in USMCA 2018. As with labor (above), the adequacy of enforcement of these provisions through intergovernmental dispute settlement under Chapter 31 of the new agreement has been challenged.

Digital Trade/Internet Providers. Digital trade, then in its infancy, was not covered under NAFTA 1994. USMCA Chapter 19 follows TPP-12 in banning data localization requirements (Canada has such rules), disallowing customs duties on digital commerce (think Netflix), limiting cross-border restrictions on data flows, and protecting consumer privacy. Source codes and algorithms are protected, as are e-signatures and electronic authentications. Internet service providers (ISPs) are protected under a "safe harbor" from copyright and criminal liability connected to unauthorized actions of their users, provided the ISPs take down copyright infringing material in a timely manner. Canada retained its "notice-and-notice" system requiring ISPs to notify customers of copyright infringement allegations.

Intellectual Property. Copyright protection is extended to life of the author plus 70 years, which will change Canada's 50-year rule, and 75 years for films and other collective works. Trademarks for sounds and scents must be allowed. Concerning geographic indicators, attempts are made at protecting trade between Mexico and the United States in arguably generic product names such as parmesan, feta and champagne. IP exceptions to promote medicines for all and compulsory patent licensing in national emergencies were retained. IP enforcement exceptions to protect public health and nutrition, and to promote development are recognized.

Pharmaceuticals and Biologics. Biologic medicines receive 10 years safety and efficacy test data exclusivity protection under USMCA 2018, more than the 8 years found in TPP-12 but less than the 12 years allowed under U.S. law. Such provisions typically delay market entry by generic firms. Biologics also enjoy linkage and patent term extension benefits. Greater transparency in pharma pricing and reimbursement rules, plus independent review procedures, are required. These provisions target single payer health care systems, such as that of Canada. They were in TPP-12 but dropped completely from TPP-11. Disputes regarding pharma transparency are excluded from USMCA dispute settlement.

Financial Services and Information. USMCA 2018 on financial services generally tracks TPP-12, including a narrowing of national treatment and MFN treatment duties in "like circumstances". In addition, USMCA governments are prohibited from preventing financial institutions from transferring personal and other information across borders by electronic or other means. Also, the governments may not restrict financial institutions from locating computing facilities abroad. In either case, regulatory authorities must have immediate, direct, complete and ongoing access to information for regulatory and supervisory purposes. Each nation must adopt or maintain "a" legal framework that provides protection for personal data.

On dispute settlement, financial services obligations are subject to USMCA investor-state arbitrations between Mexico (but not Canada) and the United States, subject to special procedures and limitations.

Trucking Services. Cross-border long-haul trucking by Mexican carriers is prohibited under a Chapter 15 Annex, effectively reversing NAFTA 1994 provisions and a unanimous NAFTA dispute panel in Mexico's favor. See Section 4.5.

Provisions Borrowed from TPP-12. New provisions in USMCA 2018, not found or heavily augmented compared to NAFTA 1994, were primarily borrowed from TPP-12. These include largely aspirational coverage of "good" regulatory practices (Chapter 28, transparency, notice and the like), advancement and protection of the interests of small and medium businesses (Chapter 25), macroeconomic policies and exchange rates (Chapter 33), competition policy (Chapter 21), and anti-corruption law (Chapter 27). More concrete provisions concern competitive neutrality for state-owned enterprises (Chapters 22, 26), customs and trade facilitation procedures (Chapter 7), and development of sectoral industry standards via Annexes (Chapter 12) to USMCA 2018.

"De Minimis" Customs Duty and Tax Free Shipments. Customs duty free shipments to Canada rise to $150 CDN, and to Mexico to $117 US, with the U.S. remaining at $800. The tax-free thresholds are lower: $50 US for Mexico, $40 CDN for Canada, and $800 US for the United States. In both cases, the U.S. amounts could be reduced to match the Canadian and Mexican sums. These duty free and tax free shipments, employing "simple" customs forms, are expected to boost cross-border e-commerce and small business trading but are hardly a victory for online trading.

Investor-state dispute settlement has been notably changed by Chapter 14 of the USMCA. See the coverage of Canada and Mexico below and Sections 4.7 and 4.8.

Sunset Clause. The United States withdrew its pressure for a five-year sunset clause. Instead, USMCA 2018 will last for 16 years. It will be reviewed every six years, triggering another 16-year period unless rejected by a partner.

As under NAFTA 1994, any Party may withdraw from the new agreement with six months' notice.

Canada under USMCA 2018

Canada is by far the largest U.S. trade partner for goods. Before NAFTA 1994, most Canadian exports went to the USA, with significant U.S. trade in services, investment and technology flowing north. By 2018, broadly speaking, Canada's economic dependence on the USA remained substantial, a bargaining lever exploited by U.S. negotiators. In the run-up to the finalization of USMCA 2018, Canada reached out for alternatives. It completed a major free trade agreement with the European Union (CETA 2017, see Section 5.4) and was a leader in developing TPP-11 (see Section 5.3).

Cultural Industries, AD and CVD Disputes, Progressive Goals, Energy. From the Canadian perspective, on the success side of the ledger, Canada retained from CUSFTA 1989 and NAFTA 1994 its cultural industry exclusion (see Section 4.1) along with utilization of binational panels (instead of judicial review) to resolve antidumping and subsidy disputes (see Section 4.11), both of which remain in force almost unchanged from NAFTA 1994.

Canada also secured recognition of the rights of indigenous peoples. The 2018 agreement further requires policies against employment discrimination on the basis of gender identity, sexual orientation, sexual harassment, pregnancy, and caregiving responsibilities, all reflecting Canada's "progressive" perspectives. Footnote 13 in Chapter 23 appears to exempt the U.S. from these duties.

Canada's much debated promise under CUSFTA 1989 and NAFTA 1994 to proportionally share energy resources (see Section 4.4) with the USA in energy crises was removed.

Agricultural Goods, Wine. On the negative side of the ledger, Canada made limited concessions allowing greater entry of U.S. dairy (milk, milk powder, milk protein, cream, butter, and cheese), margarine, whey, chicken, egg, turkey and grain products into its market, concessions broadly similar to those it had made under TPP-12. In return, Canada gained small market openings to increase exports to the U.S. of dairy, peanut and processed peanut, and sugar and sugar containing products. Dairy tariff rate quotas commitments on both sides are to be reciprocal based on tonnage. All sides committed to protecting agro-biotech, including gene editing.

Canada also agreed to open up British Columbia grocery stores to sales of U.S. wines.

Procurement. Canada and the United States have no procurement obligations under the USMCA. Hence procurement as between those countries is governed by the Enhanced WTO Procurement Agreement. Mexico (which does not participate in the optional WTO Agreement) and the United States largely retained their NAFTA 1994 procurement obligations, adopting increased thresholds under Chapter 13 of the 2018 agreement.

Investor-State Dispute Settlement. By agreement in Chapter 14, apart from legacy NAFTA 1994 claims (presented no later than three years after the new USMCA agreement enters into force), Canada and the United States *completely* removed the availability of arbitrations to resolve investor-state disputes. Compare Sections 4.7 and 4.8. In the future, such disputes will presumably be resolved by state-to-state dispute settlement or the courts of either nation.

Mexico under USMCA 2018

Before NAFTA 1994, about most Mexican exports went to the USA, with significant U.S. trade in services, investment and technology flowing south. By 2018, broadly speaking, Mexico's economic dependence on the USA remained overwhelming, a major bargaining lever exploited by U.S. negotiators. In the run-up to the finalization of USMCA 2018, Mexico also reached out for alternatives. It completed a much expanded free trade agreement with the European Union, and is a member of TPP-11. See Chapter 5.

Investor-State Dispute Settlement (ISDS). Investor-state arbitration of disputes for damages continues in full as between Mexico and Canada under TPP-11 effective Jan. 1, 2019 for all parties except those whose ratification is still pending. Such arbitrations continue under revised terms as between Mexico and the United States. U.S.-Mexico claims involving *government contracts* are limited to specified capital intensive sectors (oil and gas, telecommunications, power generation, and contracts for roads, railways, bridges or canals but not apparently dams, seaports and airports). Such government contract disputes may assert the full range of NAFTA 1994 investor rights (direct and indirect expropriation, fair and equitable treatment (minimum standard), national and MFN treatment, and more). See Section 4.7.

For claims *not* involving government contracts, limitations are placed on investor-state arbitrations by USMCA 2018. Such claims are limited to national and most-favored nation treatment, and expropriation grounds, notably dropping out fair and equitable treatment claims. In addition, borrowing from post-NAFTA 1994 U.S. free trade agreements and the TPP, "indirect" expropriation claims are also limited. Indirect expropriations are defined as situations "in which an action or series of actions by a Party has an effect equivalent to direct expropriation without formal transfer of title or outright seizure".

Further, "non-discriminatory regulatory actions by a Party that are designed and applied to protect legitimate public welfare objectives, such as health, safety and the environment, do *not* constitute indirect expropriations, except in rare circumstances." This language addresses criticisms of NAFTA 1994 investor-state arbitrations challenging environmental measures as regulatory takings and/or indirect expropriations. For examples, see Sections 4.8.

Furthermore, borrowing a TPP-12 rule, investor claimants under USMCA 2018, must first exhaust local remedies or attempt to do so for 30 months prior to seeking arbitration. This rule does not appear to apply to the select government contract claimants noted above. Investors owned or controlled by non-market economy states are barred from using arbitration remedies. Establishment claims prior to actual investment are generally excluded.

Energy. Mexico's top priority in negotiating NAFTA 1994, protection of PEMEX as a state monopoly over oil, gas and most petrochemicals (see Section 4.4) is more obliquely referenced in USMCA 2018. Explicit reference is made to Mexican direct, inalienable and imprescriptible ownership of hydrocarbon resources (which conceivably could facilitate the return of PEMEX as an absolute monopoly).

The numerous major oil companies with new wells and drilling rights in Mexico as of 2019 await with anxiety the policies of its new President, who has spoken of limiting foreign participation. That said, buried in USMCA Article 32.11, is an obligation for MFN treatment in the energy sector. Since Mexico agreed under TPP-11 Annexes to preserve the market opening reforms of its prior administration, Article 32.11 could be construed to bar backtracking on energy rules already in place that benefit U.S. and Canadian parties. (I am grateful to Professor David Gantz for this insight).

Ratification

Thirteen "side letters' that accompanied the signing of the USMCA on Nov. 30, 2018 took effect immediately. These include: Mexican and Canadian exclusions from any future U.S. tariff-rate quotas on the importation of autos (threatened by the Trump administration as a matter of national security, see Section 1.17), U.S.-Mexico agreements on biologic drugs, cheese names and auto safety standards, and U.S.-Canada agreements on wine, water and energy.

Approval and implementation of USMCA 2018 by the U.S. Congress was complicated by the takeover in November of the House of Representatives by the Democrats. Apart from not wishing to give the President a "victory", the sizeable New Democrat Coalition quickly let it be known that the new agreement's enforcement provisions on labor and the environment were, in their opinion, inadequate. Additional concerns were expressed by the Coalition about access to biologic medicines under the new agreement, and continuance of U.S. national security steel and aluminum tariffs on Canadian and Mexican exports. Republican conservatives opposed the progressive social provisions (above) secured by Canada in USMCA 2018.

President Trump has threatened to withdraw from NAFTA 1994 (with six months' notice) in order to pressure Congress to approve and implement the USMCA.

USMCA/KORUS II Overview

On balance, especially considering the rhetoric and sometimes vitriolic positions of President Trump, there are relatively few provisions of major consequence in USMCA 2018. Apart from auto rules of origin, removal of investor-state arbitrations between the U.S. and Canada, and denying entry to long-haul Mexican trucks, most of the agreement contains predictable updates largely derived from TPP-12. In sum, apart from these three areas, USMCA 2018 makes relatively modest to minor changes and additions to NAFTA 1994.

As with KORUS II, USMCA 2018 is not exactly groundbreaking. It primarily repackages free trade rules found elsewhere. That said, KORUS II and the USMCA constitute FTA models acceptable to President Trump. Of course no U.S. trade partner enjoys being "bullied" into a deal with a leader they distrust. The President seems to ignore or not understand that how you negotiate trade agreements can have long-term relationship costs.

Whether KORUS II and USMCA 2018 represent America First, Second or Third remains to be seen.

§ 6.8   Linked Contents, Annexes and Side Letters of the 2018 USMCA Agreement

Table of Contents

A.   United States-Mexico-Canada Agreement Text—Chapters

USMCA Protocol

0.   **Preamble**

1.   **Initial Provisions and General Definitions**

2.   **National Treatment and Market Access for Goods**

- **US Tariff Schedule**
  - o   **US Tariff Schedule Appendix 1**
- **MX Tariff Schedule**
  - o   **MX Tariff Schedule Appendix 1**
- **CA Tariff Schedule**
  - o   **CA Tariff Schedule Appendix 1**

3. **Agriculture**

4. **Rules of Origin**

5. **Origin Procedures**

6. **Textiles and Apparel**

7. **Customs Administration and Trade Facilitation**

8. **Recognition of Mexican Ownership of Hydrocarbons**

9. **Sanitary and Phytosanitary Measures**

10. **Trade Remedies**

11. **Technical Barriers to Trade**

12. **Sectoral Annexes**

13. **Government Procurement**

14. **Investment**

15. **Cross-Border Trade in Services**

16. **Temporary Entry**

17. **Financial Services**

18. **Telecommunications**

19. **Digital Trade**

20. **Intellectual Property**

21. **Competition Policy**

22. **State-Owned Enterprises**

23. **Labor**

24. **Environment**

25. **Small and Medium-Sized Enterprises**

26. **Competitiveness**

27. **Anticorruption**

28. **Good Regulatory Practices**

4. MX-US Side Letter on Auto Safety Standards

5. MX-US Side Letter on Biologics

6. MX-US Side Letter on Cheeses

7. MX-US Side Letter on Distilled Spirits

8. MX-US Side Letter on Prior Users

9. CA-US Side Letter on 232 Process

10. CA-US Side Letter on Wine

11. CA-US Side Letter on Natural Water Resources

12. CA-US Side Letter on Energy

13. CA-US Side Letter on Research and Development Expenditures

14. Side Letter Text on 232 CA-US Response

Source:**(https://ustr.gov/trade-agreements/free-trade-agreements/united-states-mexico-canada-agreement/agreement-between)**

Chapter 7

INVESTOR-STATE ARBITRATIONS UNDER FTAs AND BITs

Analysis

Given the absence of a cohesive body of widely accepted foreign investment law, and notably the failure of the Multilateral Agreement of Investment (MAI), nations have turned to negotiation of bilateral foreign investment treaties (BITs) and/or free trade agreements (FTAs) that contain foreign investment chapters. For detailed NAFTA 1994 coverage of foreign investor-host state rules and arbitration examples, see Chapter 4.

From the perspective of capital exporting countries, BITs and FTAs offer protection from host state actions that violate the foreign investor rights contained therein. From the perspective of capital importing countries, investment treaties and FTAs create incentives to invest in what may be perceived as high-risk markets.

There is a long history of foreign investors' purchasing political-risk insurance against expropriation, civil unrest and the like, sometimes from their home governments. See Chapter 3. In Latin America, the spread of "Calvo Doctrine" rules designed to limit foreign investors to host nations' judicial and administrative remedies increased the desire for protection. Investor-state dispute settlement (ISDS) by arbitration first appeared in a 1959 BIT treaty between Germany and Pakistan. Since the 1990s the signing of BITs and FTAs with investment arbitration provisions has proliferated.

§ 7.1   Investor-State Arbitrations

Bilateral Investment Treaties (BITs)
and Treaty Shopping

The principal focus of BITs is the protection and promotion of foreign investment. It is not only the United States which has emphasized these treaties. They are common features of most developed nations in their relations with developing host nations. Tracking its rise as a capital exporter, China has over 100 investment protection agreements, mostly with emerging economies, but also with such nations as Australia, Austria, Belgium/Luxembourg, Denmark, France, Germany, Japan, the Netherlands, and the United Kingdom. A benefit of such an agreement is that its provisions prevail over domestic law and remedies, although the agreements usually allow for exceptions to investment protection when in the interests of national security.

Approximately 3,000 bilateral investment treaties (BITs) lattice the globe. China and Germany have well over 100 BITs, France, Britain and the Netherlands about 100, India, Romania, Italy, The Czech Republic, Belgium/Luxembourg 75 to 85, Russia, Sweden, Poland 65, while Brazil has none and South Africa has said it will withdraw from all BIT treaty obligations. Singapore has a number of BITs that seem to be designed to attract foreign investors to incorporate there so as to take advantage of Singaporean subsidiaries as foreign investment vehicles in the likes of Jordan and Egypt. Investment arbitrations administered by the Singapore International Arbitration Center have skyrocketed.

The Netherlands is known for allowing "mailbox" companies to utilize their network of BITs by making foreign investments through them. Critics assert that this lattice allows foreign investors to engage in "treaty shopping", the making of investments in order to raise arbitral challenges to national laws. A prominent example is the Phillip Morris (Asia) acquisition of a Hong Kong firm to facilitate challenge of Australia's 2011 plain packaging (no brand) cigarette law under the 1993 Hong Kong-Australia Bilateral Investment Treaty. This arbitration was dismissed by the arbitrators in 2015 as an abuse of process.

Treaty shopping inside the European Union to avoid the dubious legitimacy of national courts in Poland, Hungary, and quite a few other EU states has been undertaken by making investments in those countries via U.K., Dutch and German companies benefiting from **intra-EU** BITs. Some 200 intra-EU member-state BIT arbitration provisions have effectively been invalidated by the European Court of Justice in its landmark 2018 *Slovak Republic v.*

Achmea (Case C-284/16) decision. The logic of the Court's reasoning is that such provisions interfere with the autonomy, effectiveness and primacy of the EU legal regime. As such, awards rendered thereunder are unenforceable. This decision raises questions as to whether **extra-EU** member state BIT arbitration decisions, which are numerous, may also be unenforceable. Further, it is an open question as to whether ICSID or Energy Charter investment arbitrations (see Sections 7.5, 7.6 and 7.7) are suspect under *Achmea.*

Free Trade Agreements (FTAs) with Investment Coverage

Leading nations have gathered together networks of free trade agreements under various titles, some with foreign investment dispute settlement by arbitration coverage, and some not:

(1) **Japan** has "Economic Partnership Agreements" (that is to say free trade agreements) with Mexico, Chile, Thailand, the Philippines, Malaysia, Vietnam, Switzerland, India, Indonesia, Brunei, Singapore, Peru, Mongolia, the Association of Southeast Asian Nations (ASEAN), a major 2018 FTA with the European Union (not as yet covering foreign investment), and is a leader in the Comprehensive and Progressive Trans-Pacific Partnership (TPP-11), which provides for investor-state arbitrations and took effect in 2019. See Chapter 5. Japan and its companies have rarely participated in investor-state arbitrations.

(2) **China** has free trade agreements with its own Hong Kong and Macau Special Administrative Regions, Chile, Pakistan, Costa Rica, Peru, Singapore, New Zealand, Australia, South Korea, Iceland, Maldives and ASEAN, none of which appear to cover foreign investment. Like Japan, China and its firms have only been involved in only a few investor-state arbitrations, initiated under its very large number of BITs.

(3) The **European Union** has numerous free trade agreements, including with Algeria, Chile, Egypt, Iceland, Israel, Jordan, Lebanon, Mexico, Morocco, Norway, Serbia, South Africa, Vietnam, Singapore, Japan, Canada, Tunisia and a customs union agreement with Turkey. Traditionally, EU FTAs included foreign investment law rules and dispute settlement by arbitration. But recent FTAs with Vietnam, Singapore, Mexico and the Japan-EU 2018 Economic Partnership Agreement do not. The EU's "new generation" policy for foreign investment dispute settlement anticipates using an Investment Court system instead of arbitrators. See Section 3.6.

(4) The **United States** has 12 bilateral free trade agreements with Australia (2004), Bahrain (2006), Chile (2004), Colombia (2012), Israel and the Palestinian Authority (1985), Jordan (2001), South Korea (KORUS I 2012 and II 2018), Morocco (2006), Oman (2006), Panama (2012), Peru (2012) and Singapore (2004). It also has two multilateral agreements: The NAFTA 1994 and pending USMCA 2018 agreement with Canada and Mexico, and the Central America Free Trade Agreement (CAFTA-DR 2015) which includes the Dominican Republic, Guatemala, Honduras, El Salvador, Nicaragua and Costa Rica.

All U.S. FTAs cover foreign investment dispute settlement by arbitration *except* those with Israel, Australia and Canada under the USMCA 2018. For examples of NAFTA 1994 investor-state arbitrations, the text of NAFTA 1994 Chapter 11 covering investment, and post-NAFTA foreign investment rules in later U.S. FTAs, see Chapters 4 and 5.

(5) **India** has free trade agreements with ASEAN, Sri Lanka, Malaysia, the Gulf Cooperation Council (GCC), Singapore, Korea, Japan, Afghanistan, Chile, MERCOSUR and leads the 7-nation South Asian FTA. Foreign investment arbitration coverage is limited.

(6) **South Korea** has free trade agreements with ASEAN, India, Australia, Canada, the United States (KORUS I and II), China, Chile, Colombia, EFTA, the European Union (KOREU), Turkey, Vietnam, Peru, and Singapore. Some of these FTAs cover foreign investment arbitrations, including KORUS I and II (see Section 6.6), but some do not.

(7) **Canada** has free trade agreements (in addition to NAFTA 1994 and its successor the USMCA of 2018) with Korea, the EU (CETA 2017), Chile, Peru, Colombia, Costa Rica, Israel, EFTA, Jordan, Panama, Honduras, and Ukraine, and is a leader in the TPP-11 (see Section 5.3). Virtually all have foreign investment arbitration coverage, including NAFTA 1994.

Ratification of the Canada-EU Comprehensive Economic and Trade Agreement of 2014 (CETA) was delayed primarily due foreign investor-host state issues. These were resolved by agreeing to create a new Investment Court comprised of Canadian, European and other jurists. The Court will replace party selected arbitrators. Other EU free trade agreements (above) follow this "new generation" course for investor-state dispute settlement.

CETA raised a fundamental question: Is dispute settlement by arbitration really needed when both parties have sophisticated judicial systems and/or good diplomatic relations capable of handling foreign investor disputes? *Under the pending USMCA of 2018, Canada and the United States will eliminate ISDS arbitrations.*

(8) **Mexico** has free trade agreements in addition to NAFTA and the USMCA with Chile, Colombia, Venezuela (dormant), Costa Rica, Bolivia, Nicaragua, Guatemala, Honduras, El Salvador, Peru, Uruguay, the European Union (see Chapter 3), Japan and Israel. It also has an enhanced Pacific Alliance with Chile, Peru, and Colombia, and participates in the TPP-11 (see Section 5.3). Most Mexican FTAs embrace investor-state dispute settlement by arbitration resembling NAFTA 1994.

Under NAFTA's successor, the USMCA Agreement of 2018 (ratification pending) Mexico-Canada ISDS by arbitration is governed by TPP-11, and U.S.-Mexico investor-state arbitrations are restricted. For NAFTA 1994 arbitration rules and examples involving Mexico, see Section 4.8. For USMCA arbitration rules, see Section 6.8.

§ 7.2   Foreign Investor Rights

Bilateral investment treaties and FTAs with investment coverage traditionally provide foreign investors with certain core rights:

(1) "national treatment";

(2) "most-favored-nation treatment";

(3) "fair and equitable treatment" (known as the "minimum standard);

(4) "full protection and security"; and

(5) direct and indirect expropriation rules.

Some BIT agreements also require host governments to comply with obligations undertaken with foreign investors, often via foreign investment agreements, including for example "stabilization clauses" intended to stabilize or even freeze the law of the host country at the time of the signing of the agreement. If the investor-state agreement contains a "stabilization" clause, promising no significant change in the host state's law will adversely affect the investment, such clauses may give rise to breach of contract claims which become BIT/FTA violations subject to arbitration. Veolia, a French utility, for example commenced arbitration proceedings against Egypt for raising the minimum wage.

National treatment promises nondiscriminatory, equal treatment with domestic investors. Most-favored-nation treatment means foreign investors from different nations will be treated equally, thus sometimes allowing investors to claim more generous benefits provided in other agreements. In one such dispute, an Argentinian investor in Spain obtained the benefit of a Chile-Spain BIT dispute resolution provision not requiring prior exhaustion of local judicial remedies. See *Maffenzi v. Spain*, ICSID Case No. ARB/97/7 (Jan. 25, 2000).

General exception clauses in some investment protection agreements, notably the Canada-EU Comprehensive Economic and Trade Agreement (CETA 2017), tend to mirror Article XX of the GATT and Article XIV of the GATS. Such clauses create state immunities for permissible policy objectives and acts, such as for the protection of human, animal or plant life or health, national security and the conservation of natural resources.

Fair and equitable treatment, and full protection and security, are notably open-ended "minimum standards" derived from customary international law. In determining fair and equitable treatment, the investor's legitimate expectations and the transparency, predictability, consistency and denial of justice under state rules have been evaluated as appropriate criteria. See, e.g., *Tecmed v. Mexico*, 10 ICSID Reports 133 (2004); *OEPC v. Ecuador*, Case No. UN 3467 (London Ct. Intl. Arb. July 1, 2004); *Waste Management v. Mexico*, ICSID Case No. ARB/00/0 (April 30, 2004) (NAFTA 1994 dispute).

In addition, the duty of fair and equitable treatment has frequently been construed by arbitrators as protecting the stability of the legal and business framework under which the foreign investor operates. *Id.* Fair and equitable treatment has been construed as requiring that the host state respect the basic expectations of the investor at the time of the investment. In other words, the host state may not alter rules and decisions upon which the investor relied in planning its investment. Thus unilateral changes in the legal and contractual framework existing at the time of the original investment, frustrating the investor's legitimate expectations, can and have be deemed unfair and inequitable. *Id.*

Unfair and inequitable treatment has become the primary violation found by foreign investment arbitration tribunals. For an informative review of "unfair and inequitable" conduct by Argentina in connection with emergency financial measures and judicial access to remedies, see the U.S. Supreme Court case *BG Group PLC v. Argentina,* 134 S. Ct. 1198 (2014) (litigate first requirement in UK-Argentina BIT excused in New York Convention recognition and enforcement proceedings in the USA). If the investor obtained investment rights by unlawful means, for example corruption, dismissal of its claims is appropriate as a matter of international public policy. See *World Duty Free Co. v. Kenya,* ICSID Case No. ARB/00/07 (October 4, 2006).

Beyond core foreign investor rights, some agreements broadly allow arbitration of "other claims" related to the investment. Most rules on expropriation require valid public purposes and prompt, adequate and effective compensation. NAFTA 1994 rules protect foreign investors from governmental acts "tantamount to expropriation", an ambiguous term (see Section 4.7). Acts of sub-central government authorities or state-owned companies may be attributed to the state for liability purposes. See *Tokios Tokeles v. Ukraine,* ICSID Case No. ARB/02/18 (April 29, 2004) (local government authorities); *Salini Costruttori v. Morocco,* ICSID Case No. ARB/00/04 (July 16, 2001) (state-owned company). In addition, BITs and FTAs may also protect capital movement and limit performance requirements. All of these rights may extend beyond the life of a BIT or FTA, and cannot be retroactively revoked, thus allowing for investor claims against states under "tails."

§ 7.3   Foreign Investor-Host State Dispute Settlement

BITs and FTAs covering investment provide foreign investors with designated rights, and typically establish investor-state dispute settlement procedures (ISDS) to resolve alleged violations of those rights and, if the arbitrators so rule, payment of damages by the host state. Exhaustion or at least attempted utilization of host state national legal remedies (courts, agencies) may first be required, a requirement found for example in the Trans-Pacific Partnership Agreement (TPP-12, rejected by President Trump), its TPP-11 successor and the USMCA 2018 Agreement. In some jurisdictions, notably under Calvo Clauses in Latin America, foreign investor-host state disputes can only be decided pursuant to local remedies.

A highlight of many BIT and FTA foreign investment agreements is the consent in advance of host sovereign states to arbitration of foreign investor disputes; no separate consent is required. ISDS arbitrations are subject to review in the place of arbitration *and* wherever enforcement is sought. To date, early 1,000 investor-state arbitrations have been undertaken.

Investor-State Arbitrations

Foreign investment provisions frequently establish mandatory, binding dispute settlement procedures allowing foreign investors to invoke arbitration procedures by filing claims for *damages* against host nations. The formulae for these provisions differ. Many channel investor-state disputes to the World Bank's International Centre for Settlement of Investment Disputes (ICSID) in Washington, D.C., discussed below. Some BIT arbitrations have gone to the Stockholm Chamber of Commerce, the Permanent Court of Arbitration in The Hague, the U.N. Commission on International Trade Law (UNCITRAL), and the International Chamber of Commerce (ICC) in Paris.

Hundreds of investor-state arbitration claims have been filed, the largest number against Argentina (many arising out of its sovereign debt repudiations and emergency economic measures affecting utilities). The mere filing of such claims facilitates leverage in renegotiation of investment contracts as well as compensation.

Claims have been lodged against the United States, and U.S. investors abroad have very actively pursued claims against U.S. BIT and free trade partners, notably Argentina. Exxon Mobil obtained a $1.6 billion expropriation award in ICSID proceedings under the U.S.-Venezuela BIT. Dow Chemical received a $2.2 billion award in ICC proceedings against Kuwait. Under the U.S.-Ecuador BIT, in ICSID proceedings, Occidental Petroleum won a $2.3 billion award against Ecuador for termination of an oil-concession contract.

Some investor-state claims are settled, others dismissed on technical grounds. UNCTAD data indicates that arbitrated investment disputes reaching final awards favor the state by close to two to one. That said, it is clear that investors from the developed world (notably the United States, the Netherlands, the United Kingdom and Germany) comprise a large majority of the claimants against developing nations (notably Argentina, Venezuela, Ecuador and Mexico). As a general rule, investment arbitration awards can be recognized and enforced in foreign courts under the 1958 New York Convention on the Recognition and Enforcement of Arbitral Awards. See R. Folsom, *Principles of International Arbitration and Litigation 2d* (West Academic Publishing).

The growth of investment arbitration has in many instances overrun contract-based choice of forum clauses, including alternative arbitral proceedings. When "parallel proceedings" exist arbitrators have often declined to defer to party autonomy. For example, U.S. investors in an Argentine port terminal agreed "for all purposes" in their concession contract to the jurisdiction of Argentinian courts.

They invoked instead the U.S.-Argentina BIT arbitration procedures under ICSID. The arbitrators upheld their "jurisdiction" to hear the dispute. See generally, Gus Van Harten, *Sovereign Choices and Sovereign Constraints: Judicial Restraint in Investment Treaty Arbitration* (2013).

Investor-State Arbitration Critiques

Critics of investor-state arbitrations broadly decry the creation of a private system of justice for foreign investors. Even the U.S. Congress has frequently expressed concern that ISDS arbitrations may provide foreign investors in the United States with greater remedies than U.S. investors in their home country. Critics focus particularly on the fair and equitable treatment obligation, which has been increasingly construed by arbitrators to create "legitimate expectations" (future profits), and "specific commitments" that host governments will compensate foreign investors for changes in law, notably regulatory law. This has created a degree of foreign investment "regulatory chill." Investors have also been arguing that they are entitled to the legitimate expectation that governments will adhere to their international treaty obligations, notably under the WTO TRIPs agreement concerning intellectual property rights. Investors have also used BIT and NAFTA 1994 provisions to influence and challenge proposed host state regulations.

Additional criticisms assert there is something of a "good old boy" network of inherently biased ISDS arbitrators drawn significantly from corporate legal worlds operating with relatively little transparency. Arbitrators who simultaneously act as counsel in other ongoing arbitrations, or repeat as arbitrators for the same parties, have been particularly critiqued. Most NAFTA 1994 and ICSID awards and related documents are published, and greater transparency should be forthcoming under the UNCITRAL Mauritius Convention (2015).

"Treaty shopping" to access investor-state arbitration remedies occurs, notably in connection with the formation of "mailbox companies" for that purpose. Romanian and other companies have been reported using Dutch mailbox companies as the vehicle for investments in their own home countries in order to avoid local law and asserted corrupt local courts. Philip Morris made a strategic investment in Hong Kong so as to be able to challenge anticipated (but not yet enacted) Australian no-brand, plain packaging cigarette rules under a Hong Kong-Australia BIT dating from the British era. Philip Morris feared losing Marlboro Man and other trademarked brand names. In 2015, the arbitrators dismissed this proceeding on abuse of process grounds.

Philip Morris also utilized the Swiss-Uruguay BIT to challenge Uruguay's comparable plain packaging cigarette rules. In the first "jurisdictional" round of this ICSID dispute, Philip Morris persuaded the arbitrators that an "investment" had indeed been made in Uruguay on the basis of its economic contribution to development, despite smoking's adverse effects on the people and economy of that country. This dispute was eventually settled after Philip Morris lost its treaty shopping attempt at overcoming Australian tobacco packaging rules (above). *See* generally J. Chaisse, *The Treaty Shopping Practice: Corporate Structuring and Restructuring to Gain Access to Investment Treaties and Arbitration,* 11 Hastings Bus. L.J. 225 (2015).

Rejection or Limitation of Investor-State Arbitrations

Reacting negatively to investor-state arbitrations, some developing world BITs, for example the Indian Model BIT and the Southern African Development Community (SADC) Model BIT, require foreign investors to first exhaust local remedies. The Trans-Pacific Partnership Agreements (TPP-12 and TPP-11) as well as the pending USMCA 2018 successor to NAFTA 1994 do likewise. See Chapters 5 and 6.

South Africa is actively terminating its BITs in favor of national investment code rules. Indonesia, Brazil, Bolivia, Ecuador, Nicaragua, Venezuela and others have started moving away from investor-state arbitrations and ICSID (below), replacing arbitrations with local remedies or state-to-state dispute settlement (SSDS). The latter include use of the World Court and Permanent Court of Arbitration in The Hague, Ombudsmen, conciliation, and diplomatic remedies. State-to-state remedies force foreign investors to seek remedies via their home governments, very different from investor-state arbitration mechanisms.

Foreign investors should take note that the Canada-EU FTA of 2017 (CETA) anticipates replacing traditional party-selected arbitrators with an Investment Court system comprised of judges from both sides. Recent EU FTAs with Singapore, Vietnam, Japan and Mexico may do likewise. *Under the pending USMCA of 2018, Canada and the United States will eliminate investor-state arbitrations.* They are retained, subject to limitations, for U.S-Mexico and Canada-Mexico foreign investment arbitrations. See Section 6.8.

At Australia's insistence, the United States-Australia free trade agreement does NOT contain investor-state arbitration procedures, though the Trans-Pacific Partnership (TPP-12) vetoed by President Trump would have altered that result. However, arbitration claims regarding the regulation of tobacco were specifically excluded under the TPP-12 and remain so under TPP-11.

Growing rejection and criticism of investment dispute settlement by party-selected arbitrators has led to tune ups of procedures and rules related to them. For example, TPP-12 and TPP-11 (neither of which is the United States a party) undertake material arbitration reforms. For example, financial stability regulation falls outside indirect expropriation claims, tobacco regulation may not be challenged, mere frustration of profit expectations is insufficient to pursue investor-state arbitrations, the burden of proof falls on investor claimants, no shell companies may be used to access investor-state arbitral remedies, and state-owned enterprises along with authorized government agents are made subject to the agreement's dispute settlement regime.

In addition, the TPP agreements mandate public access to hearings and documents, allow amicus briefs, facilitate expedited dismissals of frivolous claims, and generally protect existing intellectual property license royalties and durations from alteration. All of these reforms represent an effort to rehabilitate use of investor-state arbitrations.

§ 7.4   United States BITs and Model BIT

To promote national treatment and protect U.S. investors abroad, the United States embarked on a BIT program in the early 1980s. The BIT program followed earlier extensive use of Friendship, Commerce, and Navigation (FCNs) treaties, some of which provided for diplomatic state-to-state protection for U.S. foreign investors, notably regarding expropriation. Some U.S. FCNs remain in effect, *e.g.* the U.S.-Japan FCN. Unlike the FCNs, the Model U.S. BIT distinguishes treatment of foreign-owned, domestically incorporated subsidiaries and branches of foreign firms for some provisions, particularly employment. As a result of *Sumitomo Shoji America v. Avagliano,* 457 U.S. 176 (1982), the Japan-U.S. FCN treaty afforded no protection to a foreign company using its nationals in hiring inside the United States. Under the typical U.S. BIT, explicit freedom to hire nationals exists in a narrow range of management provisions.

The United States has entered into approximately 45 bilateral investment treaties (BITs). *U.S. BITs are ratified only by the Senate and, unlike U.S. FTAs, do not require implementing legislation.* Most U.S. BITs have been negotiated with small developing countries, though the United States has signed a BIT with Argentina, Egypt, Turkey and a number of Eastern European countries such as Poland. Most U.S. BITs preceded NAFTA 1994 and the 1995 WTO TRIMs Agreement regarding foreign investor performance requirements.

Earlier U.S. BITs thus placed particular emphasis on reducing performance requirements. Subsequent agreements generally reflect the foreign investor rights and investor-state claims procedures found in NAFTA 1994, which generated a large number of arbitrations and have been modified (particularly regarding indirect expropriations) by official interpretations and post-NAFTA U.S. FTAs. See Section 5.2.

Numerous U.S. investors have filed and frequently won arbitration awards for damages against Argentina. Under U.S. law, ICSID awards (below) are given full faith and credit in federal courts. The Federal Arbitration Act does not apply, and reliance on the New York Convention is not needed. Hence the enforcement rate of ICSID awards in U.S. courts is high. Argentina has as a rule unsuccessfully defended itself on foreign sovereign immunity grounds. One court held that Argentina waived its immunity by becoming a party to ICSID, and further noted that the U.S. Foreign Sovereign Immunities Act exempts arbitration awards. See *Blue Ridge Investments v. Argentina*, 902 F.Supp.2d 367 (S.D.N.Y 2012), affirmed 735 F.3d 72 (2d Cir. 2013).

United States BITs do not prohibit nations from enacting foreign investment control laws. Such laws are common in developing nations, notably in Latin America, including Mexico. But some developed nations, such as Canada, also screen foreign investments, particularly mergers and acquisitions. Most U.S. agreements provide that pre-investment laws should not interfere with any rights in the treaty, but since no rights to avoid national foreign investment controls are created, challenges to foreign investment control laws are generally not possible under U.S. BITs and FTAs.

One important provision the United States seeks to include in its BITs and FTAs is the "prompt, adequate and effective" concept of compensation subsequent to expropriation. For example, the 1994 Argentina-United States BIT uses language referring to compensation for the "fair market value. . . immediately before the expropriatory action." Many of the nations which have recently agreed to this language disputed its appropriateness during the nationalistic North-South dialogue of the 1960s and 1970s. But as they began to promote rather than restrict investment, the nations had to accept the idea that expropriated investment had to be compensated reasonably soon after the taking ("prompt"), based on a fair valuation ("adequate"), and in a realistic form ("effective").

Most U.S. BITs and FTAs do not include provisions for consultations when investment differences arise. The Argentina-United States and Sri Lanka-United States BITs are exceptions. U.S. BITs and FTAs typically provide for investor-state arbitration, sometimes with no necessary recourse to prior exhaustion of local remedies. The 2012 Model U.S. BIT is thought to have reduced the scope of foreign investor protections, but they remained very controversial in the Obama-era Trans-Pacific Partnership (TPP-12) and Transatlantic Trade and Investment (TTIP) negotiations, and in the re-negotiation of NAFTA under the Trump administration. It appears only two U.S. BITs, with Rwanda and Uruguay, have been negotiated under the 2012 Model.

The United States has considered a BIT with China, which inked a BIT with Canada in 2012 that does not cover regulatory controls over permissions to invest ("pre-investment" rules). In other words, the Canada-China BIT only concerns operational and disposal aspects of foreign investment law. This approach is common in European-based BITs, which are the most prevalent around the globe.

A linked list of U.S. BITs appears below. See: https://www.state.gov/e/eb/ifd/bit/117402.htm.

Agreement Title

Albania Bilateral Investment Treaty

Argentina Bilateral Investment Treaty

Armenia Bilateral Investment Treaty

Azerbaijan Bilateral Investment Treaty

Bahrain Bilateral Investment Treaty

Bangladesh Bilateral Investment Treaty

Bolivia Bilateral Investment Treaty

Bulgaria Bilateral Investment Treaty

Cameroon Bilateral Investment Treaty

Congo, Democratic Republic Of (Kinshasa) Bilateral Investment Treaty

Congo, Republic Of (Brazzaville) Bilateral Investment Treaty

Croatia Bilateral Investment Treaty

Czech Republic Bilateral Investment Treaty

Ecuador Bilateral Investment Treaty

Egypt Bilateral Investment Treaty

Estonia Bilateral Investment Treaty

Georgia Bilateral Investment Treaty

Grenada Bilateral Investment Treaty

Honduras Bilateral Investment Treaty

Jamaica Bilateral Investment Treaty

Jordan Bilateral Investment Treaty

Kazakhstan Bilateral Investment Treaty

Kyrgyzstan Bilateral Investment Treaty

Latvia Bilateral Investment Treaty

Lithuania Bilateral Investment Treaty

Moldova Bilateral Investment Treaty

Mongolia Bilateral Investment Treaty

Morocco Bilateral Investment Treaty

Mozambique Bilateral Investment Treaty

Panama Bilateral Investment Treaty

Poland Bilateral Investment Treaty

Poland Business and Economic Relations Treaty

Romania Bilateral Investment Treaty

Rwanda Bilateral Investment Treaty

Senegal Bilateral Investment Treaty

Slovakia Bilateral Investment Treaty

Sri Lanka Bilateral Investment Treaty

Trinidad And Tobago Bilateral Investment Treaty

Tunisia Bilateral Investment Treaty

Turkey Bilateral Investment Treaty

Ukraine Bilateral Investment Treaty

Uruguay Bilateral Investment Treaty

§ 7.5   ICSID Foreign Investment Arbitrations

Arbitration rules were adopted under the 1966 Convention on the Settlement of Investment Disputes between States and Nationals of Other States (ICSID). The text of the ICSID Convention is reproduced at the end of this chapter. Over 150 countries are parties to this Convention, but Brazil, Canada (until 2013), Mexico, Russia, Thailand and Vietnam have notably not joined the ICSID Convention. In recent years, Bolivia, Ecuador and Venezuela have withdrawn from ICSID, asserting it is biased toward investors and undermines national sovereignty.

The Convention was implemented in the United States by 22 U.S.C. § 1650 and § 1650a. An arbitral money award, rendered pursuant to the Convention, is entitled to the same full faith and credit in the United States as a final judgment of a court of general jurisdiction in a State of the United States (22 U.S.C.A.1650a).

The 1966 Convention provided for the establishment of an International Center for the Settlement of Investment Disputes (ICSID), as a non-financial organ of the World Bank (the International Bank for Reconstruction and Development). The ICSID Convention is reproduced in Appendix B of this chapter. ICSID is designed to serve as a forum for both conciliation and arbitration of disputes between private investors and host governments. It provides an institutional framework within which arbitrators, selected by the disputing parties from an ICSID Panel of Arbitrators or from elsewhere, conduct arbitration in accordance with ICSID Rules of Procedure for Arbitration Proceedings. Arbitrations are held in Washington D.C. unless agreed otherwise.

Under the 1966 Convention (Article 25), ICSID's jurisdiction extends only "to any legal dispute arising directly out of an investment, between a Contracting State or. . . any subdivision. . . and a national of another Contracting State, which the parties to the dispute consent in writing to submit to the Centre. Where the parties have given their consent, either in respect of future disputes or in respect of existing disputes, no party may withdraw its consent unilaterally." Consent by signatory states cannot unilaterally be withdrawn so long as that state is still a member of ICSID.

Thus, ICSID is an attempt to institutionalize dispute resolution between States and non-State foreign investors. The disputes often arise under contracts between foreign investors and member states. Many sovereign consents to ICSID arbitrations are found in bilateral investment treaties (BITs, see above) and free trade agreements (see for example NAFTA 1994 in Chapter 4).

Unlike international commercial arbitrations, the law of the place of arbitration generally has no influence over ICSID arbitrations, which are therefore said to be "delocalized." If one party questions such jurisdiction (predicated upon disputes arising "directly out of" an investment, between a Contracting Party and the national of another, and written consent to submission), the issue may be decided by the arbitration tribunal (Rule 41).

A party may seek annulment of any award only by an appeal to an ad hoc committee of persons drawn by the Administrative Council of ICSID from the Panel of Arbitrators under the Convention (Article 52). An ICSID award cannot be set aside by national courts or in any other way. Annulment is available only if the ICSID Tribunal was not properly constituted, exceeded its powers, seriously departed from a fundamental procedural rule, failed to state the reasons for its award, or included a member who practiced corruption.

Divergent ad hoc Annulment Committee decisions, particularly those known as the "Argentine Gas Sector Cases", have cast doubt on the legitimacy of ICSID annulment proceedings. Those cases concern challenges by foreign investors to emergency measures converting U. S. dollar bank deposits to pesos after Argentina's sovereign default in 2001. Depending on the Committee, with nearly identical facts, some investors have prevailed and others have lost arguments centered on whether Argentina was entitled to invoke public order and/or customary law of necessity defenses.

Enforcement of the award (with attachment of assets if needed) is automatically possible within ICSID signatory state courts, including those of the host state, without further review or consideration of setting aside the award. All member states must enforce ICSID awards as if they were final, binding judgments of their national courts. There is no need to go through the New York Convention procedures associated with international commercial arbitration awards.

§ 7.6   ICSID Additional Facility Arbitrations

The Convention's 1966 jurisdictional limitations have prompted the ICSID Administrative Counsel to establish an Additional Facility for conducting conciliations and arbitrations for disputes which do not arise directly out of an investment and for investment disputes in which one party is not a Contracting State to the Convention or the national of a Contracting State. The Additional Facility is intended for use by parties having long-term relationships of special economic importance to the State party to the dispute and which involve the commitment of substantial resources on the part of either party. The Facility is not designed to service disputes which fall within the 1966 Convention or which are "ordinary commercial transaction" disputes. ICSID's Secretary General must give advance approval of an agreement contemplating use of the Additional Facility.

Because the Additional Facility operates outside the scope of the 1966 Convention, the Facility has its own Arbitration Rules. Under them, ICSID Convention rules regarding exclusion of other remedies, denial of provisional relief in national courts, internal annulment review, and recognition and enforcement do not apply. Additional Facility awards are subject to the set aside rules of the arbitral seat, and enforceable under the New York Convention.

The ICSID Convention has been used under numerous bilateral investment treaties (BITs). Because neither Canada (until December 2013) nor Mexico are ICSID signatories, the Additional Facility Rules have been employed in most NAFTA 1994 investor-state arbitrations (see Section 4.8), and, more recently, in CAFTA-DR FTA investor-state arbitrations. Mexican-U.S. investor-state arbitrations under the pending USMCA 2018 Agreement are likely to follow this pattern.

§ 7.7   Energy Charter Treaty Arbitrations

Some 60 nations have signed the Energy Charter Treaty of 1991. Article 26 permits foreign investors to take to arbitration disputes with signatory states concerning investment treatment rights contained in the Charter. These rights focus on national treatment, protection from direct or indirect expropriation, and contract adherence duties of the host state. Such arbitrations can be conducted under ICSID, UNCITRAL or Stockholm Chamber of Commerce rules.

In 2009, the Permanent Court of Arbitration in The Hague held that Russia's signing of the Charter, without subsequent ratification, was sufficient to confer jurisdiction. In 2014, that body ordered Russia to pay billions to the shareholders of Yukos for what it described as Russia's "devious and calculated expropriation" of assets designed to bankrupt Yukos, which happened. Because Yukos had unclean hands as a result of tax abuses, the arbitrators reduced the award by 25% to roughly $50 billion. Collection efforts are expected to center on Russian state assets and Rosneft, the Russian company that gained control of most of these assets in a series of politically driven bankruptcy proceedings. As of 2016, some success has been had in the Dutch, French and Belgian courts.

Another controversial invocation of ISDS before the Permanent Court of Arbitration occurred in 2011 when Germany, following the Fukushima disaster, decided to close its nuclear power industry. Vattenfall, a Swedish operator of two nuclear power plants in Germany, is currently demanding billions in expropriation compensation under the Energy Charter Treaty.

§ 7.8   Link to Text of the United States Model BIT (2012)

https://www.state.gov/documents/organization/188371.pdf

§ 7.9   Link to Text of the ICSID Convention (1966)

(https://icsid.worldbank.org/en/Documents/icsiddocs/ICSID%
20Convention%20English.pdf)

Appendix A

CONSOLIDATED, EDITED TEXT OF THE USMCA 2018 AGREEMENT

(RATIFICATION PENDING AS OF APRIL 2019)

NOTE: This text was consolidated by Marina Gonzalez, faculty assistant to Professor Folsom at USD Law School, from individual USMCA Chapters 1–34 appearing on the USTR website:

(https://ustr.gov/trade-agreements/free-trade-agreements/united-states-mexico-canada-agreement/agreement-between)

For a complete consolidated version of USMCA Chapters 1–34, contact Professor Folsom at rfolsom@sandiego.edu.

AGREEMENT BETWEEN THE UNITED STATES OF AMERICA, THE UNITED MEXICAN STATES, AND CANADA

CHAPTER 1   INITIAL PROVISIONS AND GENERAL DEFINITIONS

Section A: Initial Provisions

Article 1.1:   Establishment of a Free Trade Area

The Parties, consistent with Article XXIV of the GATT 1994 and Article V of the GATS, hereby establish a free trade area.

Article 1.2:   Relation to Other Agreements

Each Party affirms its existing rights and obligations with respect to each other under the WTO Agreement and other agreements to which it and another Party are party.

Article 1.3:   Persons Exercising Delegated Governmental Authority

Each Party shall ensure that a person that has been delegated regulatory, administrative, or other governmental authority by a Party acts in accordance with the Party's obligations as set out under this Agreement in the exercise of that authority.

Section B: General Definitions

Article 1.4:   General Definitions

For the purposes of this Agreement, unless otherwise provided:

AD Agreement means the *Agreement on Implementation of Article VI of the General Agreement on Tariffs and Trade 1994*, set out in Annex 1A to the WTO Agreement;

Central level of government means:

(a)   for Canada, the Government of Canada;

(b)   for Mexico, the federal level of government; and

(c)   for the United States, the federal level of government;

Commission means the Free Trade Commission established under Article 30.1 (Establishment of the Free Trade Commission);

Covered investment means, with respect to a Party, an investment in its territory of an investor of another Party in existence as of the date of entry into force of this Agreement or established, acquired, or expanded thereafter;

Customs administration means the competent authority that is responsible under the law of a Party for the administration of customs laws and regulations or any successor of such customs administration;

Customs duty includes a duty or charge of any kind imposed on or in connection with the importation of a good, and any surtax or surcharge imposed in connection with such importation, but does not include any:

(a)   charge equivalent to an internal tax imposed consistently with Article III:2 of the GATT 1994;

(b)   fee or other charge in connection with the importation commensurate with the cost of services rendered;

(c)   antidumping or countervailing duty; and

(d)   premium offered or collected on an imported good arising out of any tendering system in respect of the administration of quantitative import restrictions, tariff rate quotas, or tariff preference levels;

Customs offense means any act committed for the purpose of, or having the effect of, avoiding a Party's laws or regulations pertaining to the provisions of this Agreement governing importations or exportations of goods between, or transit of goods through, the territories of the Parties, specifically those that violate a customs law or regulation for restrictions or prohibitions on imports or exports, duty evasion, transshipment, falsification of documents relating to the importation or exportation of goods, fraud, or smuggling of goods;

Customs Valuation Agreement means the *Agreement on Implementation of Article VII of the General Agreement on Tariffs and Trade,* set out in Annex 1A to the WTO Agreement;

Days means calendar days, including weekends and holidays;

Dispute Settlement Understanding (DSU) means the *Understanding on Rules and Procedures Governing the Settlement of Disputes*, set out in Annex 2 to the WTO Agreement;

Duty deferral program includes measures such as those governing foreign trade zones, temporary importations under bond, bonded warehouses, "maquiladoras", and inward processing programs;

Enterprise means an entity constituted or organized under applicable law, whether or not for profit, and whether privately-owned or governmentally-owned or controlled, including a corporation, trust, partnership, sole proprietorship, joint venture, association or similar organization;

Enterprise of a Party means an enterprise constituted or organized under the law of a Party;

Existing means in effect on the date of entry into force of this Agreement;

GATS means the *General Agreement on Trade in Services*, set out in Annex 1B to the WTO Agreement;

GATT 1994 means the *General Agreement on Tariffs and Trade 1994*, set out in Annex 1A to the WTO Agreement;

Goods means a merchandise, product, article, or material;

Goods of a Party means domestic products as these are understood in the GATT 1994 or such goods as the Parties may agree, and includes originating goods of a Party;

Government procurement means the process by which a government obtains the use of or acquires goods or services, or any combination thereof, for governmental purposes and not with a view to commercial sale or resale or use in the production or supply of goods or services for commercial sale or resale;

Harmonized System (HS) means the *Harmonized Commodity Description and Coding Systems*, including its General Rules of Interpretation, Section Notes, Chapter Notes, and Subheading Notes as adopted and implemented by the Parties in their respective laws;

Heading means the first four digits in the tariff classification number under the Harmonized System;

IMF Articles of Agreement means the *Articles of Agreement of the International Monetary Fund*, done at Bretton Woods, United States on July 22, 1944;

Individual means a natural person;

Measure includes any law, regulation, procedure, requirement, or practice;

NAFTA 1994 means the *North American Free Trade Agreement* that entered into force on January 1, 1994;

National means a "natural person who has the nationality of a Party" as set out below for each Party or a permanent resident of a Party:

    (a)   for Canada, a citizen of Canada;

    (b)   for Mexico, a person who has the nationality of Mexico in accordance with its applicable laws; and

    (c)   for the United States, a "national of the United States" as defined in the *Immigration and Nationality Act*;

Originating means qualifying as originating under the rules of origin set out in Chapter 4 (Rules of Origin) or Chapter 6 (Textile and Apparel Goods);

Person means a natural person or an enterprise;

Person of a Party means a national of a Party or an enterprise of a Party;

Preferential tariff treatment means the duty rate applicable to an originating good;

Publish means to disseminate information through paper or electronic means that is distributed widely and is readily accessible to the general public;

Recovered material means a material in the form of one or more individual parts that results from:

    (a)   the disassembly of a used good into individual parts; and

    (b)   the cleaning, inspecting, testing or other processing of those parts as necessary for improvement to sound working condition;

Remanufactured good means a good classified in HS Chapters 84 through 90 or under heading 94.02 except goods classified under HS headings 84.18, 85.09, 85.10, and 85.16, 87.03 or subheadings 8414.51, 8450.11, 8450.12, 8508.11, and 8517.11, that is entirely or partially composed of recovered materials and:

    (a)   has a similar life expectancy and performs the same as or similar to such a good when new; and

    (b)   has a factory warranty similar to that applicable to such a good when new;

Regional level of government means:

    (a)   for Canada, a province or territory of Canada;

    (b)   for Mexico, a state of the United Mexican States; and

    (b)   for the United States, a state of the United States, the District of Columbia, or Puerto Rico;

Safeguards Agreement means the *Agreement on Safeguards*, set out in Annex 1A to the WTO Agreement;

Sanitary or phytosanitary measure means a measure referred to in paragraph 1 of Annex A to the SPS Agreement;

SCM Agreement means the *Agreement on Subsidies and Countervailing Measures* set out in Annex 1A to the WTO Agreement;

Secretariat means the Secretariat established under Article 30.6 (The Secretariat);

SME means a small and medium-sized enterprise, including a micro-sized enterprise;

SPS Agreement means the *Agreement on the Application of Sanitary and Phytosanitary Measures*, set out in Annex 1A to the WTO Agreement;

State enterprise means an enterprise that is owned, or controlled through ownership interests, by a Party;

Subheading means the first six digits in the tariff classification number under the Harmonized System;

Territory has for each Party the meaning set out in Section C (Country-Specific Definitions);

Textile or apparel good means a textile or apparel good classified in HS subheading 4202.12, 4202.22, 4202.32, or 4202.92 (luggage, handbags and similar articles with an outer surface of textile materials), heading 50.04 through 50.07, 51.04 through 51.13, 52.04 through 52.12, 53.03 through 53.11, Chapter 54 through 63, heading 66.01 (umbrellas) or heading 70.19 (yarns and fabrics of glass fiber), subheading 9404.90 (articles of bedding and similar furnishing), or heading 96.19 (babies diapers and other sanitary textile articles);

TRIPS Agreement means the *Agreement on Trade-Related Aspects of Intellectual Property Rights*, set out in Annex 1C to the WTO Agreement;[1]

Uniform Regulations means the regulations described in Article 5.16 (Uniform Regulations);

WTO means the World Trade Organization; and

WTO Agreement means the *Marrakesh Agreement Establishing the World Trade Organization*, done at Marrakesh on April 15, 1994.

Section C: Country-Specific Definitions

For the purposes of this Agreement, unless otherwise provided:

Territory means:

    (a)   for Canada,

        (i)   the land territory, air space, internal waters, and territorial sea of Canada,

        (ii)   the exclusive economic zone of Canada, and

        (iii)   the continental shelf of Canada,

        as determined by its domestic law and consistent with international law.

---

[1]   For greater certainty, TRIPS Agreement includes any waiver in force between the Parties of any provision of the TRIPS Agreement granted by WTO Members in accordance with the WTO Agreement.

(b) for Mexico,

    (i)   the land territory, including the states of the Federation and Mexico City,

    (ii) the air space, and

    (iii) the internal waters, territorial sea, and any areas beyond the territorial seas of Mexico within which Mexico may exercise sovereign rights and jurisdiction, as determined by its domestic law, consistent with the *United Nations Convention on the Law of the Sea*, done at Montego Bay on December 10, 1982; and

(c) for the United States,

    (i)   the customs territory of the United States, which includes the 50 states, the District of Columbia, and Puerto Rico,

    (ii) the foreign trade zones located in the United States and Puerto Rico, and

    (iii) the territorial sea and air space of the United States and any area beyond the territorial sea within which, in accordance with customary international law as reflected in the *United Nations Convention on the Law of the Sea*, the United States may exercise sovereign rights or jurisdiction.

CHAPTER 2   NATIONAL TREATMENT AND MARKET ACCESS FOR GOODS

Article 2.1:   Definitions

For the purposes of this Chapter:

Advertising films and recordings means recorded visual media or audio materials that exhibit for prospective customers the nature or operation of goods or services offered for sale or lease by a person established or resident in the territory of a Party, provided that the films and recordings are not for broadcast to the general public;

Commercial samples of negligible value means commercial samples having a value, individually or in the aggregate as shipped, of not more than one U.S. dollar, or the equivalent amount in the currency of another Party, or so marked, torn, perforated, or otherwise treated that they are unsuitable for sale or use except as commercial samples;

Consular transactions means requirements that goods of a Party intended for export to the territory of another Party must first be submitted to the supervision of the consul of the importing Party in the territory of the exporting Party, or in the territory of a non-Party, for the purpose of obtaining a consular invoice or a consular visa for a commercial invoice, certificate of origin, manifest, shipper's export declaration, or any other customs documentation in connection with the importation of the good;

Consumed means:

(a)   actually consumed; or

(b)   further processed or manufactured so as to result in a substantial change in the value, form, or use of the good or in the production of another good;

Customs duty includes a duty or charge of any kind imposed on or in connection with the importation of a good, and any surtax or surcharge imposed in connection with such importation, but does not include any:

(a)   charge equivalent to an internal tax imposed consistently with Article III:2 of the GATT 1994;

(b)   fee or other charge in connection with the importation commensurate with the cost of the services rendered;

(c)   anti-dumping or countervailing duty; and

(d)   premium offered or collected on an imported good arising out of any tendering system in respect of the administration of quantitative import restrictions, tariff rate quotas, or tariff preference levels;

Distributor means a person of a Party who is responsible for the commercial distribution, agency, concession, or representation in the territory of the Party of goods of another Party;

Duty deferral program includes measures such as those governing foreign trade zones, temporary importations under bond, bonded warehouses, "maquiladoras", and inward processing programs;

Duty-free means free of customs duty;

Goods admitted for sports purposes means sports requisites admitted into the territory of the importing Party for use in sports contests, demonstrations, or training in the territory of the Party;

Import licensing means an administrative procedure requiring the submission of an application or other documentation (other than that generally required for customs clearance purposes) to the relevant administrative body as a prior condition for importation into the territory of the importing Party;

Import Licensing Agreement means the *Agreement on Import Licensing Procedures*, set out in Annex 1A to the WTO Agreement;

Performance requirement means a requirement that:

(a)   a given level or percentage of goods or services be exported;

(b)   a domestic good or service of the Party granting a waiver of a custom duty or an import license be substituted for an imported good or service;

(c)   a person benefitting from a waiver of a custom duty or a grant of an import license, purchase a good or service in the territory of the Party granting the waiver or the import license or accord a preference to a domestically produced good or service;

(d) a person benefitting from a waiver of a custom duty or a grant of an import license produce a good or provide a service, in the territory of the Party granting the waiver or import license, with a given level or percentage of domestic content; or

(e) relates in any way the volume or value of imports to the volume or value of exports or to the amount of foreign exchange inflows;

but does not include a requirement that an imported good be:

(f) subsequently exported;

(g) used as a material in the production of another good that is subsequently exported;

(h) substituted by an identical or similar good used as a material in the production of another good that is subsequently exported; or

(i) substituted by an identical or similar good that is subsequently exported;

Printed advertising materials means those goods classified in Chapter 49 of the Harmonized System, including brochures, pamphlets, leaflets, trade catalogues, yearbooks published by trade associations, tourist promotional materials, and posters, that are used to promote, publicize, or advertise a good or service, are essentially intended to advertise a good or service, and are supplied free of charge;

Satisfactory evidence means:

(a) a receipt, or a copy of a receipt, evidencing payment of a customs duty on a particular entry;

(b) a copy of the entry document with evidence that it was received by a customs administration;

(c) a copy of a final customs duty determination by a customs administration respecting the relevant entry; or

(d) any other evidence of payment of a customs duty acceptable under the Uniform Regulations; and

Used vehicle means an automobile, a truck, a bus, or a special purpose motor vehicle, not including a motorcycle, that:

(a) has been sold, leased, or loaned;

(b) has been driven for more than:

(i) 1,000 kilometers if the vehicle has a gross weight of less than five metric tons, or

    (ii)   5,000 kilometers if the vehicle has a gross weight of five metric tons or more; or

(c)   was manufactured prior to the current year and at least 90 days have elapsed since the date of manufacture.

Article 2.2:   Scope

Except as otherwise provided in this Agreement, this Chapter applies to trade in goods of a Party.

Article 2.3:   National Treatment

1.   Each Party shall accord national treatment to the goods of another Party in accordance with Article III of the GATT 1994, including its interpretative notes, and to this end, Article III of the GATT 1994 and its interpretative notes are incorporated into and made part of this Agreement, *mutatis mutandis*.

2.   The treatment to be accorded by a Party under paragraph 1 means, with respect to a regional level of government, treatment no less favorable than the most favorable treatment that regional level of government accords to any like, directly competitive, or substitutable goods, as the case may be, of the Party of which it forms a part.

3.   Paragraphs 1 and 2 do not apply to the measures set out in Annex 2-A (Exceptions to Article 2.3 (National Treatment) and Article 2.11 (Import and Export Restrictions)).

Article 2.4:   Treatment of Customs Duties

1.   Unless otherwise provided in this Agreement, no Party shall increase any existing customs duty, or adopt any new customs duty, on an originating good.

2.   Unless otherwise provided in this Agreement, each Party shall apply a customs duty on an originating good in accordance with its Schedule to Annex 2-B (Tariff Commitments).

3.   On the request of a Party, the Parties shall consult to consider accelerating or broadening the scope of the elimination of customs duties set out in their Schedules to Annex 2-B (Tariff Commitments). An agreement between two or more Parties to accelerate or broaden the scope of the elimination of a customs duty on an originating good shall supersede any customs duty rate determined pursuant to those Parties' Schedules to Annex 2-B (Tariff Commitments) for that good once approved by each Party in accordance with its applicable legal procedures.

4.   A Party may at any time unilaterally accelerate the elimination of customs duties set out in its Schedule to Annex 2-B (Tariff Commitments) on originating goods.

5.   Annex 2-C (Provisions Between Mexico and the United States on Automotive Goods) contains additional provisions between Mexico and the United States relating to customs duties on automotive goods that are not originating under Chapter 4 (Rules of Origin).

Article 2.5:   Drawback and Duty Deferral Programs

1. Except as otherwise provided in this Article, no Party shall refund the amount of customs duties paid, or waive or reduce the amount of customs duties owed, on a good imported into its territory, on condition that the good is:

    (a) subsequently exported to the territory of another Party;

    (b) used as a material in the production of another good that is subsequently exported to the territory of another Party; or

    (c) substituted by an identical or similar good used as a material in the production of another good that is subsequently exported to the territory of another Party, in an amount that exceeds the lesser of the total amount of customs duties paid or owed on the good on importation into its territory and the total amount of customs duties paid to another Party on the good that has been subsequently exported to the territory of that other Party.

2. No Party shall, on condition of export, refund, waive, or reduce:

    (a) an antidumping or countervailing duty;

    (b) a premium offered or collected on an imported good arising out of any tendering system in respect of the administration of quantitative import restrictions, or tariff rate quotas or tariff preference levels; or

    (c) customs duties paid or owed on a good imported into its territory and substituted by an identical or similar good that is subsequently exported to the territory of another Party.

3. If a good is imported into the territory of a Party pursuant to a duty deferral program and is subsequently exported to the territory of another Party, or is used as a material in the production of another good that is subsequently exported to the territory of another Party, or is substituted by an identical or similar good used as a material in the production of another good that is subsequently exported to the territory of another Party, the Party from whose territory the good is exported:

    (a) shall assess the customs duty as if the exported good had been withdrawn for domestic consumption; and

    (b) may waive or reduce such customs duty to the extent permitted under paragraph 1.

4. In determining the amount of a customs duty that may be refunded, waived, or reduced pursuant to paragraph 1 on a good imported into its territory, each Party shall require presentation of satisfactory evidence of the amount of customs duties paid to another Party on the good that has been subsequently exported to the territory of that other Party.

5. If satisfactory evidence of the customs duty paid to the Party to which a good is subsequently exported under a duty deferral program

described in paragraph 3 is not presented within 60 days after the date of exportation, the Party from whose territory the good was exported:

(a)   shall collect the customs duty as if the exported good had been withdrawn for domestic consumption; and

(b)   may refund such customs duty, to the extent permitted under paragraph 1, on the timely presentation of such evidence under its laws and regulations.

6.   This Article does not apply to:

(a)   a good entered under bond for transportation and exportation to the territory of another Party;

(b)   a good exported to the territory of another Party in the same condition as when imported into the territory of the Party from which the good was exported.[1] If that good has been commingled with fungible goods and exported in the same condition, its origin for purposes of this subparagraph may be determined on the basis of inventory management methods such as first-in, first-out or last-in, first-out. For greater certainty, nothing in this subparagraph shall be construed to permit a Party to waive, refund, or reduce a customs duty contrary to paragraph 2(c);

(c)   a good imported into the territory of a Party that is deemed to be exported from its territory, is used as a material in the production of another good that is deemed to be exported to the territory of another Party, or is substituted by an identical or similar good used as a material in the production of another good that is deemed to be exported to the territory of another Party, by reason of:

   (i)   delivery to a duty-free shop,

   (ii)   delivery for ship's stores or supplies for ships or aircraft, or

   (iii) delivery for use in joint undertakings of two or more of the Parties and that will subsequently become the property of the Party into whose territory the good was deemed to be exported;

(d)   a refund of customs duties by a Party on a particular good imported into its territory and subsequently exported to the territory of another Party, if that refund is granted by reason of the failure of that good to conform to sample or specification, or by reason of the shipment of that good without the consent of the consignee;

---

[1]   Processes such as testing, cleaning, repacking, inspecting, sorting, or marking a good, or preserving a good in its same condition, shall not be considered to change the good's condition.

(e)   an originating good that is imported into the territory of a Party and is subsequently exported to the territory of another Party, or used as a material in the production of another good that is subsequently exported to the territory of another Party, or is substituted by an identical or similar good used as a material in the production of another good that is subsequently exported to the territory of another Party;

(f)   for exports from the territory of the United States to the territory of Canada or Mexico, goods provided for in U.S. tariff items 1701.13.20 or 1701.14.20 that are imported into the territory of the United States under any re-export program or any like program and used as a material in the production of, or substituted by an identical or similar good used as a material in the production of:

     (i)   a good provided for in Canadian tariff item 1701.99.00 or Mexican tariff items 1701.99.01, 1701.99.02, and 1701.99.99 (refined sugar), or

     (ii)   sugar containing products that are prepared foodstuffs or beverages classified in headings 17.04 and 18.06 or in Chapters 19, 20, 21, or 22; or

(g)   for trade between Canada and the United States:

     (i)   imported citrus products,

     (ii)   an imported good used as a material in the production of, or substituted by an identical or similar good used as a material in the production of, a good provided for in U.S. tariff items 5811.00.20 (quilted cotton piece goods), 5811.00.30 (quilted man-made piece goods) or 6307.90.99 (furniture moving pads), or Canadian tariff items 5811.00.10 (quilted cotton piece goods), 5811.00.20 (quilted man-made piece goods) or 6307.90.30 (furniture moving pads), that are subject to the most-favored-nation rate of duty when exported to the territory of the other Party, and

     (iii)   an imported good used as a material in the production of apparel that is subject to the most-favored-nation rate of duty when exported to the territory of the other Party.

7.   For the purposes of this Article:

Identical or similar goods means "identical goods" and "similar goods," respectively, as defined in the Customs Valuation Agreement, or as otherwise provided for under the law of the importing Party;

Material means "material" as defined in Article 4.1 (Definitions);

Used means "used" as defined in Article 4.1 (Definitions).

8.   If a good referred to by a tariff item number in this Article is described in parentheses following the tariff item number, the description is provided for purposes of reference only.

Article 2.6:   Waiver of Customs Duties

No Party shall adopt or maintain any waiver of a customs duty if the waiver is conditioned, explicitly or implicitly, on the fulfillment of a performance requirement.

* * *

Article 2.10:   Most-Favored-Nation Rates of Duty on Certain Goods

1.   Each Party shall accord most-favored-nation duty-free treatment to a good provided for under the tariff provisions set out in Tables 2.10.1, 2.10.2, and 2.10.3.

2.   Notwithstanding Chapter 4 (Rules of Origin), each Party shall consider a good set out in Table 2.10.1, if imported into its territory from the territory of another Party, to be an originating good.

[Tables Omitted]

Article 2.11:   Import and Export Restrictions

1.   Except as otherwise provided in this Agreement, no Party shall adopt or maintain any prohibition or restriction on the importation of any good of another Party or on the exportation or sale for export of any good destined for the territory of another Party, except in accordance with Article XI of the GATT 1994, including its interpretative notes, and to this end Article XI of the GATT 1994 and its interpretative notes are incorporated into and made a part of this Agreement, *mutatis mutandis*.

2.   The Parties understand that GATT 1994 rights and obligations incorporated by paragraph 1 prohibit, in any circumstances in which any other form of restriction is prohibited, a Party from adopting or maintaining:

      (a)   an export or import price requirement, except as permitted in enforcement of antidumping and countervailing duty orders or price undertakings;

      (b)   import licensing conditioned on the fulfilment of a performance requirement; or

      (c)   a voluntary export restraint inconsistent with Article VI of the GATT 1994, as implemented under Article 18 of the SCM Agreement and Article 8.1 of the AD Agreement.

3.   If a Party adopts or maintains a prohibition or restriction on the importation from or exportation to a non-Party of a good, nothing in this Agreement shall be construed to prevent that Party from:

      (a)   limiting or prohibiting the importation of the good of that non-Party from the territory of another Party; or

(b)   requiring, as a condition for exporting the good of the Party to the territory of another Party, that the good not be re-exported to the non-Party, directly or indirectly, without being consumed in the territory of the other Party.

4.   If a Party adopts or maintains a prohibition or restriction on the importation of a good from a non-Party, the Parties, on the request of a Party, shall consult with a view to avoiding undue interference with or distortion of pricing, marketing, or distribution arrangements in another Party.

5.   No Party shall as a condition for engaging in importation generally, or for the importation of a particular good, require a person of another Party to establish or maintain a contractual or other relationship with a distributor in its territory.

6.   For greater certainty, paragraph 5 does not prevent a Party from requiring that a person referred to in that paragraph designate a point of contact for the purpose of facilitating communications between its regulatory authorities and that person.

7.   Paragraphs 1 through 6 do not apply to the measures set out in Annex 2-A (Exceptions to Article 2.3 (National Treatment) and Article 2.11 (Import and Export Restrictions)).

8.   For greater certainty, paragraph 1 applies to the importation of any good implementing or incorporating cryptography, if the good is not designed or modified specifically for government use and is sold or otherwise made available to the public.

9.   For greater certainty, no Party shall adopt or maintain a prohibition or restriction on the importation of originating used vehicles from the territory of another Party. This Article does not prevent a Party from applying motor vehicle safety or emissions measures, or vehicle registration requirements, of general application to originating used vehicles in a manner consistent with this Agreement.

Article 2.12:   Remanufactured Goods

1.   For greater certainty, Article 2.11.1 (Import and Export Restrictions) applies to prohibitions and restrictions on a remanufactured good.

2.   Subject to its obligations under this Agreement and the WTO Agreement, a Party may require that a remanufactured good:

(a)   be identified as such, including through labelling, for distribution or sale in its territory, and

(b)   meet all applicable technical requirements that apply to an equivalent good in new condition.

3.   If a Party adopts or maintains a prohibition or a restriction on a used good, it shall not apply the measure to a remanufactured good.

Article 2.13:   Transparency in Import Licensing Procedures

1.   Subject to paragraph 2, each Party shall notify the other Parties of its existing import licensing procedures, if any, as soon as practicable, after this Agreement enters into force. The notification shall:

   (a)   include the information specified in Article 5.2 of the Import Licensing Agreement and in the annual questionnaire on import licensing procedures described in Article 7.3 of the Import Licensing Agreement; and

   (b)   be without prejudice as to whether the import licensing procedures are consistent with this Agreement.

2.   A Party shall be deemed to be in compliance with the obligations in paragraph 1 with respect to an import licensing procedure if:

   (a)   it has notified that procedure to the Committee on Import Licensing established under Article 4 of the Import Licensing Agreement together with the information specified in Article 5.2 of that agreement; and

   (b)   it has provided the information requested in the questionnaire on import licensing procedures under Article 7.3 of the Import Licensing Agreement in its most recent submission to the Committee on Import Licensing before the entry into force of this Agreement.

3.   A Party shall publish on an official government website any new or modified import licensing procedure, including any information that it is required to be published under Article 1.4(a) of the Import Licensing Agreement. To the extent possible, the Party shall do so at least 20 days before the new procedure or modification takes effect.

4.   Each Party shall respond within 60 days to a reasonable inquiry from another Party concerning its licensing rules and its procedures for the submission of an application for an import license, including the eligibility of persons, firms, and institutions to make an application, any administrative body to be approached, and the list of products subject to the licensing requirement.

5.   If a Party denies an import license application with respect to a good of another Party, it shall, on request of the applicant and within a reasonable period after receiving the request, provide the applicant with a written explanation of the reason for the denial.

6.   No Party shall apply an import licensing procedure to a good of another Party unless the Party has complied with the requirements of paragraphs 1 or 2, and 3, with respect to that procedure.

Article 2.14:   Transparency in Export Licensing Procedures

1.   Within 30 days after the date of entry into force of this Agreement, each Party shall notify the other Parties in writing of the publications in which its export licensing procedures, if any, are set out, including addresses of relevant government websites on which the procedures are

published. Thereafter, each Party shall publish any new export licensing procedure, or any modification of an export licensing procedure, it adopts as soon as practicable but no later than 30 days after the new procedure or modification takes effect.

2.   Each Party shall ensure that it includes in the publications it has notified under paragraph 1:

(a)   the texts of its export licensing procedures, including any modifications it makes to those procedures;

(b)   the goods subject to each licensing procedure;

(c)   for each licensing procedure, a description of:

(i)   the process for applying for a license, and

(ii)   any criteria an applicant must meet to be eligible to apply for a license, such as possessing an activity license, establishing or maintaining an investment, or operating through a particular form of establishment in a Party's territory;

(d)   a contact point from which interested persons can obtain further information on the conditions for obtaining an export license;

(e)   any administrative body to which an application or other relevant documentation is to be submitted;

(f)   a description of or a citation to a publication reproducing in full any measure that the export licensing procedure implements;

(g)   the period during which each export licensing procedure will be in effect, unless the procedure will remain in effect until withdrawn or revised in a new publication;

(h)   if the Party intends to use a licensing procedure to administer an export quota, the overall quantity and, if practicable, the value of the quota, and the opening and closing dates of the quota; and

(i)   any exemptions from or exceptions to the requirement to obtain an export license that are available to the public, how to request or use these exemptions or exceptions, and the criteria for the exemptions or exceptions.

3.   Each Party shall provide another Party, upon the other Party's request and to the extent practicable, the following information regarding a particular export licensing procedure that it adopts or maintains, except when doing so would reveal business proprietary or other confidential information of a particular person:

(a)   the aggregate number of licenses the Party has granted over a recent period specified in the other Party's request; and

(b)   measures, if any, that the Party has adopted in conjunction with the licensing procedure to restrict domestic production or consumption or to stabilize production, supply, or prices for the relevant good.

4.   This Article does not require a Party to grant an export license, or prevent a Party from implementing its obligations or commitments under United Nations Security Council Resolutions, as well as multilateral non-proliferation regimes, including: the *Wassenaar Arrangement on Export Controls for Conventional Arms and Dual-Use Goods and Technologies*; Nuclear Suppliers Group; the Australia Group; *Convention on the Prohibition of the Development, Production, Stockpiling and Use of Chemical Weapons and on Their Destruction*, done at Geneva, September 3, 1992, and signed at Paris, January 13, 1993; *Convention on the Prohibition of the Development, Production and Stockpiling of Bacteriological (Biological) and Toxin Weapons and on Their Destruction*, done at Washington, London, and Moscow, April 10, 1972; *Treaty on the Non-Proliferation of Nuclear Weapons* done at Washington, London, and Moscow, July 1, 1968; and the Missile Technology Control Regime.

5.   For the purposes of this Article, export licensing procedure means a requirement that a Party adopts or maintains under which an exporter must, as a condition for exporting a good from the Party's territory, submit an application or other documentation to an administrative body or bodies, but does not include customs documentation required in the normal course of trade or any requirement that must be fulfilled prior to introduction of the good into commerce within the Party's territory.

Article 2.15:   Export Duties, Taxes, or Other Charges

No Party shall adopt or maintain any duty, tax, or other charge on the export of any good to the territory of another Party, unless the duty, tax, or charge is also applied to the good if destined for domestic consumption.

Article 2.16:   Administrative Fees and Formalities

1.   Each Party shall ensure, in accordance with Article VIII:1 of the GATT 1994 and its interpretative notes, that all fees and charges of whatever character (other than customs duties, charges equivalent to an internal tax or other internal charges applied in a manner consistent with Article III:2 of the GATT 1994, and antidumping or countervailing duties) imposed on or in connection with importation or exportation are limited in amount to the approximate cost of services rendered and do not represent an indirect protection to a domestic good or a taxation of an import or export for fiscal purposes.

2.   No Party shall require a consular transaction, including a related fee or charge, in connection with the importation of a good of another Party.[2]

---

[2]   For Mexico, this paragraph does not apply to the procedures for the duty-free entry of personal and household effects of natural persons relocating to Mexico.

3.   No Party shall adopt or maintain a customs user fee on an originating good.[3]

Article 2.17:   Committee on Trade in Goods

1.   The Parties hereby establish a Committee on Trade in Goods (Goods Committee), comprising representatives of each Party.

2.   The Goods Committee shall meet on the request of a Party or the Commission to consider any matter arising under this Chapter.

3.   The Goods Committee shall meet at a venue and time as the Parties decide or by electronic means. In-person meetings will be held alternately in the territory of each Party.

4.   The Goods Committee's functions shall include:

(a)   monitoring the implementation and administration of this Chapter;

(b)   promoting trade in goods between the Parties;

(c)   providing a forum for the Parties to consult and endeavor to resolve issues relating to this Chapter, including, as appropriate, in coordination or jointly with other Committees, working groups, or other subsidiary bodies established under this Agreement;

(d)   promptly seeking to address tariff and non-tariff barriers to trade in goods between the Parties and, if appropriate, referring the matter to the Commission for its consideration;

(e)   coordinating the exchange of information on trade in goods between the Parties;

(f)   discussing and endeavoring to resolve any difference that may arise between the Parties on matters related to the Harmonized System, including ensuring that each Party's obligations under this Agreement are not altered by its implementation of future amendments to the Harmonized System into its national nomenclature;

(g)   referring to another committee established under this Agreement those issues that may be relevant to that committee, as appropriate; and

(h)   undertaking additional work that the Commission may assign, or another committee may refer, to it.

---

[3]   The merchandise processing fee (MPF) is the only customs user fee of the United States to which this paragraph applies. The *derecho de trámite aduanero* is the only customs user fee of Mexico to which this paragraph applies.

ANNEX 2-A EXCEPTIONS TO ARTICLE 2.3 (NATIONAL TREATMENT) AND ARTICLE 2.11 (IMPORT AND EXPORT RESTRICTIONS)

Article 2.A.1: Application of Article 2.3 (National Treatment) and Article 2.11 (Import and Export Restrictions)

1. Article 2.3 (National Treatment) and Article 2.11 (Import and Export Restrictions) do not apply to the continuation, renewal, or amendment made to any law, statute, decree, or administrative regulation giving rise to a measure set out in the articles of this Annex to the extent that the continuation, renewal, or amendment does not decrease the conformity of the measure listed with Article 2.3 (National Treatment) and Article 2.11 (Import and Export Restrictions).

2. Article 2.3 (National Treatment) and Article 2.11 (Import and Export Restrictions) shall not apply to the import and export of rough diamonds (HS codes 7102.10, 7102.21, and 7102.31), pursuant to the Kimberley Process Certification Scheme and any subsequent amendments to that scheme.

Article 2.A.2: Measures of Canada

1. Article 2.3 (National Treatment) and Article 2.11 (Import and Export Restrictions) do not apply to:

    (a) the export of logs of all species;

    (b) the export of unprocessed fish pursuant to the following provincial laws and their related regulations:

        (i)   *New Brunswick Seafood Processing Act, SNB 2006, c S-5.3,* and *Fisheries and Aquaculture Development Act, SNB 2009, c F-15.001*;

        (ii) *Newfoundland and Labrador Fish Inspection Act, RSNL 1990, c F-12*;

        (iii) *Nova Scotia Fisheries and Coastal Resources Act, Chapter 25 of the Acts of 1996*;

        (iv) *Prince Edward Island Fisheries Act, R.S.P.E.I. 1988, Cap. F-13.01, and Fish Inspection Act, R.S.P.E.I. 1988, Cap. F-1*; and

        (v)   *Quebec Marine Products Processing Act, CQLR c T-11.01.*

For greater certainty, notwithstanding Article 2.A.1:1 of this Annex, Article 2.3 (National Treatment) and 2.11 (Import and Export Restrictions) shall not apply to any requirements for the export of unprocessed fish authorized under the above laws and their related regulations that are not being applied upon the entry into force of this Agreement, or that are in force upon the entry into force of this Agreement but suspended after that date, and subsequently applied;

(c)   the importation of goods of the prohibited provisions of tariff items 9897.00.00, 9898.00.00, and 9899.00.00 referred to in the Schedule of the *Customs Tariff,* except as otherwise provided;

(d)   the use of ships in the coasting trade of Canada; and

(e)   Canadian excise duties on the absolute volume of ethyl alcohol, as listed under tariff item 2207.10.90 in Canada's Schedule of Concessions annexed to GATT 1994 (Schedule V), used in manufacturing under the provisions of the *Excise Act, 2001,* Statutes of Canada 2002, c. 22, as amended.

2.   Article 2.3 (National Treatment) and Article 2.11 (Import and Export Restrictions) do not apply to quantitative import restrictions on originating goods from the United States classified in tariff headings 89.01, 89.04, and 89.05, and tariff items 8902.00.10 and 8903.99.90 (of an overall length exceeding 9.2 m only) for as long as the measures adopted under the *Merchant Marine Act of 1920* and *Passenger Vessel Services Act* and 46 U.S.C. §§ 12102, 12113, and 12116, apply with quantitative effect to comparable originating goods from Canada sold or offered for sale into the U.S. market.

Article 2.A.3:   Measures of Mexico

1.   Paragraphs 1 through 4 of Article 2.11 (Import and Export Restrictions) do not apply to:

(a)   export measures pursuant to Article 48 of the Hydrocarbons Law (*Ley de Hidrocarburos*) published in Mexico's Official Gazette (*Diario Oficial de la Federación*) on August 11, 2014, for the tariff items under the "Agreement that amends and establishes the classification and codification of Hydrocarbons and Petroleum Products subject to import and export permits by the Ministry of Energy" (*Acuerdo que modifica al diverso por el que se establece la clasificación y codificación de Hidrocarburos y Petrolíferos cuya importación y exportación está sujeta a Permiso Previo por parte de la Secretaría de Energía*) published in the Mexico's Official Gazette (*Diario Oficial de la Federación*) on December 4, 2017, subject to Mexico's rights and obligations under the WTO Agreement, including with regard to transparency and non-discriminatory treatment; and

(b)   prohibitions or restrictions on the importation into Mexico of used tyres, used apparel, non-originating used vehicles, and used chassis equipped with vehicle motors set forth in paragraphs 1(I) and 5 of Annex 2.2.1 of the Resolution through which the Ministry of the Economy establishes Rules and General Criteria on International Trade (*Acuerdo por el que la Secretaría de Economía emite reglas y criterios de carácter general en materia de Comercio Exterior*) published in Mexico's Official Gazette (*Diario Oficial de la Federación*) on December 31, 2012.

Article 2.A.4:   Measures of the United States

Article 2.3 (National Treatment) and Article 2.11 (Import and Export Restrictions) do not apply to:

(a)   controls on the export of logs of all species; and

(b)   (i) measures under existing provisions of the *Merchant Marine Act of 1920* and *Passenger Vessel Services Act* and 46 U.S.C. §§ 12102, 12113, and 12116, to the extent that such measures were mandatory legislation at the time of the accession of the United States to the General Agreement on Tariffs and Trade 1947 (GATT 1947) and have not been amended so as to decrease their conformity with Part II of the GATT 1947;

    (ii)   the continuation or prompt renewal of a non-conforming provision of any statute referred to in clause (i); and

    (iii)   the amendment to a non-conforming provision of any statute referred to in clause (i) to the extent that the amendment does not decrease the conformity of the provision with Articles 2.3 (National Treatment) and 2.11 (Import and Export Restrictions).

ANNEX 2-B   TARIFF COMMITMENTS

1.   The rate of customs duty for an originating good under this Agreement is indicated in each Party's Schedule to this Annex.

2.   Except as otherwise provided in a Party's Schedule to this Annex, and in accordance with Article 2.4 (Treatment of Customs Duties), the rate of customs duty on originating goods is designated with "0," and these goods shall be duty-free on the date of entry into force of this Agreement.

3.   For originating goods provided for in the items marked with an asterisk (*) in a Party's Schedule to this Annex, the tariff treatment set forth in Appendix 1 to that Party's Schedule applies.

[Tariff Schedule General Notes and Provisions on Tariff-Rate Quotas for United States, Mexico and Canada Omitted]

ANNEX 2-C   PROVISIONS BETWEEN MEXICO AND THE UNITED STATES ON AUTOMOTIVE GOODS

1.   This Annex does not apply to originating goods that qualify for duty free preferential tariff treatment under Chapter 4 (Rules of Origin) that are imported to the United States from Mexico and are:

(a)   passenger vehicles classified in subheadings 8703.21 through 8703.90;

(b)   light trucks classified in subheading 8704.21 or 8704.31, or

(c)   auto parts listed in the Appendix to this Annex.

2.   The customs duty applied by the United States on passenger vehicles imported from Mexico classified in subheadings 8703.21 through 8703.90 that do not qualify as originating under Chapter 4 (Rules of Origin), shall not exceed the lesser of 2.5 percent or the United States' most-favored-nation (MFN) applied rate in effect at the time of the importation of the good.

3.   The customs duty applied by the United States on light trucks imported from Mexico classified in subheadings 8704.21 or 8704.31 that do not qualify as originating under Chapter 4 (Rules of Origin), shall not exceed the lesser of 25 percent or the United States' MFN applied rate in effect at the time of the importation of the good.

4.   The customs duty applied by the United States on auto parts imported from Mexico listed in the Appendix to this Annex that do not qualify as originating under Chapter 4 (Rules of Origin), shall not exceed the lesser of the United States' MFN applied rate in effect on August 1, 2018 or the MFN applied rate in effect at the time of the importation of the good.

5.   If the United States implements any measure that increases its MFN applied rate in effect on August 1, 2018 on passenger vehicles classified in subheadings 8703.21 through 8703.90, or on auto parts listed in the Appendix to this Annex, and in order to protect Mexico's ability to export passenger vehicles and auto parts throughout the territories of the Parties at volumes that take into account Mexico's existing manufacturing capacity, the following shall apply:

(a)   The customs duty applied by the United States on a passenger vehicle classified in subheadings 8703.21 through 8703.90 imported from Mexico that does not qualify as originating under Chapter 4 (Rules of Origin) shall not exceed 2.5 percent, provided that the vehicle meets a regional value content requirement of at least 62.5 percent under the net cost method as set out under Article 4.5 (Regional Value Content). In addition, averaging provisions under Article 10.4 of the Appendix to Annex 4-B (Regional Value Content for Other Vehicles) and other provisions under Article 10.6 of the Appendix to Annex 4-B (Regional Value Content for Other Vehicles) apply. The United States may limit this treatment to 1,600,000 vehicles in any calendar year.

(b)   The customs duty applied by the United States on an auto part listed in the Appendix to this Annex imported from Mexico that do not qualify as originating under Chapter 4 (Rules of Origin) shall not exceed the United States' MFN applied rate in effect on August 1, 2018, provided that the part meets a regional value content requirement of at least 50 percent under the net cost method, or 60 percent under the transaction value method, as set out under Article 4.5 (Regional Value Content) or any non-originating materials used in the production of the auto part are classified in a different heading than the auto part. In addition, averaging provisions under Article 10.5 of the Appendix to Annex 4-B (Regional Value Content for Other Vehicles). The United States may limit this treatment to auto parts valued at 108 billion U.S. dollars in any calendar year.

(c)   Mexico shall monitor and allocate or otherwise administer quantities of passenger vehicles and auto parts eligible for this treatment under subparagraphs (a) and (b).

(d)   The customs duty applied by the United States on passenger vehicles classified in subheadings 8703.21 through 8703.90 or auto parts listed in the Appendix to this Annex that do not qualify as originating under Chapter 4 (Rules of Origin) imported from Mexico in excess of the quantities set out in subparagraphs (a) and (b) shall be the United States' MFN applied rate in effect at the time of importation of the good.

(e)   For greater certainty, goods described under subparagraphs (a) and (b) shall be subject to Chapter 5 (Origin Procedures).

[ANNEX LIST OF AUTO PARTS OMITTED]

CHAPTER 3   AGRICULTURE

Section A: General Provisions

Article 3.1:Definitions

For the purposes of this Chapter:

Agricultural good means agricultural products referred to in Article 2 of the Agreement on Agriculture;

Export subsidy has the same meaning as assigned to "export subsidies" in Article 1(e) of the Agreement on Agriculture; and

Agreement on Agriculture means the *Agreement on Agriculture,* set out in Annex 1A to the WTO Agreement.

Article 3.2:   Scope

1.   This Chapter applies to measures adopted or maintained by a Party relating to trade in agricultural goods.

2.   In the event of any inconsistency between this Chapter and another provision of this Agreement, this Chapter shall prevail to the extent of the inconsistency.

Article 3.3:   International Cooperation

The Parties shall work together at the WTO to promote increased transparency and to improve and further develop multilateral disciplines on market access, domestic support, and export competition with the objective of substantial progressive reductions in support and protection resulting in fundamental reform.

Article 3.4:   Export Competition

1. No Party shall adopt or maintain an export subsidy on any agricultural good destined for the territory of another Party.

2. If a Party considers that export financing support granted by another Party results or may result in a distorting effect on trade between the Parties, or considers that an export subsidy is being granted by another Party, with respect to an agricultural good, it may request a discussion on the matter with the other Party. The responding Party shall agree to discuss the matter with the requesting Party as soon as practicable.

Article 3.5:   Export Restrictions—Food Security

1. For the purpose of this Article, "foodstuff" includes fish and fish products intended for human consumption.

2. The Parties recognize that under Article XI:2(a) of the GATT 1994 a Party may temporarily apply an export prohibition or restriction that is otherwise prohibited under Article XI:1 of the GATT 1994 on a foodstuff to prevent or relieve a critical shortage, subject to meeting the conditions set out in Article 12.1 of the Agreement on Agriculture.

3. In addition to the conditions set out in Article 12.1 of the Agreement on Agriculture under which a Party may apply an export prohibition or restriction, other than a duty, tax, or other charge on a foodstuff, a Party that:

    (a) imposes an export prohibition or restriction on the exportation or sale for export of a foodstuff to another Party shall notify the measure to the other Parties at least 30 days prior to the date the measure takes effect, except when the critical shortage is caused by an event constituting *force majeure*, in which case the Party shall notify prior to the date the measure takes effect; or

    (b) maintains an export prohibition or restriction as of the date of entry into force of this Agreement shall notify the measure to the other Parties within 30 days of the date of entry into force of this Agreement.

4. A notification made pursuant to paragraph 3 must include: the reasons for adopting or maintaining the export prohibition or restriction, an explanation of how the measure is consistent with Article XI:2(a) of the GATT 1994, and an identification of alternative measures, if any, that the Party considered before imposing the export prohibition or restriction.

5. A Party is not required to notify an export prohibition or restriction pursuant to paragraphs 3 or 8 if the measure prohibits or restricts the exportation or sale for export only of a foodstuff that the Party has been a net importer during each of the three calendar years preceding the imposition of the measure, excluding the year in which the Party imposes the measure.

6.   If a Party that adopts or maintains a measure referred to in paragraph 3 has been a net importer of each foodstuff subject to that measure during each of the three calendar years preceding imposition of the measure, excluding the year in which the Party imposes the measure, and that

Party does not provide the other Parties with a notification pursuant to paragraph 3, the Party shall, within a reasonable period of time, provide to the other Parties trade data demonstrating that it was a net importer of the foodstuff during these three calendar years.

7.   A Party that is required to notify a measure under paragraph 3 shall:

   (a)   on the request of another Party having a substantial interest as an importer of the foodstuff subject to the measure, consult with that Party with respect to any matter relating to the measure; on the request of another Party having a substantial interest as an importer of the foodstuff subject to the measure, provide that Party with relevant economic indicators bearing on whether a critical shortage within the meaning of Article XI:2(a) of the GATT 1994 exists or is likely to occur in the absence of the measure, and on how the measure will prevent or relieve the critical shortage; and

   (b)   respond in writing to any question posed by another Party regarding the measure within 14 days of receipt of the question.

8.   A Party that considers that another Party should have notified a measure under paragraph 3 may bring the matter to the attention of that other Party. If the matter is not satisfactorily resolved promptly thereafter, the Party that considers that the measure should have been notified may itself bring the measure to the attention to the third Party.

9.   A Party should ordinarily terminate a measure subject to notification under paragraphs 3 or 8 within six months of the date it is adopted. A Party contemplating continuation of a measure beyond six months from the date it adopted the measure shall notify the other Parties no later than five months after the date it adopted the measure and provide the information identified in paragraph 3. Unless the Party has consulted with the other Parties that are net importers of the foodstuff subject to the export prohibition or restriction, the Party shall not continue the measure beyond 12 months from the date the Party adopted the measure. The Party shall immediately discontinue the measure when the critical shortage, or threat thereof, ceases to exist.

10. No Party shall apply a measure that is subject to notification under paragraphs 3 or 8 to a foodstuff purchased for a non-commercial, humanitarian purpose.

   Article 3.6:   Domestic Support

1.   The Parties recognize that domestic support measures can be of crucial importance to their agricultural sectors but may also have trade distorting effects and effects on production. If a Party supports its

agricultural producers, the Party shall consider domestic support measures that have no, or at most minimal, trade distorting effects or effects on production.

2.   If a Party raises concerns that another Party's domestic support measure has had a negative impact on trade between the Parties, the Parties shall share relevant information regarding the domestic support measure with each other and discuss the matter with a view to seeking to minimize any negative trade impact.

* * *

Article 3.9:   Agricultural Special Safeguards

Originating agricultural goods traded under preferential tariff treatment shall not be subject to any duties that the importing Party applies pursuant to a special safeguard it takes pursuant to the Agreement on Agriculture.[1]

Article 3.10:   Transparency and Consultations

1.   Each Party shall endeavor, as appropriate, to share with another Party, on request, available information regarding a measure relating to trade in agricultural goods taken by a regional level of government in its territory that may have a significant effect on trade between those Parties.

2.   At the request of another Party, a Party shall meet to discuss, and if appropriate, resolve, matters arising from grade, quality, technical specifications, and other standards as they affect trade between the Parties.

Article 3.11:   Annexes

1.   Annex 3-A applies to trade in agricultural goods between Canada and the United States.

2.   Annex 3-B applies to trade in agricultural goods between Mexico and the United States.

3.   Annex 3-C applies to trade in distilled spirits, wine, beer, and other alcohol beverages.

4.   Annex 3-D applies to proprietary formulas for prepackaged foods and food additives.

Section B: Agricultural Biotechnology

Article 3.12:   Definitions

For the purposes of this Section:

Agricultural biotechnology means technologies, including modern biotechnology, used for the deliberate manipulation of an organism to introduce, remove, or modify one or more heritable characteristics of a

---

[1]   For greater certainty, an agricultural good for which most-favored-nation tariff treatment applies may be subject to additional duties applied by a Party pursuant to a special safeguard taken under the Agreement on Agriculture.

product for agriculture and aquaculture use and that are not technologies used in traditional breeding and selection;

Low Level Presence (LLP) Occurrence means low levels of recombinant deoxyribonucleic acid (DNA) plant materials that have passed a food safety assessment according to the Codex Guideline for the Conduct of a Food Safety Assessment of Foods Derived from Recombinant-DNA Plants (CAC/GL 45-2003) in one or more countries, which may on occasion be inadvertently present in food or feed in importing countries in which the food safety of the relevant recombinant DNA plant has not been determined;

Modern biotechnology means the application of: *in vitro* nucleic acid techniques, including recombinant DNA and direct injection of nucleic acid into cells or organelles; or

(a)   fusion of cells beyond the taxonomic family,

that overcome natural physiological reproductive or recombination barriers and that are not techniques used in traditional breeding and selection;

Product of agricultural biotechnology means an agricultural good, or a fish or fish product covered by Chapter 3 of the Harmonized System, developed using agricultural biotechnology, but does not include a medicine or a medical product; and

Product of modern biotechnology means an agricultural good, or a fish or fish product covered by Chapter 3 of the Harmonized System, developed using modern biotechnology, but does not include a medicine or a medical product.

Article 3.13:   Contact Points

Each Party shall designate and notify a contact point or contact points for the sharing of information on matters related to this Section, in accordance with Article 30.5 (Agreement Coordinator and Contact Points).

Article 3.14:   Trade in Products of Agricultural Biotechnology

1.   The Parties confirm the importance of encouraging agricultural innovation and facilitating trade in products of agricultural biotechnology, while fulfilling legitimate objectives, including by promoting transparency and cooperation, and exchanging information related to the trade in products of agricultural biotechnology.

2.   This Section does not require a Party to mandate an authorization for a product of agricultural biotechnology to be on the market.

3.   Each Party shall make available to the public and, to the extent possible, online:

(a)   the information and documentation requirements for an authorization, if required, of a product of agricultural biotechnology;

(b)   any summary of any risk or safety assessment that has led to the authorization, if required, of a product of agricultural biotechnology; and

(c)   any list of the products of agricultural biotechnology that have been authorized in its territory.

4.   To reduce the likelihood of disruptions to trade in products of agricultural biotechnology:

(a)   each Party shall continue to encourage applicants to submit timely and concurrent applications to the Parties for authorization, if required, of products of agricultural biotechnology;

(b)   a Party requiring any authorization for a product of agricultural biotechnology shall:

(i)   accept and review applications for the authorization, if required, of products of agricultural biotechnology on an ongoing basis year-round,

(ii)   adopt or maintain measures that allow the initiation of the domestic regulatory authorization process of a product not yet authorized in another country,

(iii)   if an authorization is subject to expiration, take steps to help ensure that the review of the product is completed and a decision is made in a timely manner, and if possible, prior to expiration, and

(iv)   communicate with the other Parties regarding any new and existing authorizations of products of agricultural biotechnology so as to improve information exchange.

Article 3.15:   LLP Occurrence

1.   Each Party shall adopt or maintain policies or approaches designed to facilitate the management of any LLP Occurrence.

2.   To address an LLP Occurrence, and with a view to preventing future LLP Occurrences, on request of an importing Party, an exporting Party shall:

(a)   provide any summary of the specific risk or safety assessments that the exporting Party conducted in connection with any authorization of the product of modern biotechnology that is the subject of the LLP Occurrence;

(b)   provide, on receiving permission of the entity, if required, a contact point for any entity within its territory that received authorization for the product of modern biotechnology that is the subject of the LLP Occurrence and that is on the basis of this authorization, likely to possess:

(i)   any existing, validated methods for the detection of the product of modern biotechnology that is the subject of the LLP Occurrence,

(ii)   any reference sample of the product of modern biotechnology that is the subject of the LLP Occurrence necessary for the detection of the LLP Occurrence, and

(iii)   relevant information[2] that can be used by the importing Party to conduct a risk or safety assessment, if appropriate, in accordance with the relevant international standards and guidelines; and

(c)   encourage the entity in its territory that received authorization related to the product of modern biotechnology that is the subject of the LLP Occurrence to share the information referred to in paragraph 2(b) with the importing Party.

3.   In the event of an LLP Occurrence, the importing Party shall:

(a)   inform the importer or the importer's agent of the LLP Occurrence and of any additional information, including the information referenced in paragraph 2(b) of this Article, that will be required to be submitted to assist the importing Party to make a decision on the management of the LLP occurrence;

(b)   on request, and if available, provide to the exporting Party a summary of any risk or safety assessment that the importing Party has conducted in accordance with its domestic law in connection with the LLP Occurrence;

(c)   ensure that the LLP Occurrence is managed without unnecessary delay and that any measure[3] applied to manage the LLP Occurrence is appropriate to achieve compliance with the importing Party's laws and regulations and takes into account any risk posed by the LLP Occurrence; and

(d)   take into account, as appropriate, any relevant risk or safety assessment provided, and authorization granted, by another Party or non-Party when deciding how to manage the LLP Occurrence.

* * *

[ANNEX 3-A AGRICULTURAL TRADE BETWEEN CANADA AND THE UNITED STATES OMITTED]

[ANNEX 3-B AGRICULTURAL TRADE BETWEEN MEXICO AND THE UNITED STATES OMITTED]

[ANNEX 3-C DISTILLED SPIRITS, WINE, BEER, AND OTHER ALCOHOL BEVERAGES PARTIALLY OMITTED]

---

[2]   For example, relevant information includes the information contained in Annex 3 of the *Codex Guideline for the Conduct of Food Safety Assessment of Foods Derived from Recombinant-DNA Plants* (CAC/GL 45-2003).

[3]   For purposes of this paragraph, "measure" does not include penalties.

Article 3.C.2: Distinctive Products

1. Canada and Mexico shall recognize Bourbon Whiskey and Tennessee Whiskey, which is a straight Bourbon Whiskey authorized to be produced only in the State of Tennessee, as distinctive products of the United States. Accordingly, Canada and Mexico shall not permit the sale of any product as Bourbon Whiskey or Tennessee Whiskey, unless it has been manufactured in the United States in accordance with the laws and regulations of the United States governing the manufacture of Bourbon Whiskey and Tennessee Whiskey.

2. Mexico and the United States shall recognize Canadian Whisky as a distinctive product of Canada. Accordingly, Mexico and the United States shall not permit the sale of any product as Canadian Whisky, unless it has been manufactured in Canada in accordance with the laws and regulations of Canada governing the manufacture of Canadian Whisky for consumption in Canada.

3. Canada and the United States shall recognize Tequila and Mezcal as distinctive products of Mexico. Accordingly, Canada and the United States shall not permit the sale of any product as Tequila or Mezcal unless it has been manufactured in Mexico in accordance with the laws and regulations of Mexico governing the manufacture of Tequila and Mezcal.

[ANNEX 3-D PROPRIETARY FORMULAS FOR PREPACKAGED FOODS AND FOOD ADDITIVES OMITTED]

CHAPTER 4 RULES OF ORIGIN

Article 4.1: Definitions

For the purposes of this Chapter:

Aquaculture means the farming of aquatic organisms, including fish, molluscs, crustaceans, other aquatic invertebrates and aquatic plants from seed stock such as eggs, fry, fingerlings, or larvae, by intervention in the rearing or growth processes to enhance production such as regular stocking, feeding, or protection from predators;

Fungible goods or fungible materials means goods or materials that are interchangeable for commercial purposes and the properties of which are essentially identical;

Indirect material means a material used in the production, testing, or inspection of a good but not physically incorporated into the good, or a material used in the maintenance of buildings or the operation of equipment associated with the production of a good, including:

(a) fuel and energy;

(b) tools, dies, and molds;

(c) spare parts and materials used in the maintenance of equipment and buildings;

(d) lubricants, greases, compounding materials, and other materials used in production or used to operate equipment and buildings;

(e) gloves, glasses, footwear, clothing, safety equipment, and supplies;

(f) equipment, devices, and supplies used for testing or inspecting the goods;

(g) catalysts and solvents; and

(h) any other material that is not incorporated into the good but for which the use in the production of the good can reasonably be demonstrated to be a part of that production;

Intermediate material means a material that is self-produced and used in the production of a good, and designated pursuant to Article 4.8 (Intermediate Materials);

Material means a good that is used in the production of another good, and includes a part or an ingredient;

Net cost means total cost minus sales promotion, marketing and after-sales service costs, royalties, shipping and packing costs, and non-allowable interest costs that are included in the total cost;

Net cost of a good means the net cost that can be reasonably allocated to a good using one of the methods set out in Article 4.5 (Regional Value Content);

Non-allowable interest costs means interest costs incurred by a producer that exceed 700 basis points above the applicable federal government interest rate identified in the Uniform Regulations for comparable maturities;

Non-originating good or non-originating material means a good or material that does not qualify as originating under this Chapter;

Originating good or originating material means a good or material that qualifies as originating under this Chapter;

Packaging materials and containers means materials and containers in which a good is packaged for retail sale;

Packing materials and containers means materials and containers that are used to protect a good during transportation;

Producer means a person who engages in the production of a good;

Production means growing, cultivating, raising, mining, harvesting, fishing, trapping, hunting, capturing, breeding, extracting, manufacturing, processing, or assembling a good, or aquaculture;

Reasonably allocate means to apportion in a manner appropriate to the circumstances;

Royalties means payments of any kind, including payments under technical assistance or similar agreements, made as consideration for the use or right to use a copyright, literary, artistic, or scientific work, patent, trademark, design, model, plan, or secret formula or process, excluding those payments under technical assistance or similar agreements that can be related to specific services such as:

(a)   personnel training, without regard to where the training is performed; or

(b)   if performed in the territory of one or more of the Parties, engineering, tooling, die-setting, software design and similar computer services, or other services;

Sales promotion, marketing, and after-sales service costs means the following costs related to sales promotion, marketing, and after-sales service:

(a)   sales and marketing promotion; media advertising; advertising and market research; promotional and demonstration materials; exhibits; sales conferences, trade shows, and conventions; banners; marketing displays; free samples; sales, marketing, and after-sales service literature (product brochures, catalogs, technical literature, price lists, service manuals, or sales aid information); establishment and protection of logos and trademarks; sponsorships; wholesale and retail restocking charges; or entertainment;

(b)   sales and marketing incentives; consumer, retailer, or wholesaler rebates; or merchandise incentives;

(c)   salaries and wages, sales commissions, bonuses, benefits (for example, medical, insurance, or pension), travelling and living expenses, or membership and professional fees for sales promotion, marketing and after-sales service personnel;

(d)   recruiting and training of sales promotion, marketing, and after-sales service personnel, and after-sales training of customers' employees, if those costs are identified separately for sales promotion, marketing, and after-sales service of goods on the financial statements or cost accounts of the producer;

(e)   product liability insurance;

(f)   office supplies for sales promotion, marketing, and after-sales service of goods, if those costs are identified separately for sales promotion, marketing, and after-sales service of goods on the financial statements or cost accounts of the producer;

(g)   telephone, mail, and other communications, if those costs are identified separately for sales promotion, marketing, and after-sales service of goods on the financial statements or cost accounts of the producer;

(h)   rent and depreciation of sales promotion, marketing, and after-sales service offices, and distribution centers;

(i)   property insurance premiums, taxes, cost of utilities, and repair and maintenance of sales promotion, marketing, and after-sales service offices and distribution centers, if those costs are identified separately for sales promotion, marketing, and after-sales service of goods on the financial statements or cost accounts of the producer; and

(j)   payments by the producer to other persons for warranty repairs;

Self-produced material means a material that is produced by the producer of a good and used in the production of that good;

Shipping and packing costs means the costs incurred in packing a good for shipment and shipping the good from the point of direct shipment to the buyer, excluding costs of preparing and packaging the good for retail sale;

Total cost means all product costs, period costs, and other costs incurred in the territory of one or more of the Parties, where:

(a)   product costs are costs that are associated with the production of a good and include the value of materials, direct labor costs, and direct overheads;

(b)   period costs are costs, other than product costs, that are expensed in the period in which they are incurred, such as selling expenses and general and administrative expenses; and

(c)   other costs are all costs recorded on the books of the producer that are not product costs or period costs, such as interest.

Total cost does not include profits that are earned by the producer, regardless of whether they are retained by the producer or paid out to other persons as dividends, or taxes paid on those profits, including capital gains taxes;

Transaction value means the customs value as determined in accordance with the Customs Valuation Agreement, that is, the price actually paid or payable for a good or material with respect to a transaction of, except for the application of Articles 10.3(a) in the Appendix to Annex 4-B (Product-Specific Rules of Origin), the producer of the good, adjusted in accordance with the principles of Articles 8(1), 8(3), and 8(4) of the Customs Valuation Agreement, regardless of whether the good or material is sold for export;

Used means used or consumed in the production of goods; and

Value means value of a good or material for purposes of calculating customs duties or for the purposes of applying this Chapter.

Article 4.2:   Originating Goods

Except as otherwise provided in this Chapter, each Party shall provide that a good is originating if it is:

(a)   wholly obtained or produced entirely in the territory of one or more of the Parties, as defined in Article 4.3 (Wholly Obtained or Produced Goods);

(b) produced entirely in the territory of one or more of the Parties using non-originating materials provided the good satisfies all applicable requirements of Annex 4-B (Product-Specific Rules of Origin);

(c) produced entirely in the territory of one or more of the Parties exclusively from originating materials; or

(d) except for a good provided for in Chapter 61 to 63 of the Harmonized System:

(i) produced entirely in the territory of one or more of the Parties;

(ii) one or more of the non-originating materials provided for as parts under the Harmonized System used in the production of the good cannot satisfy the requirements set out in Annex 4-B (Product-Specific Rules of Origin) because both the good and its materials are classified in the same subheading or same heading that is not further subdivided into subheadings or, the good was imported into the territory of a Party in an unassembled or a disassembled form but was classified as an assembled good pursuant to rule 2(a) of the General Rules of Interpretation of the Harmonized System; and

(iii) the regional value content of the good, determined in accordance with Article 4.5 (Regional Value Content), is not less than 60 percent if the transaction value method is used, or not less than 50 percent if the net cost method is used;

and the good satisfies all other applicable requirements of this Chapter.

Article 4.3:   Wholly Obtained or Produced Goods

Each Party shall provide that, for the purposes of Article 4.2 (Originating Goods), a good is wholly obtained or produced entirely in the territory of one or more of the Parties if it is:

(a) a mineral good or other naturally occurring substance extracted or taken from there;

(b) a plant, plant good, vegetable, or fungus, grown, cultivated, harvested, picked, or gathered there;

(c) a live animal born and raised there;

(d) a good obtained from a live animal there;

(e) an animal obtained by hunting, trapping, fishing, gathering, or capturing there;

(f) a good obtained from aquaculture there;

(g) fish, shellfish, or other marine life taken from the sea, seabed or subsoil outside the territories of the Parties and, under international law, outside the territorial sea of non-Parties, by vessels that are registered, listed, or recorded with a Party and entitled to fly the flag of that Party;

(h)   a good produced from goods referred to in subparagraph (g) on board a factory ship that is registered, listed, or recorded with a Party and entitled to fly the flag of that Party;

(i)   a good other than fish, shellfish, and other marine life taken by a Party or a person of a Party from the seabed or subsoil outside the territories of the Parties, provided that Party has the right to exploit that seabed or subsoil;

(j)   waste and scrap derived from:

(i)   production there, or

(ii)   used goods collected there, provided the goods are fit only for the recovery of raw materials; and

(k)   a good produced there, exclusively from goods referred to in subparagraphs (a) through (j), or from their derivatives, at any stage of production.

Article 4.4:   Treatment of Recovered Materials Used in the Production of a Remanufactured Good

1.   Each Party shall provide that a recovered material derived in the territory of one or more of the Parties is treated as originating when it is used in the production of, and incorporated into, a remanufactured good.

2.   For greater certainty:

(a)   a remanufactured good is originating only if it satisfies the applicable requirements of Article 4.2 (Originating Goods); and

(b)   a recovered material that is not used or incorporated in the production of a remanufactured good is originating only if it satisfies the applicable requirements of Article 4.2 (Originating Goods).

Article 4.5:   Regional Value Content

1.   Except as provided in paragraph 6, each Party shall provide that the regional value content of a good shall be calculated, at the choice of the importer, exporter, or producer of the good, on the basis of either the transaction value method set out in paragraph 2 or the net cost method set out in paragraph 3.

2.   Each Party shall provide that an importer, exporter, or producer may calculate the regional value content of a good on the basis of the following transaction value method:

$$RVC = (TV\text{-}VNM)/TV \times 100$$

where

RVC is the regional value content, expressed as a percentage;

TV is the transaction value of the good, adjusted to exclude any costs incurred in the international shipment of the good; and

VNM is the value of non-originating materials including materials of undetermined origin used by the producer in the production of the good.

3. Each Party shall provide that an importer, exporter, or producer may calculate the regional value content of a good on the basis of the following net cost method:

$$RVC = (NC\text{-}VNM)/NC \times 100$$

where

RVC is the regional value content, expressed as a percentage; NC is the net cost of the good; and

VNM is the value of non-originating materials including materials of undetermined origin used by the producer in the production of the good.

4. Each Party shall provide that the value of non-originating materials used by the producer in the production of a good shall not, for the purposes of calculating the regional value content of the good under paragraph 2 or 3, include the value of non-originating materials used to produce originating materials that are subsequently used in the production of the good.

5. Each Party shall provide that if a non-originating material is used in the production of a good, the following may be counted as originating content for the purpose of determining whether the good meets a regional value content requirement:

    (a) the value of processing of the non-originating materials undertaken in the territory of one or more of the Parties; and

    (b) the value of any originating material used in the production of the non-originating material undertaken in the territory of one or more of the Parties.

6. Each Party shall provide that an importer, exporter, or producer shall calculate the regional value content of a good solely on the basis of the net cost method set out in paragraph 3 if the rule under the Annex 4-B (Product-Specific Rules of Origin) does not provide a rule based on the transaction value method.

7. If an importer, exporter, or producer of a good calculates the regional value content of the good on the basis of the transaction value method set out in paragraph 2 and a Party subsequently notifies the importer, exporter, or producer, during the course of a verification pursuant to Chapter 5 (Origin Procedures) that the transaction value of the good, or the value of material used in the production of the good, is required to be adjusted or is unacceptable under Article 1 of the Customs Valuation Agreement, the exporter, producer, or importer may then also calculate

the regional value content of the good on the basis of the net cost method set out in paragraph 3.

8. For the purposes of calculating the net cost of a good under paragraph 3, the producer of the good may:

(a) calculate the total cost incurred with respect to all goods produced by that producer, subtract any sales promotion, marketing, and after-sales service costs, royalties, shipping and packing costs, and non-allowable interest costs that are included in the total cost of all those goods, and then reasonably allocate the resulting net cost of those goods to the good;

(b) calculate the total cost incurred with respect to all goods produced by that producer, reasonably allocate the total cost to the good, and then subtract any sales promotion, marketing, and after-sales service costs, royalties, shipping and packing costs, and non-allowable interest costs that are included in the portion of the total cost allocated to the good; or

(c) reasonably allocate each cost that forms part of the total cost incurred with respect to the good so that the aggregate of these costs does not include any sales promotion, marketing, and after-sales service costs, royalties, shipping and packing costs, and non-allowable interest costs,

provided that the allocation of all those costs is consistent with the provisions regarding the reasonable allocation of costs set out in the Uniform Regulations.

Article 4.6: Value of Materials Used in Production

Each Party shall provide that, for the purposes of this Chapter, the value of a material is:

(a) for a material imported by the producer of the good, the transaction value of the material at the time of importation, including the costs incurred in the international shipment of the material;

(b) for a material acquired in the territory where the good is produced:

(i) the price paid or payable by the producer in the Party where the producer is located,

(ii) the value as determined for an imported material in subparagraph (a), or

(iii) the earliest ascertainable price paid or payable in the territory of the Party; or

(c) for a material that is self-produced:

(i)   all the costs incurred in the production of the material, which includes general expenses, and

(ii)   an amount equivalent to the profit added in the normal course of trade, or equal to the profit that is usually reflected in the sale of goods of the same class or kind as the self-produced material that is being valued.

Article 4.7:   Further Adjustments to the Value of Materials

1.   Each Party shall provide that for a non-originating material or material of undetermined origin, the following expenses may be deducted from the value of the material:

(a)   the costs of freight, insurance, packing, and all other costs incurred in transporting the material to the location of the producer of the good;

(b)   duties, taxes, and customs brokerage fees on the material paid in the territory of one or more of the Parties, other than duties and taxes that are waived, refunded, refundable, or otherwise recoverable, which include credit against duty or tax paid or payable; and

(c)   the cost of waste and spoilage resulting from the use of the material in the production of the good, less the value of reusable scrap or by-product.

2.   If the cost or expense listed in paragraph 1 is unknown or documentary evidence of the amount of the adjustment is not available, then no adjustment is allowed for that particular cost.

Article 4.8:   Intermediate Materials

Each Party shall provide that any self-produced material, other than a component identified in Table G of that Appendix, that is used in the production of a good may be designated by the producer of the good as an intermediate material for the purpose of calculating the regional value content of the good under paragraph 2 or 3 of Article 4.5 (Regional Value Content), provided that if the intermediate material is subject to a regional value content requirement, no other self-produced material subject to a regional value content requirement used in the production of that intermediate material may itself be designated by the producer as an intermediate material.

Article 4.9:   Indirect Materials

An indirect material shall be considered to be an originating material without regard to where it is produced.

Article 4.10:   Automotive Goods

The Appendix to Annex 4-B (Product-Specific Rules of Origin) includes additional provisions that apply to automotive goods.

Article 4.11:   Accumulation

1.   Each Party shall provide that a good is originating if the good is produced in the territory of one or more of the Parties by one or more producers, provided that the good satisfies the requirements of Article 4.2 (Originating Goods) and all other applicable requirements in this Chapter.

2.   Each Party shall provide that an originating good or material of one or more of the Parties is considered as originating in the territory of another Party when used as a material in the production of a good in the territory of another Party.

3.   Each Party shall provide that production undertaken on a non-originating material in the territory of one or more of the Parties may contribute toward the originating status of a good, regardless of whether that production was sufficient to confer originating status to the material itself.

Article 4.12:   *De Minimis*

1.   Except as provided in Annex 4-A (Exceptions to Article 4.12 (*De Minimis*)), each Party shall provide that a good is an originating good if the value of all non-originating materials used in the production of the good that do not undergo an applicable change in tariff classification set out in Annex 4-B (Product-Specific Rules of Origin) is not more than 10 percent:

    (a)   of the transaction value of the good adjusted to exclude any costs incurred in the international shipment of the good; or

    (b)   of the total cost of the good,

provided that the good satisfies all other applicable requirements of this Chapter.

2.   If a good described in paragraph 1 is also subject to a regional value content requirement, the value of those non-originating materials shall be included in the value of non-originating materials for the applicable regional value content requirement.

3.   A good that is otherwise subject to a regional value content requirement shall not be required to satisfy the requirement if the value of all non-originating materials used in the production of the good is not more than 10 percent of the transaction value of the good, adjusted to exclude any costs incurred in the international shipment of the good, or the total cost of the good, provided that the good satisfies all other applicable requirements of this Chapter.

4.   With respect to a textile or apparel good, Articles 6.1.2 and 6.1.3 (Rules of Origin and Related Matters) apply in place of paragraph 1.

Article 4.13:   Fungible Goods and Materials

1.   Each Party shall provide that a fungible material or good is originating if:

(a) when originating and non-originating fungible materials are used in the production of a good, the determination of whether the materials are originating is made on the basis of an inventory management method recognized in the Generally Accepted Accounting Principles of, or otherwise accepted by, the Party in which the production is performed; or

(b) when originating and non-originating fungible goods are commingled and exported in the same form, the determination of whether the goods are originating is made

on the basis of an inventory management method recognized in the Generally Accepted Accounting Principles of, or otherwise accepted by, the Party from which the good is exported.

2. The inventory management method selected under paragraph 1 must be used throughout the fiscal year of the producer or the person that selected the inventory management method.

3. For greater certainty, an importer may claim that a fungible material or good is originating if the importer, producer, or exporter has physically segregated each fungible material or good as to allow their specific identification.

Article 4.14: Accessories, Spare Parts, Tools, or Instructional or Other Information Materials

1. Each Party shall provide that:

(a) in determining whether a good is wholly obtained, or satisfies a process or change in tariff classification requirement as set out in Annex 4-B (Product-Specific Rules of Origin), accessories, spare parts, tools, or instructional or other information materials as described in paragraph 3, are to be disregarded; and

(b) in determining whether a good meets a regional value content requirement, the value of the accessories, spare parts, tools, or instructional or other information materials, as described in paragraph 3, are to be taken into account as originating or non-originating materials, as the case may be, in calculating the regional value content of the good.

2. Each Party shall provide that a good's accessories, spare parts, tools, or instructional or other information materials, as described in paragraph 3, have the originating status of the good with which they are delivered.

3. For the purposes of this Article, accessories, spare parts, tools, or instructional or other information materials are covered when:

(a) the accessories, spare parts, tools, or instructional or other information materials are classified with, delivered with, but not invoiced separately from the good; and

(b)   the types, quantities, and value of the accessories, spare parts, tools, or instructional or other information materials are customary for that good.

Article 4.15:   Packaging Materials and Containers for Retail Sale

1.   Each Party shall provide that packaging materials and containers in which a good is packaged for retail sale, if classified with the good, are disregarded in determining whether all the non-originating materials used in the production of the good have satisfied the applicable process or change in tariff classification requirement set out in Annex 4-B (Product-Specific Rules of Origin) or whether the good is wholly obtained or produced.

2.   Each Party shall provide that if a good is subject to a regional value content requirement, the value of the packaging materials and containers in which the good is packaged for retail sale, if classified with the good, are taken into account as originating or non-originating, as the case may be, in calculating the regional value content of the good.

Article 4.16:   Packing Materials and Containers for Shipment

Each Party shall provide that packing materials and containers for shipment are disregarded in determining whether a good is originating.

Article 4.17:   Sets of Goods, Kits or Composite Goods

1.   Except as provided in Annex 4-B (Product-Specific Rules of Origin), each Party shall provide that for a set classified as a result of the application of rule 3 of the General Rules for the Interpretation of the Harmonized System, the set is originating only if each good in the set is originating and both the set and the goods meet the other applicable requirements of this Chapter.

2.   Notwithstanding paragraph 1, for a set classified as a result of the application of rule 3 of the General Rules for the Interpretation of the Harmonized System, the set is originating if the value of all the non-originating goods in the set does not exceed 10 percent of the value of the set.

3.   For the purposes of paragraph 2, the value of the non-originating goods in the set and the value of the set shall be calculated in the same manner as the value of non-originating materials and the value of the good.

4.   With respect to a textile or apparel good, Articles 6.1.4 and 6.1.5 (Rules of Origin and Related Matters) apply in place of paragraph 1.

Article 4.18:   Transit and Transshipment

1.   Each Party shall provide that an originating good retains its originating status if the good has been transported to the importing Party without passing through the territory of a non-Party.

2.   Each Party shall provide that if an originating good is transported outside the territories of the Parties, the good retains its originating status if the good:

(a)   remains under customs control in the territory of a non-Party; and

(b)   does not undergo an operation outside the territories of the Parties other than: unloading; reloading; separation from a bulk shipment; storing; labeling or marking required by the importing Party; or any other operation necessary to preserve it in good condition or to transport the good to the territory of the importing Party.

Article 4.19:   Non-Qualifying Operations

Each Party shall provide that a good shall not be considered to be an originating good merely by reason of:

(a)   mere dilution with water or another substance that does not materially alter the characteristics of the good; or

(b)   a production or pricing practice in respect of which it may be demonstrated, on the basis of a preponderance of evidence, that the object was to circumvent this Chapter.

[ANNEX 4-A EXCEPTIONS TO ARTICLE 4.12 (*DE MINIMIS*) OMITTED]

[ANNEX 4-B PRODUCT-SPECIFIC RULES OF ORIGIN OMITTED]

CHAPTER 5   ORIGIN PROCEDURES

Article 5.1:   Definitions

For the purposes of this Chapter:

Exporter means an exporter located in the territory of a Party and an exporter required under this Chapter to maintain records in the territory of that Party regarding exportations of a good;

Identical goods means goods that are the same in all respects, including physical characteristics, quality, and reputation, irrespective of minor differences in appearance that are not relevant to a determination of origin of those goods under Chapter 4 (Rules of Origin) or Chapter 6 (Textile and Apparel Goods);

Importer means an importer located in the territory of a Party and an importer required under this Chapter to maintain records in the territory of that Party regarding importations of a good; and

Value means value of a good or material for purposes of calculating customs duties or for purposes of applying Chapter 4 (Rules of Origin) or Chapter 6 (Textile and Apparel Goods).

Article 5.2:   Claims for Preferential Tariff Treatment

1.   Each Party shall provide that an importer may make a claim for preferential tariff treatment, based on a certification of origin completed by the exporter, producer, or importer[1] for the purpose of

---

[1]   For Mexico, implementation of paragraph 1 with respect to a certification of origin by the importer shall be no later than three years and six months after the date of entry into force of this Agreement.

certifying that a good being exported from the territory of a Party into the territory of another Party qualifies as an originating good.

2.   An importing Party may:

    (a)   require that an importer who completes a certification of origin provide documents or other information to support the certification;

    (b)   establish in its law conditions that an importer shall meet to complete a certification of origin;

    (c)   if an importer fails to meet or no longer meets the conditions established under subparagraph (b), prohibit that importer from providing its own certification as the basis of a claim for preferential tariff treatment; or

    (d)   if a claim for preferential tariff treatment is based on a certification of origin completed by an importer, prohibit that importer from:

        (i)   issuing a certification, based on a certification of origin or a written representation completed by the exporter or producer, and

        (ii)   making a subsequent claim for preferential tariff treatment for the same importation, based on a certification of origin completed by the exporter or producer.

3.   Each Party shall provide that a certification of origin:

    (a)   need not follow a prescribed format;

    (b)   contains a set of minimum data elements as set out in Annex 5-A (Minimum Data Elements) that indicate that the good is both originating and meets the requirements of this Chapter;

    (c)   may be provided on an invoice or any other document;

    (d)   describes the originating good in sufficient detail to enable its identification; and

    (e)   meets the requirements as set out in the Uniform Regulations.

4.   A Party shall not reject a claim for preferential tariff treatment for the sole reason that the invoice was issued in a non-Party. However, a certification of origin shall not be provided on an invoice or any other commercial document issued in a non-Party.

5.   Each Party shall provide that the certification of origin for a good imported into its territory may be completed in English, French, or Spanish. If the certification of origin is not in a language of the importing Party, the importing Party may require an importer to submit, upon request, a translation into such a language.

6.   Each Party shall allow a certification of origin to be completed and submitted electronically and shall accept the certification of origin with an electronic or digital signature.

Article 5.3:   Basis of a Certification of Origin

1.   Each Party shall provide that if a producer certifies the origin of a good, the certification of origin is completed on the basis of the producer having information, including documents, that demonstrate that the good is originating.

2.   Each Party shall provide that if the exporter is not the producer of the good, the certification of origin may be completed by the exporter of the good on the basis of:

(a)   having information, including documents, that demonstrate that the good is originating; or

(b)   reasonable reliance on the producer's written representation, such as in a certification of origin, that the good is originating.

3.   Each Party shall provide that a certification of origin may be completed by the importer of the good on the basis of the importer having information, including documents, that demonstrate that the good is originating.

4.   For greater certainty, nothing in paragraph 1 or 2 shall be construed to allow a Party to require an exporter or producer to complete a certification of origin or provide a certification of origin or a written representation to another person.

5.   Each Party shall provide that a certification of origin may apply to:

(a)   a single shipment of a good into the territory of a Party; or

(b)   multiple shipments of identical goods within any period specified in the certification of origin, but not exceeding 12 months.

6.   Each Party shall provide that a certification of origin for a good imported into its territory be accepted by its customs administration for four years after the date the certification of origin was completed.

Article 5.4:   Obligations Regarding Importations

1.   Except as otherwise provided for in this Chapter, each Party shall provide that, for the purpose of claiming preferential tariff treatment, the importer shall:

(a)   make a statement forming part of the import documentation based on a valid certification of origin that the good qualifies as an originating good;

(b)   have a valid certification of origin in its possession at the time the statement referred to in subparagraph (a) is made;

(c)   provide, on the request of the importing Party's customs administration, a copy of the certification of origin, in accordance with its laws and regulations;

(d)   if a certification by the importer forms the basis for the claim, demonstrate, on request of the importing Party, that the good is originating under Article 5.3.3 (Basis of a Certification of Origin); and

(e)   if the claim for preferential tariff treatment is based on a certification of origin completed by a producer that is not the exporter of the good, demonstrate, on the request of the importing Party, that the good certified as originating did not undergo further production or any other operation other than unloading, reloading, or any other operation necessary to preserve it in good condition or to transport the good into the territory of the importing Party.

2.   Each Party shall provide that, if the importer has reason to believe that the certification of origin is based on incorrect information that could affect the accuracy or validity of the certification of origin, the importer shall promptly correct the importation document and pay any duties owing. The importer shall not be subject to penalties for making an incorrect statement that formed part of the import documentation, if it promptly corrects the importation document and pays any duties owing.

3.   A Party may require an importer to demonstrate that a good for which the importer claims preferential tariff treatment was shipped in accordance with Article 4.18 (Transit and Transshipment) by providing:

(a)   transportation documents, including the multimodal or combined transportation documents, such as bills of lading or waybills, indicating the shipping route and all points of shipment and transhipment prior to the importation of the good; and

(b)   if the good is shipped through or transhipped outside the territories of the Parties, relevant documents, such as in the case of storage, storage documents or a copy of the customs control documents, demonstrating that the good remained under customs control while outside the territories of the Parties.

Article 5.5:   Exceptions to Certification of Origin

Each Party shall provide that a certification of origin shall not be required if:

(a)   the value of the importation does not exceed US$1,000 or the equivalent amount in the importing Party's currency or any higher amount as the importing Party may establish. A Party may require a written representation certifying that the good qualifies as an originating good; or

(b)   it is an importation of a good for which the Party into whose
       territory the good is imported has waived the requirement for
       a certification of origin,

provided that the importation does not form part of a series of importations
that may reasonably be considered to have been undertaken or arranged for
the purpose of evading compliance with the importing Party's laws,
regulations, or procedures governing claims for preferential tariff treatment.

Article 5.6:   Obligations Regarding Exportations

1.   Each Party shall provide that an exporter or producer in its territory
     that completes a certification of origin shall provide a copy of the
     certification of origin to its customs administration, on its request.

2.   Each Party shall provide that if an exporter or a producer in its territory
     has provided a certification of origin and has reason to believe that it
     contains or is based on incorrect information, the exporter or producer
     shall promptly notify, in writing, every person and every Party to whom
     the exporter or producer provided the certification of origin of any
     change that could affect the accuracy or validity of the certification of
     origin.

3.   No Party shall impose penalties on an exporter or a producer in its
     territory that voluntarily provides written notification pursuant to
     paragraph 2 with respect to a certification of origin.

4.   A Party may apply measures as the circumstances may warrant when
     an exporter or a producer in its territory fails to comply with any
     requirement of this Chapter.

5.   Each Party shall allow a certification of origin to be maintained in any
     medium and submitted electronically from the exporter or producer in
     the territory of a Party to an importer in the territory of another Party.

Article 5.7:   Errors or Discrepancies

1.   Each Party shall provide that it shall not reject a certification of origin
     due to minor errors or discrepancies in it that do not create doubts
     concerning the correctness of the import documentation.

2.   Each Party shall provide that if the customs administration of the Party
     into whose territory a good is imported determines that a certification
     of origin is illegible, defective on its face, or has not been completed in
     accordance with this Chapter, the importer shall be granted a period of
     not less than five working days to provide the customs administration
     with a copy of the corrected certification of origin.

Article 5.8:   Record Keeping Requirements

1.   Each Party shall provide that an importer claiming preferential tariff
     treatment for a good imported into its territory shall maintain, for a
     period of no less than five years from the date of importation of the good:

     (a)   the documentation related to the importation, including the
           certification of origin that served as the basis for the claim;

(b)   all records necessary to demonstrate that the good is originating, if the claim was based on a certification of origin completed by the importer; and

(c)   the information, including documents, necessary to demonstrate compliance with Article 5.4.1(e) (Obligations Regarding Importations), if applicable.

2.   Each Party shall provide that an exporter or a producer in its territory that completes a certification of origin or a producer that provides a written representation shall maintain in its territory for five years after the date on which the certification of origin was completed, or for such longer period as the Party may specify, all records necessary to demonstrate that a good for which the exporter or producer provided a certification of origin or other written representation is originating, including records associated with:

(a)   the purchase of, cost of, value of, shipping of, and payment for, the good or material;

(b)   the purchase of, cost of, value of, shipping of, and payment for all materials, including indirect materials, used in the production of the good or material; and

(c)   the production of the good in the form in which the good is exported or the production of the material in the form in which it was sold.

3.   Each Party shall provide in accordance with that Party's law that an importer, exporter, or producer in its territory may choose to maintain the records or documentation specified in paragraphs 1 and 2 in any medium, including electronic, provided that the records or documentation can be promptly retrieved and printed.

4.   For greater certainty, the record keeping requirements on an importer, exporter, or producer that a Party provides for pursuant to this Article apply even if the importing Party does not require a certification of origin or if a requirement for a certification of origin has been waived.

Article 5.9:   Origin Verification

1.   For the purpose of determining whether a good imported into its territory is an originating good, the importing Party may, through its customs administration, conduct a verification of a claim for preferential tariff treatment by one or more of the following:

(a)   a written request or questionnaire seeking information, including documents, from the importer, exporter, or producer of the good;

(b)   a verification visit to the premises of the exporter or producer of the good in order to request information, including documents, and to observe the production process and the related facilities; (c) for a textile or apparel good, the procedures set out in Article 6.6 (Verification); or (d) any other procedure as may be decided by the Parties.

2. The importing Party may choose to initiate a verification under this Article to the importer or the person who completed the certification of origin.

3. If an importing Party conducts a verification under this Article it shall accept information, including documents, directly from the importer, exporter, or producer.

4. If a claim for preferential tariff treatment is based on a certification of origin completed by the exporter or producer, and in response to a request for information by an importing Party to determine whether a good is originating in verifying a claim of preferential treatment under paragraph 1(a), the importer does not provide sufficient information to demonstrate that the good is originating, the importing Party shall request information from the exporter or producer under paragraph 1 before it may deny the claim for preferential tariff treatment. The importing Party shall complete the verification, including any additional request to the exporter or producer under paragraph 1, within the time provided in paragraph 15.

5. A written request or questionnaire seeking information, including documents, or a request for a verification visit, under paragraphs 1(a) or (b) shall:

   (a) include the identity of the customs administration issuing the request;

   (b) state the object and scope of the verification, including the specific issue the requesting Party seeks to resolve with the verification;

   (c) include sufficient information to identify the good that is being verified; and

   (d) in the case of a verification visit, request the written consent of the exporter or producer whose premises are going to be visited and indicate:

       (i) the legal authority for the visit,

       (ii) the proposed date and location for the visit,

       (iii) the specific purpose of the visit, and

       (iv) the names and titles of the officials performing the visit.

6. If an importing Party has initiated a verification under paragraph 1(a) or 1(b) other than to the importer, it shall inform the importer of the initiation of the verification.

7. For a verification under paragraph 1(a) or 1(b), the importing Party shall:

   (a) ensure that the written request for information, or documentation to be reviewed, is limited to information and documentation to determine whether the good is originating;

(b) describe the information or documentation in detail to allow the importer, exporter, or producer to identify the information and documentation necessary to respond;

(c) allow the importer, exporter, or producer at least 30 days from the date of receipt of the written request or questionnaire under paragraph 1(a) to respond; and

(d) allow the exporter or producer 30 days from the date of receipt of the written request for a visit under paragraph 1(b) to consent to or refuse the request.

8. On request of the importing Party, the Party where the exporter or producer is located may, as it deems appropriate and in accordance with its laws and regulations, assist with the verification. This assistance may include providing information it has that is relevant to the origin verification. The importing Party shall not deny a claim for preferential tariff treatment solely on the grounds that the Party where the exporter or producer is located did not provide requested assistance.

9. If an importing Party initiates a verification under paragraph 1(b), it shall, at the time of the request for the visit under paragraph 5, provide a copy of the request to:

(a) the customs administration of the Party in whose territory the visit is to occur; and

(b) if requested by the Party in whose territory the visit is to occur, the embassy of that Party in the territory of the Party proposing to conduct the visit.

10. Each Party shall provide that, when the exporter or producer receives notification pursuant to paragraph 5, the exporter or producer may, on a single occasion, within 15 days of receipt of the notification, request the postponement of the proposed verification visit for a period not exceeding 30 days from the proposed date of the visit.

11. Each Party shall provide that, when its customs administration receives notification pursuant to paragraph 9, the customs administration may, within 15 days of receipt of the notification, postpone the proposed verification visit for a period not exceeding 60 days from the proposed date of the visit, or for a longer period as the relevant Parties may decide.

12. A Party shall not deny preferential tariff treatment to a good based solely on the postponement of a verification visit pursuant to paragraphs 10 or 11.

13. Each Party shall permit an exporter or a producer whose good is subject to a verification visit by another Party to designate two observers to be present during the visit, provided that:

(a) the observers do not participate in a manner other than as observers;

(b)   the failure of the exporter or producer to designate observers
does not result in the postponement of the visit; and

(c)   an exporter or producer of a good identifies to the customs
administration conducting a verification visit any observers
designated to be present during the visit.

14.   The importing Party shall provide the importer, exporter, or producer
that certified that the good was originating and is the subject of a
verification, with a written determination of origin that includes the
findings of facts and the legal basis for the determination. If the
importer is not the certifier, the importing Party shall also provide that
written determination to the importer.

15.   The Party conducting a verification shall, as expeditiously as possible
and within 120 days after it has received all the information necessary[2]
to make the determination, provide the written determination under
paragraph 14. Notwithstanding the foregoing, the Party may extend
this period, in exceptional cases, for up to 90 days after notifying the
importer, and any exporter or producer who is subject to the verification
or provided information during the verification.

16.   Prior to issuing a written determination under paragraph 14, if the
importing Party intends to deny preferential tariff treatment, the
importing Party shall inform the importer, and any exporter or
producer who is subject to the verification and provided information
during the verification, of the preliminary results of the verification and
provide those persons with a notice of intent to deny that includes when
the denial would be effective and a period of at least 30 days for the
submission of additional information, including documents, related to
the originating status of the good.

17.   If verifications by a Party indicate a pattern of conduct by an importer,
exporter, or a producer of false or unsupported representations that a
good imported into its territory qualifies as an originating good, the
Party may withhold preferential tariff treatment to identical goods
imported, exported, or produced by such person until that person
establishes compliance with this Chapter, Chapter 4 (Rules of Origin),
and Chapter 6 (Textile and Apparel Goods).

18.   For the purposes of this Article and relevant articles of the Uniform
Regulations, all communication to the exporter or producer and to the
customs administration of the Party of export will be sent by any means
that can produce any confirmation of receipt. The specified time periods
will begin from the date of receipt.

Article 5.10:   Determinations of Origin

1.   Except as otherwise provided in paragraph 2 or Article 6.7
(Determinations), each Party shall grant a claim for preferential tariff

---

[2]   This includes any information collected pursuant to a verification request to
an exporter or producer.

treatment made under this Chapter on or after the date of entry into force of this Agreement.

2.   The importing Party may deny a claim for preferential tariff treatment if:

(a)   it determines that the good does not qualify for preferential treatment;

(b)   pursuant to a verification under Article 5.9 (Origin Verification), it has not received sufficient information to determine that the good qualifies as originating;

(c)   the exporter, producer, or importer fails to respond to a written request or questionnaire for information, including documents, under Article 5.9 (Origin Verification);

(d)   the exporter or producer fails to provide its written consent for a verification visit, in accordance with Article 5.9 (Origin Verification);

(e)   the importer, exporter, or producer fails to comply with the requirements of this Chapter; or

(f)   the exporter, producer, or importer of the good that is required to maintain records or documentation in accordance with this Chapter:

(i)   fails to maintain records or documentation, or

(ii)   denies access, if requested by a Party, to those records or documentation.

Article 5.11:   Refunds and Claims for Preferential Tariff Treatment after Importation

1.   Each Party shall provide that an importer may apply for preferential tariff treatment and a refund of any excess duties paid for a good if the importer did not make a claim for preferential tariff treatment at the time of importation, provided that the good would have qualified for preferential tariff treatment when it was imported into the territory of the Party.

2.   The importing Party may, for the purposes of paragraph 1, require that the importer:

(a)   make a claim for preferential tariff treatment;

(b)   provide a statement that the good was originating at the time of importation;

(c)   provide a copy of the certification of origin; and

(d)   provide any other documentation relating to the importation of the good as the importing Party may require,

no later than one year after the date of importation or a longer period if specified in the importing Party's law.

Article 5.12:   Confidentiality

1. If a Party provides information to another Party in accordance with this Chapter and designates the information as confidential or it is confidential under the receiving Party's law, the receiving Party shall keep the information confidential in accordance with its law.

2. A Party may decline to provide information requested by another Party if that Party has failed to act in accordance with paragraph 1.

3. A Party may use or disclose confidential information received from another Party under this Chapter but only for the purposes of administration or enforcement of its customs laws or as otherwise provided under the Party's law, including in an administrative, quasi-judicial, or judicial proceeding.

4. When a Party collects information from a trader under this Chapter, that Party shall apply the provisions set out in Article 7.24 (Protection of Trader Information) to keep the information confidential.

Article 5.13:   Penalties

Each Party shall maintain criminal, civil, or administrative penalties for violations of its laws and regulations related to this Chapter.

Article 5.14:   Advance Rulings Relating to Origin

1. In accordance with Article 7.5 (Advance Rulings), each Party, through its customs administration, shall, on request, provide for the issuance of a written advance ruling on origin under this Agreement.

2. Each Party shall adopt or maintain uniform procedures throughout its territory for the issuance of advance rulings on origin under this Agreement, including the common standards set out in the Uniform Regulations regarding the information required to process an application for a ruling.

Article 5.15:   Review and Appeal

1. Each Party shall grant substantially the same rights of review and appeal of determinations of origin and advance rulings by its customs administration related to origin under this Agreement as it provides to importers in its territory, to an exporter or producer:

    (a) that completes a certification of origin for a good that has been the subject of a determination of origin under this Agreement; or

    (b) that has received an advance ruling on origin under this Agreement pursuant to Article 5.14 (Advance Rulings Relating to Origin), and Article 7.5 (Advance Rulings).

Article 5.16:   Uniform Regulations

1. The Parties shall, by entry into force of this Agreement, adopt or maintain through their respective laws or regulations, Uniform Regulations regarding the interpretation, application, and administration of this Chapter, Chapter 4 (Rules of Origin), Chapter 6

(Textile and Apparel Goods), Chapter 7 (Customs Administration and Trade Facilitation) and other matters as may be decided by the Parties.

2. The Committee on Rules of Origin and Origin Procedures (Origin Committee) shall consult to discuss possible amendments or modifications to the Uniform Regulations.

3. In particular, the Origin Committee shall consult regularly to consider modifications or additions to the Uniform Regulations to reduce their complexity and provide practical and useful guidance to ensure better compliance with the rules and procedures of this Chapter, Chapter 4 (Rules of Origin), and Chapter 6 (Textile and Apparel Goods), including examples or guidance that would be of particular assistance to SMEs in the territories of the Parties.

4. The Origin Committee shall notify the Commission of any modification of or addition to the Uniform Regulations it decides.

5. Each Party shall implement any modification of or addition to the Uniform Regulations within a period that the Parties decide.

6. Each Party shall apply the Uniform Regulations in addition to the obligations in the Chapter.

Article 5.17:   Notification of Treatment

1. Each Party shall notify the other Parties of the following determinations, measures, and rulings, including to the extent practicable those that are prospective in application:

(a) a determination of origin issued as the result of a verification conducted pursuant to Article 5.9 (Origin Verification);

(b) a determination of origin that the Party is aware is contrary to:

(i) a ruling issued by the customs administration of another Party, or

(ii) consistent treatment given by the customs administration of another Party with respect to the tariff classification or value of a good, or of materials used in the production of a good, or the reasonable allocation of costs when calculating the net cost of a good, that has been the subject of a determination of origin;

(c) a measure establishing or significantly modifying an administrative policy that is likely to affect a future determination of origin; and

(d) an advance ruling, or a ruling modifying or revoking an advance ruling, on origin under this Agreement, pursuant to Article 5.14 (Advance Rulings Relating to Origin), and Article 7.5 (Advance Rulings).

Article 5.18:   Committee on Rules of Origin and Origin Procedures

1.   The Parties hereby establish a Committee on Rules of Origin and Origin
      Procedures   (Origin   Committee),   composed   of   government
      representatives of each Party, to consider any matters arising under
      this Chapter or Chapter 4 (Rules of Origin).

2.   The Origin Committee shall consult regularly to ensure that this
      Chapter and Chapter 4 (Rules of Origin) are administered effectively,
      uniformly, and consistently with the spirit and objectives of this
      Agreement.

3.   The Origin Committee shall consult to discuss possible amendments or
      modifications to this Chapter or Chapter 4 (Rules of Origin), and in
      particular to the Product-Specific Rules of Origin in Annex 4-B, except
      Product-Specific Rules for textile and apparel goods, taking into account
      developments in technology, production processes, or other related
      matters. A Party may submit a proposed modification, along with
      supporting rationale and any studies to the other Parties for
      consideration. In particular, the Committee shall consider the
      possibility of cumulation with non-parties with which the Parties have
      trade agreements on a product by product basis.

4.   Prior to the entry into force of an amended version of the Harmonized
      System, the Origin Committee shall consult to prepare updates to this
      Chapter and Chapter 4 (Rules of Origin), and in particular to the
      Product-Specific Rules of Origin in Annex 4-B, except for textiles and
      apparel goods, that are necessary to reflect changes to the Harmonized
      System.

5.   With respect to a textile or apparel good, Article 6.8 (Committee on
      Textile and Apparel Trade Matters) applies in place of this Article.

Article 5.19:   Sub-Committee on Origin Verification

1.   The Parties hereby establish a Sub-Committee on Origin Verification,
      composed of government representatives of each Party, which will be a
      subcommittee of the Origin Committee.

2.   The Sub-Committee shall meet at least once within one year of the date
      of entry into force of this Agreement, and thereafter at such times as
      the Parties decide or on request of the Commission or the Origin
      Committee.

3.   The Sub-Committee's functions shall include:

      (a)   discussing and developing technical papers and sharing
            technical advice related to this Chapter or Chapter 4 (Rules
            of Origin) for the purposes of conducting verifications of
            origin;

      (b)   developing and improving the NAFTA 1994 Audit Manual
            and recommending verification procedures;

      (c)   developing and improving verification questionnaires, forms,
            or brochures; and

(d)   providing a forum for the Parties to consult and endeavor to resolve issues relating to origin verification.

[ANNEX 5-A MINIMUM DATA ELEMENTS OMITTED]

CHAPTER 6   TEXTILE AND APPAREL GOODS

Article 6.1:   Rules of Origin and Related Matters

Application of Chapters 4 (Rules of Origin) and 5 (Origin Procedures)

1.   Except as provided in this Chapter, Chapters 4 (Rules of Origin) and 5 (Origin Procedures) apply to textile and apparel goods.

De Minimis

2.   A textile or apparel good classified in Chapters 50 through 60 or heading 96.19 of the Harmonized System that contains non-originating materials that do not satisfy the applicable change in tariff classification requirement specified in Annex 4-B (Product-Specific Rules of Origin), shall nonetheless be considered to be an originating good if the total weight of all those materials is not more than 10 percent of the total weight of the good, of which the total weight of elastomeric content may not exceed 7 percent of the total weight of the good, and the good meets all the other applicable requirements of this Chapter and Chapter 4 (Rules of Origin).

* * *

Article 6.6:   Verification

1.   An importing Party may, through its customs administration, conduct a verification with respect to a textile or apparel good pursuant to Article 5.9 (Origin Verification), and the associated manner and prior to the date of the first visit to an exporter or producer under paragraph 2, to facilitate coordination, logistical support, and scheduling of the site visit.

2.   The host Party shall promptly acknowledge receipt of the notification of a proposed site visit under paragraph 2, and may request information from the importing Party to facilitate planning of the site visit, such as logistical arrangements or provision of requested assistance.

3.   If an importing Party seeks to conduct a site visit under paragraph 2:

(a)   officials of the customs administration of the host Party may accompany the officials of the importing Party during the site visit;

(b)   officials of the customs administration of the host Party may, in accordance with its laws and regulations, on request of the importing Party or on its own initiative, assist the officials of the importing Party during the site visit and provide, to the extent practicable, information relevant to conduct the site visit;

(c)   the importing and the host Party shall limit communication regarding the site visit to relevant government officials and shall not inform any person outside the government of the host Party in advance of a site visit or provide any other verification or other information not publicly available the disclosure of which could undermine the effectiveness of the action;

(d)   the importing Party shall request permission from the exporter, producer, or a person having capacity to consent on behalf of the exporter or producer, either prior to the site visit if this would not undermine the effectiveness of the site visit or at the time of the site visit, to access the relevant records or facilities; and

(e)   if the exporter, producer, or person having the capacity to consent on behalf of the exporter or producer denies permission or access to the records or facilities, the site visit will not occur. If the exporter, producer, or a person having the capacity to consent on behalf of the exporter or producer is not able to receive the importing Party to carry out the site visit, the site visit shall be conducted on the following working day unless:

(i)   the importing Party agrees otherwise, or

(ii)   the exporter, producer, or person having the capacity to consent on behalf of the exporter or producer, substantiates a valid reason acceptable to the importing Party that the site visit cannot occur at that time.

If the exporter, producer, or person having the capacity to consent on behalf of the exporter or producer, does not have a valid reason acceptable to the importing Party that the site visit cannot take place on the following working day, the importing Party may deem permission for the site visit or access to the records or facilities to be denied. The importing Party shall give consideration to any reasonable alternative proposed dates, taking into account the availability of relevant employees or facilities of the person visited.

* * *

Article 6.7:   Determinations

The importing Party may deny a claim for preferential tariff treatment for a textile or apparel good:

(a)   for a reason listed in Article 5.10 (Determinations of Origin);

(b)   if, pursuant to a site visit under Article 6.6.2 (Verification), it has not received sufficient information to determine that the textile or apparel good qualifies for preferential tariff treatment; or

(c)   if, pursuant to a request for a site visit under Article 6.6.2 (Verification), a the importing Party is unable to conduct a site visit as access or permission for the site visit is denied, the importing Party is prevented from completing the site visit, or the exporter, producer, or person having the capacity to consent on behalf of the exporter or producer does not provide access to the relevant records or facilities during a site visit.

* * *

CHAPTER 7   CUSTOMS ADMINISTRATION
AND TRADE FACILITATION

Section A: Trade Facilitation

Article 7.1:   Trade Facilitation

1.   The Parties affirm their rights and obligations under the *Agreement on Trade Facilitation*, set out in Annex 1A to the WTO Agreement.

2.   With a view to minimizing the costs incurred by traders through the importation, exportation, or transit of a good, each Party shall administer its customs procedures in a manner that facilitates the importation, exportation, or transit of a good, and supports compliance with its law.

*   *   *

Article 7.8:   Express Shipments

1.   Each Party shall adopt or maintain specific expedited customs procedures for express shipments while maintaining appropriate customs controls. These procedures shall:

(a)   provide for information required to release an express shipment to be submitted and processed before the shipment arrives;

(b)   allow a single submission of information, such as a manifest, covering all goods contained in an express shipment, through, if possible, electronic means;

(c)   expedite the release of these shipments based on, to the extent possible, minimum documentation or a single submission of information;

(d)   provide for these shipments, under normal circumstances, to be released immediately after arrival, provided that all required documentation and data are submitted;

(e)   apply to shipments of any weight or value, recognizing that a Party may require formal entry procedures as a condition for release, including a declaration and supporting documentation and payment of customs duties, based on the good's weight or value; and

(f)   provide that, under normal circumstances, no customs duties or taxes will be assessed at the time or point of importation or formal entry procedures required,[2] on express shipments of a Party valued at or below a fixed amount set out under the Party's law, provided that the shipment does not form part of a series of shipments carried out or planned for the purpose of evading duties or taxes, or avoiding any regulation

---

[2]   For greater certainty, this subparagraph shall not prevent a Party from requiring informal entry procedures, including applicable supporting documents.

applicable to the formal entry procedures required by the importing Party. The fixed amount set out under the Party's law shall be at least[3]:

(i)   for the United States, US$800,

(ii)   for Mexico, US$117 for customs duties and US$50 for taxes, and

(iii)   for Canada, C$150 for customs duties and C$40 for taxes.

For these shipments, each Party shall allow for the periodic assessment and payment of duties and taxes applicable at the time or point of importation.

2.   Each Party shall adopt or maintain procedures that apply fewer customs formalities than those applied under formal entry procedures, to shipments valued at less than CAD$3,300 for Canada and US$2,500 for the United States and Mexico, provided that the shipments do not form part of a series of importations that may be reasonably considered to have been undertaken or arranged for the purpose of avoiding compliance by an importer with the importing Party's laws, regulations, or procedures related to formal entry.

3.   Nothing in this Article prevents a Party from requiring the necessary information and documents as a condition for the release of goods, and from assessing customs duties or taxes for restricted or controlled goods.

Article 7.9:   Use of Information Technology

Each Party shall:

(a)   use information technology that expedites procedures for the release of goods;

(b)   make available by electronic means any declaration or other form that is required for import, export, or transit of goods through its territory;

(c)   allow a customs declaration and related documentation to be submitted in electronic format;

(d)   make electronic systems accessible to importers, exporters, persons engaged in the transit of goods through its territory, and other customs users in order to submit and receive information;

(e)   promote the use of its electronic systems to facilitate the communication between traders and its customs administration and other related agencies;

(f)   adopt or maintain procedures allowing for the electronic payment of customs duties, taxes, fees, or charges imposed

---

[3]   Notwithstanding the amounts set out under this subparagraph, a Party may impose a reciprocal amount that is lower for shipments from another Party if the amount provided for under that other Party's law is lower than that of the Party.

on or in connection with importation or exportation and collected by customs and other related agencies;

(g) use electronic risk management systems in accordance with Article 7.12 (Risk Management); and

(h) endeavor to allow an importer, through its electronic systems, to correct multiple import declarations previously submitted to the Party involving the same issue through a single submission.

Article 7.10:   Single Window

1. Each Party shall establish or maintain a single window system that enables the electronic submission through a single entry point of the documentation and data the Party requires for importation into its territory.

2. Each Party shall review the operations of its single window system with a view to expanding its functionality to cover all its import, export, and transit transactions.

3. Each Party shall, in a timely manner, inform a person that is using its single window system of the status of the release of goods, through the single window system.

4. If a Party receives documentation or data for a good or shipment of goods through its single window system, the Party shall not request the same documentation or data for that good or shipment of goods, except in urgent circumstances or pursuant to other limited exceptions set out in its laws, regulations, or procedures. Each Party shall minimize the extent to which paper documents are required if electronic copies are provided.

5. In building and maintaining its single window system, each Party shall:

(a) incorporate, as appropriate, the World Customs Organization Data Model for data elements;

(b) endeavor to implement standards and data elements for import, export, and transit that are the same as the other Parties' single window system; and

(c) on an ongoing basis, streamline its single window system, including by adding functionality to facilitate trade, improve transparency, and reduce release times and costs.

6. In implementing paragraph 5, the Parties shall:

(a) share with each other their respective experiences in developing and maintaining their single window system; and

(b) work towards a harmonization, to the extent possible, of data elements and customs processes that facilitate use of a single transmission of information to both the exporting and importing Party.

* * *

CHAPTER 8   RECOGNITION OF THE UNITED MEXICAN STATES' DIRECT, INALIENABLE, AND IMPRESCRIPTIBLE OWNERSHIP OF HYDROCARBONS

Article 8.1:   Recognition of the United Mexican States' Direct, Inalienable, and Imprescriptible Ownership of Hydrocarbons

1.   As provided for in this Agreement, the Parties confirm their full respect for sovereignty and their sovereign right to regulate with respect to matters addressed in this Chapter in accordance with their respective Constitutions and domestic laws, in the full exercise of their democratic processes.

2.   In the case of Mexico, and without prejudice to their rights and remedies available under this Agreement, the United States and Canada recognize that:

   (a)   Mexico reserves its sovereign right to reform its Constitution and its domestic legislation; and

   (b)   Mexico has the direct, inalienable, and imprescriptible ownership of all hydrocarbons in the subsoil of the national territory, including the continental shelf and the exclusive economic zone located outside the territorial sea and adjacent thereto, in strata or deposits, regardless of their physical conditions pursuant to Mexico's Constitution (*Constitución Política de los Estados Unidos Mexicanos*).

CHAPTER 9   SANITARY AND PHYTOSANITARY MEASURES

Article 9.1:   Definitions

1.   The definitions in Annex A of the SPS Agreement are incorporated into and made part of this Chapter, *mutatis mutandis*, except as otherwise provided for in paragraph 2.

2.   For the purposes of this Chapter:

Competent authority means a government body of a Party responsible for measures or matters referred to in this Chapter;

Import check means an inspection, examination, sampling, review of documentation, test, or procedure, including laboratory, organoleptic, or identity, conducted at the border or otherwise during the entry process by an importing Party or its representative to determine if a consignment complies with the sanitary or phytosanitary requirements of the importing Party;

Relevant international organizations means the Codex Alimentarius Commission, the World Organization for Animal Health, the International Plant Protection Convention, and other international organizations as decided by the Committee on Sanitary and Phytosanitary Measures established under Article 9.17 (SPS Committee);

Relevant international standards, guidelines, or recommendations means those defined in paragraph 3(a) through (c) of Annex A of the SPS Agreement and standards, guidelines, or recommendations of other international organizations as decided by the SPS Committee;

risk management means the weighing of policy alternatives in light of the results of risk assessment and, if required, selecting and implementing appropriate controls, which may include sanitary or phytosanitary measures;

WTO SPS Committee means the WTO Committee on Sanitary and Phytosanitary Measures established under Article 12 of the SPS Agreement.

Article 9.2:   Scope

This Chapter applies to all sanitary and phytosanitary measures of a Party that may, directly or indirectly, affect trade between the Parties.

Article 9.3:   Objectives

1.   The objectives of this Chapter are to:

(a)   protect human, animal, or plant life or health in the territories of the Parties while facilitating trade between them;

(b)   reinforce and build upon the SPS Agreement;

(c)   strengthen communication, consultation, and cooperation between the Parties, and particularly between the Parties' competent authorities;

(d)   ensure that sanitary or phytosanitary measures implemented by a Party do not create unnecessary barriers to trade;

(e)   enhance transparency in and understanding of the application of each Party's sanitary and phytosanitary measures;

(f)   encourage the development and adoption of science-based international standards, guidelines, and recommendations, and promote their implementation by the Parties;

(g)   enhance compatability of sanitary or phytosanitary measures as appropriate; and

(h)   advance science-based decision making.

Article 9.4:   General Provisions

1.   The Parties affirm their rights and obligations under the SPS Agreement.

2.   Sanitary or phytosanitary measures which conform to the relevant provisions of this Chapter are presumed to be consistent with the obligations of the Parties under Chapter 2 (National Treatment and

Market Access for Goods), which relate to the use of sanitary or phytosanitary measures, and Article XX(b) of the GATT 1994 as incorporated into Article 32.1 (General Exceptions).

3. Sanitary or phytosanitary measures which conform to relevant international standards, guidelines, and recommendations are deemed to be necessary to protect human, animal, or plant life or health, and presumed to be consistent with the relevant provisions of this Chapter, Chapter 2 (National Treatment and Market Access for Goods), which relate to the use of sanitary or phytosanitary measures, and Article XX(b) of the GATT 1994 as incorporated into Article 32.1 (General Exceptions).

Article 9.5:   Competent Authorities and Contact Points

1. Each Party shall provide to the other Parties a list of its central level of government competent authorities. On request of a Party, and, if applicable, a Party shall provide contact information or written descriptions of the sanitary and phytosanitary responsibilities of its competent authorities.

2. Each Party shall designate and notify a contact point for matters arising under this Chapter, in accordance with Article 30.5 (Agreement Coordinator and Contact Points).

3. Each Party shall promptly inform the other Parties of any change in its competent authorities or contact points.

Article 9.6:   Science and Risk Analysis

1. The Parties recognize the importance of ensuring that their respective sanitary and phytosanitary measures are based on scientific principles.

2. Each Party has the right to adopt or maintain sanitary and phytosanitary measures necessary for the protection of human, animal, or plant life or health, provided that those measures are not inconsistent with the provisions of this Chapter.

3. Each Party shall base its sanitary and phytosanitary measures on relevant international standards, guidelines, or recommendations provided that doing so meets the Party's appropriate level of sanitary or phytosanitary protection (appropriate level of protection). If a sanitary or phytosanitary measure is not based on relevant international standards, guidelines, or recommendations, or if relevant international standards, guidelines, or recommendations do not exist, the Party shall ensure that its sanitary or phytosanitary measure is based on an assessment, as appropriate to the circumstances, of the risk to human, animal, or plant life or health.

4. Recognizing the Parties' rights and obligations under the relevant provisions of the SPS Agreement, this Chapter does not prevent a Party from:

    (a) establishing the level of protection it determines to be appropriate;

(b)   establishing or maintaining an approval procedure that requires a risk assessment to be conducted before the Party grants a product access to its market; or

(c)   adopting or maintaining a sanitary or phytosanitary measure on a provisional basis if relevant scientific evidence is insufficient.

5.   If a Party adopts or maintains a provisional sanitary or phytosanitary measure if relevant scientific evidence is insufficient, the Party shall within a reasonable period of time:

(a)   seek to obtain the additional information necessary for a more objective assessment of risk;

(b)   complete the risk assessment after obtaining the requisite information; and

(c)   review and, if appropriate, revise the provisional measure in light of the risk assessment.

6.   Each Party shall ensure that its sanitary and phytosanitary measures:

(a)   are applied only to the extent necessary to protect human, animal, or plant life or health;

(b)   are based on relevant scientific principles, taking into account relevant factors, including, if appropriate, different geographic conditions;

(c)   are not maintained if there is no longer a scientific basis;

(d)   do not arbitrarily or unjustifiably discriminate between Parties where identical or similar conditions prevail, including between its own territory and that of other Parties; and

(e)   are not applied in a manner that constitutes a disguised restriction on trade between the Parties.

7.   Each Party shall conduct its risk assessment and risk management with respect to a sanitary or phytosanitary regulation within the scope of Annex B of the SPS Agreement in a manner that is documented and provides the other Parties and persons of the Parties an opportunity to comment, in a manner to be determined by that Party.

8.   In conducting its risk assessment and risk management, each Party shall:

(a)   ensure that each risk assessment it conducts is appropriate to the circumstances of the risk to human, animal, or plant life or health, and takes into account the available relevant scientific evidence, including qualitative and quantitative data and information; and

(b)   take into account relevant guidance of the WTO SPS Committee and the relevant international standards, guidelines, and recommendations of the relevant international organization.

9. Each Party shall consider, as a risk management option, taking no measure if that would achieve the Party's appropriate level of protection.

10. Without prejudice to Article 9.4 (General Provisions), each Party shall select a sanitary or phytosanitary measure that is not more trade restrictive than required to achieve the level of protection that the Party has determined to be appropriate. For greater certainty, a sanitary or phytosanitary measure is not more trade restrictive than required unless there is another option that is reasonably available, taking into account technical and economic feasibility, that achieves the Party's appropriate level of protection and is significantly less restrictive to trade.

11. If an importing Party requires a risk assessment to evaluate a request from an exporting Party to authorize importation of a good of that exporting Party, the importing Party shall provide, on request of the exporting Party, an explanation of the information required for the risk assessment. On receipt of the requisite information from the exporting Party, the importing Party shall endeavor to facilitate the evaluation of the request for authorization by scheduling work on this request in accordance with the procedures, policies, resources, laws, and regulations of the importing Party.

12. On request of the exporting Party, the importing Party shall inform the exporting Party of the status of a request to authorize trade, including the status of any risk assessment or other evaluation the Party requires to authorize trade, and of any delay that occurs during the process.

13. If the importing Party, as a result of a risk assessment, adopts a sanitary or phytosanitary measure that may facilitate trade between the Parties, the importing Party shall implement the measure without undue delay.

14. If a Party has reason to believe that a specific sanitary or phytosanitary measure adopted or maintained by another Party is constraining, or has the potential to constrain, its exports and the measure is not based on a relevant international standard, guideline, or recommendation, or a relevant standard, guideline, or recommendation does not exist, the Party adopting or maintaining the measure shall provide an explanation of the reasons and pertinent relevant information regarding the measure upon request by the other Party.

15. Without prejudice to Article 9.14 (Emergency Measures), no Party shall stop the importation of a good of another Party for the reason that the importing Party is undertaking a review of its sanitary or phytosanitary

measure, if the importing Party permitted the importation of that good of the other Party when the review was initiated.[1]

Article 9.7:   Enhancing   Compatibility   of   Sanitary   and Phytosanitary Measures

1.   Each Party recognizes that enhancing the compatibility of its sanitary and phytosanitary measures with the measures of another Party may facilitate trade while maintaining each Party's right to determine its appropriate level of protection.

2.   To reduce unnecessary obstacles to trade, each Party shall endeavor to enhance the compatibility of its sanitary and phytosanitary measures with the sanitary and phytosanitary measures of the other Parties, provided that doing so does not reduce each Party's appropriate level of protection. In so doing, each Party:

(a)   is encouraged to consider relevant actual or proposed sanitary or phytosanitary measures of the other Parties in the development, modification, or adoption of their sanitary or phytosanitary measures; and

(b)   shall have the objective, among others, of making its sanitary and phytosanitary measures equivalent or, if appropriate, identical to those of the other Parties, but only to the extent that doing either does not reduce the Party's appropriate level of protection.

Article 9.8:   Adaptation to Regional Conditions, Including Pest- or Disease-Free Areas and Areas of Low Pest or Disease Prevalence

1.   The Parties recognize that adaptation to regional conditions, including regionalization, zoning, and compartmentalization, is an important means to facilitate trade.

2.   The Parties shall endeavor to cooperate on the recognition of pest- or disease-free areas, and areas of low pest or disease prevalence with the objective of acquiring confidence in the procedures followed by each Party for the recognition of pest- or disease-free areas, and areas of low pest or disease prevalence.

3.   In making a determination regarding regional conditions, each Party shall take into account the relevant guidance of the WTO SPS Committee and relevant international standards, guidelines, and recommendations.

4.   If an importing Party receives from an exporting Party a request for a determination of regional conditions and determines that the exporting Party has provided sufficient information, the importing Party shall initiate an assessment without undue delay. For this purpose, each

---

[1]   For greater certainty, a Party is not stopping imports because it is undertaking a review if the Party stops imports on the basis that the review identifies that the information necessary to permit the importation of a good is lacking.

exporting Party shall provide reasonable access in its territory to the importing Party for inspection, testing, and other relevant procedures.

5. The importing Party shall inform the exporting Party of receipt of information provided by the exporting Party under paragraph 4. The importing Party shall evaluate the information provided by the exporting Party and shall inform the exporting Party whether the information is sufficient to evaluate a request for adaptation to regional conditions. The importing Party may request additional relevant information or an on-site verification, if justified, based on the results of the ongoing evaluation.

6. When an importing Party initiates an evaluation of a request for a determination of regional conditions under paragraph 4, that Party shall explain, on request of the exporting Party, its process for making the determination of regional conditions without undue delay.

7. On request from the exporting Party, the importing Party's competent authority shall consider whether a streamlined process may be used for the determination of regional conditions.

8. If the importing and exporting Parties' competent authorities decide that a request for a determination of regional conditions is a priority, and the importing Party has received sufficient information, as referenced in paragraph 4, the competent authorities involved shall establish reasonable timeframes based on the circumstances and may establish a work plan under which the importing Party, under normal circumstances[2], may finalize the determination. The determination may be positive or negative.

9. On request of the exporting Party, the importing Party shall inform the exporting Party of the status of the evaluation of the exporting Party's request for a determination of regional conditions.

10. The importing Party shall finalize the evaluation and all necessary stages involved for the determination of regional conditions of the exporting Party without undue delay once the importing Party's competent authority determines that it has received sufficient information from the exporting Party.

11. If the evaluation results in the recognition of specific regional conditions of an exporting Party, the importing Party shall communicate this determination to the exporting Party in writing and shall apply this recognition without undue delay.

12. If the evaluation of the evidence provided by the exporting Party does not result in a determination to recognize pest- or disease-free areas or areas of low pest and disease prevalence, the importing Party shall provide in writing to the exporting Party with the rationale for its determination.

---

[2] For the purposes of this paragraph, "normal circumstances" do not include any extraordinary or unanticipated situations, such as unanticipated risks to human, animal, or plant life or health, or resource or regulatory constraints.

13. The importing and exporting Parties involved in a particular determination of regional conditions may also decide in advance the risk management measures that will apply to trade between them in the event of a change in the status.

14. If there is an incident that results in a change of status, the exporting Party shall inform the importing Party. If the importing Party modifies or revokes the determination recognizing regional conditions as a result of the change in status, on request of the exporting Party, the Parties involved shall cooperate to assess whether the determination can be reinstated.

15. The Parties involved in a determination recognizing regional conditions shall, if mutually decided, report the outcome to the SPS Committee.

Article 9.9:   Equivalence

1. The Parties recognize that a positive determination of equivalence of sanitary and phytosanitary measures is an important means to facilitate trade.

2. Further to Article 4 of the SPS Agreement, the Parties shall apply a recognition of equivalence to a specific sanitary or phytosanitary measure, or to the extent feasible and appropriate, to a group of measures or on a systems-wide basis. In determining the equivalence of a specific sanitary or phytosanitary measure, group of measures, or measures on a systems-wide basis, each Party shall take into account the relevant guidance of the WTO SPS Committee and relevant international standards, guidelines, and recommendations.

3. On request of the exporting Party, the importing Party shall explain the objective and rationale of its sanitary or phytosanitary measure and identify the risk the sanitary or phytosanitary measure is intended to address.

4. When an importing Party receives a request for a determination of equivalence from an exporting Party and determines that the exporting Party has provided sufficient information, the importing Party shall initiate an assessment without undue delay.

5. When an importing Party initiates an equivalence assessment, the importing Party shall explain, on request of the exporting Party, and without undue delay, its process for making the determination of equivalence, and, if the determination results in recognition, its plan for enabling trade.

6. On request of the exporting Party, the importing Party's competent authority shall consider whether a streamlined process may be used to determine equivalence.

7. If the importing and exporting Parties' competent authorities decide that a request for a determination of equivalence is a priority, and the importing Party has received sufficient information, as referenced in paragraph 4, the competent authorities involved shall establish reasonable timeframes based on the circumstances and may establish

a work plan under which the importing Party, under normal circumstances[3], may finalize the determination. The determination may be positive or negative.

8.   On request of the exporting Party, the importing Party shall inform the exporting Party of the status of the equivalence assessment.

9.   Once the importing Party determines that the information provided by the exporting Party is sufficient to finalize the assessment, the importing Party shall finalize the assessment and communicate the results of the assessment to the exporting Party without undue delay.

10. In determining equivalence, an importing Party shall take into account available knowledge, information, and relevant experience, including knowledge acquired through experience with the exporting Party's relevant competent authority.

11. An importing Party shall recognize the equivalence of a sanitary or phytosanitary measure, group of measures, or system, even if the measure, group of measures, or system differs from its own, if the exporting Party objectively demonstrates to the importing Party that the exporting Party's measure achieves the importing Party's appropriate level of protection, taking into account outcomes that the exporting Party's measure, group of measures, or system achieves.

12. If an importing Party adopts a measure that recognizes the equivalence of an exporting Party's specific sanitary or phytosanitary measure, group of measures, or measures on a systems-wide basis, the importing Party shall communicate that measure to the exporting Party in writing and implement the measure without undue delay.

13. The Parties involved in an equivalence determination that results in recognition shall, if mutually decided, report the outcome to the SPS Committee.

14. If an assessment does not result in the recognition of equivalence, the importing Party shall communicate that determination and its rationale to the exporting Party without undue delay.

15. If a Party plans to adopt, modify, or repeal a measure that is the subject of a sanitary or phytosanitary equivalence recognition, the following applies:

   (a) The Party shall notify the other Party involved in the recognition of its plan. The notification should take place at an early appropriate stage where any comments submitted by the other Party can be taken into account, including by revising its plan. Upon request of a Party involved in the recognition, the Parties involved shall discuss whether the adoption, modification, or repeal of the measure may affect the equivalence recognition.

---

[3]   For the purposes of this paragraph, "normal circumstances" do not include any extraordinary or unanticipated situations, such as unanticipated risks to human, animal or plant life or health, or resource or regulatory constraints.

(b) The Party shall, upon request of the other Party, provide information and rationale concerning its planned adoption, modification, or repeal. The other Party shall review any information provided to it and submit any comments to the Party that plans to adopt, modify, or repeal the measure, without undue delay.

(c) The importing Party shall not revoke its recognition of equivalence on the basis that an adoption, modification, or repeal of the measure is pending.

16. If a Party adopts, modifies, or repeals a measure that is the subject of a sanitary or phytosanitary recognition of equivalence, the importing Party shall maintain its recognition of equivalence provided that the exporting Party's measures concerning the good continue to achieve the appropriate level of protection of the importing Party. Upon request of a Party, the Parties involved in the recognition shall promptly discuss the determination made by the importing Party.

17. If a Party adopts, modifies, or repeals a measure that is the subject of a sanitary or phytosanitary recognition of equivalence, the importing Party shall:

(a) continue to accept the recognition of equivalence until it has communicated to the exporting Party whether other requirements must be met to maintain equivalence; and

(b) if other requirements under subparagraph (a) must be met, upon request, discuss those requirements with the exporting Party.

Article 9.10:   Audits[4]

1. To determine an exporting Party's ability to comply with the importing Party's sanitary or phytosanitary requirements or to verify an exporting Party's compliance with its sanitary or phytosanitary requirements that the importing Party has determined to be equivalent, the importing Party shall have the right to audit the exporting Party's competent authorities, including associated or designated inspection systems in accordance with this Article. That audit may include an assessment of the competent authorities' control programs, including, if appropriate and feasible, the inspection programs, audit programs, or on-site inspections of facilities or other agriculture production areas.

2. An audit must be systems-based and designed to check the effectiveness of the regulatory controls of the competent authorities of the exporting Party.

---

[4]   For greater certainty, the Parties recognize that an inspection of a facility and other premises relevant to the inspection in a Party's territory in order to verify compliance with applicable sanitary or phytosanitary measures is a distinct activity from an audit and the provisions of this Article do not apply to that inspection.

3.   In undertaking an audit, a Party shall take into account relevant guidance of the WTO SPS Committee and relevant international standards, guidelines, and recommendations.

4.   Prior to the commencement of an audit, the auditing and audited Parties shall discuss: the rationale, objectives, and scope of the audit; and the criteria or requirements against which the audited Party will be assessed. Also at that time, the auditing and audited Parties shall decide the itinerary and procedures for conducting the audit.

5.   Unless the auditing and audited Parties decide otherwise, the auditing Party shall hold an exit meeting at the end of the audit that includes an opportunity for the competent authority of the audited Party to raise questions or seek clarification on the preliminary findings and observations provided at the meeting.

6.   The auditing Party shall provide the audited Party the draft written audit report, including its initial findings. The auditing Party shall provide the audited Party the opportunity to comment on the accuracy of the draft audit report and shall take any such comments into account before the auditing Party finalizes its report. The auditing Party shall provide a final audit report setting out its conclusions in writing to the audited Party within a reasonable period of time.

7.   In undertaking an audit in cases in which an importing Party has recognized equivalence on a system-wide basis, the importing Party shall:

   (a)   conduct the audit to verify that the audited Party's system achieves an equivalent outcome to the sanitary or phytosanitary appropriate level of protection of the importing Party; and

   (b)   audit against the exporting Party's implementation of the equivalent oversight and control system.

8.   If a Party has recognized another Party's system as equivalent, the competent authorities of the Parties involved in the recognition may discuss schedules of the audits of that system.

9.   A decision or action taken by the auditing Party as a result of the audit must be supported by objective evidence and data that can be verified, taking into account the auditing Party's knowledge of, relevant experience with, and confidence in, the audited Party's regulatory controls. The auditing Party shall, on request of the audited Party, provide this objective evidence and data.

10.   The costs incurred by the auditing Party shall be borne by the auditing Party, unless the auditing and audited Parties decide otherwise.

11.   The auditing Party and audited Party shall each ensure that procedures are in place to prevent the disclosure of confidential information that is acquired during the audit process.

12.   If the auditing Party makes a final audit report publicly available, the final audit report must incorporate, or be accompanied by, the

comments or written response to the draft report provided by the competent authority of the audited Party.

13. The Parties may decide, if possible, to:

(a) collaborate on audits of non-Parties; or

(b) share the results of audits of non-Parties.

Article 9.11: Import Checks

1. An importing Party may use import checks to assess compliance with its sanitary and phytosanitary measures and to obtain information to assess risk or to determine the need for, develop, or periodically review a risk-based import check.

2. Each Party shall ensure that its import checks are based on the risks associated with importations, and that its import checks are carried out without undue delay.

3. A Party shall make available to another Party, on request, information on its import procedures and its basis for determining the nature and frequency of import checks, including the factors it considers to determine the risks associated with importations.

4. A Party may change the frequency of its import checks as a result of experience gained through import checks or as a result of actions or discussions provided for in this Chapter.

5. An importing Party shall provide to another Party, on request, information regarding the analytical methods, quality controls, sampling procedures, and facilities that the importing Party uses to test a good. The importing Party shall ensure that any testing is conducted using appropriate and validated methods under a quality assurance program that is consistent with international laboratory standards. The importing Party shall maintain physical or electronic documentation regarding the identification, collection, sampling, transportation and storage of the test sample, and the analytical methods used on the test sample.

6. Each Party, with respect to any import check that it conducts, shall:

(a) limit any requirements regarding individual specimens or samples of an import to those that are reasonable and necessary;

(b) ensure that any fees imposed for the procedures on imported products are equitable in relation to any fees charged on like domestic products or products originating in any other Party or non-Party and should be no higher than the actual cost of the service;

(c) use criteria for selecting facilities at which an import check is conducted:

(i) so that the location does not cause unnecessary inconvenience to an applicant or its agent, and

(ii)   so that the integrity of the good is preserved, except for the individual specimens or samples obtained pursuant to the requirements referred to in subparagraph (a).

7.   An importing Party shall ensure that its final decision in response to a finding of non-conformity with the importing Party's sanitary or phytosanitary measure is limited to what is reasonable and necessary in response to the non-conformity.

8.   If an importing Party prohibits or restricts the importation of a good of another Party on the basis of an adverse result of an import check, the importing Party shall provide a notification, if practicable by electronic means, about the adverse result to at least one of the following: the importer or its agent; the exporter; or the manufacturer.

9.   When the importing Party provides a notification pursuant to paragraph 8, the Party shall:

(a)   include in its notification:

(i)   the reason for the prohibition or restriction,

(ii)   the legal basis or authorization for the action, and

(iii)   information on the status of the affected goods including, if applicable:

(A)   relevant laboratory results and laboratory methodologies, if requested and possible to include;

(B)   in the case of pest interceptions, an identification of the pests at the species level, if available; and

(C)   information on the disposition of goods, if appropriate; and

(b)   transmit the notification as soon as possible, and, in any event, under normal circumstances no later than five days after the date of the decision to prohibit or restrict, unless the good is seized by a customs administration or subject to ongoing law enforcement action.

10.   An importing Party that prohibits or restricts the importation of a good of another Party on the basis of an adverse result of an import check shall provide an opportunity for a review of the decision and consider any relevant information submitted to assist in the review.[5] The review request and information should be submitted to the importing Party within a reasonable period of time.

11.   Paragraph 9 does not prevent an importing Party from disposing of goods which are found to have an infectious pathogen or pest that, if

---

[5]   For greater certainty, a Party shall provide an opportunity for review to at least one of the following: the importer or its agent, the exporter, or the manufacturer of the good, and the review shall be conducted by the customs administration or the relevant competent authority.

urgent action is not taken, can spread and cause damage to human, animal, or plant life or health in the Party's territory.

12. If an importing Party determines that there is a significant, sustained or recurring pattern of non-conformity with a sanitary or phytosanitary measure, the importing Party shall notify the exporting Party of the pattern of non-conformity.

13. On request, an importing Party shall provide to the exporting Party available information on goods of the exporting Party that were found not to conform to a sanitary or phytosanitary measure of the importing Party.

Article 9.12:   Certification

1. The Parties recognize that assurances with respect to sanitary or phytosanitary requirements may be provided through means other than certificates.

2. Each Party shall ensure that at least one of the following conditions is satisfied before imposing a sanitary or phytosanitary certification requirement:

   (a) the certification requirement is based on the relevant international standards; or

   (b) the certification requirement is appropriate to the circumstances of risks to human, animal, or plant life or health at issue.[6]

3. If an importing Party requires certification for trade in a good, that Party shall ensure that the certification requirement is applied only to the extent necessary to meet its appropriate level of protection.

4. In applying certification requirements, an importing Party shall take into account relevant guidance of the WTO SPS Committee and relevant international standards, guidelines, and recommendations.

5. An importing Party shall limit attestations and information it requires on the certificates to essential information that is necessary to provide assurances to the importing Party that its appropriate level of protection has been met.

6. An importing Party shall provide to another Party, on request, the rationale for any attestations or information that the importing Party requires to be included on a certificate.

7. The Parties may decide to work cooperatively to develop model certificates to accompany specific goods traded between the Parties, taking into account relevant guidance of the WTO SPS Committee and relevant international standards, guidelines, and recommendations.

---

[6] For greater certainty, a certification requirement concerning non-sanitary or phytosanitary requirements, including the quality of a product or information relating to consumer preferences, does not constitute a certification requirement appropriate to the circumstances of a risk to human, animal, or plant life or health.

8.   The Parties shall promote the implementation of electronic certification and other technologies to facilitate trade.

Article 9.13:   Transparency

1.   This Article applies to sanitary or phytosanitary measures that constitute sanitary or phytosanitary regulations for the purposes of Annex B of the SPS Agreement.

2.   The Parties recognize the value of sharing information about their sanitary and phytosanitary measures on an ongoing basis, and of providing other Parties and persons of the Parties with the opportunity to comment on their proposed sanitary or phytosanitary measures.

3.   In implementing this Article, each Party shall take into account relevant guidance of the WTO SPS Committee and relevant international standards, guidelines, and recommendations.

4.   A Party shall notify a proposed sanitary or phytosanitary measure that may have an effect on the trade of another Party, including any that conforms to international standards, guidelines, or recommendations, by using the WTO SPS notification submission system as a means of notifying the other Parties.

5.   Unless urgent problems of human, animal, or plant life or health protection arise or threaten to arise requiring the adoption of an emergency measure, or the measure is of a trade-facilitating nature, a Party shall normally allow at least 60 days for the other Parties or persons of the Parties to provide written comments on the proposed measure, other than proposed legislation, after it makes the notification under paragraph 4. The Party shall consider any reasonable request from another Party or persons of the Parties to extend the comment period. On request of another Party, the Party shall respond to the written comments of the other Party in an appropriate manner.

6.   The Party shall make available on a free, publicly available website or official journal, the proposed sanitary or phytosanitary measure notified under paragraph 4, the legal basis for the measure, and the written comments or a summary of the written comments that the Party has received from the public on the proposed measure.

7.   If a Party proposes a sanitary or phytosanitary measure that does not conform to a relevant international standard, guideline, or recommendation, the Party shall provide to another Party, on request, the relevant documentation that the Party considered in developing the proposed measure, including documented and objective scientific evidence related to the measure, such as risk assessments, relevant studies, and expert opinions.

8.   A Party that proposes to adopt a sanitary or phytosanitary measure shall discuss with another Party, on request and when appropriate during its regulatory process, any scientific or trade concerns that the other Party may raise regarding the proposed measure and the availability of alternative, less trade-restrictive approaches for achieving the Party's appropriate level of protection.

9. Each Party shall publish, preferably by electronic means, notices of final sanitary or phytosanitary measures in an official journal or website.

10. Each Party shall notify the other Parties of final sanitary or phytosanitary measures through the WTO SPS notification submission system. Each Party shall ensure that the text or the notice of a final sanitary or phytosanitary measure specifies the date on which the measure takes effect and the legal basis for the measure. A Party shall also make available to another Party, on request, and to the extent permitted by the confidentiality and privacy requirements of the Party's law, significant written comments and relevant documentation considered to support the measure that were received during the comment period.

11. If a final sanitary or phytosanitary measure is substantively altered from the proposed measure, a Party shall also include in the notice of the final sanitary or phytosanitary measure that it publishes, an explanation of:

    (a) the objective and rationale of the measure and how the measure advances that objective and rationale; and

    (b) any substantive revisions that it made to the proposed measure.

12. An exporting Party shall notify the importing Party through the contact points referred to in Article 9.5 (Competent Authorities and Contact Points) in a timely and appropriate manner:

    (a) if it has knowledge of a significant sanitary or phytosanitary risk related to the export of a good from its territory;

    (b) of urgent situations where a change in animal or plant health status in the territory of the exporting Party may affect current trade;

    (c) of significant changes in the status of a regionalized pest or disease;

    (d) of new scientific findings of importance which affect the regulatory response with respect to food safety, pests, or diseases; and

    (e) of significant changes in food safety, pest, or disease management, control or eradication policies or practices that may affect trade.

13. If feasible and appropriate, a Party shall normally provide an interval of not less than six months between the date it publishes a final sanitary or phytosanitary measure and the date on which the measure takes effect, unless the measure is intended to address an urgent problem of human, animal, or plant life or health protection or the measure facilitates trade.

14. A Party shall make available to another Party, on request, all sanitary or phytosanitary measures related to the importation of a good into that Party's territory.

Article 9.14:   Emergency Measures

1.   If an importing Party adopts an emergency measure to address an urgent problem of human, animal or plant life or health that arises or threatens to arise, and applies it to the exports of another Party the importing Party shall promptly notify in writing each affected Party of that measure through the normal channels. The importing Party shall take into consideration any information provided by an affected Party in response to the notification.

2.   If an importing Party adopts an emergency measure under paragraph 1, it shall review the scientific basis of that measure within six months and make available the results of the review to any Party on request. If the emergency measure is maintained after the review, because the reason for its adoption remains, the Party should review the measure periodically.

Article 9.15:   Information Exchange

A Party may request information from another Party on a matter arising under this Chapter. A Party that receives a request for information shall endeavor to provide available information to the requesting Party within a reasonable period of time, and if possible, by electronic means.

Article 9.16:   Cooperation

1.   The Parties shall explore opportunities for further cooperation, collaboration, and information exchange between the Parties on sanitary and phytosanitary matters of mutual interest, consistent with this Chapter. Those opportunities may include trade facilitation initiatives and technical assistance. The Parties shall cooperate to facilitate the implementation of this Chapter.

2.   The Parties shall cooperate and may work, as mutually decided, on sanitary and phytosanitary matters, including to develop as appropriate, common principles, guidelines, and approaches on matters covered by this Chapter, with the goal of eliminating unnecessary obstacles to trade between the Parties.

3.   If mutually decided, the Parties shall share information on their respective approaches to risk management with the objective of enhancing the compatibility of their risk management approaches.

4.   The Parties are encouraged to create and develop initiatives to facilitate and promote the compatibility of their sanitary or phytosanitary measures.

5.   If there is mutual interest and with the objective of establishing a common scientific foundation for each Party's risk management approach, the competent authorities of the Parties are encouraged to:

(a) share best practices on their respective approaches to risk analysis;

(b) cooperate on joint scientific data collection;

(c) if feasible and appropriate, undertake science-based joint risk assessments;

(d) if applicable and in accordance with the procedures, policies, resources, laws, and regulations of each Party, provide access to their respective completed risk assessments and the data used to develop risk assessments; or

(e) if appropriate, cooperate on aligning data requirements for risk assessments.

Article 9.17:   Committee on Sanitary and Phytosanitary Measures

1. For the purposes of the effective implementation and operation of this Chapter, the Parties hereby establish a Committee on Sanitary and Phytosanitary Measures, composed of government representatives of each Party responsible for sanitary and phytosanitary matters.

2. The SPS Committee shall serve as a forum:

(a) to consider any matter related to this Chapter, including relating to its implementation;

(b) to improve the Parties' understanding of sanitary or phytosanitary issues that relate to the implementation of the SPS Agreement or this Chapter;

(c) to enhance mutual understanding of each Party's sanitary or phytosanitary measures or the regulatory processes that relate to those measures;

(d) to enhance communication and cooperation among the Parties related to sanitary or phytosanitary matters;

(e) to identify and discuss, at an early appropriate stage, proposed sanitary or phytosanitary measures or revisions to existing sanitary or phytosanitary measures that may have a significant effect on trade in North America including for the purposes of issue avoidance and facilitating greater alignment of sanitary or phytosanitary measures; and

(f) for a Party to share information, as appropriate, on a sanitary or phytosanitary matter that has arisen between it and another Party or Parties.

3. The SPS Committee may serve as a forum:

(a) if appropriate, to identify and develop technical assistance and cooperation projects between the Parties on sanitary and phytosanitary measures;

(b) to consult on matters and positions for meetings of the WTO SPS Committee, and meetings held under the auspices of the

Codex Alimentarius Commission, the World Organisation for Animal Health, the International Plant Protection Convention, and other international organizations as appropriate;

(c) to identify, prioritize, manage, and resolve bilateral or trilateral issues;

(d) to review progress on addressing specific trade concerns related to the application of a sanitary or phytosanitary measure, with a view to facilitating mutually acceptable solution;

(e) to establish and, as appropriate, determine the scope and mandate of technical working groups in areas such as, animal health, plant health, food safety, or pesticides, taking into account existing mechanisms, to undertake work related to the implementation of this Chapter;

(f) to provide guidance to technical working groups, as needed and appropriate, for the identification, prioritization, and management of sanitary or phytosanitary matters;

(g) to request updates and discuss the work of the technical working groups;

(h) to review the recommendation from a technical working group regarding whether it should be continued, suspended, or dissolved;

(i) to seek, to the extent practicable, the assistance of relevant international or regional organizations, such as the North American Plant Protection Organization, to obtain available scientific and technical advice and minimize duplication of effort; and

(j) to facilitate the development, as appropriate, of common principles, guidelines and approaches on matters covered by this Chapter.

4. The SPS Committee shall establish its terms of reference at its first meeting and may revise those terms of reference as needed.

5. The SPS Committee shall meet within one year of the date of entry into force of this Agreement and once a year thereafter unless the Parties decide otherwise.

6. The SPS Committee shall report annually to the Commission on the implementation of this Chapter.

Article 9.18:   Technical Working Groups

1. A technical working group may function on an on-going or *ad hoc* basis.

2. Any on-going technical working group shall meet on an annual basis unless otherwise decided by the Parties participating in the technical working group. Any *ad hoc* technical working group shall meet as

frequently as decided by the Parties participating in the technical working group.

3. At the first meeting of a technical working group, the participating Parties shall establish the working group's terms of reference, unless the Parties decide otherwise.

4. Any technical working group established under Article 9.17.3(e) (Committee on Sanitary and Phytosanitary Measures) may:

   (a) engage, at the earliest appropriate stage, in scientific or technical exchange and cooperation regarding sanitary or phytosanitary matters;

   (b) consider any sanitary or phytosanitary measure or set of measures identified by any Party that are likely to affect, directly or indirectly, trade, and provide technical advice with a view to facilitating the resolution of specific trade concerns relating to those measures;

   (c) serve as a forum to facilitate discussion and consideration of specific risk assessments and possible risk management options;

   (d) provide an opportunity for Parties to discuss developments relevant to the work of the technical working group;

   (e) discuss other issues related to this Chapter; and

   (f) report to the SPS Committee on progress of work, as appropriate.

5. A technical working group may provide the SPS Committee with the recommendation that it be continued, suspended, or dissolved.

6. Each technical working group shall be co-chaired by representatives of the participating Parties.

7. The Parties may seek to resolve any specific trade concern through the relevant technical working group.

Article 9.19: Technical Consultations

1. Recognizing that trade matters arising under this Chapter are best resolved by the appropriate competent authority, if a Party has concerns regarding any matter arising under this Chapter with respect to another Party, the Party shall endeavor to resolve the matter through available administrative procedures of the relevant competent authority or through a relevant technical working group established by the SPS Committee, if it considers that it is appropriate to do so. A Party may have recourse to technical consultations set out in paragraph 2 at any time it considers that the use of the relevant administrative procedures, the relevant technical working group, or other mechanisms would not resolve the matter.

2. A Party (requesting Party) may initiate technical consultations with another Party (responding Party) to discuss any matter arising under

this Chapter that may adversely affect its trade by delivering a written request to the Contact Point of the responding Party. The request shall identify the reason for the request, including a description of the requesting Party's concerns about the matter.

3.   The requesting and responding Parties shall meet within 30 days of the responding Party's receipt of the request, with the aim of resolving the matter cooperatively within 180 days of the request if possible.

4.   The requesting and responding Parties shall ensure the appropriate involvement of relevant trade representatives and competent authorities in meetings held pursuant to this Article.

5.   Recognizing that Parties may decide to engage in consultations pursuant to this Article for any length of time, the requesting Party may cease technical consultations under this Article and have recourse to dispute settlement under Chapter 31 (Dispute Settlement) following the meeting referred to in paragraph 3 or if the meeting is not held within 30 days as specified in paragraph 3.

6.   No Party shall have recourse to dispute settlement under Chapter 31 (Dispute Settlement) for a matter arising under this Chapter without first seeking to resolve the matter through technical consultations in accordance with this Article.

Article 9.20:   Dispute Settlement

In a dispute under this Chapter that involves scientific or technical issues, a panel should seek advice from experts chosen by the panel in consultation with the disputing Parties. To this end, the panel may, if it deems appropriate, establish an advisory technical experts group, or consult the relevant international standard setting organizations, at the request of a disputing Party or on its own initiative.

CHAPTER 10   TRADE REMEDIES

Section A: Safeguards

Article 10.1:   Definitions

For the purposes of this Section:

Competent investigating authority means:

(a)   for Canada, the Canadian International Trade Tribunal, or its successor;

(b)   for Mexico, the International Trade Practices Unit of the *Secretaría de Economía*, or its successor; and

(c)   for the United States, the United States International Trade Commission, or its successor.

Article 10.2:   Rights and Obligations

1.   Each Party retains its rights and obligations under Article XIX of the GATT 1994 and the Safeguards Agreement except those regarding compensation or retaliation and exclusion from an action to the extent

that such rights or obligations are inconsistent with this Article. Any Party taking an emergency action under Article XIX and the Safeguards Agreement shall exclude imports of a good from each other Party from the action unless:

(a)   imports from a Party, considered individually, account for a substantial share of total imports; and

(b)   imports from a Party considered individually, or in exceptional circumstances imports from Parties considered collectively, contribute importantly to the serious injury, or threat thereof, caused by imports.

2.   In determining whether:

(a)   imports from a Party, considered individually, account for a substantial share of total imports, those imports normally shall not be considered to account for a substantial share of total imports if that Party is not among the top five suppliers of the good subject to the proceeding, measured in terms of import share during the most recent three-year period; and

(b)   imports from a Party or Parties contribute importantly to the serious injury, or threat thereof, the competent investigating authority shall consider such factors as the change in the import share of each Party, and the level and change in the level of imports of each Party. In this regard, imports from a Party normally shall not be deemed to contribute importantly to serious injury, or the threat thereof, if the growth rate of imports from a Party during the period in which the injurious surge in imports occurred is appreciably lower than the growth rate of total imports from all sources over the same period.

3.   A Party taking such action, from which a good from another Party or Parties is initially excluded pursuant to paragraph 1, shall have the right subsequently to include that good from the other Party or Parties in the action in the event that the competent investigating authority determines that a surge in imports of such good from the other Party or Parties undermines the effectiveness of the action.

4.   A Party shall, without delay, deliver written notice to the other Parties of the institution of a proceeding that may result in emergency action under paragraph 1 or 3.

5.   No Party may impose restrictions on a good in an action under paragraph 1 or 3:

(a)   without delivery of prior written notice to the Commission, and without adequate opportunity for consultation with the Party or Parties against whose good the action is proposed to be taken, as far in advance of taking the action as practicable; and

(b)   that would have the effect of reducing imports of such good from a Party below the trend of imports of the good from that Party over a recent representative base period with allowance for reasonable growth.

6.   The Party taking an action pursuant to this Article shall provide to the Party or Parties against whose good the action is taken mutually agreed trade liberalizing compensation in the form of concessions having substantially equivalent trade effects or equivalent to the value of the additional duties expected to result from the action. If the Parties concerned are unable to agree on compensation, the Party against whose good the action is taken may take action having trade effects substantially equivalent to the action taken under paragraph 1 or 3.

Article 10.3:   Administration of Emergency Action Proceedings

Each Party shall entrust determinations of serious injury, or threat thereof, in emergency action proceedings to a competent investigating authority, subject to review by judicial or administrative tribunals, to the extent provided by domestic law. Negative injury determinations shall not be subject to modification, except by such review. The competent investigating authority empowered under domestic law to conduct such proceedings should be provided with the necessary resources to enable it to fulfill its duties.

Section B: Antidumping and Countervailing Duties Article 10.4: Definitions

For purposes of this Section and Annex 10-A (Practices Relating to Antidumping and Countervailing Duty Proceedings):

confidential information means information that is provided to an investigating authority on a confidential basis and that is by its nature confidential (for example, because its disclosure would be of significant competitive advantage to a competitor or because its disclosure would have a significantly adverse effect upon a person supplying the information or upon a person from whom that person acquired the information), whether in its original form or in a form other than the one in which it was originally provided;

Interested party[1] means:

(a)   an exporter, foreign producer, or importer of a product subject to a proceeding, or a trade or business association a majority of the members of which are producers, exporters, or importers of such product;

(b)   the government of the exporting Party;

(c)   a producer of the like product in the territory of the importing Party, or a trade and business association a majority of the members of which produce the like product in the territory of the importing Party; or

---

[1]   For greater certainty, an entity or person may be an interested party as long as they fulfill all the corresponding requirements, if any, provided in the law of the importing Party.

(d)   any other person treated as an interested party by the investigating authority of the importing Party;

Investigating authority means any authority of a Party that conducts antidumping or countervailing duty proceedings;

(a)   for Mexico, an antidumping or countervailing duty investigation, review, or other relevant set of formalities and acts provided by the legal system which precede the issuance of the administrative act conducted by an investigating authority; and

(b)   for Canada and the United States, all segments of a proceeding, and begins on the date of the formal filing of an antidumping or countervailing duty application, or the publication of a notice of initiation in a self-initiated investigation, and ends with the conclusion of all administrative action pertaining to the product under consideration. For Canada, the formal filing of an antidumping or countervailing duty application corresponds to the determination that a complaint is properly documented;

Responding party means:

(a)   for Canada and Mexico, a person or entity that an investigating authority of a Party requires to respond to an antidumping or countervailing duty questionnaire or any other request; and

(b)   for the United States, a producer, manufacturer, exporter, importer, or, where appropriate, a government or government entity, that an investigating authority of a Party requires to respond to an antidumping or countervailing duty questionnaire; and

segment of a proceeding means for Canada and the United States,[2] an antidumping or countervailing duty investigation, review, or other relevant action conducted by an investigating authority. For Canada, relevant actions conducted by an investigating authority do not cover duty assessment and related procedures.

Article 10.5:   Rights and Obligations

1.   Each Party retains its rights and obligations under Article VI of GATT 1994, the AD Agreement, and the SCM Agreement.

2.   Except as provided in Annex 10-A (Practices Relating to Antidumping and Countervailing Duty Proceedings), nothing in this Agreement shall be construed to confer any rights or impose any obligations on the Parties with respect to antidumping or countervailing duty proceedings or measures taken pursuant to Article VI of GATT 1994, the AD Agreement, or the SCM Agreement.

---

[2]   For Mexico, "segment of a proceeding" does not apply.

3.   No Party shall have recourse to dispute settlement under this Agreement for any matter arising under this Section or Annex 10-A (Practices Relating to Antidumping and Countervailing Duty Proceedings).

Section C: Cooperation on Preventing Duty Evasion of Trade Remedy Laws

Article 10.6:   General

1.   The Parties recognize their shared concerns regarding duty evasion[3] of antidumping, countervailing, and safeguard duties, and the importance of cooperation, including through information sharing, to combat duty evasion.

2.   The Parties agree to strengthen and expand their customs and trade enforcement efforts in matters related to duty evasion, and to strengthen their cooperation as set out in the Article 10.7 (Duty Evasion Cooperation).

Article 10.7:   Duty Evasion Cooperation

1.   Each Party shall, in accordance with its law cooperate with the other Parties for the purposes of enforcing or assisting in the enforcement of their respective measures concerning duty evasion.

2.   Each Party shall, subject to its law, share customs information with the other Parties pertaining to imports, exports, and transit transactions, to help enable the Parties to combat duty evasion and conduct joint or coordinated analysis and investigations of suspected duty evasion. In addition, each Party shall maintain a mechanism through which it can share information with the other Parties regarding entries that may involve evasion of antidumping, countervailing, or safeguard duties, including the information described in paragraph 3. The information referred to in this paragraph may be trader-specific or it may include an industry sector or group of traders.

3.   Each Party shall, subject to its law and on the request of another Party, provide the requesting Party with information collected in connection with the imports, exports and transit, and other relevant information that it has or can reasonably obtain, that will help enable the requesting Party to determine whether an entry into its territory is subject to antidumping, countervailing, or safeguard duties imposed by the requesting Party.[4]

A request for information described in paragraph 3 shall be made in writing, by the customs administration of the requesting Party to the customs authority of the requested Party, by electronic means or any other acceptable method, and shall include sufficient information for the requested Party to respond.

---

     [3]   For purposes of this Section, "duty evasion" refers to evasion of antidumping, countervailing, or safeguards duties.

     [4]   For greater certainty, nothing in this Section shall be construed as an obligation on the requested Party to provide an original or copy of an export declaration submitted to its customs administration.

A Party may request in writing that another Party conduct a duty evasion verification[5] in the requested Party's territory for the purposes of obtaining information, including documents, from an exporter or producer, to enable the requesting Party to determine whether a particular entry into the requesting Party's territory is subject to antidumping, countervailing, or safeguard duties imposed by the requesting Party. The requested Party shall respond to the request promptly and in any case no later than 30 days after the date it receives the request. The response must include whether it will conduct the duty evasion verification. If the Party does not intend to conduct the duty evasion verification, the response must indicate the basis for refusal. If a Party will conduct the duty evasion verification, the response must indicate the intended timing and other relevant details.

4.   If the requested Party conducts a duty evasion verification under paragraph 5 it shall provide the requesting Party promptly on completing the duty evasion verification a report containing the relevant information including data and documents, obtained during its duty evasion verification.

5.   Regardless of whether a request to conduct a verification was made under paragraph 5, a duty evasion verification may be conducted in the relevant facilities located in the territory of the requested Party, as a result of a request. The requested Party normally shall grant the other Party access to its territory to participate in the duty evasion verification, absent extraordinary circumstances, provided that:

   (a)   the duty evasion verification is subject to mutually agreed conditions and procedures between the Parties;[6]

   (b)   the requesting Party gives reasonable advance notice to the requested Party before the proposed date of the duty evasion verification; and

   (c)   the parties to be verified in the requested Party consent to the duty evasion verification.

6.   Each Party shall maintain procedures that permit the sharing of confidential information with the other Parties, as a result of a request under paragraph 3 or a duty evasion verification

Section B: Antidumping and Countervailing Duties

   Article 10.4:   Definitions

For purposes of this Section and Annex 10-A (Practices Relating to Antidumping and Countervailing Duty Proceedings):

Confidential information means information that is provided to an investigating authority on a confidential basis and that is by its nature confidential (for example, because its disclosure would be of significant competitive advantage to a competitor or because its disclosure would have

---

   [5]   For greater certainty, a duty evasion verification visit to facilities located in the territory of a requested Party shall be subject to paragraph 7.

   [6]   For the purposes of subparagraph (a), the Parties may agree to use any applicable mechanism, including existing bilateral cooperation mechanisms.

a significantly adverse effect upon a person supplying the information or upon a person from whom that person acquired the information), whether in its original form or in a form other than the one in which it was originally provided;

Interested party[1] means:

(a)   an exporter, foreign producer, or importer of a product subject to a proceeding, or a trade or business association a majority of the members of which are producers, exporters, or importers of such product;

(b)   the government of the exporting Party;

(c)   a producer of the like product in the territory of the importing Party, or a trade and business association a majority of the members of which produce the like product in the territory of the importing Party; or

(d)   any other person treated as an interested party by the investigating authority of the importing Party;

Investigating authority means any authority of a Party that conducts antidumping or countervailing duty proceedings;

Proceeding means:

(a)   for Mexico, an antidumping or countervailing duty investigation, review, or other relevant set of formalities and acts provided by the legal system which precede the issuance of the administrative act conducted by an investigating authority; and

(b)   for Canada and the United States, all segments of a proceeding, and begins on the date of the formal filing of an antidumping or countervailing duty application, or the publication of a notice of initiation in a self-initiated investigation, and ends with the conclusion of all administrative action pertaining to the product under consideration. For Canada, the formal filing of an antidumping or countervailing duty application corresponds to the determination that a complaint is properly documented;

Responding party means:

(a)   for Canada and Mexico, a person or entity that an investigating authority of a Party requires to respond to an antidumping or countervailing duty questionnaire or any other request; and

(b)   for the United States, a producer, manufacturer, exporter, importer, or, where appropriate, a government or

---

[1]   For greater certainty, an entity or person may be an interested party as long as they fulfill all the corresponding requirements, if any, provided in the law of the importing Party.

government entity, that an investigating authority of a Party requires to respond to an antidumping or countervailing duty questionnaire; and

Segment of a proceeding means for Canada and the United States,[2] an antidumping or countervailing duty investigation, review, or other relevant action conducted by an investigating authority. For Canada, relevant actions conducted by an investigating authority do not cover duty assessment and related procedures.

Article 10.5:   Rights and Obligations

1. Each Party retains its rights and obligations under Article VI of GATT 1994, the AD Agreement, and the SCM Agreement.

2. Except as provided in Annex 10-A (Practices Relating to Antidumping and Countervailing Duty Proceedings), nothing in this Agreement shall be construed to confer any rights or impose any obligations on the Parties with respect to antidumping or countervailing duty proceedings or measures taken pursuant to Article VI of GATT 1994, the AD Agreement, or the SCM Agreement.

3. No Party shall have recourse to dispute settlement under this Agreement for any matter arising under this Section or Annex 10-A (Practices Relating to Antidumping and Countervailing Duty Proceedings).

Section C: Cooperation on Preventing Duty Evasion of Trade Remedy Laws

Article 10.6:   General

1. The Parties recognize their shared concerns regarding duty evasion[3] of antidumping, countervailing, and safeguard duties, and the importance of cooperation, including through information sharing, to combat duty evasion.

2. The Parties agree to strengthen and expand their customs and trade enforcement efforts in matters related to duty evasion, and to strengthen their cooperation as set out in the Article 10.7 (Duty Evasion Cooperation).

Article 10.7:   Duty Evasion Cooperation

1. Each Party shall, in accordance with its law cooperate with the other Parties for the purposes of enforcing or assisting in the enforcement of their respective measures concerning duty evasion.

2. Each Party shall, subject to its law, share customs information with the other Parties pertaining to imports, exports, and transit transactions, to help enable the Parties to combat duty evasion and conduct joint or coordinated analysis and investigations of suspected duty evasion. In addition, each Party shall maintain a mechanism through which it can share information with the other Parties regarding entries that may

---

[2]   For Mexico, "segment of a proceeding" does not apply.

[3]   For purposes of this Section, "duty evasion" refers to evasion of antidumping, countervailing, or safeguards duties.

involve evasion of antidumping, countervailing, or safeguard duties, including the information described in paragraph 3. The information referred to in this paragraph may be trader-specific or it may include an industry sector or group of traders.

3. Each Party shall, subject to its law and on the request of another Party, provide the requesting Party with information collected in connection with the imports, exports and transit, and other relevant information that it has or can reasonably obtain, that will help enable the requesting Party to determine whether an entry into its territory is subject to antidumping, countervailing, or safeguard duties imposed by the requesting Party.[4]

4. A request for information described in paragraph 3 shall be made in writing, by the customs administration of the requesting Party to the customs authority of the requested Party, by electronic means or any other acceptable method, and shall include sufficient information for the requested Party to respond.

5. A Party may request in writing that another Party conduct a duty evasion verification[5] in the requested Party's territory for the purposes of obtaining information, including documents, from an exporter or producer, to enable the requesting Party to determine whether a particular entry into the requesting Party's territory is subject to antidumping, countervailing, or safeguard duties imposed by the requesting Party. The requested Party shall respond to the request promptly and in any case no later than 30 days after the date it receives the request. The response must include whether it will conduct the duty evasion verification. If the Party does not intend to conduct the duty evasion verification, the response must indicate the basis for refusal. If a Party will conduct the duty evasion verification, the response must indicate the intended timing and other relevant details.

6. If the requested Party conducts a duty evasion verification under paragraph 5 it shall provide the requesting Party promptly on completing the duty evasion verification a report containing the relevant information including data and documents, obtained during its duty evasion verification.

7. Regardless of whether a request to conduct a verification was made under paragraph 5, a duty evasion verification may be conducted in the relevant facilities located in the territory of the requested Party, as a result of a request. The requested Party normally shall grant the other Party access to its territory to participate in the duty evasion verification, absent extraordinary circumstances, provided that:

---

[4] For greater certainty, nothing in this Section shall be construed as an obligation on the requested Party to provide an original or copy of an export declaration submitted to its customs administration.

[5] For greater certainty, a duty evasion verification visit to facilities located in the territory of a requested Party shall be subject to paragraph 7.

(a)   the duty evasion verification is subject to mutually agreed conditions and procedures between the Parties;[6]

(b)   the requesting Party gives reasonable advance notice to the requested Party before the proposed date of the duty evasion verification; and

(c)   the parties to be verified in the requested Party consent to the duty evasion verification.

8.   Each Party shall maintain procedures that permit the sharing of confidential information with the other Parties, as a result of a request under paragraph 3 or a duty evasion verification

Section D: Review And Dispute Settlement In Antidumping And Countervailing Duty Matters

Article 10.8:   Definitions

For purposes of this Section and Annex 10-B.1 (Establishment of Binational Panels), Annex 10-B.2 (Panel Procedures under Article 10.11), Annex 10-B.3 (Extraordinary Challenge Procedure), Annex 10-B.4 (Special Committee Procedures), and Annex 10-B.5 (Amendments to Domestic Laws):

Administrative record means, unless otherwise agreed by the Parties and the other persons appearing before a panel:

(a)   all documentary or other information presented to or obtained by the competent investigating authority in the course of the administrative proceeding, including any governmental memoranda pertaining to the case, and including any record of *ex parte* meetings as may be required to be kept;

(b)   a copy of the final determination of the competent investigating authority, including reasons for the determination;

(c)   all transcripts or records of conferences or hearings before the competent investigating authority; and

(d)   all notices published in the official journal of the importing Party in connection with the administrative proceeding;

Antidumping statute means:

(a)   in the case of Canada, the relevant provisions of the *Special Import Measures Act*, as amended, and any successor statutes;

(b)   in the case of Mexico, the relevant provisions of the *Foreign Trade Act* (*Ley de Comercio Exterior*), as amended, and any successor statutes;

---

[6]   For the purposes of subparagraph (a), the Parties may agree to use any applicable mechanism, including existing bilateral cooperation mechanisms.

(c)   in the case of the United States, the relevant provisions of Title VII of the *Tariff Act of 1930*, as amended, and any successor statutes; and

(d)   the provisions of any other statute that provides for judicial review of final determinations under subparagraph (a), (b), or (c), or indicates the standard of review to be applied to such determinations;

Competent investigating authority means:

(a)   in the case of Canada:

   (i)   the President of the Canada Border Services Agency as defined in the *Special Import Measures Act*, as amended, or the President's successor; or

   (ii) the Canadian International Trade Tribunal, or its successor;

(b)   in the case of Mexico, the designated authority within the Secretariat of Economy (*Secretaría de Economía*), or its successor; and

(c)   in the case of the United States:

   (i)   the International Trade Administration of the United States Department of Commerce, or its successor, or

   (ii) the United States International Trade Commission, or its successor;

Countervailing duty statute means:

(a)   in the case of Canada, the relevant provisions of the *Special Import Measures Act*, as amended, and any successor statutes;

(b)   in the case of Mexico, the relevant provisions of the Foreign Trade Act (*Ley de Comercio Exterior*), as amended, and any successor statutes;

(c)   in the case of the United States, section 303 and the relevant provisions of Title VII of the *Tariff Act of 1930*, as amended, and any successor statutes; and

(d)   the provisions of any other statute that provides for judicial review of final determinations under subparagraph (a), (b), or (c), or indicates the standard of review to be applied to such determinations;

Domestic law for purposes of Article 10.13.1 (Safeguarding the Panel Review System) means a Party's constitution, statutes, regulations and judicial decisions to the extent they are relevant to the antidumping and countervailing duty laws;

Final determination means:

(a)   in the case of Canada:

(i)   an order or finding of the Canadian International Trade Tribunal under subsection 43(1) of the *Special Import Measures Act,*

(ii)   an order by the Canadian International Trade Tribunal under subsection 76(4) of the *Special Import Measures Act,* as amended, continuing an order or finding made under subsection 43(1) of the Act with or without amendment,

(iii) a determination by the President of the Canada Border Services Agency pursuant to section 41 of the *Special Import Measures Act,* as amended,

(iv)   a redetermination by the President pursuant to section 59 of the *Special Import Measures Act,* as amended,

(v)   a decision by the Canadian International Trade Tribunal pursuant to subsection 76(3) of the *Special Import Measures Act,* as amended, not to initiate a review,

(vi)   a reconsideration by the Canadian International Trade Tribunal pursuant to subsection 91(3) of the *Special Import Measures Act,* as amended, and

(vii) a review by the President of an undertaking pursuant to subsection 53(1) of the *Special Import Measures Act,* as amended; and

(b) in the case of Mexico:

(i)   a final resolution regarding antidumping or countervailing duties investigations by the Secretariat of Economy (*Secretaría de Economía*), pursuant to Article 59 of the Foreign Trade Act (*Ley de Comercio Exterior*), as amended,

(ii)   a final resolution regarding an annual administrative review of antidumping or countervailing duties by the Secretariat of Economy (*Secretaría deEconomía*), as described in subparagraph (*o*) of its Schedule to Annex 10-B.5 (Amendments to Domestic Laws), and

(iii) (iii) a final resolution by the Secretariat of Economy (*Secretaría de Economía*), as to whether a particular type of merchandise is within the class or kind of merchandise described in an existing antidumping or countervailing duty resolution; and

(c) in the case of the United States:

(i)   a final affirmative determination by the International Trade Administration of the United States Department of Commerce or by the United States International Trade Commission under section 705 or 735 of the

Tariff Act of 1930, as amended, including any negative part of such a determination,

(ii)   a final negative determination by the International Trade Administration of the United States Department of Commerce or by the United States International Trade Commission under section 705 or 735 of the *Tariff Act of 1930*, as amended, including any affirmative part of such a determination,

(iii)   a final determination, other than a determination in (iv), under section 751 of the *Tariff Act of 1930*, as amended,

(iv)   a determination by the United States International Trade Commission under section 751(b) of the *Tariff Act of 1930*, as amended, not to review a determination based on changed circumstances, and

(v)   a final determination by the International Trade Administration of the United States Department of Commerce as to whether a particular type of merchandise is within the class or kind of merchandise described in an existing finding of dumping or antidumping or countervailing duty order;

Foreign interests includes exporters or producers of the Party whose goods are the subject of the proceeding or, in the case of a countervailing duty proceeding, the government of the Party whose goods are the subject of the proceeding;

General legal principles includes principles such as standing, due process, rules of statutory construction, mootness and exhaustion of administrative remedies;

Goods of a Party means domestic products as these are understood in the GATT 1994;

Importing Party means the Party that issued the final determination;

Interested parties includes foreign interests;

Involved Party means:

(a)   the importing Party; or

(b)   a Party whose goods are the subject of the final determination;

Remand means a referral back for a determination not inconsistent with the panel or committee decision; and

Standard of review means the following standards, as may be amended from time to time by the relevant Party:

(a)   in the case of Canada, the grounds set out in subsection 18.1(4) of the *Federal Court Act*, as amended, with respect to all final determinations;

(b)   in the case of Mexico, the standard set out in Article 51 of the Federal Act of Administrative Litigation Procedure (*Ley Federal de Procedimiento Contencioso Administrativo*), or any successor statutes, based solely on the administrative record; and

(c)   in the case of the United States;

(i)   the standard set out in section 516A(b)(*l*)(B) of the *Tariff Act of 1930*, as amended, with the exception of a determination referred to in (ii); and

(ii)   the standard set out in section 516A(b)(*l*)(A) of the *Tariff Act of 1930*, as amended, with respect to a determination by the United States International Trade Commission not to initiate a review pursuant to section 751(b) of the *Tariff Act of 1930*, as amended.

Article 10.9:   General Provisions

1.   Article 10.12 (Review of Final Antidumping Law and Countervailing Duty Law) applies only with respect to goods that the competent investigating authority of the importing Party, applying the importing Party's antidumping or countervailing duty law to the facts of a specific case, determines are goods of another Party.

2.   For purposes of Article 10.11 (Review of Statutory Amendments) and Article 10.12 (Review of Final Antidumping Law and Countervailing Duty Law), panels shall be established in accordance with the provisions of Annex 10-B.1 (Establishment of Binational Panels).

3.   Except for Article 34.5 (Entry into Force), no provision of any other Chapter of this Agreement shall be construed as imposing obligations on a Party with respect to the Party's antidumping law or countervailing duty law.

Article 10.10:   Retention   of   Domestic   Antidumping   Law   and Countervailing Duty Law

1.   Each Party reserves the right to apply its antidumping law and countervailing duty law to goods imported from the territory of any other Party. Antidumping law and countervailing duty law include, as appropriate for each Party, relevant statutes, legislative history, regulations, administrative practice, and judicial precedents.

2.   Each Party reserves the right to change or modify its antidumping law or countervailing duty law, provided that in the case of an amendment to a Party's antidumping or countervailing duty statute:

(a)   such amendment shall apply to goods from another Party only if the amending statute specifies that it applies to goods from that Party or from the Parties to this Agreement;

(b)   the amending Party notifies in writing the Parties to which the amendment applies of the amending statute as far in advance as possible of the date of enactment of such statute;

(c)   following notification, the amending Party, on request of any Party to which the amendment applies, consults with that Party prior to the enactment of the amending statute; and

(d)   such amendment, as applicable to that other Party, is not inconsistent with:

   (i)   GATT 1994, the AD Agreement or the SCM Agreement, or any successor agreement to which the Parties are party, or

   (ii)   the object and purpose of this Agreement and this Chapter, which is to establish fair and predictable conditions for the progressive liberalization of trade between the Parties to this Agreement while maintaining effective and fair disciplines on unfair trade practices, such object and purpose to be ascertained from the provisions of this Agreement, its preamble and objectives, and the practices of the Parties.

Article 10.11:   Review of Statutory Amendments

1.   A Party to which an amendment of another Party's antidumping or countervailing duty statute applies may request in writing that such amendment be referred to a binational panel for a declaratory opinion as to whether:

(a)   the amendment does not conform to the provisions of Article 10.10(2)(d)(i) or (ii) (Retention of Domestic Antidumping Law and Countervailing Duty Law); or

(b)   such amendment has the function and effect of overturning a prior decision of a panel made pursuant to Article 10.12 (Review of Final Antidumping and Countervailing Duty Determinations) and does not conform to the provisions of Article 10.10(2)(d)(i) or (ii) (Retention of Domestic Antidumping Law and Countervailing Duty Law).

Such declaratory opinion shall have force or effect only as provided in this Article.

2.   The panel shall conduct its review in accordance with the procedures of Annex 10-B.2 (Panel Procedures under Article 10.11).

3.   In the event that the panel recommends modifications to the amending statute to remedy a non-conformity that it has identified in its opinion:

(a)   the two Parties shall immediately begin consultations and shall seek to achieve a mutually satisfactory solution to the matter within 90 days of the issuance of the panel's final declaratory opinion. Such solution may include seeking corrective legislation with respect to the statute of the amending Party;

(b) if corrective legislation is not enacted within nine months from the end of the 90 day consultation period referred to in subparagraph (a) and no other mutually satisfactory solution has been reached, the Party that requested the panel may:

  (i) take comparable legislative or equivalent executive action, or

  (ii) terminate this Agreement with regard to the amending Party on 60 day written notice to that Party.

Article 10.12:   Review of Final Antidumping and Countervailing Duty Determinations

1. As provided in this Article, each Party shall replace judicial review of final antidumping and countervailing duty determinations with binational panel review.

2. An involved Party may request that a panel review, based on the administrative record, a final antidumping or countervailing duty determination of a competent investigating authority of an importing Party to determine whether such determination was in accordance with the antidumping or countervailing duty law of the importing Party. For this purpose, the antidumping or countervailing duty law consists of the relevant statutes, legislative history, regulations, administrative practice, and judicial precedents to the extent that a court of the importing Party would rely on such materials in reviewing a final determination of the competent investigating authority. Solely for purposes of the panel review provided for in this Article, the antidumping and countervailing duty statutes of the Parties, as those statutes may be amended from time to time, are incorporated into and made a part of this Section.

3. The panel shall apply the standard of review set out in Article 10.8 (Definitions) and the general legal principles that a court of the importing Party otherwise would apply to a review of a determination of the competent investigating authority.

4. A request for a panel shall be made in writing to the other involved Party within 30 days following the date of publication of the final determination in question in the official journal of the importing Party. In the case of final determinations that are not published in the official journal of the importing Party, the importing Party shall immediately notify the other involved Party of such final determination where it involves goods from the other involved Party, and the other involved Party may request a panel within 30 days of receipt of such notice. Where the competent investigating authority of the importing Party has imposed provisional measures in an investigation, the other involved Party may provide notice of its intention to request a panel under this Article, and the Parties shall begin to establish a panel at that time. Failure to request a panel within the time specified in this paragraph shall preclude review by a panel.

5.   An involved Party on its own initiative may request review of a final determination by a panel and shall, on request of a person who would otherwise be entitled under the law of the importing Party to commence domestic procedures for judicial review of that final determination, request such review.

6.   The panel shall conduct its review in accordance with the procedures established by the Parties pursuant to paragraph 14. Where both involved Parties request a panel to review a final determination, a single panel shall review that determination.

7.   The competent investigating authority that issued the final determination in question shall have the right to appear and be represented by counsel before the panel. Each Party shall provide that other persons who, pursuant to the law of the importing Party, otherwise would have had the right to appear and be represented in a domestic judicial review proceeding concerning the determination of the competent investigating authority, shall have the right to appear and be represented by counsel before the panel.

8.   The panel may uphold a final determination, or remand it for action not inconsistent with the panel's decision. Where the panel remands a final determination, the panel shall establish as brief a time as is reasonable for compliance with the remand, taking into account the complexity of the factual and legal issues involved and the nature of the panel's decision. In no event shall the time permitted for compliance with a remand exceed an amount of time equal to the maximum amount of time (counted from the date of the filing of a petition, complaint or application) permitted by statute for the competent investigating authority in question to make a final determination in an investigation. If review of the action taken by the competent investigating authority on remand is needed, such review shall be before the same panel, which shall normally issue a final decision within 90 days of the date on which such remand action is submitted to it.

9.   The decision of a panel under this Article shall be binding on the involved Parties with respect to the particular matter between the Parties that is before the panel.

10.   This Agreement shall not affect:

      (a)   the judicial review procedures of any Party; or

      (b)   cases appealed under those procedures,

with respect to determinations other than final determinations.

11.   A final determination shall not be reviewed under any judicial review procedures of the importing Party if an involved Party requests a panel with respect to that determination within the time limits set out in this Article. No Party may provide in its domestic legislation for an appeal from a panel decision to its domestic courts.

12.   This Article shall not apply where:

(a)   neither involved Party seeks panel review of a final determination;

(b)   a revised final determination is issued as a direct result of judicial review of the original final determination by a court of the importing Party in cases where neither involved Party sought panel review of that original final determination; or

(c)   a final determination is issued as a direct result of judicial review that was commenced in a court of the importing Party before the date of entry into force of this Agreement.

13.   Where, within a reasonable time after the panel decision is issued, an involved Party alleges that:

(a)   (i) a member of the panel was guilty of gross misconduct, bias, or a serious conflict of interest, or otherwise materially violated the rules of conduct,

(ii)   the panel seriously departed from a fundamental rule of procedure, or

(iii)   the panel manifestly exceeded its powers, authority or jurisdiction set out in this Article, for example by failing to apply the appropriate standard of review, and

(b)   any of the actions set out in subparagraph (a) has materially affected the panel's decision and threatens the integrity of the binational panel review process,

that Party may avail itself of the extraordinary challenge procedure set out in Annex 10-B.3 (Extraordinary Challenge Procedure).

14.   For purposes of this Article, the Parties shall adopt or maintain rules of procedure based, where appropriate, on judicial rules of appellate procedure, and shall include rules concerning: the content and service of requests for panels; a requirement that the competent investigating authority transmit to the panel the administrative record of the proceeding; the protection of business proprietary, government classified, and other privileged information (including sanctions against persons participating before panels for improper release of such information); participation by private persons; limitations on panel review to errors alleged by the Parties or private persons; filing and service; computation and extensions of time; the form and content of briefs and other papers; pre- and post-hearing conferences; motions; oral argument; requests for rehearing; and voluntary terminations of panel reviews. The rules shall be designed to result in final decisions within 315 days of the date on which a request for a panel is made, and shall allow:

(a)   30 days for the filing of the complaint;

(b)   30 days for designation or certification of the administrative record and its filing with the panel;

(c)   60 days for the complainant to file its brief;

(d)   60 days for the respondent to file its brief;

(e)   15 days for the filing of reply briefs;

(f)   15 to 30 days for the panel to convene and hear oral argument; and

(g)   90 days for the panel to issue its written decision.

15.   In order to achieve the objectives of this Article, the Parties shall maintain or amend their antidumping and countervailing duty statutes and regulations with respect to antidumping or countervailing duty proceedings involving goods of the other Parties, and other statutes and regulations to the extent that they apply to the operation of the antidumping and countervailing duty laws. In particular, without limiting the generality of the foregoing, each Party shall:

(a)   maintain or amend its statutes or regulations to ensure that existing procedures concerning the refund, with interest, of antidumping or countervailing duties operate to give effect to a final panel decision that a refund is due;

(b)   maintain or amend its statutes or regulations to ensure that its courts shall give full force and effect, with respect to any person within its jurisdiction, to all sanctions imposed pursuant to the laws of the other Parties to enforce provisions of any protective order or undertaking that such other Party has promulgated or accepted in order to permit access for purposes of panel review or of the extraordinary challenge procedure to confidential, personal, business proprietary or other privileged information;

(c)   maintain or amend its statutes or regulations to ensure that:

(i)   domestic procedures for judicial review of a final determination may not be commenced until the time for requesting a panel under paragraph 4 has expired, and

(ii)   as a prerequisite to commencing domestic judicial review procedures to review a final determination, a Party or other person intending to commence such procedures shall provide notice of such intent to the Parties concerned and to other persons entitled to commence such review procedures of the same final determination no later than 10 days prior to the latest date on which a panel may be requested; and

(d)   maintain the amendments set out in its Schedule to Annex 1904.15 of the NAFTA 1994, as reproduced in Annex 10-B.5 (Amendments to Domestic Laws), and make any conforming amendments necessary.

Article 10.13:   Safeguarding the Panel Review System

1.   Where a Party alleges that the application of another Party's domestic law:

(a)   has prevented the establishment of a panel requested by the complaining Party;

(b)   has prevented a panel requested by the complaining Party from rendering a final decision;

(c)   has prevented the implementation of the decision of a panel requested by the complaining Party or denied it binding force and effect with respect to the particular matter that was before the panel; or

(d)   has resulted in a failure to provide opportunity for review of a final determination by a panel or court of competent jurisdiction that is independent of the competent investigating authorities, that examines the basis for the competent investigating authority's determination and whether the competent investigating authority properly applied domestic antidumping and countervailing duty law in reaching the challenged determination, and that employs the relevant standard of review identified in Article 10.8 (Definitions);

the Party may request in writing consultations with the other Party regarding the allegations. The consultations shall begin within 15 days of the date of the request.

2.   If the matter has not been resolved within 45 days of the request for consultations, or such other period as the consulting Parties may agree, the complaining Party may request the establishment of a special committee.

3.   Unless otherwise agreed by the disputing Parties, the special committee shall be established within 15 days of a request and perform its functions in a manner consistent with this Section.

4.   The roster for special committees shall be that established under Annex 10-B.3 (Extraordinary Challenge Procedure).

5.   The special committee shall comprise three members selected in accordance with the procedures set out in Annex 10-B.3 (Extraordinary Challenge Procedure).

6.   The Parties shall establish or maintain rules of procedure in accordance with the principles set out in Annex 10-B.4 (Special Committee Procedures).

7.   Where the special committee makes an affirmative finding with respect to one of the grounds specified in paragraph 1, the complaining Party and the Party complained against shall begin consultations within 10 days thereafter and shall seek to achieve a mutually satisfactory solution within 60 days of the issuance of the committee's report.

8.   If, within the 60-day period, the Parties are unable to reach a mutually satisfactory solution to the matter, or the Party complained against has not demonstrated to the satisfaction of the special committee that it has

corrected the problem or problems with respect to which the committee
has made an affirmative finding, the complaining Party may suspend:

(a) the operation of Article 10.12 (Review of Final Antidumping
and Countervailing Duty Determinations) with respect to the
Party complained against; or

(b) the application to the Party complained against of such
benefits under this Agreement as may be appropriate under
the circumstances.

If the complaining Party decides to take action under this paragraph, it shall
do so within 30 days after the end of the 60-day consultation period.

9. In the event that a complaining Party suspends the operation of Article
10.12 (Review of Final Antidumping and Countervailing Duty
Determinations) with respect to the Party complained against, the
latter Party may reciprocally suspend the operation of Article 10.12
(Review of Final Antidumping and Countervailing Duty
Determinations) within 30 days after the suspension of the operation of
Article 10.12 (Review of Final Antidumping and Countervailing Duty
Determinations) by the complaining Party. If either Party decides to
suspend the operation of Article 10.12 (Review of Final Antidumping
and Countervailing Duty Determinations), it shall provide written
notice of such suspension to the other Party.

10. On the request of the Party complained against, the special committee
shall reconvene to determine whether:

(a) the suspension of benefits by the complaining Party pursuant
to paragraph 8(b) is manifestly excessive; or

(b) the Party complained against has corrected the problem or
problems with respect to which the committee has made an
affirmative finding.

The special committee shall, within 45 days of the request, present a report
to both Parties containing its determination. Where the special committee
determines that the Party complained against has corrected the problem or
problems, any suspension effected by the complaining Party or the Party
complained against, or both, pursuant to paragraph 8 or 9 shall be
terminated.

11. If the special committee makes an affirmative finding with respect to
one of the grounds specified in paragraph 1, then effective as of the day
following the date of issuance of the special committee's report:

(a) binational panel or extraordinary challenge committee
review under Article 10.12 (Review of Final Antidumping
and Countervailing Duty Determinations) shall be stayed

(i) in the case of review of any final determination of the
complaining Party requested by the Party complained
against, if such review was requested after the date on
which consultations were requested pursuant to

paragraph 1, and in no case more than 150 days prior
to an affirmative finding by the special committee, or

(ii)   in the case of review of any final determination of the
Party complained against requested by the complaining
Party, at the request of the complaining Party; and

(b)   the time set out in Article 10.12(4) (Review of Final
Antidumping and Countervailing Duty Determinations) or
Annex 10-B.3 (Extraordinary Challenge Procedure) for
requesting panel or committee review shall not run unless
and until resumed in accordance with paragraph 12.

12.   If either Party suspends the operation of Article 10.12 (Review of Final
Antidumping and Countervailing Duty Determinations) pursuant to
paragraph 8(a), the panel or committee review stayed under paragraph
11(a) shall be terminated and the challenge to the final determination
shall be irrevocably referred to the appropriate domestic court for
decision, as provided below:

(a)   in the case of review of any final determination of the
complaining Party requested by the Party complained
against, at the request of either Party, or of a party to the
panel review under Article 10.12 (Review of Final
Antidumping and Countervailing Duty Determinations); or

(b)   in the case of review of any final determination of the Party
complained against requested by the complaining Party, at
the request of the complaining Party, or of a person of the
complaining Party that is a party to the panel review under
Article 10.12 (Review of Final Antidumping and
Countervailing Duty Determinations).

13.   If either Party suspends the operation of Article 10.12 (Review of
Antidumping Law and Countervailing Duty Law) pursuant to
paragraph 8(a), any running of time suspended under paragraph 11(b)
shall resume.

14.   If the suspension of the operation of Article 10.12 (Review of
Antidumping Law and Countervailing Duty Law) does not become
effective, panel or committee review stayed under paragraph 11(a), and
any running of time suspended under paragraph 11(b), shall resume.

15.   If the complaining Party suspends the application to the Party
complained against of such benefits under the Agreement as may be
appropriate under the circumstances pursuant to paragraph 8(b), panel
or committee review stayed under paragraph 11(a), and any running of
time suspended under paragraph 11(b), shall resume.

16.   Each Party shall provide in its domestic legislation that, in the event of
an affirmative finding by the special committee, the time for requesting
judicial review of a final antidumping or countervailing duty
determination shall not run unless and until the Parties concerned
have negotiated a mutually satisfactory solution under paragraph 7,
have suspended the operation of Article 10.12 (Review of Antidumping

Law and Countervailing Duty Law) or the application of other benefits under paragraph 8.

Article 10.14:   Prospective Application

This Section shall apply only prospectively to:

(a)   final determinations of a competent investigating authority made after the date of entry into force of this Agreement; and

(b)   with respect to declaratory opinions under Article 10.11 (Review of Statutory Amendments), amendments to antidumping or countervailing duty statutes enacted after the date of entry into force of this Agreement.

Article 10.15:   Consultations

1.   The Parties shall consult annually, or on the request of any Party, to consider any problems that may arise with respect to the implementation or operation of this Section and recommend solutions, where appropriate. The Parties shall each designate one or more officials, including officials of the competent investigating authorities, to be responsible for ensuring that consultations occur, when required, so that the provisions of this Section are carried out expeditiously.

2.   The Parties further agree to consult on:

(a)   the potential to develop more effective rules and disciplines concerning the use of government subsidies; and

(b)   the potential for reliance on a substitute system of rules for dealing with unfair transborder pricing practices and government subsidization.

3.   The competent investigating authorities of the Parties shall consult annually, or on the request of any Party, and may submit reports to the Commission, where appropriate. In the context of these consultations, the Parties agree that it is desirable in the administration of antidumping and countervailing duty laws to:

(a)   publish notice of initiation of investigations in the importing Party's official journal, setting forth the nature of the proceeding, the legal authority under which the proceeding is initiated, and a description of the goods at issue;

(b)   provide notice of the times for submissions of information and for decisions that the competent investigating authorities are expressly required by statute or regulations to make;

(c)   provide explicit written notice and instructions as to the information required from interested parties and reasonable time to respond to requests for information;

(d)   accord reasonable access to information, noting that in this context

(i) "reasonable access" means access during the course of the investigation, to the extent practicable, so as to permit an opportunity to present facts and arguments as set out in paragraph (e); when it is not practicable to provide access to information during the investigation in such time as to permit an opportunity to present facts and arguments, reasonable access shall mean in time to permit the adversely affected party to make an informed decision as to whether to seek judicial or panel review, and

(ii) "access to information" means access to representatives determined by the competent investigating authority to be qualified to have access to information received by that competent investigating authority, including access to confidential (business proprietary) information, but does not include information of such high degree of sensitivity that its release would lead to substantial and irreversible harm to the owner or which is required to be kept confidential in accordance with domestic law of a Party; any privileges arising under the domestic law of the importing Party relating to communications between the competent investigating authorities and a lawyer in the employ of, or providing advice to, those authorities may be maintained;

(e) provide an opportunity for interested parties to present facts and arguments, to the extent time permits, including an opportunity to comment on the preliminary determination of dumping or of subsidization;

(f) protect confidential (business proprietary) information received by the competent investigating authority to ensure that there is no disclosure except to representatives determined by the competent investigating authority to be qualified;

(g) prepare administrative records, including recommendations of official advisory bodies that may be required to be kept, and any record of *ex parte* meetings that may be required to be kept;

(h) provide disclosure of relevant information, including an explanation of the calculation or the methodology used to determine the margin of dumping or the amount of the subsidy, on which any preliminary or final determination of dumping or of subsidization is based, within a reasonable time after a request by interested parties;

(i) provide a statement of reasons concerning the final determination of dumping or subsidization; and

(j)   provide a statement of reasons for final determinations concerning material injury to a domestic industry, threat of material injury to a domestic industry or material retardation of the establishment of such an industry.

Inclusion of an item in subparagraphs (a) through (j) is not intended to serve as guidance to a binational panel reviewing a final antidumping or countervailing duty determination pursuant to Article 10.12 (Review of Final Antidumping and Countervailing Duty Determinations) in determining whether such determination was in accordance with the antidumping or countervailing duty law of the importing Party.

Article 10.16:   Special Secretariat Provisions

1.   Each Party shall maintain a Secretariat to facilitate the operation of this Section, including the work of panels or committees that may be convened pursuant to this Section.

2.   The Secretaries of the Secretariat shall act jointly to provide administrative assistance to all panels or committees established pursuant to this Section. The Secretary for the Section of the Party in which a panel or committee proceeding is held shall prepare a record thereof and shall preserve an authentic copy of the same in that Party's Section office. Such Secretary shall, on request, provide to the Secretary for the Section of another Party a copy of such portion of the record as is requested, except that only public portions of the record shall be provided to the Secretary for the Section of any Party that is not an involved Party.

3.   Each Secretary shall receive and file all requests, briefs and other papers properly presented to a panel or committee in any proceeding before it that is instituted pursuant to this Section and shall number in numerical order all requests for a panel or committee. The number given to a request shall be the file number for briefs and other papers relating to such request.

4.   The Secretary for the Section of the Party in which a panel or committee proceeding is held shall forward to the Secretary for the Section of the other involved Party copies of all official letters, documents or other papers received or filed with that Party's Section office pertaining to any proceeding before a panel or committee, except for the administrative record, which shall be handled in accordance with paragraph 2. The Secretary for the Section of an involved Party shall provide on request to the Secretary for the Section of a Party that is not an involved Party in the proceeding a copy of such public documents as are requested.

Article 10.17:   Code of Conduct

The Parties shall exchange letters establishing or maintaining a code of conduct for panelists and members of committees established pursuant to Article 10.11 (Review of Statutory Amendments), Article 10.12 (Review of Final Antidumping and Countervailing Duty Determinations), and Article 10.13 (Safeguarding the Panel Review System).

Article 10.18: Miscellaneous

On request of another Party, the competent investigating authority of a Party shall provide to the other Party copies of all public information submitted to it for purposes of an antidumping or countervailing duty investigation with respect to goods of that other Party.

ANNEX 10-A PRACTICES RELATING TO ANTIDUMPING AND COUNTERVAILING DUTY PROCEEDINGS

The Parties recognize the right to apply trade remedy measures consistent with Article VI of GATT 1994, the AD Agreement, and the SCM Agreement, and the importance of promoting transparency in antidumping and countervailing duty proceedings and of ensuring the opportunity of all interested parties to participate meaningfully in such proceedings.[7]

1.   To facilitate access to information relevant to antidumping and countervailing duty proceedings, a Party shall publish online the following:

    (a)   laws and regulations that pertain to its antidumping and countervailing duty proceedings; and

    (b)   sample questionnaires that it would issue in a typical antidumping proceeding.

In publishing information online, a Party shall endeavor to minimize the number of webpages on which it provides such information. A Party shall also endeavor to publish online other information relevant to antidumping and countervailing duty proceedings such as manuals, guidelines, templates, and other reference and orientation materials, where applicable.[8]

2.   For each antidumping and countervailing duty proceeding which involves imports of another Party, initiated[9] after the date of entry into force of this Agreement, each investigating authority of a Party shall maintain and make available without charge online for all interested parties:[10]

    (a)   a file that contains:

        (i)   all non-confidential documents that are part of its administrative record for each segment of a proceeding, or proceeding in the case of Mexico, and

---

[7]   With regards to the provisions in this Annex, the Parties shall protect the confidentiality of the information pursuant to each Party's law.

[8]   For greater certainty, the documents listed in this paragraph are not intended to constitute a comprehensive list of documents relating to antidumping and countervailing duty proceedings and no inference shall be drawn from this list's inclusion or exclusion of a particular document. Such documents may be published online to the extent that they are available.

[9]   For greater certainty, when the proceedings involve imports from other countries of the same subject merchandise and are initiated on the same date, this paragraph also applies.

[10]   For greater certainty, for the United States, this paragraph shall not impact information and data already made publicly available pursuant to its law.

(ii) to the extent feasible without revealing confidential information, non-confidential summaries of confidential information contained in its administrative record;[11] and

(b) a listing of all documents that are part of its administrative record for each segment of a proceeding, or proceeding in the case of Mexico, in a manner that enables any interested party to identify and locate particular documents in the file.

If technical constraints prevent online access to a document that is part of its administrative record for each segment of a proceeding, or proceeding in the case of Mexico, the investigating authority may instead make the document available for all interested parties, pursuant to the domestic legislation of the Party, by means of physical inspection during the investigating authority's normal business hours.

3. Each investigating authority of a Party shall maintain or establish a system through which interested parties participating in an antidumping or countervailing duty segment of a proceeding, or proceeding in the case of Mexico, shall submit documents electronically in such a segment of a proceeding, or proceeding in the case of Mexico. Notwithstanding the previous sentence, each investigating authority of a Party may require manual submission of a petition, or of other documents in exceptional circumstances, including where technical constraints may impact the ability of interested parties to submit certain documents electronically.

4. For the purposes of paragraphs 2 and 3, the online access point and the system for submitting documents electronically shall be established or maintained beginning no later than five years after the date of entry into force of this Agreement.

(a) If a Party requests assistance with implementation of these obligations from another Party, that Party may provide assistance to the extent practicable. The Parties recognize that a need for assistance may necessitate additional flexibility in implementing the systems set forth in paragraphs 2 and 3, pursuant to the provisions in paragraph 4(b).

(b) The Parties are aware of the technical and financial difficulties of establishing and maintaining the systems set forth in paragraphs 2 and 3, and may consult to discuss additional flexibility regarding the establishment and maintenance of such systems, as necessary.

---

[11] To the extent that individual information is not susceptible of summarization without disclosing confidential information, it may be aggregated. Nothing in this paragraph shall require an investigating authority to make publicly available a non-confidential summary of a questionnaire response that the investigating authority treats as confidential in its entirety.

5. On receipt of a formally filed antidumping or countervailing duty application with respect to imports of another Party, and normally no later than seven days prior to the date on which the investigating authority issues a determination on the application, the Party shall notify the other Party or Parties that it received the application.[12]

6. In any segment of a proceeding, or proceeding in the case of Mexico, in which an investigating authority of a Party determines to conduct an in-person verification of information provided by a responding party and pertinent to the calculation of an antidumping duty margin or the level of a countervailable subsidy, the investigating authority shall promptly notify the responding party of its intent to do so, and normally shall:

    (a) provide the responding party advance notice of the dates on which the investigating authority intends to conduct any such in-person verification of information;

    (b) prior to any such in-person verification, provide the responding party a document that sets forth the topics the responding party should be prepared to address during the verification and describes the types of supporting documentation the responding party should make available for review;

    (c) after the verification is completed prepare a written report describing the methods and procedures that it followed in carrying out the verification and the results of the verification; and

    (d) make the report available to all interested parties, without disclosing confidential information, in sufficient time for the interested parties to defend their interests in the segment of a proceeding, or proceeding in the case of Mexico.

7. An investigating authority of a Party shall disclose, among other things, for each interested party for whom the investigating authority has determined an individual rate of duty, the calculations used to determine the rate of dumping or countervailable subsidization and, if different, the calculations used to determine the rate of duty to be applied to imports of the interested party. The disclosure and explanation shall be in sufficient detail so as to permit the interested party to reproduce the calculations without undue difficulty. Such disclosure shall include, whether in electronic format, such as a computer program or spreadsheet, or in any other medium, a detailed explanation of the information the investigating authority used, the sources of that information, and any adjustments it made to the information when used in the calculations.[13] The investigating

---

[12] For Mexico, this notification shall apply only to an affirmative determination on the application.

[13] When making such disclosure, the disclosing Party shall protect the confidentiality of the information in the disclosure pursuant its law.

authority shall provide interested parties adequate opportunity to respond to the disclosure.

8. On receipt of a formally filed antidumping or countervailing duty application by the investigating authority of a Party against imports of goods from a non-Party, the investigating authorities of the other Parties may consider the information and data in the application and make a determination as to whether self-initiation of an antidumping or countervailing duty investigation or other relevant action is warranted.

9. To the extent feasible, Parties may exchange non-Parties' subsidy information and consider whether self-initiation of a countervailing duty investigation or other relevant action is warranted.

ANNEX 10-B.1   ESTABLISHMENT OF BINATIONAL PANELS

1. On the date of entry into force of this Agreement, the Parties shall establish or maintain a roster of individuals to serve as panelists in disputes under Section D. The roster shall include judges or former judges to the fullest extent practicable. The Parties shall consult in developing the roster, which shall include at least 75 candidates. Each Party shall select at least 25 candidates, and all candidates shall be citizens of Canada, Mexico, or the United States. Candidates shall be of good character, high standing and repute, and shall be chosen strictly on the basis of objectivity, reliability, sound judgment and general familiarity with international trade law. Candidates shall not be affiliated with a Party, and in no event shall a candidate take instructions from a Party. The Parties shall maintain the roster, and may amend it, when necessary, after consultations.

2. A majority of the panelists on each panel shall be lawyers in good standing. Within 30 days of a request for a panel, each involved Party shall appoint two panelists, in consultation with the other involved Party. The involved Parties normally shall appoint panelists from the roster. If a panelist is not selected from the roster, the panelist shall be chosen in accordance with and be subject to the criteria of paragraph 1. Each involved Party shall have the right to exercise four peremptory challenges, to be exercised simultaneously and in confidence, disqualifying from appointment to the panel up to four candidates proposed by the other involved Party. Peremptory challenges and the selection of alternative panelists shall occur within 45 days of the request for the panel. If an involved Party fails to appoint its members to a panel within 30 days or if a panelist is struck and no alternative panelist is selected within 45 days, such panelist shall be selected by lot on the 31st or 46th day, as the case may be, from that Party's candidates on the roster.

3. Within 55 days of the request for a panel, the involved Parties shall agree on the selection of a fifth panelist. If the involved Parties are unable to agree, they shall decide by lot which of them shall select, by the 61st day, the fifth panelist from the roster, excluding candidates eliminated by peremptory challenges.

4.   On appointment of the fifth panelist, the panelists shall promptly appoint a chair from among the lawyers on the panel by majority vote of the panelists. If there is no majority vote, the chair shall be appointed by lot from among the lawyers on the panel.

5.   Decisions of the panel shall be by majority vote and based on the votes of all members of the panel. The panel shall issue a written decision with reasons, together with any dissenting or concurring opinions of panelists.

6.   Panelists shall be subject to the code of conduct established pursuant to Article 10.17 (Code of Conduct). If an involved Party believes that a panelist is in violation of the code of conduct, the involved Parties shall consult and if they agree, the panelist shall be removed and a new panelist shall be selected in accordance with the procedures of this Annex.

7.   When a panel is convened pursuant to Article 10.12 (Review of Final Antidumping and Countervailing Duty Determinations) each panelist shall be required to sign:

    (a)   an application for protective order for information supplied by the United States or its persons covering business proprietary and other privileged information;

    (b)   an undertaking for information supplied by Canada or its persons covering confidential, personal, business proprietary and other privileged information; or

    (c)   an undertaking for information supplied by Mexico or its persons covering confidential, business proprietary and other privileged information.

8.   On a panelist's acceptance of the obligations and terms of an application for protective order or disclosure undertaking, the importing Party shall grant access to the information covered by such order or disclosure undertaking. Each Party shall establish appropriate sanctions for violations of protective orders or disclosure undertakings issued by or given to any Party. Each Party shall enforce such sanctions with respect to any person within its jurisdiction. Failure by a panelist to sign an application for a protective order or disclosure undertaking shall result in disqualification of the panelist.

9.   If a panelist becomes unable to fulfill panel duties or is disqualified, proceedings of the panel shall be suspended pending the selection of a substitute panelist in accordance with the procedures of this Annex.

10.   Subject to the code of conduct established pursuant to Article 10.17 (Code of Conduct), and provided that it does not interfere with the performance of the duties of such panelist, a panelist may engage in other business during the term of the panel.

11.   While acting as a panelist, a panelist may not appear as counsel before another panel.

12. With the exception of violations of protective orders or disclosure undertakings, signed pursuant to paragraph 7, panelists shall be immune from suit and legal process relating to acts performed by them in their official capacity.

ANNEX 10-B.2   PANEL PROCEDURES UNDER ARTICLE 10.11

1. The panel shall establish its own rules of procedure unless the Parties otherwise agree prior to the establishment of that panel. The procedures shall ensure a right to at least one hearing before the panel, as well as the opportunity to provide written submissions and rebuttal arguments. The proceedings of the panel shall be confidential, unless the two Parties otherwise agree. The panel shall base its decisions solely on the arguments and submissions of the two Parties.

2. Unless the Parties to the dispute otherwise agree, the panel shall, within 90 days after its chair is appointed, present to the two Parties an initial written declaratory opinion containing findings of fact and its determination pursuant to Article 10.11 (Review of Statutory Amendments).

3. If the findings of the panel are affirmative, the panel may include in its report its recommendations as to the means by which the amending statute could be brought into conformity with the provisions of Article 10.10(2)(d) (Retention of Domestic Antidumping Law and Countervailing Duty Law). In determining what, if any, recommendations are appropriate, the panel shall consider the extent to which the amending statute affects interests under this Agreement. Individual panelists may provide separate opinions on matters not unanimously agreed. The initial opinion of the panel shall become the final declaratory opinion, unless a Party to the dispute requests a reconsideration of the initial opinion pursuant to paragraph 4.

4. Within 14 days of the issuance of the initial declaratory opinion, a Party to the dispute disagreeing in whole or in part with the opinion may present a written statement of its objections and the reasons for those objections to the panel. In such event, the panel shall request the views of both Parties and shall reconsider its initial opinion. The panel shall conduct any further examination that it deems appropriate, and shall issue a final written opinion, together with dissenting or concurring views of individual panelists, within 30 days of the request for reconsideration.

5. Unless the Parties to the dispute otherwise agree, the final declaratory opinion of the panel shall be made public, along with any separate opinions of individual panelists and any written views that either Party may wish to be published.

6. Unless the Parties to the dispute otherwise agree, meetings and hearings of the panel shall take place at the office of the amending Party's Section of the Secretariat.

ANNEX 10-B.3 EXTRAORDINARY CHALLENGE PROCEDURE

1. The involved Parties shall establish an extraordinary challenge committee, composed of three members, within 15 days of a request pursuant to Article 10.12.13 (Review of Final Antidumping and Countervailing Duty Determinations). The members shall be selected from a 15-person roster comprised of judges or former judges of a federal judicial court of the United States or a judicial court of superior jurisdiction of Canada or a federal judicial or quasi-judicial tribunal of Mexico. Each Party shall name five persons to this roster. Each involved Party shall select one member from this roster and the involved Parties shall decide by lot which of them shall select the third member from the roster.

2. The Parties shall establish or maintain rules of procedure for committees. The rules shall provide for a decision of a committee within 90 days of its establishment.

3. Committee decisions shall be binding on the Parties with respect to the particular matter between the Parties that was before the panel. After examination of the legal and factual analysis underlying the findings and conclusions of the panel's decision in order to determine whether one of the grounds set out in Article 10.12.13 (Review of Final Antidumping and Countervailing Duty Determinations) has been established, and on finding that one of those grounds has been established, the committee shall vacate the original panel decision or remand it to the original panel for action not inconsistent with the committee's decision; if the grounds are not established, it shall deny the challenge and, therefore, the original panel decision shall stand affirmed. If the original decision is vacated, a new panel shall be established pursuant to Annex 10-B.1 (Establishment of Binational Panels).

ANNEX 10-B.4 SPECIAL COMMITTEE PROCEDURES

By the date of entry into force of this Agreement the Parties shall establish or maintain rules of procedure in accordance with the following principles:

(a) the procedures shall assure a right to at least one hearing before the special committee as well as the opportunity to provide initial and rebuttal written submissions;

(b) the procedures shall assure that the special committee shall prepare an initial report typically within 60 days of the appointment of the last member, and shall afford the Parties 14 days to comment on that report prior to issuing a final report 30 days after presentation of the initial report;

(c) the special committee's hearings, deliberations, and initial report, and all written submissions to and communications with the special committee shall be confidential;

(d) unless the Parties to the dispute otherwise agree, the decision of the special committee shall be published 10 days after it is transmitted to the disputing Parties, along with any separate opinions of individual members and any written views that either Party may wish to be published; and

(e)   unless the Parties to the dispute otherwise agree, meetings and hearings of the special committee shall take place at the office of the Section of the Secretariat of the Party complained against.

ANNEX 10-B.5   AMENDMENTS TO DOMESTIC LAWS

Schedule of Canada

1.   Canada shall amend sections 56 and 58 of the *Special Import Measures Act*, as amended, to allow the United States with respect to goods of the United States or Mexico with respect to goods of Mexico or a United States or a Mexican manufacturer, producer, or exporter, without regard to payment of duties, to make a written request for a redetermination; and section 59 to require the Deputy Minister to make a ruling on a request for a redetermination within one year of a request to a designated officer or other customs officer.

2.   Canada shall amend section 18.3(1) of the *Federal Court Act*, as amended, to render that section inapplicable to the United States and to Mexico; and shall provide in its statutes or regulations that persons (including producers of goods subject to an investigation) have standing to ask Canada to request a panel review where such persons would be entitled to commence domestic procedures for judicial review if the final determination were reviewable by the Federal Court pursuant to section 18.1(4).

3.   Canada shall amend the *Special Import Measures Act*, as amended, and any other relevant provisions of law, to provide that the following actions of the President shall be deemed for the purposes of Section D to be final determinations subject to judicial review:

(a)   a determination by the President pursuant to section 41;

(b)   a redetermination by the President pursuant to section 59; and

(c)   a review by the President of an undertaking pursuant to section 53(1).

4.   Canada shall amend Part II of the *Special Import Measures Act*, as amended, to provide for binational panel review respecting goods of Mexico and the United States.

5.   Canada shall amend Part II of the *Special Import Measures Act*, as amended, to provide for definitions related to Section D, as may be required.

6.   Canada shall amend Part II of the *Special Import Measures Act*, as amended, to permit the governments of Mexico and the United States to request binational panel review of final determinations respecting goods of Mexico and the United States.

7.   Canada shall amend Part II of the *Special Import Measures Act*, as amended, to provide for the establishment of binational panels requested to review final determinations in respect of goods of Mexico and the United States.

8.   Canada shall amend Part II of the *Special Import Measures Act*, as amended, to provide that binational panel review of a final determination shall be conducted in accordance with this Chapter.

9.   Canada shall amend Part II of the *Special Import Measures Act*, as amended, to provide that an extraordinary challenge proceeding shall be requested and conducted in accordance with Article10.12 (Review of Final Antidumping and Countervailing Duty Determinations) and Annex 10-B.3 (Extraordinary Challenge Procedure).

10. Canada shall amend Part II of the *Special Import Measures Act*, as amended, to provide for a code of conduct, immunity for anything done or omitted to be done during the course of panel proceedings, the signing of and compliance with disclosure undertakings respecting confidential information, and remuneration for members of panels and committees established pursuant to this Chapter.

11. Canada shall make such amendments as are necessary to establish a Canadian Secretariat for this Agreement and generally to facilitate the operation of Section D and the work of the binational panels, extraordinary challenge committees and special committees convened under this Chapter.

Schedule of Mexico

Mexico shall amend its antidumping and countervailing duty statutes and regulations, and other statutes and regulations to the extent that they apply to the operation of the antidumping and countervailing duty laws, to provide the following:

(a)   elimination of the possibility of imposing duties within the five-day period after the acceptance of a petition;

(b)   substitution of the term Initial Resolution (*Resolución de Inicio*) for the term Provisional Resolution (*Resolución Provisional*) and the term Provisional Resolution (*Resolución Provisional*) for the term Resolution Reviewing the Provisional Resolution (*Resolución que revisa a la Resolución Provisional*);

(c)   full participation in the administrative process for interested parties, as well as the right to administrative appeal and judicial review of final determinations of investigations, reviews, product coverage or other final decisions affecting them;

(d)   elimination of the possibility of imposing provisional duties before the issuance of a preliminary determination;

(e) the right to immediate access to review of final determinations by binational panels for interested parties, without the need to exhaust first the administrative appeal;

(f) explicit and adequate timetables for determinations of the competent investigating authority and for the submission of questionnaires, evidence and comments by interested parties, as well as an opportunity for them to present facts and arguments in support of their positions prior to any final determination, to the extent time permits, including an opportunity to be adequately informed in a timely manner of and to comment on all aspects of preliminary determinations of dumping or subsidization;

(g) written notice to interested parties of any of the actions or resolutions rendered by the competent investigating authority, including initiation of an administrative review as well as its conclusion;

(h) disclosure meetings with interested parties by the competent investigating authority conducting its investigations and reviews, within seven calendar days after the date of publication in the Federal Official Journal (*Diario Oficial de la Federación*) of preliminary and final determinations, to explain the margins of dumping and the amount of subsidies calculations and to provide the interested parties with copies of sample calculations and, if used, computer programs;

(i) timely access by eligible counsel of interested parties during the course of the proceeding (including disclosure meetings) and on appeal, either before a national tribunal or a panel, to all information contained in the administrative record of the proceeding, including confidential information, excepting proprietary information of such a high degree of sensitivity that its release would lead to substantial and irreversible harm to the owner as well as government classified information, subject to an undertaking for confidentiality that strictly forbids use of the information for personal benefit and its disclosure to persons who are not authorized to receive such information; and for sanctions that are specific to violations of undertakings in proceedings before national tribunals or panels;

(j) timely access by interested parties during the course of the proceeding, to all non-confidential information contained in the administrative record and access to such information by interested parties or their representatives in any proceeding after 90 days following the issuance of the final determination;

(k) a mechanism requiring that any person submitting documents to the competent investigating authority shall simultaneously serve on interested persons, including foreign interests, any submissions after the complaint;

(*l*) preparation of summaries of *ex parte* meetings held between the competent investigating authority and any interested party and the inclusion in the administrative record of such summaries, which shall be made available to parties to the proceeding; if such summaries contain business proprietary information, the documents must be disclosed to a party's representative under an undertaking to ensure confidentiality;

(m) maintenance by the competent investigating authority of an administrative record as defined in Article 10.8 (Definitions) and a requirement that the final determination be based solely on the administrative record;

(n) informing interested parties in writing of all data and information the administering authority requires them to submit for the investigation, review, product coverage proceeding, or other antidumping or countervailing duty proceeding;

(o) the right to an annual individual review on request by the interested parties through which they can obtain their own dumping margin or countervailing duty rate, or can change the margin or rate they received in the investigation or a previous review, reserving to the competent investigating authority the ability to initiate a review, at any time, on its own motion and requiring that the competent investigating authority issue a notice of initiation within a reasonable period of time after the request;

(p) application of determinations issued as a result of judicial, administrative, or panel review, to the extent they are relevant to interested parties in addition to the plaintiff, so that all interested parties will benefit;

(q) issuance of binding decisions by the competent investigating authority if an interested party seeks clarification outside the context of an antidumping or countervailing duty investigation or review with respect to whether a particular product is covered by an antidumping or countervailing duty order;

(r) a detailed statement of reasons and the legal basis for final determinations in a manner sufficient to permit interested parties to make an informed decision as to whether to seek judicial or panel review, including an explanation of methodological or policy issues raised in the calculation of dumping or subsidization;

(s) written notice to interested parties and publication in the Federal Official Journal (*Diario Oficial de la Federación*) of initiation of investigations setting forth the nature of the proceeding, the legal authority under which the proceeding is initiated, and a description of the product at issue;

(t) documentation in writing of all advisory bodies' decisions or recommendations, including the basis for the decisions, and release of such written decisions to parties to the proceeding; all decisions or recommendations of any advisory body shall be placed in the administrative record and made available to parties to the proceeding; and

(u) a standard of review to be applied by binational panels as set out in subparagraph (b) of the definition of "standard of review" in Article 10.8 (Definitions).

Schedule of the United States

1. The United States shall amend section 301 of the *Customs Courts Act of 1980*, as amended, and any other relevant provisions of law, to eliminate the authority to issue declaratory judgments in any civil action involving an antidumping or countervailing duty proceeding regarding a class or kind of Canadian or Mexican merchandise.

2. The United States shall amend section 405(a) of the *United States-Canada Free-Trade Agreement Implementation Act of 1988*, to provide that the interagency group established under section 242 of the *Trade Expansion Act of 1962* shall prepare a list of individuals qualified to serve as members of binational panels, extraordinary challenge committees and special committees convened under this Chapter.

3. The United States shall amend section 405(b) of the *United States-Canada Free-Trade Agreement Implementation Act of 1988*, to provide that panelists selected to serve on panels or committees convened pursuant to this Chapter, and individuals designated to assist such appointed individuals, shall not be considered employees of the United States.

4. The United States shall amend section 405(c) of the *United States-Canada Free-Trade Agreement Implementation Act of 1988*, to provide that panelists selected to serve on panels or committees convened pursuant to this Chapter, and individuals designated to assist the individuals serving on such panels or committees, shall be immune from suit and legal process relating to acts performed by such individuals in their official capacity and within the scope of their functions as such panelists or committee members, except with respect to the violation of protective orders described in section 777f(d)(3) of the *Tariff Act of 1930*, as amended.

5. The United States shall amend section 405(d) of the *United States-Canada Free-Trade Agreement Implementation Act of 1988*, to establish a United States Secretariat to facilitate the operation of Section D and the work of the binational panels, extraordinary challenge committees and special committees convened under this Chapter.

6. The United States shall amend section 407 of the *United States-Canada Free-Trade Agreement Implementation Act of 1988*, to provide that an extraordinary challenge committee convened pursuant to Article 10.12 (Review of Final Antidumping and Countervailing Duty Determinations) and Annex 10-B.3 (Extraordinary Challenge Procedure) shall have authority to obtain information in the event of an allegation that a member of a binational panel was guilty of gross misconduct, bias, or a serious conflict of interest, or otherwise materially violated the rules of conduct, and for the committee to summon the attendance of witnesses, order the taking of depositions and obtain the assistance of any district or territorial court of the United States in aid of the committee's investigation.

7. The United States shall amend section 408 of the *United States-Canada Free-Trade Agreement Implementation Act of 1988*, to provide that, in the case of a final determination of a competent investigating authority of Mexico, as well as Canada, the filing with the United States Secretary of a request for binational panel review by a person described in Article 10.12.5 (Review of Final Antidumping and Countervailing Duty Determinations) shall be deemed, on receipt of the request by the Secretary, to be a request for binational panel review within the meaning of Article 10.12.4 (Review of Final Antidumping and Countervailing Duty Determinations).

8. The United States shall amend section 516A of the *Tariff Act of 1930*, as amended, to provide that judicial review of antidumping or countervailing duty cases regarding Mexican, as well as Canadian, merchandise shall not be commenced in the Court of International Trade if binational panel review is requested.

9. The United States shall amend section 516A(a) of the *Tariff Act of 1930*, as amended, to provide that the time limits for commencing an action in the Court of International Trade with regard to antidumping or countervailing duty proceedings involving Mexican or Canadian merchandise shall not begin to run until the 31st day after the date of publication in the *Federal Register* of notice of the final determination or the antidumping duty order.

10. The United States shall amend section 516A(g) of the *Tariff Act of 1930*, as amended, to provide, in accordance with the terms of this Chapter, for binational panel review of antidumping and countervailing duty cases involving Mexican or Canadian merchandise. Such amendment shall provide that if binational panel review is requested such review will be exclusive.

11. The United States shall amend section 516A(g) of the *Tariff Act of 1930*, as amended, to provide that the competent investigating authority shall, within the period specified by any panel formed to review a final determination regarding Mexican or Canadian merchandise, take action not inconsistent with the decision of the panel or committee.

12. The United States shall amend section 777 of the *Tariff Act of 1930*, as amended, to provide for the disclosure to authorized persons under

protective order of proprietary information in the administrative record, if binational panel review of a final determination regarding Mexican or Canadian merchandise is requested.

13.   The United States shall amend section 777 of the *Tariff Act of 1930*, as amended, to provide for the imposition of sanctions on any person who the competent investigating authority finds to have violated a protective order issued by the competent investigating authority of the United States or disclosure undertakings entered into with an authorized agency of Mexico or with a competent investigating authority of Canada to protect proprietary material during binational panel review.

CHAPTER 11   TECHNICAL BARRIERS TO TRADE

Article 11.1:   Definitions

1.   Annex 1 of the TBT Agreement, including the chapeau and explanatory notes, is incorporated into and made part of this Chapter, *mutatis mutandis*.

2.   For the purposes of this Chapter:

International conformity assessment systems means systems that facilitate voluntary recognition or acceptance of the results of conformity assessment or accreditation bodies by the authorities of another Party based on compliance with international standards for conformity assessment;

International standard means a standard that is consistent with the TBT Committee Decision on International Standards;

Mutual recognition agreement means an intergovernmental agreement that specifies the conditions by which a Party will recognize the results of conformity assessment procedures produced by another Party's conformity assessment bodies that demonstrate fulfillment of appropriate standards or technical regulations;[1]

Mutual recognition arrangement or multilateral recognition arrangement means an international or regional arrangement among accreditation bodies in the territories of the Parties, in which the accreditation bodies, on the basis of peer evaluation, accept the results of each other's accredited conformity assessment bodies or among conformity assessment bodies in the territories of the Parties recognizing the results of conformity assessment;

Proposed technical regulation or conformity assessment procedure means the entirety of the text setting forth: (a) a proposed technical regulation or conformity assessment procedure; or (b) a

---

[1]   For greater certainty, mutual recognition agreements include agreements to implement the *APEC Mutual Recognition Arrangement for Conformity Assessment of Telecommunications Equipment* of May 8, 1998 and the *Electrical and Electronic Equipment Mutual Recognition Arrangement* of July 7, 1999.

significant amendment to an existing technical regulation or conformity assessment procedure;

TBT Agreement means the *Agreement on Technical Barriers to Trade*, set out in Annex 1A to the WTO Agreement; and

TBT Committee Decision on International Standards means Annex 2 to Part 1 (*Decision of the Committee on Principles for the Development of International Standards, Guides and Recommendations with relation to Articles 2, 5 and Annex 3 of the Agreement*) in the *Decisions and Recommendations adopted by the WTO Committee on Technical Barriers to Trade Since 1 January 1995* (G/TBT/1/Rev.13), as may be revised, issued by the WTO Committee on Technical Barriers to Trade.

Article 11.2:   Scope

1. This Chapter applies to the preparation, adoption and application of standards, technical regulations, and conformity assessment procedures, including any amendments, of central level of government bodies, which may affect trade in goods between the Parties.

2. Notwithstanding paragraph 1, this Chapter does not apply to:

    (a) technical specifications prepared by a governmental body for production or consumption requirements of a governmental body; or

    (b) sanitary or phytosanitary measures.

Article 11.3:   Incorporation of the TBT Agreement

1. The following provisions of the TBT Agreement are incorporated into and made part of this Agreement, *mutatis mutandis*:

    (a) Articles 2.1, 2.2, 2.3, 2.4, 2.5, 2.9, 2.10, 2.11, and 2.12;

    (b) Articles 3.1, 4.1, and 7.1;

    (c) Articles 5.1, 5.2, 5.3, 5.4, 5.6, 5.7, 5.8, and 5.9; and

    (d) Paragraphs D, E, F, and J of Annex 3.

2. No Party shall have recourse to dispute settlement under Chapter 31 (Dispute Settlement) for a matter arising under this Chapter if the dispute concerns:

    (a) exclusively claims made under the provisions of the TBT Agreement incorporated under paragraph 1; or

    (b) a measure that a Party alleges to be inconsistent with this Chapter that:

        (i) was referred or is subsequently referred to a WTO dispute settlement panel,

        (ii) was taken to comply in response to the recommendations or rulings from the WTO Dispute Settlement Body, or

(iii) bears a close nexus, such as in terms of nature, effects, and timing, with respect to a measure described in subparagraph (ii).

Article 11.4:   International   Standards,   Guides   and Recommendations

1. The Parties recognize the important role that international standards, guides, and recommendations can play in supporting greater regulatory alignment and good regulatory practices, and in reducing unnecessary barriers to trade.

2. To determine whether there is an international standard, guide, or recommendation within the meaning of Articles 2 and 5 and Annex 3 of the TBT Agreement, each Party shall apply the TBT Committee Decision on International Standards.

3. Each Party shall apply no additional principles or criteria other than those in the TBT Committee Decision on International Standards in order to recognize a standard as an international standard. For greater certainty, criteria that are not relevant to determining whether a standard is an international standard include:

    (a) the domicile of the standards body;

    (b) whether the standards body is non-governmental or inter-governmental; and

    (c) whether the standards body limits participation to delegations.

4. The Parties shall cooperate with each other in appropriate circumstances to ensure that international standards, guides, and recommendations that are likely to become a basis for technical regulations and conformity assessment procedures do not create unnecessary obstacles to international trade.

5. No Party shall accord any preference to the consideration or use of standards that are developed through processes that:

    (a) are inconsistent with the TBT Committee Decision on International Standards; or

    (b) treat persons of any of the Parties less favorably than persons whose domicile is the same as the standardization body.

6. With respect to any agreement or understanding establishing a customs union or free-trade area or providing trade-related technical assistance, each Party shall encourage the adoption, and use as the basis for standards, technical regulations, and conformity assessment procedures, of any relevant standards, guides, or recommendations developed in accordance with the TBT Committee Decision on International Standards.

7. Recognizing the importance of maintaining North American commercial integration and maintaining market access for producers in

North America, each Party shall ensure that any obligation or understanding it has with a non-Party does not facilitate or require the withdrawal or limitation on the use or acceptance of any relevant standard, guide, or recommendation developed in accordance with the TBT Committee Decision on International Standards or the relevant provisions of this Chapter.

Article 11.5:   Technical Regulations

Preparation and Review of Technical Regulations

1.   Each Party shall conduct an appropriate assessment concerning any major technical regulations it proposes to adopt. An assessment can include:

   (a)   a regulatory impact analysis of the technical regulation's potential impacts; or

   (b)   an analysis that requires evaluation of alternative measures, if any, including voluntary actions that are brought to the Party's attention in a timely manner.

Each Party shall maintain discretion in deciding if a proposed technical regulation is major under this paragraph.

2.   Each Party shall:

   (a)   periodically review technical regulations and conformity assessment procedures in order to:

      (i)   examine increasing alignment with relevant international standards, including by reviewing any new developments in the relevant international standards and whether the circumstances that have given rise to divergences from any relevant international standard continue to exist, and

      (ii)   consider the existence of any less trade-restrictive approaches; or

   (b)   maintain a process whereby a person of another Party may directly petition the Party's regulatory authorities to review a technical regulation or conformity assessment procedure on the grounds that:

      (i)   circumstances that were relevant to the content of the technical regulation have changed, or

      (ii)   a less trade-restrictive method to fulfil the technical regulation's objective exists, such as a technical regulation based on the international standard.

Use of Standards in Technical Regulations

3.   If there are multiple international standards that would be effective and appropriate to fulfil the Party's legitimate objectives of a technical regulation or conformity assessment procedure, the Party shall:

(a) consider using as a basis for the technical regulation or conformity assessment procedure each of the international standards that fulfill the legitimate objectives of the technical regulation or conformity assessment procedure; and

(b) if the Party has rejected an international standard that was brought to its attention, issue a written explanation wherever practicable.

The written explanation provided for in subparagraph (b) must include the reasons for the Party's decision to reject an international standard and shall be provided directly to the person that proposed a particular international standard or in a document that is published at the same time that the Party publishes the final technical regulation or conformity assessment procedure.

4. If no international standard is available that fulfils the legitimate objectives of the technical regulation or conformity assessment procedure, each Party shall consider whether a standard developed by a standardizing body domiciled in any of the Parties can fulfill its legitimate objectives. To that end, each Party shall:

(a) consider and decide whether to accept the standard developed by a standardizing body domiciled in any of the Parties fulfils its legitimate objectives; and

(b) if the Party has rejected a standard that was brought to its attention, issue a written explanation wherever practicable.

The written explanation provided for in subparagraph (b) must include the reasons for the Party's decision to reject an international standard and shall be provided directly to the person that proposed a particular standard or in a document that is published at the same time the Party publishes the final technical regulation or conformity assessment procedure.

5. In order for a Party to consider accepting or using a standard as provided for in paragraphs 4 and 5, the Parties recognize that a standard must be brought to the attention of a Party, in a language the Party utilizes for the publication of technical regulations and conformity assessment procedures. This must be done during the Party's planning stage or when the proposed technical regulation or conformity assessment procedure is published for comment as provided for in Article 11.7 (Transparency).

Information Exchange

6. If a Party has not used an international standard as a basis for a technical regulation, a Party shall, on request from another Party, explain why it has not used a relevant international standard or has substantially deviated from an international standard. The explanation shall address why the standard has been judged inappropriate or ineffective for the objective pursued, and identify the scientific or technical evidence on which this assessment is based. To facilitate an appropriate explanation, the requesting Party shall in its request:

(a)   identify a relevant international standard that the technical regulation has purportedly not used as its basis; and

(b)   describe how the technical regulation is constraining or has the potential to constraint its exports.

The requesting Party shall also endeavour to indicate whether the international standard was brought to the responding Party's attention when it was developing the technical regulation.

7.   In addition to Article 2.7 of the TBT Agreement, a Party shall, on request of another Party,[2] provide the reasons why it has not or cannot accept a technical regulation of that Party as equivalent to its own. The Party to which the request is made should provide its response within a reasonable period of time.

Labeling

8.   In order to avoid disrupting North American trade, and consistent with the obligations contained in Article 11.3 (Incorporation of the TBT Agreement), each Party shall ensure that its technical regulations concerning labels:

(a)   accord treatment no less favorable than that accorded to like goods of national origin; and

(b)   do not create unnecessary obstacles to trade between the Parties.

Article 11.6:   Conformity Assessment

National Treatment

1.   In addition to Article 6.4 of the TBT Agreement, each Party shall accord to conformity assessment bodies located in the territory of another Party treatment no less favorable than that it accords to conformity assessment bodies located in its own territory or in the territory of the other Party. Treatment under this paragraph includes procedures, criteria, fees, and other conditions relating to accrediting, approving, licensing, or otherwise recognizing conformity assessment bodies.

2.   In addition to Article 6.4 of the TBT Agreement, if a Party maintains procedures, criteria or other conditions as set out in paragraph 1 and requires conformity assessment results, including test results, certifications, technical reports or inspections as positive assurance that a product conforms to a technical regulation or standard, it shall:

(a)   not require the conformity assessment body to be located within its territory;

(b)   not effectively require the conformity assessment body to operate an office within its territory; and

---

2   The Party's request should identify with precision the respective technical regulations it considers to be equivalent and any data or evidence that supports its position.

(c)   permit conformity assessment bodies in other Parties' territories to apply to the Party, or any body that it has recognized or approved for this purpose, for a determination that they comply with any procedures, criteria and other conditions the Party requires to deem them competent or to otherwise approve them to test or certify the product or conduct an inspection.

Explanations and Information

3.   If a Party undertakes conformity assessment procedures in relation to specific products by specified government bodies located in its own territory or in another Party's territory, the Party shall, on the request of another Party or if practicable, an applicant of another Party, explain:

(a)   how the information it requires is necessary to assess conformity;

(b)   the sequence in which a conformity assessment procedure is undertaken and completed;

(c)   how the Party ensures that confidential business information is protected; and

(d)   the procedure to review complaints concerning the operation of the conformity assessment procedure and to take corrective action when a complaint is justified.

4.   Each Party shall explain, on the request of another Party, the reasons for its decision, whenever it declines to:

(a)   accredit, approve, license, or otherwise recognize a conformity assessment body;

(b)   recognize the results from a conformity assessment body that is a signatory to a mutual recognition arrangement;

(c)   accept the results of a conformity assessment procedure conducted in the territory of another Party; or

(d)   continue negotiations for a mutual recognition agreement.

Subcontracting

5.   If a Party requires conformity assessment as a positive assurance that a product conforms with a technical regulation or standard, it shall not prohibit a conformity assessment body from using subcontractors, or refuse to accept the results of conformity assessment on account of the conformity assessment body using subcontractors, to perform testing or inspections in relation to the conformity assessment, including subcontractors located in the territory of another Party,[3] provided that the subcontractors are accredited and approved in the Party's territory, when required.

---

[3]   For greater certainty, this paragraph does not prohibit a Party from taking steps to ensure the performance of the subcontractor meets its requirements.

Accreditation

6.   In addition to Article 9.2 of the TBT Agreement, no Party shall refuse to accept, or take actions that have the effect of, directly or indirectly, requiring or encouraging the refusal of acceptance of conformity assessment results performed by a conformity assessment body located in the territory of another Party because the accreditation body that accredited the conformity assessment body:

   (a)   operates in the territory of a Party where there is more than one accreditation body;

   (b)   is a non-governmental body;

   (c)   is domiciled in the territory of a Party that does not maintain a procedure for recognizing accreditation bodies, provided that the accreditation body is recognized internationally, consistent with paragraph 7;

   (d)   does not operate an office in the Party's territory; or

   (e)   is a for-profit entity.

7.   In addition to Article 9.1 of the TBT Agreement, each Party shall:

   (a)   adopt or maintain measures to facilitate and encourage its authorities to rely on mutual or multilateral recognition arrangements to accredit, approve, license or otherwise recognize conformity assessment bodies where effective and appropriate to fulfill the Party's legitimate objectives; and

   (b)   consider approving or recognizing accredited conformity assessment bodies for its technical regulations or standards, by an accreditation body that is a signatory to a mutual or multilateral recognition arrangement, for example, the International Laboratory Accreditation Cooperation (ILAC) and the International Accreditation Forum (IAF).

The Parties recognize that the arrangements referenced in subparagraph (b) can address considerations in approving conformity assessment bodies, including technical competence, independence, and the avoidance of conflicts of interest.

Choice of Conformity Assessment

8.   The Parties recognize that the choice of conformity assessment procedures in relation to a specific product covered by a technical regulation or standard should include an evaluation of the risks involved, the need to adopt procedures to address those risks, relevant scientific and technical information, incidence of non-compliant products, and possible alternative approaches for establishing that the technical regulation or standard has been met.

Fees

9.   Nothing in this Article precludes a Party from requesting that conformity assessment procedures in relation to specific products are

performed by specified government authorities of the Party. In those cases, the Party conducting the conformity assessment procedures shall:

(a) limit any fees it imposes for conformity assessment procedures on products from the other Parties to the costs of services rendered;

(b) not impose fees on an applicant of another Party to deliver conformity assessment services, except to recover costs incurred from services rendered;

(c) make the amounts of any fees for conformity assessment procedures publicly available;

(d) not apply a new or modified fee for conformity assessment procedures until the fee and the method for assessing the fee are published and, if practicable, the Party has provided an opportunity for interested persons to comment on the proposed introduction or modification of a conformity assessment fee.

10. On request of a Party, or an applicant's request if practicable, a Party shall explain how:

(a) any fees it imposes for such conformity assessment are no higher than the cost of services rendered;

(b) fees for its conformity assessment procedures are calculated; and

(c) any information it requires is necessary to calculate fees.

Exceptions

11. For greater certainty, nothing in paragraphs 1 or 2 precludes a Party from taking actions to verify the results from a conformity assessment procedure, including requesting information from the conformity assessment or accreditation body. These actions shall not subject a product to duplicative conformity assessment procedures, except when necessary to address non-compliance. The verifying Party may share information it has requested with another Party, provided it protects confidential information.

12. Paragraphs 2(b) and 5 do not apply to any requirement a Party may have concerning the use of products, conformity assessment procedures or related services in the commercial maritime or civil aviation sectors.

Article 11.7:   Transparency

1. Each Party shall allow persons of another Party to participate in the development of technical regulations, standards and conformity

assessment procedures[4] by its central government bodies on terms no less favorable than those that it accords to its own persons.

2.   Further to Articles 2.9 and 5.6 of the TBT Agreement, if a Party prepares or proposes to adopt a technical regulation or conformity assessment procedure that is not in response to an urgent situation as referred to in Article 2.10 and Article 5.7 of the TBT Agreement, the Party shall:

     (a)   publish the proposed technical regulation or conformity assessment procedure;

     (b)   allow persons of another Party to submit written comments during a public consultation period on no less favorable terms than it provides to its own persons;

     (c)   publish and allow for written comment in accordance with subparagraphs (a) and (b) at a time when the authority proposing the measure has sufficient time to review those comments and, as appropriate, to revise the measure to take them into account;

     (d)   consider the written comments from a person of another Party on no less favorable terms than it considers those submitted by its own persons; and

     (e)   if practicable,[5] accept a written request from another Party to discuss written comments that the other Party has submitted.

The Party requested under subparagraph (e) to discuss its proposed technical regulation or conformity assessment procedure shall ensure that it has appropriate personnel to participate in the discussions, such as from the competent authority that has proposed the technical regulation or conformity assessment procedure, in order to confirm that the written comments are fully taken into account.

3.   Each Party shall endeavor to promptly make publicly available any written comments it receives under paragraph 2(c), except to the extent necessary to protect confidential information or withhold personal identifying information or inappropriate content. If it is impracticable to post these comments on a single website, the regulatory authority of a Party shall endeavor to make these comments available via its own website.

---

     [4]   A Party satisfies this obligation by, for example, providing interested persons a reasonable opportunity to provide comments on the measure it proposes to develop and by taking those comments into account in the development of the measure.

     [5]   Circumstances when discussions are not practicable include where the Party requesting discussions has failed to submit its comments in a timely manner or if discussions would need to take place after the deadline to submit written comments has passed.

4. Each Party shall publish the final technical regulation or conformity assessment procedure and an explanation of how it has addressed substantive issues raised in comments submitted in a timely manner.

5. If appropriate, each Party shall encourage non-governmental bodies including standardization bodies in its territory to act consistently with the obligations in paragraphs 1 and 7, in developing standards and voluntary conformity assessment procedures.

6. Each Party shall ensure that its central government standardizing body's work program, containing the standards it is currently preparing and the standards it has adopted, is published:

    (a) on the central government standardizing body's website;

    (b) in its official gazette; or

    (c) on the website referred to in paragraph 10.

Stakeholder Participation in Developing Technical Regulations and Mandatory Conformity Assessment Procedures

7. Each Party shall encourage consideration of methods to provide additional transparency in the development of technical regulations, standards and conformity assessment procedures, including the use of electronic tools and public outreach or consultations.

8. If a Party requests a body within its territory to develop a standard for use as a technical regulation or conformity assessment procedure, the Party shall require the body to allow persons of another Party to participate on no less favorable terms than its own persons in groups or committees of the body that is developing the standard, and apply Annex 3 of the TBT Agreement.

9. Each Party shall take such reasonable measures as may be available to it to ensure proposed and final technical regulations and conformity assessment procedures of regional governments are published.[6]

10. Each Party shall publish online and make freely accessible, preferably on a single website, all proposed and final technical regulations and mandatory conformity assessment procedures, except with respect to any standards that are:

    (a) developed by non-governmental organizations; and

    (b) have been incorporated by reference into a technical regulation or conformity assessment procedure.

Notification of Technical Regulations and Conformity Assessment

11. In accordance with the procedures established under Article 2.9 or Article 5.6 of the TBT Agreement, each Party shall notify proposed technical regulations and conformity assessment procedures that are in accordance with the technical content of relevant international

---

[6]   For greater certainty, a Party may comply with this obligation by ensuring that the proposed and final measures in this paragraph are published on, or otherwise accessible through, the official website of the WTO.

standards, guides, or recommendations if they may have a significant effect on trade. The Party's notification shall identify the precise international standards, guides or recommendations with which the proposal is in accordance.

12. In accordance with the procedures under Article 2.10 or Article 5.7 of the TBT Agreement, and notwithstanding paragraph 11, if urgent problems of safety, health, environmental protection, or national security arise or threaten to arise for a Party, that Party shall notify a technical regulation or conformity assessment procedure that is in accordance with the technical content of relevant international standards, guides or recommendations. In its notification, the Party shall identify the precise international standards, guides, or recommendations with which the proposal is in accordance.

13. In accordance with the procedures established under Article 2.9 or Article 5.6 of the TBT Agreement, each Party shall endeavor to notify, proposed technical regulations and conformity assessment procedures of regional level of governments that may have a significant effect on trade and that are in accordance with the technical content of relevant international standards, guides, and recommendations.

14. With respect to notifications made under Articles 2.9 and 5.6 of the TBT Agreement and paragraph 11 of this Chapter, each Party shall notify proposed technical regulations and conformity assessment procedures at an early appropriate stage by:

(a) ensuring the notification is made at a time when the authority developing the measure can introduce amendments, including in response to any comments submitted as set out in subparagraph (d);

(b) including with its notification:

(i) any objective for the proposed technical regulation or conformity assessment procedure and its legal basis,

(ii) an explanation of how the proposed technical regulation or conformity assessment procedure would fulfill the identified objectives, and

(iii) a copy of the proposed technical regulation or conformity assessment procedure or an online address at which the proposed measure can be accessed;

(c) transmitting the notification electronically to the other Parties through their enquiry points established in accordance with Article 10 of the TBT Agreement, contemporaneously with the submission of the notification to the WTO Secretariat; and

(d) providing sufficient time between the end of the comment period and the adoption of the notified technical regulation or conformity assessment procedure to ensure that the responsible authority can fully consider the submitted comments and the Party can issue its responses to the comments.

Each Party shall normally allow 60 days from the date it transmits a proposal under subparagraph (b) for another Party or an interested person of a Party to provide comments in writing on the proposal. A Party shall consider any reasonable request from another Party or an interested person of a Party to extend the comment period. A Party that is able to extend a time limit beyond 60 days, for example 90 days, shall consider doing so.

15. Each Party, when making a notification under Article 2.10 or Article 5.7 of the TBT Agreement, shall at the same time transmit electronically the notification and text of the technical regulation or conformity assessment procedure, or an online address where the text of the measure can be viewed, to the Parties' contact points referred to in Article 11.12 (Contact Points).

16. If a Party is notifying a proposed technical regulation or conformity assessment procedure to the WTO TBT Committee and the other Parties for the first time,[7] the Party shall notify it to the WTO TBT Committee and the other Parties as a regular notification.[8] Each Party shall endeavor to identify the scope of its proposed technical regulation or conformity assessment procedure in its notification by reference to the specific Harmonized System heading, subheading, or tariff item for the products that would be affected by the proposal.

17. If a Party is notifying a proposed technical regulation or conformity assessment procedure that is related to a measure that was previously notified, including because it is an revision, amendment, or replacement to the previously notified measure, the Party shall provide the WTO notification symbol for the previously notified measure.[9] Each Party shall endeavor to submit a revision to a notification if the notified measure has been substantially redrafted prior to its entry into force. If the Party files a revision or the circumstances in paragraph 18(e) arise, the Party shall endeavor to allow either a new or extended period of time for interested persons to submit comments to the Party.

18. Each Party shall submit an addendum to a notification it has previously made to the WTO TBT Committee and the Parties in any of the following circumstances:

    (a) the period of time to submit comments on the proposed measure has changed;

---

[7]   The Parties shall follow the recommendation set forth in G/TBT/35, Coherent Use of Notification Formats.

[8]   A notification is a document that is circulated by the WTO Secretariat, or submitted to the WTO Secretariat for the purposes of circulation, under the prefix "G/TBT/N."

[9]   The Parties agree the appropriate place to make the identification is in field 8 of a document produced consistent with the Format and Guidelines for Notification Procedures for Draft Technical Regulations and Conformity Assessment Procedures.

(b) the notified measure has been adopted or otherwise entered into force;

(c) the compliance dates for the final measure have changed;

(d) the notified measure has been withdrawn, revoked, or replaced;[10]

(e) the content or scope of the notified measure is partially changed or amended;

(f) any interpretive guidance for a notified measure that has been issued; or

(g) the final text of the notified measure is published or adopted or otherwise enters into force.

19. Each Party shall endeavor to submit a corrigendum to a notification if it subsequently determines there are minor administrative or clerical errors in:

(a) a notification or subsequent related addendum or revision; or

(b) the text of the notified measure.

20. If a Party obtains a translation of a measure notified to the WTO TBT Committee, whether official or unofficial, in an official WTO language other than the language of the notification, it shall endeavor to send the translation to the Parties' contact points referred to in Article 11.12 (Contact Points).

21. For the purposes of determining whether a proposed technical regulation or conformity assessment procedure may have a significant effect on trade and is subject to notification in accordance with Articles 2.9, 2.10, 3.2, 5.6, 5.7, or 7.2 of the TBT Agreement and this Chapter, a Party shall consider, among other things, the relevant guidance in the *Decisions and Recommendations Adopted by the WTO Committee on Technical Barriers to Trade Since 1 January 1995* (G/TBT/1/Rev.13), as may be revised.

22. When a Party has adopted a technical regulation or conformity assessment procedure that may have a significant effect on trade, the Party shall promptly publish online:

(a) an explanation of how the technical regulation or conformity assessment procedure achieves the Party's objectives;

(b) a description of alternative approaches, if any, that the Party considered in developing the adopted technical regulation or conformity assessment procedure and the explanation of why it chose one approach over the others it considered;

---

[10] The Party shall provide the WTO document number identifying the notification of a measure that replaces or has been proposed as a replacement for a withdrawn or revoked measure.

(c) its views on any substantive issues raised in timely submitted comments on the proposed technical regulation or conformity assessment procedure;

(d) any impact assessment it has undertaken;

(e) if not addressed by an impact assessment, an explanation of the relationship between the regulation and the key evidence, data, and other information the regulatory authority considered in finalizing its work on the regulation; and

(f) the date by which compliance is required.

Article 11.8: Compliance Period for Technical Regulations and Conformity Assessment Procedures

1. For the purposes of Articles 2.12 and 5.9 of the TBT Agreement, the term "reasonable interval" means normally a period of not less than six months, except when this would be ineffective in fulfilling the legitimate objectives pursued by the technical regulation or the conformity assessment procedure.

2. If feasible and appropriate, each Party shall endeavor to provide an interval of more than six months between the publication of a final technical regulation or conformity assessment procedure and its entry into force.

3. In addition to paragraphs 1 and 2, in setting a "reasonable interval" for a specific technical regulation or conformity assessment procedure, each Party provide suppliers with a reasonable period of time, under the circumstances, to be able to demonstrate the conformity of their products with the relevant requirements of the technical regulation by the date of entry into force of the specific technical regulation or conformity assessment procedure. In doing so, each Party shall endeavor to take into account the resources available to suppliers.

* * *

CHAPTER 12 SECTORAL ANNEXES

* * *

ANNEX 12-C INFORMATION AND COMMUNICATION TECHNOLOGY

Article 12.C.1: Definitions

For the purposes of this Annex:

Cipher or cryptographic algorithm means a mathematical procedure or formula for combining a key with plaintext to create a ciphertext;

Cryptography means the principles, means or methods for the transformation of data in order to conceal or disguise its content, prevent its undetected modification, or prevent its unauthorized use; and is limited to the transformation of information using one or more secret parameters, for example, crypto variables, or associated key management;

Electromagnetic compatibility means the ability of a system or equipment to function satisfactorily in its electromagnetic environment without introducing intolerable electromagnetic disturbances with respect to any other device or system in that environment;

Electronic labeling means the electronic display of information, including required compliance information;

Encryption means the conversion of data (plaintext) through the use of a cryptographic algorithm into a form that cannot be easily understood without subsequent re-conversion (ciphertext) and the appropriate cryptographic key;

Information and communication technology good (ICT good) means a product whose intended function is information processing and communication by electronic means, including transmission and display, or electronic processing applied to determine or record physical phenomena, or to control physical processes;

Information technology equipment product (ITE product) means a device, system, or component thereof for which the primary function is the entry, storage, display, retrieval, transmission, processing, Switching, or control (or combinations thereof) of data or telecommunication messages by means other than radio transmission or reception;

Key means a parameter used in conjunction with a cryptographic algorithm that determines its operation in such a way that an entity with knowledge of the key can reproduce or reverse the operation, while an entity without knowledge of the key cannot;

Supplier's declaration of conformity means an attestation by a supplier that a product meets a specified standard or technical regulation based on an evaluation of the results of conformity assessment procedures; and

Terminal equipment means a digital or analog device capable of processing, receiving, switching, signaling, or transmitting signals by electromagnetic means and that is connected by radio or wire to a public telecommunications transport network at a termination point.

Article 12.C.2: ICT Goods that Use Cryptography

1.   This Article applies to ICT goods that use cryptography.[6] This Article does not apply to:

     (a)   a Party's law enforcement authorities requiring service suppliers using encryption they control to provide unencrypted communications pursuant to that Party's legal procedures;

     (b)   the regulation of financial instruments;

---

[6]   For greater certainty, for the purposes of this Annex, an ICT good does not include a financial instrument.

(c)   a requirement that a Party adopts or maintains relating to access to networks, including user devices, that are owned or controlled by the government of that Party, including those of central banks;

(d)   a measure taken by a Party pursuant to supervisory, investigatory, or examination authority relating to financial institutions or financial markets; or

(e)   the manufacture, sale, distribution, import, or use of the good by or for the government of the Party.

2.   With respect to an ICT good that uses cryptography and is designed for commercial applications, no Party shall require a manufacturer or supplier of the good, as a condition of the manufacture, sale, distribution, import, or use of the good, to:

(a)   transfer or provide access to any proprietary information relating to cryptography, including by disclosing a particular technology or production process or other information, for example, a private key or other secret parameter, algorithm specification, or other design detail, to the Party or a person in the Party's territory;

(b)   partner or otherwise cooperate with a person in its territory in the development, manufacture, sale, distribution, import, or use of the product; or

(c)   use or integrate a particular cryptographic algorithm or cipher.

Article 12.C.3: Electromagnetic Compatibility of ITE Products

1.   This Article applies to requirements regarding the electromagnetic compatibility of ITE products.

2.   This Article does not apply to a product:

(a)   that a Party regulates as a medical device, a medical device system, or a component of a medical device or medical device system; or

(b)   for which the Party demonstrates that there is a high risk that the product will cause harmful electromagnetic interference with a safety or radio transmission or reception device or system.

3.   If a Party requires positive assurance that an ITE product meets a standard or technical regulation for electromagnetic compatibility, it shall accept a supplier's declaration of conformity,[7] provided that the declaration satisfies the Party's requirements regarding testing, such as testing by an accredited laboratory, in support of a supplier's declaration of conformity, registration of the supplier's declaration of

---

[7]   For greater certainty, this paragraph does not apply to requirements a Party has adopted for certification by a conformity assessment body.

conformity, or the submission of evidence necessary to support the supplier's declaration of conformity.

Article 12.C.4: Regional Cooperation Activities on Telecommunications Equipment

1. This Article applies to telecommunications equipment.

2. The Parties are encouraged to implement the APEC *Mutual Recognition Arrangement for Conformity Assessment of Telecommunications Equipment* of May 8, 1998 (MRA-TEL) and, with respect to each other, the APEC *Mutual Recognition Arrangement for Equivalence of Technical Requirements* of October 31, 2010 (MRA-ETR), and to consider other arrangements to facilitate trade in telecommunications equipment.

3. In accordance with the *Mutual Recognition Agreement between the Government of the United States and the Government of the United Mexican States for the Conformity Assessment of Telecommunications Equipment*, done on May 26, 2011 at Paris, France the United States and Mexico shall accept test reports provided by a recognized testing laboratory designated by the other Party under terms and conditions no less favorable than those it accords to test reports produced by testing laboratories in its territory, and without regard to the nationality of the supplier or manufacturer of the telecommunications equipment, or the country of origin of the equipment for which a test report has been produced.

4. In accordance with the *Mutual Recognition Agreement between the Government of Canada and the Government of the United Mexican States for the Conformity Assessment of Telecommunications Equipment*, done at Honolulu on 12 November 2011, Canada and Mexico shall accept test reports provided by a recognized testing laboratory designated by the other Party under terms and conditions no less favorable than those it accords to test reports produced by testing laboratories in its territory, and without regard to the nationality of the supplier or manufacturer of the telecommunications equipment, or the country of origin of the equipment for which a test report has been produced.

5. If a Party requires equipment subject to electromagnetic compatibility and radio frequency requirements to include a label containing compliance information about the equipment, it shall permit this information to be provided through an electronic label. The Parties shall exchange information, as appropriate, about their respective electronic labeling requirements with a view to facilitate compatible approaches to electronic labeling.

Article 12.C.5: Terminal Equipment

1. This Article applies to terminal equipment.

2. Each Party shall ensure that its technical regulations, standards, and conformity assessment procedures relating to the attachment of terminal equipment to the public telecommunications networks,

including those measures relating to the use of testing and measuring equipment for conformity assessment procedures, are adopted or maintained only to the extent necessary to:

(a)   prevent damage to public telecommunications networks;

(b)   prevent degradation of public telecommunications services;

(c)   prevent electromagnetic interference, and ensure compatibility, with other uses of the electromagnetic spectrum;

(d)   prevent billing equipment malfunction; or

(e)   ensure safety of and access to public telecommunications or services, including for the hearing impaired or other disabled persons.

3.   Each Party shall ensure that the network termination points for its public telecommunications networks are established on a reasonable and transparent basis.

4.   Each Party shall permit any recognized[8] conformity assessment body to perform the testing required under the Party's conformity assessment procedures for terminal equipment to be attached to the public telecommunications network, subject to the Party's right to review the accuracy and completeness of the test results.

* * *

ANNEX 12-F   PHARMACEUTICALS

Article 12.F.1:   Definitions

For the purposes of this Annex:

Marketing authorization means the process or processes by which a Party approves or registers a pharmaceutical product in order to authorize the marketing, distribution, or sale of the product in its territory on the basis of the Party's safety, efficacy, and quality requirements; and

Pharmaceutical product means:

(a)   for Canada, a product destined for human use that constitutes a "drug" as defined under section 2 of the *Food and Drugs Act*, R.S.C., 1985, c. F-27, as amended, and that is regulated as a "drug" under the *Food and Drug Regulations* C.R.C., c. 870, as amended;

(b)   for Mexico, a product covered as human "drugs," "biologics," and "biotechnology" under articles 221, 222 bis, 224, and 224 bis of the *Ley General de Salud* (General Heath Law) as amended; and

---

[8]   "Recognized" means recognized pursuant to an act by a regulatory authority under which a conformity assessment body is approved to perform conformity assessment.

(c) for the United States, a product for human use covered as a "drug" under 21 U.S.C. § 321(g)(1), as amended, or as a "biologic" under 42 U.S.C. § 262(i), as amended.

Article 12.F.2: Scope

This Annex applies to the preparation, adoption, and application of technical regulations, standards, conformity assessment procedures, marketing authorization, and notification procedures of a Party's central level of government that may affect trade in pharmaceutical products between the Parties, other than sanitary or phytosanitary measures or technical specifications prepared by a government body for production or consumption requirements of that body.

Article 12.F.3: Competent Authorities

1. Each Party shall make available online the following information with respect to each of its competent authorities at its central level of government that has responsibility for implementing and enforcing measures regulating pharmaceutical products:

    (a) a description of each authority, including the authority's specific responsibilities; and

    (b) a point of contact within each authority.

2. Each Party shall promptly notify the other Parties of any material changes to this information and update the information online.

3. Each Party shall avoid adopting or maintaining unnecessarily duplicative regulatory requirements with respect to pharmaceutical products, including by periodically examining whether its authorities are engaged in duplicative activities.

Article 12.F.4: Enhancing Regulatory Compatibility

The Parties shall seek to collaborate to improve the alignment of their respective regulations and regulatory activities for pharmaceutical products through work in relevant international initiatives as appropriate, such as those aimed at harmonization, as well as regional initiatives that support those international initiatives.

Article 12.F.5: Application of Regulatory Controls

1. Each Party shall ensure that for a measure it applies to ensure the safety, effectiveness, or quality of pharmaceutical products, including marketing authorizations, notification procedures, and elements of either, products imported from the territory of another Party be accorded treatment no less favorable than that accorded to like products of national origin and to like products originating in any other country, in a comparable situation.

2. When developing a regulatory requirement for a pharmaceutical product, each Party shall consider its available resources and technical capacity in order to minimize the likelihood of implementing requirements that could:

    (a)   inhibit the efficacy of procedures for ensuring the safety, effectiveness, or quality of pharmaceutical products; or

    (b)   lead to substantial delays for pharmaceutical products becoming available in that Party's market.

3.   The Parties shall seek to improve their collaboration on pharmaceutical inspections. Accordingly, each Party shall, with respect to a good manufacturing practice surveillance inspection of a manufacturing facility for pharmaceutical products within the territory of another Party:

    (a)   notify the other Party prior to conducting an inspection, unless there are reasonable grounds to believe that doing so could prejudice the effectiveness of the inspection;

    (b)   if practicable, permit representatives of the other Party's competent authority to observe the inspection; and

    (c)   notify the other Party of its findings as soon as possible following the inspection and, if the findings will be publicly released, no later than a reasonable time before release.

With respect to subparagraph (c), the inspecting Party is not required to notify the other Party of a finding that is subject to treatment as confidential information under the inspecting Party's law.

4.   Upon certification by the competent authority in the United States, the competent authorities of Canada and the United States shall establish mechanisms to permit the exchange of confidential information relevant to pharmaceutical inspections, including unredacted Good Manufacturing Practice inspection reports.

5.   Upon certification by the competent authority in the United States, the competent authorities of Mexico and the United States shall establish mechanisms to permit the exchange of confidential information relevant to pharmaceutical inspections, including unredacted Good Manufacturing Practice inspection reports.

6.   To facilitate the exchange of information pursuant to paragraphs 4 and 5, each Party shall maintain procedures to prevent the disclosure of confidential information that may be necessary for the Parties to permit the exchange.

7.   Competent authorities in Mexico and Canada shall strengthen their cooperation in the exchange of information, including through multilateral fora in existence. To that end, Mexico and Canada shall increase collaboration and confidence building exercises in the regulation of pharmaceutical products.

8.   When developing or implementing regulations with respect to inspection of pharmaceutical products, each Party shall consider relevant scientific or technical guidance documents developed through international collaborative efforts.

Article 12.F.6:　　Marketing Authorizations

1. When developing or implementing a regulation for the marketing authorization of a pharmaceutical product, each Party shall consider relevant scientific or technical guidance documents developed through international collaborative efforts. Each Party is further encouraged to consider regionally-developed scientific or technical guidance documents that are aligned with international collaborative efforts.

2. Each Party shall make a determination whether to grant marketing authorization for a specific pharmaceutical product on the basis of information that is necessary to evaluate the safety, effectiveness, and quality of the pharmaceutical product. This information may include:

    (a) clinical data and information on safety and effectiveness of the product;

    (b) information on the quality of the product, including manufacturing controls for the ingredients of the product; and

    (c) labeling information related to the safety, effectiveness, quality, and use of the product.

3. No Party shall require sales data, or other financial data concerning the marketing of the product in making the determination referred to in paragraph 2. Further, each Party shall endeavor not to require pricing data in making the determination.

4. Each Party shall administer its marketing authorizations:

    (a) reasonably, including by:

        (i) avoiding duplicative requests or requests for unnecessary information from the applicant,

        (ii) promptly communicating any deficiencies, and the reasons for the deficiencies, to the applicant, if the deficiency would prevent or delay consideration of the application, and

        (iii) providing an applicant that requests marketing authorization for a pharmaceutical product with a determination within a reasonable period of time;[14]

    (b) objectively, through application of published criteria;

    (c) impartially, including by adopting or maintaining procedures to manage any conflicts of interest; and

    (d) transparently, including by publishing a checklist or other guidance concerning the information that must be provided in any application.

---

[14] For greater certainty, the reasonable period of time required to make a marketing authorization determination may be affected by factors such as the novelty of a product or regulatory implications that may arise.

5. Each Party shall ensure that it adopts or maintains measures that permit an applicant for a marketing authorization to seek review or reconsideration if the application is denied.

6. Paragraph 5 does not preclude a Party from imposing a deadline by which review must be sought.

7. If a Party requires periodic re-authorization for a pharmaceutical product that has previously received marketing authorization from the Party, the Party shall allow the pharmaceutical product to remain on its market under the conditions of the previous marketing authorization pending a decision on the periodic reauthorization, unless the Party identifies a significant safety, effectiveness, or quality concern.[15]

8. No Party shall require that a pharmaceutical product receive marketing authorization from a regulatory authority in the country of manufacture as a condition for the product to receive marketing authorization from that Party.

9. A Party may accept a prior marketing authorization that is issued by another regulatory authority as evidence that a pharmaceutical product meets its requirements. Notwithstanding paragraph 6, if the Party faces regulatory resource limitations that restrict its ability to provide marketing authorizations, a Party may require a marketing authorization from a reference country as a condition for the marketing authorization, provided that the Party has established and published a list of those countries from which it will accept a marketing authorization as evidence that a pharmaceutical product meets its requirements.

10. Each Party shall review the safety, effectiveness, and quality information submitted by the applicant requesting marketing authorization in a format that is consistent with the specifications set forth in the Common Technical Document (CTD) of the *International Conference on Harmonisation of Technical Requirements for Registration of Pharmaceuticals for Human Use*, as amended.[16]

CHAPTER 13   GOVERNMENT PROCUREMENT

Article 13.1:   Definitions

For the purposes of this Chapter:

Build-operate-transfer contract and public works concession contract means a contractual arrangement the primary purpose of which is to provide for the construction or rehabilitation of physical infrastructure, plants, buildings, facilities, or other government-owned works and under which, as

---

[15]   For greater certainty, an application for reauthorization that is not filed in a timely manner, that contains insufficient information, or that is otherwise inconsistent with a Party's requirements, is deficient for the purposes of the reauthorization decision.

[16]   For greater certainty, the CTD may not address all aspects relevant to a Party's determination to approve marketing authorization for a particular product.

consideration for a supplier's execution of a contractual arrangement, a procuring entity grants to the supplier, for a specified period of time, temporary ownership or a right to control and operate, and demand payment for the use of those works for the duration of the contract;

Commercial goods or services means goods or services of a type generally sold or offered for sale in the commercial marketplace to, and customarily purchased by, non-governmental buyers for non-governmental purposes;

Construction service means a service that has as its objective the realization by whatever means of civil or building works, based on Division 51 of the United Nations Provisional Central Product Classification (CPC);

In writing or written means any worded or numbered expression that can be read, reproduced and may be later communicated, and may include electronically transmitted and stored information;

Limited tendering means a procurement method whereby the procuring entity contacts a supplier or suppliers of its choice;

Multi-use list means a list of suppliers that a procuring entity has determined satisfy the conditions for participation in that list, and that the procuring entity intends to use more than once;

Notice of intended procurement means a notice published by a procuring entity inviting interested suppliers to submit a request for participation, a tender, or both;

Offset means any condition or undertaking that requires the use of domestic content, a domestic supplier, the licensing of technology, technology transfer, investment, counter-trade, or similar action to encourage local development or to improve a Party's balance of payments accounts;

Open tendering means a procurement method whereby all interested suppliers may submit a tender;

Procuring entity means an entity listed in Annex 13-A;

Qualified supplier means a supplier that a procuring entity recognizes as having satisfied the conditions for participation;

Selective tendering means a procurement method whereby the procuring entity invites only qualified suppliers to submit a tender;

Services includes construction services, unless otherwise specified;

Supplier means a person or group of persons that provides or could provide a good or service to a procuring entity; and

Technical specification means a tendering requirement that:

    (a)   sets out the characteristics of:

        (i)   goods to be procured, including quality, performance, safety, and dimensions, or the processes and methods for their production, or

      (ii)   services to be procured, or the processes or methods for their provision, including any applicable administrative provisions; or

  (b)   addresses terminology, symbols, packaging, marking, or labelling requirements, as they apply to a good or service.

Article 13.2:   Scope

Application of Chapter

1.   This Chapter applies to any measure regarding covered procurement.

2.   For the purposes of this Chapter, covered procurement means government procurement:

  (a)   of a good, service, or any combination thereof as specified in each Party's Schedule to Annex 13-A;

  (b)   by any contractual means, including: purchase; rental or lease, with or without an option to buy; build-operate-transfer contracts and public works concessions contracts;

  (c)   for which the value, as estimated in accordance with paragraphs 9 and 10, equals or exceeds the relevant threshold specified in a Party's Schedule to Annex 13-A, at the time of publication of a notice of intended procurement;

  (d)   by a procuring entity; and

  (e)   that is not otherwise excluded from coverage under this Agreement.

3.   **This Chapter applies only as between Mexico and the United Sates (emphasis added).** Accordingly, for the purposes of this Chapter, "Party" or "Parties" means Mexico or the United States, singly or collectively.

Activities Not Covered

4.   Unless otherwise provided in a Party's Schedule to Annex 13-A, this Chapter does not apply to:

  (a)   the acquisition or rental of land, existing buildings or other immovable property or the rights thereon;

  (b)   non-contractual agreements or any form of assistance that a Party, including its procuring entities, provides, including cooperative agreements, grants, loans, equity infusions, guarantees, subsidies, fiscal incentives, and sponsorship arrangements;

  (c)   the procurement or acquisition of: fiscal agency or depository services; liquidation and management services for regulated financial institutions; or services related to the sale, redemption and distribution of public debt, including loans and government bonds, notes and other securities;

  (e)   public employment contracts; and

(f)   procurement conducted:

    (i)   for the specific purpose of providing international assistance, including development aid,

    (ii)   under the particular procedure or condition of an international agreement relating to the stationing of troops or relating to the joint implementation by the signatory countries of a project, or

    (iii)   under the particular procedure or condition of an international organization, or funded by international grants, loans, or other assistance if the applicable procedure or condition would be inconsistent with this Chapter.

Schedules

5.   Each Party shall specify the following information in its Schedule to Annex 13-A:

(a)   in Section A, the central government entities for which procurement is covered by this Chapter;

(b)   in Section B, other entities for which procurement is covered by this Chapter;

(c)   in Section C, the goods covered by this Chapter;

(d)   in Section D, the services, other than construction services, covered by this Chapter;

(e)   in Section E, the construction services covered by this Chapter;

(f)   in Section F, any General Notes;

(g)   in Section G, the applicable Threshold Adjustment Formula; and

(h)   in Section H, the publication information required under Article 13.5.2 (Publication of Procurement Information).

Compliance

6.   Each Party shall ensure that its procuring entities comply with this Chapter in conducting covered procurements.

7.   No procuring entity shall prepare or design a procurement, or otherwise structure or divide a procurement into separate procurements in any stage of the procurement, or use a particular method to estimate the value of a procurement, in order to avoid the obligations of this Chapter.

8.   Nothing in this Chapter shall be construed to prevent a Party, including its procuring entities, from developing new procurement policies, procedures or contractual means, provided that they are not inconsistent with this Chapter.

Valuation

9.   In estimating the value of a procurement for the purposes of ascertaining whether it is a covered procurement, a procuring entity shall include the estimated maximum total value of the procurement over its entire duration, taking into account:

   (a)   all forms of remuneration, including any premium, fee, commission, interest or other revenue stream that may be provided for under the contract;

   (b)   the value of any option clause; and

   (c)   any contract awarded at the same time or over a given period to one or more suppliers under the same procurement.

10. If the total estimated maximum value of a procurement over its entire duration is not known, the procurement shall be deemed a covered procurement, unless otherwise excluded under this Agreement.

   Article 13.3:   Exceptions

1.   Subject to the requirement that the measure is not applied in a manner that would constitute a means of arbitrary or unjustifiable discrimination between Parties where the same conditions prevail, or a disguised restriction on international trade between the Parties, nothing in this Chapter shall be construed to prevent a Party, including its procuring entities, from adopting or maintaining a measure:

   (a)   necessary to protect public morals, order, or safety;

   (b)   necessary to protect human, animal, or plant life or health;

   (c)   necessary to protect intellectual property; or

   (d)   relating to the good or service of a person with disabilities, of philanthropic or not-for-profit institutions, or of prison labor.

2.   The Parties understand that subparagraph 1(b) includes environmental measures necessary to protect human, animal, or plant life or health.

   Article 13.4:   General Principles

National Treatment and Non-Discrimination

1.   With respect to any measure regarding covered procurement, each Party, including its procuring entities, shall accord immediately and unconditionally to the goods and services of the other Party and to the suppliers of the other Party, treatment no less favorable than the treatment that the Party, including its procuring entities, accords to domestic goods, services, and suppliers.

2.   With respect to a measure regarding covered procurement, no Party, including its procuring entities, shall:

   (a)   treat a locally established supplier less favorably than another locally established supplier on the basis of degree of foreign affiliation or ownership; or

(b)   discriminate against a locally established supplier on the basis that the good or service offered by that supplier for a particular procurement is a good or service of the other Party.

3.   All orders under contracts awarded for covered procurement shall be subject to paragraphs 1 and 2 of this Article.

Procurement Methods

4.   A procuring entity shall use an open tendering procedure for covered procurement unless Article 13.8 (Qualification of Suppliers) or Article 13.9 (Limited Tendering) applies.

Rules of Origin

5.   For the purposes of covered procurement, a Party shall not apply rules of origin to goods or services imported from or supplied from the other Party that are different from the rules of origin the Party applies at the same time in the normal course of trade to imports or supplies of the same goods or services from the same Party.

Offsets

6.   With regard to covered procurement, no Party, including its procuring entities, shall seek, take account of, impose, or enforce any offset, at any stage of a procurement.

Measures Not Specific to Procurement

7.   Paragraphs 1 and 2 shall not apply to customs duties and charges of any kind imposed on or in connection with importation, the method of levying such duties and charges, other import regulations or formalities, and measures affecting trade in services other than measures governing covered procurement.

Use of Electronic Means

8.   The Parties shall seek to provide opportunities for covered procurement to be undertaken through electronic means, including for the publication of procurement information, notices, and tender documentation, and for the receipt of tenders.

9.   When conducting covered procurement by electronic means, a procuring entity shall:

(a)   ensure that the procurement is conducted using information technology systems and software, including those related to authentication and encryption of information, that are generally available and interoperable with other generally available information technology systems and software; and

(b)   establish and maintain mechanisms that ensure the integrity of information provided by suppliers, including requests for participation and tenders.

Article 13.5:   Publication of Procurement Information

1. Each Party shall promptly publish any measure of general application relating to covered procurement, and any change or addition to this information.

2. Each Party shall list in Section I of its Schedule to Annex 13-A the paper or electronic means through which the Party publishes the information described in paragraph 1 and the notices required by Article 13.6 (Notices of Intended Procurement), Article 13.8.3 (Qualification of Suppliers), and Article 13.15.3 (Transparency and Post-Award Information).

3. Each Party shall, on request, provide an explanation in response to an inquiry relating to the information referred to in paragraph 1.

Article 13.6:   Notices of Intended Procurement

1. For each covered procurement, except in the circumstances described in Article 13.9 (Limited Tendering), a procuring entity shall publish a notice of intended procurement through the appropriate paper or electronic means listed in Annex 13-A. The notices shall remain readily accessible to the public until at least the expiration of the time period for responding to the notice or the deadline for submission of the tender.

2. The notices shall, if accessible by electronic means, be provided free of charge:

    (a) for central government entities that are covered under Annex 13-A, through a single point of access; and

    (b) for other entities covered under Annex 13-A, through links in a single electronic portal.

3. Unless otherwise provided in this Chapter, each notice of intended procurement shall include the following information, unless that information is provided in the tender documentation that is made available free of charge to all interested suppliers at the same time as the notice of intended procurement:

    (a) the name and address of the procuring entity and other information necessary to contact the procuring entity and obtain all relevant documents relating to the procurement, and the cost and terms of payment to obtain the relevant documents, if any;

    (b) a description of the procurement, including, if appropriate, the nature and quantity of the goods or services to be procured and a description of any options, or the estimated quantity if the quantity is not known;

    (c) if applicable, the time-frame for delivery of goods or services or the duration of the contract;

    (d) if applicable, the address and any final date for the submission of requests for participation in the procurement;

(e)   the address and the final date for the submission of tenders;

(f)   the language or languages in which tenders or requests for participation may be submitted, if other than an official language of the Party of the procuring entity;

(g)   a list and a brief description of any conditions for participation of suppliers, that may include any related requirements for specific documents or certifications that suppliers must provide;

(h)   if, pursuant to Article 13.8 (Qualification of Suppliers), a procuring entity intends to select a limited number of qualified suppliers to be invited to tender, the criteria that will be used to select them and, if applicable, any limitation on the number of suppliers that will be permitted to tender; and

(i)   an indication that the procurement is covered by this Chapter.

4.   For greater certainty, paragraph 3 does not preclude a Party from charging a fee for tender documentation if the notice of intended procurement includes all of the information set out in paragraph 3.

Notice of Planned Procurement

5.   Procuring entities are encouraged to publish as early as possible in each fiscal year a notice regarding their future procurement plans (notice of planned procurement) which should include the subject matter of the procurement and the planned date of publication of the notice of intended procurement.

Article 13.7:   Conditions for Participation

1.   A procuring entity shall limit any conditions for participation in a covered procurement to those conditions that ensure that a supplier has the legal and financial capacities and the commercial and technical abilities to fulfil the requirements of that procurement.

2.   In establishing the conditions for participation, a procuring entity:

(a)   shall not impose the condition that, in order for a supplier to participate in a procurement, the supplier has previously been awarded one or more contracts by a procuring entity of a given Party or that the supplier has prior work experience in the territory of that Party; and

(b)   may require relevant prior experience if essential to meet the requirements of the procurement.

3.   In assessing whether a supplier satisfies the conditions for participation, a procuring entity shall:

(a)   evaluate the financial capacity and the commercial and technical abilities of a supplier on the basis of that supplier's business activities both inside and outside the territory of the Party of the procuring entity; and

(b) base its evaluation solely on the conditions that the procuring entity has specified in advance in notices or tender documentation.

4. If there is supporting evidence, a Party, including its procuring entities, may exclude a supplier on grounds such as:

(a) bankruptcy or insolvency;

(b) false declarations;

(c) significant or persistent deficiencies in the performance of any substantive requirement or obligation under a prior contract or contracts;

(d) final judgments in respect of serious crimes or other serious offences;

(e) professional misconduct or actions or omissions that adversely reflect on the commercial integrity of the supplier; or

(f) failure to pay taxes.

5. For greater certainty, this Article is not intended to preclude a procuring entity from promoting compliance with laws in the territory in which the good is produced or the service is performed relating to labor rights as recognized by the Parties and set forth in Article 23.3 (Labor Rights), provided that such measures are applied in a manner consistent with Chapter 29 (Publication and Administration), and are not applied in a manner that constitutes a means of arbitrary or unjustifiable discrimination between the Parties or a disguised restriction on trade between the Parties.[1]

Article 13.8:   Qualification of Suppliers

Registration Systems and Qualification Procedures

1. A Party, including its procuring entities, may maintain a supplier registration system under which interested suppliers are required to register and provide certain information.

2. No Party, including its procuring entities, shall:

(a) adopt or apply any registration system or qualification procedure with the purpose or the effect of creating unnecessary obstacles to the participation of suppliers of the other Party in its procurement; or

(b) use such registration system or qualification procedure to prevent or delay the inclusion of suppliers of the other Party

---

[1]   The adoption and maintenance of these measures by a Party should not be construed as evidence that the other Party has breached the obligations under Chapter 23 (Labor) with respect to labor.

on a list of suppliers or prevent those suppliers from being considered for a particular procurement.

Selective Tendering

3. If a procuring entity intends to use selective tendering, the procuring entity shall:

    (a) publish a notice of intended procurement that invites suppliers to submit a request for participation in a covered procurement; and

    (b) include in the notice of intended procurement the information specified in Article 13.6.3(a), (b), (d), (g), (h), and (i) (Notices of Intended Procurement).

4. The procuring entity shall:

    (a) publish the notice sufficiently in advance of the procurement to allow interested suppliers to request participation in the procurement;

    (b) provide, by the commencement of the time period for tendering, at least the information in Article 13.6.3 (c), (e), and (f) (Notices of Intended Procurement) to the qualified suppliers that it notifies as specified in Article 13.13.3(b) (Time Periods); and

    (c) allow all qualified suppliers to submit a tender, unless the procuring entity stated in the notice of intended procurement a limitation on the number of suppliers that will be permitted to tender and the criteria or justification for selecting the limited number of suppliers.

5. If the tender documentation is not made publicly available from the date of publication of the notice referred to in paragraph 3, the procuring entity shall ensure that the tender documentation is made available at the same time to all the qualified suppliers selected in accordance with paragraph 4(c).

Multi-Use Lists

6. A Party, including its procuring entities, may establish or maintain a multi-use list provided that it publishes annually, or otherwise makes continuously available by electronic means, a notice inviting interested suppliers to apply for inclusion on the list. The notice shall include:

    (a) a description of the goods and services, or categories thereof, for which the list may be used;

    (b) the conditions for participation to be satisfied by suppliers for inclusion on the list and the methods that the procuring entity or other government agency will use to verify a supplier's satisfaction of those conditions;

    (c) the name and address of the procuring entity or other government agency and other information necessary to contact the procuring entity and to obtain all relevant documents relating to the list;

(d) the period of validity of the list and the means for its renewal or termination or, if the period of validity is not provided, an indication of the method by which notice will be given of the termination of use of the list;

(e) the deadline for submission of applications for inclusion on the list, if applicable; and

(f) an indication that the list may be used for procurement covered by this Chapter, unless that indication is publicly available through information published pursuant to Article 13.5.2 (Publication of Procurement Information).

7. A Party, including its procuring entities, that establishes or maintains a multi-use list, shall include on the list, within a reasonable period of time, all suppliers that satisfy the conditions for participation set out in the notice referred to in paragraph 6.

8. If a supplier that is not included on a multi-use list submits a request for participation in a procurement based on the multi-use list and submits all required documents, within the time period provided for in Article 13.13.2 (Time Periods), a procuring entity shall examine the request. The procuring entity shall not exclude the supplier from consideration in respect of the procurement unless the procuring entity is not able to complete the examination of the request within the time period allowed for the submission of tenders.

Information on Procuring Entity Decisions

9. A procuring entity or other entity of a Party shall promptly inform any supplier that submits a request for participation in a procurement or application for inclusion on a multi-use list of the decision with respect to the request or application.

10. If a procuring entity or other entity of a Party rejects a supplier's request for participation or application for inclusion on a multi-use list, ceases to recognize a supplier as qualified, or removes a supplier from a multi-use list, the entity shall promptly inform the supplier and on request of the supplier, promptly provide the supplier with a written explanation of the reason for its decision.

Article 13.9:   Limited Tendering

1. Provided that it does not use this provision for the purpose of avoiding competition between suppliers, to protect domestic suppliers, or in a manner that discriminates against suppliers of the other Party, a procuring entity may use limited tendering.

2. If a procuring entity uses limited tendering, it may choose, according to the nature of the procurement, not to apply Article 13.6 (Notices of Intended Procurement), Article 13.7 (Conditions for Participation), Article 13.8 (Qualification of Suppliers), Article 13.10 (Negotiations), Article 13.11 (Technical Specifications), Article 13.12 (Tender

Documentation), Article 13.13 (Time Periods), or Article 13.14 (Treatment of Tenders and Awarding of Contracts). A procuring entity may use limited tendering only under the following circumstances:

(a)   if, in response to a prior notice, invitation to participate, or invitation to tender:

    (i)   no tenders were submitted or no suppliers requested participation,

    (ii)   no tenders were submitted that conform to the essential requirements in the tender documentation,

    (iii)   no suppliers satisfied the conditions for participation, or

    (iv)   the tenders submitted were collusive,

provided that the procuring entity does not substantially modify the essential requirements set out in the notices or tender documentation;

(b)   if the good or service can be supplied only by a particular supplier and no reasonable alternative or substitute good or service exists for any of the following reasons:

    (i)   the requirement is for a work of art,

    (ii)   the protection of patents, copyrights, or other exclusive rights, or

    (iii)   due to an absence of competition for technical reasons;

(c)   for additional deliveries by the original supplier or its authorized agents, of goods or services that were not included in the initial procurement if a change of supplier for such additional goods or services:

    (i)   cannot be made for technical reasons such as requirements of interchangeability or interoperability with existing equipment, software, services, or installations procured under the initial procurement, or due to conditions under original supplier warranties, and

    (ii)   would cause significant inconvenience or substantial duplication of costs for the procuring entity;

(d)   for a good purchased on a commodity market or exchange;

(e)   if a procuring entity procures a prototype or a first good or service that is intended for limited trial or that is developed at its request in the course of, and for, a particular contract for research, experiment, study, or original development. Original development of a prototype or a first good or service may include limited production or supply in order to incorporate the results of field testing and to demonstrate that the prototype or the first good or service is suitable for production or supply in quantity to acceptable quality standards, but does not include quantity production or supply to establish commercial viability or to recover research and development costs;

(f)   for purchases made under exceptionally advantageous conditions that only arise in the very short term, such as from unusual disposals, liquidation, bankruptcy, or receivership, but not for routine purchases from regular suppliers;

(g)   if a contract is awarded to the winner of a design contest, provided that:

(i)   the contest has been organized in a manner that is consistent with this Chapter, and

(ii) the contest is judged by an independent jury with a view to award a design contract to the winner; or

(h)   in so far as is strictly necessary if, for reasons of extreme urgency brought about by events unforeseeable by the procuring entity, the good or service could not be obtained in time by means of open or selective tendering.

3.   For each contract awarded in accordance with paragraph 2, a procuring entity shall prepare a report in writing, or maintain a record, that includes the name of the procuring entity, the value and kind of good or service procured, and a statement that indicates the circumstances and conditions described in paragraph 2 that justified the use of limited tendering.

Article 13.10:   Negotiations

1.   A Party may provide for its procuring entities to conduct negotiations in the context of covered procurement if:

(a)   the procuring entity has indicated its intent to conduct negotiations in the notice of intended procurement required under Article 13.6 (Notices of Intended Procurement); or

(b)   it appears from the evaluation that no tender is obviously the most advantageous in terms of the specific evaluation criteria set out in the notice of intended procurement or tender documentation.

2.   A procuring entity shall:

(a)   ensure that any elimination of suppliers participating in negotiations is carried out in accordance with the evaluation criteria set out in the notice of intended procurement or tender documentation; and

(b)   when negotiations are concluded, provide a common deadline for the remaining participating suppliers to submit any new or revised tenders.

Article 13.11:   Technical Specifications

1.   A procuring entity shall not prepare, adopt, or apply any technical specification or prescribe any conformity assessment procedure with

the purpose or effect of creating an unnecessary obstacle to trade between the Parties.

2.   In prescribing the technical specifications for the good or service being procured, a procuring entity shall, if appropriate:

   (a)   set out the technical specifications in terms of performance and functional requirements, rather than design or descriptive characteristics; and

   (b)   base the technical specifications on international standards, if these exist; otherwise, on national technical regulations, recognized national, standards or building codes.

3.   A procuring entity shall not prescribe technical specifications that require or refer to a particular trademark or trade name, patent, copyright, design, type, specific origin, producer, or supplier, unless there is no other sufficiently precise or intelligible way of describing the procurement requirements and provided that, in these cases, the procuring entity includes words such as "or equivalent" in the tender documentation.

4.   A procuring entity shall not seek or accept, in a manner that would have the effect of precluding competition, advice that may be used in the preparation or adoption of any technical specification for a specific procurement from a person that may have a commercial interest in the procurement.

5.   For greater certainty, a procuring entity may conduct market research in developing specifications for a particular procurement.

6.   For greater certainty, this Article is not intended to preclude a procuring entity from preparing, adopting, or applying technical specifications to promote the conservation of natural resources or the protection of the environment.

7.   For greater certainty, this Chapter is not intended to preclude a Party, or its procuring entities, from preparing, adopting, or applying technical specifications required to protect sensitive government information, including specifications that may affect or limit the storage, hosting, or processing of such information outside the territory of the Party.

Article 13.12:   Tender Documentation

1.   A procuring entity shall promptly make available or provide on request to any interested supplier tender documentation that includes all information necessary to permit the supplier to prepare and submit a responsive tender. Unless already provided in the notice of intended procurement, that tender documentation shall include a complete description of:

   (a)   the procurement, including the nature, scope and, if known, the quantity of the good or service to be procured or, if the quantity is not known, the estimated quantity and any requirements to be fulfilled, including any technical specifications, conformity certification, plans, drawings, or instructional materials;

(b)   any conditions for participation, including any financial guarantees, information, and documents that suppliers are required to submit;

(c)   all criteria to be considered in the awarding of the contract and the relative importance of those criteria;

(d)   if there will be a public opening of tenders, the date, time, and place for the opening;

(e)   any other terms or conditions relevant to the evaluation of tenders; and

(f)   any date for delivery of a good or supply of a service.

2.   In establishing any date for the delivery of a good or the supply of a service being procured, a procuring entity shall take into account factors such as the complexity of the procurement, the extent of subcontracting anticipated, and the realistic time required for production, de-stocking, and transport of goods from the point of supply or for supply of services.

3.   A procuring entity shall promptly reply to any reasonable request for relevant information by an interested or participating supplier, provided that the information does not give that supplier an advantage over other suppliers.

Modifications

4.   If, prior to the award of a contract, a procuring entity modifies the evaluation criteria or requirements set out in a notice of intended procurement or tender documentation provided to a participating supplier, or amends, or re-issues a notice or tender documentation, it shall publish or provide those modifications, or the amended or re-issued notice or tender documentation:

(a)   to all suppliers that are participating in the procurement at the time of the modification, amendment, or re-issuance, if those suppliers are known to the procuring entity, and in all other cases, in the same manner as the original information was made available; and

(b)   in adequate time to allow those suppliers to modify and re-submit their initial tender, if appropriate.

Article 13.13:   Time Periods

General

1.   A procuring entity shall, consistent with its own reasonable needs, provide sufficient time for a supplier to obtain the tender documentation and to prepare and submit a request for participation and a responsive tender, taking into account factors such as:

(a)   the nature and complexity of the procurement; and

(b)   the time necessary for transmitting tenders by non-electronic means from foreign as well as domestic points if electronic means are not used.

Deadlines

2.   A procuring entity that uses selective tendering shall establish that the final date for the submission of a request for participation shall not, in principle, be less than 25 days from the date of publication of the notice of intended procurement. If a state of urgency duly substantiated by the procuring entity renders this time period impracticable, the time period may be reduced to no less than 10 days.

3.   Except as provided in paragraphs 4 and 5, a procuring entity shall establish that the final date for the submission of tenders shall not be less than 40 days from the date on which:

(a)   in the case of open tendering, the notice of intended procurement is published; or

(b)   in the case of selective tendering, the procuring entity notifies the suppliers that they will be invited to submit tenders, whether or not it uses a multi-use list.

4.   A procuring entity may reduce the time period for tendering set out in paragraph 3 by five days for each one of the following circumstances:

(a)   the notice of intended procurement is published by electronic means;

(b)   the tender documentation is made available by electronic means from the date of the publication of the notice of intended procurement; and

(c)   the procuring entity accepts tenders by electronic means.

5.   A procuring entity may reduce the time period for tendering set out in paragraph 3 to no less than 10 days if:

(a)   the procuring entity has published a notice of planned procurement under Article 13.6 (Notices of Intended Procurement) at least 40 days and no more than 12 months in advance of the publication of the notice of intended procurement, and the notice of planned procurement contains:

(i)   a description of the procurement,

(ii)   the approximate final dates for the submission of tenders or requests for participation,

(iii) the address from which documents relating to the procurement may be obtained, and

(iv)   as much of the information that is required for the notice of intended procurement as is available;

(b)   a state of urgency duly substantiated by the procuring entity renders impracticable the time period for tendering set out in paragraph 3; or

(c)   the procuring entity procures commercial goods or services.

6.   The use of paragraph 4, in conjunction with paragraph 5, shall in no case result in the reduction of the time periods for tendering set out in paragraph 3 to less than 10 days.

7.   A procuring entity shall require all interested or participating suppliers to submit requests for participation or tenders in accordance with a common deadline. These time periods, and any extension of these time periods, shall be the same for all interested or participating suppliers.

Article 13.14:   Treatment of Tenders and Awarding of Contracts

Treatment of Tenders

1.   A procuring entity shall receive, open and treat all tenders under procedures that guarantee the fairness and impartiality of the procurement process and the confidentiality of tenders.

2.   If the tender of a supplier is received after the time specified for receiving tenders, the procuring entity shall not penalize that supplier if the delay is due solely to the mishandling on the part of the procuring entity.

3.   If a procuring entity provides a supplier with an opportunity to correct unintentional errors of form between the opening of tenders and the awarding of the contract, the procuring entity shall provide the same opportunity to all participating suppliers.

Awarding of Contracts

4.   To be considered for an award, a tender shall be submitted in writing and shall, at the time of opening, comply with the essential requirements set out in the notice and tender documentation and be submitted by a supplier who satisfies the conditions for participation.

5.   Unless a procuring entity determines that it is not in the public interest to award a contract, it shall award the contract to the supplier that the procuring entity has determined to be fully capable of fulfilling the terms of the contract and that, based solely on the evaluation criteria specified in the notice and tender documentation, submits:

(a)   the most advantageous tender; or

(b)   if price is the sole criterion, the lowest price.

6.   If a procuring entity received a tender with a price that is abnormally lower than the prices in other tenders submitted, it may verify with the supplier that it satisfies the conditions for participation and is capable of fulfilling the terms of the contract.

7.   A procuring entity shall not use options, cancel a covered procurement, or modify or terminate awarded contracts in order to avoid the obligations of this Chapter.

Article 13.15:   Transparency and Post-Award Information

Information Provided to Suppliers

1. A procuring entity shall promptly inform suppliers that have submitted a tender of the contract award decision. The procuring entity may do so in writing or through the prompt publication of the notice in paragraph 3, provided that the notice includes the date of award. If a supplier has requested the information in writing, the procuring entity shall provide it in writing.

2. Subject to Article 13.16 (Disclosure of Information), a procuring entity shall, on request, provide an unsuccessful supplier with an explanation of the reasons why the procuring entity did not select the unsuccessful supplier's tender or an explanation of the relative advantages of the successful supplier's tender.

Publication of Award Information

3. A procuring entity shall, promptly after the award of a contract for a covered procurement, publish in an officially designated publication a notice containing at least the following information:

    (a) a description of the good or service procured;

    (b) the name and address of the procuring entity;

    (c) the name and address of the successful supplier;

    (d) the value of the contract award;

    (e) the date of award or, if the procuring entity has already informed suppliers of the date of the award under paragraph 1, the contract date; and

    (f) the procurement method used and, if a procedure was used pursuant to Article 13.9 (Limited Tendering), a brief description of the circumstances justifying the use of that procedure.

Maintenance of Records

4. A procuring entity shall maintain the documentation, records and reports relating to tendering procedures and contract awards for covered procurement, including the records and reports provided for in Article 13.9.3 (Limited Tendering), for at least three years after the award of a contract.

Collection and Reporting of Statistics

5. Each Party shall prepare a statistical report on its covered procurement, and make such report publicly available on an official website. Each report shall cover one year and be available within two years of the end of the reporting period, and shall contain:

    (a) for Section A procuring entities:

        (i) the number and total value, for all such entities, of all contracts covered by this Chapter,

    (ii)   the number and total value of all contracts covered by this Chapter awarded by each such entity, broken down by categories of goods and services according to an internationally recognized uniform classification system, and

    (iii) the number and total value of all contracts covered by this Chapter awarded by each such entity under limited tendering;

(b)   for Section B procuring entities, the number and total value of contracts covered by this Chapter awarded by all such entities; and

(c)   estimates for the data required under subparagraphs (a) and (b), with an explanation of the methodology used to develop the estimates, if it is not feasible to provide the data.

Article 13.16:   Disclosure of Information

Provision of Information to Parties

1.   On request of the other Party, a Party shall provide promptly information sufficient to demonstrate whether a procurement was conducted fairly, impartially and in accordance with this Chapter, including, if applicable, information on the characteristics and relative advantages of the successful tender, without disclosing confidential information. The Party that receives the information shall not disclose it to any supplier, except after consulting with, and obtaining the agreement of, the Party that provided the information.

Non-Disclosure of Information

2.   Notwithstanding any other provision of this Chapter, a Party, including its procuring entities, shall not, except to the extent required by law or with the written authorization of the supplier that provided the information, disclose information that would prejudice legitimate commercial interests of a particular supplier or that might prejudice fair competition between suppliers.

3.   Nothing in this Chapter shall be construed to require a Party, including its procuring entities, authorities, and review bodies, to disclose confidential information if that disclosure:

(a)   would impede law enforcement;

(b)   might prejudice fair competition between suppliers;

(c)   would prejudice the legitimate commercial interests of particular persons, including the protection of intellectual property; or

(d)   would otherwise be contrary to the public interest.

Article 13.17:   Ensuring Integrity in Procurement Practices

1.   Each Party shall ensure that criminal, civil, or administrative measures exist that can address corruption, fraud, and other wrongful acts in its government procurement.

2.   These measures may include procedures to debar, suspend, or declare ineligible from participation in the Party's procurements, for a stated period of time, a supplier that the Party has determined to have engaged in corruption, fraud, or other wrongful acts relevant to a supplier's eligibility to participate in a Party's government procurement. Each Party:

   (a)   may consider the seriousness of the supplier's acts or omissions and any remedial measures or mitigating factors in making any decisions on debarment or suspension, including in making a decision on whether to reduce the period or extent of debarment or suspension at the supplier's request pursuant to paragraph 2(b)(ii); and

   (b)   shall provide a supplier of the other Party directly implicated by a proceeding applying procedures adopted or maintained under paragraph 2:

      (i)   reasonable notice that the proceeding was initiated, including a description of the nature of the proceeding, a statement of the authority under which the proceeding was initiated, and the reasons for the proceeding, and

      (ii)   reasonable opportunity to present facts and arguments in support of its position; and

   (c)   shall publish and update a list of enterprises and, subject to its law, natural persons it has debarred, suspended, or declared ineligible.

3.   Each Party shall ensure that it has in place policies or procedures to address potential conflicts of interest on the part of those engaged in or having influence over a procurement.

4.   Each Party may also put in place policies or procedures, including provisions in tender documentation, that require successful suppliers to maintain and enforce effective internal controls, business ethics, and compliance programs, taking into account the size of the supplier, particularly SMEs, and other relevant factors, for preventing and detecting corruption, fraud, and other wrongful acts.

Article 13.18:   Domestic Review

1.   Each Party shall maintain, establish, or designate at least one impartial administrative or judicial authority (review authority) that is independent of its procuring entities to review, in a non-discriminatory, timely, transparent, and effective manner, a challenge or complaint (complaint) by a supplier that there has been:

(a) a breach of this Chapter; or

(b) if the supplier does not have a right to directly challenge a breach of this Chapter under the law of a Party, a failure of a procuring entity to comply with the Party's measures implementing this Chapter,

arising in the context of a covered procurement, in which the supplier has, or had, an interest. The procedural rules for these complaints shall be in writing and made generally available.

2. In the event of a complaint by a supplier, arising in the context of covered procurement in which the supplier has, or had, an interest, that there has been a breach or a failure as referred to in paragraph 1, the Party of the procuring entity conducting the procurement shall encourage, if appropriate, the procuring entity and the supplier to seek resolution of the complaint through consultations. The procuring entity shall accord impartial and timely consideration to the complaint in a manner that is not prejudicial to the supplier's participation in ongoing or future procurement or to its right to seek corrective measures under the administrative or judicial review procedure. Each Party shall make information on its complaint mechanisms generally available.

3. If a body other than the review authority initially reviews a complaint, a Party shall ensure that the supplier may appeal the initial decision to the review authority that is independent of the procuring entity that is the subject of the complaint.

4. If the review authority has determined that there has been a breach or a failure as referred to in paragraph 1, a Party may limit compensation for the loss or damages suffered to either the costs reasonably incurred in the preparation of the tender or in bringing the complaint, or both.

5. Each Party shall ensure that, if the review authority is not a court, its review procedures are conducted in accordance with the following procedures:

(a) a supplier shall be allowed sufficient time to prepare and submit a complaint in writing, which in no case shall be less than 10 days from the time when the basis of the complaint became known or reasonably should have become known to the supplier;

(b) a procuring entity shall respond in writing to a supplier's complaint and provide all relevant documents to the review authority;

(c) a supplier that initiates a complaint shall be provided an opportunity to reply to the procuring entity's response before the review authority takes a decision on the complaint; and

(d) the review authority shall provide its decision on a supplier's complaint in a timely manner, in writing, with an explanation of the basis for the decision.

6.   Each Party shall adopt or maintain procedures that provide for:

(a)   prompt interim measures, pending the resolution of a complaint, to preserve the supplier's opportunity to participate in the procurement and to ensure that the procuring entities of the Party comply with its measures implementing this Chapter; and

(b)   corrective action that may include compensation under paragraph 4.

The procedures may provide that overriding adverse consequences for the interests concerned, including the public interest, may be taken into account when deciding whether those measures should be applied. Just cause for not acting shall be provided in writing.

Article 13.19:   Modifications and Rectifications of Annex

1.   A Party shall notify any proposed modification or rectification (modification) to its Schedule to Annex 13-A by circulating a notice in writing to the other Party through the Agreement Coordinator designated under Article 30.5 (Agreement Coordinator and Contact Points). A Party shall provide compensatory adjustments for a change in coverage if necessary to maintain a level of coverage comparable to the coverage that existed prior to the modification. The Party may include the offer of compensatory adjustment in its notice.

2.   A Party is not required to provide compensatory adjustments to the other Party if the proposed modification concerns one of the following:

(a)   a procuring entity over which the Party has effectively eliminated its control or influence in respect of covered procurement by that procuring entity; or

(b)   rectifications of a purely formal nature and minor modifications to its Schedule to Annex 13-A, such as:

(i)   changes in the name of a procuring entity,

(ii)   the merger of one or more procuring entities listed in its Schedule,

(iii) the separation of a procuring entity listed in its Schedule into two or more procuring entities that are all added to the procuring entities listed in the same Section of the Annex, or

(iv)   changes in website references,

and the other Party does not object under paragraph 3 on the basis that the proposed modification does not concern subparagraph (a) or (b).

3.   A Party whose rights under this Chapter may be affected by a proposed modification that is notified under paragraph 1 shall notify the other Party of any objection to the proposed modification within 45 days of the date of circulation of the notice.

4.   If a Party objects to a proposed modification, including a modification regarding a procuring entity on the basis that government control or influence over the entity's covered procurement has been effectively eliminated, that Party may request additional information, including information on the nature of any government control or influence, with a view to clarifying and reaching agreement on the proposed modification, including the procuring entity's continued coverage under this Chapter. The modifying Party and the objecting Party shall make every attempt to resolve the objection through consultations.

5.   The Commission shall modify Annex 13-A to reflect any agreed modification.

Article 13.20:   Facilitation of Participation by SMEs

1.   The Parties recognize the important contribution that SMEs can make to economic growth and employment and the importance of facilitating the participation of SMEs in government procurement.

2.   If a Party maintains a measure that provides preferential treatment for SMEs, the Party shall ensure that the measure, including the criteria for eligibility, is transparent.

3.   To facilitate participation by SMEs in covered procurement, each Party shall, to the extent possible and if appropriate:

(a)   provide comprehensive procurement-related information that includes a definition of SMEs in a single electronic portal;

(b)   endeavor to make all tender documentation available free of charge;

(c)   conduct procurement by electronic means or through other new information and communication technologies; and

(d)   consider the size, design, and structure of the procurement, including the use of subcontracting by SMEs.

Article 13.21:   Committee on Government Procurement

1.   The Parties hereby establish a Committee on Government Procurement (Government Procurement Committee), composed of government representatives of each Party. On request of a Party, the Government Procurement Committee shall meet to address matters related to the implementation and operation of this Chapter, such as:

(a)   facilitation of participation by SMEs in covered procurement, as provided for in Article 13.20 (Facilitation of Participation by SMEs);

(b)   experiences and best practices in the use and adoption of information technology in conducting covered procurement. This could include topics such as the use of digital modeling in construction services; and

(c) experiences and best practices in the use and adoption of measures to promote opportunities for socially or economically disadvantaged people when conducting covered procurement.

CHAPTER 14   INVESTMENT

Article 14.1:   Definitions

For the purposes of this Chapter:

Covered investment means, with respect to a Party, an investment in its territory of an investor of another Party in existence as of the date of entry into force of this Agreement or established, acquired, or expanded thereafter;

Enterprise means an enterprise as defined in Article 1.4 (General Definitions), and a branch of an enterprise;

Enterprise of a Party means an enterprise constituted or organized under the law of a Party, or a branch located in the territory of a Party and carrying out business activities there;

Freely usable currency means "freely usable currency" as determined by the International Monetary Fund under its *Articles of Agreement*;

Investment means every asset that an investor owns or controls, directly or indirectly, that has the characteristics of an investment, including such characteristics as the commitment of capital or other resources, the expectation of gain or profit, or the assumption of risk. An investment may include:

(a) an enterprise;

(b) shares, stock and other forms of equity participation in an enterprise;

(c) bonds, debentures, other debt instruments, and loans;[1]

(d) futures, options, and other derivatives;

(e) turnkey, construction, management, production, concession, revenue-sharing, and other similar contracts;

(f) intellectual property rights;

(g) licenses, authorizations, permits, and similar rights conferred pursuant to a Party's law;[2] and

---

[1] Some forms of debt, such as bonds, debentures, and long-term notes or loans, are more likely to have the characteristics of an investment, while other forms of debt, such as claims to payment that are immediately due, are less likely to have these characteristics.

[2] Whether a particular type of license, authorization, permit, or similar instrument (including a concession to the extent that it has the nature of such an instrument) has the characteristics of an investment depends on such factors as the nature and extent of the rights that the holder has under a Party's law. For greater certainty, among such instruments that do not have the characteristics of an investment are those that do not create any rights protected under the Party's law.

(h)   other tangible or intangible, movable or immovable property, and related property rights, such as liens, mortgages, pledges, and leases,

but investment does not mean:

(i)   an order or judgment entered in a judicial or administrative action;

(j)   claims to money that arise solely from:

(i)   commercial contracts for the sale of goods or services by a natural person or enterprise in the territory of a Party to an enterprise in the territory of another Party, or

(ii)   the extension of credit in connection with a commercial contract referred to in subparagraph (j)(i);

Investor of a non-Party means, with respect to a Party, an investor that attempts to make,[3] is making, or has made an investment in the territory of that Party, that is not an investor of a Party; and

Investor of a Party means a Party, or a national or an enterprise of a Party, that attempts to make, is making, or has made an investment in the territory of another Party, provided however that:

(a)   a natural person who is a dual citizen is deemed to be exclusively a national of the State of his or her dominant and effective citizenship; and

(b)   a natural person who is a citizen of a Party and a permanent resident of another Party is deemed to be exclusively a national of the Party of which that natural person is a citizen.

Article 14.2:   Scope

1.   This Chapter applies to measures adopted or maintained by a Party relating to:

(a)   investors of another Party;

(b)   covered investments; and

(c)   with respect to Article 14.10 (Performance Requirements) and Article 14.16 (Investment and Environmental, Health, Safety, and other Regulatory Objectives), all investments in the territory of that Party.

2.   A Party's obligations under this Chapter apply to measures adopted or maintained by:

For greater certainty, the foregoing is without prejudice to whether any asset associated with such instruments has the characteristics of an investment.

   [3]   For greater certainty, the Parties understand that, for the purposes of the definitions of "investor of a non-Party" and "investor of a Party", an investor "attempts to make" an investment when that investor has taken concrete action or actions to make an investment, such as channeling resources or capital in order to set up a business, or applying for a permit or license.

    (a)   the central, regional, or local governments or authorities of that Party;[4] and

    (b)   a person, including a state enterprise or another body, when it exercises any governmental authority delegated to it by central, regional, or local governments or authorities of that Party.[5]

3.   For greater certainty, this Chapter, except as provided for in Annex 14-C (Legacy Investment Claims and Pending Claims) does not bind a Party in relation to an act or fact that took place or a situation that ceased to exist before the date of entry into force of this Agreement.

4.   For greater certainty, an investor may only submit a claim to arbitration under this Chapter as provided under Annex 14-C (Legacy Investment Claims and Pending Claims), Annex 14-D (Mexico-United States Investment Disputes), or Annex 14-E (Mexico-United States Investment Disputes Related to Covered Government Contracts).

Article 14.3:   Relation to Other Chapters

1.   In the event of any inconsistency between this Chapter and another Chapter of this Agreement, the other Chapter shall prevail to the extent of the inconsistency.

2.   This Chapter does not apply to measures adopted or maintained by a Party to the extent that they are covered by Chapter 17 (Financial Services).

3.   A requirement of a Party that a service supplier of another Party post a bond or other form of financial security as a condition for the cross-border supply of a service does not of itself make this Chapter applicable to measures adopted or maintained by the Party relating to the cross-border supply of the service. This Chapter applies to measures adopted or maintained by the Party relating to the posted bond or financial security, to the extent that the bond or financial security is a covered investment.

4.   For greater certainty, consistent with Article 15.2.2(a) (Scope), Article 15.5 (Market Access), and Article 15.8 (Development and Administration of Measures) apply to measures adopted or maintained by a Party relating to the supply of a service in its territory by a covered investment.

Article 14.4:   National Treatment

1.   Each Party shall accord to investors of another Party treatment no less favorable than that it accords, in like circumstances, to its own

---

[4]   For greater certainty, the term "governments or authorities" means the organs of a Party, consistent with the principles of attribution under customary international law.

[5]   For greater certainty, governmental authority is delegated to any person under the Party's law, including through a legislative grant or a government order, directive, or other act transferring or authorizing the exercise **of** governmental authority.

investors with respect to the establishment, acquisition, expansion, management, conduct, operation, and sale or other disposition of investments in its territory.

2.   Each Party shall accord to covered investments treatment no less favorable than that it accords, in like circumstances, to investments in its territory of its own investors with respect to the establishment, acquisition, expansion, management, conduct, operation, and sale or other disposition of investments.

3.   The treatment accorded by a Party under paragraphs 1 and 2 means, with respect to a government other than at the central level, treatment no less favorable than the most favorable treatment accorded, in like circumstances, by that government to investors, and to investments of investors, of the Party of which it forms a part.

4.   For greater certainty, whether treatment is accorded in "like circumstances" under this Article depends on the totality of the circumstances, including whether the relevant treatment distinguishes between investors or investments on the basis of legitimate public welfare objectives.

Article 14.5:   Most-Favored-Nation Treatment

1.   Each Party shall accord to investors of another Party treatment no less favorable than the treatment it accords, in like circumstances, to investors of any other Party or of any non-Party with respect to the establishment, acquisition, expansion, management, conduct, operation, and sale or other disposition of investments in its territory.

2.   Each Party shall accord to covered investments treatment no less favorable than that it accords, in like circumstances, to investments in its territory of investors of any other Party or of any non-Party with respect to the establishment, acquisition, expansion, management, conduct, operation, and sale or other disposition of investments.

3.   The treatment accorded by a Party under paragraphs 1 and 2 means, with respect to a government other than at the central level, treatment no less favorable than the most favorable treatment accorded, in like circumstances, by that government to investors in its territory, and to investments of those investors, of any other Party or of any non-Party.

4.   For greater certainty, whether treatment is accorded in "like circumstances" under this Article depends on the totality of the circumstances, including whether the relevant treatment distinguishes between investors or investments on the basis of legitimate public welfare objectives.

Article 14.6:   Minimum Standard of Treatment[6]

1. Each Party shall accord to covered investments treatment in accordance with customary international law, including fair and equitable treatment and full protection and security.

2. For greater certainty, paragraph 1 prescribes the customary international law minimum standard of treatment of aliens as the standard of treatment to be afforded to covered investments. The concepts of "fair and equitable treatment" and "full protection and security" do not require treatment in addition to or beyond that which is required by that standard, and do not create additional substantive rights. The obligations in paragraph 1 to provide:

    (a) "fair and equitable treatment" includes the obligation not to deny justice in criminal, civil, or administrative adjudicatory proceedings in accordance with the principle of due process embodied in the principal legal systems of the world; and

    (b) "full protection and security" requires each Party to provide the level of police protection required under customary international law.

3. A determination that there has been a breach of another provision of this Agreement, or of a separate international agreement, does not establish that there has been a breach of this Article.

4. For greater certainty, the mere fact that a Party takes or fails to take an action that may be inconsistent with an investor's expectations does not constitute a breach of this Article, even if there is loss or damage to the covered investment as a result.

Article 14.7:   Treatment in Case of Armed Conflict or Civil Strife

1. Notwithstanding Article 14.12.5(b) (Non-Conforming Measures), each Party shall accord to investors of another Party and to covered investments non-discriminatory treatment with respect to measures it adopts or maintains relating to losses suffered by investments in its territory owing to armed conflict or civil strife.

2. Notwithstanding paragraph 1, if an investor of a Party, in a situation referred to in paragraph 1, suffers a loss in the territory of another Party resulting from:

    (a) requisitioning of its covered investment or part thereof by the latter's forces or authorities; or

    (b) destruction of its covered investment or part thereof by the latter's forces or authorities, which was not required by the necessity of the situation,

the latter Party shall provide the investor restitution, compensation, or both, as appropriate, for that loss.

---

[6]   This Article shall be interpreted in accordance with Annex 14-A (Customary International Law).

3. Paragraph 1 does not apply to existing measures relating to subsidies or grants that would be inconsistent with Article 14.4 (National Treatment) but for Article 14.12.5(b) (Non-Conforming Measures).

Article 14.8:   Expropriation and Compensation[7]

1. No Party shall expropriate or nationalize a covered investment either directly or indirectly through measures equivalent to expropriation or nationalization (expropriation), except:

    (a)   for a public purpose;

    (b)   in a non-discriminatory manner;

    (c)   on payment of prompt, adequate, and effective compensation in accordance with paragraphs 2, 3, and 4; and

    (d)   in accordance with due process of law.

2. Compensation shall:

    (a)   be paid without delay;

    (b)   be equivalent to the fair market value of the expropriated investment immediately before the expropriation took place (the date of expropriation);

    (c)   not reflect any change in value occurring because the intended expropriation had become known earlier; and

    (d)   be fully realizable and freely transferable.

3. If the fair market value is denominated in a freely usable currency, the compensation paid shall be no less than the fair market value on the date of expropriation, plus interest at a commercially reasonable rate for that currency, accrued from the date of expropriation until the date of payment.

4. If the fair market value is denominated in a currency that is not freely usable, the compensation paid—converted into the currency of payment at the market rate of exchange prevailing on the date of payment[8]— shall be no less than:

    (a)   the fair market value on the date of expropriation, converted into a freely usable currency at the market rate of exchange prevailing on that date; plus

    (b)   interest, at a commercially reasonable rate for that freely usable currency, accrued from the date of expropriation until the date of payment.

---

[7]   This Article shall be interpreted in accordance with Annex 14-B (Expropriation).

[8]   For greater certainty, for the purposes of this paragraph, the currency of payment may be the same as the currency in which the fair market value is denominated.

5.   For greater certainty, whether an action or series of actions by a Party constitutes an expropriation shall be determined in accordance with paragraph 1 of this Article and Annex 14-B (Expropriation).

6.   This Article does not apply to the issuance of compulsory licenses granted in relation to intellectual property rights in accordance with the TRIPS Agreement, or to the revocation, limitation, or creation of intellectual property rights, to the extent that the issuance, revocation, limitation, or creation is consistent with Chapter 20 (Intellectual Property) and the TRIPS Agreement.[9]

Article 14.9:   Transfers

1.   Each Party shall permit all transfers relating to a covered investment to be made freely and without delay into and out of its territory. These transfers include:

   (a)   contributions to capital;[10]

   (b)   profits, dividends, interest, capital gains, royalty payments, management fees, technical assistance, and other fees;

   (c)   proceeds from the sale of all or any part of the covered investment or from the partial or complete liquidation of the covered investment;

   (d)   payments made under a contract entered into by the investor, or the covered investment, including payments made pursuant to a loan agreement or employment contract; and

   (e)   payments made pursuant to Article 14.7 (Treatment in Case of Armed Conflict or Civil Strife) and Article 14.8 (Expropriation and Compensation).

2.   Each Party shall permit transfers relating to a covered investment to be made in a freely usable currency at the market rate of exchange prevailing at the time of transfer.

3.   A Party shall not require its investors to transfer, or penalize its investors that fail to transfer, the income, earnings, profits, or other amounts derived from, or attributable to, investments in the territory of another Party.

4.   Each Party shall permit returns in kind relating to a covered investment to be made as authorized or specified in a written agreement between the Party and a covered investment or an investor of another Party.

---

[9]   For greater certainty, the Parties recognize that, for the purposes of this Article, the term "revocation" of an intellectual property right includes the cancellation or nullification of that right, and the term "limitation" of an intellectual property right includes exceptions to that right.

[10]   For greater certainty, contributions to capital include the initial contribution.

5.   Notwithstanding paragraphs 1, 2, and 4, a Party may prevent or delay a transfer through the equitable, non-discriminatory, and good faith application of its laws[11] relating to:

    (a)   bankruptcy, insolvency, or the protection of the rights of creditors;

    (b)   issuing, trading, or dealing in securities or derivatives;

    (c)   criminal or penal offenses;

    (d)   financial reporting or record keeping of transfers when necessary to assist law enforcement or financial regulatory authorities; or

    (e)   ensuring compliance with orders or judgments in judicial or administrative proceedings.

6.   Notwithstanding paragraph 4, a Party may restrict transfers of returns in kind in circumstances where it could otherwise restrict those transfers under this Agreement, including as set out in paragraph 5.

Article 14.10:   Performance Requirements

1.   No Party shall, in connection with the establishment, acquisition, expansion, management, conduct, operation, or sale or other disposition of an investment of an investor of a Party or of a non-Party in its territory, impose or enforce any requirement, or enforce any commitment or undertaking:[12]

    (a)   to export a given level or percentage of goods or services;

    (b)   to achieve a given level or percentage of domestic content;

    (c)   to purchase, use, or accord a preference to a good produced or a service supplied in its territory, or to purchase a good or a service from a person in its territory;

    (d)   to regulate in any way the volume or value of imports to the volume or value of exports or to the amount of foreign exchange inflows associated with the investment;

    (e)   to restrict sales of a good or a service in its territory that the investment produces or supplies by relating those sales in any way to the volume or value of its exports or foreign exchange earnings;

    (f)   to transfer a technology, a production process, or other proprietary knowledge to a person in its territory;

---

[11]   For greater certainty, this Article does not preclude the equitable, non-discriminatory, and good faith application of a Party's laws relating to its social security, public retirement, or compulsory savings programs.

[12]   For greater certainty, a condition for the receipt or continued receipt of an advantage referred to in paragraph 2 does not constitute a "requirement" or a "commitment or undertaking" for the purposes of paragraph 1.

(g)   to supply exclusively from the territory of the Party a good that the investment produces or a service that it supplies to a specific regional market or to the world market;

(h)   (i) to purchase, use, or accord a preference to, in its territory, technology of the Party or of a person of the Party,[13] or

        (ii)   that prevents the purchase or use of, or the according of a preference to, in its territory, a technology; or

(i)   to adopt:

        (i)   a given rate or amount of royalty under a license contract, or

        (ii)   a given duration of the term of a license contract,

        in regard to any license contract in existence at the time the requirement is imposed or enforced, or any commitment or undertaking is enforced, or any future license contract[14] freely entered into between the investor and a person in its territory, provided that the requirement is imposed or the commitment or undertaking is enforced in a manner that constitutes direct interference with that license contract by an exercise of non-judicial governmental authority of a Party. For greater certainty, paragraph 1(i) does not apply when the license contract is concluded between the investor and a Party.

2.   No Party shall condition the receipt or continued receipt of an advantage, in connection with the establishment, acquisition, expansion, management, conduct, operation, or sale or other disposition of an investment of an investor of a Party or of a non-Party in its territory, on compliance with any requirement:

(a)   to achieve a given level or percentage of domestic content;

(b)   to purchase, use, or accord a preference to a good produced in its territory, or to purchase a good from a person in its territory;

(c)   to relate in any way the volume or value of imports to the volume or value of exports or to the amount of foreign exchange inflows associated with the investment;

(d)   to restrict sales of goods or services in its territory that the investment produces or supplies by relating those sales in any way to the volume or value of its exports or foreign exchange earnings; or

---

[13]   For the purposes of this Article, the term "technology of the Party or of a person of the Party" includes technology that is owned by the Party or a person of the Party, and technology for which the Party or a person of the Party holds an exclusive license.

[14]   A "license contract" referred to in this subparagraph means a contract concerning the licensing of technology, a production process, or other proprietary knowledge.

(e) (i) to purchase, use or accord a preference to, in its territory, technology of the Party or of a person of the Party, or

    (ii) that prevents the purchase or use of, or the according of a preference to, in its territory, a technology.

3. In relation to paragraphs 1 and 2:

(a) Nothing in paragraph 2 shall be construed to prevent a Party from conditioning the receipt or continued receipt of an advantage, in connection with an investment of an investor of a Party or of a non-Party in its territory, on compliance with a requirement to locate production, supply a service, train or employ workers, construct or expand particular facilities, or carry out research and development, in its territory.

(b) Paragraphs 1(f), 1(h), 1(i), and 2(e) do not apply:

    (i) if a Party authorizes use of an intellectual property right in accordance with Article 31[15] of the TRIPS Agreement, or to a measure requiring the disclosure of proprietary information that fall within the scope of, and is consistent with, Article 39 of the TRIPS Agreement, or

    (ii) if the requirement is imposed or the commitment or undertaking[16] is enforced by a court, administrative tribunal, or competition authority, after judicial or administrative process, to remedy an alleged violation of competition laws.[17]

(c) Provided that such measures are not applied in an arbitrary or unjustifiable manner, or do not constitute a disguised restriction on international trade or investment, paragraphs 1(b), 1(c), 1(f), 2(a), and 2(b) shall not be construed to prevent a Party from adopting or maintaining measures:

    (i) necessary to secure compliance with laws and regulations that are not inconsistent with this Agreement,

    (ii) necessary to protect human, animal or plant life or health, or

    (iii) related to the conservation of living or non-living exhaustible natural resources.

---

[15] The reference to "Article 31" includes any waiver or amendment to the TRIPS Agreement implementing paragraph 6 of the *Doha Declaration on the TRIPS Agreement and Public Health* (WT/MIN (01)/DEC/2).

[16] For greater certainty, for the purposes of this subparagraph, a commitment or undertaking includes a consent agreement.

[17] The Parties recognize that a patent does not necessarily confer market power.

(d)   Paragraphs 1(a), 1(b), 1(c), 2(a), and 2(b) do not apply to qualification requirements for a good or a service with respect to export promotion and foreign aid programs.

(e)   Paragraphs 1(b), 1(c), 1(f), 1(g), 1(h), 1(i), 2(a), 2(b), and 2(e) do not apply to government procurement.

(f)   Paragraphs 2(a) and 2(b) do not apply to requirements imposed by an importing Party relating to the content of a good necessary to qualify for preferential tariffs or preferential quotas.

(g)   Paragraphs 1(h), 1(i), and 2(e) shall not be construed to prevent a Party from adopting or maintaining measures to protect legitimate public welfare objectives, provided that such measures are not applied in an arbitrary or unjustifiable manner, or in a manner that constitutes a disguised restriction on international trade or investment.

4.   For greater certainty, paragraphs 1 and 2 do not apply to any commitment, undertaking, or requirement other than those set out in those paragraphs.

5.   This Article does not preclude enforcement of any commitment, undertaking, or requirement between private parties, if a Party did not impose or require the commitment, undertaking, or requirement.

Article 14.11:   Senior Management and Boards of Directors

1.   No Party shall require that an enterprise of that Party that is a covered investment appoint to senior management positions a natural person of a particular nationality.

2.   A Party may require that a majority of the board of directors, or any committee thereof, of an enterprise of that Party that is a covered investment, be of a particular nationality, or resident in the territory of the Party, provided that the requirement does not materially impair the ability of the investor to exercise control over its investment.

Article 14.12:   Non-Conforming Measures

1.   Article 14.4 (National Treatment), Article 14.5 (Most-Favored-Nation Treatment), Article 14.10 (Performance Requirements), and Article 14.11 (Senior Management and Boards of Directors) do not apply to:

(a)   any existing non-conforming measure that is maintained by a Party at:

(i)   the central level of government, as set out by that Party in its Schedule to Annex I,

(ii)   a regional level of government, as set out by that Party in its Schedule to Annex I, or

(iii)   a local level of government;

(b)   the continuation or prompt renewal of any non-conforming measure referred to in subparagraph (a); or

(c)   an amendment to any non-conforming measure referred to in subparagraph (a) to the extent that the amendment does not decrease the conformity of the measure, as it existed immediately before the amendment, with Article 14.4 (National Treatment), Article 14.5 (Most-Favored-Nation Treatment), Article 14.10 (Performance Requirements), or Article 14.11 (Senior Management and Boards of Directors).

2.   Article 14.4 (National Treatment), Article 14.5 (Most-Favored-Nation Treatment), Article 14.10 (Performance Requirements), and Article 14.11 (Senior Management and Boards of Directors) do not apply to any measure that a Party adopts or maintains with respect to sectors, sub-sectors, or activities, as set out by that Party in its Schedule to Annex II.

3.   No Party shall, under any measure adopted after the date of entry into force of this Agreement and covered by its Schedule to Annex II, require an investor of another Party, by reason of its nationality, to sell or otherwise dispose of an investment existing at the time the measure becomes effective.

4.   (a)   Article 14.4 (National Treatment) does not apply to any measure that falls within an exception to, or derogation from, the obligations imposed by:

      (i)   Article 20.8 (National Treatment), or

      (ii)   Article 3 of the TRIPS Agreement, if the exception or derogation relates to matters not addressed by Chapter 20 (Intellectual Property Rights);

   (b)   Article 14.5 (Most-Favored-Nation Treatment) does not apply to any measure that falls within Article 5 of the TRIPS Agreement, or an exception to, or derogation from, an obligation imposed by:

      (i)   Article 20.8 (National Treatment), or

      (ii)   Article 4 of the TRIPS Agreement.

5.   Article 14.4 (National Treatment), Article 14.5 (Most-Favored-Nation Treatment), and Article 14.11 (Senior Management and Boards of Directors) do not apply to:

   (a)   government procurement; or

   (b)   subsidies or grants provided by a Party, including government-supported loans, guarantees, and insurance.

Article 14.13:   Special Formalities and Information Requirements

1.   Nothing in Article 14.4 (National Treatment) shall be construed to prevent a Party from adopting or maintaining a measure that prescribes special formalities in connection with covered investments, such as a requirement that investors be residents of the Party or that covered investments be legally constituted under the laws or regulations of the Party, provided that these formalities do not

materially impair the protections afforded by the Party to investors of another Party and covered investments pursuant to this Chapter.

2.   Notwithstanding Article 14.4 (National Treatment) and Article 14.5 (Most-Favored-Nation Treatment), a Party may require an investor of another Party or its covered investment to provide information concerning that investment solely for informational or statistical purposes. The Party shall protect such information that is confidential from any disclosure that would prejudice the competitive position of the investor or its covered investment. Nothing in this paragraph shall be construed to prevent a Party from otherwise obtaining or disclosing information in connection with the equitable and good faith application of its law.

Article 14.14:   Denial of Benefits

1.   A Party may deny the benefits of this Chapter to an investor of another Party that is an enterprise of that other Party and to investments of that investor if the enterprise:

(a)   is owned or controlled by a person of a non-Party or of the denying Party; and

(b)   has no substantial business activities in the territory of any Party other than the denying Party.

2.   A Party may deny the benefits of this Chapter to an investor of another Party that is an enterprise of that other Party and to investments of that investor if persons of a non-Party own or control the enterprise and the denying Party adopts or maintains measures with respect to the non-Party or a person of the non-Party that prohibit transactions with the enterprise or that would be violated or circumvented if the benefits of this Chapter were accorded to the enterprise or to its investments.

Article 14.15:   Subrogation

If a Party, or an agency of a Party, makes a payment to an investor of the Party under a guarantee, a contract of insurance, or other form of indemnity that it has entered into with respect to a covered investment, the other Party in whose territory the covered investment was made shall recognize the subrogation or transfer of any right the investor would have possessed with respect to the covered investment but for the subrogation, and the investor shall be precluded from pursuing that right to the extent of the subrogation, unless a Party or an agency of a Party authorizes the investor to act on its behalf.

Article 14.16:   Investment and Environmental, Health, Safety, and other Regulatory Objectives

Nothing in this Chapter shall be construed to prevent a Party from adopting, maintaining, or enforcing any measure otherwise consistent with this Chapter that it considers appropriate to ensure that investment activity in its territory is undertaken in a manner sensitive to environmental, health, safety, or other regulatory objectives.

Article 14.17:   Corporate Social Responsibility

The Parties reaffirm the importance of each Party encouraging enterprises operating within its territory or subject to its jurisdiction to voluntarily incorporate into their internal policies those internationally recognized standards, guidelines, and principles of corporate social responsibility that have been endorsed or are supported by that Party, which may include the OECD Guidelines for Multinational Enterprises. These standards, guidelines, and principles may address areas such as labor, environment, gender equality, human rights, indigenous and aboriginal peoples' rights, and corruption.

ANNEX 14-A CUSTOMARY INTERNATIONAL LAW

The Parties confirm their shared understanding that "customary international law" generally and as specifically referenced in Article 14.6 (Minimum Standard of Treatment) results from a general and consistent practice of States that they follow from a sense of legal obligation. The customary international law minimum standard of treatment of aliens refers to all customary international law principles that protect the investments of aliens.

ANNEX 14-B EXPROPRIATION

The Parties confirm their shared understanding that:

1.   An action or a series of actions by a Party cannot constitute an expropriation unless it interferes with a tangible or intangible property right[18] or property interest in an investment.

2.   Article 14.8.1 (Expropriation and Compensation) addresses two situations. The first is direct expropriation, in which an investment is nationalized or otherwise directly expropriated through formal transfer of title or outright seizure.

3.   The second situation addressed by Article 14.8.1 (Expropriation and Compensation) is indirect expropriation, in which an action or series of actions by a Party has an effect equivalent to direct expropriation without formal transfer of title or outright seizure.

   (a)   The determination of whether an action or series of actions by a Party, in a specific fact situation, constitutes an indirect expropriation, requires a case-by-case, fact-based inquiry that considers, among other factors:

      (i)   the economic impact of the government action, although the fact that an action or series of actions by a Party has an adverse effect on the economic value of an investment, standing alone, does not establish that an indirect expropriation has occurred,

---

[18]   For greater certainty, the existence of a property right is determined with reference to a Party's law.

(ii)   the extent to which the government action interferes with distinct, reasonable investment-backed expectations,[19] and

(iii) the character of the government action, including its object, context, and intent.

(b)   Non-discriminatory regulatory actions by a Party that are designed and applied to protect legitimate public welfare objectives, such as health, safety and the environment, do not constitute indirect expropriations, except in rare circumstances.

ANNEX 14C-LEGACY INVESTMENT CLAIMS AND PENDING CLAIMS

1.   Each Party consents, with respect to a legacy investment, to the submission of a claim to arbitration in accordance with Section B of Chapter 11 (Investment) of NAFTA 1994 and this Annex alleging breach of an obligation under:

(a)   Section A of Chapter 11 (Investment) of NAFTA 1994;

(b)   Article 1503(2) (State Enterprises) of NAFTA 1994; and

(c)   Article 1502(3)(a) (Monopolies and State Enterprises) of NAFTA 1994 where the monopoly has acted in a manner inconsistent with the Party's obligations under Section A of Chapter 11 (Investment) of NAFTA 1994.[20],[21]

2.   The consent under paragraph 1 and the submission of a claim to arbitration in accordance with Section B of Chapter 11 (Investment) of NAFTA 1994 and this Annex shall satisfy the requirements of:

---

[19]   For greater certainty, whether an investor's investment-backed expectations are reasonable depends, to the extent relevant, on factors such as whether the government provided the investor with binding written assurances and the nature and extent of governmental regulation or the potential for government regulation in the relevant sector. ANNEX 14-C

[20]   For greater certainty, the relevant provisions in Chapter 2 (General Definitions), Chapter 11 (Section A) (Investment), Chapter 14 (Financial Services), Chapter 15 (Competition Policy, Monopolies and State Enterprises), Chapter 17 (Intellectual Property), Chapter 21 (Exceptions), and Annexes I-VII (Reservations and Exceptions to Investment, Cross-Border Trade in Services and Financial Services Chapters) of NAFTA 1994 apply with respect to such a claim.

[21]   Mexico and the United States do not consent under paragraph 1 with respect to an investor of the other Party that is eligible to submit claims to arbitration under paragraph 2 of Annex 14-E (Mexico-United States Investment Disputes Related to Covered Government Contracts).For greater certainty, an arbitration initiated pursuant to the submission of a claim under Section B of Chapter 11 (Investment) of NAFTA 1994 while NAFTA 1994 is in force may proceed to its conclusion in accordance with Section B of Chapter 11 (Investment) of NAFTA 1994, the Tribunal's jurisdiction with respect to such a claim is not affected by the termination of NAFTA 1994, and Article 1136 of NAFTA 1994 (excluding paragraph 5) applies with respect to any award made by the Tribunal.

(a) Chapter II of the ICSID Convention (Jurisdiction of the Centre) and the ICSID Additional Facility Rules for written consent of the parties to the dispute;

(b) Article II of the New York Convention for an "agreement in writing"; and

(c) Article I of the Inter-American Convention for an "agreement".

3. A Party's consent under paragraph 1 shall expire three years after the termination of NAFTA 1994.

4. For greater certainty, an arbitration initiated pursuant to the submission of a claim under paragraph 1 may proceed to its conclusion in accordance with Section B of Chapter 11 (Investment) of NAFTA 1994, the Tribunal's jurisdiction with respect to such a claim is not affected by the expiration of consent referenced in paragraph 3, and Article 1136 (Finality and Enforcement of an Award) of NAFTA 1994 (excluding paragraph 5) applies with respect to any award made by the Tribunal.

5. For the purposes of this Annex:

(a) "legacy investment" means an investment of an investor of another Party in the territory of the Party established or acquired between January 1, 1994, and the date of termination of NAFTA 1994, and in existence on the date of entry into force of this Agreement;

(b) "investment", "investor", and "Tribunal" have the meanings accorded in Chapter 11 (Investment) of NAFTA 1994; and

(c) "ICSID Convention", "ICSID Additional Facility Rules", "New York Convention", and "Inter-American Convention" have the meanings accorded in Article 14.D.1 (Definitions).

ANNEX 14-D MEXICO-UNITED STATES INVESTMENT DISPUTES

Article 14.D.1: Definitions

For the purposes of this Annex:

Annex Party means Mexico or the United States;

Centre means the International Centre for Settlement of Investment Disputes (ICSID) established by the ICSID Convention;

Claimant means an investor of an Annex Party that is a party to a qualifying investment dispute, excluding an investor that is owned or controlled by a person of a non-Annex Party that, on the date of signature of this Agreement, the other Annex Party has determined to be a non-market economy for purposes of its trade remedy laws and with which no Party has a free trade agreement;

Disputing parties means the claimant and the respondent;

Disputing party means either the claimant or the respondent;

ICSID Additional Facility Rules means the *Rules Governing the Additional Facility for the Administration of Proceedings by the Secretariat of the International Centre for Settlement of Investment Disputes;*

ICSID Convention means the *Convention on the Settlement of Investment Disputes between States and Nationals of other States,* done at Washington, March 18, 1965;

Inter-American Convention means the *Inter-American Convention on International Commercial Arbitration,* done at Panama, January 30, 1975;

New York Convention means the *Convention on the Recognition and Enforcement of Foreign Arbitral Awards,* done at New York, June 10, 1958;

Non-disputing Annex Party means the Annex Party that is not a party to a qualifying investment dispute;

Protected information means confidential business information or information that is privileged or otherwise protected from disclosure under a Party's law, including classified government information;

Qualifying investment dispute means an investment dispute between an investor of an Annex Party and the other Annex Party; Respondent means the Annex Party that is a party to a qualifying investment dispute;

Secretary-General means the Secretary-General of ICSID; and

UNCITRAL Arbitration Rules means the arbitration rules of the United Nations Commission on International Trade Law.

Article 14.D.2: Consultation and Negotiation

1. In the event of a qualifying investment dispute, the claimant and the respondent should initially seek to resolve the dispute through consultation and negotiation, which may include the use of non-binding, third party procedures, such as good offices, conciliation, or mediation.

2. For greater certainty, the initiation of consultations and negotiations shall not be construed as recognition of the jurisdiction of the tribunal.

Article 14.D.3: Submission of a Claim to Arbitration

1. In the event that a disputing party considers that a qualifying investment dispute cannot be settled by consultation and negotiation:

    (a) the claimant, on its own behalf, may submit to arbitration under this Annex a claim:

        (i) that the respondent has breached:

            (A) Article 14.4 (National Treatment) or Article 14.5 (Most-Favored-Nation Treatment),[22] except with

---

[22] For the purposes of this paragraph: (i) the "treatment" referred to in Article 14.5 (Most-Favored-Nation Treatment) excludes provisions in other international trade or investment agreements that establish international dispute resolution procedures or impose substantive obligations; and (ii) the "treatment" referred to in Article 14.5 only encompasses measures adopted or maintained by the other Annex Party, which for greater clarity may include measures adopted in connection with the

respect to the establishment or acquisition of an
investment, or

(B) Article 14.8 (Expropriation and Compensation),
except with respect to indirect expropriation, and

(ii) that the claimant has incurred loss or damage by reason
of, or arising out of, that breach; and

(b) the claimant, on behalf of an enterprise of the respondent
that is a juridical person that the claimant owns or controls
directly or indirectly, may submit to arbitration under this
Annex a claim:

(i) that the respondent has breached:

(A) Article 14.4 (National Treatment) or Article 14.5
(Most-Favored-Nation Treatment), except with
respect to the establishment or acquisition of an
investment, or

(B) Article 14.8 (Expropriation and Compensation),
except with respect to indirect expropriation, and

(ii) that the enterprise has incurred loss or damage by
reason of, or arising out of, that breach.[23]

2. At least 90 days before submitting any claim to arbitration under this
Annex, the claimant shall deliver to the respondent a written notice of
its intention to submit a claim to arbitration (notice of intent). The
notice shall specify:

(a) the name and address of the claimant and, if a claim is
submitted on behalf of an enterprise, the name, address, and
place of incorporation of the enterprise;

(b) for each claim, the provision of this Agreement alleged to
have been breached and any other relevant provisions;

(c) the legal and factual basis for each claim; and

(d) the relief sought and the approximate amount of damages
claimed.

3. The claimant may submit a claim referred to in paragraph 1 under one
of the following alternatives:

(a) the ICSID Convention and the ICSID *Rules of Procedure for
Arbitration Proceedings*, provided that both the respondent

---

implementation of substantive obligations in other international trade or investment
agreements.

[23] For greater certainty, in order for a claim to be submitted to arbitration under
subparagraph (b), an investor of the Party of the claimant must own or control the
enterprise on the date of the alleged breach and the date on which the claim is
submitted to arbitration.

and the Party of the claimant are parties to the ICSID Convention;[24]

(b)   the ICSID Additional Facility Rules, provided that either the respondent or the Party of the claimant is a party to the ICSID Convention;

(c)   the UNCITRAL Arbitration Rules; or

(d)   if the claimant and respondent agree, any other arbitral institution or any other arbitration rules.

(e)   referred to in the ICSID Convention is received by the Secretary-General;

(f)   referred to in the ICSID Additional Facility Rules is received by the Secretary-General;

(g)   referred to in the UNCITRAL Arbitration Rules, together with the statement of claim referred to therein, are received by the respondent; or

(h)   referred to under any arbitral institution or arbitration rules selected under paragraph 3(d) is received by the respondent.

A claim asserted by the claimant for the first time after such notice of arbitration is submitted shall be deemed submitted to arbitration under this Annex on the date of its receipt under the applicable arbitration rules.

4.   The arbitration rules applicable under paragraph 3 that are in effect on the date the claim or claims were submitted to arbitration under this Annex shall govern the arbitration except to the extent modified by this Agreement.

5.   The claimant shall provide with the notice of arbitration:

(a)   the name of the arbitrator that the claimant appoints; or

(b)   the claimant's written consent for the Secretary-General to appoint that arbitrator.

Article 14.D.4: Consent to Arbitration

1.   Each Annex Party consents to the submission of a claim to arbitration under this Annex in accordance with this Agreement.

2.   The consent under paragraph 1 and the submission of a claim to arbitration under this Annex shall be deemed to satisfy the requirements of:

(a)   Chapter II of the ICSID Convention (Jurisdiction of the Centre) and the ICSID Additional Facility Rules for written consent of the parties to the dispute;

---

[24]   For greater certainty, if a claimant submits a claim under this subparagraph, any award made by the tribunal under Article 14.D.13 (Awards) constitutes an award under Chapter IV of the ICSID Convention (Arbitration).A claim shall be deemed submitted to arbitration under this Annex when the claimant's notice of or request for arbitration (notice of arbitration):

(b) Article II of the New York Convention for an "agreement in writing"; and

(c) Article I of the Inter-American Convention for an "agreement".

Article 14.D.5: Conditions and Limitations on Consent

1. No claim shall be submitted to arbitration under this Annex unless:

(a) the claimant (for claims brought under Article 14.D.3.1(a) (Submission of a Claim to Arbitration)) and the claimant or the enterprise (for claims brought under Article 14.D.3.1(b)) first initiated a proceeding before a competent court or administrative tribunal of the respondent with respect to the measures alleged to constitute a breach referred to in Article 14.D.3;

(b) the claimant or the enterprise obtained a final decision from a court of last resort of the respondent or 30 months have elapsed from the date the proceeding in subparagraph (a) was initiated;[25]

(c) no more than four years have elapsed from the date on which the claimant first acquired, or should have first acquired, knowledge of the breach alleged under Article 14.D.3.1 (Submission of a Claim to Arbitration) and knowledge that the claimant (for claims brought under Article 14.D.3.1(a)) or the enterprise (for claims brought under Article 14.D.3.1(b)) has incurred loss or damage;

(d) the claimant consents in writing to arbitration in accordance with the procedures set out in this Agreement; and

(e) the notice of arbitration is accompanied:

(i) for claims submitted to arbitration under Article 14.D.3.1(a) (Submission of a Claim to Arbitration), by the claimant's written waiver, and

(ii) for claims submitted to arbitration under Article 14.D.3.1(b) (Submission of a Claim to Arbitration), by the claimant's and the enterprise's written waivers,

of any right to initiate or continue before any court or administrative tribunal under the law of an Annex Party, or any other dispute settlement procedures, any proceeding with respect to any measure alleged to constitute a breach referred to in Article 14.D.3 (Submission of a Claim to Arbitration).

2. Notwithstanding paragraph 1(e), the claimant (for claims brought under Article 14.D.3.1(a) (Submission of a Claim to Arbitration)) and the claimant or the enterprise (for claims brought under Article 14.D.3.1(b)) may initiate or continue an action that seeks interim injunctive relief and does not involve the payment of monetary damages

---

[25] The provisions in subparagraphs (a) and (b) do not apply to the extent recourse to domestic remedies was obviously futile.

before a judicial or administrative tribunal of the respondent, provided that the action is brought for the sole purpose of preserving the claimant's or the enterprise's rights and interests during the pendency of the arbitration.

Article 14.D.6: Selection of Arbitrators

1. Unless the disputing parties agree otherwise, the tribunal shall comprise three arbitrators, one arbitrator appointed by each of the disputing parties and the third, who shall be the presiding arbitrator, appointed by agreement of the disputing parties.

2. The Secretary-General shall serve as appointing authority for an arbitration under this Annex.

3. If a tribunal has not been constituted within a period of 75 days after the date that a claim is submitted to arbitration under this Annex, the Secretary-General, on the request of a disputing party, shall appoint, in his or her discretion, the arbitrator or arbitrators not yet appointed. The Secretary-General shall not appoint a national of either the respondent or the Party of the claimant as the presiding arbitrator unless the disputing parties agree otherwise.

4. For the purposes of Article 39 of the ICSID Convention and Article 7 of Schedule C to the ICSID Additional Facility Rules, and without prejudice to an objection to an arbitrator on a ground other than nationality:

    (a) the respondent agrees to the appointment of each individual member of a tribunal established under the ICSID Convention or the ICSID Additional Facility Rules;

    (b) a claimant referred to in Article 14.D.3.1(a) (Submission of a Claim to Arbitration) may submit a claim to arbitration under this Annex, or continue a claim, under the ICSID Convention or the ICSID Additional Facility Rules, only on condition that the claimant agrees in writing to the appointment of each individual member of the tribunal; and

    (c) a claimant referred to in Article 14.D.3.1(b) (Submission of a Claim to Arbitration) may submit a claim to arbitration under this Annex, or continue a claim, under the ICSID Convention or the ICSID Additional Facility Rules, only on condition that the claimant and the enterprise agree in writing to the appointment of each individual member of the tribunal.

5. Arbitrators appointed to a tribunal for claims submitted under Article 14.D.3.1 shall:

    (a) comply with the International Bar Association Guidelines on Conflicts of Interest in International Arbitration, including guidelines regarding direct or indirect conflicts of interest, or any supplemental guidelines or rules adopted by the Annex Parties;

(b)   not take instructions from any organization or government regarding the dispute; and not, for the duration of the proceedings, act as counsel or as party-appointed expert or witness in any pending arbitration under the annexes to this Chapter.

6.   Challenges to arbitrators shall be governed by the procedures in the UNCITRAL Arbitration Rules.

Article 14.D.7: Conduct of the Arbitration

1.   The disputing parties may agree on the legal place of any arbitration under the arbitration rules applicable under Article 14.D.3.3 (Submission of a Claim to Arbitration). If the disputing parties fail to reach agreement, the tribunal shall determine the place in accordance with the applicable arbitration rules, provided that the place shall be in the territory of a State that is a party to the New York Convention.

2.   The non-disputing Annex Party may make oral and written submissions to the tribunal regarding the interpretation of this Agreement.

3.   After consultation with the disputing parties, the tribunal may accept and consider written *amicus curiae* submissions regarding a matter of fact or law within the scope of the dispute that may assist the tribunal in evaluating the submissions and arguments of the disputing parties from a person or entity that is not a disputing party but has a significant interest in the arbitral proceedings. Each submission shall identify the author; disclose any affiliation, direct or indirect, with any disputing party; and identify any person, government, or other entity that has provided, or will provide, any financial or other assistance in preparing the submission. Each submission shall be in a language of the arbitration and comply with any page limits and deadlines set by the tribunal. The tribunal shall provide the disputing parties with an opportunity to respond to such submissions. The tribunal shall ensure that the submissions do not disrupt or unduly burden the arbitral proceedings, or unfairly prejudice any disputing party.

4.   Without prejudice to a tribunal's authority to address other objections as a preliminary question, such as an objection that a dispute is not within the competence of the tribunal, including an objection to the tribunal's jurisdiction, a tribunal shall address and decide as a preliminary question any objection by the respondent that, as a matter of law, a claim submitted is not a claim for which an award in favor of the claimant may be made under Article 14.D.13 (Awards) or that a claim is manifestly without legal merit.

(a)   An objection under this paragraph shall be submitted to the tribunal as soon as possible after the tribunal is constituted, and in no event later than the date the tribunal fixes for the respondent to submit its counter-memorial or, in the case of an amendment to the notice of arbitration, the date the tribunal fixes for the respondent to submit its response to the amendment.

(b) On receipt of an objection under this paragraph, the tribunal shall suspend any proceedings on the merits, establish a schedule for considering the objection consistent with any schedule it has established for considering any other preliminary question, and issue a decision or award on the objection, stating the grounds therefor.

(c) In deciding an objection under this paragraph that a claim submitted is not a claim for which an award in favor of the claimant may be made under Article 14.D.13 (Awards), the tribunal shall assume to be true the claimant's factual allegations in support of any claim in the notice of arbitration (or any amendment thereof) and, in disputes brought under the UNCITRAL Arbitration Rules, the statement of claim referred to in the relevant article of the UNCITRAL Arbitration Rules. The tribunal may also consider any relevant facts not in dispute.

(d) The respondent does not waive any objection as to competence, including an objection to jurisdiction, or any argument on the merits merely because the respondent did or did not raise an objection under this paragraph or make use of the expedited procedure set out in paragraph 5.

5. In the event that the respondent so requests within 45 days after the tribunal is constituted, the tribunal shall decide on an expedited basis an objection under paragraph 4 or any objection that the dispute is not within the tribunal's competence, including an objection that the dispute is not within the tribunal's jurisdiction. The tribunal shall suspend any proceedings on the merits and issue a decision or award on the objection, stating the grounds therefor, no later than 150 days after the date of the request. However, if a disputing party requests a hearing, the tribunal may take an additional 30 days to issue the decision or award. Regardless of whether a hearing is requested, a tribunal may, on a showing of extraordinary cause, delay issuing its decision or award by an additional brief period, which may not exceed 30 days.

6. When the tribunal decides a respondent's objection under paragraph 4 or 5, it may, if warranted, award to the prevailing disputing party reasonable costs and attorney's fees incurred in submitting or opposing the objection. In determining whether such an award is warranted, the tribunal shall consider whether either the claimant's claim or the respondent's objection was frivolous, and shall provide the disputing parties a reasonable opportunity to comment.

7. For greater certainty, if an investor of an Annex Party submits a claim under this Annex, the investor has the burden of proving all elements of its claims, consistent with general principles of international law applicable to international arbitration.

8.   A respondent may not assert as a defense, counterclaim, right of set-off, or for any other reason, that the claimant has received or will receive indemnification or other compensation for all or part of the alleged damages pursuant to an insurance or guarantee contract.

9.   A tribunal may order an interim measure of protection to preserve the rights of a disputing party, or to ensure that the tribunal's jurisdiction is made fully effective, including an order to preserve evidence in the possession or control of a disputing party or to protect the tribunal's jurisdiction. A tribunal may not order attachment or enjoin the application of a measure alleged to constitute a breach referred to in Article 14.D.3 (Submission of a Claim to Arbitration). For the purposes of this paragraph, an order includes a recommendation.

10.   The tribunal and the disputing parties shall endeavor to conduct the arbitration in an expeditious and cost-effective manner.

11.   Following the submission of a claim to arbitration under this Annex, if the disputing parties fail to take any steps in the proceedings for more than 150 days, or such period as they may agree with the approval of the tribunal, the tribunal shall notify the disputing parties that they shall be deemed to have discontinued the proceedings if the parties fail to take any steps within 30 days after the notice is received. If the parties fail to take any steps within that time period, the tribunal shall take note of the discontinuance in an order. If a tribunal has not yet been constituted, the Secretary-General shall assume these responsibilities.

12.   In any arbitration conducted under this Annex, at the request of a disputing party, a tribunal shall, before issuing a decision or award on liability, transmit its proposed decision or award to the disputing parties. Within 60 days after the tribunal transmits its proposed decision or award, the disputing parties may submit written comments to the tribunal concerning any aspect of its proposed decision or award. The tribunal shall consider any comments and issue its decision or award no later than 45 days after the expiration of the 60-day comment period.

Article 14.D.8: Transparency of Arbitral Proceedings

1.   Subject to paragraphs 2 and 4, the respondent shall, after receiving the following documents, promptly transmit them to the non-disputing Annex Party and make them available to the public:

   (a)   the notice of intent;

   (b)   the notice of arbitration;

   (c)   pleadings, memorials, and briefs submitted to the tribunal by a disputing party and any written submissions submitted pursuant to Article 14.D.7.2 and 14.D.7.3 (Conduct of the Arbitration), and Article 14.D.12 (Consolidation);

   (d)   minutes or transcripts of hearings of the tribunal, if available; and

(e)   orders, awards, and decisions of the tribunal.

2.   The tribunal shall conduct hearings open to the public and shall determine, in consultation with the disputing parties, the appropriate logistical arrangements. If a disputing party intends to use information in a hearing that is designated as protected information or otherwise subject to paragraph 3 it shall so advise the tribunal. The tribunal shall make appropriate arrangements to protect such information from disclosure which may include closing the hearing for the duration of the discussion of that information.

3.   Nothing in this Annex, including paragraph 4(d), requires a respondent to make available to the public or otherwise disclose during or after the arbitral proceedings, including the hearing, protected information, or to furnish or allow access to information that it may withhold in accordance with Article 32.2 (Essential Security) or Article 32.5 (Disclosure of Information).[26]

4.   Any protected information that is submitted to the tribunal shall be protected from disclosure in accordance with the following procedures:

(a)   subject to subparagraph (d), neither the disputing parties nor the tribunal shall disclose to the non-disputing Annex Party or to the public any protected information if the disputing party that provided the information clearly designates it in accordance with subparagraph (b);

(b)   any disputing party claiming that certain information constitutes protected information shall clearly designate the information according to any schedule set by the tribunal;

(c)   a disputing party shall, according to any schedule set by the tribunal, submit a redacted version of the document that does not contain the protected information.

Only the redacted version shall be disclosed in accordance with paragraph 1; and

(d)   the tribunal, subject to paragraph 3, shall decide any objection regarding the designation of information claimed to be protected information. If the tribunal determines that the information was not properly designated, the disputing party that submitted the information may:

(i)   withdraw all or part of its submission containing that information, or

(ii)   agree to resubmit complete and redacted documents with corrected designations in accordance with the tribunal's determination and subparagraph (c).

---

[26]   For greater certainty, when a respondent chooses to disclose to the tribunal information that may be withheld in accordance with Article 32.2 (Essential Security) or Article 32.5 (Disclosure of Information), the respondent may still withhold that information from disclosure to the public.

In either case, the other disputing party shall, whenever necessary, resubmit complete and redacted documents which either remove the information withdrawn under subparagraph (d)(i) by the disputing party that first submitted the information or redesignate the information consistent with the designation under subparagraph (d)(ii) of the disputing party that first submitted the information.

5.   Nothing in this Annex requires a respondent to withhold from the public information required to be disclosed by its laws. The respondent should endeavor to apply those laws in a manner sensitive to protecting from disclosure information that has been designated as protected information.

Article 14.D.9: Governing Law

1.   Subject to paragraph 2, when a claim is submitted under Article 14.D.3.1 (Submission of a Claim to Arbitration), the tribunal shall decide the issues in dispute in accordance with this Agreement and applicable rules of international law.

2.   A decision of the Commission on the interpretation of a provision of this Agreement under Article 30.2 (Functions of the Commission) shall be binding on a tribunal, and any decision or award issued by a tribunal must be consistent with that decision.

Article 14.D.10:   Interpretation of Annexes

1.   If a respondent asserts as a defense that the measure alleged to be a breach is within the scope of a non-conforming measure set out in Annex I or Annex II, the tribunal shall, on request of the respondent, request the interpretation of the Commission on the issue. The Commission shall submit in writing any decision on its interpretation under Article 30.2 (Functions of the Commission) to the tribunal within 90 days of delivery of the request.

2.   A decision issued by the Commission under paragraph 1 shall be binding on the tribunal, and any decision or award issued by the tribunal must be consistent with that decision. If the Commission fails to issue such a decision within 90 days, the tribunal shall decide the issue.

Article 14.D.11:   Expert Reports

Without prejudice to the appointment of other kinds of experts when authorized by the applicable arbitration rules, a tribunal, on request of a disputing party or, unless the disputing parties disapprove, on its own initiative, may appoint one or more experts to report to it in writing on any factual issue concerning scientific matters raised by a disputing party in a proceeding, subject to any terms and conditions that the disputing parties may agree.

Article 14.D.12:   Consolidation

1.   If two or more claims have been submitted separately to arbitration under Article 14.D.3.1 (Submission of a Claim to Arbitration) and the claims have a question of law or fact in common and arise out of the

same events or circumstances, any disputing party may seek a consolidation order in accordance with the agreement of all the disputing parties sought to be covered by the order or the terms of paragraphs 2 through 10.

(a)   A disputing party that seeks a consolidation order under this Article shall deliver, in writing, a request to the Secretary-General and to all the disputing parties sought to be covered by the order and shall specify in the request: the names and addresses of all the disputing parties sought to be covered by the order;

(b)   the nature of the order sought; and

(c)   the grounds on which the order is sought.

2.   Unless the Secretary-General finds within a period of 30 days after the date of receiving a request under paragraph 2 that the request is manifestly unfounded, a tribunal shall be established under this Article.

3.   Unless all the disputing parties sought to be covered by the order agree otherwise, a tribunal established under this Article shall comprise three arbitrators:

(a)   one arbitrator appointed by agreement of the claimants;

(b)   one arbitrator appointed by the respondent; and

(c)   the presiding arbitrator appointed by the Secretary-General, provided that the presiding arbitrator is not a national of the respondent or of the Party of the claimants.

4.   If, within a period of 60 days after the date when the Secretary-General receives a request made under paragraph 2, the respondent fails or the claimants fail to appoint an arbitrator in accordance with paragraph 4, the Secretary-General, on request of any disputing party sought to be covered by the order, shall appoint, in his or her discretion, the arbitrator or arbitrators not yet appointed.

5.   If a tribunal established under this Article is satisfied that two or more claims that have been submitted to arbitration under Article 14.D.3.1 (Submission of a Claim to Arbitration) have a question of law or fact in common, and arise out of the same events or circumstances, the tribunal may, in the interest of fair and efficient resolution of the claims, and after hearing the disputing parties, by order:

(a)   assume jurisdiction over, and hear and determine together, all or part of the claims;

(b)   assume jurisdiction over, and hear and determine one or more of the claims, the determination of which it believes would assist in the resolution of the others; or

(c)   instruct a tribunal previously established under Article 14.D.6 (Selection of Arbitrators) to assume jurisdiction over, and hear and determine together, all or part of the claims, provided that:

(i)   that tribunal, on request of a claimant that was not previously a disputing party before that tribunal, shall be reconstituted with its original members, except that the arbitrator for the claimants shall be appointed pursuant to paragraphs 4(a) and 5, and

(ii) that tribunal shall decide whether a prior hearing shall be repeated.

6.   If a tribunal has been established under this Article, a claimant that has submitted a claim to arbitration under Article 14.D.3.1 (Submission of a Claim to Arbitration) and that has not been named in a request made under paragraph 2 may make a written request to the tribunal that it be included in any order made under paragraph 6. The request shall specify:

(a)   the name and address of the claimant;

(b)   the nature of the order sought; and

(c)   the grounds on which the order is sought.

The claimant shall deliver a copy of its request to the Secretary-General.

7.   A tribunal established under this Article shall conduct its proceedings in accordance with the UNCITRAL Arbitration Rules, except as modified by this Annex.

8.   A tribunal established under Article 14.D.6 (Selection of Arbitrators) shall not have jurisdiction to decide a claim, or a part of a claim, over which a tribunal established or instructed under this Article has assumed jurisdiction.

9.   On the application of a disputing party, a tribunal established under this Article, pending its decision under paragraph 6, may order that the proceedings of a tribunal established under Article 14.D.6 (Selection of Arbitrators) be stayed, unless the latter tribunal has already adjourned its proceedings.

Article 14.D.13:   Awards

1.   When a tribunal makes a final award, the tribunal may award, separately or in combination, only:

(a)   monetary damages and any applicable interest; and

(b)   restitution of property, in which case the award shall provide that the respondent may pay monetary damages and any applicable interest in lieu of restitution.[27]

---

[27]   For greater certainty, in the final award the tribunal may not order the respondent to take or not to take other actions, including the amendment, repeal, adoption, or implementation of a law or regulation.

2.   For greater certainty, if an investor of an Annex Party submits a claim to arbitration under Article 14.D.3.1 (Submission of a Claim to Arbitration), it may recover only for loss or damage that is established on the basis of satisfactory evidence and that is not inherently speculative.

3.   For greater certainty, if an investor of an Annex Party submits a claim to arbitration under Article 14.D.3.1(a) (Submission of a Claim to Arbitration), it may recover only for loss or damage incurred in its capacity as an investor of an Annex Party.

4.   A tribunal may also award costs and attorney's fees incurred by the disputing parties in connection with the arbitral proceedings, and shall determine how and by whom those costs and attorney's fees shall be paid, in accordance with this Annex and the applicable arbitration rules.

5.   Subject to paragraph 1, if a claim is submitted to arbitration under Article 14.D.3.1(b) (Submission of a Claim to Arbitration) and an award is made in favor of the enterprise:

(a)   an award of restitution of property shall provide that restitution be made to the enterprise;

(b)   an award of monetary damages and any applicable interest shall provide that the sum be paid to the enterprise; and

(c)   the award shall provide that it is made without prejudice to any right that any person may have under applicable domestic law with respect to the relief provided in the award.

6.   A tribunal shall not award punitive damages.

7.   An award made by a tribunal has no binding force except between the disputing parties and in respect of the particular case.

8.   Subject to paragraph 9 and the applicable review procedure for an interim award, a disputing party shall abide by and comply with an award without delay.

9.   A disputing party shall not seek enforcement of a final award until:

(a)   in the case of a final award made under the ICSID Convention:

(i)   120 days have elapsed from the date the award was rendered and no disputing party has requested revision or annulment of the award, or

(ii)   revision or annulment proceedings have been completed; and

(b)   in the case of a final award under the ICSID Additional Facility Rules, the UNCITRAL Arbitration Rules, or the rules selected pursuant to Article 14.D.3.3(d) (Submission of a Claim to Arbitration):

    (i)   90 days have elapsed from the date the award was rendered and no disputing party has commenced a proceeding to revise, set aside or annul the award, or

    (ii)   a court has dismissed or allowed an application to revise, set aside or annul the award and there is no further appeal.

10. Each Annex Party shall provide for the enforcement of an award in its territory.

11. If the respondent fails to abide by or comply with a final award, on delivery of a request by the Party of the claimant, a panel shall be established under Article 31.6 (Establishment of a Panel). The requesting Party may seek in those proceedings:

    (a)   a determination that the failure to abide by or comply with the final award is inconsistent with the obligations of this Agreement; and

    (b)   in accordance with Article 31.17 (Panel Report), a recommendation that the respondent abide by or comply with the final award.

12. A disputing party may seek enforcement of an arbitration award under the ICSID Convention, the New York Convention, or the Inter-American Convention regardless of whether proceedings have been taken under paragraph 11.

13. A claim that is submitted to arbitration under this Annex shall be considered to arise out of a commercial relationship or transaction for the purposes of Article I of the New York Convention and Article I of the Inter-American Convention.

    Article 14.D.14:   Service of Documents

Delivery of notice and other documents to an Annex Party shall be made to the place named for that Annex Party in Appendix 1 (Service of Documents on an Annex Party). An Annex Party shall promptly make publicly available and notify the other Annex Party of any change to the place referred to in that Appendix.

* * *

APPENDIX 2   PUBLIC DEBT

1. For greater certainty, no award shall be made in favor of a claimant for a claim under Article 14.D.3.1 (Submission of a Claim to Arbitration) with respect to default or non-payment of debt issued by a Party[28] unless the claimant meets its burden of proving that such default or non-payment constitutes a breach of a relevant obligation in the Chapter.

---

[28] For purposes of this Annex, "debt issued by a Party" includes, in the case of Mexico, "public debt" of Mexico as defined in Article 1 of the Federal Law on Public Debt (*Ley Federal de Deuda Pública*).

2. No claim that a restructuring of debt issued by a Party, standing alone, breaches an obligation in this Chapter shall be submitted to arbitration under Article 14.D.3.1 (Submission of a Claim to Arbitration), provided that the restructuring is effected as provided for under the debt instrument's terms, including the debt instrument's governing law.

APPENDIX 3   SUBMISSION OF A CLAIM TO ARBITRATION

An investor of the United States may not submit to arbitration a claim that Mexico has breached an obligation under this Chapter either:

(a) on its own behalf under Article 14.D.3.1(a) (Submission of a Claim to Arbitration); or

(b) on behalf of an enterprise of Mexico that is a juridical person that the investor owns or controls directly or indirectly under Article 14.D.3.1(b) (Submission of a Claim to Arbitration),

if the investor or the enterprise, respectively, has alleged that breach of an obligation under this Chapter, as distinguished from breach of other obligations under Mexican law, in proceedings before a court or administrative tribunal of Mexico.

ANNEX 14-E

MEXICO-UNITED STATES INVESTMENT DISPUTES RELATED TO COVERED GOVERNMENT CONTRACTS

1. Annex 14-D (Mexico-United States Investment Disputes) applies as modified by this Annex to the settlement of a qualifying investment dispute under this Chapter in the circumstances set out in paragraph 2.[29]

2. In the event that a disputing party considers that a qualifying investment dispute cannot be settled by consultation and negotiation:

(a) the claimant, on its own behalf, may submit to arbitration under Annex 14-D (Mexico-United States Investment Disputes) a claim:

   (i) that the respondent has breached any obligation under this Chapter,[30] provided that:

      (A) the claimant is:

         (1) a party to a covered government contract, or

---

[29] For greater certainty, Annex 14-D (Mexico-United States Investment Disputes) includes its appendices.

[30] For the purposes of this paragraph: (i) the "treatment" referred to in Article 14.5 (Most-Favored-Nation Treatment) excludes provisions in other international trade or investment agreements that establish international dispute resolution procedures or impose substantive obligations; (ii) the "treatment" referred to in Article 14.5 only encompasses measures adopted or maintained by the other Annex Party, which for greater clarity may include measures adopted in connection with the implementation of substantive obligations in other international trade or investment agreements.

(2)   engaged in activities in the same covered sector in the territory of the respondent as an enterprise of the respondent that the claimant owns or controls directly or indirectly and that is a party to a covered government contract, and

(B)   the respondent is a party to another international trade or investment agreement that permits investors to initiate dispute settlement procedures to resolve an investment dispute with a government, and

(ii)   that the claimant has incurred loss or damage by reason of, or arising out of, that breach;

(b)   the claimant, on behalf of an enterprise of the respondent that is a juridical person that the claimant owns or controls directly or indirectly, may submit to arbitration under Annex 14-D (Mexico-United States Investment Disputes) a claim:

(i)   that the respondent has breached any obligation under this Chapter, provided that:

(A)   the enterprise is:

(1)   a party to a covered government contract,

(2)   engaged in activities in the same covered sector in the territory of the respondent as the claimant and the claimant is a party to a covered government contract, or

(3)   engaged in activities in the same covered sector in the territory of the respondent as another enterprise of the respondent that the claimant owns or controls directly or indirectly and that is a party to a covered government contract, and

(B)   the respondent is a party to another international trade or investment agreement that permits investors to initiate dispute settlement procedures to resolve an investment dispute with a government, and

(ii)   that the enterprise has incurred loss or damage by reason of, or arising out of, that breach.[31]

3.   For the purposes of paragraph 2, if a covered government contract is terminated in a manner inconsistent with an obligation under this

---

[31]   For greater certainty, in order for a claim to be submitted to arbitration under subparagraph (b), an investor of the Party of the claimant must own or control the enterprise on the date of the alleged breach and the date on which the claim is submitted to arbitration.

Chapter, the claimant or enterprise that was previously a party to the contract shall be deemed to remain a party for the duration of the contract, as if it had not been terminated.

4.   No claim shall be submitted to arbitration under paragraph 2 if:

   (a)   less than six months have elapsed from the events giving rise to the claim; and

   (b)   more than three years have elapsed from the date on which the claimant first acquired, or should have first acquired, knowledge of the breach alleged under paragraph 2 and knowledge that the claimant (for claims brought under paragraph 2(a)) or the enterprise (for claims brought under paragraph 2(b)) has incurred loss or damage.[32]

5.   For greater certainty, the Annex Parties may agree to modify or eliminate this Annex.

6.   For the purposes of this Annex:

   (a)   "covered sector" means:

      (i)   activities with respect to oil and natural gas that a national authority of an Annex Party controls, such as exploration, extraction, refining, transportation, distribution, or sale,

      (ii)   the supply of power generation services to the public on behalf of an Annex Party,

      (iii) the supply of telecommunications services to the public on behalf of an Annex Party,

      (iv)   the supply of transportation services to the public on behalf of an Annex Party, or

      (v)   the ownership or management of roads, railways, bridges, or canals that are not for the exclusive or predominant use and benefit of the government of an Annex Party;

   (b)   "national authority" means an authority at the central level of government;[33] and

---

   [32]   For greater certainty, Article 14.D.5.1(a)–(c) does not apply to claims under paragraph 2."covered government contract" means a written agreement between a national authority of an Annex Party and a covered investment or investor of the other Annex Party, on which the covered investment or investor relies in establishing or acquiring a covered investment other than the written agreement itself, that grants rights to the covered investment or investor in a covered sector;

   [33]   For greater certainty, an authority at the central level of government includes any person, including a state enterprise or another body, when it exercises governmental authority delegated to it by an authority at the central level of government.

(c)   "written agreement" means an agreement in writing, negotiated, and executed by two or more parties, whether in a single instrument or in multiple instruments.[34]

CHAPTER 15   CROSS-BORDER TRADE IN SERVICES

Article 15.1:   Definitions

For the purposes of this Chapter:

Cross-border trade in services or cross-border supply of services means the supply of a service:

(a)   from the territory of a Party into the territory of another Party;

(b)   in the territory of a Party by a person of that Party to a person of another Party; or

(c)   by a national of a Party in the territory of another Party,

but does not include the supply of a service in the territory of a Party by a covered investment;

Enterprise means an enterprise as defined in Article 1.4 (General Definitions), or a branch of an enterprise;

Professional service means a service, the supply of which requires specialized post-secondary education, or equivalent training or experience, and for which the right to practice is granted or restricted by a Party, but does not include a service provided by a tradesperson, or a vessel or aircraft crew member;

Service supplied in the exercise of governmental authority means, for a Party, a service that is supplied neither on a commercial basis nor in competition with one or more service suppliers;

Service supplier of another Party means a person of a Party that seeks to supply or supplies a service; and

Specialty air service means a specialized commercial operation using an aircraft whose primary purpose is not the transportation of goods or passengers, such as aerial fire-fighting, flight training, sightseeing, spraying, surveying, mapping, photography, parachute jumping, glider towing, and helicopter-lift for logging and construction, and other airborne agricultural, industrial, and inspection services.

Article 15.2:   Scope

1.   This Chapter applies to measures adopted or maintained by a Party relating to cross-border trade in services by a service supplier of another Party, including a measure relating to:

---

[34]   For greater certainty, (a) a unilateral act of an administrative or judicial authority, such as a permit, license, certificate, approval, or similar instrument issued by an Annex Party in its regulatory capacity, or a subsidy or grant, or a decree, order or judgment, standing alone; and (b) an administrative or judicial consent decree or order, shall not be considered a written agreement.

(a) the production, distribution, marketing, sale or delivery of a service;[1]

(b) the purchase or use of, or payment for, a service;[2]

(c) the access to or use of distribution, transport, or telecommunications networks or services in connection with the supply of a service;

(d) the presence in the Party's territory of a service supplier of another Party; or

(e) the provision of a bond or other form of financial security as a condition for the supply of a service.

2. In addition to paragraph 1:

(a) Article 15.5 (Market Access) and Article 15.8 (Development and Administration of Measures) apply to measures adopted or maintained by a Party relating to the supply of a service in its territory by a covered investment; and

(b) Annex 15-A (Delivery Services) applies to measures adopted or maintained by a Party relating to the supply of delivery services, including by a covered investment.

3. This Chapter does not apply to:

(a) a financial service as defined in Article 17.1 (Definitions), except that paragraph 2(a) applies if the financial service is supplied by a covered investment that is not a covered investment in a financial institution as defined in Article 17.1 (Definitions) in the Party's territory;

(b) government procurement;

(c) a service supplied in the exercise of governmental authority; or

(d) a subsidy or grant provided by a Party or a state enterprise, including government-supported loans, guarantees, or insurance.

4. This Chapter does not apply to air services, including domestic and international air transportation services, whether scheduled or non-scheduled, or to related services in support of air services, other than the following:

(a) aircraft repair or maintenance services during which an aircraft is withdrawn from service, excluding so-called line maintenance; and

(b) specialty air services.

---

[1]   For greater certainty, subparagraph (a) includes the production, distribution, marketing, sale or delivery of a service by electronic means.

[2]   For greater certainty, subparagraph (b) includes the purchase or use of, or payment for, a service by electronic means.

5.   This Chapter does not impose an obligation on a Party with respect to a national of another Party who seeks access to its employment market or who is employed on a permanent basis in its territory, and does not confer any right on that national with respect to that access or employment.

6.   Annex 15-B (Committee on Transportation Services) and Annex 15-D (Programming Services) include additional provisions related to this Chapter.

Article 15.3:   National Treatment

1.   Each Party shall accord to services or service suppliers of another Party treatment no less favorable than that it accords, in like circumstances, to its own services and service suppliers.

2.   The treatment to be accorded by a Party under paragraph 1 means, with respect to a government other than at the central level, treatment no less favorable than the most favorable treatment accorded, in like circumstances, by that government to services and service suppliers of the Party of which it forms a part.

3.   For greater certainty, whether treatment referred to in paragraph 1 is accorded in "like circumstances" depends on the totality of the circumstances, including whether the relevant treatment distinguishes between services or service suppliers on the basis of legitimate public welfare objectives.

Article 15.4:   Most-Favored-Nation Treatment

1.   Each Party shall accord to services or service suppliers of another Party treatment no less favorable than that it accords, in like circumstances, to services and service suppliers of another Party or a non-Party.

2.   The treatment to be accorded by a Party under paragraph 1 means, with respect to a government other than at the central level, treatment no less favorable than the most favorable treatment accorded, in like circumstances, by that government to services and service suppliers of another Party or a non-Party.

3.   For greater certainty, whether treatment referred to in paragraph 1 is accorded in "like circumstances" depends on the totality of the circumstances, including whether the relevant treatment distinguishes between services or services suppliers on the basis of legitimate public welfare objectives.

Article 15.5:   Market Access

1.   No Party shall adopt or maintain, either on the basis of a regional subdivision or on the basis of its entire territory, a measure that:

   (a)   imposes a limitation on:

      (i)   the number of service suppliers, whether in the form of a numerical quota, monopoly, exclusive service suppliers, or the requirement of an economic needs test,

      (ii)   the total value of service transactions or assets in the form of a numerical quota or the requirement of an economic needs test,

      (iii) the total number of service operations or the total quantity of service output expressed in terms of a designated numerical unit in the form of a quota or the requirement of an economic needs test,[3] or

      (iv) the total number of natural persons that may be employed in a particular service sector or that a service supplier may employ and who are necessary for, and directly related to, the supply of a specific service in the form of a numerical quota or the requirement of an economic needs test; or

  (b)   restricts or requires a specific type of legal entity or joint venture through which a service supplier may supply a service.

Article 15.6:   Local Presence

No Party shall require a service supplier of another Party to establish or maintain a representative office or an enterprise, or to be resident, in its territory as a condition for the cross-border supply of a service.

Article 15.7:   Non-Conforming Measures

1.   Article 15.3 (National Treatment), Article 15.4 (Most-Favored-Nation Treatment), Article 15.5 (Market Access), and Article 15.6 (Local Presence) do not apply to:

  (a)   an existing non-conforming measure that is maintained by a Party at:

      (i)   the central level of government, as set out by that Party in its Schedule to Annex I,

      (ii) a regional level of government, as set out by that Party in its Schedule to Annex I, or

      (iii) a local level of government;

  (b)   the continuation or prompt renewal of a non-conforming measure referred to in subparagraph (a); or

  (c)   an amendment to a non-conforming measure referred to in subparagraph (a), to the extent that the amendment does not decrease the conformity of the measure, as it existed immediately before the amendment, with Article 15.3 (National Treatment), Article 15.4 (Most-Favored-Nation Treatment), Article 15.5 (Market Access), or Article 15.6 (Local Presence).

---

[3]   Subparagraph (a)(iii) does not cover measures of a Party which limit inputs for the supply of services.

2. Article 15.3 (National Treatment), Article 15.4 (Most-Favored-Nation Treatment), Article 15.5 (Market Access), and Article 15.6 (Local Presence) do not apply to a measure that a Party adopts or maintains with respect to sectors, sub-sectors or activities, as set out by that Party in its Schedule to Annex II.

3. If a Party considers that a non-conforming measure applied by a regional level of government of another Party, as referred to in sub-paragraph 1(a)(ii), creates a material impediment to the cross-border supply of services in relation to the former Party, it may request consultations with regard to that measure. These Parties shall enter into consultations with a view to exchanging information on the operation of the measure and to considering whether further steps are necessary and appropriate.

4. For greater certainty, a Party may request consultations with another Party regarding non-conforming measures applied by the central level of government, as referred to in subparagraph 1(a)(i).

Article 15.8:   Development and Administration of Measures

1. Each Party shall ensure that a measure of general application affecting trade in services is administered in a reasonable, objective, and impartial manner.

2. If a Party adopts or maintains a measure relating to licensing requirements and procedures, or qualification requirements and procedures, affecting trade in services, the Party shall, with respect to that measure:

    (a) ensure that the requirement or procedure is based on criteria that are objective and transparent. For greater certainty, these criteria may include competence or ability to supply a service, or potential health or environmental impacts of an authorization, and competent authorities may assess the weight given to such criteria;

    (b) ensure that the competent authority reaches and administers a decision in an independent manner;

    (c) ensure that the procedure does not in itself prevent fulfilment of a requirement; and

    (d) to the extent practicable, avoid requiring an applicant to approach more than one competent authority for each application for authorization.[4]

3. If a Party requires an authorization for the supply of a service, it shall ensure that each of its competent authorities:

    (a) to the extent practicable, permits an applicant to submit an application at any time;

---

[4]   For greater certainty, a Party may require multiple applications for authorization if a service is within the jurisdiction of multiple competent authorities.

(b) if a specific time period for applications exists, allows a reasonable period for the submission of an application;

(c) if an examination is required, schedules the examination at reasonably frequent intervals and provides a reasonable period of time to enable an applicant to request to take the examination;

(d) endeavors to accept an application electronically;

(e) to the extent practicable, provides an indicative timeframe for processing an application;

(f) to the extent practicable, ascertains without undue delay the completeness of an application for processing under the Party's law;

(g) accepts copies of documents that are authenticated in accordance with the Party's law, in place of original documents, unless the competent authority requires original documents to protect the integrity of the authorization process;

(h) at the request of the applicant, provides without undue delay information concerning the status of the application;

(i) if an application is considered complete under the Party's law, within a reasonable period of time after the submission of the application, ensures that the processing of the application is completed, and that the applicant is informed of the decision concerning the application, to the extent possible in writing;[5]

(j) if an application is considered incomplete for processing under the Party's law, within a reasonable period of time, to the extent practicable:

    (i) informs the applicant that the application is incomplete,

    (ii) if the applicant requests, provides guidance on why the application is considered incomplete,

    (iii) provides the applicant with an opportunity[6] to provide the additional information that is required for the application to be considered complete, and

---

[5] A competent authority can meet this requirement by informing an applicant in advance in writing, including through a published measure, that lack of response after a specified period of time from the date of submission of the application indicates either acceptance or rejection of the application. For greater certainty, "in writing" includes in electronic form.

[6] For greater certainty, providing this opportunity does not require a competent authority to provide extensions of deadlines.

if none of the above is practicable, and the application is rejected due to incompleteness, ensures that the applicant is informed of the rejection within a reasonable period of time;

(k) if an application is rejected, to the extent possible, either upon its own initiative or upon the request of the applicant, informs the applicant of the reasons for rejection and, if applicable, the timeframe for an appeal or review of the decision to reject the application and the procedures for resubmission of an application; and

(l) ensures that authorization, once granted, enters into effect without undue delay, subject to the applicable terms and conditions.

4. Each Party shall ensure that any authorization fee charged by any of its competent authorities is reasonable, transparent, and does not, in itself, restrict the supply of the relevant service. For the purposes of this paragraph, an authorization fee does not include a fee for the use of natural resources, payments for auction, tendering, or other non-discriminatory means of awarding concessions, or mandated contributions to the provision of universal service.

5. Each Party shall encourage its competent authorities, when adopting a technical standard, to adopt technical standards developed through an open and transparent process, and shall encourage a body designated to develop a technical standard to use an open and transparent process.

6. If a Party requires authorization for the supply of a service, the Party shall provide to a service supplier or person seeking to supply a service the information necessary to comply with requirements or procedures for obtaining, maintaining, amending, and renewing that authorization. That information must include:

(a) any fee;

(b) the contact information of a relevant competent authority;

(c) any procedure for appeal or review of a decision concerning an application;

(d) any procedure for monitoring or enforcing compliance with the terms and conditions of licenses;

(e) any opportunities for public involvement, such as through hearings or comments;

(f) any indicative timeframe for processing of an application;

(g) any requirement or procedure; and

(h) any technical standard.

7. Paragraphs 1 through 6 do not apply to the aspects of a measure set out in an entry to a Party's Schedule to Annex I, or to a measure that a Party adopts or maintains with respect to sectors, sub-sectors, or activities as set out by that Party in its Schedule to Annex II.

Article 15.9:   Recognition

1. For the purposes of the fulfilment, in whole or in part, of a Party's standards or criteria for the authorization, licensing, or certification of a service supplier, and subject to the requirements of paragraph 4, a Party may recognize any education or experience obtained, requirements met, or licenses or certifications granted, in the territory of another Party or a non-Party. That recognition, which may be achieved through harmonization or otherwise, may be based on an agreement or arrangement with the Party or non-Party concerned, or may be accorded autonomously.

2. If a Party recognizes, autonomously or by agreement or arrangement, the education or experience obtained, requirements met, or licenses or certifications granted, in the territory of another Party or a non-Party, Article 15.4 (Most-Favored-Nation Treatment) does not require the Party to accord recognition to the education or experience obtained, requirements met, or licenses or certifications granted, in the territory of another Party.

3. If a Party is a party to an agreement or arrangement of the type referred to in paragraph 1, whether existing or future, the Party shall afford adequate opportunity to another Party, on request, to negotiate its accession to that agreement or arrangement, or to negotiate a comparable agreement or arrangement. If a Party accords recognition of the type referred to in paragraph 1 autonomously, the Party shall afford adequate opportunity to another Party to demonstrate that education or experience obtained, requirements met, or licenses or certifications granted, in that other Party's territory should be recognized.

4. A Party shall not accord recognition in a manner that would constitute a means of discrimination between Parties or between a Party and a non-Party in the application of its standards or criteria for the authorization, licensing, or certification of a service supplier, or a disguised restriction on trade in services.

5. The Parties shall endeavor to facilitate trade in professional services as set out in Annex 15-C (Professional Services).

Article 15.10:   Small and Medium-Sized Enterprises

1. With a view to enhancing commercial opportunities in services for SMEs, and further to Chapter 25 (Small and Medium-Sized Enterprises), each Party shall endeavor to support the development of SME trade in services and SME-enabling business models, such as direct selling services,[7] including through measures that facilitate SME access to resources or protect individuals from fraudulent practices.

---

[7]   Direct selling is the retail distribution of goods by an independent sales representative, and for which the representative is compensated based exclusively on the value of goods sold either by the representative or additional representatives recruited, trained, or otherwise supported by the representative. These goods include any product that may be distributed by other retail distribution service suppliers

2.   Further to Chapter 28 (Good Regulatory Practices), each Party shall endeavor to adopt or maintain appropriate mechanisms that consider the effects of regulatory actions on SME service suppliers and that enable small businesses to participate in regulatory policy development.

3.   Further to Article 15.8 (Development and Administration of Measures), each Party shall endeavor to ensure that authorization procedures for a service sector do not impose disproportionate burdens on SMEs.

Article 15.11:   Denial of Benefits

1.   A Party may deny the benefits of this Chapter to a service supplier of another Party if the service supplier is an enterprise owned or controlled by a person of a non-Party, and the denying Party adopts or maintains a measure with respect to the non-Party or a person of the non-Party that prohibits a transaction with that enterprise or that would be violated or circumvented if the benefits of this Chapter were accorded to that enterprise.

2.   A Party may deny the benefits of this Chapter to a service supplier of another Party if the service supplier is an enterprise owned or controlled by a person of a non-Party, or by a person of the denying Party, that has no substantial business activities in the territory of any Party other than the denying Party.

Article 15.12:   Payments and Transfers

1.   Each Party shall permit all transfers and payments that relate to the cross-border supply of services to be made freely and without delay into and out of its territory.

2.   Each Party shall permit transfers and payments that relate to the cross-border supply of services to be made in a freely usable currency at the market rate of exchange that prevails at the time of transfer.

3.   Notwithstanding paragraphs 1 and 2, a Party may prevent or delay a transfer or payment through the equitable, non-discriminatory, and good faith application of its laws that relate to:

   (a)   bankruptcy, insolvency, or the protection of the rights of creditors;

   (b)   issuing, trading, or dealing in securities or derivatives;[8]

   (c)   financial reporting or record keeping of transfers when necessary to assist law enforcement or financial regulatory authorities;

---

without a prescription or other special authorization, and may include food products, such as food and nutritional supplements in tablet, powder, or liquid capsule form;

[8]   cosmetics; common consumer products for which medical expertise is not required, such as cotton swabs; and other hygiene and cleaning products. The term "nutritional supplement" applies to all health-maintenance products not intended to cure or treat a disease, and that are sold without prescription or other special authorization.

(d)   criminal or penal offenses; or

(e)   ensuring compliance with orders or judgments in judicial or administrative proceedings.

4.   For greater certainty, this Article does not preclude the equitable, non-discriminatory, and good faith application of a Party's laws relating to its social security, public retirement, or compulsory savings programs.

ANNEX 15-A   DELIVERY SERVICES

1.   For the purposes of this Annex:

Delivery services means the collection, sorting, transport, and delivery of documents, printed matter, parcels, goods, or other items;

Postal monopoly means the exclusive right accorded to an operator within a Party's territory to supply specified delivery services pursuant to a measure of the Party; and

universal service means a delivery service that is made available to all users in a designated territory in accordance with standards of price and quality as defined by each Party.

2.   For greater certainty, this Annex does not apply to maritime, internal waterway, air, rail, or road transportation services, including cabotage.

3.   Each Party that maintains a postal monopoly shall define the scope of the monopoly on the basis of objective criteria, including quantitative criteria such as price or weight thresholds.

4.   For greater certainty, each Party has the right to define the kind of universal service obligation it wishes to adopt or maintain. Each Party that maintains a universal service obligation shall administer it in a transparent, non-discriminatory, and impartial manner with regard to all service suppliers subject to the obligation.

5.   No Party shall allow a supplier of a delivery service covered by a postal monopoly to:

(a)   use revenues derived from the supply of such services to cross-subsidize the supply of a delivery service not covered by a postal monopoly;[8] or

(b)   unjustifiably differentiate among mailers in like circumstances or consolidators in like circumstances with respect to tariffs or other terms and conditions for the supply of a delivery service covered by a postal monopoly.

---

[8]   A Party shall be deemed in compliance with this paragraph if an independent audit (which, for greater certainty, means for the United States a finding by the Postal Regulatory Commission) determines on an annual basis that the Party's supplier of a delivery service covered by a postal monopoly has not used revenues derived from that monopoly to cross-subsidize its delivery services not covered by a postal monopoly. For greater certainty, this paragraph does not require a Party to ensure that a supplier of a delivery service covered by a postal monopoly maintain accounts in a sufficiently detailed manner to show the costs and revenues of each of its delivery services.

6.   Each Party shall ensure that a supplier of services covered by a postal monopoly does not abuse its monopoly position to act in the Party's territory in a manner inconsistent with the Party's commitments under Article 14.4 (National Treatment), Article 15.3 (National Treatment), or Article 15.5 (Market Access) with respect to the supply of delivery services outside of the postal monopoly.

7.   No Party shall:

   (a)   require the supply of a delivery service on a universal basis as a condition for an authorization or license to supply a delivery service not covered by a postal monopoly; or

   (b)   assess fees or other charges exclusively on the supply of any delivery service that is not a universal service for the purpose of funding the supply of a universal service.

8.   Each Party shall ensure that the authority primarily responsible for regulating delivery services is not accountable to any supplier of delivery services, and that the decisions and procedures that the authority adopts are impartial, non-discriminatory, and transparent with respect to all delivery services not covered by a postal monopoly in its territory.[9]

9.   No Party may require a supplier of a delivery service not covered by a postal monopoly to contract, or prevent such a supplier from contracting, with another service supplier to supply a segment of the delivery service.

ANNEX 15-B COMMITTEE ON TRANSPORTATION SERVICES [Omitted]

ANNEX 15-C PROFESSIONAL SERVICES [Omitted]

APPENDIX 1 GUIDELINES FOR MUTUAL RECOGNITION AGREEMENTS OR ARRANGEMENTS FOR THE PROFESSIONAL SERVICES SECTOR

Introductory Notes

This Appendix provides practical guidance for governments, negotiating entities or other entities entering into mutual recognition negotiations for the professional services sector. These guidelines are non-binding and are intended to be used by the Parties on a voluntary basis. They do not modify or affect the rights and obligations of the Parties under this Agreement.

The objective of these guidelines is to facilitate the negotiation of mutual recognition agreements or arrangements (MRAs).

The examples listed under this Appendix are provided by way of illustration. The listing of these examples is indicative and is intended neither to be exhaustive, nor as an endorsement of the application of such measures by the Parties.

---

[9]   For greater certainty, and for the purposes of this paragraph, an "authority responsible for regulating delivery services" does not mean a customs administration.

Section A: Conduct of Negotiations and Relevant Obligations Opening of Negotiations

1. Parties intending to enter into negotiations towards an MRA are encouraged to inform the Professional Services Working Group established under Annex 15-C. The following information may be supplied:

    (a) the entities involved in discussions (for example, governments, national organizations in the professional services sector or institutes which have authority, statutory or otherwise, to enter into such negotiations);

    (b) a contact point to obtain further information;

    (c) the subject of the negotiations (specific activity covered); and

    (d) the expected time of the start of negotiations.

Single Negotiating Entity

2. If no single negotiating entity exists, the Parties are encouraged to establish one.

Results

3. Upon the conclusion of an MRA, parties to the MRA are encouraged to inform the Professional Services Working Group, and may supply the following information in its notification:

    (a) the content of a new MRA; or

    (b) the significant modifications to an existing MRA.

Follow-up Actions

4. As a follow-up action to a conclusion of an MRA, parties to the MRA are encouraged to inform the Professional Services Working Group of the following:

    (a) that the MRA comply with the provisions of this Chapter;

    (b) measures and actions taken regarding the implementation and monitoring of the MRA; and

    (c) that the text of the MRA is publicly available.

Section B: Form and Content of MRAs

Introductory Note

This Section sets out various issues that may be addressed in MRA negotiations and, if so agreed during the negotiations, included in the MRA. It includes some basic ideas on what a Party might require of foreign professionals seeking to take advantage of an MRA.

Participants

5. The MRA should identify clearly:

    (a) the parties to the MRA (for example, governments, national professional organisations, or institutes);

(b) competent authorities or organizations other than the parties to the MRA, if any, and their position in relation to the MRA; and

(c) the status and area of competence of each party to the MRA.

Purpose of the MRA

6. The purpose of the MRA should be clearly stated.

Scope of the MRA

7. The MRA should set out clearly:

(a) its scope in terms of the specific profession or titles and professional activities it covers in the territories of the parties;

(b) who is entitled to use the professional titles concerned;

(c) whether the recognition mechanism is based on qualifications, on the license obtained in the country of origin or on some other requirement; and

(d) whether it covers temporary access, permanent access, or both, to the profession concerned.

MRA Provisions

8. The MRA should clearly specify the conditions to be met for recognition in the territories of each Party and the level of equivalence agreed between the parties to the MRA. The precise terms of the MRA depend on the basis on which the MRA is founded, as discussed above. If the requirements of the various sub-national jurisdictions of a party to an MRA are not identical, the difference should be clearly presented. The MRA should address the applicability of the recognition granted by one sub-national jurisdiction in the other sub-national jurisdictions of the party to the MRA.

9. The Parties should seek to ensure that recognition does not require citizenship or any form of residency, or education, experience, or training in the territory of the host jurisdiction.

Eligibility for Recognition—Qualifications

10. If the MRA is based on recognition of qualifications, then it should, where applicable, state:

(a) the minimum level of education required (including entry requirements, length of study, and subjects studied);

(b) the minimum level of experience required (including location, length, and conditions of practical training or supervised professional practice prior to licensing, and framework of ethical and disciplinary standards);

(c) examinations passed, especially examinations of professional competence;

(d)   the extent to which home country qualifications are recognised in the host country; and

(e)   the qualifications which the parties to the MRA are prepared to recognize, for instance, by listing particular diplomas or certificates issued by certain institutions, or by reference to particular minimum requirements to be certified by the authorities of the country of origin, including whether the possession of a certain level of qualification would allow recognition for some activities but not others.

Eligibility for Recognition—Registration

11.   If the MRA is based on recognition of the licensing or registration decision made by regulators in the country of origin, it should specify the mechanism by which eligibility for such recognition may be established.

12.   If it is considered necessary to provide for additional requirements in order to ensure the quality of the service, the MRA should set out the conditions under which those requirements may apply, for example, in case of shortcomings in relation to qualification requirements in the host country or knowledge of local law, practice, standards, and regulations. This knowledge should be essential for practice in the host country or required because there are differences in the scope of licensed practice.

13.   If additional requirements are deemed necessary, the MRA should set out in detail what they entail (for example, examination, aptitude test, additional practice in the host country or in the country of origin, practical training, and language used for examination).

Mechanisms for Implementation

14.   The MRA could state:

(a)   the rules and procedures to be used to monitor and enforce the provisions of the MRA;

(b)   the mechanisms for dialogue and administrative cooperation between the parties to the MRA; and

(c)   the means of arbitration for disputes under the MRA.

15.   As a guide to the treatment of individual applicants, the MRA could include details on:

(a)   the focal point of contact in each party to the MRA for information on all issues relevant to the application (such as the name and address of competent authorities, licensing formalities, and information on additional requirements which need to be met in the host country);

(b)   the duration of procedures for the processing of applications by the relevant authorities of the host country;

(c)   the documentation required of applicants and the form in which it should be presented and any time limits for applications;

(d)   acceptance of documents and certificates issued in the country of origin in relation to qualifications and licensing;

(e)   the procedures of appeal to or review by the relevant authorities; and

(f)   the fees that might be reasonably required.

16.   The MRA could also include the following commitments:

(a)   that requests about the measures will be promptly dealt with;

(b)   that adequate preparation time will be provided where necessary;

(c)   that any exams or tests will be arranged with reasonable periodicity;

(d)   that fees to applicants seeking to take advantage of the terms of the MRA will be in proportion to the cost to the host country or organisation; and

(e)   that information on any assistance programmes in the host country for practical training, and any commitments of the host country in that context, be supplied.

Licensing and Other Provisions in the Host Country

17.   If applicable:

(a)   the MRA could also set out the means by which, and the conditions under which, a license is actually obtained following the establishment of eligibility, and what such license entails (such as a license and its content, membership of a professional body, and use of professional or academic titles);

(b)   a licensing requirement, other than qualifications, should include, for example:

(i)   an office address, an establishment requirement, or a residency requirement,

(ii)   a language requirement,

(iii) proof of good conduct and financial standing,

(iv)   professional indemnity insurance,

(v)   compliance with host country's requirements for use of trade or firm names, and

(vi)   compliance with host country ethics, for instance independence and incompatibility.

Revision of the MRA

18. If the MRA includes terms under which it can be reviewed or revoked, the details of such terms should be clearly stated.

ANNEX 15-D PROGRAMMING SERVICES

Simultaneous Substitution

1. Canada shall rescind Broadcasting Regulatory Policy CRTC 2016-334 and Broadcasting Order CRTC 2016-335. With respect to simultaneous substitution of signals during the retransmission in Canada of the program referenced in those measures, Canada may not accord the program treatment less favorable than the treatment accorded to other programs originating in the United States retransmitted in Canada.

2. The United States and Canada shall each provide in its copyright law that:

   (a) retransmission to the public of program signals not intended in the original transmission for free, over-the-air reception by the general public shall be permitted only with the authorization of the holder of the copyright in the program; and

   (b) if the original transmission of the program is carried in signals intended for free, over-the-air reception by the general public, willful retransmission in altered form or non-simultaneous retransmission of signals carrying a copyright holder's program shall be permitted only with the authorization of the holder of the copyright in the program.

3. Other than as provided for in paragraph 1, nothing in subparagraph 2 (b) shall be construed to prevent a Party from maintaining existing measures relating to retransmission of a program carried in signals intended for free, over-the-air reception by the general public; or introducing measures to enable the local licensee of the copyrighted program to exploit fully the commercial value of its license.

Home Shopping Programming Services

4. Canada shall ensure that U.S. programming services specializing in home shopping, including modified versions of these U.S. programming services for the Canadian market, are authorized for distribution in Canada and may negotiate affiliation agreements with Canadian cable, satellite, and IPTV distributors.

ANNEX 15-E MEXICO'S CULTURAL EXCEPTIONS

Recognizing that culture is an important component of the creative, symbolic and economic dimension of human development,

Affirming the fundamental right of freedom of expression and the right to plural and diverse information,

Recognizing that states have the sovereign right to preserve, develop and implement their cultural policies, to support their cultural industries for the purpose of strengthening the diversity of cultural expressions, and to preserve their cultural identity, and

In order to preserve and promote the development of Mexican culture, Mexico has negotiated reservations in its schedules to Annex I and Annex II for certain obligations in Chapter 14 (Investment) and Chapter 15 (Cross-Border Trade in Services), which are summarized below.

In Annex I:

Broadcasting (radio and free-to-air television):

Reservations taken against:

- National Treatment obligations for Investment and Cross-Border Trade in Services Chapters

- Local Presence obligation for Cross-Border Trade in Services Chapter

- Sole concessions and frequency band concessions will be granted only to Mexican nationals or enterprises constituted under Mexican laws and regulations.

- Investors of a Party or their investments may participate up to 49 per cent in concessionaire enterprises providing broadcasting services. This maximum foreign investment will be applied according to the reciprocity existent with the country in which the investor or trader who ultimately controls it, directly or indirectly, is constituted.

- Concessions for indigenous social use shall be granted to indigenous people and indigenous communities of Mexico, with the objective to promote, develop and preserve languages, culture, knowledge, traditions, identity and their internal rules that, under principles of gender equality, enable the integration of indigenous women in the accomplishment of the purposes for which the concession is granted.

- Under no circumstances may a concession, the rights conferred therein, facilities, auxiliary services, offices or accessories and properties affected thereto, be assigned, encumbered, pledged or given in trust, mortgaged, or transferred totally or partially to any foreign government or state.

- The State shall guarantee that broadcasting promotes the values of national identity.

- The broadcasting concessionaires shall use and stimulate local and national artistic values and expressions of Mexican culture, according to the characteristics of its programming.

- The daily programming with personal performances shall include more time covered by Mexicans.

Newspaper publishing

Reservation taken against:

- National Treatment obligation for Investment Chapter

- Investors of another Party or their investments may only own, directly or indirectly, up to 49 per cent of the ownership interest in an enterprise established or to be established in the territory of Mexico engaged in the printing or publication of daily newspapers written primarily for a Mexican audience and distributed in the territory of Mexico.

Cinema services

Reservation taken against:

- National Treatment obligation for Investment Chapter

- Most-Favored-Nation Treatment obligation for Investment and Cross-Border Trade in Services Chapters

- Exhibitors shall reserve 10 per cent of the total screen time to the projection of national films.

In Annex II:

Audiovisual services

Reservation taken against:

- Market Access obligation for Cross-Border Trade in Services Chapter

- Mexico is taking only limited commitments in the Market Access obligation with respect to the audiovisual services sectors.

CHAPTER 16   TEMPORARY ENTRY
FOR BUSINESS PERSONS

Article 16.1:   Definitions

For the purposes of this Chapter:

Business person means a citizen of a Party who is engaged in trade in goods, the supply of services or the conduct of investment activities;

Citizen means, with respect to Mexico, a national or a citizen according to the provisions of Articles 30 and 34, respectively, of the Mexico's Constitution (*Constitución Política de los Estados Unidos Mexicanos*); and

Temporary entry means entry into the territory of a Party by a business person of another Party without the intent to establish permanent residence.

Article 16.2:   Scope

1.   This Chapter applies to measures affecting the temporary entry of business persons of a Party into the territory of another Party.

2.   This Chapter does not apply to measures affecting natural persons seeking access to the employment market of another Party, nor does it

apply to measures regarding citizenship, nationality, residence or employment on a permanent basis.

3. Nothing in this Agreement prevents a Party from applying measures to regulate the entry of natural persons of another Party into, or their temporary stay in, its territory, including those measures necessary to protect the integrity of, and to ensure the orderly movement of natural persons across, its borders, provided that those measures are not applied in a manner as to nullify or impair the benefits accruing to any Party under this Chapter.

Article 16.3:   General Obligations

1. Each Party shall apply its measures relating to this Chapter expeditiously so as to avoid unduly impairing or delaying trade in goods or services or the conduct of investment activities under this Agreement.

2. The Parties shall endeavor to develop and adopt common criteria, definitions and interpretations for the implementation of this Chapter.

Article 16.4:   Grant of Temporary Entry

1. Each Party shall grant temporary entry to a business person who is otherwise qualified for entry under its measures relating to public health and safety and national security, in accordance with this Chapter, including Annex 16-A (Temporary Entry for Business Persons).

2. A Party may refuse to grant temporary entry or issue an immigration document authorizing employment to a business person where the temporary entry of that person might adversely affect:

    (a) the settlement of a labor dispute that is in progress at the place or intended place of employment; or

    (b) the employment of a person who is involved in that dispute.

3. If a Party refuses pursuant to paragraph 2 to grant temporary entry or issue an immigration document authorizing employment, it shall:

    (a) provide written notice to the business person of the reasons for the refusal; and

    (b) promptly provide written notice to the Party whose business person has been refused entry of the reasons for the refusal.

4. Each Party shall limit any fees for processing applications for temporary entry of business persons to the approximate cost of services rendered.

5. The sole fact that a Party grants temporary entry to a business person of another Party pursuant to this Chapter does not exempt that business person from meeting any applicable licensing or other requirements, including any mandatory codes of conduct, to practice a profession or otherwise engage in business activities.

Article 16.5:   Provision of Information

1.   Further to Article 29.2 (Publication), each Party shall publish online or otherwise make publicly available explanatory material regarding the requirements for temporary entry under this Chapter that will enable a business person of another Party to become acquainted with them.

2.   Each Party shall collect and maintain, and make available to the other Parties in accordance with its law, data respecting the granting of temporary entry under this Chapter to business persons of the other Parties who have been issued immigration documentation, including, if practicable, data specific to each occupation, profession, or activity.

Article 16.6:   Temporary Entry Working Group

1.   The Parties hereby establish a Temporary Entry Working Group, comprising representatives of each Party, including representatives of immigration authorities.

2.   The Working Group shall meet at least once each year to consider:

(a)   the implementation and administration of this Chapter;

(b)   the development of measures to further facilitate temporary entry of business persons on a reciprocal basis;

(c)   the waiving of labor certification tests or procedures of similar effect for spouses of business persons who have been granted temporary entry for more than one year under Section B, C or D of Annex 16-A (Temporary Entry for Business Persons);

(d)   proposed modifications of or additions to this Chapter; and

(e)   issues of common interest related to the temporary entry of business persons, such as the use of technologies related to processing of applications, that can be further explored among the Parties in other fora.

Article 16.7:   Dispute Settlement

1.   A Party may not initiate proceedings under Article 31.5 (Commission Good Offices, Conciliation, and Mediation) regarding a refusal to grant temporary entry under this Chapter or a particular case arising under Article 16.3(1) unless:

(a)   the matter involves a pattern of practice; and

(b)   the business person has exhausted the available administrative remedies regarding the particular matter.

2.   The remedies referred to in paragraph (1)(b) will be deemed to be exhausted if a final determination in the matter has not been issued by the competent authority within one year of the institution of an administrative proceeding, and the failure to issue a determination is not attributable to delay caused by the business person.

Article 16.8:   Relation to Other Chapters

Except for this Chapter, Chapter 1 (Initial Provisions and General Definitions), Chapter 30 (Administrative and Institutional Provisions), Chapter 31 (Dispute Settlement), Chapter 34 (Final Provisions), Article 29.2 (Publication), and Article 29.3 (Administrative Proceedings), this Agreement does not impose an obligation on a Party regarding its immigration measures.

ANNEX 16-A TEMPORARY ENTRY FOR BUSINESS PERSONS

Section A: Business Visitors

1.   Each Party shall grant temporary entry to a business person seeking to engage in a business activity set out in Appendix 1, without requiring that person to obtain an employment authorization, provided that the business person otherwise complies with the Party's measures applicable to temporary entry, on presentation of:

   (a)   proof of citizenship of a Party;

   (b)   documentation demonstrating that the business person will be so engaged and describing the purpose of entry; and

   (c)   evidence demonstrating that the proposed business activity is international in scope and that the business person is not seeking to enter the local labor market.

2.   Each Party shall provide that a business person may satisfy the requirements of paragraph 1(c) by demonstrating that:

   (a)   the primary source of remuneration for the proposed business activity is outside the territory of the Party granting temporary entry; and

   (b)   the business person's principal place of business and the actual place of accrual of profits, at least predominantly, remain outside that Party's territory.

A Party shall normally accept an oral declaration as to the principal place of business and the actual place of accrual of profits. Where the Party requires further proof, it shall normally consider a letter from the employer attesting to these matters as sufficient proof.

3.   Paragraph 1 does not limit the ability of a business person seeking to engage in a business activity other than those set out in Appendix 1 to seek temporary entry under a Party's measures relating to the entry of business persons.

4.   No Party shall:

   (a)   as a condition for temporary entry under paragraph 1, require prior approval procedures, petitions, labor certification tests or other procedures of similar effect; or

   (b)   impose or maintain a numerical restriction relating to temporary entry under paragraph 1.

5.   Notwithstanding paragraph 4, a Party may require a business person seeking temporary entry under this Section to obtain a visa or its equivalent prior to entry. Before imposing a visa requirement, the Party shall consult, on request, with a Party whose business persons would be affected with a view to avoiding the imposition of the requirement. With respect to an existing visa requirement, a Party shall consult, on request, with a Party whose business persons are subject to the requirement with a view to its removal.

Section B: Traders and Investors

1.   Each Party shall grant temporary entry and provide confirming documentation to a business person seeking to:

   (a)   carry on substantial trade in goods or services principally between the territory of the Party of which the business person is a citizen and the territory of the Party into which entry is sought; or

   (b)   establish, develop, administer or provide advice or key technical services to the operation of an investment to which the business person or the business person's enterprise has committed, or is in the process of committing, a substantial amount of capital,

in a capacity that is supervisory, executive or involves essential skills, provided that the business person otherwise complies with the Party's measures applicable to temporary entry.

2.   No Party shall:

   (a)   as a condition for temporary entry under paragraph 1, require labor certification tests or other procedures of similar effect; or

   (b)   impose or maintain a numerical restriction relating to temporary entry under paragraph 1.

3.   Notwithstanding paragraph 2, a Party may require a business person seeking temporary entry under this Section to obtain a visa or its equivalent prior to entry. Before imposing a visa requirement, the Party shall consult with a Party whose business persons would be affected with a view to avoiding the imposition of the requirement. With respect to an existing visa requirement, a Party shall consult, on request, with a Party whose business persons are subject to the requirement with a view to its removal.

Section C: Intra-Company Transferees

1.   Each Party shall grant temporary entry and provide confirming documentation to a business person employed by an enterprise who seeks to render services to that enterprise or a subsidiary or affiliate thereof, in a capacity that is managerial, executive or involves specialized knowledge, provided that the business person otherwise complies with the Party's measures applicable to temporary entry. A Party may require the business person to have been employed

continuously by the enterprise for one year within the three-year period immediately preceding the date of the application for admission.

2.   No Party shall:

   (a)   as a condition for temporary entry under paragraph 1, require labor certification tests or other procedures of similar effect; or

   (b)   impose or maintain a numerical restriction relating to temporary entry under paragraph 1.

3.   Notwithstanding paragraph 2, a Party may require a business person seeking temporary entry under this Section to obtain a visa or its equivalent prior to entry. Before imposing a visa requirement, the Party shall consult with a Party whose business persons would be affected with a view to avoiding the imposition of the requirement. With respect to an existing visa requirement, a Party shall consult, on request, with a Party whose business persons are subject to the requirement with a view to its removal.

Section D: Professionals

1.   Each Party shall grant temporary entry and provide confirming documentation to a business person seeking to engage in a business activity at a professional level in a profession set out in Appendix 2, if the business person otherwise complies with the Party's measures applicable to temporary entry, on presentation of:

   (a)   proof of citizenship of a Party; and

   (b)   documentation demonstrating that the business person will be so engaged and describing the purpose of entry.

2.   No Party shall:

   (a)   as a condition for temporary entry under paragraph 1, require prior approval procedures, petitions, labor certification tests or other procedures of similar effect; or

   (b)   impose or maintain a numerical restriction relating to temporary entry under paragraph 1.

3.   Notwithstanding paragraph 2, a Party may require a business person seeking temporary entry under this Section to obtain a visa or its equivalent prior to entry. Before imposing a visa requirement, the Party shall consult with a Party whose business persons would be affected with a view to avoiding the imposition of the requirement. With respect to an existing visa requirement, a Party shall consult, on request, with a Party whose business persons are subject to the requirement with a view to its removal.

APPENDIX 1   BUSINESS VISITORS

Section A: Definitions

For the purposes of this Appendix:

Territory of another Party means the territory of a Party other than the territory of the Party into which temporary entry is sought;

Tour bus operator means a natural person, including relief personnel accompanying or following to join, necessary for the operation of a tour bus for the duration of a trip; and

Transportation operator means a natural person, other than a tour bus operator, including relief personnel accompanying or following to join, necessary for the operation of a vehicle for the duration of a trip.

Section B: Business Activities

Research and Design

☐ Technical, scientific and statistical researchers conducting independent research or research for an enterprise located in the territory of another Party.

Growth, Manufacture, and Production

☐ Harvester owner supervising a harvesting crew admitted under a Party's law.

☐ Purchasing and production management personnel conducting commercial transactions for an enterprise located in the territory of another Party.

Marketing

☐ Market researchers and analysts conducting independent research or analysis or research or analysis for an enterprise located in the territory of another Party.

☐ Trade fair and promotional personnel attending a trade convention.

Sales

☐ Sales representatives and agents taking orders or negotiating contracts for goods or services for an enterprise located in the territory of another Party but not delivering goods or supplying services.

☐ Buyers purchasing for an enterprise located in the territory of another Party.

Distribution

☐ Transportation operators transporting goods or passengers to the territory of a Party from the territory of another Party or loading and transporting goods or passengers from the territory of a Party, with no unloading in that territory, to the territory of another Party.

☐ With respect to temporary entry into the territory of the United States, Canadian customs brokers performing brokerage duties relating to the export of goods from the territory of the United States to or through the territory of Canada.

☐ With respect to temporary entry into the territory of Canada, United States customs brokers performing brokerage duties relating to the export of goods from the territory of Canada to or through the territory of the United States.

☐ Customs brokers providing consulting services regarding the facilitation of the import or export of goods.

After Sales Services

☐ Installers, repair and maintenance personnel, and supervisors, possessing specialized knowledge essential to a seller's contractual obligation, performing services or training workers to perform services, pursuant to a warranty or other service contract incidental to the sale of commercial or industrial equipment or machinery, including computer software, purchased from an enterprise located outside the territory of the Party into which temporary entry is sought, during the life of the warranty or service agreement.

General Service

☐ Professionals engaging in a business activity at a professional level in a profession set out in Appendix 2

Commercial Transactions

☐ Management and supervisory personnel engaging in a commercial transaction for an enterprise located in the territory of another Party.

☐ Financial services personnel (insurers, bankers or investment brokers) engaging in commercial transactions for an enterprise located in the territory of another Party.

Public Relations and Advertising

☐ Public relations and advertising personnel consulting with business associates, or attending or participating in conventions.

Tourism

☐ Tourism personnel (tour and travel agents, tour guides or tour operators) attending or participating in conventions or conducting a tour that has begun in the territory of another Party.

Tour Bus Operation

☐ Tour bus operators entering the territory of a Party:

   (a) with a group of passengers on a bus tour that has begun in, and will return to, the territory of another Party;

   (b) to meet a group of passengers on a bus tour that will end, and the predominant portion of which will take place, in the territory of another Party; or

   (c) with a group of passengers on a bus tour to be unloaded in the territory of the Party into which temporary entry is sought, and returning with no passengers or reloading with the group for transportation to the territory of another Party.

Translation

☐   Translators or interpreters performing services as employees of an enterprise located in the territory of another Party.

APPENDIX 2   PROFESSIONALS

PROFESSION[1]	MINIMUM EDUCATION REQUIREMENTS AND ALTERNATIVE CREDENTIALS
General	
Accountant	Baccalaureate or Licenciatura Degree; or C.P.A., C.A., C.G.A. or C.M.A.
Architect	Baccalaureate or Licenciatura Degree; or state/provincial license[2]
Computer Systems Analyst	Baccalaureate or Licenciatura Degree; or Post-Secondary Diploma[3] or Post-Secondary Certificate,[4] and three years experience
Disaster Relief Insurance Claims Adjuster (claims Adjuster employed by an insurance company located in the territory of a Party, or an independent claims adjuster)	Baccalaureate or Licenciatura Degree, and successful completion of training in the appropriate areas of insurance adjustment pertaining to disaster relief claims; or three years experience in claims adjustment and successful completion of training in the appropriate areas of insurance adjustment pertaining to disaster relief claims
Economist	Baccalaureate or Licenciatura Degree

----

[1]   A business person seeking temporary entry under this Appendix may also perform training functions relating to the profession, including conducting seminars.

[2]   "State/provincial license" and "state/provincial/federal license" mean a document issued by a state, provincial, or federal government, as the case may be, or under its authority, but not by a local government, that permits a person to engage in a regulated activity or profession.

[3]   "Post-Secondary Diploma" means a credential issued, on completion of two or more years of postsecondary education, by an accredited academic institution in Canada or the United States.

[4]   "Post-Secondary Certificate" means a certificate issued, on completion of two or more years of postsecondary education at an academic institution, by the federal government of Mexico or a state government in Mexico, an academic institution recognized by the federal government or a state government, or an academic institution created by federal or state law.

Engineer	Baccalaureate or Licenciatura Degree; or state/provincial license
Forester	Baccalaureate or Licenciatura Degree; or state/provincial license
Graphic Designer	Baccalaureate or Licenciatura Degree; or Post-Secondary Diploma or Post-Secondary Certificate, and three years experience
Hotel Manager	Baccalaureate or Licenciatura Degree in hotel/restaurant management; or Post-Secondary Diploma or Post-Secondary Certificate in hotel/restaurant management, and three years experience in hotel/restaurant management
Industrial Designer	Baccalaureate or Licenciatura Degree; or Post-Secondary Diploma or Post-Secondary Certificate, and three years experience
Interior Designer	Baccalaureate or Licenciatura Degree; or Post-Secondary Diploma or Post-Secondary Certificate, and three years experience
Land Surveyor	Baccalaureate or Licenciatura Degree; or state/provincial/federal license
Landscape Architect	Baccalaureate or Licenciatura Degree
Lawyer (including Notary in the Province of Quebec)	LL.B., J.D., LL.L., B.C.L. or Licenciatura Degree (five years); or membership in a state/provincial bar
Librarian	M.L.S. or B.L.S. (for which another Baccalaureate or Licenciatura Degree was a prerequisite)
Management Consultant	Baccalaureate or Licenciatura Degree; or equivalent professional experience as established by statement or professional credential attesting to five years experience as a management consultant, or five years experience in a field of specialty related to the consulting agreement

Mathematician (including Statistician)[5]	Baccalaureate or Licenciatura Degree
Range Manager/Range Conservationalist	Baccalaureate or Licenciatura Degree
Research Assistant (working in a post-secondary educational institution)	Baccalaureate or Licenciatura Degree
Scientific Technician/ Technologist[6]	Possession of (a) theoretical knowledge of any of the following disciplines: agricultural sciences, astronomy, biology, chemistry, engineering, forestry, geology, geophysics, meteorology or physics; and (b) the ability to solve practical problems in any of those disciplines, or the ability to apply principles of any of those disciplines to basic or applied research
Social Worker	Baccalaureate or Licenciatura Degree
Sylviculturist (including Forestry Specialist)	Baccalaureate or Licenciatura Degree
Technical Publications Writer	Baccalaureate or Licenciatura Degree; or Post-Secondary Diploma or Post-Secondary Certificate, and three years experience
Urban Planner (including Geographer)	Baccalaureate or Licenciatura Degree
Vocational Counsellor	Baccalaureate or Licenciatura Degree
Medical/Allied Professional	Baccalaureate or Licenciatura Degree
Dentist	D.D.S., D.M.D., Doctor en Odontologia or Doctor en Cirugia Dental; or state/provincial license
Dietitian	Baccalaureate or Licenciatura Degree; or state/provincial license

---

[5]   In accordance with the NAFTA 1994 Commission decision of October 7, 2003, the term "Mathematician" includes the profession of Actuary.

[6]   A business person in this category must be seeking temporary entry to work in direct support of professionals in agricultural sciences, astronomy, biology, chemistry, engineering, forestry, geology, geophysics, meteorology, or physics

Medical Laboratory Technologist (Canada)/ Medical Technologist (Mexico and the United States)[7]	Baccalaureate or Licenciatura Degree; or Post-Secondary Diploma or Post-Secondary Certificate, and three years experience
Nutritionist	Baccalaureate or Licenciatura Degree
Occupational Therapist	Baccalaureate or Licenciatura Degree; or state/provincial license
Pharmacist	Baccalaureate or Licenciatura Degree; or state/provincial license
Physician (teaching or research only)	M.D. or Doctor en Medicina; or state/provincial license
Physiotherapist/Physical Therapist	Baccalaureate or Licenciatura Degree; or state/provincial license
Psychologist	State/provincial license; or Licenciatura Degree
Recreational Therapist	Baccalaureate or Licenciatura Degree
Registered Nurse	State/provincial license; or Licenciatura Degree
Veterinarian	D.V.M., D.M.V. or Doctor en Veterinaria; or state/provincial license

Scientist

Agriculturist (including Agronomist)	Baccalaureate or Licenciatura Degree
Animal Breeder	Baccalaureate or Licenciatura Degree
Animal Scientist	Baccalaureate or Licenciatura Degree
Apiculturist	Baccalaureate or Licenciatura Degree
Astronomer	Baccalaureate or Licenciatura Degree
Biochemist	Baccalaureate or Licenciatura Degree

---

[7]   A business person in this category must be seeking temporary entry to perform in a laboratory chemical, biological, hematological, immunologic, microscopic, or bacteriological tests and analyses for diagnosis, treatment or prevention of disease.

Biologist[8]	Baccalaureate or Licenciatura Degree
Chemist	Baccalaureate or Licenciatura Degree
Dairy Scientist	Baccalaureate or Licenciatura Degree
Entomologist	Baccalaureate or Licenciatura Degree
Epidemiologist	Baccalaureate or Licenciatura Degree
Geneticist	Baccalaureate or Licenciatura Degree
Geologist	Baccalaureate or Licenciatura Degree
Geochemist	Baccalaureate or Licenciatura Degree
Geophysicist	(including Oceanographer in Mexico Baccalaureate or Licenciatura Degree and the United States)
Horticulturist	Baccalaureate or Licenciatura Degree
Meteorologist	Baccalaureate or Licenciatura Degree
Pharmacologist	Baccalaureate or Licenciatura Degree Physicist (including Oceanographer in Canada) Baccalaureate or Licenciatura Degree
Plant Breeder	Baccalaureate or Licenciatura Degree
Poultry Scientist	Baccalaureate or Licenciatura Degree
Soil Scientist	Baccalaureate or Licenciatura Degree
Zoologist	Baccalaureate or Licenciatura Degree
Teacher	Baccalaureate or Licenciatura Degree
College	Baccalaureate or Licenciatura Degree
Seminary	Baccalaureate or Licenciatura Degree
University	Baccalaureate or Licenciatura Degree

---

[8]   In accordance with the NAFTA 1994 Commission decision of October 7, 2003, the term "Biologist" includes the profession of Plant Pathologist.

CHAPTER 17   FINANCIAL SERVICES

Article 17.1:   Definitions

For the purposes of this Chapter:

Computing facility means a computer server or storage device for the processing or storage of information for the conduct of business within the scope of the license, authorization, or registration of a covered person, but does not include a computer server or storage device of or those used to access:

    (a)   financial market infrastructures;

    (b)   exchanges or markets for securities or for derivatives such as futures, options, and swaps; or

    (c)   non-governmental bodies that exercise regulatory or supervisory authority over covered persons;

Covered person means

    (a)   a financial institution of another Party; or

    (b)   a cross-border financial service supplier of another Party that is subject to regulation, supervision, and licensing, authorization, or registration by a financial regulatory authority of the Party;[1]

Cross-border financial service supplier of a Party means a person of a Party that is engaged in the business of supplying a financial service within the territory of the Party and that seeks to supply or supplies a financial service through the cross-border supply of that service;

Cross-border trade in financial services or cross-border supply of financial services means the supply of a financial service:

    (a)   from the territory of a Party into the territory of another Party;

    (b)   in the territory of a Party by a person of that Party to a person of another Party; or

    (c)   by a national of a Party in the territory of another Party,

but does not include the supply of a financial service in the territory of a Party by a covered investment;

---

[1]   For greater certainty, whenever a cross-border financial service supplier of another Party is subject to regulation, supervision, and licensing, authorization, or registration by a financial regulatory authority of the Party, that supplier is a covered person for the purposes of this Chapter. For greater certainty, if a financial regulatory authority of the Party foregoes imposition of certain regulatory or supervisory requirements on the condition that a cross-border financial service supplier of another Party comply with certain regulatory or supervisory requirements imposed by a financial regulatory authority of the other Party, that supplier is a covered person.

Financial institution means a financial intermediary or other enterprise that is authorized to do business and is regulated or supervised as a financial institution under the law of the Party in whose territory it is located;

Financial institution of another Party means a financial institution, including a branch, located in the territory of a Party that is controlled by a person of another Party;

Financial market infrastructure means a multi-participant system in which a covered person participates with other financial service suppliers, including the operator of the system, used for the purposes of clearing, settling, or recording payments, securities, derivatives, or other financial transactions;

Financial service means a service of a financial nature. Financial services include all insurance and insurance-related services, and all banking and other financial services (excluding insurance), as well as services incidental or auxiliary to a service of a financial nature. Financial services include the following activities:

Insurance and insurance-related services

(a)   direct insurance (including co-insurance):

   (i)   life,

   (ii) non-life;

(b)   reinsurance and retrocession;

(c)   insurance intermediation, such as brokerage and agency; and

(d)   services auxiliary to insurance, such as consultancy, actuarial, risk assessment, and claim settlement services;

Banking and other financial services (excluding insurance)

(e)   acceptance of deposits and other repayable funds from the public;

(f)   lending of all types, including consumer credit, mortgage credit, factoring, and financing of commercial transactions;

(g)   financial leasing;

(h)   all payment and money transmission services, including credit, charge and debit cards, travelers checks, and bankers drafts;

(i)   guarantees and commitments;

(j)   trading for own account or for account of customers, whether on an exchange, in an over-the-counter market or otherwise, the following:

   (i)   money market instruments (including checks, bills, certificates of deposits),

   (ii) foreign exchange,

    (iii)   derivative products, including futures and options,

    (iv)   exchange rate and interest rate instruments, including products such as swaps and forward rate agreements,

    (v)   transferable securities, and

    (vi)   other negotiable instruments and financial assets, including bullion;

(k)   participation in issues of all kinds of securities, including underwriting and placement as agent (whether publicly or privately) and supply of services related to these issues;

(l)   money broking;

(m)   asset management, such as cash or portfolio management, all forms of collective investment management, pension fund management, custodial, depository, and trust services;

(n)   settlement and clearing services for financial assets, including securities, derivative products, and other negotiable instruments;

(o)   provision and transfer of financial information, and financial data processing and related software by suppliers of other financial services; and

(p)   advisory, intermediation and other auxiliary financial services on all the activities listed in subparagraphs (e) through (o), including credit reference and analysis,

Investment and portfolio research and advice, advice on acquisitions, and on corporate restructuring and strategy;

Financial service supplier of a Party means a person of a Party that is engaged in the business of supplying a financial service within the territory of that Party;

Investment means "investment" as defined in Article 14.1 (Definitions), except that with respect to "loans" and "debt instruments" referred to in that Article:

(a)   a loan to or debt instrument issued by a financial institution is an investment only if it is treated as regulatory capital by the Party in whose territory the financial institution is located; and

(b)   a loan granted by or debt instrument owned by a financial institution, other than a loan to or debt instrument issued by a financial institution referred to in subparagraph (a), is not an investment;

For greater certainty, a loan granted, or debt instrument owned, by a cross-border financial service supplier, other than a loan to or debt instrument issued by a financial institution, is an investment for the purposes of Chapter 14 (Investment), if that loan or debt instrument meets the criteria for investments set out in Article 14.1 (Definitions); investor of a Party means a

Party, or a person of a Party, that attempts to make,[2] is making, or has made an investment in the territory of another Party;

New financial service means a financial service not supplied in the Party's territory that is supplied within the territory of another Party, and includes any new form of delivery of a financial service or the sale of a financial product that is not sold in the Party's territory;

Person of a Party means "person of a Party" as defined in Article 1.4 (General Definitions) and, for greater certainty, does not include a branch of an enterprise of a non-Party;

public entity means a central bank or monetary authority of a Party, or a financial institution that is owned or controlled by a Party; and

Self-regulatory organization means a non-governmental body, including a securities or futures exchange or market, clearing agency, or other organization or association, that exercises regulatory or supervisory authority over financial service suppliers or financial institutions by statute or delegation from a central or regional government.

Article 17.2:   Scope

1. This Chapter applies to a measure adopted or maintained by a Party relating to:

    (a)   a financial institution of another Party;

    (b)   an investor of another Party, and an investment of that investor, in a financial institution in the Party's territory; and

    (c)   cross-border trade in financial services.

2. Chapter 14 (Investment) and Chapter 15 (Cross-Border Trade in Services) apply to a measure described in paragraph 1 only to the extent that those Chapters are incorporated into this Chapter.

    (a)   Article 14.6 (Minimum Standard of Treatment), Article 14.7 (Treatment in Case of Armed Conflict or Civil Strife), Article 14.8 (Expropriation and Compensation), Article 14.9 (Transfers), Article 14.13 (Special Formalities and Information Requirements), Article 14.14 (Denial of Benefits), Article 14.16 (Investment and Environmental, Health, Safety, and other Regulatory Objectives), and Article 15.11 (Denial of Benefits) are incorporated into and made a part of this Chapter.

    (b)   Article 15.12 (Payments and Transfers) is incorporated into and made a part of this Chapter to the extent that cross-border trade in financial services is subject to obligations

---

[2]   For greater certainty, the Parties understand that an investor "attempts to make" an investment when that investor has taken concrete action or actions to make an investment, such as channeling resources or capital in order to set up a business, or applying for permits or licenses.

pursuant to Article 17.3.3 (National Treatment), Article 17.5.1(b) and

(c)   (Market Access), and Article 17.6 (Cross-Border Trade Standstill).

3.   This Chapter does not apply to a measure adopted or maintained by a Party relating to:

(a)   an activity or a service forming part of a public retirement plan or statutory system of social security; or

(b)   an activity or a service conducted for the account or with the guarantee or using the financial resources of the Party, including its public entities,

except that this Chapter applies to the extent that a Party allows an activity or service referred to in subparagraph (a) or (b) to be conducted by its financial institutions in competition with a public entity or a financial institution.

4.   This Chapter does not apply to government procurement of financial services.

5.   This Chapter does not apply to a subsidy or a grant provided by a Party, including a government supported loan, guarantee, and insurance, with respect to the cross-border supply of financial services by a cross-border supplier of another Party.

Article 17.3:   National Treatment

1.   Each Party shall accord to investors of another Party treatment no less favorable than that it accords to its own investors, in like circumstances, with respect to the establishment, acquisition, expansion, management, conduct, operation, and sale or other disposition of financial institutions, and investments in financial institutions in its territory.

2.   Each Party shall accord to financial institutions of another Party, and to investments of investors of another Party in financial institutions, treatment no less favorable than that it accords to its own financial institutions, and to investments of its own investors in financial institutions, in like circumstances, with respect to the establishment, acquisition, expansion, management, conduct, operation, and sale or other disposition of financial institutions and investments.

3.   Each Party shall accord to:

(a)   financial services or cross-border financial service suppliers of another Party seeking to supply or supplying the financial services as specified by the Party in Annex 17-A (Cross-Border Trade); and

(b)   financial services or cross-border financial service suppliers of another Party seeking to supply or supplying financial services subject to paragraph 4, treatment no less favorable than that it accords to its own financial services and financial service suppliers, in like circumstances.

4. Subparagraph 3(b) does not require a Party to permit a cross-border financial service supplier of another Party to do business or solicit in the Party's territory. A Party may define "doing business" and "solicitation" in its law for the purposes of this paragraph.

5. The treatment to be accorded by a Party under paragraphs 1, 2, and 3 means, with respect to a government other than at the central level, treatment no less favorable than the most favorable treatment accorded, in like circumstances, by that government to financial institutions of the Party, investors of the Party, and investments of those investors, in financial institutions; or financial services or financial service suppliers, of the Party.

6. For greater certainty, whether treatment is accorded in "like circumstances" under this Article depends on the totality of the circumstances, including whether the relevant treatment distinguishes between investors in financial institutions, investments in financial institutions, financial institutions, or financial services or financial service suppliers on the basis of legitimate public welfare objectives.

Article 17.4:   Most-Favored-Nation Treatment

1. Each Party shall accord to:

    (a) investors of another Party, treatment no less favorable than that it accords to investors of any other Party or of a non-Party, in like circumstances;

    (b) financial institutions of another Party, treatment no less favorable than that it accords to financial institutions of any other Party or of a non-Party, in like circumstances;

    (c) investments of investors of another Party in a financial institution, treatment no less favorable than that it accords to investments of investors of any other Party or of a non-Party in financial institutions, in like circumstances; and

    (d) financial services or cross-border financial service suppliers of another Party, treatment no less favorable than that it accords to financial services and cross-border financial service suppliers of any other Party or of a non-Party, in like circumstances.

2. The treatment to be accorded by a Party under paragraph 1 means, with respect to a government other than at the central level, treatment no less favorable than the most favorable treatment accorded, in like circumstances, by that government to financial institutions of another Party or a non-Party; investors of another Party or a non-Party, and investments of those investors, in financial institutions; or financial services or cross-border financial service suppliers of another Party or non-Party.

3. For greater certainty, whether treatment is accorded in "like circumstances" under this Article depends on the totality of the circumstances, including whether the relevant treatment distinguishes between investors in financial institutions, investments in financial institutions, financial institutions, or financial services or financial service suppliers on the basis of legitimate public welfare objectives.

Article 17.5:   Market Access

1. No Party shall adopt or maintain with respect to:

    (a) a financial institution of another Party or, an investor of another Party seeking to establish those institutions;

    (b) a cross-border financial service supplier of another Party seeking to supply or supplying the financial services as specified by the Party in Annex 17-A (Cross-Border Trade); or

    (c) a cross-border financial service supplier of another Party seeking to supply or supplying financial services, subject to paragraph 2,

either on the basis of a regional subdivision or on the basis of its entire territory, a measure that:

    (d) imposes a limitation on:

        (i)   the number of financial institutions or cross-border financial service suppliers, whether in the form of numerical quotas, monopolies, exclusive service suppliers or the requirement of an economic needs test,

        (ii) the total value of financial service transactions or assets in the form of numerical quotas or the requirement of an economic needs test,

        (iii) the total number of financial service operations or the total quantity of financial services output expressed in terms of designated numerical units in the form of quotas or the requirement of an economic needs test,[3] or

        (iv) the total number of natural persons that may be employed in a particular financial service sector or that a financial institution or cross-border f i n an ci al service supplier may employ and who are necessary for, and directly related to, the supply of a specific financial service in the form of numerical quotas or the requirement of an economic needs test; or

---

[3]   Subparagraph (d)(iii) does not cover measures of a Party that limit inputs for the supply of financial services.

(e)   restricts or requires specific types of legal entity or joint venture through which a financial institution or cross-border financial service supplier may supply a service.

2.   Subparagraph 1(c) does not require a Party to permit a cross-border financial service supplier of another Party to do business or solicit in the Party's territory. A Party may define "doing business" and "solicitation" in its law for the purposes of this paragraph.

3.   No Party shall require a cross-border financial service supplier of another Party to establish or maintain a representative office or an enterprise, or to be resident, in its territory as a condition for the cross-border supply of a financial service, with respect to the financial services referred to in Article 17.6 (Cross-Border Trade Standstill) and the financial services as specified by the Party in Annex 17-A (Cross-Border Trade).

4.   For greater certainty, a Party may require the registration or authorization of a cross-border financial service supplier of another Party or of a financial instrument.

Article 17.6:   Cross-Border Trade Standstill

No Party shall adopt a measure restricting any type of cross-border trade in financial services by cross-border financial service suppliers of another Party that the Party permitted on January 1, 1994, or that is inconsistent with Article 17.3.3 (National Treatment), with respect to the supply of those services.

Article 17.7:   New Financial Services[4]

Each Party shall permit a financial institution of another Party to supply a new financial service that the Party would permit its own financial institutions, in like circumstances, to supply without adopting a law or modifying an existing law.[5] Notwithstanding Article 17.5.1(a) and(e) (Market Access), a Party may determine the institutional and juridical form through which the new financial service may be supplied and may require authorization for the supply of the service. If a Party requires a financial institution to obtain authorization to supply a new financial service, the Party shall decide within a reasonable period of time whether to issue the authorization and may refuse the authorization only for prudential reasons.

Article 17.8:   Treatment of Customer Information

This Chapter does not require a Party to disclose information related to the financial affairs or accounts of individual customers of financial institutions or cross-border financial service suppliers.

---

[4]   The Parties understand that nothing in this Article prevents a financial institution of a Party from applying to another Party to request that it authorize the supply of a financial service that is not supplied in the territory of any Party. That application will be subject to the law of the Party to which the application is made and, for greater certainty, is not subject to this Article.

[5]   For greater certainty, a Party may issue a new regulation or other subordinate measure in permitting the supply of the new financial service.

Article 17.9:   Senior Management and Boards of Directors

1.   No Party shall require a financial institution of another Party to engage a natural person of a particular nationality as senior managerial or other essential personnel.

2.   No Party shall require that more than a simple majority of the board of directors of a financial institution of another Party be composed of nationals of the Party, persons residing in the territory of the Party, or a combination thereof.

Article 17.10:   Non-Conforming Measures

1.   Article 17.3 (National Treatment), Article 17.4 (Most-Favored-Nation Treatment), Article 17.5 (Market Access), and Article 17.9 (Senior Management and Boards of Directors) do not apply to:

  (a)   an existing non-conforming measure that is maintained by a Party at:

      (i)   the central level of government, as set out by that Party in Section A of its Schedule to Annex III,

      (ii)   a regional level of government, as set out by that Party in Section A of its Schedule to Annex III, or

      (iii) a local level of government;

  (b)   the continuation or prompt renewal of a non-conforming measure referred to in subparagraph (a); or

  (c)   an amendment to a non-conforming measure referred to in subparagraph (a) to the extent that the amendment does not decrease the conformity of the measure as it existed:

      (i)   immediately before the amendment, with Articles 17.3.1 and 17.3.2 (National Treatment), Article 17.4 (Most-Favored-Nation Treatment), Article 17.5.1(a) (Market Access), or Article 17.9 (Senior Management and Boards of Directors), or

      (ii)   on the date of entry into force of this Agreement for the Party applying the non-conforming measure with Article 17.3.3 (National Treatment), Article 17.5.1(b) (Market Access), or Article 17.5.1(c) (Market Access).

2.   Article 17.3 (National Treatment), Article 17.4 (Most-Favored-Nation Treatment), Article 17.5 (Market Access), Article 17.6 (Cross-Border Trade Standstill), and Article 17.9 (Senior Management and Boards of Directors) do not apply to a measure that a Party adopts or maintains with respect to a sector, subsector, or an activity, as set out by that Party in Section B of its Schedule to Annex III.

3.   A non-conforming measure, set out in a Party's Schedule to Annex I or II as not subject to Article 1 4.4 (National Treatment), Article 14.5 (Most-Favored-Nation Treatment), Article 14.11 (Senior Management and Boards of Directors), Article 15.3 (National Treatment) or Article

15. 4 (Most-Favored-Nation Treatment), shall be treated as a non-conforming measure not subject to Article 17.3 (National Treatment), Article 17.4 (Most-Favored-Nation Treatment) or Article 17.9 (Senior Management and Boards of Directors), as the case may be, to the extent that the measure, sector, subsector or activity set out in the Party's schedule to Annex I or II is covered by this Chapter.

4.   (a) Article 17.3 (National Treatment) does not apply to a measure that falls within an exception to, or derogation from, the obligations which are imposed by:

        (i)   Article 20.8 (National Treatment), or

        (ii)   Article 3 of the TRIPS Agreement, if the exception or derogation relates to matters not addressed by Chapter 20 (Intellectual Property Rights).

    (b)   Article 17.4 (Most-Favored-Nation Treatment) does not apply to a measure that falls within Article 5 of the TRIPS Agreement, or an exception to, or derogation from, the obligations which are imposed by:

        (i)   Article 20.8 (National Treatment), or

        (ii)   Article 4 of the TRIPS Agreement.

Article 17.11:   Exceptions

1.   Notwithstanding the other provisions of this Agreement except for Chapter 2 (National Treatment and Market Access for Goods), Chapter 3 (Agriculture), Chapter 4 (Rules of Origin), Chapter 5 (Origin Procedures), Chapter 6 (Textiles and Apparel), Chapter 7 (Customs Administration and Trade Facilitation), Chapter 9 (Sanitary and Phytosanitary Measures), Chapter 10 (Trade Remedies), and Chapter 11 (Technical Barriers to Trade), a Party is not prevented from adopting or maintaining a measure for prudential reasons,[6] including for the protection of investors, depositors, policy holders, or persons to whom a fiduciary duty is owed by a financial institution or cross-border financial service supplier, or to ensure the integrity and stability of the financial system. If the measure does not conform with the provisions of this Agreement to which this exception applies, the measure must not be used as a means of avoiding the Party's commitments or obligations under those provisions.

Nothing in this Chapter, Chapter 14 (Investment), Chapter 15 (Cross-Border Trade in Services), Chapter 18 (Telecommunications) including specifically Article 18.26 (Relation to Other Chapters), or Chapter 19 (Digital Trade), applies to a non-discriminatory measure of general application taken by a public entity in pursuit of monetary and related credit policies or exchange rate policies. This paragraph does not affect a Party's obligations under

---

6   The Parties understand that the term "prudential reasons" includes the maintenance of the safety, soundness, integrity, or financial responsibility of individual financial institutions or cross-border financial service suppliers as well as the safety, and financial and operational integrity of payment and clearing systems.

Article 14.10 (Performance Requirements) with respect to a measure covered by Chapter 14 (Investment), under Article 14.9 (Transfers) or Article 15.12 (Cross Border Trade in Services, Payments and Transfers).

2.   Notwithstanding Article 14.9 (Transfers) and Article 15.12 (Payments and Transfers), as incorporated into this Chapter, a Party may prevent or limit a transfer by a financial institution or a cross-border financial service supplier to, or for the benefit of, an affiliate of or person related to that institution or supplier, through the equitable, non-discriminatory and good faith application of a measure relating to maintenance of the safety, soundness, integrity, or financial responsibility of financial institutions or cross-border financial service suppliers. This paragraph does not prejudice any other provision of this Agreement that permits a Party to restrict transfers.

3.   For greater certainty, nothing in this Chapter shall be construed to prevent a Party from adopting or maintaining a measure necessary to secure compliance with laws or regulations that are not inconsistent with this Chapter, including those relating to the prevention of deceptive and fraudulent practices or to deal with the effects of a default on financial services contracts, subject to the requirement that the measure is not applied in a manner that would constitute a means of arbitrary or unjustifiable discrimination between Parties or between Parties and non-Parties where like conditions prevail, or a disguised restriction on investment in financial institutions or cross-border trade in financial services as covered by this Chapter.

Article 17.12:   Recognition

1.   A Party may recognize prudential measures of another Party or a non-Party in the application of a measure covered by this Chapter. That recognition may be:

(a)   accorded autonomously;

(b)   achieved through harmonization or other means; or

(c)   based upon an agreement or arrangement with another Party or a non-Party.

2.   A Party that accords recognition of prudential measures under paragraph 1 shall provide adequate opportunity to another Party to demonstrate that circumstances exist in which there are or would be equivalent regulation, oversight, implementation of regulation and, if appropriate, procedures concerning the sharing of information between the relevant Parties.

3.   If a Party accords recognition of prudential measures under paragraph 1(c) and the circumstances set out in paragraph 2 exist, that Party shall provide adequate opportunity to another Party to negotiate accession to the agreement or arrangement, or to negotiate a comparable agreement or arrangement.

4.   For greater certainty, nothing in Article 17.4 (Most-Favored-Nation Treatment) requires a Party to accord recognition to prudential measures of any other Party.

Article 17.13:   Transparency and Administration of Certain Measures

1.   Chapter 28 (Good Regulatory Practices) and Chapter 29 (Publication and Administration) do not apply to a measure relating to this Chapter.

2.   Each Party shall ensure that all measures of general application to which this Chapter applies are administered in a reasonable, objective and impartial manner.

3.   Each Party shall, to the extent practicable:

(a)   publish in advance any regulation that it proposes to adopt and the purpose of the regulation; and

(b)   provide interested persons and other Parties with a reasonable opportunity to comment on that proposed regulation.

4.   At the time that it adopts a final regulation, a Party should, to the extent practicable, address in writing the substantive comments received from interested persons and other Parties with respect to the proposed regulation. For greater certainty, a Party may address those comments collectively on an official government website.

5.   To the extent practicable, each Party should allow a reasonable period of time between publication of a final regulation of general application and the date when it enters into effect.

6.   Each Party shall establish or maintain appropriate mechanisms for responding to inquiries from interested persons and other Parties regarding measures of general application covered by this Chapter.

7.   If a Party requires authorization for the supply of a financial service, it shall ensure that its financial regulatory authorities:

(a)   to the extent practicable, permit an applicant to submit an application at any time;

(b)   allow a reasonable period for the submission of an application if specific time periods for applications exist;

(c)   provide to service suppliers and persons seeking to supply a service the information necessary to comply with the requirements and procedures for obtaining, maintaining, amending, and renewing such authorization;

(d)   to the extent practicable, provide an indicative timeframe for processing of an application;

(e)   endeavor to accept applications in electronic format;

(f)   accept copies of documents that are authenticated in accordance with the Party's law, in place of original documents, unless the financial regulatory authorities require original documents to protect the integrity of the authorization process;

(g)   at the request of the applicant, provide without undue delay information concerning the status of the application;

(h)   in the case of an application considered complete under the Party's laws and regulations, within a reasonable period of time taking into account the available resources of the competent authority after the submission of the application, ensure that the processing of an application is completed, and that the applicant is informed of the decision concerning the application, to the extent possible in writing;

   (i)   in the case of an application considered incomplete under the Party's law, within a reasonable period of time, to the extent practicable:

   (i)   inform the applicant that the application is incomplete,

   (ii)   at the request of the applicant, provide guidance on why the application is considered incomplete, and

   (iii)   provide the applicant with the opportunity[7] to provide the additional information that is required to complete the application; and

if none of the actions in subparagraphs (i) through (iii) is practicable, and the application is rejected due to incompleteness, ensure that the applicant is informed within a reasonable period of time;

(j)   in the case of a rejected application, to the extent practicable, either on its own initiative or upon the request of the applicant, inform the applicant of the reasons for rejection and, if applicable, the procedures for resubmission of an application;

(k)   with respect to an authorization fee[8] charged by financial regulatory authorities:

   (i)   provide applicants with a schedule of fees or information on how fee amounts are calculated, and

   (ii)   do not use the fees as a means of avoiding the Party's commitments or obligations under this Chapter; and

(l)   ensure that authorization, once granted, enters into effect without undue delay.

---

[7]   For greater certainty, this opportunity does not require a competent authority to provide extensions of deadlines.

[8]   An authorization fee includes a licensing fee and fees relating to qualification procedures but does not include a fee for the use of natural resources, payments for auction, tendering or other non-discriminatory means of awarding concessions, or mandated contributions to universal service provision.

Article 17.14: Self-Regulatory Organizations

If a Party requires a financial institution or a cross-border financial service supplier of another Party to be a member of, participate in, or have access to, a self-regulatory organization in order to provide a financial service in or into its territory, it shall ensure that the self-regulatory organization observes the obligations contained in this Chapter.

Article 17.15: Payment and Clearing Systems

Under terms and conditions that accord national treatment, each Party shall grant financial institutions of another Party established in its territory access to payment and clearing systems operated by public entities, and to official funding and refinancing facilities available in the normal course of ordinary business. This Article does not confer or require access to the Party's lender of last resort facilities.

Article 17.16: Expedited Availability of Insurance Services

The Parties recognize the importance of maintaining and developing regulatory procedures to expedite the offering of insurance services by licensed suppliers. These procedures may include: allowing introduction of products unless those products are disapproved within a reasonable period of time; not requiring product approval or authorization of insurance lines for insurance other than insurance sold to individuals or compulsory insurance; or not imposing limitations on the number or frequency of product introductions. If a Party maintains regulatory product approval procedures, that Party shall endeavor to maintain or improve those procedures, as appropriate, to expedite availability of insurance services by licensed suppliers.

Article 17.17: Transfer of Information

No Party shall prevent a covered person from transferring information, including personal information, into and out of the Party's territory by electronic or other means when this activity is for the conduct of business within the scope of the license, authorization, or registration of that covered person. Nothing in this Article restricts the right of a Party to adopt or maintain measures to protect personal data, personal privacy and the confidentiality of individual records and accounts, provided that such measures are not used to circumvent this Article.

Article 17.18: Location of Computing Facilities

1. The Parties recognize that immediate, direct, complete, and ongoing access by a Party's financial regulatory authorities to information of covered persons, including information underlying the transactions and operations of such persons, is critical to financial regulation and supervision, and recognize the need to eliminate any potential limitations on that access.

2. No Party shall require a covered person to use or locate computing facilities in the Party's territory as a condition for conducting business in that territory, so long as the Party's financial regulatory authorities, for regulatory and supervisory purposes, have immediate, direct,

complete, and ongoing access to information processed or stored on computing facilities that the covered person uses or locates outside the Party's territory.[9]

3.   Each Party shall, to the extent practicable, provide a covered person with a reasonable opportunity to remediate a lack of access to information as described in paragraph 2 before the Party requires the covered person to use or locate computing facilities in the Party's territory or the territory of another jurisdiction.[10]

4.   Nothing in this Article restricts the right of a Party to adopt or maintain measures to protect personal data, personal privacy and the confidentiality of individual records and accounts, provided that these measures are not used to circumvent the commitments or obligations of this Article.

Article 17.19:   Committee on Financial Services

1.   The Parties hereby establish a Committee on Financial Services (Financial Services Committee). The principal representative of each Party must be an official of the Party's authority responsible for financial services set out in Annex 17-B (Authorities Responsible for Financial Services).

2.   The Financial Services Committee shall supervise the implementation of this Chapter and its further elaboration, including by considering issues regarding financial services that are referred to it by a Party.

3.   The Financial Services Committee shall meet as the Parties decide to assess the functioning of this Agreement as it applies to financial services. The Financial Services Committee shall inform the Commission of the results of any meeting. The Parties may invite, as appropriate, representatives of their domestic financial regulatory authorities to attend meetings of the Committee.

Article 17.20:   Consultations

1.   A Party may request, in writing, consultations with another Party regarding any matter arising under this Agreement that affects financial services. The other Party shall give sympathetic consideration

---

[9]   For greater certainty, access to information includes access to information of a covered person that is processed or stored on computing facilities of the covered person or on computing facilities of a third-party service supplier. For greater certainty, a Party may adopt or maintain a measure that is not inconsistent with this Agreement, including any measure consistent with Article 17.11.1 (Exceptions), such as a measure requiring a covered person to obtain prior authorization from a financial regulatory authority to designate a particular enterprise as a recipient of that information, or a measure adopted or maintained by a financial regulatory authority in the exercise of its authority over a covered person's business continuity planning practices with respect to maintenance of the operation of computing facilities.

[10]   For greater certainty, so long as a Party's financial regulatory authorities do not have access to information as described in paragraph 2, the Party may, subject to paragraph 3, require a covered person to use or locate computing facilities either in the territory of the Party or the territory of another jurisdiction where the Party has that access.

to this request. The consulting Parties shall report the results of their consultations to the Financial Services Committee.

2.   A Party may request information on an existing non-conforming measure of another Party as referred to in Article 17.10.1 (Non-Conforming Measures). Each Party's financial authorities specified in Annex 17-B (Authorities Responsible for Financial Services) shall be the contact point to respond to those requests and to facilitate the exchange of information regarding the operation of measures covered by those requests.

3.   For greater certainty, nothing in this Article shall be construed to require a Party to derogate from its law regarding sharing of information between financial regulatory authorities or the requirements of an agreement or arrangement between financial regulatory authorities of the Parties, or to require a financial regulatory authority to take any action that would interfere with specific regulatory, supervisory, administrative or enforcement matters.

Article 17.21:   Dispute Settlement

1.   Chapter 31 (Dispute Settlement) applies as modified by this Article to the settlement of disputes arising under this Chapter.

2.   For disputes arising under this Chapter or a dispute in which a Party invokes Article 17.11 (Exceptions), when selecting panelists to compose a panel under Article 31.9 (Panel Composition), each disputing Party shall select panelists so that:

(a)   the chairperson has expertise or experience in financial services law or practice, such as the regulation of financial institutions, and meets the qualifications set out in Article 31.8.2 (Roster and Qualifications of Panelists); and

(b)   each of the other panelists:

(i)   has expertise or experience in financial services law or practice, such as the regulation of financial institutions, and meets the qualifications set out in paragraph (2)(b) through (2)(d) of Article 31.8.2 (Roster and Qualifications of Panelists); or

(ii)   meets the qualifications set out in Article 31.8.2 (Roster and Qualification of Panelists).

3.   If a Party seeks to suspend benefits in the financial services sector, a panel that reconvenes to make a determination on the proposed suspension of benefits, in accordance with Article 31.19 (Non-Implementation—Suspension of Benefits), shall seek the views of financial services experts, as necessary.

4.   Notwithstanding Article 31.19 (Non-Implementation—Suspension of Benefits), when a panel's determination is that a Party's measure is inconsistent with this Agreement and the measure affects:

(a)   only a sector other than the financial services sector, the complaining Party may not suspend benefits in the financial services sector; or

(b)   the financial services sector and another sector, the complaining Party may not suspend benefits in the financial services sector that have an effect that exceeds the effect of the measure in the complaining Party's financial services sector.

ANNEX 17-A   CROSS-BORDER TRADE

Canada[11]

Insurance and Insurance-Related Services

1.   Articles 17.3.3 (National Treatment) and 17.5.1 (Market Access) apply to the cross-border supply of or trade in financial services, as defined in subparagraph (a) of the definition of "cross-border supply of financial services" in Article 17.1 (Definitions), with respect to:

(a)   insurance of risks relating to:

(i)   maritime transport and commercial aviation and space launching and freight (including satellites), with such insurance to cover any or all of the following: the goods being transported, the vehicle transporting the goods, and any liability deriving therefrom, and

(ii)   goods in international transit;

(b)   reinsurance and retrocession;

(c)   services auxiliary to insurance as described in subparagraph (d) of the definition of "financial service" in Article 17.1 (Definitions); and

(d)   insurance intermediation such as brokerage and agency, as referred to in subparagraph (c) of the definition of "financial service" in Article 14.1 (Definitions) of insurance of risks related to services listed in subparagraphs (a) and (b) of this paragraph.

Banking and Other Financial Services (excluding insurance)

2.   Articles 17.3.3 (National Treatment) and 17.5.1 (Market Access) apply to the cross-border supply of or trade in financial services, as defined in subparagraphs (a) of the definition of "cross-border supply of financial services" in Article 17.1 (Definitions), with respect to:

(a)   the provision and transfer of financial information and financial data processing as described in subparagraph (o) of the definition of "financial service" in Article 14.1 (Definitions);

---

[11]   For greater certainty, Canada requires that a cross-border financial services supplier appoint a local agent in Canada that is provided with power of attorney.

(b)   advisory and other auxiliary financial services, and credit reference and analysis, excluding intermediation, relating to banking and other financial services as described in subparagraph (p) of the definition of financial service" in Article 14.1 (Definitions); and

(c)   electronic payment services for payment card transactions falling within subparagraph (h) of the definition of "financial service" in Article 14.1 (Definitions), and within subcategory 71593 of the United Nations Central Product Classification, Version 2.1, and including only:

   (i)   the processing of financial transactions, such as verification of financial balances, authorization of transactions, notification of banks (or credit card issuers) of individual transactions and provision of daily summaries and instructions regarding the net financial position of relevant institutions for authorized transactions, and

   (ii) those services that are provided on a business-to-business basis and use proprietary networks to process payment transactions,

but not including the transfer of funds to and from transactors' accounts.[12]

(d)   the following services if they are provided to a collective investment scheme located in Canada:

   (i)   investment advice, and

   (ii) portfolio management services, excluding:

      (A)   trustee services, and

      (B)   custodial services and execution services that are not related to managing a collective investment scheme.

3.   For the purposes of paragraph 3, in Canada:

(a)   payment card means a "payment card" as defined under the Payment Card Networks Act as of January 1, 2015. For greater certainty, physical and electronic forms of credit and debit cards are included in the definition. For greater certainty, credit cards include pre-paid cards.

---

[12]   Nothing in this subparagraph prevents a Party from adopting or maintaining measures to protect personal data, personal privacy, and the confidentiality of individual records and accounts, provided that these measures are not used to circumvent the commitments or obligations of this subparagraph. For greater certainty, nothing in this subparagraph prevents a Party from adopting or maintaining measures that regulate fees, such as interchange or switching fees, or that impose fees.

(b)   a collective investment scheme means, an *"investment fund"*[13] as defined under the relevant Securities Act.

Mexico

Insurance and insurance-related services

1.   Article 17.3.3 (National Treatment) and Article 17.5.1 (Market Access) shall apply to the cross-border supply of or trade in financial services, as defined in subparagraph (a) of the definition of "cross-border supply of financial services" in Article 17.1 (Definitions), with respect to:

   (a)   insurance of risks relating to:

      (i)   maritime shipping and commercial aviation, space launching and freight (including satellites), with such insurance to cover all or any of the following: the goods being transported; and the vehicle transporting the goods, when such vehicles have foreign registration or are property of persons domiciled abroad, and

      (ii)   goods in international transit;

   (b)   any other insurance of risks, if the person seeking to purchase the insurance demonstrates that none of the insurance companies authorized to operate in Mexico is able or deems convenient to enter into such insurance proposed to it;

   (c)   reinsurance and retrocession; and

   (d)   insurance intermediation, as referred to in subparagraph (c) of the definition of "financial service" in Article 17.1 (Definitions), and services auxiliary to insurance, as referred to in subparagraph (d) of the definition of "financial service" in Article 17.1 (Definitions), only in respect of insurance referred to in the section of Mexico in this Annex.

Banking and other financial services (excluding insurance)

2.   Article 17.3.3 (National Treatment) and Article 17.5.1 (Market Access) shall apply to the cross-border supply of or trade in financial services, as defined in subparagraph (a) of the definition of "cross-border supply of financial services" in Article 17.1 (Definitions), with respect to:

   (a)   provision and transfer of financial information, and financial data processing and related software, as referred to in subparagraph (*o*) of the definition of "financial service" in Article 14.1 (Definitions);

---

[13]   In Canada, a financial institution organized in the territory of another Party can only provide custodial services to a collective investment scheme located in Canada if the financial institution has shareholders' equity equivalent to at least $100 million.

(b) advisory and other auxiliary services,[14] excluding intermediation, and credit reference and analysis, relating to banking and other financial services, as referred to in subparagraph (p) of the definition of "financial service" in Article 17.1 (Definitions);

(c) the following services if they are provided to a collective investment scheme in Mexico:

    (i) investment advice, and

    (ii) portfolio management services, excluding:

        (A) trustee services, and

        (B) custodial services and execution services that are not related to managing a collective investment scheme; and

(d) electronic payment services for payment card transactions falling within subparagraph (h) of the definition of "financial service" in Article 17.1 (Definitions), and within subcategory 71593 of the United Nations Central Product Classification, Version 2.1, and including only:

    (i) receiving and sending messages for: authorization requests, authorization responses (approvals or declines), stand-in authorizations, adjustments, refunds, returns, retrievals, charge backs and related administrative messages,

    (ii) calculation of fees and balances derived from transactions of acquirers and issuers, and receiving and sending messages related to this process to acquirers and issuers, and their agents and representatives,

    (iii) the provision of periodic reconciliation, summaries and instructions regarding the net financial position of acquirers and issuers, and their agents and representatives for approved transactions,

    (iv) value-added services related to the main processing activities referred to in subparagraphs (i), (ii), and (iii), such as fraud prevention and mitigation activities, and administration of loyalty programs, and

    (v) those services that are provided on a business-to-business basis and use proprietary networks to process payment transactions, as referenced in subparagraphs (i)–(iv),

---

[14] The Parties understand that advisory and other auxiliary financial services do not include those services referred to in subparagraphs (e) through (o) of the definition of "financial service" in Article 17.1 (Definitions).

but not including the transfer of funds to and from transactors' accounts. For Mexico, a payment card means a credit card, debit card, and reloadable card in physical form or electronic format, as defined under Mexican law.[15]

3. For the purposes of paragraph 2(b) and 2(c), in Mexico a collective investment scheme means the "Managing Companies of Investment Funds (*Sociedades Operadoras de Fondos de Inversión*)" established under the Investment Funds Law (*Ley de Fondos de Inversión*). A financial institution organized in the territory of another Party will only be authorized to provide portfolio management services to a collective investment scheme located in Mexico if it provides the same services in the territory of the Party where it is established.

United States

Insurance and insurance-related services

1. Article 17.3.3 (National Treatment) and Article 17.5.1 (Market Access) shall apply to the cross-border supply of or trade in financial services, as defined in subparagraph (a) of the definition of "cross-border supply of financial services" in Article 17.1 (Definitions), with respect to:

    (a) insurance of risks relating to:

        (i)   maritime shipping and commercial aviation and space launching and freight (including satellites), with that insurance to cover any or all of the following: the goods being transported, the vehicle transporting the goods, and any liability arising therefrom, and

        (ii) goods in international transit; and

    (b) reinsurance and retrocession; services auxiliary to insurance, as referred to in subparagraph (d) of the definition of "financial service" in Article 17.1 (Definitions); and insurance intermediation, such as brokerage and agency, as referred to in subparagraph (c) of the definition of "financial service" in Article 17.1 (Definitions).

Banking and other financial services (excluding insurance)

2. Article 17.3.3 (National Treatment) and 17.5.1 (Market Access) shall apply to the cross-border supply of or trade in financial services, as defined in subparagraph (a) of the definition of "cross-border supply of financial services" in Article 17.1 (Definitions), with respect to:

    (a) provision and transfer of financial information, and financial data processing and related software, as referred to in

---

[15] Nothing in this subparagraph prevents a Party from adopting or maintaining measures to protect personal data, personal privacy, and the confidentiality of individual records and accounts, provided that these measures are not used to circumvent the commitments or obligations of this subparagraph. For greater certainty, nothing in this subparagraph prevents a Party from adopting or maintaining measures that regulate fees, such as interchange or switching fees, or that impose fees.

subparagraph (*o*) of the definition of "financial service" in Article 17.1 (Definitions);

(b) advisory and other auxiliary services, excluding intermediation, relating to banking and other financial services, as referred to in subparagraph (p) of the definition of "financial service" in Article 17.1 (Definitions);

(c) investment advice to a collective investment scheme located in the Party's territory;

(d) portfolio management services, excluding

  (i) trustee services, and

  (ii) custodial services and execution services that are not related to managing a collective investment scheme; and

(e) electronic payment services for payment card transactions falling within subparagraph (h) of the definition of "financial service" in Article 17.1 (Definitions), and within subcategory 71593 of the United Nations Central Product Classification, Version 2.1, and including only:

  (i) the processing of financial transactions such as verification of financial balances, authorization of transactions, notification of banks (or credit card issuers) of individual transactions and provision of daily summaries and instructions regarding the net financial position of relevant institutions for authorized transactions, and

  (ii) those services that are provided on a business-to-business basis and use proprietary networks to process payment transactions,

but not including the transfer of funds to and from transactors' accounts.

For the United States, a payment card means a credit card, charge card, debit card, check card, automated teller machine (ATM) card, prepaid card, and other physical or electronic products or services for performing similar functions as these cards, and the unique account number associated with that card, product, or service.[16]

3. For the purposes of subparagraphs 2(c) and 2(d), for the United States, a collective investment scheme means an investment company

---

[16] Nothing in this subparagraph prevents a Party from adopting or maintaining measures to protect personal data, personal privacy, and the confidentiality of individual records and accounts, provided that these measures are not used to circumvent the commitments or obligations of this subparagraph. For greater certainty, nothing in this subparagraph prevents a Party from adopting or maintaining measures that regulate fees, such as interchange or switching fees, or that impose fees.

registered with the Securities and Exchange Commission under the *Investment Company Act of 1940*.[17]

ANNEX 17-B AUTHORITIES RESPONSIBLE FOR FINANCIAL SERVICES

The authorities for each Party responsible for financial services are:

(a)   for Canada, the Department of Finance of Canada;

(b)   for Mexico, the Ministry of Finance and Public Credit (*Secretaría de Hacienda y Crédito Público*); and

(c)   for the United States, the Department of the Treasury for the purposes of Annex 17-C (Mexico-United States Investment Disputes in Financial Services) and for all matters involving banking, securities, and financial services other than insurance, and the Department of the Treasury, in cooperation with the Office of the U.S. Trade Representative, for insurance matters.

ANNEX 17-C   MEXICO-UNITED STATES INVESTMENT DISPUTES IN FINANCIAL SERVICES

1.   Annex 14-D (Mexico-United States Investment Disputes) applies as modified by this Annex to the settlement of a qualifying investment dispute under this Chapter.

2.   In the event that a disputing party considers that a qualifying investment dispute under this Chapter cannot be settled by consultation and negotiation:

(a)   the claimant, on its own behalf, may submit to arbitration under Annex 14-D a claim:

(i)   that the respondent has breached:

(A)   Article 17.3.1 (National Treatment), Article 17.3.2 (National Treatment), Article 17.4.1(a) (Most-Favored-Nation Treatment), Article 17.4.1(b) (Most-Favored-Nation Treatment), or Article 17.4.1(c) (Most-Favored-Nation Treatment)[18] except with respect to the establishment or acquisition of an investment; or

---

[17]   Custodial services are included in the scope of the commitment made by the United States under this Annex only with respect to investments for which the primary market is outside the territory of the Party.

[18]   For the purposes of this paragraph:(i) the "treatment" referred to in Article 17.4.1(a) (Most-Favored-Nation Treatment), Article 17.4.1(b) (Most-Favored-Nation Treatment), and Article 17.4.1(c) (Most-Favored-Nation Treatment) excludes provisions in other international trade or investment agreements that establish international dispute resolution procedures or impose substantive obligations; and (ii) the "treatment" referred to in these subparagraphs only encompasses measures adopted or maintained by the other Annex Party, which for greater clarity may include measures adopted in connection with the implementation of substantive obligations in other international trade or investment agreements

   (B)   Article 14.8 (Expropriation and Compensation) as
         incorporated into this Chapter under Article
         17.2.2(a) (Scope), except with respect to indirect
         expropriation; and

   (ii) that the claimant has incurred loss or damage by reason
         of, or arising out of, that breach; and

(b)   the claimant, on behalf of a financial institution of the
      respondent that is a juridical person that the claimant owns
      or controls directly or indirectly, may submit to arbitration
      under Annex 14-D a claim:

   (i)   that the respondent has breached:

      (A)   Article 17.3.1 (National Treatment), Article 17.3.2
            (National Treatment), Article 17.4.1(a) (Most-
            Favored-Nation Treatment),

      (B)   Article 14.8 (Expropriation and Compensation) as
            incorporated into this Chapter under Article
            17.2.2(a), except with respect to indirect
            expropriation; and

   (ii) that the financial institution has incurred loss or
         damage by reason of, or arising out of, that breach.

3.   If an investor of an Annex Party submits a claim to arbitration under
     Annex 14-D (Mexico-United States Investment Disputes) as modified
     by this Annex:

   (a)   the presiding arbitrator and the other arbitrators shall be
         selected so that the presiding arbitrator has expertise or
         experience in financial services law or practice such as the
         regulation of financial institutions, and, to the extent
         practicable, the other arbitrators have expertise or
         experience in financial services law or practice such as the
         regulation of financial institutions; and

   (b)   the respondent shall endeavor to consult with its domestic
         financial regulatory authorities on the claim.

4.   No claim shall be submitted to arbitration under Annex 14-D (Mexico-
     United States Investment Disputes) as modified by this Annex unless
     the conditions in Article 14.D.5.1 (Conditions and Limitations on
     Consent) of Annex 14-D (Mexico-United States Investment Disputes)
     are satisfied, except the relevant time period in subparagraph (b) is 18
     months.

5.   If an investor of an Annex Party submits a claim to arbitration under
     Annex 14-D (Mexico-United States Investment Disputes) as modified
     by this Annex, and the respondent invokes Article 17.11 (Exceptions)
     as a defense, the following provisions of this Article apply:

   (a)   The respondent shall, no later than the date the tribunal
         fixes for the respondent to submit its counter-memorial, or in

the case of an amendment to the notice of arbitration, the date the tribunal fixes for the respondent to submit its response to the amendment, submit in writing to the authorities responsible for financial services of the Annex Party of the claimant, as set out in Annex 17-B (Authorities Responsible for Financial Services), a request for a joint determination by the authorities of the respondent and the Annex Party of the claimant on the issue of whether and to what extent Article 17.11 (Exceptions) is a valid defense to the claim.

(i)   The respondent shall set out in the request the text of a proposed joint determination that specifies the claims to which it considers Article 17.11 (Exceptions) a valid defense.

(ii)   The respondent shall promptly provide the tribunal, if constituted, a copy of the request.

(iii)   The authorities of the Annex Party of the claimant shall notify the authorities of the respondent in writing that the request has been received.

(iv)   The arbitration may proceed with respect to the claim only as provided in subparagraph (g).[19]

(b)   The authorities referred to in subparagraph (a) shall attempt in good faith to make a joint determination as described in that subparagraph within 120 days after the date of the written request for that determination. The authorities may, in extraordinary circumstances, agree to extend the date for a joint determination for up to 60 additional days.

(c)   The authorities of the Annex Party of the claimant shall notify the authorities of the respondent within 120 days after the date of the written request for a joint determination under subparagraph (a), or within the period agreed under subparagraph (b), whichever is longer, whether the authorities of the Annex Party of the claimant agree to the proposed joint determination submitted under subparagraph (a)(i), propose an alternative joint determination, or will not, for any reason, agree to a joint determination.

(d)   If the authorities of the Annex Party of the claimant make no notification under subparagraph (c), they shall be presumed to take a position that is consistent with that of the authorities of the respondent, and a joint determination shall deemed to be made regarding the issue of whether and to what extent Article 17.11 (Exceptions) is a valid defense to

---

[19]   The term "joint determination" as used in this subparagraph refers to a determination by the authorities responsible for financial services of the respondent and of the Annex Party of the claimant, as set out in Annex 17-B (Authorities Responsible for Financial Services).

the claim as set out in the proposed joint determination submitted under subparagraph (a)(i).

(e) Any joint determination made or deemed to be made shall be transmitted promptly to the disputing parties, the Committee and, if constituted, to the tribunal. The joint determination shall be binding on the tribunal and any decision or award issued by the tribunal must be consistent with that determination.

(f) If the authorities referred to in subparagraph (a), within 120 days after the date of the written request for a joint determination under subparagraph (a) or within the date agreed under subparagraph (b), whichever is longer, have not made a determination as described in subparagraph (a), the tribunal shall decide the issue left unresolved by the authorities.

(i) The tribunal shall draw no inference regarding the application of Article 17.11 (Exceptions) from the fact that the competent authorities have not made a determination as described in subparagraph (a).

(ii) The Annex Party of the claimant may make oral and written submissions to the tribunal regarding the issue of whether and to what extent Article 17.11 (Exceptions) is a valid defense to the claim. Unless it makes such a submission, the Annex Party of the claimant shall be presumed, for purposes of the arbitration, to take a position on Article 17.11 (Exceptions) not inconsistent with that of the respondent.

* * *

ANNEX 17-D LOCATION OF COMPUTING FACILITIES

Article 17.18 (Location of Computing Facilities) does not apply to existing measures of Canada for one year after the entry into force of this Agreement.

CHAPTER 18   TELECOMMUNICATIONS

Article 18.1:   Definitions

For the purposes of this Chapter:

Cost-oriented means based on cost, and may include a reasonable profit, and may involve different cost methodologies for different facilities or services;

Dialing parity means the ability of an end-user to use an equal number of digits to access a particular public telecommunications service, regardless of which public telecommunications services supplier the end-user chooses;

End-user means a final consumer of or subscriber to a public telecommunications service, including a service supplier other than a supplier of public telecommunications services;

Enterprise means an enterprise as defined in Article 1.4 (General Definitions) and a branch of an enterprise;

Essential facilities means facilities of a public telecommunications network or service that:

(a) are exclusively or predominantly provided by a single or limited number of suppliers; and

(b) cannot feasibly be economically, or technically substituted in order to supply a service;

Interconnection means linking suppliers providing public telecommunications services in order to allow a user of one supplier to communicate with a user of another supplier and to access services provided by another supplier;

Leased circuit means a telecommunications facility between two or more designated points that is set aside for the dedicated use of, or availability to, a user and supplied by a supplier of a fixed telecommunications service;

License means any authorization that a Party may require of a person, in accordance with its laws and regulations, in order for that person to offer a telecommunications service, including concessions, permits or registrations;

Major supplier means a supplier of public telecommunications services that has the ability to materially affect the terms of participation (having regard to price and supply) in the relevant market for public telecommunications services as a result of:

(a) control over essential facilities; or

(b) use of its position in the market[1]

Mobile service means a public telecommunications service supplied through mobile wireless means;

Network element means a facility or equipment used in supplying a fixed public telecommunications service, including features, functions and capabilities provided by means of that facility or equipment;

Non-discriminatory means according treatment no less favorable than that accorded to another user of like public telecommunications services in like circumstances, including with respect to timeliness;

Number portability means the ability of an end-user of public telecommunications services to retain the same telephone numbers when switching between suppliers of public telecommunications services;

---

[1] For Mexico, a major supplier includes a preponderant economic agent deemed as such by virtue of its national share in the supply of telecommunication services, when it directly or indirectly holds more than fifty percent national share. This percentage shall be measured either by the number of users, subscribers, traffic on their networks or the utilized capacity of said networks, according to the information held by the Federal Telecommunications Institute.

Physical co-location means physical access to and control over space in order to install, maintain or repair equipment, at premises owned or controlled and used by a major supplier to provide public telecommunications services;

Public telecommunications network means telecommunications infrastructure used to provide public telecommunications services between defined network termination points;

Public telecommunications service means a telecommunications service that a Party requires, explicitly or in effect, to be offered to the public generally that typically involves the transmission of customer-supplied information between two or more points without an end-to-end change in the form or content of the customer's information. This service may include telephone and data transmission;

Reference interconnection offer means an interconnection offer extended by a major supplier and filed with, approved by or determined by a telecommunications regulatory body that sufficiently details the terms, rates, and conditions for interconnection so that a supplier of a public telecommunications service that is willing to accept it may obtain interconnection with the major supplier on that basis, without having to engage in negotiations with the major supplier concerned;

Roaming service means a mobile service provided pursuant to an agreement between suppliers of public telecommunications services that enables an end-user to use their mobile handset or other device for voice, data, or messaging services while outside the home public telecommunications network of the mobile handset or other device;

Telecommunications means the transmission and reception of signals by any electromagnetic means;

Telecommunications regulatory body means a body or bodies responsible for the regulation of telecommunications;

User means a service consumer or a service supplier;

Value-added service means a telecommunications service employing a computer processing application that:

(a) acts on the format, content, code, protocol or similar aspects of a customer's transmitted information;

(b) provides a customer with additional, different or restructured information; or

(c) involves customer interaction with stored information; and

Virtual co-location means an arrangement whereby a requesting supplier that seeks co-location may specify equipment to be used in the premises of a major supplier but does not obtain physical access to those premises and allows the major supplier to install, maintain, and repair that equipment.

Article 18.2:   Scope

1. This Chapter applies to a measure affecting trade in telecommunications services, including:

(a) a measure relating to access to and use of public telecommunications networks or services;

(b) a measure relating to obligations of suppliers of public telecommunications services;

(c) a measure relating to the supply of value-added services; and

(d) any other measure relating to public telecommunications networks or services.

2. This Chapter does not apply to a measure relating to broadcast or cable distribution of radio or television programming, except to ensure that an enterprise operating a broadcast station or cable system has continued access to and use of public telecommunications networks and services, as provided under Article 18.3 (Access and Use).[2]

3. Nothing in this Chapter shall be construed to require a Party:

(a) to establish, construct, acquire, lease, operate, or provide a telecommunications network or service not offered to the public generally, or require a Party to compel an enterprise to do so; or

(b) to compel an enterprise exclusively engaged in the broadcast or cable distribution of radio or television programming to make available its broadcast or cable facilities as a public telecommunications network.

4. Annex 18-A (Rural Telephone Suppliers) includes additional provisions relating to the scope of this Chapter.

Article 18.3: Access and Use

1. Each Party shall ensure that any enterprise of another Party has access to and use of any public telecommunications network or service, including leased circuits, offered in its territory or across its borders, on reasonable and non-discriminatory terms and conditions. This obligation shall be applied, *inter alia*, to paragraphs 2 through 6.[3]

2. Each Party shall ensure that any enterprise of another Party is permitted to:

(a) purchase or lease, and attach terminal or other equipment that interfaces with a public telecommunications network;

(b) provide services to individual or multiple end-users over leased or owned circuits;

---

[2] For greater certainty, to the extent that a services supplier engaged in the broadcast or cable distribution of radio or television programming is also engaged in the supply of public telecommunications services, measures relating to the supply of those public telecommunications by that services supplier are covered by this Chapter.

[3] For greater certainty, this Article does not prohibit any Party from requiring an enterprise to obtain a license to supply a public telecommunications service within its territory.

(c)   connect leased or owned circuits with public telecommunications networks and services or with circuits leased or owned by another enterprise;

(d)   perform switching, signaling, processing, and conversion functions; and

(e)   use operating protocols of its choice.

3.   Each Party shall ensure that any enterprise of another Party may use public telecommunications networks or services for the movement of information in its territory or across its borders, including for intra-corporate communications, and to access information contained in databases or otherwise stored in machine-readable form in the territory of a Party.

4.   Notwithstanding paragraph 3, a Party may take measures necessary to ensure the security and confidentiality of messages or to protect the privacy of personal data of end-users of public telecommunications networks or services, provided that those measures are not applied in a manner that would constitute a means of arbitrary or unjustifiable discrimination or disguised restriction on trade in services.

5.   Each Party shall ensure that no condition is imposed on access to and use of public telecommunications networks and services, other than as necessary to:

(a)   safeguard the public service responsibilities of suppliers of public telecommunications networks and services, in particular their ability to make their networks or services available to the public generally; or

(b)   protect the technical integrity of public telecommunications networks or services.

6.   Provided that the conditions for access to and use of public telecommunications networks and services satisfy the criteria set out in paragraph 5, those conditions may include:

(a)   a requirement to use a specified technical interface, including an interface protocol, for connection with those networks or services;

(b)   a requirement, if necessary, for the interoperability of those networks and services;

(c)   type approval of terminal or other equipment that interfaces with the network and technical requirements relating to the attachment of that equipment to those networks; and

(d)   notification, registration, and licensing which, if adopted or maintained, is transparent and provides for processing applications filed thereunder in accordance with a Party's laws or regulations.

Article 18.4: Obligations Relating to Suppliers of Public Telecommunications Services

Interconnection

1. Each Party shall ensure that a supplier of public telecommunications services in its territory provides, directly or indirectly within its territory, interconnection with a supplier of public telecommunications services of another Party.

2. Each Party shall provide its telecommunications regulatory body with the authority to require interconnection at reasonable rates.

3. Further to paragraph 1, each Party shall ensure that a supplier of public telecommunications services in its territory takes reasonable steps to protect the confidentiality of commercially sensitive information of, or relating to, suppliers and end-users of public telecommunications services obtained as a result of interconnection arrangements and only uses that information for the purpose of providing these services.

Resale

4. No Party shall prohibit the resale of a public telecommunications service.

Roaming

5. No Party shall prohibit a supplier of public telecommunications services from entering into an agreement to provide roaming services, including an agreement to provide roaming services to devices that is not limited to a transient presence in a Party's territory.

Number Portability

6. Each Party shall ensure that a supplier of public telecommunications services in its territory provides number portability without impairment to quality and reliability, on a timely basis, and on reasonable and non-discriminatory terms and conditions.[4]

Dialing Parity

7. Each Party shall ensure that a supplier of public telecommunications services in its territory provides dialing parity within the same category of service to suppliers of public telecommunications services of another Party.[5]

---

[4] With respect to Mexico, this obligation shall apply only to end-users switching suppliers within the same category of service until such time as Mexico determines, pursuant to periodic review, that it is economically and technically feasible to implement number portability without that restriction. With respect to the United States and Canada, this obligation is limited to the ability of end-users to retain at the same location the same telephone numbers, until such time as the Party determines, pursuant to periodic review, that it is economically and technically feasible to implement number portability without that restriction in its territory.

[5] For greater certainty, this paragraph shall not be construed to apply to pre-subscribed long distance service.

Access to Numbers

8. Each Party shall ensure that a supplier of public telecommunications services of another Party established in its territory is afforded access to telephone numbers on a non-discriminatory basis.

Article 18.5:   Treatment   by   Major   Suppliers   of   Public Telecommunications Services

Each Party shall ensure that a major supplier in its territory accords a supplier of public telecommunications services of another Party treatment no less favorable than that major supplier accords in like circumstances to itself, its subsidiaries, its affiliates, or non-affiliated service suppliers regarding:

(a)   the availability, provisioning, rates, or quality of like public telecommunications services; and

(b)   the availability of technical interfaces necessary for interconnection.

Article 18.6:   Competitive Safeguards

1. Each Party shall maintain appropriate measures for the purpose of preventing suppliers of public telecommunications services that, alone or together, are a major supplier in its territory from engaging in or continuing anti-competitive practices.[6]

2. The anti-competitive practices referred to in paragraph 1 include in particular:

(a)   engaging in anti-competitive cross-subsidization;

(b)   using information obtained from competitors with anti-competitive results; and

(c)   not making available, on a timely basis, to suppliers of public telecommunications services, technical information about essential facilities and commercially relevant information that are necessary for them to provide services.

---

[6]   Mexico reaffirms the principles underlying the Decree amending and supplementing certain provisions of the Articles 6, 7, 27, 28, 73, 78, 94 and 105 of Mexico's Constitution (*Constitución Política de los Estados Unidos Mexicanos*), in telecommunications, *Diario Oficial de la Federació*n, June 11, 2013 and, as set out therein, shall impose on a major supplier the necessary measures to prevent impairment of competition. For Mexico, any changes to the measures concerning the rates, terms, and conditions of access to and use of the networks, facilities, and services of a major supplier shall be consistent with the objective of advancing effective competition and preventing monopolistic practices and shall not impair the conditions of competition in the corresponding market.

Article 18.7:   Resale[7]

Each Party shall ensure that a major supplier in its territory does not impose unreasonable or discriminatory conditions or limitations on the resale of its public telecommunications services.

Article 18.8:   Unbundling of Network Elements

Each Party shall provide its telecommunications regulatory body with the authority to require a major supplier in its territory to offer public telecommunications service suppliers access to network elements on an unbundled basis on terms and conditions, and at cost-oriented rates, that are reasonable, non-discriminatory, and transparent for the supply of public telecommunications services. A Party may determine, in accordance with its laws and regulations, the network elements required to be made available in its territory, and the suppliers that may obtain those elements.

Article 18.9:   Interconnection with Major Suppliers

General Terms and Conditions

1.   Each Party shall ensure that a major supplier in its territory provides interconnection for the facilities and equipment of suppliers of public telecommunications services of another Party:

   (a)   at any technically feasible point in the major supplier's network;

   (b)   under non-discriminatory terms, conditions (including technical standards and specifications), and rates;

   (c)   of a quality no less favorable than that provided by the major supplier for its own like services, for like services of non-affiliated service suppliers, or for its subsidiaries or other affiliates;

   (d)   in a timely manner, on terms and conditions (including technical standards and specifications), and at cost-oriented rates, that are transparent, reasonable, having regard to economic feasibility, and sufficiently unbundled so that the suppliers do not have to pay for network components or facilities that they do not require for the service to be provided; and

   (e)   on request, at points in addition to the network termination points made generally available to users, subject to charges that reflect the cost of construction of necessary additional facilities.

Options for Interconnecting with Major Suppliers

2.   Each Party shall ensure that a major supplier in its territory provides suppliers of public telecommunications services of another Party the

---

[7]   For the purposes of this Article, a supplier of mobile services in a Party's territory is not a major supplier unless a Party determines that the supplier meets the definition of "major supplier" set out in Article 18.1 (Definitions).

opportunity to interconnect their facilities and equipment with those of the major supplier through:

(a) a reference interconnection offer containing the rates, terms, and conditions that the major supplier offers generally to suppliers of public telecommunications services; or

(b) the terms and conditions of an interconnection agreement in effect.

3. In addition to the options provided in paragraph 2, each Party shall ensure that suppliers of public telecommunications services of another Party have the opportunity to interconnect their facilities and equipment with those of the major supplier through the negotiation of a new interconnection agreement.

Public Availability of Interconnection Offers and Agreements

4. Each Party shall make publicly available the applicable procedures for interconnection negotiations with a major supplier in its territory.

5. Each Party shall provide means for suppliers of another Party to obtain the rates, terms, and conditions necessary for interconnection offered by a major supplier. Those means include, at a minimum, ensuring the public availability of:

(a) rates, terms and conditions for interconnection with a major supplier set by the telecommunications regulatory body;

(b) interconnection agreements that are in effect between a major supplier in its territory and other suppliers of public telecommunications services in its territory; and

(c) any reference interconnection offer.

Article 18.10:   Provisioning and Pricing of Leased Circuits Services

1. Each Party shall ensure that a major supplier in its territory provides service suppliers of another Party leased circuits services that are public telecommunications services in a reasonable period of time on terms and conditions, and at rates, that are reasonable and non-discriminatory, and based on a generally available offer.

2. Further to paragraph 1, each Party shall provide its telecommunications regulatory body with the authority to require a major supplier in its territory to offer leased circuits services that are public telecommunications services to service suppliers of another Party at capacity-based, cost-oriented prices.

Article 18.11:   Co-Location[8]

1. Subject to paragraphs 2 and 3, each Party shall ensure that a major supplier in its territory provides to suppliers of public telecommunications services of another Party in the Party's territory

---

[8]   For the purposes of this Article, a supplier of mobile services in a Party's territory is not a major supplier unless a Party determines that the supplier meets the definition of "major supplier" set out in Article 18.1 (Definitions).

physical co-location of equipment necessary for interconnection or access to unbundled network elements based on a generally available offer, on a timely basis, and on terms and conditions and at cost-oriented rates, that are reasonable, non-discriminatory, and transparent.

2.   Where physical co-location is not practical for technical reasons or because of space limitations, each Party shall ensure that a major supplier in its territory provides an alternative solution, such as virtual co-location or some other arrangement that facilitates interconnection or access to unbundled network elements, based on a generally available offer, on a timely basis, and on terms and conditions, and at cost-oriented rates, that are reasonable, non-discriminatory, and transparent.

3.   A Party may determine, in accordance with its laws and regulations, which premises owned or controlled by major suppliers in its territory are subject to paragraphs 1 and 2. If a Party makes this determination, it shall take into account factors such as the state of competition in the market where co-location is required, whether those premises can be substituted in an economically or technically feasible manner in order to provide a competing service, or other specified public interest factors.

4.   Even if a Party does not require that a major supplier offer co-location at certain premises, it shall allow a service supplier to request that those premises be offered for co-location consistent with paragraph 1, without prejudice to the Party's decision on that request.

Article 18.12:   Access to Poles, Ducts, Conduits, and Rights-of-Way[9]

Each Party shall ensure that a major supplier in its territory provides access, subject to technical feasibility, to poles, ducts, conduits, rights-of-way, and any other structures as determined by the Party, owned or controlled by the major supplier, to suppliers of public telecommunications services of another Party in the Party's territory on a timely basis, on terms and conditions and at rates, that are reasonable, non-discriminatory, and transparent.

Article 18.13:   Submarine Cable Systems

Each Party shall ensure that a major supplier that controls international submarine cable landing stations in the Party's territory for which there are no economically or technically feasible alternatives provides access to those landing stations consistent with Article 18.9 (Interconnection with Major Suppliers), Article 18.10 (Provisioning and Pricing of Leased Circuits Services), and Article 18.11 (Co-Location), to public telecommunications suppliers of another Party.[10]

---

[9]   For the purposes of this Article, a supplier of mobile services in a Party's territory is not a major supplier unless a Party determines that the supplier meets the definition of "major supplier" set out in Article 18.1 (Definitions).

[10]   Mexico, based on its evaluation of the state of competition of the Mexican submarine cable systems market, has not applied major supplier-related measures to submarine cable landing stations pursuant to this Article.

Article 18.14:   Conditions for the Supply of Value-Added Services[11]

1.   The Parties recognize the importance of value-added services to innovation, competition, and consumer welfare. If a Party engages in direct regulation of value-added services, it should not impose on a supplier of value-added services requirements applicable to a supplier of public telecommunications services without due consideration of the legitimate public policy objectives, the technical feasibility of the requirements, and the characteristics of the value-added services at issue.

2.   Further to paragraph 1, each Party shall:

   (a)   ensure that:

      (i)   any licensing, permit, registration, or notification procedure that it adopts or maintains relating to the supply of value-added services is transparent and non-discriminatory, and that applications filed thereunder are processed expeditiously, and

      (ii)   information required under that procedure is limited to that necessary to demonstrate that the applicant has the financial solvency to begin providing services or to assess conformity of the applicant's terminal or other equipment with the Party's applicable standards or technical regulations, and

   (b)   not require an enterprise in its territory that supplies value-added services to:

      (i)   supply those services to the public generally,

      (ii)   cost-justify its rates for those services,

      (iii)   file a tariff for those services,

      (iv)   connect its networks with a particular customer or network for the supply of those services or

      (v)   conform with a particular standard or technical regulation of the telecommunications regulatory body for connecting to any other network, other than a public telecommunications network.

3.   Notwithstanding paragraphs 2(a)(ii) and 2(b), a Party may take the actions described in paragraphs 2(a)(ii) and 2(b) to remedy a practice of a supplier of value-added services that the Party has found in a particular case to be anticompetitive under its law, or to otherwise promote competition or safeguard the interests of consumers.

---

[11]   For greater certainty, this Article should not be understood to reflect a Party's view on whether a service should be categorized as a value-added service or a public telecommunications service.

Article 18.15:   Flexibility in the Choice of Technology

1.   No Party shall prevent a supplier of public telecommunications services from choosing the technologies it wishes to use to supply its services, subject to requirements necessary to satisfy legitimate public policy interests, provided that any measure restricting that choice is not prepared, adopted, or applied in a manner that creates an unnecessary obstacle to trade.

2.   For greater certainty, if a Party adopts a measure restricting choice referred to in paragraph 1, it shall do so consistent with Article 18.24 (Transparency).

Article 18.16:   Approaches to Regulation

1.   The Parties recognize the value of competitive markets to deliver a wide choice in the supply of telecommunications services and to enhance consumer welfare, and that economic regulation may not be needed if there is effective competition or if a service is new to a market. Accordingly, the Parties recognize that regulatory needs and approaches differ by market, and that each Party may determine how to implement its obligations under this Chapter.

2.   In this respect, the Parties recognize that a Party may:

(a)   engage in direct regulation either in anticipation of an issue that the Party expects may arise or to resolve an issue that has arisen in the market;

(b)   rely on the role of market forces, particularly with respect to market segments that are, or are likely to be, competitive or that have low barriers to entry, such as services provided by telecommunications suppliers that do not own network facilities;[12] or

(c)   use other appropriate means that benefit the long-term interest of end-users.

3.   If a Party engages in direct regulation, it may nonetheless forbear, to the extent provided for in its law, from applying that regulation to a service that the Party classifies as a public telecommunications service, if its telecommunications regulatory body determines that:

(a)   enforcement of the regulation is not necessary to prevent unreasonable or discriminatory practices;

(b)   enforcement of the regulation is not necessary for the protection of consumers; and

---

[12]   Consistent with this subparagraph, the United States, based on its evaluation of the state of competition of the U.S. commercial mobile market, has not applied major supplier-related measures pursuant to Article 18.5 (Treatment by Major Suppliers of Public Telecommunications Services), Article 18.7 (Resale), Article 18.9 (Interconnection with Major Suppliers), Article 18.11 (Co-Location), or Article 18.12 (Access to Poles, Ducts, Conduits, and Rights-of Way) to the commercial mobile market.

(c)   forbearance is consistent with the public interest, including promoting and enhancing competition between suppliers of public telecommunications services.

Article 18.17:   Telecommunications Regulatory Bodies

1.   Each Party shall ensure that its telecommunications regulatory body is separate from, and not accountable to, a supplier of public telecommunications services. With a view to ensuring the independence and impartiality of telecommunications regulatory bodies, each Party shall ensure that its telecommunications regulatory body does not hold a financial interest[13] or maintain an operating or management role in a supplier of public telecommunications services.[14]

2.   Each Party shall ensure that its regulatory decisions and procedures, including decisions and procedures relating to licensing, interconnection with public telecommunications networks and services, tariffs, and assignment or allocation of spectrum for commercial telecommunications services, are impartial with respect to market participants.

3.   Each Party shall ensure that its telecommunications regulatory body has the authority to impose requirements on a major supplier that are additional to or different from requirements imposed on other suppliers in the telecommunications sector.

Article 18.18:   State Enterprises

No Party shall accord more favorable treatment to a supplier of telecommunications services in its territory than that accorded to a like service supplier of another Party on the basis that the supplier receiving more favorable treatment is owned or controlled by the central level of government of the Party.

Article 18.19:   Universal Services

Each Party has the right to define the kind of universal service obligation it wishes to maintain. Each Party shall administer any universal service obligation that it maintains in a transparent, non-discriminatory, and competitively neutral manner and shall ensure that its universal service obligation is not more burdensome than necessary for the kind of universal service that it has defined.

Article 18.20:   Licensing Process

1.   If a Party requires a supplier of public telecommunications services to have a license, the Party shall make publicly available:

---

[13]   For greater certainty, this paragraph shall not be construed to prohibit a government entity of a Party other than the telecommunications regulatory body from owning equity in a supplier of public telecommunications services.

[14]   For Mexico, the telecommunications regulatory body is autonomous from the Executive Branch of government, is independent regarding its decisions and functioning, and has the purpose of regulating and promoting competition and efficient development of telecommunications, as set out in existing Mexican law.

(a) applicable licensing criteria and procedures;

(b) the period that it normally requires to reach a decision concerning an application for a license; and

(c) the terms and conditions of licenses in effect.

2. Each Party shall ensure that, on request, an applicant or licensee receives the reasons for the:

(a) denial of a license;

(b) imposition of supplier-specific conditions on a license;

(c) revocation of a license; or

(d) refusal to renew a license.

Article 18.21:   Allocation and Use of Scarce Resources

1. Each Party shall administer its procedures for the allocation and use of scarce telecommunications resources, including frequencies, numbers and rights-of-way, in an objective, timely, transparent, and non-discriminatory manner.

2. Each Party shall make publicly available the current state of frequency bands allocated and assigned to specific suppliers but retains the right not to provide detailed identification of frequencies that are allocated or assigned for specific government uses.

3. For greater certainty, a measure of a Party that allocates or assigns spectrum or manages frequency is not in itself inconsistent with Article 15.5 (Market Access) either as it applies to cross-border trade in services or through the operation of Article 15.2 (Scope) to an investor or covered investment of another Party. Accordingly, each Party retains the right to establish and apply spectrum and frequency management policies that may have the effect of limiting the number of suppliers of public telecommunications services, provided that the Party does so in a manner that is consistent with this Agreement. This includes the ability to allocate frequency bands, taking into account current and future needs and spectrum availability.

4. When making a spectrum allocation for commercial telecommunications services, each Party shall endeavor to rely on an open and transparent process that considers the public interest, including the promotion of competition.

5. Each Party shall endeavor to rely generally on market-based approaches in assigning spectrum for terrestrial commercial telecommunications services. To this end, each Party may use mechanisms such as auctions, if appropriate, to assign spectrum for commercial use.

Article 18.22:   Enforcement

Each Party shall provide its competent authority the authority to enforce the Party's measures relating to the obligations set out in Article 18.3 (Access and Use), Article 18.4. (Obligations Relating to Suppliers of Public

Telecommunications Services), Article 18.5 (Treatment by Major Suppliers of Public Telecommunications Services), Article 18.6 (Competitive Safeguards), Article 18.7 (Resale), Article 18.8 (Unbundling of Network Elements), Article 18.9 (Interconnection with Major Suppliers), Article 18.10 (Provisioning and Pricing of Leased Circuits Services), Article 18.11 (Co-Location), Article 18.12 (Access to Poles, Ducts, Conduits, and Rights-of-Way) and Article 18.13 (Submarine Cable Systems). That authority shall include the ability to impose effective sanctions, which may include financial penalties, injunctive relief (on an interim or final basis), corrective orders, or the modification, suspension, or revocation of licenses.

Article 18.23:   Resolution of Disputes

1.   Further to Article 29.3 (Administrative Proceedings) and Article 29.4 (Review and Appeal), each Party shall ensure that:

Recourse

(a)   enterprises have recourse to the telecommunications regulatory body of the Party to resolve disputes with a supplier of public telecommunications services regarding the Party's measures relating to matters set out in Article 18.3 (Access and Use), Article 18.4 (Obligations Relating to Suppliers of Public Telecommunications Services), Article 18.5 (Treatment by Major Suppliers of Public Telecommunications Services), Article 18.6 (Competitive Safeguards), Article 18.7 (Resale), Article 18.8 (Unbundling of Network Elements), Article 18.9 (Interconnection with Major Suppliers), Article 18.10 (Provisioning and Pricing of Leased Circuits Services), Article 18.11 (Co-Location), Article 18.12 (Access to Poles, Ducts, Conduits, and Rights-of-Way), and Article 18.13 (Submarine Cable Systems);

(b)   if the telecommunications regulatory body declines to initiate action on a request to resolve a dispute, it shall, on request, provide a written explanation for its decision within a reasonable period of time;[15]

(c)   a supplier of public telecommunications services of another Party that has requested interconnection with a major supplier in the Party's territory has, within a reasonable and publicly specified period of time after the supplier requests interconnection, recourse to its telecommunications regulatory body to resolve disputes regarding the appropriate terms, conditions and rates for interconnection with that major supplier; and

---

[15]   For the United States, this subparagraph applies only to the national regulatory body.

Reconsideration[16]

 (d) an enterprise whose legally protected interests are adversely affected by a determination or decision of the Party's telecommunications regulatory body may appeal to or petition the body to reconsider that determination or decision. No Party shall permit the making of an application for reconsideration to constitute grounds for non-compliance with the determination or decision of the telecommunications regulatory body, unless the regulatory body issues an order that the determination or decision not be enforced while the proceeding is pending. A Party may limit the circumstances under which reconsideration is available, in accordance with its laws and regulations.

Judicial Review

2. No Party shall permit the making of an application for judicial review to constitute grounds for non-compliance with the determination or decision of the telecommunications regulatory body, unless the judicial body issues an order that the determination or decision not be enforced while the proceeding is pending.

Article 18.24: Transparency

1. Further to Article 29.2 (Publication), each Party shall ensure that when its telecommunications regulatory body seeks input[17] for a proposal for a regulation, that body:

 (a) makes the proposal public or otherwise available to any interested persons;

 (b) includes an explanation of the purpose of and reasons for the proposal;

 (c) provides interested persons with adequate public notice of the ability to comment and reasonable opportunity for comment;

 (d) to the extent practicable, makes publicly available all relevant comments filed with it; and

 (e) responds to all significant and relevant issues raised in comments filed, in the course of issuance of the final regulation.[18]

---

 [16] This subparagraph does not apply to Mexico. For Mexico, the general rules, acts or omissions of the Federal Telecommunications Institute may only be challenged through an indirect *amparo* trial before federal courts specialized in competition, broadcasting, and telecommunications and shall not be subject to injunction (*suspensión*).

 [17] For greater certainty, seeking input does not include internal governmental deliberations.

 [18] For greater certainty, a Party may consolidate its responses to the comments received from interested persons.

2. Further to Article 29.2 (Publication), each Party shall ensure that its measures relating to public telecommunications services are publicly available, including:

    (a) tariffs and other terms and conditions of service;

    (b) specifications of technical interfaces;

    (c) conditions for attaching terminal or other equipment to the public telecommunications network;

    (d) licensing, permit, registration, or notification requirements, if any;

    (e) general procedures relating to resolution of telecommunications disputes provided for in Article 18.23 (Resolution of Disputes); and

    (f) any measures of the telecommunications regulatory body if the government delegates to other bodies the responsibility for preparing, amending, and adopting standards-related measures affecting access and use.

Article 18.25: International Roaming Services

1. The Parties shall endeavor to cooperate on promoting transparent and reasonable rates for international mobile roaming services that can help promote the growth of trade between the Parties and enhance consumer welfare.

2. A Party may take steps to enhance transparency and competition with respect to international mobile roaming rates and technological alternatives to roaming services, such as:

    (a) ensuring that information regarding retail rates is easily accessible to consumers; and

    (b) minimizing impediments to the use of technological alternatives to roaming, whereby consumers can access telecommunications services using the device of their choice when visiting the territory of a Party from the territory of another Party.

Article 18.26: Relation to Other Chapters

If there is an inconsistency between this Chapter and another Chapter of this Agreement, this Chapter shall prevail to the extent of the inconsistency.

* * *

ANNEX 18-A RURAL TELEPHONE SUPPLIERS

United States

The United States may exempt rural local exchange carriers and rural telephone companies, as defined, respectively, in sections 251(f)(2) and 3(44) of the Communications Act of 1934, as amended, (47 U.S.C. Section 251(f)(2) and Section 153(44)), from the obligations contained in Article 18.4.6

(Obligations Relating to Suppliers of Public Telecommunications Services—Number Portability), Article 18.4.7 (Obligations Relating to Suppliers of Public Telecommunications Services—Dialing Parity), Article 18.7 (Resale), Article 18.8 (Unbundling of Network Elements), Article 18.9 (Interconnection with Major Suppliers), and Article 18.11 (Co-Location).

CHAPTER 19 DIGITAL TRADE

Article 19.1: Definitions

For the purposes of this Chapter:

Algorithm means a defined sequence of steps, taken to solve a problem or obtain a result;

Computing facility means a computer server or storage device for processing or storing information for commercial use;

Covered person means:

 (a) a covered investment as defined in 1.4 (General Definitions);

 (b) an investor of a Party as defined in Article 14.1 (Definitions); or

 (c) a service supplier of a Party as defined in Article 15.1 (Definitions), but does not include a covered person as defined in Article 17.1 (Definitions);

Digital product means a computer program, text, video, image, sound recording, or other product that is digitally encoded, produced for commercial sale or distribution, and that can be transmitted electronically. For greater certainty, digital product does not include a digitized representation of a financial instrument, including money;[1]

Electronic authentication means the process or act of verifying the identity of a party to an electronic communication or transaction and ensuring the integrity of an electronic communication;

Electronic signature means data in electronic form that is in, affixed to, or logically associated with, an electronic document or message, and that may be used to identify the signatory in relation to the electronic document or message and indicate the signatory's approval of the information contained in the electronic document or message;

Government information means non-proprietary information, including data, held by the central government;

Information content provider means a person or entity that creates or develops, in whole or in Part, information provided through the Internet or another interactive computer service;

Interactive computer service means a system or service that provides or enables electronic access by multiple users to a computer server;

---

[1] This definition should not be understood to reflect a Party's view that digital products are a good or are a service.

Personal information means information, including data, about an identified or identifiable natural person;

Trade administration document means a form issued or controlled by a Party that must be completed by or for an importer or exporter in connection with the import or export of goods; and

Unsolicited commercial electronic communication means an electronic message, which is sent to an electronic address of a person for commercial or marketing purposes without the consent of the recipient or despite the explicit rejection of the recipient.[2]

Article 19.2:   Scope and General Provisions

1. The Parties recognize the economic growth and opportunities provided by digital trade and the importance of frameworks that promote consumer confidence in digital trade and of avoiding unnecessary barriers to its use and development.

2. This Chapter applies to measures adopted or maintained by a Party that affect trade by electronic means.

3. This Chapter does not apply:

    (a) to government procurement; or

    (b) except for Article 19.18 (Open Government Data), to information held or processed by or on behalf of a Party, or measures related to that information, including measures related to its collection.

4. For greater certainty, a measure that affects the supply of a service delivered or performed electronically is subject to Chapter 14 (Investment), Chapter 15 (Cross-Border Trade in Services), and Chapter 17 (Financial Services), including any exception or non-conforming measure set out in this Agreement that is applicable to the obligations contained in those Chapters.

Article 19.3:   Customs Duties

1. No Party shall impose customs duties, fees, or other charges on or in connection with the importation or exportation of digital products transmitted electronically, between a person of one Party and a person of another Party.

2. For greater certainty, paragraph 1 does not preclude a Party from imposing internal taxes, fees, or other charges on a digital product transmitted electronically, provided that those taxes, fees, or charges are imposed in a manner consistent with this Agreement.

Article 19.4:   Non-Discriminatory Treatment of Digital Products

1. No Party shall accord less favorable treatment to a digital product created, produced, published, contracted for, commissioned, or first

---

    [2] For the United States, an unsolicited commercial electronic communication does not include an electronic message sent primarily for purposes other than commercial or marketing purposes.

made available on commercial terms in the territory of another Party, or to a digital product of which the author, performer, producer, developer, or owner is a person of another Party, than it accords to other like digital products.[3]

2.   This Article does not apply to a subsidy or grant provided by a Party, including a government-supported loan, guarantee, or insurance.

Article 19.5:   Domestic Electronic Transactions Framework

1.   Each Party shall maintain a legal framework governing electronic transactions consistent with the principles of the *UNCITRAL Model Law on Electronic Commerce 1996.*

2.   Each Party shall endeavor to:

   (a)   avoid unnecessary regulatory burden on electronic transactions; and

   (b)   facilitate input by interested persons in the development of its legal framework for electronic transactions.

Article 19.6:   Electronic Authentication and Electronic Signatures

1.   Except in circumstances provided for under its law, a Party shall not deny the legal validity of a signature solely on the basis that the signature is in electronic form.

2.   No Party shall adopt or maintain measures for electronic authentication and electronic signatures that would:

   (a)   prohibit parties to an electronic transaction from mutually determining the appropriate authentication methods or electronic signatures for that transaction; or

   (b)   prevent parties to an electronic transaction from having the opportunity to establish before judicial or administrative authorities that their transaction complies with any legal requirements with respect to authentication or electronic signatures.

3.   Notwithstanding paragraph 2, a Party may require that, for a particular category of transactions, the electronic signature or method of authentication meets certain performance standards or is certified by an authority accredited in accordance with its law.

4.   Each Party shall encourage the use of interoperable electronic authentication.

Article 19.7:   Online Consumer Protection

1.   The Parties recognize the importance of adopting and maintaining transparent and effective measures to protect consumers from

---

[3]   For greater certainty, to the extent that a digital product of a non-Party is a "like digital product," it will qualify as an "other like digital product" for the purposes of Article 19.4.1 (Non-Discriminatory Treatment of Digital Products).

fraudulent or deceptive commercial activities as referred to in Article 21.4.2 (Consumer Protection) when they engage in digital trade.

2.   Each Party shall adopt or maintain consumer protection laws to proscribe fraudulent and deceptive commercial activities that cause harm or potential harm to consumers engaged in online commercial activities.

3.   The Parties recognize the importance of, and public interest in, cooperation between their respective national consumer protection agencies or other relevant bodies on activities related to cross-border digital trade in order to enhance consumer welfare. To this end, the Parties affirm that cooperation under paragraphs 21.4.3 through 21.4.5 (Consumer Protection) includes cooperation with respect to online commercial activities.

Article 19.8:   Personal Information Protection

1.   The Parties recognize the economic and social benefits of protecting the personal information of users of digital trade and the contribution that this makes to enhancing consumer confidence in digital trade.

2.   To this end, each Party shall adopt or maintain a legal framework that provides for the protection of the personal information of the users of digital trade. In the development of this legal framework, each Party should take into account principles and guidelines of relevant international bodies,[4] such as the *APEC Privacy Framework* and the *OECD Recommendation of the Council concerning Guidelines governing the Protection of Privacy and Transborder Flows of Personal Data (2013).*

3.   The Parties recognize that pursuant to paragraph 2, key principles include: limitation on collection; choice; data quality; purpose specification; use limitation; security safeguards; transparency; individual participation; and accountability. The Parties also recognize the importance of ensuring compliance with measures to protect personal information and ensuring that any restrictions on cross-border flows of personal information are necessary and proportionate to the risks presented.

4.   Each Party shall endeavor to adopt non-discriminatory practices in protecting users of digital trade from personal information protection violations occurring within its jurisdiction.

5.   Each Party shall publish information on the personal information protections it provides to users of digital trade, including how:

(a)   a natural person can pursue a remedy; and

(b)   an enterprise can comply with legal requirements.

---

[4]   For greater certainty, a Party may comply with the obligation in this paragraph by adopting or maintaining measures such as a comprehensive privacy, personal information or personal data protection laws, sector-specific laws covering privacy, or laws that provide for the enforcement of voluntary undertakings by enterprises relating to privacy.

6.   Recognizing that the Parties may take different legal approaches to protecting personal information, each Party should encourage the development of mechanisms to promote compatibility between these different regimes. The Parties shall endeavor to exchange information on the mechanisms applied in their jurisdictions and explore ways to extend these or other suitable arrangements to promote compatibility between them. The Parties recognize that the *APEC Cross-Border Privacy Rules* system is a valid mechanism to facilitate cross-border information transfers while protecting personal information.

Article 19.9:   Paperless Trading

Each Party shall endeavor to accept a trade administration document submitted electronically as the legal equivalent of the paper version of that document.

Article 19.10:   Principles on Access to and Use of the Internet for Digital Trade

The Parties recognize that it is beneficial for consumers in their territories to be able to:

(a)   access and use services and applications of a consumer's choice available on the Internet, subject to reasonable network management;

(b)   connect the end-user devices of a consumer's choice to the Internet, provided that such devices do not harm the network; and

(c)   access information on the network management practices of a consumer's Internet access service supplier.

Article 19.11:   Cross-Border Transfer of Information by Electronic Means

1.   No Party shall prohibit or restrict the cross-border transfer of information, including personal information, by electronic means if this activity is for the conduct of the business of a covered person.

2.   This Article does not prevent a Party from adopting or maintaining a measure inconsistent with paragraph 1 that is necessary to achieve a legitimate public policy objective, provided that the measure:

(a)   is not applied in a manner which would constitute a means of arbitrary or unjustifiable discrimination or a disguised restriction on trade; and

(b)   does not impose restrictions on transfers of information greater than are necessary to achieve the objective.[5]

---

[5]   A measure does not meet the conditions of this paragraph if it accords different treatment to data transfers solely on the basis that they are cross-border in a manner that modifies the conditions of competition to the detriment of service suppliers of another Party.

Article 19.12:   Location of Computing Facilities

No Party shall require a covered person to use or locate computing facilities in that Party's territory as a condition for conducting business in that territory.

Article 19.13:   Unsolicited Commercial Electronic Communications

1.   Each Party shall adopt or maintain measures providing for the limitation of unsolicited commercial electronic communications.

2.   Each Party shall adopt or maintain measures regarding unsolicited commercial electronic communications sent to an electronic mail address that:

(a)   require suppliers of unsolicited commercial electronic messages to facilitate the ability of recipients to prevent ongoing reception of those messages; or

(b)   require the consent, as specified in the laws and regulations of each Party, of recipients to receive commercial electronic messages.

3.   Each Party shall endeavor to adopt or maintain measures that enable consumers to reduce or prevent unsolicited commercial electronic communications sent other than to an electronic mail address.

4.   Each Party shall provide recourse in its law against suppliers of unsolicited commercial electronic communications that do not comply with a measure adopted or maintained pursuant to paragraph 2 or 3.

5.   The Parties shall endeavor to cooperate in appropriate cases of mutual concern regarding the regulation of unsolicited commercial electronic communications.

Article 19.14:   Cooperation

1.   Recognizing the global nature of digital trade, the Parties shall endeavor to:

(a)   exchange information and share experiences on regulations, policies, enforcement and compliance relating to digital trade, including:

(i)   personal information protection, particularly with a view to strengthening existing international mechanisms for cooperation in enforcing laws protecting privacy,

(ii)   security in electronic communications,

(iii)   authentication, and

(iv)   government use of digital tools and technologies to achieve better government performance;

(b)   cooperate and maintain a dialogue on the promotion and development of mechanisms, including the *APEC Cross-*

Border Privacy Rules, that further global interoperability of privacy regimes;

(c) actively participate in regional and multilateral fora to promote the development of digital trade;

(d) encourage development by the private sector of methods of self-regulation that foster digital trade, including codes of conduct, model contracts, guidelines, and enforcement mechanisms;

(e) promote access for persons with disabilities to information and communications technologies; and

(f) promote, through international cross-border cooperation initiatives, the development of mechanisms to assist users in submitting cross-border complaints regarding personal information protection.

2. The Parties shall consider establishing a forum to address any of the issues listed above, or any other matter pertaining to the operation of this Chapter.

Article 19.15: Cybersecurity

1. The Parties recognize that threats to cybersecurity undermine confidence in digital trade. Accordingly, the Parties shall endeavor to:

(a) build the capabilities of their respective national entities responsible for cybersecurity incident response; and

(b) strengthen existing collaboration mechanisms for cooperating to identify and mitigate malicious intrusions or dissemination of malicious code that affect electronic networks, and use those mechanisms to swiftly address cybersecurity incidents, as well as for the sharing of information for awareness and best practices.

2. Given the evolving nature of cybersecurity threats, the Parties recognize that risk-based approaches may be more effective than prescriptive regulation in addressing those threats. Accordingly, each Party shall endeavor to employ, and encourage enterprises within its jurisdiction to use, risk-based approaches that rely on consensus-based standards and risk management best practices to identify and protect against cybersecurity risks and to detect, respond to, and recover from cybersecurity events.

Article 19.16: Source Code

1. No Party shall require the transfer of, or access to, a source code of software owned by a person of another Party, or to an algorithm expressed in that source code, as a condition for the import, distribution, sale or use of that software, or of products containing that software, in its territory.

2. This Article does not preclude a regulatory body or judicial authority of a Party from requiring a person of another Party to preserve and make

available the source code of software, or an algorithm expressed in that source code, to the regulatory body for a specific investigation, inspection, examination, enforcement action, or judicial proceeding,[6] subject to safeguards against unauthorized disclosure.

Article 19.17:   Interactive Computer Services

1. The Parties recognize the importance of the promotion of interactive computer services, including for small and medium-sized enterprises, as vital to the growth of digital trade.

2. To that end, other than as provided in paragraph 4, no Party shall adopt or maintain measures that treat a supplier or user of an interactive computer service as an information content provider in determining liability for harms related to information stored, processed, transmitted, distributed, or made available by the service, except to the extent the supplier or user has, in whole or in part, created, or developed the information.[7]

3. No Party shall impose liability on a supplier or user of an interactive computer service on account of:

    (a) any action voluntarily taken in good faith by the supplier or user to restrict access to or availability of material that is accessible or available through its supply or use of the interactive computer services and that the supplier or user considers to be harmful or objectionable; or

    (b) any action taken to enable or make available the technical means that enable an information content provider or other persons to restrict access to material that it considers to be harmful or objectionable.

4. Nothing in this Article shall:

    (a) apply to any measure of a Party pertaining to intellectual property, including measures addressing liability for intellectual property infringement; or

    (b) be construed to enlarge or diminish a Party's ability to protect or enforce an intellectual property right; or

    (c) be construed to prevent:

        (i) a Party from enforcing any criminal law, or

        (ii) a supplier or user of an interactive computer service from complying with a specific, lawful order of a law enforcement authority.[8]

---

[6]   This disclosure shall not be construed to negatively affect the software source code's status as a trade secret, if such status is claimed by the trade secret owner.

[7]   For greater certainty, a Party may comply with this Article through its laws, regulations, or application of existing legal doctrines as applied through judicial decisions.

[8]   The Parties understand that measures referenced in paragraph 4(c)(ii) shall be not inconsistent with paragraph 2 in situations where paragraph 2 is applicable.

5.   This Article is subject to Annex 19-A.

Article 19.18:   Open Government Data

1.   The Parties recognize that facilitating public access to and use of government information fosters economic and social development, competitiveness, and innovation.

2.   To the extent that a Party chooses to make government information, including data, available to the public, it shall endeavor to ensure that the information is in a machine-readable and open format and can be searched, retrieved, used, reused, and redistributed.

3.   The Parties shall endeavor to cooperate to identify ways in which each Party can expand access to and use of government information, including data, that the Party has made public, with a view to enhancing and generating business opportunities, especially for SMEs.

ANNEX 19-A

1.   Article 19.17 (Interactive Computer Services) shall not apply with respect to Mexico until the date of three years after entry into force of this Agreement.

2.   The Parties understand that Articles 145 and 146 of Mexico's *Ley Federal de Telecomunicaciones y Radiodifusión*, as in force on the date of entry into force of this Agreement, are not inconsistent with Article 19.17.3 (Interactive Computer Services). In a dispute with respect to this article, subordinate measures adopted or maintained under the authority of and consistent with Articles 145 and 146 of Mexico's *Ley Federal de Telecomunicaciones y Radiodifusión* shall be presumed to be not inconsistent with Article 19.17.3 (Interactive Computer Services).

3.   The Parties understand that Mexico will comply with the obligations in Article 19.17.3 (Interactive Computer Services) in a manner that is both effective and consistent with Mexico's Constitution (*Constitución Política de los Estados Unidos Mexicanos*), specifically Articles 6 and 7.

4.   For greater certainty, Article 19.17 (Interactive Computer Services) is subject to Article 32.1 (General Exceptions), which, among other things, provides that, for purposes of Chapter 19, the exception for measures necessary to protect public morals pursuant to paragraph (a) of Article XIV of GATS is incorporated into and made part of this Agreement, *mutatis mutandis*. The Parties agree that measures necessary to protect against online sex trafficking, sexual exploitation of children, and prostitution, such as Public Law 115–164, the "Allow States and Victims to Fight Online Sex Trafficking Act of 2017," which amends the Communications Act of 1934, and any relevant provisions of *Ley General para Prevenir, Sancionar y Erradicar los Delitos en Materia de Trata de Personas y para la Protección y Asistencia a las Víctimas de estos delitos*, are measures necessary to protect public morals.

CHAPTER 20   INTELLECTUAL PROPERTY RIGHTS

Section A: General Provisions

Article 20.1:   Definitions

1.   For the purposes of this Chapter:

Berne Convention means the *Berne Convention for the Protection of Literary and Artistic Works*, done at Berne on September 9, 1886, as revised at Paris on July 24, 1971;

Brussels Convention means the *Convention Relating to the Distribution of Programme-Carrying Signals Transmitted by Satellite*, done at Brussels on May 21, 1974;

Budapest Treaty means the *Budapest Treaty on the International Recognition of the Deposit of Microorganisms for the Purposes of Patent Procedure* (1977), done at Budapest on April 28, 1977, as amended on September 26, 1980;

Declaration on TRIPS and Public Health means the *Declaration on the TRIPS Agreement and Public Health* (WT/MIN(01)/DEC/2), adopted on November 14, 2001;

Geographical indication means an indication that identifies a good as originating in the territory of a Party, or a region or locality in that territory, where a given quality, reputation, or other characteristic of the good is essentially attributable to its geographical origin;

Hague Agreement means the *Geneva Act of the Hague Agreement Concerning the International Registration of Industrial Designs*, done at Geneva on July 2, 1999;

Intellectual property refers to all categories of intellectual property that are the subject of Sections 1 through 7 of Part II of the TRIPS Agreement;

Madrid Protocol means the *Protocol Relating to the Madrid Agreement Concerning the International Registration of Marks*, done at Madrid on June 27, 1989;

Paris Convention means the *Paris Convention for the Protection of Industrial Property,* done at Paris on March 20, 1883 as revised at Stockholm on July 14, 1967;

Performance means a performance fixed in a phonogram, unless otherwise specified with respect to copyright and related rights, right to authorize or prohibit refers to exclusive rights;

PLT means the *Patent Law Treaty* adopted by the WIPO Diplomatic Conference done at Geneva on June 1, 2000;

Singapore Treaty means the *Singapore Treaty on the Law of Trademarks*, done at Singapore on March 27, 2006;

UPOV 1991 means the *International Convention for the Protection of New Varieties of Plants*, done at Paris on December 2, 1961, as revised at Geneva on March 19, 1991;

WCT means the *WIPO Copyright Treaty*, done at Geneva on December 20, 1996;

WIPO means the World Intellectual Property Organization;

For greater certainty, Work includes a cinematographic work, photographic work, and computer program; and

WPPT means the *WIPO Performances and Phonograms Treaty*, done at Geneva on December 20, 1996.

2. For the purposes of Article 20.8 (National Treatment), Article 20.30 (Administrative Procedures for the Protection or Recognition of Geographical Indications), and Article 20.62 (Related Rights):

a national means, in respect of the relevant right, a person of a Party that would meet the criteria for eligibility for protection provided for in the agreements listed in Article 20.7 (International Agreements) or the TRIPS Agreement.

Article 20.2:   Objectives

The protection and enforcement of intellectual property rights should contribute to the promotion of technological innovation and to the transfer and dissemination of technology, to the mutual advantage of producers and users of technological knowledge and in a manner conducive to social and economic welfare, and to a balance of rights and obligations.

Article 20.3:   Principles

1. A Party may, in formulating or amending its laws and regulations, adopt measures necessary to protect public health and nutrition, and to promote the public interest in sectors of vital importance to their socio-economic and technological development, provided that those measures are consistent with the provisions of this Chapter.

2. Appropriate measures, provided that they are consistent with the provisions of this Chapter, may be needed to prevent the abuse of intellectual property rights by right holders or the resort to practices which unreasonably restrain trade or adversely affect the international transfer of technology.

Article 20.4:   Understandings in Respect of this Chapter

Having regard to the underlying public policy objectives of national systems, the Parties recognize the need to:

(a) promote innovation and creativity;

(b) facilitate the diffusion of information, knowledge, technology, culture, and the arts; and

(c) foster competition and open and efficient markets;

through their respective intellectual property systems, while respecting the principles of transparency and due process, and taking into account the interests of relevant stakeholders, including right holders, service providers, users, and the public.

Article 20.5:   Nature and Scope of Obligations

1.   Each Party shall provide in its territory to the nationals of another Party adequate and effective protection and enforcement of intellectual property rights, while ensuring that measures to enforce intellectual property rights do not themselves become barriers to legitimate trade.

2.   A Party may, but shall not be obliged to, provide more extensive protection for, or enforcement of, intellectual property rights under its law than is required by this Chapter, provided that such protection or enforcement does not contravene this Chapter. Each Party shall be free to determine the appropriate method of implementing the provisions of this Chapter within its own legal system and practice.

Article 20.6:   Understandings Regarding Certain Public Health Measures

The Parties affirm their commitment to the Declaration on TRIPS and Public Health. In particular, the Parties have reached the following understandings regarding this Chapter:

(a)   The obligations of this Chapter do not and should not prevent a Party from taking measures to protect public health. Accordingly, while reiterating their commitment to this Chapter, the Parties affirm that this Chapter can and should be interpreted and implemented in a manner supportive of each Party's right to protect public health and, in particular, to promote access to medicines for all. Each Party has the right to determine what constitutes a national emergency or other circumstances of extreme urgency, it being understood that public health crises, including those relating to HIV/AIDS, tuberculosis, malaria, and other epidemics, can represent a national emergency or other circumstances of extreme urgency.

(b)   In recognition of the commitment to access to medicines that are supplied in accordance with the Decision of the WTO General Council of August 30, 2003 on the *Implementation of Paragraph Six of the Doha Declaration on the TRIPS Agreement and Public Health* (WT/L/540) and the WTO General Council Chairman's Statement Accompanying the Decision (JOB(03)/177, WT/GC/M/82), as well as the Decision of the WTO General Council of December 6, 2005 on the *Amendment of the TRIPS Agreement,* (WT/L/641) and the WTO General Council Chairperson's Statement Accompanying the Decision (JOB(05)/319 and Corr. 1,WT/GC/M/100) (collectively, the "TRIPS/health solution"), this Chapter does not and should not prevent the effective utilization of the TRIPS/health solution.

(c)   With respect to the aforementioned matters, if any waiver of a provision of the TRIPS Agreement, or any amendment of the TRIPS Agreement, enters into force with respect to the

Parties, and a Party's application of a measure in conformity with that waiver or amendment is contrary to the obligations of this Chapter, the Parties shall immediately consult in order to adapt this Chapter as appropriate in the light of the waiver or amendment.

Article 20.7:   International Agreements

1. Each Party affirms that it has ratified or acceded to the following agreements:

    (a) *Patent Cooperation Treaty,* as amended on September 28, 1979, and modified on February 3, 1984;

    (b) Paris Convention;

    (c) Berne Convention;

    (d) WCT; and

    (e) WPPT.

2. Each Party shall ratify or accede to each of the following agreements, if it is not already a party to that agreement, by the date of entry into force of this Agreement:

    (a) Madrid Protocol;

    (b) Budapest Treaty;

    (c) Singapore Treaty;[1]

    (d) UPOV 1991;

    (e) Hague Agreement; and

    (f) Brussels Convention.

3. Each Party shall give due consideration to ratifying or acceding to the PLT, or, in the alternative, shall adopt or maintain procedural standards consistent with the objective of the PLT.

Article 20.8:   National Treatment

1. In respect of all categories of intellectual property covered in this Chapter, each Party shall accord to nationals of another Party treatment no less favorable than it accords to its own nationals with regard to the protection[2] of intellectual property rights.

---

[1] A Party may satisfy the obligations in paragraphs 2(a) and 2(c) by ratifying or acceding to either the Madrid Protocol or the Singapore Treaty.

[2] For the purposes of this paragraph, "protection" shall include matters affecting the availability, acquisition, scope, maintenance and enforcement of intellectual property rights as well as matters affecting the use of intellectual property rights specifically covered by this Chapter. Further, for the purposes of this paragraph, "protection" also includes the prohibition on the circumvention of effective technological measures set out in Article 20.67 (Technological Protection Measures) and the provisions concerning rights management information set out in Article 20.68 (Rights Management Information). For greater certainty, "matters affecting the use of intellectual property rights specifically covered by this Chapter" in respect of works,

2.   A Party may derogate from paragraph 1 in relation to its judicial and administrative procedures, including requiring a national of another Party to designate an address for service of process in its territory, or to appoint an agent in its territory, provided that this derogation is:

     (a)   necessary to secure compliance with laws or regulations that are not inconsistent with this Chapter; and

     (b)   not applied in a manner that would constitute a disguised restriction on trade.

3.   Paragraph 1 does not apply to procedures provided in multilateral agreements concluded under the auspices of WIPO relating to the acquisition or maintenance of intellectual property rights.

Article 20.9:   Transparency

1.   Further to Article 20.81 (Enforcement Practices with Respect to Intellectual Property Rights), each Party shall endeavor to publish online its laws, regulations, procedures, and administrative rulings of general application concerning the protection and enforcement of intellectual property rights.

2.   Each Party shall, subject to its law, endeavor to publish online information that it makes public concerning applications for trademarks, geographical indications, designs, patents, and plant variety rights.[3],[4]

3.   Each Party shall, subject to its law, publish online information that it makes public concerning registered or granted trademarks, geographical indications, designs, patents, and plant variety rights, sufficient to enable the public to become acquainted with those registered or granted rights.[5]

Article 20.10:   Application of Chapter to Existing Subject Matter and Prior Acts

1.   Unless otherwise provided in this Chapter, including in Article 20.64 (Application of Article 18 of the Berne Convention and Article 14.6 of the TRIPS Agreement), this Chapter gives rise to obligations in respect of all subject matter existing at the date of entry into force of this Agreement and that is protected on that date in the territory of a Party where protection is claimed, or that meets or comes subsequently to meet the criteria for protection under this Chapter.

---

performances, and phonograms, include any form of payment, such as licensing fees, royalties, equitable remuneration, or levies, in respect of uses that fall under the copyright and related rights in this Chapter. The preceding sentence is without prejudice to a Party's interpretation of "matters affecting the use of intellectual property rights" in footnote 3 of the TRIPS Agreement.

[3]   For greater certainty, paragraphs 2 and 3 are without prejudice to a Party's obligations under Article 20.23 (Electronic Trademarks System).

[4]   For greater certainty, paragraph 2 does not require a Party to publish online the entire dossier for the relevant application.

[5]   For greater certainty, paragraph 3 does not require a Party to publish online the entire dossier for the relevant registered or granted intellectual property right.

2.   Unless provided in Article 20.64 (Application of Article 18 of the Berne Convention and Article 14.6 of the TRIPS Agreement), a Party shall not be required to restore protection to subject matter that on the date of entry into force of this Agreement has fallen into the public domain in its territory.

3.   This Chapter does not give rise to obligations in respect of acts that occurred before the date of entry into force of this Agreement.

Article 20.11:   Exhaustion of Intellectual Property Rights

Nothing in this Agreement prevents a Party from determining whether or under what conditions the exhaustion of intellectual property rights applies under its legal system.[6]

* * *

Section C: Trademarks

Article 20.17:   Types of Signs Registrable as Trademarks

No Party shall require, as a condition of registration, that a sign be visually perceptible, nor shall a Party deny registration of a trademark only on the ground that the sign of which it is composed is a sound. Additionally, each Party shall make best efforts to register scent marks.

A Party may require a concise and accurate description, or graphical representation, or both, as applicable, of the trademark.

Article 20.18:   Collective and Certification Marks

Each Party shall provide that trademarks include collective marks and certification marks. A Party is not required to treat certification marks as a separate category in its law, provided that those marks are protected. Each Party shall also provide that signs that may serve as geographical indications are capable of protection under its trademark system.[8]

Article 20.19:   Use of Identical or Similar Signs

Each Party shall provide that the owner of a registered trademark has the exclusive right to prevent third parties that do not have the owner's consent from using in the course of trade identical or similar signs, including subsequent geographical indications[9] for goods or services that are related to those goods or services in respect of which the owner's trademark is registered, if that use would result in a likelihood of confusion. In the case of

---

[6]   For greater certainty, this Article is without prejudice to any provisions addressing the exhaustion of intellectual property rights in international agreements to which a Party is a party.

[8]   Consistent with the definition of a geographical indication in Article 20.1 (Definitions), any sign, or combination of signs, shall be eligible for protection under one or more of the legal means for protecting geographical indications, or a combination of those means.

[9]   For greater certainty, the Parties understand that this Article should not be interpreted to affect their rights and obligations under Articles 22 and 23 of the TRIPS Agreement.

the use of an identical sign for identical goods or services, a likelihood of confusion shall be presumed.

Article 20.20: Exceptions

A Party may provide limited exceptions to the rights conferred by a trademark, such as fair use of descriptive terms, provided that those exceptions take account of the legitimate interests of the owner of the trademark and of third parties.

Article 20.21: Well-Known Trademarks

1. No Party shall require as a condition for determining that a trademark is well-known that the trademark has been registered in the Party or in another jurisdiction, included on a list of well-known trademarks, or given prior recognition as a well-known trademark.

2. Article 6*bis* of the Paris Convention shall apply, *mutatis mutandis*, to goods or services that are not identical or similar to those identified by a well-known trademark,[10] whether registered or not, provided that use of that trademark in relation to those goods or services would indicate a connection between those goods or services and the owner of the trademark, and provided that the interests of the owner of the trademark are likely to be damaged by that use.

3. The Parties recognize the importance of the *Joint Recommendation Concerning Provisions on the Protection of Well-Known Marks* as adopted by the Assembly of the Paris Union for the Protection of Industrial Property and the General Assembly of WIPO at the Thirty-Fourth Series of Meetings of the Assemblies of the Member States of WIPO September 20 to 29, 1999.

4. Each Party shall provide for appropriate measures to refuse the application or cancel the registration and prohibit the use of a trademark that is identical or similar to a well-known trademark,[11] for identical or similar goods or services, if the use of that trademark is likely to cause confusion with the prior well-known trademark. A Party may also provide those measures including in cases in which the subsequent trademark is likely to deceive.

Article 20.22: Procedural Aspects of Examination, Opposition, and Cancellation

Each Party shall provide a system for the examination and registration of trademarks that includes among other things:

(a) communicating to the applicant in writing, which may be by electronic means, the reasons for any refusal to register a trademark;

---

[10] In determining whether a trademark is well-known in a Party, that Party need not require that the reputation of the trademark extend beyond the sector of the public that normally deals with the relevant goods or services.

[11] The Parties understand that a well-known trademark is one that was already well-known before, as determined by a Party, the application for, registration of, or use of the first-mentioned trademark.

    (b)   providing the applicant with an opportunity to respond to communications from the competent authorities, to contest any initial refusal, and to make a judicial appeal of any final refusal to register a trademark;

    (c)   providing an opportunity to oppose the registration of a trademark and an opportunity to seek cancellation[12] of a trademark through, at a minimum, administrative procedures; and

    (d)   requiring administrative decisions in opposition and cancellation proceedings to be reasoned and in writing, which may be provided by electronic means.

Article 20.23:   Electronic Trademarks System

Further to Article 20.9.3 (Transparency), each Party shall provide a:

    (a)   system for the electronic application for, and maintenance of, trademarks; and

    (b)   publicly available electronic information system, including an online database, of trademark applications and of registered trademarks.

Article 20.24:   Classification of Goods and Services

Each Party shall adopt or maintain a trademark classification system that is consistent with the *Nice Agreement Concerning the International Classification of Goods and Services for the Purposes of the Registration of Marks,* done at Nice, June 15, 1957, as revised and amended (Nice Classification). Each Party shall provide that:

    (a)   registrations and the publications of applications indicate the goods and services by their names, grouped according to the classes established by the Nice Classification;[13] and

    (b)   goods or services may not be considered as being similar to each other on the ground that, in any registration or publication, they are classified in the same class of the Nice Classification. Conversely, each Party shall provide that goods or services may not be considered as being dissimilar from each other on the ground that, in any registration or publication, they are classified in different classes of the Nice Classification.

Article 20.25:   Term of Protection for Trademarks

Each Party shall provide that initial registration and each renewal of registration of a trademark is for a term of no less than 10 years.

---

   [12]   For greater certainty, cancellation for the purposes of this Section may be implemented through a nullification or revocation proceeding.

   [13]   A Party that relies on translations of the Nice Classification shall follow updated versions of the Nice Classification to the extent that official translations have been issued and published.

Article 20.26: Non-Recordal of a License

No Party shall require recordal of trademark licenses:

(a) to establish the validity of the licenses; or

(b) as a condition for use of a trademark by a licensee to be deemed to constitute use by the holder in a proceeding that relates to the acquisition, maintenance, or enforcement of trademarks.

Article 20.27: Domain Names

1. In connection with each Party's system for the management of its country-code top-level domain (ccTLD) domain names, the following shall be available:

(a) an appropriate procedure for the settlement of disputes that, based on, or modelled along the same lines as, the principles established in the *Uniform Domain-Name Dispute-Resolution Policy*, or that:

(i) is designed to resolve disputes expeditiously and at low cost,

(ii) is fair and equitable,

(iii) is not overly burdensome, and

(iv) does not preclude resort to judicial proceedings; and

(b) online public access to a reliable and accurate database of contact information concerning domain name registrants,

in accordance with each Party's law and, if applicable, relevant administrator policies regarding protection of privacy and personal data.

2. In connection with each Party's system for the management of ccTLD domain names, appropriate remedies shall be available at least in cases in which a person registers or holds, with a bad faith intent to profit, a domain name that is identical or confusingly similar to a trademark. The Parties understand that those remedies may, but need not, include revocation, cancellation, transfer, damages, or injunctive relief.

Section D: Country Names

Article 20.28: Country Names

Each Party shall provide the legal means for interested persons to prevent commercial use of the country name of a Party in relation to a good in a manner that misleads consumers as to the origin of that good.

Section E: Geographical Indications Article 20.29: Recognition of Geographical Indications

The Parties recognize that geographical indications may be protected through a trademark or a *sui generis* system or other legal means.

Article 20.30: Administrative Procedures for the Protection or Recognition of Geographical Indications

If a Party provides administrative procedures for the protection or recognition of geographical indications, whether through a trademark or a *sui generis* system, with respect to applications for that protection or petitions for that recognition, that Party shall:

(a) accept those applications or petitions without requiring intercession by a Party on behalf of its nationals;[15]

(b) process those applications or petitions without imposing overly burdensome formalities;

(c) ensure that its laws and regulations governing the filing of those applications or petitions are readily available to the public and clearly set out the procedures for these actions;

(d) make available information sufficient to allow the general public to obtain guidance concerning the procedures for filing applications or petitions and the processing of those applications or petitions in general; and allow an applicant, a petitioner, or their representative to ascertain the status of specific applications and petitions;

(e) require that applications or petitions may specify particular translation or transliteration for which protection is being sought;

(f) examine applications or petitions;

(g) ensure that those applications or petitions are published for opposition and provide procedures for opposing geographical indications that are the subject of applications or petitions;

(h) provide a reasonable period of time during which an interested person may oppose the application or petition;

(i) require that administrative decisions in opposition proceedings be reasoned and in writing, which may be provided by electronic means;

(j) require that administrative decisions in cancellation proceedings be reasoned and in writing, which may be provided by electronic means; and

(k) provide for cancellation[16] of the protection or recognition afforded to a geographical indication.

---

[15] This subparagraph also applies to judicial procedures that protect or recognize a geographical indication.

[16] For greater certainty, for the purposes of this Section, cancellation may be implemented through nullification or revocation proceedings.

Article 20.31:   Grounds of Denial, Opposition, and Cancellation[17]

1.   If a Party protects or recognizes a geographical indication through the procedures referred to in Article 20.30 (Administrative Procedures for the Protection or Recognition of Geographical Indications), that Party shall provide procedures that allow interested persons to object to the protection or recognition of a geographical indication, and that allow for that protection or recognition to be refused or otherwise not afforded, at least, on the grounds that the geographical indication is:

   (a)   likely to cause confusion with a trademark that is the subject of a pre-existing good faith pending application or registration in the territory of the Party;

   (b)   likely to cause confusion with a pre-existing trademark, the rights to which have been acquired in accordance with the Party's law; and

   (c)   a term customary in common language as the common name[18],[19],[20] for the relevant good in the territory of the Party.

2.   If a Party has protected or recognized a geographical indication through the procedures referred to in Article 20.30 (Administrative Procedures for the Protection or Recognition of Geographical Indications), that Party shall provide procedures that allow for interested persons to seek the cancellation of a geographical indication, and that allow for the protection or recognition to be cancelled, at least, on the grounds listed in paragraph 1. A Party may provide that the grounds listed in paragraph 1 apply as of the time of filing the request for protection or recognition of a geographical indication in the territory of the Party.[21]

---

[17]   A Party is not required to apply this Article to geographical indications for wines and spirits or to applications or petitions for those geographical indications.

[18]   If a Party refuses to protect or recognize a compound geographical indication on the grounds that an individual term of that geographical indication is the common name for the relevant good in the territory of a Party, the Party may withdraw its refusal of protection or recognition if the applicant or registrant agrees to disclaim any claim of exclusive rights to the particular individual term that was the basis for the refusal.

[19]   For greater certainty, if a Party provides for the procedures in Article 20.30 (Administrative Procedures for the Protection or Recognition of Geographical Indications) and this Article to be applied to geographical indications for wines and spirits or applications or petitions for those geographical indications, that Party is not required to protect or recognize a geographical indication of any other Party with respect to products of the vine for which the relevant indication is identical with the customary name of a grape variety existing in the territory of that Party.

[20]   For greater certainty, a term customary in common language as the common name may refer to a single-component term or individual components of a multi-component term.

[21]   For greater certainty, if the grounds listed in paragraph 1 did not exist in a Party's law as of the time of filing of the request for protection or recognition of a geographical indication under Article 20.30 (Administrative Procedures for the Protection or Recognition of Geographical Indications), that Party is not required to apply those grounds for the purposes of paragraphs 2 or 4 of this Article in relation to that geographical indication.

3.   No Party shall preclude the possibility that the protection or recognition of a geographical indication may be cancelled, or otherwise cease, on the basis that the protected or recognized term has ceased meeting the conditions upon which the protection or recognition was originally granted in that Party.

4.   If a Party has in place a *sui generis* system for protecting unregistered geographical indications by means of judicial procedures, that Party shall provide that its judicial authorities have the authority to deny the protection or recognition of a geographical indication if any circumstance identified in paragraph 1 has been established.[22] That Party shall also provide a process that allows interested persons to commence a proceeding on the grounds identified in paragraph 1.

5.   If a Party provides protection or recognition of a geographical indication through the procedures referred to in Article 20.30 (Administrative Procedures for the Protection or Recognition of Geographical Indications) to the translation or transliteration of that geographical indication, that Party shall make available procedures that are equivalent to, and grounds that are the same as, those referred to in paragraphs 1 and 2 with respect to that translation or transliteration.

Article 20.32: Guidelines for Determining Whether a Term is the Term Customary in the Common Language

With respect to the procedures in Article 20.30 (Administrative Procedures for the Protection or Recognition of Geographical Indications) and Article 20.31 (Grounds of Denial, Opposition, and Cancellation), in determining whether a term is the term customary in common language as the common name for the relevant good in the territory of a Party, that Party's authorities shall have the authority to take into account how consumers understand the term in the territory of that Party. Factors relevant to that consumer understanding may include:

(a)   whether the term is used to refer to the type of good in question, as indicated by competent sources such as dictionaries, newspapers, and relevant websites;

(b)   how the good referenced by the term is marketed and used in trade in the territory of that Party;

(c)   whether the term is used, as appropriate, in relevant international standards recognized by the Parties to refer to a type or class of good in the territory of the Party, such as pursuant to a standard promulgated by the Codex Alimentarius; and

---

[22]   As an alternative to this paragraph, if a Party has in place a *sui generis* system of the type referred to in this paragraph as of the applicable date under Article 20.35.6 (International Agreements), that Party shall at least provide that its judicial authorities have the authority to deny the protection or recognition of a geographical indication if the circumstances identified in paragraph 1(c) have been established.

(d)   whether the good in question is imported into the Party's territory, in significant quantities,[23] from a place other than the territory identified in the application or petition, and whether those imported goods are named by the term.

Article 20.33:   Multi-Component Terms

With respect to the procedures in Article 20.30 (Administrative Procedures for the Protection or Recognition of Geographical Indications) and Article 20.31 (Grounds of Denial, Opposition, and Cancellation), an individual component of a multi-component term that is protected as a geographical indication in the territory of a Party shall not be protected in that Party if that individual component is a term customary in the common language as the common name for the associated good.

Article 20.34:   Date of Protection of a Geographical Indication

If a Party grants protection or recognition to a geographical indication through the procedures referred to in Article 20.30 (Administrative Procedures for the Protection or Recognition of Geographical Indications), that protection or recognition shall commence no earlier than the filing date[24] in the Party or the registration date in the Party, as applicable.

Article 20.35:   International Agreements

1.   If a Party protects or recognizes a geographical indication pursuant to an international agreement, as of the applicable date under paragraph 6, involving a Party or a non-Party and that geographical indication is not protected through the procedures referred to in Article 20.30 (Administrative Procedures for the Protection or Recognition of Geographical Indications)[25] or Article 20.31 (Grounds of Denial, Opposition, and Cancellation), that Party at least shall apply procedures and grounds that are equivalent to those in Article 20.30(f), (g), (h), and (i) (Administrative Procedures for the Protection or Recognition of Geographical Indications) and Article 20.31.1 (Grounds of Denial, Opposition, and Cancellation), as well as:

(a)   make available information sufficient to allow the general public to obtain guidance concerning the procedures for protecting or recognizing the geographical indication and

---

[23]   In determining whether the good in question is imported in significant quantities, a Party may consider the amount of importation at the time of the application or petition.

[24]   For greater certainty, the filing date referred to in this paragraph includes, as applicable, the priority filing date under the Paris Convention. No Party shall use the date of protection in a country of origin of a geographical indication to establish a priority date in the territory of the Party, unless filed within the Paris Convention priority period.

[25]   Each Party shall apply Article 20.32 (Guidelines for Determining Whether a Term is the Term Customary in the Common Language) and Article 20.33 (Multi-Component Terms) in determining whether to grant protection or recognition of a geographical indication pursuant to this paragraph. That period shall allow for a meaningful opportunity for any interested person to participate in an opposition process; and

allow interested persons to ascertain the status of requests for protection or recognition;

(b) to publish online details regarding the terms that the Party is considering protecting or recognizing through an international agreement involving a Party or a non-Party, including specifying whether the protection or recognition is being considered for any translations or transliterations of those terms, and with respect to multi-component terms, specifying the components, if any, for which protection or recognition is being considered, or the components that are disclaimed;

(c) in respect of opposition procedures, provide a reasonable period of time for interested persons to oppose the protection or recognition of the terms referred to in

(d) inform the other Parties of the opportunity to oppose, no later than the commencement of the opposition period.

2. In respect of international agreements referred to in paragraph 6 that permit the protection or recognition of a new geographical indication, a Party shall:[26],[27]

(a) apply paragraph 1(b) and apply at least procedures and grounds that are equivalent to those in Article 20.30(f), (g), (h), and (i) (Administrative Procedures for the Protection or Recognition of Geographical Indications) and Article 20.31.1 (Grounds of Denial, Opposition, and Cancellation);

(b) provide an opportunity for interested persons to comment regarding the protection or recognition of the new geographical indication for a reasonable period of time before that term is protected or recognized; and

(c) inform the other Parties of the opportunity to comment, no later than the commencement of the period for comment.

3. For the purposes of this Article, a Party shall not preclude the possibility that the protection or recognition of a geographical indication could cease.

4. For the purposes of this Article, a Party is not required to apply Article 20.31 (Grounds of Denial, Opposition, and Cancellation), or obligations equivalent to Article 20.31, to geographical indications for wines and spirits or applications for those geographical indications.

---

[26] In respect of an international agreement referred to in paragraph 6 that has geographical indications that have been identified, but have not yet received protection or recognition in the territory of the Party that is a party to that agreement, that Party may fulfil the obligations of paragraph 2 by complying with the obligations of paragraph 1.

[27] A Party may comply with this Article by applying Article 20.30 (Administrative Procedures for the Protection or Recognition of Geographical Indications) and Article 20.31 (Grounds of Denial, Opposition, and Cancellation).

5.   The protection or recognition that each Party provides pursuant to paragraph 1 shall commence no earlier than the date on which that agreement enters into force or, if that Party grants that protection or recognition on a date after the entry into force of that agreement, on that later date.

6.   No Party shall be required to apply this Article to geographical indications that have been specifically identified in, and that are protected or recognized pursuant to, an international agreement involving a Party or a non-Party, provided that the agreement:

   (a)   was concluded, or agreed in principle,[28] prior to the date of conclusion, or agreement in principle, of this Agreement;

   (b)   was ratified by a Party prior to the date of ratification of this Agreement by that Party; or

   (c)   entered into force for a Party prior to the date of entry into force of this Agreement.

Section E: Patents and Undisclosed Test or Other Data

Subsection A: General Patents

Article 20.36:   Patentable Subject Matter

1.   Subject to paragraphs 3 and 4, each Party shall make patents available for any invention, whether a product or process, in all fields of technology, provided that the invention is new, involves an inventive step, and is capable of industrial application.[29]

2.   Subject to paragraphs 3 and 4 and consistent with paragraph 1, each Party confirms that patents are available for inventions claimed as at least one of the following: new uses of a known product, new methods of using a known product, or new processes of using a known product.

3.   A Party may exclude from patentability inventions, the prevention within their territory of the commercial exploitation of which is necessary to protect *ordre public* or morality, including to protect human, animal, or plant life or health or to avoid serious prejudice to nature or the environment, provided that such exclusion is not made merely because the exploitation is prohibited by its law. A Party may also exclude from patentability:

   (a)   diagnostic, therapeutic, and surgical methods for the treatment of humans or animals;

---

   [28]   For the purpose of this Article, an agreement "agreed in principle" means an agreement involving another government, government entity, or international organization in respect of which a political understanding has been reached and the negotiated outcomes of the agreement have been publicly announced.

   [29]   For the purposes of this Section, a Party may deem the terms "inventive step" and "capable of industrial application" to be synonymous with the terms "non-obvious" and "useful", respectively. In determinations regarding inventive step, or non-obviousness, each Party shall consider whether the claimed invention would have been obvious to a person skilled in the art, or having ordinary skill in the art, having regard to the prior art.

(b)   animals other than microorganisms, and essentially biological processes for the production of plants or animals, other than non-biological and microbiological processes.

4.   A Party may also exclude from patentability plants other than microorganisms. However, consistent with paragraph 1 and subject to paragraph 3, each Party confirms that patents are available at least for inventions that are derived from plants.

Article 20.37:   Grace Period

Each Party shall disregard at least information contained in public disclosures used to determine if an invention is novel or has an inventive step, if the public disclosure:[30]

(a)   was made by the patent applicant or by a person that obtained the information directly or indirectly from the patent applicant; and

(b)   occurred within twelve months prior to the filing date in the territory of the Party.

Article 20.38:   Patent Revocation

1.   Each Party shall provide that a patent may be cancelled, revoked, or nullified only on grounds that would have justified a refusal to grant the patent. A Party may also provide that fraud, misrepresentation, or inequitable conduct may be the basis for cancelling, revoking, or nullifying a patent or holding a patent unenforceable.

2.   Notwithstanding paragraph 1, a Party may provide that a patent may be revoked, provided it is done in a manner consistent with Article 5A of the Paris Convention and the TRIPS Agreement.

Article 20.39:   Exceptions

A Party may provide limited exceptions to the exclusive rights conferred by a patent, provided that those exceptions do not unreasonably conflict with a normal exploitation of the patent and do not unreasonably prejudice the legitimate interests of the patent owner, taking account of the legitimate interests of third parties.

Article 20.40:   Other Use Without Authorization of the Right Holder

The Parties understand that nothing in this Chapter limits a Party's rights and obligations under Article 31 of the TRIPS Agreement, and any waiver of or amendment to that Article that the Parties accept.

---

[30]   For greater certainty, a Party may limit the application of this Article to disclosures made by, or obtained directly or indirectly from, the inventor or joint inventor. For greater certainty, a Party may provide that, for the purposes of this Article, information obtained directly or indirectly from the patent applicant may be information contained in the public disclosure that was authorized by, or derived from, the patent applicant.

Article 20.41:   Amendments, Corrections, and Observations

Each Party shall provide a patent applicant with at least one opportunity to make amendments, corrections, and observations in connection with its application.[31]

Article 20.42:   Publication of Patent Applications

1. Recognizing the benefits of transparency in the patent system, each Party shall endeavor to publish unpublished pending patent applications promptly after the expiration of 18 months from the filing date or, if priority is claimed, from the earliest priority date.

2. If a pending application is not published promptly in accordance with paragraph 1, a Party shall publish that application or the corresponding patent, as soon as practicable.

3. Each Party shall provide that an applicant may request the early publication of an application prior to the expiration of the period referred to in paragraph 1.

Article 20.43:   Information Relating to Published Patent Applications and Granted Patents

For published patent applications and granted patents, and in accordance with the Party's requirements for prosecution of those applications and patents, each Party shall make available to the public at least the following information, to the extent that this information is in the possession of the competent authorities and is generated on, or after, the date of the entry into force of this Agreement:

(a) search and examination results, including details of, or information related to, relevant prior art searches;

(b) as appropriate, non-confidential communications from applicants; and

(c) patent and non-patent related literature citations submitted by applicants and relevant third parties.

Article 20.44:   Patent Term Adjustment for Unreasonable Granting Authority Delays

1. Each Party shall make best efforts to process patent applications in an efficient and timely manner, with a view to avoiding unreasonable or unnecessary delays.

2. A Party may provide procedures for a patent applicant to request to expedite the examination of its patent application.

3. If there are unreasonable delays in a Party's issuance of a patent, that Party shall provide the means to, and at the request of the patent owner shall, adjust the term of the patent to compensate for those delays.

---

[31]   A Party may provide that those amendments or corrections must not exceed the scope of the disclosure of the invention, as of the filing date.

4.   For the purposes of this Article, an unreasonable delay at least shall include a delay in the issuance of a patent of more than five years from the date of filing of the application in the territory of the Party, or three years after a request for examination of the application has been made, whichever is later. A Party may exclude, from the determination of those delays, periods of time that do not occur during the processing[32] of, or the examination of, the patent application by the granting authority; periods of time that are not directly attributable[33] to the granting authority; as well as periods of time that are attributable to the patent applicant.[34]

Subsection B: Measures Relating to Agricultural Chemical Products

Article 20.45:   Protection of Undisclosed Test or Other Data for Agricultural Chemical Products

1.   If a Party requires, as a condition for granting marketing approval[35] for a new agricultural chemical product, the submission of undisclosed test or other data concerning the safety and efficacy of the product,[36] that Party shall not permit third persons, without the consent of the person that previously submitted that information, to market the same or a similar[37] product on the basis of that information or the marketing approval granted to the person that submitted that test or other data for at least 10 years[38] from the date of marketing approval of the new agricultural chemical product in the territory of the Party.

2.   If a Party permits, as a condition of granting marketing approval for a new agricultural chemical product, the submission of evidence of a prior marketing approval of the product in another territory, that Party shall not permit third persons, without the consent of the person that previously submitted undisclosed test or other data concerning the safety and efficacy of the product in support of that prior marketing

---

[32]   For the purposes of this paragraph, a Party may interpret processing to mean initial administrative processing and administrative processing at the time of grant.

[33]   A Party may treat delays "that are not directly attributable to the granting authority" as delays that are outside the direction or control of the granting authority.

[34]   Notwithstanding Article 20.10 (Application of Chapter to Existing Subject Matter and Prior Acts), this Article shall apply to all patent applications filed after the date of entry into force of this Agreement, or the date two years after the signing of this Agreement, whichever is later.

[35]   For the purposes of this Chapter, the term "marketing approval" is synonymous with "sanitary approval" under a Party's law.

[36]   Each Party confirms that the obligations of this Article apply to cases in which the Party requires the submission of undisclosed test or other data concerning: (a) only the safety of the product, (b) only the efficacy of the product, or (c) both.

[37]   For greater certainty, for the purposes of this Section, an agricultural chemical product is "similar" to a previously approved agricultural chemical product if the marketing approval, or, in the alternative, the applicant's request for that approval, of that similar agricultural chemical product is based upon the undisclosed test or other data concerning the safety and efficacy of the previously approved agricultural chemical product, or the prior approval of that previously approved product.

[38]   For greater certainty, a Party may limit the period of protection under this Article to 10 years.

approval, to market the same or a similar product based on that undisclosed test or other data, or other evidence of the prior marketing approval in the other territory, for at least 10 years from the date of marketing approval of the new agricultural chemical product in the territory of the Party.

3. For the purposes of this Article, a new agricultural chemical product is one that contains a chemical entity that has not been previously approved in the territory of the Party for use in an agricultural chemical product.

Subsection C: Measures Relating to Pharmaceutical Products

Article 20.46: Patent   Term   Adjustment   for   Unreasonable Curtailment

1. Each Party shall make best efforts to process applications for marketing approval of pharmaceutical products in an efficient and timely manner, with a view to avoiding unreasonable or unnecessary delays.

2. With respect to a pharmaceutical product that is subject to a patent, each Party shall make available an adjustment[39] of the patent term to compensate the patent owner for unreasonable curtailment of the effective patent term as a result of the marketing approval process.

3. For greater certainty, in implementing the obligations of this Article, each Party may provide for conditions and limitations, provided that the Party continues to give effect to this Article.

4. With the objective of avoiding unreasonable curtailment of the effective patent term, a Party may adopt or maintain procedures that expedite the processing of marketing approval applications.

Article 20.47: Regulatory Review Exception

Without prejudice to the scope of, and consistent with, Article 20.39 (Exceptions), each Party shall adopt or maintain a regulatory review exception for pharmaceutical products.

Article 20.48: Protection of Undisclosed Test or Other Data

1. (a) If a Party requires, as a condition for granting marketing approval for a new pharmaceutical product, the submission of undisclosed test or other data concerning the safety and efficacy of the product,[40] that Party shall not permit third persons, without the consent of the person

---

[39] For greater certainty, a Party may alternatively make available a period of additional *sui generis* protection to compensate for unreasonable curtailment of the effective patent term as a result of the marketing approval process. The *sui generis* protection must confer the rights conferred by the patent, subject to any conditions and limitations pursuant to paragraph 3.

[40] Each Party confirms that the obligations of this Article and Article 20.49 (Biologics) apply to cases in which the Party requires the submission of undisclosed test or other data concerning: (i) only the safety of the product, (ii) only the efficacy of the product, or (iii) both.

that previously submitted that information, to market the same or a similar[41] product on the basis of:

    (i)   that information, or

    (ii)   the marketing approval granted to the person that submitted that information, for at least five years[42] from the date of marketing approval of the new pharmaceutical product in the territory of the Party;

    (b)   If a Party permits, as a condition of granting marketing approval for a new pharmaceutical product, the submission of evidence of prior marketing approval of the product in another territory, that Party shall not permit third persons, without the consent of a person that previously submitted the information concerning the safety and efficacy of the product, to market a same or a similar product based on evidence relating to prior marketing approval in the other territory for at least five years from the date of marketing approval of the new pharmaceutical product in the territory of that Party.

2.   Each Party shall:[43]

    (a)   apply paragraph 1, *mutatis mutandis*, for a period of at least three years with respect to new clinical information submitted as required in support of a marketing approval of a previously approved pharmaceutical product covering a new indication, new formulation, or new method of administration; or, alternatively,

    (b)   apply paragraph 1, *mutatis mutandis*, for a period of at least five years to new pharmaceutical products that contain a chemical entity that has not been previously approved in that Party.[44]

3.   Notwithstanding paragraphs 1 and 2 and Article 20.49 (Biologics), a Party may take measures to protect public health in accordance with:

    (a)   the Declaration on TRIPS and Public Health;

---

[41]   For greater certainty, for the purposes of this Section, a pharmaceutical product is "similar" to a previously approved pharmaceutical product if the marketing approval, or, in the alternative, the applicant's request for that approval, of that similar pharmaceutical product is based upon the undisclosed test or other data concerning the safety and efficacy of the previously approved pharmaceutical product, or the prior approval of that previously approved product.

[42]   For greater certainty, a Party may limit the period of protection under paragraph 1 to five years, and the period of protection under Article 20.49.1 (Biologics) to 10 years.

[43]   A Party that provides a period of at least eight years of protection under paragraph 1 is not required to apply paragraph 2.

[44]   For the purposes of Article 20.48.2(b) (Protection of Undisclosed Test or Other Data), a Party may choose to protect only the undisclosed test or other data concerning the safety and efficacy relating to the chemical entity that has not been previously approved.

(b) any waiver of a provision of the TRIPS Agreement granted by WTO Members in accordance with the WTO Agreement to implement the Declaration on TRIPS and Public Health and that is in force between the Parties; or

(c) any amendment of the TRIPS Agreement to implement the Declaration on TRIPS and Public Health that enters into force with respect to the Parties.

Article 20.49:   Biologics

1. With regard to protecting new biologics, a Party shall, with respect to the first marketing approval in a Party of a new pharmaceutical product that is, or contains, a biologic,[45],[46] provide effective market protection through the implementation of Article 20.48.1 (Protection of Undisclosed Test or Other Data) and Article 20.48.3 (Protection of Undisclosed Test or Other Data), *mutatis mutandis*, for a period of at least ten years from the date of first marketing approval of that product in that Party.

2. Each Party shall apply this Article to, at a minimum,[47] a product that is produced using biotechnology processes and that is, or contains, a virus, therapeutic serum, toxin, antitoxin, vaccine, blood, blood component or derivative, allergenic product, protein, or analogous product, for use in human beings for the prevention, treatment, or cure of a disease or condition.

Article 20.50:   Definition of New Pharmaceutical Product

For the purposes of Article 20.48.1 (Protection of Undisclosed Test or Other Data), a new pharmaceutical product means a pharmaceutical product that does not contain a chemical entity that has been previously approved in that Party.

Article 20.51:   Measures Relating to the Marketing of Certain Pharmaceutical Products

1. If a Party permits, as a condition of approving the marketing of a pharmaceutical product, persons, other than the person originally

---

[45] Nothing requires a Party to extend the protection of this paragraph to:

(a) any second or subsequent marketing approval of such a pharmaceutical product; or

(b) a pharmaceutical product that is, or contains, a previously approved biologic.

[46] Each Party may provide that an applicant may request approval of a pharmaceutical product that is, or contains, a biologic under the procedures set forth in Article 20.48.1(a) (Protection of Undisclosed Test or Other Data) and Article 20.48.1(b) (Protection of Undisclosed Test or Other Data) on or before March 23, 2020, provided that other pharmaceutical products in the same class of products have been approved by that Party under the procedures set forth in in Article 20.48.1(a) (Protection of Undisclosed Test or Other Data) and Article 20.48.1(b) (Protection of Undisclosed Test or Other Data) before the date of entry into force of this Agreement.

[47] For greater certainty, for the purposes of this Article, the Parties understand that "at a minimum" means that a Party may limit the application to the scope specified in this paragraph.

submitting the safety and efficacy information, to rely on evidence or information concerning the safety and efficacy of a product that was previously approved, such as evidence of prior marketing approval by the Party or in another territory, that Party shall provide:

(a) a system to provide notice to a patent holder[48] or to allow for a patent holder to be notified prior to the marketing of such a pharmaceutical product, that such other person is seeking to market that product during the term of an applicable patent claiming the approved product or its approved method of use;

(b) adequate time and sufficient opportunity for such a patent holder to seek, prior to the marketing of an allegedly infringing product, available remedies in subparagraph (c); and

(c) procedures, such as judicial or administrative proceedings, and expeditious remedies, such as preliminary injunctions or equivalent effective provisional measures, for the timely resolution of disputes concerning the validity or infringement of an applicable patent claiming an approved pharmaceutical product or its approved method of use.

2. As an alternative to paragraph 1, a Party shall instead adopt or maintain a system other than judicial proceedings that precludes, based upon patent-related information submitted to the marketing approval authority by a patent holder or the applicant for marketing approval, or based on direct coordination between the marketing approval authority and the patent office, the issuance of marketing approval to any third person seeking to market a pharmaceutical product subject to a patent claiming that product, unless by consent or acquiescence of the patent holder.

Article 20.52:   Alteration of Period of Protection

Subject to Article 20.48.3 (Protection of Undisclosed Test or Other Data), if a product is subject to a system of marketing approval in the territory of a Party pursuant to Article 20.45 (Protection of Undisclosed Test or Other Data for Agricultural Chemical Products), Article 20.48, or Article 20.49 (Biologics) and is also covered by a patent in the territory of that Party, that Party shall not alter the period of protection that it provides pursuant to Article 20.45, Article 20.48, or Article 20.49 in the event that the patent protection terminates on a date earlier than the end of the period of protection specified in Article 20.45, Article 20.48, or Article 20.49.

---

[48] For greater certainty, for the purposes of this Article, a Party may provide that a "patent holder" includes a patent licensee or the authorized holder of marketing approval.

Section G: Industrial Designs

Article 20.53:   Protection

1.   Each Party shall ensure adequate and effective protection of industrial designs consistent with Articles 25 and 26 of the TRIPS Agreement.

2.   Consistent with paragraph 1, each Party confirms that protection is available for designs embodied in a part of an article.

Article 20.54:   Non-Prejudicial Disclosures/Grace Period[49]

Each Party shall disregard at least information contained in public disclosures used to determine if an industrial design is new, original, or, where applicable, non-obvious, if the public disclosure:[50]

   (a)   was made by the design applicant or by a person that obtained the information directly or indirectly from the design applicant; and

   (b)   occurred within 12 months prior to the filing date in the territory of the Party.

Article 20.55:   Electronic Industrial Design System

Each Party shall provide a:

   (a)   system for the electronic application for industrial design rights; and

   (b)   publicly available electronic information system, which must include an online database of protected industrial designs.

Article 20.56:   Term of Protection

Each Party shall provide a term of protection for industrial designs of at least 15 years from either: (a) the date of filing, or (b) the date of grant or registration.

Section H: Copyright and Related Rights Article 20.57: Definitions

For the purposes of Article 20.58 (Right of Reproduction) and Article 20.60 (Right of Distribution) through Article 20.69 (Collective Management), the following definitions apply with respect to performers and producers of phonograms:

Broadcasting means the transmission by wireless means for public reception of sounds or of images and sounds or of the representations thereof; such transmission by satellite is also "broadcasting"; transmission of encrypted signals is "broadcasting" if the means for decrypting are provided to the public by the broadcasting organization or with its consent; "broadcasting"

---

[49]   Articles 20.54 (Non-Prejudicial Disclosures/Grace Period) and 20.55 (Electronic Industrial Design System) apply with respect to industrial design patent systems or industrial design registration systems.

[50]   For greater certainty, a Party may limit the application of this Article to disclosures made by, or obtained directly or indirectly from, the creator or co-creator and provide that, for the purposes of this Article, information obtained directly or indirectly from the design applicant may be information contained in the public disclosure that was authorized by, or derived from, the design applicant.

does not include transmission over computer networks or any transmissions where the time and place of reception may be individually chosen by members of the public;

Communication to the public of a performance or a phonogram means the transmission to the public by any medium, other than by broadcasting, of sounds of a performance or the sounds or the representations of sounds fixed in a phonogram;

Fixation means the embodiment of sounds, or of the representations thereof, from which they can be perceived, reproduced, or communicated through a device;

Performers means actors, singers, musicians, dancers, and other persons who act, sing, deliver, declaim, play in, interpret, or otherwise perform literary or artistic works or expressions of folklore;

Phonogram means the fixation of the sounds of a performance or of other sounds, or of a representation of sounds, other than in the form of a fixation incorporated in a cinematographic or other audio-visual work;

Producer of a phonogram means a person that takes the initiative and has the responsibility for the first fixation of the sounds of a performance or other sounds, or the representations of sounds; and

Publication of a performance or phonogram means the offering of copies of the performance or the phonogram to the public, with the consent of the right holder, and provided that copies are offered to the public in reasonable quantity.

Article 20.58: Right of Reproduction

Each Party shall provide[51] to authors, performers, and producers of phonograms[52] the exclusive right to authorize or prohibit all reproduction of their works, performances, or phonograms in any manner or form, including in electronic form.

Article 20.59: Right of Communication to the Public

Without prejudice to Article 11(1)(ii), Article 11bis(1)(i) and (ii), Article 11ter(1)(ii), Article 14(1)(ii), and Article 14bis(1) of the Berne Convention, each Party shall provide to authors the exclusive right to authorize or prohibit the communication to the public of their works, by wire or wireless means, including the making available to the public of their works in such a way that members of the public may access these works from a place and at a time individually chosen by them.[53]

---

[51] For greater certainty, the Parties understand that it is a matter for each Party's law to prescribe that works, performances, or phonograms in general or any specified categories of works, performances and phonograms are not protected by copyright or related rights unless the work, performance, or phonogram has been fixed in some material form.

[52] References to "authors, performers, and producers of phonograms" refer also to any of their successors in interest.

[53] The Parties understand that the mere provision of physical facilities for enabling or making a communication does not in itself amount to communication

Article 20.60:   Right of Distribution

Each Party shall provide to authors, performers, and producers of phonograms the exclusive right to authorize or prohibit the making available to the public of the original and copies[54] of their works, performances, and phonograms through sale or other transfer of ownership.

Article 20.61:   No Hierarchy

Each Party shall provide that, in cases in which authorization is needed from both the author of a work embodied in a phonogram and a performer or producer that owns rights in the phonogram, the need for the authorization of the:

(a)   author does not cease to exist because the authorization of the performer or producer is also required; and

(b)   performer or producer does not cease to exist because the authorization of the author is also required.

Article 20.62:   Related Rights

1.   Further to the protection afforded to performers and producers of phonograms as "nationals" under Article 20.8 (National Treatment), each Party shall accord the rights provided for in this Chapter to performances and phonograms first published or first fixed[55] in the territory of another Party.[56] A performance or phonogram is considered first published in the territory of a Party if it is published in the territory of that Party within 30 days of its original publication.

2.   Each Party shall provide to performers the exclusive right to authorize or prohibit:

(a)   the broadcasting and communication to the public of their unfixed performances, unless the performance is already a broadcast performance; and

(b)   the fixation of their unfixed performances.

3.   (a) Each Party shall provide to performers and producers of phonograms the exclusive right to authorize or prohibit the broadcasting or any communication to the public of their performances

---

within the meaning of this Chapter or the Berne Convention. The Parties further understand that nothing in this Article precludes a Party from applying Article 11*bis*(2) of the Berne Convention.

[54]   The expressions "copies" and "original and copies", that are subject to the right of distribution in this Article, refer exclusively to fixed copies that can be put into circulation as tangible objects.

[55]   For the purposes of this Article, fixation means the finalization of the master tape or its equivalent.

[56]   For greater certainty, consistent with Article 20.8 (National Treatment), each Party shall accord to performances and phonograms first published or first fixed in the territory of another Party treatment no less favorable than it accords to performances or phonograms first published or first fixed in its own territory.

or phonograms, by wire or wireless means[57] and the making available to the public of those performances or phonograms in such a way that members of the public may access them from a place and at a time individually chosen by them.

(b)   Notwithstanding subparagraph (a) and Article 20.65 (Limitations and Exceptions), the application of the right referred to in subparagraph (a) to analog transmissions and non-interactive free over-the-air broadcasts, and exceptions or limitations to this right for those activities, is a matter of each Party's law.[58]

(c)   Each Party may adopt limitations to this right in respect of other non-interactive transmissions in accordance with Article 20.65.1 (Limitations and Exceptions), provided that the limitations do not prejudice the right of the performer or producer of phonograms to obtain equitable remuneration.

Article 20.63:   Term of Protection for Copyright and Related Rights

Each Party shall provide that in cases in which the term of protection of a work, performance, or phonogram is to be calculated:

(a)   on the basis of the life of a natural person, the term shall be not less than the life of the author and 70 years after the author's death;[59] and

(b)   on a basis other than the life of a natural person, the term shall be:

    (i)   not less than 75 years from the end of the calendar year of the first authorized publication[60] of the work, performance, or phonogram, or

    (ii)   failing such authorized publication within 25 years from the creation of the work, performance, or

---

[57]   For greater certainty, the obligation under this paragraph does not include broadcasting or communication to the public, by wire or wireless means, of the sounds or representations of sounds fixed in a phonogram that are incorporated in a cinematographic or other audio-visual work.

[58]   For the purposes of this subparagraph the Parties understand that a Party may provide for the retransmission of non-interactive, free over-the-air broadcasts, provided that these retransmissions are lawfully permitted by that Party's government communications authority; any entity engaging in these retransmissions complies with the relevant rules, orders, or regulations of that authority; and these retransmissions do not include those delivered and accessed over the Internet. For greater certainty this footnote does not limit a Party's ability to avail itself of this subparagraph.

[59]   The Parties understand that if a Party provides its nationals a term of copyright protection that exceeds life of the author plus 70 years, nothing in this Article or Article 20.8 (National Treatment) precludes that Party from applying Article 7(8) of the Berne Convention with respect to the term in excess of the term provided in this subparagraph of protection for works of another Party.

[60]   For greater certainty, for the purposes of subparagraph (b), if a Party's law provides for the calculation of term from fixation rather than from the first authorized publication that Party may continue to calculate the term from fixation.

phonogram, not less than 70 years from the end of the calendar year of the creation of the work, performance, or phonogram.

Article 20.64:   Application of Article 18 of the Berne Convention and Article 14.6 of the TRIPS Agreement

Each Party shall apply Article 18 of the Berne Convention and Article 14.6 of the TRIPS Agreement, *mutatis mutandis*, to works, performances, and phonograms, and the rights in and protections afforded to that subject matter as required by this Section.

Article 20.65:   Limitations and Exceptions

1.   With respect to this Section, each Party shall confine limitations or exceptions to exclusive rights to certain special cases that do not conflict with a normal exploitation of the work, performance, or phonogram, and do not unreasonably prejudice the legitimate interests of the right holder.

2.   This Article does not reduce or extend the scope of applicability of the limitations and exceptions permitted by the TRIPS Agreement, the Berne Convention, the WCT, or the WPPT.

Article 20.66:   Contractual Transfers

Each Party shall provide that for copyright and related rights, any person acquiring or holding an economic right[61] in a work, performance, or phonogram:

(a)   may freely and separately transfer that right by contract; and

(b)   by virtue of contract, including contracts of employment underlying the creation of works, performances, or phonograms, must be able to exercise that right in that person's own name and enjoy fully the benefits derived from that right.[62]

Article 20.67:   Technological Protection Measures[63]

1.   In order to provide adequate legal protection and effective legal remedies against the circumvention of effective technological measures that authors, performers, and producers of phonograms use in connection with the exercise of their rights and that restrict

---

[61]   For greater certainty, this Article does not affect the exercise of moral rights.

[62]   Nothing in this Article affects a Party's ability to establish: (i) which specific contracts underlying the creation of works, performances, or phonograms shall, in the absence of a written agreement, result in a transfer of economic rights by operation of law; and (ii) reasonable limits to protect the interests of the original right holders, taking into account the legitimate interests of the transferees.

[63]   Nothing in this Agreement requires a Party to restrict the importation or domestic sale of a device that does not render effective a technological measure the only purpose of which is to control market segmentation for legitimate physical copies of a cinematographic film, and is not otherwise a violation of its law.

unauthorized acts in respect of their works, performances, and phonograms, each Party shall provide[64] that a person who:

(a)   knowingly, or having reasonable grounds to know,[65] circumvents without authority an effective technological measure that controls access to a protected work, performance, or phonogram;[66] or

(b)   manufactures, imports, distributes, offers for sale or rental to the public, or otherwise provides devices, products, or components, or offers to the public or provides services, that:

   (i)   are promoted, advertised, or otherwise marketed by that person for the purpose of circumventing any effective technological measure,

   (ii)   have only a limited commercially significant purpose or use other than to circumvent any effective technological measure, or

   (iii)   are primarily designed, produced, or performed for the purpose of circumventing any effective technological measure,

is liable and subject to the remedies provided for in Article 20.82.18 (Civil and Administrative Procedures and Remedies).[67]

Each Party shall provide for criminal procedures and penalties to be applied when a person, other than a non-profit library, archive,[68] educational institution, or public non-commercial broadcasting entity, is found to have engaged willfully and for the purposes of commercial advantage or financial gain in any of the foregoing activities.

Criminal procedures and penalties listed in subparagraphs (a), (c), and (f) of Article 20.85.6 (Criminal Procedures and Penalties) shall apply, as applicable to infringements *mutatis mutandis*, to the activities described in subparagraphs (a) and (b) of this paragraph.

---

[64]   A Party that, prior to the date of entry into force of this Agreement, maintains legal protections for technological protection measures consistent with Article 20.67.1 (Technological Protection Measures), may maintain its current scope of limitations, exceptions, and regulations regarding circumvention.

[65]   For greater certainty, for the purposes of this subparagraph, a Party may provide that reasonable grounds to know may be demonstrated through reasonable evidence, taking into account the facts and circumstances surrounding the alleged illegal act.

[66]   For greater certainty, no Party is required to impose civil or criminal liability under this subparagraph for a person that circumvents any effective technological measure that protects any of the exclusive rights of copyright or related rights in a protected work, performance, or phonogram, but does not control access to that work, performance, or phonogram.

[67]   For greater certainty, no Party is required to impose liability under this Article and Article 20.68 (Rights Management Information) for actions taken by that Party or a third person acting with authorization or consent of the Party.

[68]   For greater certainty, a Party may treat a non-profit museum as a non-profit archive.

2.   In implementing paragraph 1, no Party shall be obligated to require that the design of, or the design and selection of parts and components for, a consumer electronics, telecommunications, or computing product provide for a response to any particular technological measure, so long as the product does not otherwise violate any measure implementing paragraph 1.

3.   Each Party shall provide that a violation of a measure implementing this Article is a separate cause of action, independent of any infringement that might occur under the Party's law on copyright and related rights.

4.   Each Party shall confine exceptions and limitations to measures implementing paragraph 1 to the following activities, which shall be applied to relevant measures in accordance with paragraph 5:[69]

(a)   non-infringing reverse engineering activities with regard to a lawfully obtained copy of a computer program, carried out in good faith with respect to particular elements of that computer program that have not been readily available to the person engaged in those activities, for the sole purpose of achieving interoperability of an independently created computer program with other programs;

(b)   non-infringing good faith activities, carried out by an appropriately qualified researcher who has lawfully obtained a copy, unfixed performance, or display of a work, performance, or phonogram and who has made a good faith effort to obtain authorization for those activities, to the extent necessary for the sole purpose of research consisting of identifying and analyzing flaws and vulnerabilities of technologies for scrambling and descrambling of information;

(c)   the inclusion of a component or part for the sole purpose of preventing the access of minors to inappropriate online content in a technology, product, service, or device that itself is not prohibited under the measures implementing paragraph (1)(b);

(d)   non-infringing good faith activities that are authorized by the owner of a computer, computer system, or computer network for the sole purpose of testing, investigating, or correcting the security of that computer, computer system, or computer network;

(e)   non-infringing activities for the sole purpose of identifying and disabling a capability to carry out undisclosed collection or dissemination of personally identifying information reflecting the online activities of a natural person in a way

---

[69]   A Party may request consultations with the other Parties to consider how to address, under paragraph 4, activities of a similar nature that a Party identifies after the date this Agreement enters into force.

that has no other effect on the ability of any person to gain access to any work;

(f) lawfully authorized activities carried out by government employees, agents, or contractors for the purpose of law enforcement, intelligence, essential security, or similar governmental purposes;

(g) access by a nonprofit library, archive, or educational institution to a work, performance, or phonogram not otherwise available to it, for the sole purpose of making acquisition decisions; and

(h) in addition, a Party may provide additional exceptions or limitations for non-infringing uses of a particular class of works, performances, or phonograms, when an actual or likely adverse impact on those non-infringing uses is demonstrated by substantial evidence in a legislative, regulatory, or administrative proceeding in accordance with the Party's law.

5. The exceptions and limitations to measures implementing paragraph 1 for the activities set forth in paragraph 4 may only be applied as follows, and only to the extent that they do not impair the adequacy of legal protection or the effectiveness of legal remedies against the circumvention of effective technological measures under the Party's legal system:

(a) measures implementing paragraph (1)(a) may be subject to exceptions and limitations with respect to each activity set forth in paragraph (4);

(b) measures implementing paragraph (1)(b), as they apply to effective technological measures that control access to a work, performance, or phonogram, may be subject to exceptions and limitations with respect to activities set forth in paragraphs (4)(a), (b), (c), (d), and (f); and

(c) measures implementing paragraph (1)(b), as they apply to effective technological measures that protect any copyright or any rights related to copyright, may be subject to exceptions and limitations with respect to activities set forth in paragraphs (4)(a) and (f).

6. Effective technological measure means a technology, device, or component that, in the normal course of its operation, controls access to a protected work, performance, or phonogram, or protects copyright or rights related to copyright.[70]

---

[70] For greater certainty, a technological measure that can, in a usual case, be circumvented accidentally is not an "effective" technological measure.

Article 20.68:   Rights Management Information[71]

1. In order to provide adequate and effective legal remedies to protect rights management information (RMI), each Party shall provide that any person that, without authority, and knowing, or having reasonable grounds to know, that it would induce, enable, facilitate, or conceal an infringement of the copyright or related right of authors, performers, or producers of phonograms, knowingly:[72]

    (a) removes or alters any RMI;

    (b) distributes or imports for distribution RMI knowing that the RMI has been altered without authority;[73] or

    (c) distributes, imports for distribution, broadcasts, communicates, or makes available to the public copies of works, performances, or phonograms, knowing that RMI has been removed or altered without authority, is liable and subject to the remedies set out in Article 20.82 (Civil and Administrative Procedures and Remedies).

2. Each Party shall provide for criminal procedures and penalties to be applied if a person is found to have engaged willfully and for purposes of commercial advantage or financial gain in any of the activities referred to in paragraph 1.

3. A Party may provide that the criminal procedures and penalties do not apply to a non-profit library, museum, archive, educational institution or public non-commercial broadcasting entity.[74]

4. For greater certainty, nothing prevents a Party from excluding from a measure that implements paragraphs 1 through 3 a lawfully authorized activity that is carried out for the purpose of law enforcement, essential security interests, or other related governmental purposes, such as the performance of a statutory function.

5. For greater certainty, nothing in this Article obligates a Party to require a right holder in a work, performance, or phonogram to attach RMI to copies of the work, performance, or phonogram, or to cause RMI to appear in connection with a communication of the work, performance, or phonogram to the public.

---

[71]   A Party may comply with the obligations in this Article by providing legal protection only to electronic rights management information.

[72]   For greater certainty, a Party may extend the protection afforded by this paragraph to circumstances in which a person engages without knowledge in the acts in subparagraphs (a), (b), and (c), and to other related right holders.

[73]   A Party may meet its obligation under this subparagraph if it provides effective protection for original compilations, provided that the acts described in this subparagraph are treated as infringements of copyright in those original compilations.

[74]   For greater certainty, a Party may treat a broadcasting entity established without a profit-making purpose under its law as a public non-commercial broadcasting entity.

6. RMI means:

(a) information that identifies a work, performance, or phonogram, the author of the work, the performer of the performance, or the producer of the phonogram; or the owner of a right in the work, performance, or phonogram;

(b) information about the terms and conditions of the use of the work, performance, or phonogram; or

(c) any numbers or codes that represent the information referred to in subparagraphs (a) and (b),

if any of these items is attached to a copy of the work, performance, or phonogram or appears in connection with the communication or making available of a work, performance, or phonogram to the public.

Article 20.69: Collective Management

The Parties recognize the important role of collective management societies for copyright and related rights in collecting and distributing royalties[75] based on practices that are fair, efficient, transparent, and accountable, which may include appropriate record keeping and reporting mechanisms.

Section I: Trade Secrets[76],[77]

Article 20.70: Protection of Trade Secrets

In the course of ensuring effective protection against unfair competition as provided in Article 10bis of the Paris Convention, each Party shall ensure that persons have the legal means to prevent trade secrets lawfully in their control from being disclosed to, acquired by, or used by others (including state-owned enterprises) without their consent in a manner contrary to honest commercial practices.

Article 20.71: Civil Protection and Enforcement

In fulfilling its obligation under paragraphs 1 and 2 of Article 39 of the TRIPS Agreement, each Party shall:

(a) provide civil judicial procedures[78] for any person lawfully in control of a trade secret to prevent, and obtain redress for, the misappropriation of the trade secret by any other person; and

(b) not limit the duration of protection for a trade secret, so long as the conditions in Article 20.73 (Definitions) exist.

---

[75] For greater certainty, royalties may include equitable remuneration.

[76] For greater certainty, the enforcement obligations and principles set forth in Section J also apply to the obligations in this section, as relevant.

[77] For greater certainty, this Section is without prejudice to a Party's measures protecting good faith lawful disclosures to provide evidence of a violation of that Party's law.

[78] For greater certainty, civil judicial procedures do not have to be federal provided that those procedures are available.

Article 20.72:   Criminal Enforcement

1.   Subject to paragraph 2, each Party shall provide for criminal procedures and penalties for the unauthorized and willful misappropriation[79] of a trade secret.

2.   With respect to the acts referred to in paragraph 1, a Party may, as appropriate, limit the availability of its procedures, or limit the level of penalties available, to one or more of the following cases in which the act is:

 (a)   for the purposes of commercial advantage or financial gain;

 (b)   related to a product or service in national or international commerce; or

 (c)   intended to injure the owner of that trade secret.

Article 20.73:   Definitions

For the purposes of this Section:

Trade secret means information that:

 (a)   is secret in the sense that it is not, as a body or in the precise configuration and assembly of its components, generally known among or readily accessible to persons within the circles that normally deal with the kind of information in question;

 (b)   has actual or potential commercial value because it is secret; and

 (c)   has been subject to reasonable steps under the circumstances, by the person lawfully in control of the information, to keep it secret;

Misappropriation means the acquisition, use, or disclosure of a trade secret in a manner contrary to honest commercial practices, including the acquisition, use, or disclosure of a trade secret by a third party that knew, or had reason to know, that the trade secret was acquired in a manner contrary to honest commercial practices.[80] Misappropriation does not include situations in which a person:

 (a)   reverse engineered an item lawfully obtained;

 (b)   independently discovered information claimed as a trade secret; or

 (c)   acquired the subject information from another person in a legitimate manner without an obligation of confidentiality or knowledge that the information was a trade secret; and

---

[79]   For the purposes of this Article, "willful misappropriation" requires a person to have known that the trade secret was acquired in a manner contrary to honest commercial practices.

[80]   For greater certainty, "misappropriation" as defined in this paragraph includes cases in which the acquisition, use, or disclosure involves a computer system.

manner contrary to honest commercial practices means at least practices such as breach of contract, breach of confidence, and inducement to breach, and includes the acquisition of undisclosed information by third parties that knew, or were grossly negligent in failing to know, that those practices were involved in the acquisition.

Article 20.74:   Provisional Measures

In the civil judicial proceedings described in Article 20.71 (Civil Protection and Enforcement), each Party shall provide that its judicial authorities have the authority to order prompt and effective provisional measures, such as orders to prevent the misappropriation of the trade secret and to preserve relevant evidence.

Article 20.75:   Confidentiality

In connection with the civil judicial proceedings described in Article 20.71 (Civil Protection and Enforcement), each Party shall provide that its civil judicial authorities have the authority to:

(a)   order specific procedures to protect the confidentiality of any trade secret, alleged trade secret, or any other information asserted by an interested party to be confidential; and

(b)   impose sanctions on parties, counsel, expert, or other person subject to those proceedings, related to violation of orders concerning the protection of a trade secret or alleged trade secret produced or exchanged in that proceeding, as well as other information asserted by an interested party to be confidential.

Each Party shall further provide in its law that, in cases in which an interested party asserts information to be a trade secret, its judicial authorities shall not disclose that information without first providing that person with an opportunity to make a submission under seal that describes the interest of that person in keeping the information confidential.

Article 20.76:   Civil Remedies

In connection with the civil judicial proceedings described in Article 20.71 (Civil Protection and Enforcement), each Party shall provide that its judicial authorities have the authority at least to order:

(a)   injunctive relief that conforms to Article 44 of the TRIPS Agreement against a person that misappropriated a trade secret; and

(b)   a person that misappropriated a trade secret to pay damages adequate to compensate the person lawfully in control of the trade secret for the injury suffered because of the misappropriation of the trade secret[81] and, if appropriate, because of the proceedings to enforce the trade secret.

---

[81]   For greater certainty, a Party may provide that the determination of damages is carried out after the determination of misappropriation.

Article 20.77:   Licensing and Transfer of Trade Secrets

No Party shall discourage or impede the voluntary licensing of trade secrets by imposing excessive or discriminatory conditions on those licenses or conditions that dilute the value of the trade secrets.

Article 20.78:   Prohibition of Unauthorized Disclosure or Use of a Trade Secret by Government Officials Outside the Scope of Their Official Duties

1.   In civil, criminal, and regulatory proceedings in which trade secrets may be submitted to a court or government entity, each Party shall prohibit the unauthorized disclosure of a trade secret by a government official at the central level of government outside the scope of that person's official duties.

2.   Each Party shall provide for in its law deterrent level penalties, including monetary fines, suspension or termination of employment, and imprisonment, to guard against the unauthorized disclosure of a trade secret described in paragraph 1.

Section J: Enforcement

Article 20.79:   General Obligations

1.   Each Party shall ensure that enforcement procedures as specified in this Section are available under its law so as to permit effective action against an act of infringement of intellectual property rights covered by this Chapter, including expeditious remedies to prevent infringements and remedies that constitute a deterrent to future infringements.[82] These procedures shall be applied in such a manner as to avoid the creation of barriers to legitimate trade and to provide for safeguards against their abuse.

2.   Each Party confirms that the enforcement procedures set forth in Article 20.82 (Civil and Administrative Procedures and Remedies), Article 20.83 (Provisional Measures), and Article 20.85 (Criminal Procedures and Penalties) shall be available to the same extent with respect to acts of trademark infringement, as well as copyright or related rights infringement, in the digital environment.

3.   Each Party shall ensure that its procedures concerning the enforcement of intellectual property rights are fair and equitable. These procedures shall not be unnecessarily complicated or costly, or entail unreasonable time-limits or unwarranted delays.

4.   This Section does not create any obligation:

   (a)   to put in place a judicial system for the enforcement of intellectual property rights distinct from that for the

---

[82]   For greater certainty, and subject to Article 44 of the TRIPS Agreement and this Agreement, each Party confirms that it makes those remedies available with respect to enterprises, regardless of whether the enterprises are private or state-owned.

enforcement of law in general, nor does it affect the capacity of each Party to enforce its law in general; or

(b)   with respect to the distribution of resources as between the enforcement of intellectual property rights and the enforcement of law in general.

5.   In implementing this Section in its intellectual property system, each Party shall take into account the need for proportionality between the seriousness of the infringement of the intellectual property right and the applicable remedies and penalties, as well as the interests of third parties.

Article 20.80:   Presumptions

1.   In civil, criminal, and, if applicable, administrative proceedings involving copyright or related rights, each Party shall provide for a presumption[83] that, in the absence of proof to the contrary:

(a)   the person whose name is indicated in the usual manner[84] as the author, performer, or producer of the work, performance, or phonogram, or if applicable the publisher, is the designated right holder in that work, performance, or phonogram; and

(b)   the copyright or related right subsists in that subject matter.

2.   In connection with the commencement of a civil, administrative, or criminal enforcement proceeding involving a registered trademark that has been substantively examined by its competent authority, each Party shall provide that the trademark be considered *prima facie* valid.

3.   In connection with the commencement of a civil or administrative enforcement proceeding involving a patent that has been substantively examined and granted by the competent authority of a Party, that Party shall provide that each claim in the patent be considered *prima facie* to satisfy the applicable criteria of patentability in its territory.[85],[86]

---

[83]   For greater certainty, a Party may implement this Article on the basis of sworn statements or documents having evidentiary value, such as statutory declarations. A Party may also provide that these presumptions are rebuttable presumptions that may be rebutted by evidence to the contrary.

[84]   For greater certainty, a Party may establish the means by which it shall determine what constitutes the "usual manner" for a particular physical support.

[85]   For greater certainty, if a Party provides its administrative authorities with the exclusive authority to determine the validity of a registered trademark or patent, nothing in paragraphs 2 and 3 shall prevent that Party's competent authority from suspending enforcement procedures until the validity of the registered trademark or patent is determined by the administrative authority. In those validity procedures, the party challenging the validity of the registered trademark or patent shall be required to prove that the registered trademark or patent is not valid. Notwithstanding this requirement, a Party may require the trademark holder to provide evidence of first use.

[86]   A Party may provide that this paragraph applies only to those patents that have been applied for, examined, and granted after the entry into force of this Agreement.

Article 20.81: Enforcement Practices with Respect to Intellectual Property Rights

1. Each Party shall provide that final judicial decisions and administrative rulings of general application pertaining to the enforcement of intellectual property rights:

    (a) are in writing and preferably state any relevant findings of fact and the reasoning or the legal basis on which the decisions and rulings are based; and

    (b) are published[87] or, if publication is not practicable, otherwise made available to the public in a national language in such a manner as to enable interested persons and Parties to become acquainted with them.

2. Each Party recognizes the importance of collecting and analyzing statistical data and other relevant information concerning infringements of intellectual property rights as well as collecting information on best practices to prevent and combat infringements.

3. Each Party shall publish or otherwise make available to the public information on its efforts to provide effective enforcement of intellectual property rights in its civil, administrative, and criminal systems, such as statistical information that the Party may collect for those purposes.

Article 20.82: Civil and Administrative Procedures and Remedies

1. Each Party shall make available to right holders civil judicial procedures concerning the enforcement of any intellectual property right covered in this Chapter.[88]

2. Each Party shall provide that its judicial authorities have the authority to order injunctive relief that conforms to Article 44 of the TRIPS Agreement, including to prevent goods that involve the infringement of an intellectual property right under the law of the Party providing that relief from entering into the channels of commerce.

3. Each Party shall provide[89] that, in civil judicial proceedings, its judicial authorities have the authority at least to order the infringer to pay the right holder damages adequate to compensate for the injury the right holder has suffered because of an infringement of that person's intellectual property right by an infringer who knowingly, or with reasonable grounds to know, engaged in infringing activity.

---

[87] For greater certainty, a Party may satisfy the requirement for publication by making the decision or ruling available to the public online.

[88] For the purposes of this Article, the term "right holders" includes those authorized licensees, federations, and associations that have the legal standing and authority to assert those rights. The term "authorized licensee" includes the exclusive licensee of any one or more of the exclusive intellectual property rights encompassed in a given intellectual property.

[89] A Party may also provide that the right holder may not be entitled to any of the remedies set out in paragraphs 3, 5, and 7 if there is a finding of non-use of a trademark. For greater certainty, there is no obligation for a Party to provide for the possibility of any of the remedies in paragraphs 3, 5, 6, and 7 to be ordered in parallel.

4.   In determining the amount of damages under paragraph 3, each Party's judicial authorities shall have the authority to consider, among other things, any legitimate measure of value the right holder submits, which may include lost profits, the value of the infringed goods or services measured by the market price, or the suggested retail price.

5.   At least in cases of copyright or related rights infringement and trademark counterfeiting, each Party shall provide that, in civil judicial proceedings, its judicial authorities have the authority to order the infringer, at least in cases described in paragraph 3, to pay the right holder the infringer's profits that are attributable to the infringement.[90]

6.   In civil judicial proceedings with respect to the infringement of copyright or related rights protecting works, phonograms, or performances, each Party shall establish or maintain a system that provides for one or more of the following:

   (a)   pre-established damages, which shall be available on the election of the right holder; or

   (b)   additional damages.[91]

7.   In civil judicial proceedings with respect to trademark counterfeiting, each Party shall also establish or maintain a system that provides for one or more of the following:

   (a)   pre-established damages, which shall be available on the election of the right holder; or

   (b)   additional damages.[92]

8.   Pre-established damages referred to in paragraphs 6 and 7 shall be in an amount sufficient to constitute a deterrent to future infringements and to compensate fully the right holder for the harm caused by the infringement.

9.   In awarding additional damages referred to in paragraphs 6 and 7, judicial authorities shall have the authority to award those additional damages as they consider appropriate, having regard to all relevant matters, including the nature of the infringing conduct and the need to deter similar infringements in the future.

10.   Each Party shall provide that its judicial authorities, if appropriate, have the authority to order, at the conclusion of civil judicial proceedings concerning infringement of at least copyright or related rights, patents, and trademarks, that the prevailing party be awarded payment by the losing party of court costs or fees and appropriate

---

[90]   A Party may comply with this paragraph by presuming those profits to be the damages referred to in paragraph 3.

[91]   For greater certainty, additional damages may include exemplary or punitive damages.

[92]   For greater certainty, additional damages may include exemplary or punitive damages.

attorney's fees, or any other expenses as provided for under the Party's law.

11. If a Party's judicial or other authorities appoint a technical or other expert in a civil proceeding concerning the enforcement of an intellectual property right and require that the parties in the proceeding pay the costs of that expert, that Party should seek to ensure that those costs are reasonable and related appropriately, among other things, to the quantity and nature of work to be performed and do not unreasonably deter recourse to those proceedings.

12. Each Party shall provide that in civil judicial proceedings:

    (a) at least with respect to pirated copyright goods and counterfeit trademark goods, its judicial authorities have the authority, at the right holder's request, to order that the infringing goods be destroyed, except in exceptional circumstances, without compensation of any sort;

    (b) its judicial authorities have the authority to order that materials and implements that have been used in the manufacture or creation of the infringing goods be, without compensation of any sort, promptly destroyed or, in exceptional circumstances, without compensation of any sort, disposed of outside the channels of commerce in such a manner as to minimize the risk of further infringement; and

    (c) in regard to counterfeit trademark goods, the simple removal of the trademark unlawfully affixed is not sufficient, other than in exceptional circumstances, to permit the release of goods into the channels of commerce.

13. Without prejudice to its law governing privilege, the protection of confidentiality of information sources, or the processing of personal data, each Party shall provide that, in civil judicial proceedings concerning the enforcement of an intellectual property right, its judicial authorities have the authority, on a justified request of the right holder, to order the infringer or the alleged infringer, as applicable, to provide to the right holder or to the judicial authorities, at least for the purpose of collecting evidence, relevant information as provided for in its applicable laws and regulations that the infringer or alleged infringer possesses or controls. This information may include information regarding any person involved in any aspect of the infringement or alleged infringement and the means of production or the channels of distribution of the infringing or allegedly infringing goods or services, including the identification of third persons alleged to be involved in the production and distribution of the goods or services and of their channels of distribution.

14. In cases in which a party in a proceeding voluntarily and without good reason refuses access to, or otherwise does not provide relevant evidence under its control within a reasonable period, or significantly impedes a proceeding relating to an enforcement action, each Party

shall provide that its judicial authorities shall have the authority to make preliminary and final determinations, affirmative or negative, on the basis of the evidence presented, including the complaint or the allegation presented by the party adversely affected by the denial of access to evidence, subject to providing the parties an opportunity to be heard on the allegations or evidence.

15. Each Party shall ensure that its judicial authorities have the authority to order a party at whose request measures were taken and that has abused enforcement procedures to provide to a party wrongfully enjoined or restrained adequate compensation for the injury suffered because of that abuse. The judicial authorities shall also have the authority to order the applicant to pay the defendant expenses, which may include appropriate attorney's fees.

16. Each Party shall provide that in relation to a civil judicial proceeding concerning the enforcement of an intellectual property right, its judicial or other authorities have the authority to impose sanctions on a party, counsel, expert, or other person subject to the court's jurisdiction for violation of judicial orders concerning the protection of confidential information produced or exchanged in that proceeding.

17. To the extent that a civil remedy can be ordered as a result of administrative procedures on the merits of a case, each Party shall provide that those procedures conform to principles equivalent in substance to those set out in this Article.

18. In civil judicial proceedings concerning the acts described in Article 20.67 (Technological Protection Measures) and Article 20.68 (Rights Management Information):

   (a) each Party shall provide that its judicial authorities have the authority at least to:[93]

      (i) impose provisional measures, including seizure or other taking into custody of devices and products suspected of being involved in the prohibited activity,

      (ii) order the type of damages available for copyright infringement, as provided under its law in accordance with this Article,

      (iii) order court costs, fees or expenses as provided for under paragraph 10, and

      (iv) order the destruction of devices and products found to be involved in the prohibited activity; and

   (b) a Party may provide that damages are not available against a non-profit library, museum, archive, educational institution, or public non-commercial broadcasting entity, if

---

[93] For greater certainty, a Party may, but is not required to, put in place separate remedies in respect of Article 20.67 (Technological Protection Measures) and 20.68 (Rights Management Information), if those remedies are available under its copyright law.

it sustains the burden of proving that it was not aware or had no reason to believe that its acts constituted a prohibited activity.

Article 20.83:   Provisional Measures

1.   Each Party's authorities shall act on a request for relief in respect of an intellectual property right *inaudita altera parte* expeditiously in accordance with that Party's judicial rules.

2.   Each Party shall provide that its judicial authorities have the authority to require the applicant for a provisional measure in respect of an intellectual property right to provide any reasonably available evidence in order to satisfy the judicial authority, with a sufficient degree of certainty, that the applicant's right is being infringed or that the infringement is imminent, and to order the applicant to provide security or equivalent assurance set at a level sufficient to protect the defendant and to prevent abuse. That security or equivalent assurance shall not unreasonably deter recourse to those procedures.

3.   In civil judicial proceedings concerning copyright or related rights infringement and trademark counterfeiting, each Party shall provide that its judicial authorities have the authority to order the seizure or other taking into custody of suspected infringing goods, materials, and implements relevant to the infringement, and, at least for trademark counterfeiting, documentary evidence relevant to the infringement.

Article 20.84:   Special Requirements Related to Border Measures

1.   Each Party shall provide for applications to suspend the release of, or to detain, suspected counterfeit or confusingly similar trademark or pirated copyright goods that are imported into the territory of the Party.[94]

2.   Each Party shall provide that a right holder, submitting an application referred to in paragraph 1, to initiate procedures for the Party's competent authorities[95] to suspend release into free circulation of, or to

---

[94]   For the purposes of this Article:

    (a) "counterfeit trademark goods" means goods, including packaging, bearing without authorization a trademark that is identical to the trademark validly registered in respect of those goods, or that cannot be distinguished in its essential aspects from such a trademark, and that thereby infringes the rights of the owner of the trademark in question under the law of the Party providing the procedures under this Section; and

    (b) "pirated copyright goods" means goods that are copies made without the consent of the right holder or person duly authorized by the right holder in the country of production and that are made directly or indirectly from an article when the making of that copy would have constituted an infringement of a copyright or a related right under the law of the Party providing the procedures under this Section.

[95]   For the purposes of this Article, unless otherwise specified, competent authorities may include the appropriate judicial, administrative, or law enforcement authorities under a Party's law.

detain, suspected counterfeit or confusingly similar trademark or pirated copyright goods, is required to:

(a)   provide adequate evidence to satisfy the competent authorities that, under the law of the Party providing the procedures, there is *prima facie* an infringement of the right holder's intellectual property right; and

(b)   supply sufficient information that may reasonably be expected to be within the right holder's knowledge to make the suspect goods reasonably recognizable by its competent authorities.

The requirement to provide that information shall not unreasonably deter recourse to these procedures.

3.   Each Party shall provide that its competent authorities have the authority to require a right holder submitting an application referred to in paragraph 1 to provide a reasonable security or equivalent assurance sufficient to protect the defendant and the competent authorities, and to prevent abuse. Each Party shall provide that such security or equivalent assurance does not unreasonably deter recourse to these procedures. A Party may provide that the security may be in the form of a bond conditioned to hold the defendant harmless from any loss or damage resulting from any suspension of the release of goods in the event the competent authorities determine that the article is not an infringing good.

4.   Without prejudice to a Party's law pertaining to privacy or the confidentiality of information:

(a)   if a Party's competent authorities have detained or suspended the release of goods that are suspected of being counterfeit trademark or pirated copyright goods, that Party may provide that its competent authorities have the authority to inform the right holder without undue delay of the names and addresses of the consignor, exporter, consignee, or importer; a description of the goods; the quantity of the goods; and, if known, the country of origin of the goods;[96] or

(b)   if a Party does not provide its competent authority with the authority referred to in subparagraph (a) when suspect goods are detained or suspended from release, it shall provide, at least in cases of imported goods, its competent authorities with the authority to provide the information specified in subparagraph (a) to the right holder normally within 30 working days of the seizure or determination that the goods are counterfeit trademark goods or pirated copyright goods.

---

[96]   For greater certainty, a Party may establish reasonable procedures to receive or access that information.

5. Each Party shall provide that its competent authorities may initiate border measures *ex officio* against suspected counterfeit trademark goods or pirated copyright goods under customs control[97] that are:

    (a) imported;

    (b) destined for export;

    (c) in transit;[98] and

    (d) admitted into or exiting from a free trade zone or a bonded warehouse.

6. Nothing in this Article precludes a Party from exchanging, if appropriate and with a view to eliminating international trade in counterfeit trademarked goods or pirated copyrighted goods, available information to another Party in respect of goods that it has examined without a local consignee and that are transshipped through its territory and are destined for the territory of the other Party, to inform that other Party's efforts to identify suspect goods upon arrival in its territory.

7. Each Party shall adopt or maintain a procedure by which its competent authorities may determine within a reasonable period of time after the initiation of the procedures described in paragraphs 1 and 5, whether the suspect goods infringe an intellectual property right. If a Party provides administrative procedures for the determination of an infringement, it may also provide its authorities with the authority to impose administrative penalties or sanctions, which may include fines or the seizure of the infringing goods following a determination that the goods are infringing.

8. Each Party shall provide that its competent authorities have the authority to order the destruction of goods following a determination that the goods are infringing. In cases in which the goods are not destroyed, each Party shall ensure that, except in exceptional circumstances, the goods are disposed of outside the channels of commerce in such a manner as to avoid harm to the right holder. In regard to counterfeit trademark goods, the simple removal of the trademark unlawfully affixed shall not be sufficient, other than in exceptional cases, to permit the release of the goods into the channels of commerce.

9. If a Party establishes or assesses, in connection with the procedures described in this Article, an application fee, storage fee, or destruction fee, that Party shall not set the fee at an amount that unreasonably deters recourse to these procedures.

---

[97] For the purposes of this Article, "goods under customs control" means goods that are subject to a Party's customs procedures.

[98] For the purposes of this Article, an "in-transit" good means a good that is under "Customs transit" or "transshipped," as defined in the *International Convention on the Simplification and Harmonization of Customs Procedures* (as amended), done at Kyoto on May 18, 1973, as amended at Brussels on June 26, 1999.

10. This Article applies to goods of a commercial nature sent in small consignments. A Party may exclude from the application of this Article small quantities of goods of a non-commercial nature contained in travelers' personal luggage.[99]

Article 20.85:   Criminal Procedures and Penalties

1. Each Party shall provide for criminal procedures and penalties to be applied at least in cases of willful trademark counterfeiting or copyright or related rights piracy on a commercial scale. In respect of willful copyright or related rights piracy, "on a commercial scale" includes:

   (a)   acts carried out for commercial advantage or financial gain; and

   (b)   significant acts, not carried out for commercial advantage or financial gain, that have a substantial prejudicial impact on the interests of the copyright or related rights holder in relation to the marketplace.[100],[101]

2. Each Party shall treat willful importation or exportation of counterfeit trademark goods or pirated copyright goods on a commercial scale as unlawful activities subject to criminal penalties.[102]

3. Each Party shall provide for criminal procedures and penalties to be applied in cases of willful importation[103] and domestic use, in the course of trade and on a commercial scale, of a label or packaging:

   (a)   to which a trademark has been applied without authorization that is identical to, or cannot be distinguished from, a trademark registered in its territory; and

   (b)   that is intended to be used in the course of trade on goods or in relation to services that are identical to goods or services for which that trademark is registered.

---

[99]   For greater certainty, a Party may also exclude from the application of this Article small quantities of goods of a non-commercial nature sent in small consignments.

[100]   The Parties understand that a Party may comply with subparagraph (b) by addressing those significant acts under its criminal procedures and penalties for non-authorized uses of protected works, performances and phonograms in its law.

[101]   A Party may provide that the volume and value of any infringing items may be taken into account in determining whether the act has a substantial prejudicial impact on the interests of the copyright or related rights holder in relation to the marketplace.

[102]   The Parties understand that a Party may comply with its obligation under this paragraph by providing that distribution or sale of counterfeit trademark goods or pirated copyright goods on a commercial scale is an unlawful activity subject to criminal penalties. The Parties understand that criminal procedures and penalties as specified in paragraphs 1, 2, and 3 are applicable in any free trade zones in a Party.

[103]   A Party may comply with its obligation relating to importation of labels or packaging through its measures concerning distribution.

4.   Each Party shall provide for criminal procedures to be applied against a person who, willfully and without the authorization of the holder[104] of copyright or related rights in a cinematographic work, knowingly uses or attempts to use an audiovisual recording device to transmit or make a copy of the cinematographic work or any part thereof, from a performance of the motion picture or other audiovisual work in a movie theater or other venue that is being used primarily for the exhibition of a copyrighted motion picture. In addition to the criminal procedures, a Party may provide for administrative enforcement procedures.

5.   With respect to the offenses for which this Article requires a Party to provide for criminal procedures and penalties, each Party shall ensure that criminal liability for aiding and abetting is available under its law.

6.   With respect to the offenses described in paragraphs 1 through 5, each Party shall provide:

(a)   penalties that include sentences of imprisonment as well as monetary fines sufficiently high to provide a deterrent to future acts of infringement, consistent with the level of penalties applied for crimes of a corresponding gravity;[105]

(b)   that its judicial authorities have the authority, in determining penalties, to account for the seriousness of the circumstances, which may include circumstances that involve threats to, or effects on, health or safety;[106]

(c)   that its judicial or other competent authorities have the authority to order the seizure of suspected counterfeit trademark goods or pirated copyright goods, any related materials and implements used in the commission of the alleged offense, documentary evidence relevant to the alleged offense, and assets derived from, or obtained through the alleged infringing activity. If a Party requires identification of items subject to seizure as a prerequisite for issuing a judicial order referred to in this subparagraph, that Party shall not require the items to be described in greater detail than necessary to identify them for the purpose of seizure;

(d)   that its judicial authorities have the authority to order the forfeiture, at least for serious offenses, of any assets derived from or obtained through the infringing activity;

---

[104]   For greater certainty, the theater or venue owner or operator shall be entitled to contact the criminal law enforcement authorities with respect to the suspected commission of the acts referred to in this provision. For greater certainty, nothing in this paragraph expands or diminishes the existing rights and obligations of a theater or venue owner or operator with respect to the cinematographic work.

[105]   The Parties understand that there is no obligation for a Party to provide for the possibility of imprisonment and monetary fines to be imposed in parallel.

[106]   A Party may also account for those circumstances through a separate criminal offense.

    (e)   that its judicial authorities have the authority to order the forfeiture or destruction of:

        (i)   all counterfeit trademark goods or pirated copyright goods,

        (ii) materials and implements that have been predominantly used in the creation of pirated copyright goods or counterfeit trademark goods, and

        (iii) any other labels or packaging to which a counterfeit trademark has been applied and that have been used in the commission of the offense,

In cases in which counterfeit trademark goods and pirated copyright goods are not destroyed, the judicial or other competent authorities shall ensure that, except in exceptional circumstances, those goods are disposed of outside the channels of commerce in such a manner as to avoid causing any harm to the right holder. Each Party shall further provide that forfeiture or destruction under this subparagraph and subparagraph (d) occur without compensation of any kind to the defendant;

    (f)   that its judicial or other competent authorities have the authority to release or, in the alternative, provide access to, goods, material, implements, and other evidence held by the relevant authority to a right holder for civil[107] infringement proceedings; and

    (g)   that its competent authorities may act upon their own initiative to initiate legal action without the need for a formal complaint by a third person or right holder.

7.   With respect to the offenses described in paragraphs 1 through 5, a Party may provide that its judicial authorities have the authority to order the seizure or forfeiture of assets, or alternatively, a fine, the value of which corresponds to the assets derived from, or obtained directly or indirectly through, the infringing activity.

    Article 20.86: Protection of Encrypted Program-Carrying Satellite and Cable Signals

1.   Each Party shall make it a criminal offense to:

    (a)   manufacture, assemble,[108] modify, import, export,[109] sell, or otherwise distribute a tangible or intangible device or system knowing or having reason to know[110] that the device or system meets at least one of the following conditions:

---

[107]   A Party may also provide this authority in connection with administrative infringement proceedings.

[108]   For greater certainty, a Party may treat "assemble" as incorporated in "manufacture."

[109]   The obligation regarding export may be met by making it a criminal offense to possess and distribute a device or system described in this paragraph.

[110]   For the purposes of this paragraph, a Party may provide that "having a reason to know" may be demonstrated through reasonable evidence, taking into account the

    (i)   it is intended to be used to assist, or

    (ii) it is primarily of assistance,

> in decoding an encrypted program-carrying satellite signal without the authorization of the lawful distributor[111] of that signal;[112] and

  (b) with respect to an encrypted program-carrying satellite signal, willfully:

    (i)   receive[113] that signal, or

    (ii) further distribute[114] that signal,

knowing that it has been decoded without the authorization of the lawful distributor of the signal.

2.   Each Party shall provide for civil remedies for a person that holds an interest in an encrypted program-carrying satellite signal or its content and that is injured by an activity described in paragraph 1.

3.   Each Party shall provide for criminal penalties and civil[115] remedies for willfully:

  (a) manufacturing or distributing equipment knowing that the equipment is intended to be used in the unauthorized reception of any encrypted program-carrying cable signal; and

  (b) receiving, or assisting another to receive,[116] an encrypted program-carrying cable signal without authorization of the lawful distributor of the signal.

Article 20.87: Government Use of Software

1.   Each Party recognizes the importance of promoting the adoption of measures to enhance government awareness of respect for intellectual

---

facts and circumstances surrounding the alleged illegal act, as part of the Party's "knowledge" requirements. A Party may treat "having reason to know" as meaning "willful negligence".

[111] With regard to the criminal offenses and penalties in paragraphs 1 and 3, a Party may require a demonstration of intent to avoid payment to the lawful distributor, or a demonstration of intent to otherwise secure a pecuniary benefit to which the recipient is not entitled.

[112] For the purposes of this Article, a Party may provide that a "lawful distributor" means a person that has the lawful right in that Party's territory to distribute the encrypted program carrying signal and authorize its decoding.

[113] For greater certainty and for the purposes of paragraphs 1(b) and 3(b), a Party may provide that willful receipt of an encrypted program carrying satellite or cable signal means receipt and use of the signal, or means receipt and decoding of the signal.

[114] For greater certainty, a Party may interpret "further distribute" as "retransmit to the public".

[115] In providing for civil remedies, a Party may require a demonstration of injury.

[116] A Party may comply with its obligation in respect of "assisting another to receive" by providing for criminal penalties to be available against a person willfully publishing any information in order to enable or assist another person to receive a signal without authorization of the lawful distributor of the signal.

property rights and of the detrimental effects of the infringement of intellectual property rights.

2. Each Party shall adopt or maintain appropriate laws, regulations, policies, orders, government-issued guidelines, or administrative or executive decrees that provide that its central government agencies use only non-infringing computer software protected by copyright and related rights, and, if applicable, only use that computer software in a manner authorized by the relevant license. These measures apply to the acquisition and management of the software for government use.

Article 20.88:   Internet Service Providers

1. For the purpose of Article 20.89 (Legal Remedies and Safe Harbors), an Internet Service Provider is:

    (a) a provider of services for the transmission, routing, or providing of connections for digital online communications without modification of their content, between or among points specified by a user, of material of the user's choosing, undertaking the function in Article 20.89.2(a) (Legal Remedies and Safe Harbors); or

    (b) a provider of online services undertaking the functions in Article 20.89.2(b), Article 20.89.2(c), or Article 20.89.2(d) (Legal Remedies and Safe Harbors).

2. For the purposes of Article 20.89 (Legal Remedies and Safe Harbors), "copyright" includes related rights.

Article 20.89:   Legal Remedies and Safe Harbors[117]

1. The Parties recognize the importance of facilitating the continued development of legitimate online services operating as intermediaries and, in a manner consistent with Article 41 of the TRIPS Agreement, providing enforcement procedures that permit effective and expeditious action by right holders against copyright infringement covered under this Chapter that occurs in the online environment. Accordingly, each Party shall ensure that legal remedies are available for right holders to address that copyright infringement and shall establish or maintain appropriate safe harbors in respect of online services that are Internet Service Providers. This framework of legal remedies and safe harbors shall include:

    (a) legal incentives for Internet Service Providers to cooperate with copyright owners to deter the unauthorized storage and transmission of copyrighted materials or, in the alternative, to take other action to deter the unauthorized storage and transmission of copyrighted materials; and

    (b) limitations in its law that have the effect of precluding monetary relief against Internet Service Providers for

---

[117]   Annex 20-A (Annex to Section J) applies to Articles 20.89.3, 20.89.4, and 20.89.6.

copyright infringements that they do not control, initiate or direct, and that take place through systems or networks controlled or operated by them or on their behalf.

2. The limitations described in paragraph 1(b) shall include limitations in respect of the following functions:

    (a) transmitting, routing, or providing connections for material without modification of its content or the intermediate and transient storage of that material done automatically in the course of such a technical process;[118]

    (b) caching carried out through an automated process;

    (c) storage, at the direction of a user, of material residing on a system or network controlled or operated by or for the Internet Service Provider; and

    (d) referring or linking users to an online location by using information location tools, including hyperlinks and directories.

3. To facilitate effective action to address infringement, each Party shall prescribe in its law conditions for Internet Service Providers to qualify for the limitations described in paragraph 1(b), or, alternatively, shall provide for circumstances under which Internet Service Providers do not qualify for the limitations described in paragraph 1(b):[119]

    (a) With respect to the functions referred to in paragraphs 2(c) and 2(d), these conditions shall include a requirement for Internet Service Providers to expeditiously remove or disable access to material residing on their networks or systems upon obtaining actual knowledge of the copyright infringement or becoming aware of facts or circumstances from which the infringement is apparent, such as through receiving a notice[120] of alleged infringement from the right holder or a person authorized to act on its behalf.

---

[118] The Parties understand that these limitations shall apply only where the Internet Service Provider does not initiate the chain of transmission of the materials, and does not select the material or its recipients.

[119] The Parties understand that a Party that has yet to implement the obligations in paragraphs 3 and 4 will do so in a manner that is both effective and consistent with that Party's existing constitutional provisions. To that end, a Party may establish an appropriate role for the government that does not impair the timeliness of the process provided in paragraphs 3 and 4, and does not entail advance government review of each individual notice.

[120] For greater certainty, a notice of alleged infringement, as may be set out under a Party's law, must contain information that:

    (a) is reasonably sufficient to enable the Internet Service Provider to identify the work, performance or phonogram claimed to be infringed, the alleged infringing material, and the online location of the alleged infringement; and

    (b) has a sufficient indicia of reliability with respect to the authority of the person sending the notice.

(b)   An Internet Service Provider that removes or disables access to material in good faith under subparagraph (a) shall be exempt from any liability for having done so, provided that it takes reasonable steps in advance or promptly after to notify the person whose material is removed or disabled.[121]

4.   For the purposes of the functions referred to in paragraphs 2(c) and 2(d), each Party shall establish appropriate procedures in its laws or regulations for effective notices of claimed infringement, and effective counter-notices by those whose material is removed or disabled through mistake or misidentification. If material has been removed or access has been disabled in accordance with paragraph 3, that Party shall require that the Internet Service Provider restores the material that is the subject of a counter-notice, unless the person giving the original notice seeks relief through civil judicial proceedings within a reasonable period of time as set forth in that Party's laws or regulations.

5.   Each Party shall ensure that monetary remedies are available in its legal system against a person that makes a knowing material misrepresentation in a notice or counter-notice that causes injury to any interested party[122] as a result of an Internet Service Provider relying on the misrepresentation.

6.   Eligibility for the limitations in paragraph 1 shall be conditioned on the Internet Service Provider:

(a)   adopting and reasonably implementing a policy that provides for termination in appropriate circumstances of the accounts of repeat infringers;

(b)   accommodating and not interfering with standard technical measures accepted in the Party's territory that protect and identify copyrighted material, that are developed through an open, voluntary process by a broad consensus of copyright owners and service providers, that are available on reasonable and nondiscriminatory terms, and that do not impose substantial costs on service providers or substantial burdens on their systems or networks; and

(c)   with respect to the functions identified in paragraphs 2(c) and 2(d), not receiving a financial benefit directly attributable to the infringing activity, in circumstances where it has the right and ability to control such activity.

7.   Eligibility for the limitations identified in paragraph 1 shall not be conditioned on the Internet Service Provider monitoring its service or affirmatively seeking facts indicating infringing activity, except to the

---

[121]   With respect to the function in paragraph 2(b), a Party may limit the requirements of paragraph 3 related to an Internet Service Provider removing or disabling access to material to circumstances in which the Internet Service Provider becomes aware or receives notification that the cached material has been removed or access to it has been disabled at the originating site.

[122]   For greater certainty, the Parties understand that, "any interested party" may be limited to those with a legal interest recognized under that Party's law.

extent consistent with the technical measures identified in paragraph 6(b).

8.   Each Party shall provide procedures, whether judicial or administrative, in accordance with its legal system, and consistent with principles of due process and privacy, that enable a copyright owner that has made a legally sufficient claim of copyright infringement to obtain expeditiously from an Internet Service Provider information in the provider's possession identifying the alleged infringer, in cases in which that information is sought for the purpose of protecting or enforcing that copyright.

9.   The Parties understand that the failure of an Internet Service Provider to qualify for the limitations in paragraph 1(b) does not itself result in liability. Further, this Article is without prejudice to the availability of other limitations and exceptions to copyright, or any other defenses under a Party's legal system.

10. The Parties recognize the importance, in implementing their obligations under this Article, of taking into account the impact on the right holders and Internet Service Providers.

Section K: Final Provisions

Article 20.90:   Final Provisions

1.   Except as otherwise provided in Article 20.10 (Application of Chapter to Existing Subject Matter and Prior Acts) and paragraphs 2 and 3, each Party shall implement the provisions of this Chapter on the date of entry into force of this Agreement.

2.   During the relevant periods set out below, a Party shall not amend an existing measure or adopt a new measure that is less consistent with its obligations under the Articles referred to below for that Party than relevant measures that are in effect on the date of signature of this Agreement.

3.   With regard to obligations subject to a transition period, Mexico shall fully implement its obligations under the provisions of this Chapter no later than the expiration of the relevant time period specified below, which begins on the date of entry into force of this Agreement:

   (a)   Article 20.7 (International Agreements), UPOV 1991, four years;

   (b)   Article 20.45 (Protection of Undisclosed Test or Other Data for Agricultural Chemical Products), five years;

   (c)   Article 20.46 (Patent Term Adjustment for Unreasonable Curtailment), 4.5 years;

   (d)   Article 20.48 (Protection of Undisclosed Test or Other Data), five years;

   (e)   Article 20.49 (Biologics), five years;

(f) Article 20.71 (Civil Protection and Enforcement), Article 20.74 (Provisional Measures) and Article 20.76 (Civil Remedies), five years; and

(g) Articles 20.88 (Internet Service Providers) and 20.89 (Legal Remedies and Safe Harbors), three years.

4. With regard to obligations subject to a transition period, Canada shall fully implement its obligations under the provisions of this Chapter no later than the expiration of the relevant time period specified below, which begins on the date of entry into force of this Agreement.

(a) Article 20.7.2(f) (International Agreements), four years;

(b) Article 20.44 (Patent Term Adjustment for Unreasonable Granting Authority Delays), 4.5 years;

(c) Article 20.49 (Biologics), five years; and

(d) Article 20.63(a) (Term of Protection for Copyright and Related Rights), 2.5 years.

ANNEX 20-A ANNEX TO SECTION J

1. In order to facilitate the enforcement of copyright online and to avoid unwarranted market disruption in the online environment, Articles 20.89.3, 20.89.4, and 20.89.6 (Legal Remedies and Safe Harbors) shall not apply to a Party provided that, as from the date of agreement in principle of this Agreement, the Party continues to:

(a) prescribe in its law circumstances under which Internet Service Providers do not qualify for the limitations described in Article 20.89.1(b) (Legal Remedies and Safe Harbors);

(b) provide statutory secondary liability for copyright infringement in cases in which a person, by means of the Internet or another digital network, provides a service primarily for the purpose of enabling acts of copyright infringement, in relation to factors set out in its law, such as:

(i) whether the person marketed or promoted the service as one that could be used to enable acts of copyright infringement;

(ii) whether the person had knowledge that the service was used to enable a significant number of acts of copyright infringement;

(iii) whether the service has significant uses other than to enable acts of copyright infringement;

(iv) the person's ability, as part of providing the service, to limit acts of copyright infringement, and any action taken by the person to do so;

(v) any benefits the person received as a result of enabling the acts of copyright infringement; and

(vi) the economic viability of the service if it were not used to enable acts of copyright infringement;

(c) require Internet Service Providers carrying out the functions referred to in Article 20.89.2(a) and (c) (Legal Remedies and Safe Harbors) to participate in a system for forwarding notices of alleged infringement, including if material is made available online, and if the Internet Service Provider fails to do so, subjecting that provider to pre-established monetary damages for that failure;

(d) induce Internet Service Providers offering information location tools to remove within a specified period of time any reproductions of material that they make, and communicate to the public, as part of offering the information location tool upon receiving a notice of alleged infringement and after the original material has been removed from the electronic location set out in the notice; and

(e) induce Internet Service Providers carrying out the function referred to in Article 20.89.2(c) (Legal Remedies and Safe Harbors) to remove or disable access to material upon becoming aware of a decision of a court of that Party to the effect that the person storing the material infringes copyright in the material.

2. For a Party to which Articles 20.89.3, 20.89.4, and 20.89.6 (Legal Remedies and Safe Harbors) do not apply pursuant to paragraph 1, and in light of, among other things, paragraph 1(b), for the purposes of Article 20.89.1(a), legal incentives shall not mean the conditions for Internet Service Providers to qualify for the limitations provided for in Article 20.89.1(b), as set out in Article 20.89.3.

3. Pursuant to paragraph 1, for a Party to which Articles 20.89.3, 20.89.4, and 20.89.6 (Legal Remedies and Safe Harbors) do not apply:

(a) the term "modification" in paragraphs 20.88.1(a) and 20.89.2(a) does not include modifications made for solely technical reasons such as division into packets; and

(b) with regard to paragraph 20.89.7, "except to the extent consistent with the technical measures identified in paragraph 6(b)" does not apply.

CHAPTER 21 COMPETITION POLICY

Article 21.1: Competition Law and Authorities

1. Each Party shall maintain national competition laws that proscribe anticompetitive business conduct to promote competition in order to increase economic efficiency and consumer welfare, and shall take appropriate action with respect to that conduct.

2. Each Party shall endeavor to apply its national competition laws to all commercial activities in its territory. This does not prevent a Party from

applying its national competition laws to commercial activities outside its borders that have an appropriate nexus to its jurisdiction.

3. Each Party may provide for certain exemptions from the application of its national competition laws provided that those exemptions are transparent, established in its law, and based on public interest or public policy grounds.

4. Each Party shall maintain a national competition authority or authorities (national competition authorities) responsible for the enforcement of its national competition laws.

5. Each Party shall ensure that the enforcement policies of its national competition authorities include:

    (a) treating persons of another Party no less favorably than persons of the Party in like circumstances;

    (b) considering, if applicable, the effect of enforcement activities on related enforcement activities by a national competition authority of another Party; and

    (c) limiting remedies relating to conduct or assets outside the Party's territory to situations in which there is an appropriate nexus to harm or threatened harm affecting the Party's territory or commerce.

Article 21.2:   Procedural Fairness in Competition Law Enforcement

1. For the purposes of this Article, "enforcement proceeding" means a judicial or administrative proceeding following an investigation into the alleged violation of the national competition laws and does not include matters occurring before a grand jury.

2. Each Party shall ensure that its national competition authorities:

    (a) provide transparency, including in writing, regarding the applicable competition laws, regulations, and procedural rules pursuant to which national competition law investigations and enforcement proceedings are conducted;

    (b) conduct their investigations subject to definitive deadlines or within a reasonable time frame, if the investigations are not subject to definitive deadlines;

    (c) afford to a person a reasonable opportunity to be represented by legal counsel, including by:

        (i) allowing, at the person's request, counsel's participation in all meetings or proceedings between the national competition authority and the person. This sub-subparagraph does not apply to matters occurring before a grand jury, ex parte proceedings, or to searches conducted pursuant to judicial warrants, and

        (ii) recognizing a privilege, as acknowledged by its law, if not waived, for lawful confidential communications between the counsel and the person if the communications concern the soliciting or rendering of legal advice; and

(d) with respect to reviews of merger transactions, permit early consultations between the national competition authority and the merging persons to provide their views concerning the transaction, including on potentially dispositive issues.

3. Each Party shall ensure that all information that its national competition authorities obtain during investigations and reviews, and that its law protects as confidential or privileged is not disclosed, subject to applicable legal exceptions.

4. Each Party shall ensure that its national competition authorities do not state or imply in any public notice confirming or revealing the existence of a pending or ongoing investigation against a particular person that that person has in fact violated the Party's national competition laws.

5. Each Party shall ensure that its national competition authorities1 have the ultimate burden of establishing the legal and factual basis for an alleged violation in an enforcement proceeding; however, a Party may require that a person against whom that allegation is made be responsible for establishing certain defenses to the allegation.

6. Each Party shall ensure that all final decisions in contested civil or administrative matters finding a violation of its national competition laws are in writing and set out the findings of fact and conclusions of law on which they are based. Each Party shall make public those final decisions, with the exception of any confidential material contained therein.

7. Each Party shall ensure that before it imposes a sanction or remedy against a person for a violation of its national competition laws, it affords the person a reasonable opportunity to:

(a) obtain information regarding the national competition authority's concerns, including identification of the specific competition laws alleged to have been violated;

(b) engage with the relevant national competition authority at key points on significant legal, factual, and procedural issues;

(c) have access to information that is necessary to prepare an adequate defense if the person contests the allegations in an enforcement proceeding; however, a national competition authority is not obliged to produce information that is not already in its possession. If a Party's national competition authority2 introduces or will introduce confidential information in an enforcement proceeding, the Party shall, as permissible under its law, allow the person under investigation or its legal counsel timely access to that information;

(d) be heard and present evidence in its defense, including rebuttal evidence, and, whenever relevant, the analysis of a properly qualified expert;

(e) cross-examine any witness testifying in an enforcement proceeding; and

(f) contest an allegation that the person has violated national competition laws before an impartial judicial or administrative authority, provided that in the case of an administrative authority, the decision-making body must be independent of the unit offering evidence in support of the allegation;

except that a Party may provide for these opportunities within a reasonable time after it imposes an interim measure.

8. Each Party shall provide a person that is subject to the imposition of a fine, sanction, or remedy for violation of its national competition laws with the opportunity to seek judicial review by a court or independent tribunal, including review of alleged substantive or procedural errors, unless the person voluntarily agreed to the imposition of the fine, sanction, or remedy.

9. Each Party shall ensure that criteria used for calculating a fine for a violation of national competition laws are transparent. If a Party imposes a fine as a penalty for a non-criminal violation of its national competition laws that is based on the person's revenue or profit, it shall ensure that the calculation considers revenue or profit relating to the Party's territory.

10. Each Party's national competition authority shall maintain measures to preserve all relevant evidence, including exculpatory evidence, that it collected as part of an enforcement proceeding until the review is exhausted.

* * *

Article 21.4:   Consumer Protection

1. The Parties recognize the importance of consumer protection policy and enforcement to creating efficient and competitive markets, and enhancing consumer welfare in the free trade area.

2. Each Party shall adopt or maintain national consumer protection laws or other laws or regulations that proscribe fraudulent and deceptive commercial activities, recognizing that the enforcement of those laws and regulations is in the public interest. The laws and regulations a Party adopts or maintains to proscribe these activities may be civil or criminal in nature.

3. The Parties recognize that fraudulent and deceptive commercial activities increasingly transcend national borders and that cooperation and coordination between the Parties to address these activities effectively is important and in the public interest.

4.   The Parties shall promote, as appropriate, cooperation and coordination on matters of mutual interest related to fraudulent and deceptive commercial activities, including in the enforcement of their consumer protection laws through activities such as the exchange of consumer complaints and other enforcement information. That cooperation and coordination may be based on cooperation mechanisms in existence. Each Party shall protect confidential information in accordance with its law, including business information.

5.   The Parties shall endeavor to cooperate and coordinate on the matters set out in this Article through the relevant national public bodies or officials responsible for consumer protection policy, law, or enforcement, as determined by each Party and compatible with their respective law and important interests, and within their reasonably available resources.

Article 21.5:   Transparency

1.   The Parties recognize the value of making competition enforcement and advocacy policies as transparent as possible.

2.   On request of another Party, a Party shall make available to the requesting Party public information concerning:

(a)   its national competition law enforcement policies and practices; and

(b)   exemptions and immunities to its national competition laws, provided that the request specifies the particular good or service and market of concern and includes information explaining how the exemption or immunity may hinder trade or investment between the Parties.

* * *

Article 21.7:   Non-Application of Dispute Settlement

No Party shall have recourse to dispute settlement under Chapter 14 (Investment) or Chapter 31 (Dispute Settlement) for a matter arising under this Chapter.

CHAPTER 22 STATE-OWNED ENTERPRISES AND DESIGNATED MONOPOLIES

Article 22.1:   Definitions

For the purposes of this Chapter:

Arrangement means the *Arrangement on Officially Supported Export Credits,* developed within the framework of the Organization for Economic Co-operation and Development (OECD), or a successor undertaking, whether developed within or outside of the OECD framework, that has been adopted by at least 12 original WTO Members that were Participants to the Arrangement as of January 1, 1979;

Commercial activities means activities that an enterprise undertakes with an orientation toward profit-making[1] and that result in the production of a good or supply of a service that will be sold to a consumer in the relevant market in quantities and at prices determined by the enterprise;[2]

Commercial considerations means price, quality, availability, marketability, transportation, and other terms and conditions of purchase or sale, or other factors that would normally be taken into account in the commercial decisions of a privately owned enterprise in the relevant business or industry;

Designate means to establish, name, or authorize a monopoly, or to expand the scope of a monopoly to cover an additional good or service;

Designated monopoly means a privately owned monopoly that is designated after the date of entry into force of this Agreement and a government monopoly that a Party designates or has designated;

Financial services supplier, financial institution, and financial services have the same meaning as in Article 17.1 (Definitions);

Government monopoly means a monopoly that is owned, or controlled through ownership interests, by a Party or by another government monopoly;

Independent pension fund means an enterprise that is owned, or controlled through ownership interests, by a Party that:

(a)   is engaged exclusively in the following activities:

   (i)   administering or providing a plan for pension, retirement, social security, disability, death, or employee benefits, or any combination thereof solely for the benefit of natural persons who are contributors to such a plan or their beneficiaries, or

   (ii)   investing the assets of these plans;

(b)   has a fiduciary duty to the natural persons referred to in subparagraph (a)(i); and

(c)   is not subject to investment direction by the government of the Party;[3]

Market means the geographical and commercial market for a good or service;

Monopoly means an entity, including a consortium or government agency that, in a relevant market in the territory of a Party, is designated as the

---

[1]   For greater certainty, activities undertaken by an enterprise that operates on a not-for-profit basis or on a cost-recovery basis are not activities undertaken with an orientation toward profit-making.

[2]   For greater certainty, measures of general application to the relevant market shall not be construed as the determination by a Party of pricing, production, or supply decisions of an enterprise.

[3]   Investment direction from the government of a Party does not include general guidance with respect to risk management and asset allocation that is not inconsistent with usual investment practice and is not demonstrated solely by the presence of government officials on the enterprise's board of directors or investment panel.

sole provider or purchaser of a good or service, but does not include an entity that has been granted an exclusive intellectual property right solely by reason of the grant;

Non-commercial assistance[4] means assistance that is limited to certain enterprises, and:

(a) "assistance" means the following forms of assistance:

    (i) direct transfers of funds or potential direct transfers of funds or liabilities, such as:

        (A) grants or debt forgiveness,

        (B) loans, loan guarantees, or other types of financing on terms more favorable than those commercially available to that enterprise, or

        (C) equity capital inconsistent with the usual investment practice (including for the provision of risk capital) of private investors,

    (ii) the provision of goods or the supply of services other than general infrastructure, on terms more favorable than those commercially available to the enterprise, or

    (iii) the purchase of goods on terms more favorable than those commercially available to the enterprise;

(b) "certain enterprises" means an enterprise or industry or group of enterprises or industries;

(c) "limited to certain enterprises" means that the Party or any of the Party's state enterprises or state-owned enterprises, or a combination thereof:

    (i) explicitly limits access to the assistance to certain enterprises,

    (ii) provides assistance to a limited number of certain enterprises,

    (iii) provides assistance which is predominantly used by certain enterprises,

    (iv) provides a disproportionately large amount of the assistance to certain enterprises, or

---

[4] For greater certainty, non-commercial assistance does not include a Party's transfer of funds, collected from contributors to a plan for pension, retirement, social security, disability, death or employee benefits, or any combination thereof, to an independent pension fund for investment on behalf of the contributors and their beneficiaries.

    (v)   otherwise favors certain enterprises through the use of its discretion in the provision of assistance;[5] and

  (d)   assistance that falls under Article 22.6.1, Article 22.6.2, or Article 22.6.3 (Non-Commercial Assistance) shall be deemed to be "limited to certain enterprises";

Public service mandate means a government mandate pursuant to which a state-owned enterprise makes available a service, directly or indirectly, to the general public in its territory;[6]

State-owned enterprise means an enterprise that is principally engaged in commercial activities, and in which a Party:

  (a)   directly or indirectly[7] owns more than 50 percent of the share capital;

  (b)   controls, through direct or indirect ownership interests, the exercise of more than 50 percent of the voting rights;

  (c)   holds the power to control the enterprise through any other ownership interest, including indirect or minority ownership;[8] or

  (d)   holds the power to appoint a majority of members of the board of directors or any other equivalent management body.

    Article 22.2:   Scope

1.   This Chapter applies to the activities of state-owned enterprises, state enterprises, or designated monopolies of a Party that affect or could affect trade or investment between Parties within the free trade area. This Chapter also applies to the activities of state-owned enterprises of a Party that cause adverse effects in the market of a non-Party as provided in Article 22.7 (Adverse Effects).

2.   This Chapter does not apply to:

---

   [5]   For greater certainty, assistance that is limited, in law or fact, to state enterprises or state-owned enterprises of a Party, or a combination thereof, is "limited to certain enterprises".

   [6]   For greater certainty, a service to the general public includes the distribution of goods and the supply of general infrastructure services.

   [7]   For the purposes of this definition, the term "indirectly" refers to situations in which a Party holds an ownership interest in an enterprise through one or more state enterprises of that Party. At each level of the ownership chain, the state enterprise—either alone or in combination with other state enterprises—must own, or control through ownership interests, another enterprise.

   [8]   For the purposes of this subparagraph, a Party holds the power to control the enterprise if, through an ownership interest, it can determine or direct important matters affecting the enterprise, excluding minority shareholder protections. In determining whether a Party has this power, all relevant legal and factual elements shall be taken into account on a case-by-case basis. Those elements may include the power to determine or direct commercial operations, including major expenditures or investments; issuances of equity or significant debt offerings; or the restructuring, merger, or dissolution of the enterprise.

(a) the regulatory or supervisory activities, or monetary and related credit policy and exchange rate policy, of a central bank or monetary authority of a Party;

(b) the regulatory or supervisory activities of a financial regulatory body of a Party, including a non-governmental body, such as a securities or futures exchange or market, clearing agency, or other organization or association, that exercises regulatory or supervisory authority over financial services suppliers; or

(c) activities undertaken by a Party or one of its state enterprises or state-owned enterprises for the purpose of the resolution of a failing or failed financial institution or any other failing or failed enterprise principally engaged in the supply of financial services.

3. This Chapter does not apply to:

(a) an independent pension fund of a Party; or

(b) an enterprise owned or controlled by an independent pension fund of a Party, except:

    (i) Article 22.6.1, Article 22.6.2, Article 22.6.4, and Article 22.6.6 (Non-Commercial Assistance) apply only to a Party's direct or indirect provision of non-commercial assistance to an enterprise owned or controlled by an independent pension fund, and

    (ii) Article 22.6.1, Article 22.6.2, Article 22.6.4, and Article 22.6.6 (Non-Commercial Assistance) apply only to a Party's indirect provision of non-commercial assistance through an enterprise owned or controlled by an independent pension fund.

4. This Chapter does not apply to government procurement.

5. Nothing in this Chapter shall be construed to prevent a Party from:

(a) establishing or maintaining a state enterprise or a state-owned enterprise; or

(b) designating a monopoly.

6. Article 22.4 (Non-Discriminatory Treatment and Commercial Considerations), Article 22.6 (Non-Commercial Assistance), and Article 22.10 (Transparency) do not apply to a service supplied in the exercise of governmental authority.[9]

7. Article 22.4.1(b), Article 22.4.1(c), Article 22.4.2(b), and Article 22.4.2(c) (Non-Discriminatory Treatment and Commercial Considerations) do not apply to the extent that a Party's state-owned enterprise or

---

[9] For the purposes of this paragraph, "a service supplied in the exercise of governmental authority" has the same meaning as in the GATS, including the meaning in its Financial Services Annex if applicable.

designated monopoly makes purchases and sales of goods or services pursuant to:

(a) an existing non-conforming measure that the Party maintains, continues, renews or amends in accordance with Article 14.12.1 (Non-Conforming Measures), Article 15.7.1 (Non-Conforming Measures) or Article 17.10.1 (Non-Conforming Measures), as set out in its Schedule to Annex I or in Section A of its Schedule to Annex III; or

(b) a non-conforming measure that the Party adopts or maintains with respect to sectors, subsectors, or activities in accordance with Article 14.12.2 (Non-Conforming Measures), Article 15.7.2 (Non-Conforming Measures) or Article 17.10.2 (Non-Conforming Measures), as set out in its Schedule to Annex II or in Section B of its Schedule to Annex III.

Article 22.3: Delegated Authority

Consistent with Article 1.3 (Persons Exercising Delegated Governmental Authority), each Party shall ensure that if its state-owned enterprises, state enterprises, or designated monopolies exercise regulatory, administrative, or other governmental authority that the Party has directed or delegated to those entities to carry out, those entities act in a manner that is not inconsistent with that Party's obligations under this Agreement.[10]

Article 22.4: Non-Discriminatory Treatment and Commercial Considerations

1. Each Party shall ensure that each of its state-owned enterprises, when engaging in commercial activities:

(a) acts in accordance with commercial considerations in its purchase or sale of a good or service, except to fulfil the terms of its public service mandate that are not inconsistent with subparagraphs (b) or (c)(ii);

(b) in its purchase of a good or service:

(i) accords to a good or service supplied by an enterprise of another Party treatment no less favorable than it accords to a like good or a like service supplied by enterprises of the Party, of any other Party or of a non-Party, and

(ii) accords to a good or service supplied by an enterprise that is a covered investment in the Party's territory treatment no less favorable than it accords to a like good or a like service supplied by enterprises in the relevant market in the Party's territory that are investments of

---

[10] Examples of regulatory, administrative, or other governmental authority include the power to expropriate, grant licenses, approve commercial transactions, or impose quotas, fees, or other charges.

investors of the Party, of another Party or of a non-Party; and

(c)   in its sale of a good or service:

   (i)   accords to an enterprise of another Party treatment no less favorable than it accords to enterprises of the Party, of any other Party or of a non-Party, and

   (ii)   accords to an enterprise that is a covered investment in the Party's territory treatment no less favorable than it accords to enterprises in the relevant

market in the Party's territory that are investments of investors of the Party, of another Party or of a non-Party.[11]

2.   Each Party shall ensure that each of its designated monopolies:

(a)   acts in accordance with commercial considerations in its purchase or sale of the monopoly good or service in the relevant market, except to fulfil any terms of its designation that are not inconsistent with subparagraphs (b), (c), or (d);

(b)   in its purchase of the monopoly good or service:

   (i)   accords to a good or service supplied by an enterprise of another Party treatment no less favorable than it accords to a like good or a like service supplied by enterprises of the Party, of any other Party or of a non-Party, and

   (ii)   accords to a good or service supplied by an enterprise that is a covered investment in the Party's territory treatment no less favorable than it accords to a like good or a like service supplied by enterprises in the relevant market in the Party's territory that are investments of investors of the Party, of another Party or of a non-Party; and

(c)   in its sale of the monopoly good or service:

   (i)   accords to an enterprise of another Party treatment no less favorable than it accords to enterprises of the Party, of any other Party or of a non-Party, and

   (ii)   accords to an enterprise that is a covered investment in the Party's territory treatment no less favorable than it accords to enterprises in the relevant market in the Party's territory that are investments of investors of the Party, of another Party or of a non-Party; and

---

[11]   Article 22.4.1 (Non-Discriminatory Treatment and Commercial Considerations) does not apply with respect to the purchase or sale of shares, stock, or other forms of equity by a state-owned enterprise as a means of its equity participation in another enterprise.

(d)   does not use its monopoly position to engage in, either directly or indirectly, including through its dealings with its parent, subsidiaries, or other entities the Party or the designated monopoly owns, anticompetitive practices in a non-monopolized market in its territory that negatively affect trade or investment between the Parties.

3.   Paragraphs 1(b) and 1(c) and paragraphs 2(b) and 2(c) do not preclude a state-owned enterprise or designated monopoly from:

(a)   purchasing or selling goods or services on different terms or conditions including those relating to price; or

(b)   refusing to purchase or sell goods or services,

provided that this differential treatment or refusal is undertaken in accordance with commercial considerations.

Article 22.5:   Courts and Administrative Bodies

1.   Each Party shall provide its courts with jurisdiction over civil claims against an enterprise owned or controlled through ownership interests by a foreign government based on a commercial activity carried on in its territory.[12] This shall not be construed to require a Party to provide jurisdiction over those claims if it does not provide jurisdiction over similar claims against enterprises that are not owned or controlled through ownership interests by a foreign government.

2.   Each Party shall ensure that any administrative body that the Party establishes or maintains that regulates a state-owned enterprise exercises its regulatory discretion in an impartial manner with respect to enterprises that it regulates, including enterprises that are not state-owned enterprises.

Article 22.6:   Non-Commercial Assistance

1.   The following forms of non-commercial assistance, if provided to a state-owned enterprise primarily engaged in the production or sale of goods other than electricity, are prohibited:[13]

---

[12]   This paragraph shall not be construed to preclude a Party from providing its courts with jurisdiction over claims against enterprises owned or controlled through ownership interests by a foreign government other than those claims referred to in this paragraph.

[13]   Article 22.6.1, Article 22.6.2, and Article 22.6.3 (Non-Commercial Assistance) do not apply to state-owned enterprises of a Party that are primarily engaged in the construction of general infrastructure such as bridges, highways, ports, or railways (including intercity or urban railways), if (i) the infrastructure is located, in whole or in part, within the territory of the Party; and (ii) neither access to nor use of the infrastructure is limited to certain enterprises, unless those enterprises access or use the infrastructure primarily to supply a service to the general public within the territory of the Party.

(a)   loans or loan guarantees provided by a state enterprise or state-owned enterprise of a Party to an uncreditworthy state-owned enterprise of that Party;[14]

(b)   non-commercial assistance provided by a Party or a state enterprise or state-owned enterprise of a Party to a state-owned enterprise of that Party, in circumstances where the recipient is insolvent[15] or on the brink of insolvency,[16] without a credible restructuring plan designed to return the state-owned enterprise within a reasonable period of time to long-term viability; or

(c)   conversion by a Party or a state enterprise or state-owned enterprise of a Party of the outstanding debt of a state-owned enterprise of that Party to equity, in circumstances where this would be inconsistent with the usual investment practice of a private investor.[17]

2.   No Party shall provide, either directly or indirectly,[18] non-commercial assistance referred to in paragraphs 1(b) and 1(c).

3.   Each Party shall ensure that its state enterprises and state-owned enterprises do not provide, either directly or indirectly, non-commercial assistance referred to in paragraphs 1(a), 1(b), and 1(c).

4.   No Party shall cause[19] adverse effects to the interests of another Party through the use of non-commercial assistance that it provides, either

---

[14]   A state-owned enterprise is "uncreditworthy" if, at the time the terms of the financing were agreed upon, the state-owned enterprise's financial position would preclude it from obtaining long-term financing from conventional commercial sources (that is, bank loans and non-speculative grade bond issues). To determine whether a state-owned enterprise is creditworthy, all relevant legal and factual elements must be taken into consideration on a case-by-case basis. These elements may include whether a creditor would have reasonable assurance of repayment of contractual

[15]   A state-owned enterprise is "insolvent" if it is unable to meet its debt obligations as they become due. Insolvency exists, for example, where (i) the state-owned enterprise has failed to make required payments due to an inability to service the debt obligations; or (ii) the state-owned enterprise has filed for bankruptcy, has been determined by a court to be bankrupt or insolvent, or is subject to court supervision, for purposes of either reorganization or liquidation of the enterprise.

[16]   A state-owned enterprise is "on the brink of insolvency" if it will likely be unable to meet its debt obligations at any point over the next 12 months. To determine whether a state-owned enterprise is on the brink of insolvency, primary consideration shall be given to opinions of independent credit rating agencies and independent accounting firms issued in the ordinary course of business, if available. To the extent relevant, additional factual evidence concerning the ability of the state-owned enterprise to meet its debt obligations may also be taken into account.

[17]   With respect to Mexico, the obligations set out in Article 22.6.1, Article 22.6.2, and Article 22.6.3 (Non-Commercial Assistance) are subject to the additional provisions of Annex 22-F (Non-Commercial Assistance to Certain State Productive Enterprises).

[18]   For greater certainty, indirect provision includes the situation in which a Party entrusts or directs an enterprise that is not a state-owned enterprise to provide non-commercial assistance.

[19]   For the purposes of paragraphs 4 and 5, it must be demonstrated that the adverse effects claimed have been caused by the non-commercial assistance. Thus, the

directly or indirectly, to its state-owned enterprises with respect to debt obligations in a timely manner, for instance, from the cash flow and assets of the business.

(a) the production and sale of a good by the state-owned enterprise;

(b) the supply of a service by the state-owned enterprise from the territory of the Party into the territory of another Party; or

(c) the supply of a service in the territory of another Party through an enterprise that is a covered investment in the territory of that other Party or any other Party.

5. Each Party shall ensure that its state enterprises and state-owned enterprises do not cause adverse effects to the interests of another Party through the use of non-commercial assistance that the state enterprise or state-owned enterprise provides to a state-owned enterprise of the Party with respect to:

(a) the production and sale of a good by the state-owned enterprise;

(b) the supply of a service by the state-owned enterprise from the territory of the Party into the territory of another Party; or

(c) the supply of a service in the territory of another Party through an enterprise that is a covered investment in the territory of that other Party or any other Party.

6. No Party shall cause injury to a domestic industry[20] of another Party through the use of non-commercial assistance that it provides, either directly or indirectly, to any of its state-owned enterprises that is a covered investment in the territory of that other Party in circumstances in which:

(a) the non-commercial assistance is provided with respect to the production and sale of a good by the state-owned enterprise in the territory of the other Party; and

(b) a like good is produced and sold in the territory of the other Party by the domestic industry of that other Party.[21]

---

non-commercial assistance must be examined within the context of other possible causal factors to ensure an appropriate attribution of causality.

[20] The term "domestic industry" refers to the domestic producers as a whole of the like good, or to those domestic producers whose collective output of the like good constitutes a major proportion of the total domestic production of the like good, excluding the state-owned enterprise that is a covered investment that has received the non-commercial assistance referred to in this paragraph.

[21] In situations of material retardation of the establishment of a domestic industry, it is understood that a domestic industry may not yet produce and sell the like good. However, in these situations, there must be evidence that a prospective domestic producer has made a substantial commitment to commence production and sales of the like good.

7.   A service supplied by a state-owned enterprise of a Party within that Party's territory shall be deemed not to cause adverse effects.[22]

Article 22.7:   Adverse Effects

1.   For the purposes of Article 22.6.4 and Article 22.6.5 (Non-Commercial Assistance), adverse effects arise if the effect of the non-commercial assistance is:

(a)   that the production and sale of a good by a Party's state-owned enterprise that has received the non-commercial assistance displaces or impedes from the Party's market imports of a like good of another Party or sales of a like good produced by an enterprise that is a covered investment in the territory of the Party;

(b)   that the production and sale of a good by a Party's state-owned enterprise that has received the non-commercial assistance displaces or impedes from:

(i)   the market of another Party sales of a like good produced by an enterprise that is a covered investment in the territory of that other Party, or imports of a like good of any other Party, or

(ii)   the market of a non-Party imports of a like good of another Party;

(c)   a significant price undercutting by a good produced by a Party's state-owned enterprise that has received the non-commercial assistance and sold by the enterprise in:

(i)   the market of a Party as compared with the price in the same market of imports of a like good of another Party or a like good that is produced by an enterprise that is a covered investment in the territory of the Party, or significant price suppression, price depression or lost sales in the same market, or

(ii)   the market of a non-Party as compared with the price in the same market of imports of a like good of another Party, or significant price suppression, price depression or lost sales in the same market.

(d)   that services supplied by a Party's state-owned enterprise that has received the non-commercial assistance displace or impede from the market of another Party a like service supplied by a service supplier of that other Party or any other Party; or

a significant price undercutting by a service supplied in the market of another Party by a Party's state-owned enterprise that has received the non-commercial assistance as compared with the price in the same market of a

---

[22]   For greater certainty, this paragraph shall not be construed to apply to a service that itself is a form of non-commercial assistance.

like service supplied by a service supplier of that other Party or any other Party, or significant price suppression, price depression or lost sales in the same market.[23]

2. For the purposes of paragraphs l(a), l(b), and 1 (d), the displacing or impeding of a good or service includes a case in which it has been demonstrated that there has been a significant change in relative shares of the market to the disadvantage of the like good or like service. "Significant change in relative shares of the market" includes the following situations:

   (a) there is a significant increase in the market share of the good or service of the Party's state-owned enterprise;

   (b) the market share of the good or service of the Party's state-owned enterprise remains constant in circumstances in which, in the absence of the non-commercial assistance, it would have declined significantly; or

   (c) the market share of the good or service of the Party's state-owned enterprise declines, but at a significantly slower rate than would have been the case in the absence of the non-commercial assistance.

The change must manifest itself over an appropriately representative period sufficient to demonstrate clear trends in the development of the market for the good or service concerned, which, in normal circumstances, is at least one year.

3. For the purposes of paragraphs l(c) and l(e), price undercutting includes a case in which such price undercutting has been demonstrated through a comparison of the prices of the good or service of the state-owned enterprise with the prices of the like good or service.

4. Comparisons of the prices in paragraph 3 must be made at the same level of trade and at I comparable times, and due account must be taken for factors affecting price comparability. If a direct comparison of transactions is not possible, the existence of price undercutting may be demonstrated on some other reasonable basis, such as, in the case of goods, a comparison of unit values.

5. Non-commercial assistance that a Party provides before the signing of this Agreement shall be deemed not to cause adverse effects.

---

[23] The purchase or sale of shares, stock or other forms of equity by a state-owned enterprise that has received non-commercial assistance as a means of its equity participation in another enterprise shall not, in and of itself, be construed to give rise to adverse effects as provided for in Article 22.7.1 (Adverse Effects). Consistent with Article 22.6.5 (Non-Commercial Assistance), if the state-owned enterprise provides equity capital to another state-owned enterprise, and the equity capital is a form of non-commercial assistance, then, depending on the facts, the production and sale of a good or the supply of a service by the recipient enterprise could give rise to adverse effects.

Article 22.8:   Injury

1.   For the purposes of Article 22.6.6 (Non-Commercial Assistance), the term "injury" means material injury to a domestic industry, threat of material injury to a domestic industry, or material retardation of the establishment of such an industry. A determination of material injury shall be based on positive evidence and involve an objective examination of the relevant factors, including the volume of production by the covered investment that has received non-commercial assistance, the effect of that production on prices for like goods produced and sold by the domestic industry, and the effect of that production on the domestic industry producing like goods.[24]

2.   With regard to the volume of production by the covered investment that has received non-commercial assistance, consideration shall be given as to whether there has been a significant increase in the volume of production, either in absolute terms or relative to production or consumption in the territory of the Party in which injury is alleged to have occurred. With regard to the effect of the production by the covered investment on prices, consideration shall be given as to whether there has been a significant price undercutting by the goods produced and sold by the covered investment as compared with the price of like goods produced and sold by the domestic industry, or whether the effect of production by the covered investment is otherwise to depress prices to a significant degree or to prevent price increases, which otherwise would have occurred, to a significant degree. No one or several of these factors can necessarily give decisive guidance.

3.   The examination of the impact on the domestic industry of the goods produced and sold by the covered investment that received the non-commercial assistance must include an evaluation of all relevant economic factors and indices having a bearing on the state of the industry, such as actual and potential decline in output, sales, market share, profits, productivity, return on investments, or utilization of capacity; factors affecting domestic prices; actual and potential negative effects on cash flow, inventories, employment, wages, growth, ability to raise capital or investments and, in the case of agriculture, whether there has been an increased burden on government support programs. This list is not exhaustive, nor can one or several of these factors necessarily give decisive guidance.

4.   It must be demonstrated that the goods produced and sold by the covered investment are, through the effects of the non-commercial assistance, set out in paragraphs 2 and 3, causing injury within the meaning of this Article. The demonstration of a causal relationship between the goods produced and sold by the covered investment and the injury to the domestic industry shall be based on an examination of all relevant evidence. Any known factors other than the goods produced by

---

[24]   The periods for examination of the non-commercial assistance and injury shall be reasonably established and shall end as closely as practical to the date of initiation of the proceeding before the panel.

the covered investment which at the same time are injuring the domestic industry must be examined, and the injuries caused by these other factors must not be attributed to the goods produced and sold by the covered investment that has received non-commercial assistance. Factors that may be relevant in this respect include the volumes and prices of other like goods in the market in question, contraction in demand or changes in the patterns of consumption, and developments in technology and the export performance and productivity of the domestic industry.

5.   A determination of a threat of material injury shall be based on facts and not merely on allegation, conjecture or remote possibility and shall be considered with special care. The change in circumstances that would create a situation in which non-commercial assistance to the covered investment would cause injury must be clearly foreseen and imminent. In making a determination regarding the existence of a threat of material injury, there should be consideration of relevant factors[25] and of whether the totality of the factors considered lead to the conclusion that further availability of goods produced by the covered investment is imminent and that, unless protective action is taken, material injury would occur.

Article 22.9:   Party-Specific Annexes

1.   Article 22.4 (Non-Discriminatory Treatment and Commercial Considerations) and Article 22.6 (Non-Commercial Assistance) do not apply with respect to the non-conforming activities of state-owned enterprises or designated monopolies that a Party lists in its Schedule to Annex IV in accordance with the terms of the Party's Schedule.

2.   Article 22.4 (Non-Discriminatory Treatment and Commercial Considerations), Article 22.5 (Courts and Administrative Bodies), Article 22.6 (Non-Commercial Assistance), and Article 22.10 (Transparency) do not apply to a Party's state-owned enterprises or designated monopolies as set out in Annex 22-D (Application to Sub-Central State-Owned Enterprises and Designated Monopolies).

Article 22.10:   Transparency

1.   Each Party shall provide to the other Parties or publish on an official website a list of its state-owned enterprises no later than six months

---

[25]   In making a determination regarding the existence of a threat of material injury, a panel established pursuant to Chapter 31 (Dispute Settlement) should consider, among other things, such factors as: (i) the nature of the non-commercial assistance in question and the trade effects likely to arise therefrom; (ii) a significant rate of increase in sales in the domestic market by the covered investment, indicating a likelihood of substantially increased sales; (iii) sufficient freely disposable, or an imminent, substantial increase in, capacity of the covered investment indicating the likelihood of substantially increased production of the good by that covered investment, taking into account the availability of export markets to absorb additional production; (iv) whether prices of goods sold by the covered investment will have a significant depressing or suppressing effect on the price of like goods; and (v) inventories of like goods.

after the date of entry into force of this Agreement, and thereafter shall update the list annually.

2. Each Party shall promptly notify the other Parties or publish on an official website the designation of a monopoly or expansion of the scope of an existing monopoly and the terms of its designation.

3. On the written request of another Party, a Party shall promptly provide the following information in writing concerning a state-owned enterprise or a government monopoly, provided that the request includes a reasoned explanation of how the activities of the entity affect or could affect trade or investment between the Parties:

    (a) the percentage of shares that the Party, its state enterprises, state-owned enterprises, or designated monopolies cumulatively own, and the percentage of votes that they cumulatively hold, in the entity;

    (b) a description of any special shares or special voting or other rights that the Party, its state enterprises, state-owned enterprises, or designated monopolies hold, to the extent these rights are different from the rights attached to the general common shares of the entity;

    (c) the government titles of any government official serving as an officer or member of the entity's board of directors;

    (d) the entity's annual revenue and total assets over the most recent three year period for which information is available;

    (e) any exemptions and immunities from which the entity benefits under the Party's law; and

    (f) any additional information regarding the entity that is publicly available, including annual financial reports and third-party audits, and that is sought in the written request.

4. On the written request of another Party, a Party shall promptly provide, in writing, information regarding any policy or program that the Party has adopted or maintains that provides for the provision of either non-commercial assistance or any equity capital (regardless of whether the equity infusion also constitutes non-commercial assistance) to its state-owned enterprises.

5. When a Party provides a response pursuant to paragraph 4, the information it provides must be sufficiently specific to enable the requesting Party to understand the operation of the policy or program and evaluate its effects or potential effects on trade or investment between the Parties. The Party responding to a request shall ensure that the response that it provides contains the following information:

    (a) the form of the non-commercial assistance provided under the policy or program, for example, grant or loan;

    (b) the names of the government agencies, state enterprises, or state-owned enterprises providing the non-commercial assistance or equity capital and the names of the state-owned enterprises that have received or are eligible to receive the non-commercial assistance;

(c) the legal basis and policy objective of the policy or program providing for the non-commercial assistance or equity infusion;

(d) with respect to goods, the amount per unit of the non-commercial assistance or, in cases if it is not possible to provide a per unit amount, the total amount of or the annual amount budgeted for the non-commercial assistance, indicating, if possible, the average amount per unit in the previous year;

(e) with respect to services, the total amount of or the annual amount budgeted for the non-commercial assistance, indicating, if possible, the total amount in the previous year;

(f) with respect to policies or programs providing for non-commercial assistance in the form of loans or loan guarantees, the amount of the loan or amount of the loan guaranteed, interest rates, and fees charged;

(g) with respect to policies or programs providing for non-commercial assistance in the form of the provision of goods or the supply of services, the prices charged, if any, for those goods and services;

(h) with respect to policies or programs for the provision of equity capital, the amount invested, the number and a description of the shares received, and any assessment of the enterprise's financial health and prospects that is conducted with respect to the underlying investment decision;

(i) duration of the policy or program or any other time-limits attached to it; and

(j) statistical data permitting an assessment of the effects of the non-commercial assistance on trade or investment between the Parties.

6. In response to a request made pursuant to paragraph 4, if a Party considers that it has not adopted or does not maintain any policies or programs referred to in paragraph 4, it shall promptly provide a reasoned explanation of this in writing to the requesting Party.

7. If any relevant points in paragraph 5 have not been addressed in the written response, that Party shall provide a reasoned explanation of this in the written response.

8. The Parties recognize that the provision of information under paragraphs 5 and 7 does not prejudge the legal status of the assistance that was the subject of the request under paragraph 4 or the effects of that assistance under this Agreement.

9. When a Party responds to a request for information under this Article, and informs the requesting Party that it considers certain information to be confidential, the Party shall provide a reasoned explanation for its determination. The requesting Party shall not disclose this information without the prior consent of the Party that provided it. To the maximum extent possible under its law, the Party should not consider the amount of the financial contribution associated with the non-commercial assistance or equity capital to be confidential.

Article 22.11:   Technical Cooperation

The Parties shall, if appropriate and subject to available resources, engage in mutually decided upon technical cooperation activities, including:

(a) exchanging information regarding Parties' experiences in improving the corporate governance and operation of their state-owned enterprises;

(b) sharing best practices on policy approaches to ensure a level playing field between state-owned and privately owned enterprises, including policies related to competitive neutrality; and

(c) organizing international seminars, workshops or any other appropriate forum for sharing technical information and expertise related to the governance and operations of state-owned enterprises.

Article 22.12:   Committee   on   State-Owned   Enterprises   and Designated Monopolies

1. The Parties hereby establish a Committee on State-owned Enterprises and Designated Monopolies (SOE Committee), composed of government representatives of each Party.

2. The SOE Committee's functions include:

(a) reviewing and considering the operation and implementation of this Chapter;

(b) at a Party's request, consulting on a matter arising under this Chapter;

(c) developing cooperative efforts, as appropriate, to promote the principles underlying the disciplines contained in this Chapter in the free trade area and to contribute to the development of similar disciplines in other regional and multilateral institutions in which two or more Parties participate; and

(d) undertaking other activities as the SOE Committee may decide.

3. The SOE Committee shall meet within one year after the date of entry into force of this Agreement, and at least annually thereafter, unless the Parties decide otherwise.

Article 22.13:   Exceptions

1.   Nothing in Article 22.4 (Non-Discriminatory Treatment and Commercial Considerations) or Article 22.6 (Non-Commercial Assistance) shall be construed to:

(a)   prevent the adoption or enforcement by a Party of measures to respond temporarily to a national or global economic emergency; or

(b)   apply to a state-owned enterprise with respect to which a Party has adopted or enforced measures on a temporary basis in response to a national or global economic emergency, for the duration of that emergency.

2.   Article 22.4.1 (Non-Discriminatory Treatment and Commercial Considerations) does not apply to the supply of financial services by a state-owned enterprise pursuant to a government mandate if that supply of financial services:

(a)   supports exports or imports, provided that these services are:

(i)   not intended to displace commercial financing, or

(ii)   offered on terms no more favorable than those that could be obtained for comparable financial services in the commercial market;[26]

(b)   supports private investment outside the territory of the Party, provided that these services are:

(i)   not intended to displace commercial financing, or

(ii)   offered on terms no more favorable than those that could be obtained for comparable financial services in the commercial market; or

(c)   is offered on terms consistent with the Arrangement, provided that it falls within the scope of the Arrangement.

3.   The supply of financial services by a state-owned enterprise pursuant to a government mandate shall be deemed not to give rise to adverse effects under Article 22.6.4(b) (Non-Commercial Assistance) or Article 22.6.5(b), or under Article 22.6.4(c) or Article 22.6.5(c) if the Party in which the financial service is supplied requires a local presence in order to supply those services, if that supply of financial services:[27]

---

[26]   In circumstances in which no comparable financial services are offered in the commercial market: (a) for the purposes of paragraphs 2(a)(ii), 2(b)(ii), 3(a)(ii), and 3(b)(ii), the state-owned enterprise may rely as necessary on available evidence to establish a benchmark of the terms on which such services would be offered in the commercial market; and (b) for the purposes of paragraphs 2(a)(i), 2(b)(i), 3(a)(i), and 3(b)(i), the supply of the financial services is deemed not to be intended to displace commercial financing.

[27]   For the purposes of this paragraph, in cases where the Party in which the financial service is supplied requires a local presence in order to supply those services, the supply of the financial services identified in this paragraph through an enterprise that is a covered investment shall be deemed to not give rise to adverse effects.

(a) supports exports or imports, provided that these services are:

    (i) not intended to displace commercial financing, or

    (ii) offered on terms no more favorable than those that could be obtained for comparable financial services in the commercial market;

(b) supports private investment outside the territory of the Party, provided that these services are:

    (i) not intended to displace commercial financing, or

    (ii) offered on terms no more favorable than those that could be obtained for comparable financial services in the commercial market; or

(c) is offered on terms consistent with the Arrangement, provided that it falls within the scope of the Arrangement.

4. Article 22.6 (Non-Commercial Assistance) does not apply with respect to an enterprise located outside the territory of a Party over which a state-owned enterprise of that Party has assumed temporary ownership as a consequence of foreclosure or a similar action in connection with defaulted debt, or payment of an insurance claim by the state-owned enterprise, associated with the supply of the financial services referred to in paragraphs 2 and 3, provided that any support the Party, a state enterprise, or state-owned enterprise of the Party provides to the enterprise during the period of temporary ownership is provided in order to recoup the state-owned enterprise's investment in accordance with a restructuring or liquidation plan that will result in the ultimate divestiture from the enterprise.

5. Article 22.4 (Non-Discriminatory Treatment and Commercial Considerations), Article 22.6 (Non-Commercial Assistance), Article 22.10 (Transparency), and Article 22.12 (Committee on State-Owned Enterprises and Designated Monopolies) do not apply with respect to a state-owned enterprise or designated monopoly if in any one of the three previous consecutive fiscal years, the annual revenue derived from the commercial activities of the state-owned enterprise or designated monopoly was less than a threshold amount which shall be calculated in accordance with Annex 22-A (Threshold Calculation).[28]

Article 22.14:   Further Negotiations

Within six months of the date of entry into force of this Agreement, the Parties shall begin further negotiations so as to extend the application of the disciplines in this Chapter in accordance with Annex 22-C (Further Negotiations).

---

[28] When a Party invokes this exception during consultations under Article 31.4 (Consultations), the consulting Parties should exchange and discuss available evidence concerning the annual revenue of the state-owned enterprise or the designated monopoly derived from the commercial activities during the three previous consecutive fiscal years in an effort to resolve during the consultations period any disagreement regarding the application of this exception.

Article 22.15:   Process for Developing Information

Annex 22-B (Process for Developing Information Concerning State-Owned Enterprises and Designated Monopolies) applies in any dispute under Chapter 31 (Dispute Settlement) regarding a Party's conformity with Article 22.4 (Non-Discriminatory Treatment and Commercial Considerations) or Article 22.6 (Non-Commercial Assistance).

ANNEX 22-A   THRESHOLD CALCULATION

1.   On the date of entry into force of this Agreement, the threshold referred to in Article 22.13.5 (Exceptions) shall be 175 million Special Drawing Rights (SDRs).

2.   The amount of the threshold shall be adjusted at three-year intervals with each adjustment taking effect on 1 January. The first adjustment must take place on the first 1 January following the entry into force of this Agreement, in accordance with the formula set out in this Annex.

3.   The threshold shall be adjusted for changes in general price levels using a composite SDR inflation rate, calculated as a weighted sum of cumulative per cent changes in the Gross Domestic Product (GDP) deflators of SDR component currencies over the three-year period ending 30 June of the year prior to the adjustment taking effect * * *.

4.   Each Party shall convert the threshold into national currency terms where the conversion rates are the average of monthly values of that Party's national currency in SDR terms over the three-year period to 30 June of the year before the threshold is to take effect. Each Party shall notify the other Parties of their applicable threshold in their respective national currencies.

5.   For the purposes of this Chapter, all data shall be drawn from the International Monetary Fund's *International Financial Statistics* database.

6.   The Parties shall consult if a major change in a national currency *vis-à-vis* the SDR were to create a significant problem with regard to the application of this Chapter.

ANNEX 22-B   PROCESS   FOR   DEVELOPING   INFORMATION CONCERNING STATE-OWNED ENTERPRISES AND DESIGNATED MONOPOLIES

1.   If a panel has been established pursuant to Chapter 31 (Dispute Settlement) to examine a complaint arising under Article 22.4 (Non-Discriminatory Treatment and Commercial Considerations) or Article 22.6 (Non-Commercial Assistance), the disputing Parties may exchange written questions and responses, as set forth in paragraphs 2, 3, and 4, to obtain information relevant to the complaint that is not otherwise readily available.

2.   A disputing Party (questioning Party) may provide written questions to another disputing Party (answering Party) within 15 days of the date the panel is established. The answering Party shall provide its

responses to the questions to the questioning Party within 30 days of the date it receives the questions.

3. The questioning Party may provide any follow-up written questions to the answering Party within 15 days of the date it receives the responses to the initial questions. The answering Party shall provide its responses to the follow-up questions to the questioning Party within 30 days of the date it receives the follow-up questions.

4. If the questioning Party considers that the answering Party has failed to cooperate in the information-gathering process under this Annex, the questioning Party shall inform the panel and the answering Party in writing within 30 days of the date the responses to the questioning Party's final questions are due, and provide the basis for its view. The panel shall afford the answering Party an opportunity to reply in writing.

5. A disputing Party that provides written questions or responses to another disputing Party pursuant to the procedures set out in this Annex shall, on the same day, provide the questions or answers to the panel. In the event that a panel has not yet been composed, each disputing Party shall, upon the composition of the panel, promptly provide the panel with any questions or responses it has provided to the other disputing Party.

6. The answering Party may designate information in its responses as confidential information in accordance with the procedures set out in the Rules of Procedure established under Article 30.2.1 (e) (Functions of the Commission) or other rules of procedure agreed to by the disputing Parties.

7. The time periods in paragraphs 2, 3, and 4 may be modified upon agreement of the disputing Parties or approval by the panel.

8. In determining whether a disputing Party has failed to cooperate in the information-gathering process, the panel shall take into account the reasonableness of the questions and the efforts the answering Party has made to respond to the questions in a cooperative and timely manner.

9. In making findings of fact and its initial report, the panel should draw adverse inferences from instances of non-cooperation by a disputing Party in the information-gathering process.

10. The panel may deviate from the time period set out in Chapter 31 (Dispute Settlement) for the issuance of the initial report if necessary to accommodate the information-gathering process.

11. The panel may seek additional information from a disputing Party that was not provided to the panel through the information-gathering process if the panel considers the information necessary to resolve the dispute. However, the panel shall not request additional information to complete the record if the information would support a Party's position and the absence of that information in the record is the result of that Party's non-cooperation in the information-gathering process.

ANNEX 22-C FURTHER NEGOTIATIONS

Within six months of the date of entry into force of this Agreement, the Parties shall begin further negotiations so as to extend the application of:

(a) the obligations in this Chapter to the activities of state-owned enterprises that are owned or controlled by a sub-central level of government, and designated monopolies designated by a sub-central level of government, if these obligations are listed in Annex 22-D (Application to Sub-Central State-Owned Enterprises and Designated Monopolies); and

(b) the disciplines of Article 22.6 (Non-Commercial Assistance) and Article 22.7 (Adverse Effects) to address effects caused in a market of a non-Party through the supply of services by a state-owned enterprise.

The Parties shall meet on a quarterly basis, and shall endeavor to conclude these further negotiations within three years after entry into force of this Agreement.

ANNEX 22-D APPLICATION TO SUB-CENTRAL STATE-OWNED ENTERPRISES AND DESIGNATED MONOPOLIES

Pursuant to Article 22.9.2 (Party-Specific Annexes), the following provisions do not apply with respect to a state-owned enterprise owned or controlled by a sub-central level of government or a designated monopoly designated by a sub-central level of government:[29]

(a) For Canada:

(i) Article 22.4.1(a) (Non-Discriminatory Treatment and Commercial Considerations),

(ii) Article 22.4.1(b) (Non-Discriminatory Treatment and Commercial Considerations), with respect to purchases of a good or service,

(iii) Article 22.4.1(c)(i) (Non-Discriminatory Treatment and Commercial Considerations),

(iv) Article 22.4.2 (Non-Discriminatory Treatment and Commercial Considerations), with respect to designated monopolies designated by a sub-central level of government,

(v) Article 22.5.2 (Courts and Administrative Bodies), with respect to administrative regulatory bodies established or maintained by a sub-central level of government,

(vi) Article 22.6.1, Article 22.6.2, and Article 22.6.3 (Non-commercial Assistance),

---

[29] For the purposes of this Annex, "sub-central level of government" means the regional level of government and the local level of government of a Party.

(vii) Article 22.6.4(a) (Non-commercial Assistance) and Article 22.6.5(a) (Non-commercial Assistance), with respect to the production and sale of a good in competition with a like good produced and sold by a covered investment,

(viii) Article 22.6.4(b) and (c) (Non-commercial Assistance) and Article 22.6.5(b) and (c) (Non-commercial Assistance),

(ix) Article 22.6.6 (Non-Commercial Assistance),

(x) Article 22.10.1 (Transparency), and

(xi) Article 22.10.4 (Transparency) with respect to a policy or program adopted or maintained by a sub-central level of government.

(b) For Mexico:

(i) Article 22.4.1(a) (Non-Discriminatory Treatment and Commercial Considerations),

(ii) Article 22.4.1(b) (Non-Discriminatory Treatment and Commercial Considerations), with respect to purchases of a good or service,

(iii) Article 22.4.1(c)(i) (Non-Discriminatory Treatment and Commercial Considerations),

(iv) Article 22.4.2 (Non-Discriminatory Treatment and Commercial Considerations), with respect to designated monopolies designated by a sub-central level of government,

(v) Article 22.5.2 (Courts and Administrative Bodies), with respect to administrative regulatory bodies established or maintained by a sub-central level of government,

(vi) Article 22.6.1, Article 22.6.2, and Article 22.6.3 (Non-Commercial Assistance),

(vii) Article 22.6.4(a) (Non-Commercial Assistance) and Article 22.6.5(a) (Non-Commercial Assistance), with respect to the production and sale of a good in competition with a like good produced and sold by a covered investment in the territory of Mexico,

(viii) Article 22.6.4(b) and (c) (Non-Commercial Assistance) and Article 22.6.5(b) and (c) (Non-Commercial Assistance), and

(ix) Article 22.10.1 (Transparency).

(c) For the United States:

(i) Article 22.4.1(a) (Non-Discriminatory Treatment and Commercial Considerations),

(ii)   Article 22.4.1(b) (Non-Discriminatory Treatment and Commercial Considerations), with respect to purchases of a good or service,

(iii) Article 22.4.1(c)(i) (Non-Discriminatory Treatment and Commercial Considerations),

(iv)   Article 22.4.2 (Non-Discriminatory Treatment and Commercial Considerations), with respect to designated monopolies designated by a sub-central level of government,

(v)   Article 22.5.2 (Courts and Administrative Bodies), with respect to administrative regulatory bodies established or maintained by a sub-central level of government,

(vi)   Article 22.6.1, Article 22.6.2, and Article 22.6.3 (Non-Commercial Assistance),

(vii) Article 22.6.4(a) (Non-Commercial Assistance) and Article 22.6.5(a) (Non-Commercial Assistance), with respect to the production and sale of a good in competition with a like good produced and sold by a covered investment in the territory of the United States,

(viii) Article 22.6.4(b) and (c) (Non-Commercial Assistance) and Article 22.6.5(b) and (c) (Non-Commercial Assistance), and

(ix)   Article 22.10.1 (Transparency).

ANNEX 22-E SPECIAL PURPOSE VEHICLES OF STATE PRODUCTIVE ENTERPRISES

1.   This Chapter applies to the State Productive Enterprises ("SPEs") referred to in the Decree amending the Political Constitution of the United Mexican States on December 20, 2013 as published in the Official Gazette ("the Decree"), and to the subsidiaries and affiliates of the SPEs.

2.   This Chapter does not apply to Special Purpose Vehicles, with the exception of paragraphs 3 and 4 of this Annex. For the purposes of this Annex, the term "Special Purpose Vehicle" means a private legal entity established by the SPEs, their subsidiaries and affiliates, as a result of a venture with private investors, created to perform, develop, own, or operate a specific project.[30]

3.   Mexico shall ensure that Special Purpose Vehicles:

   (a)   be established as a result of competitive processes under the laws and regulations of Mexico applicable to the SPE;

---

[30]   For greater certainty, any contractual agreement, including a joint venture or partnership, between an SPE and another enterprise, which does not constitute an entity constituted or organized under applicable law, is not an "enterprise" as defined in Article 1.4 (General Definitions) or a "monopoly" as defined in Article 22.1 (Definitions), and falls outside the scope of this Chapter.

(b)   pursue the performance of commercial activities on equal circumstances and conditions available to competitors on a level playing field, with no intention of displacing or impeding competitors from the relevant market;

(c)   be aimed at generating economic value and profitability under commercial conditions;

(d)   follow generally accepted accounting principles and generally accepted international corporate governance rules such as the G20/OECD Principles of Corporate Governance;

(e)   act in accordance with Article 22.4 (Non-Discriminatory Treatment and Commercial Considerations), Article 22.5 (Courts and Administrative Bodies), and Article 22.6 (Non-Commercial Assistance).

4.   Mexico shall provide information concerning the SPV and any assistance provided to it, to the extent reasonably available, if it is requested in accordance with the relevant provisions of Article 22.10 (Transparency).

ANNEX 22-F NON-COMMERCIAL ASSISTANCE TO CERTAIN STATE PRODUCTIVE ENTERPRISES

1.   With respect to Article 22.6.1, Article 22.6.2, and Article 22.6.3 (Non-Commercial Assistance), Mexico or its state enterprises or state-owned enterprises may provide non-commercial assistance to an SPE referred to in Annex 22-E (Special Purpose Vehicles of State Productive Enterprises) (including the SPE's affiliates and subsidiaries) that is primarily engaged in oil and gas activities, in circumstances that jeopardize the continued viability of the recipient enterprise, and for the sole purpose of enabling the enterprise to return to viability and fulfil its mandate under the Decree and Article 25 of Mexico's Constitution (*Constitución Política de los Estados Unidos Mexicanos*).

2.   At the request of a Party, the Parties may consult regarding whether this Annex should be amended or eliminated. This Annex should only be maintained if Mexico considers that circumstances continue to require the possibility of providing non-commercial assistance to an SPE to ensure its continued viability.

CHAPTER 23   LABOR

Article 23.1:   Definitions

For the purposes of this Chapter:

ILO Declaration on Rights at Work means the International Labor Organization (ILO)

Declaration on Fundamental Principles and Rights at Work and its Follow-Up (1998);

Labor laws means statutes and regulations, or provisions of statutes and regulations, of a Party that are directly related to the following internationally recognized labor rights:

(a) freedom of association and the effective recognition of the right to collective bargaining;

(b) the elimination of all forms of forced or compulsory labor;

(c) the effective abolition of child labor, a prohibition on the worst forms of child labor, and other labor protections for children and minors;

(d) the elimination of discrimination in respect of employment and occupation; and

(e) acceptable conditions of work with respect to minimum wages,[1] hours of work, and occupational safety and health;

Statutes and regulations and statutes or regulations means:[2]

(a) for Mexico, Acts of Congress or regulations and provisions promulgated pursuant to Acts of Congress and, for the purposes of this Chapter, includes the Constitution of the United Mexican States; and

(b) for the United States, Acts of Congress or regulations promulgated pursuant to Acts of Congress and, for the purposes of this Chapter, includes the Constitution of the United States.

Article 23.2:   Statement of Shared Commitments

1. The Parties affirm their obligations as members of the ILO, including those stated in the ILO Declaration on Rights at Work and the ILO *Declaration on Social Justice for a Fair Globalization (2008)*.

2. The Parties recognize the important role of workers' and employers' organizations in protecting internationally recognized labor rights.

3. The Parties also recognize the goal of trading only in goods produced in compliance with this Chapter.

Article 23.3:   Labor Rights

1. Each Party shall adopt and maintain in its statutes and regulations, and practices thereunder, the following rights, as stated in the ILO Declaration on Rights at Work:[3],[4]

---

[1] For greater certainty, a Party's labor laws regarding "acceptable conditions of work with respect to minimum wages" include requirements under that Party's labor laws to provide wage-related benefit payments to, or on behalf of, workers, such as those for profit sharing, bonuses, retirement, and healthcare.

[2] For greater certainty, for each Party setting out a definition, which has a federal form of government, its definition provides coverage for substantially all workers.

[3] The obligations set out in this Article, as they relate to the ILO, refer only to the ILO Declaration on Rights at Work

[4] To establish a violation of an obligation under paragraphs 1 or 2, a Party must demonstrate that the other Party has failed to adopt or maintain a statute, regulation, or practice in a manner affecting trade or investment between the Parties. For greater

(a)   freedom of association[5] and the effective recognition of the right to collective bargaining;[6]

(b)   the elimination of all forms of forced or compulsory labor;

(c)   the effective abolition of child labor and, for the purposes of this Agreement, a prohibition on the worst forms of child labor; and

(d)   the elimination of discrimination in respect of employment and occupation.

2.   Each Party shall adopt and maintain statutes and regulations, and practices thereunder, governing acceptable conditions of work with respect to minimum wages, hours of work, and occupational safety and health.

Article 23.4:   Non-Derogation

The Parties recognize that it is inappropriate to encourage trade or investment by weakening or reducing the protections afforded in each Party's labor laws. Accordingly, no Party shall waive or otherwise derogate from, or offer to waive or otherwise derogate from, its statutes or regulations:

(a)   implementing Article 23.3.1 (Labor Rights), if the waiver or derogation would be inconsistent with a right set out in that paragraph; or

(b)   implementing Article 23.3.1 or Article 23.3.2 (Labor Rights), if the waiver or derogation would weaken or reduce adherence to a right set out in Article 23.3.1 (Labor Rights), or to a condition of work referred to in Article 23.3.2 (Labor Rights), in a special trade or customs area, such as an export processing zone or foreign trade zone, in the Party's territory;

in a manner affecting trade or investment between the Parties.[7]

---

certainty, a failure is "in a manner affecting trade or investment between the Parties" if it involves:

   (i) a person or industry that produces a good or supplies a service traded between the Parties or has an investment in the territory of the Party that has failed to comply with this obligation; or (ii) a person or industry that produces a good or supplies a service that competes in the territory of a Party with a good or a service of another Party.

[5]   For greater certainty, the right to strike is linked to the right to freedom of association, which cannot be realized without protecting the right to strike.

[6]   Annex 23-A (Worker Representation in Collective Bargaining in Mexico) sets out obligations with regard to worker representation in collective bargaining.

[7]   For greater certainty, a waiver or derogation is "in a manner affecting trade or investment between the Parties" if it involves: (i) a person or industry that produces a good or supplies a service traded between the Parties or has an investment in the territory of the Party that has failed to comply with this obligation; or (ii) a person or industry that produces a good or supplies a service that competes in the territory of a Party with a good or a service of another Party.

Article 23.5:   Enforcement of Labor Laws

1. No Party shall fail to effectively enforce its labor laws through a sustained or recurring course of action or inaction[8] in a manner affecting trade or investment between the Parties[9] after the date of entry into force of this Agreement.

2. Each Party shall promote compliance with its labor laws through appropriate government action, such as by:

    (a) appointing and training inspectors;

    (b) monitoring compliance and investigating suspected violations, including through unannounced on-site inspections, and giving due consideration to requests to investigate an alleged violation of its labor laws;

    (c) seeking assurances of voluntary compliance;

    (d) requiring record keeping and reporting;

    (e) encouraging the establishment of labor-management committees to address labor regulation of the workplace;

    (f) providing or encouraging mediation, conciliation, and arbitration services;

    (g) initiating, in a timely manner, proceedings to seek appropriate sanctions or remedies for violations of its labor laws; and

    (h) implementing remedies and sanctions imposed for noncompliance with its labor laws, including timely collection of fines and reinstatement of workers.

3. If a Party fails to comply with an obligation under this Chapter, a decision made by that Party on the provision of enforcement resources shall not excuse that failure. Each Party retains the right to exercise reasonable enforcement discretion and to make *bona fide* decisions with regard to the allocation of enforcement resources between labor enforcement activities among the fundamental labor rights and acceptable conditions of work enumerated in Article 23.3.1 and Article 23.3.2 (Labor Rights), provided that the exercise of that discretion, and those decisions, are not inconsistent with its obligations under this Chapter.

---

[8]   For greater certainty, a "sustained or recurring course of action or inaction" is "sustained" if the course of action or inaction is consistent or ongoing, and is "recurring" if the course of action or inaction occurs periodically or repeatedly and when the occurrences are related or the same in nature. A course of action or inaction does not include an isolated instance or case.

[9]   For greater certainty, a "course of action or inaction" is "in a manner affecting trade or investment between the Parties" if the course involves: (i) a person or industry that produces a good or supplies a service traded between the Parties or has an investment in the territory of the Party that has failed to comply with this obligation; or (ii) a person or industry that produces a good or supplies a service that competes in the territory of a Party with a good or a service of another Party.

4.   Nothing in this Chapter shall be construed to empower a Party's authorities to undertake labor law enforcement activities in the territory of another Party.

Article 23.6:   Forced or Compulsory Labor

1.   The Parties recognize the goal of eliminating all forms of forced or compulsory labor, including forced or compulsory child labor. Accordingly, each Party shall prohibit, through measures it considers appropriate, the importation of goods into its territory from other sources produced in whole or in part by forced or compulsory labor, including forced or compulsory child labor.[10]

2.   To assist in the implementation of paragraph 1, the Parties shall establish cooperation for the identification and movement of goods produced by forced labor as provided for under Article 23.12.5(c) (Cooperation).

Article 23.7:   Violence Against Workers

The Parties recognize that workers and labor organizations must be able to exercise the rights set out in Article 23.3 (Labor Rights) in a climate that is free from violence, threats, and intimidation, and the imperative of governments to effectively address incidents of violence, threats, and intimidation against workers. Accordingly, no Party shall fail to address cases of violence or threats of violence against workers, directly related to exercising or attempting to exercise the rights set out in Article 23.3 (Labor Rights), through a sustained or recurring course of action or inaction[11] in a manner affecting trade or investment between the Parties.[12]

Article 23.8:   Migrant Workers

The Parties recognize the vulnerability of migrant workers with respect to labor protections. Accordingly, in implementing Article 23.3 (Labor Rights), each Party shall ensure that migrant workers are protected under its labor laws, whether they are nationals or non-nationals of the Party.

Article 23.9:   Discrimination in the Workplace

The Parties recognize the goal of eliminating discrimination in employment and occupation, and support the goal of promoting equality of women in the

---

[10]   For greater certainty, nothing in this Article authorizes a Party to take measures that would be inconsistent with its obligations under this Agreement, the WTO Agreement, or other international trade agreements.

[11]   For greater certainty, a "sustained or recurring course of action or inaction" is "sustained" if the course of action or inaction is consistent or ongoing, and is "recurring" if the course of action or inaction occurs periodically or repeatedly and when the occurrences are related or the same in nature. A course of action or inaction does not include an isolated instance or case.

[12]   For greater certainty, a "course of action or inaction" is "in a manner affecting trade or investment between the Parties" if the course involves: (i) a person or industry that produces a good or supplies a service traded between the Parties or has an investment in the territory of the Party that has failed to comply with this obligation; or (ii) a person or industry that produces a good or supplies a service that competes in the territory of a Party with a good or a service of another Party.

workplace. Accordingly, each Party shall implement policies[13] that it considers appropriate to protect workers against employment discrimination on the basis of sex (including with regard to sexual harassment), pregnancy, sexual orientation, gender identity, and caregiving responsibilities; provide job-protected leave for birth or adoption of a child and care of family members; and protect against wage discrimination.

Article 23.10:   Public Awareness and Procedural Guarantees

1. Each Party shall promote public awareness of its labor laws, including by ensuring that information related to its labor laws and enforcement and compliance procedures is publicly available.

2. Each Party shall ensure that a person with a recognized interest under its law in a particular matter has appropriate access to tribunals for the enforcement of its labor laws. These tribunals may include administrative tribunals, quasi-judicial tribunals, judicial tribunals, or labor tribunals, as provided for in each Party's law.

3. Each Party shall ensure that proceedings before these tribunals for the enforcement of its labor laws:

    (a)   are fair, equitable and transparent;

    (b)   comply with due process of law;

    (c)   do not entail unreasonable fees or time limits or unwarranted delay; and

    (d)   that any hearings in these proceedings are open to the public, except where the administration of justice otherwise requires, and in accordance with its applicable laws.

4. Each Party shall ensure that:

    (a)   the parties to these proceedings are entitled to support or defend their respective positions, including by presenting information or evidence; and

    (b)   final decisions on the merits of the case:

    (i)   are based on information or evidence in respect of which the parties were offered the opportunity to be heard,

        (ii)   state the reasons on which they are based, and

        (iii) are available in writing without undue delay to the parties to the proceedings and, consistent with its law, to the public.

---

[13] The United States' existing federal agency policies regarding the hiring of federal workers are sufficient to fulfill the obligations set forth in this Article. The Article thus requires no additional action on the part of the United States, including any amendments to Title VII of the Civil Rights Act of 1964, in order for the United States to be in compliance with the obligations set forth in this Article.

5.   Each Party shall provide, as appropriate, that parties to these proceedings have the right to seek review and, if warranted, correction of decisions issued in these proceedings.

6.   Each Party shall ensure that tribunals that conduct or review these proceedings are impartial and independent.

7.   Each Party shall ensure that the parties to these proceedings have access to remedies under its law for the effective enforcement of their rights under its labor laws and that these remedies are executed in a timely manner.

8.   Each Party shall provide procedures to effectively enforce the final decisions of its tribunals in these proceedings.

9.   For greater certainty, and without prejudice to whether a tribunal's decision is inconsistent with a Party's obligations under this Chapter, nothing in this Chapter shall be construed to require a tribunal of a Party to reopen a decision that it has made in a particular matter.

10.   Each Party shall ensure that other types of proceedings within its labor bodies for the implementation of its labor laws:

     (a)   are fair and equitable;

     (b)   are conducted by officials who meet appropriate guarantees of impartiality;

     (c)   do not entail unreasonable fees or time limits or unwarranted delay; and

     (d)   document and communicate decisions to persons directly affected by these proceedings.

Article 23.11:   Public Submissions

1.   Each Party, through its contact point designated under Article 23.15 (Contact Points), shall provide for the receipt and consideration of written submissions from persons of a Party on matters related to this Chapter in accordance with its domestic procedures. Each Party shall make readily accessible and publicly available its procedures, including timelines, for the receipt and consideration of written submissions.

2.   Each Party shall:

     (a)   consider matters raised by the submission and provide a timely response to the submitter, including in writing as appropriate; and

     (b)   make the submission and the results of its consideration available to the other Parties and the public, as appropriate, in a timely manner.

3.   A Party may request from the person or organization that made the submission additional information that is necessary to consider the substance of the submission.

Article 23.12:   Cooperation

1. The Parties recognize the importance of cooperation as a mechanism for effective implementation of this Chapter, to enhance opportunities to improve labor standards, and to further advance common commitments regarding labor matters, including the principles and rights stated in the ILO Declaration on Rights at Work.

2. The Parties may, commensurate with the availability of resources, cooperate through:

    (a) exchanging of information and sharing of best practices on issues of common interest, including through seminars, workshops, and online fora;

    (b) study trips, visits, and research studies to document and study policies and practices;

    (c) collaborative research and development related to best practices in subjects of mutual interest;

    (d) specific exchanges of technical expertise and assistance, as appropriate; and

    (e) other forms as the Parties may decide.

3. In undertaking cooperative activities, the Parties shall consider each Party's priorities and complementarity with initiatives in existence, with the aim to achieve mutual benefits and measurable labor outcomes.

4. Each Party shall invite the views and, as appropriate, participation of its stakeholders, including worker and employer representatives, in identifying potential areas for cooperation and undertaking cooperative activities.

5. The Parties may develop cooperative activities in the following areas:

    (a) labor laws and practices, including the promotion and effective implementation of the principles and rights as stated in the ILO Declaration on Rights at Work;

    (b) labor laws and practices related to compliance with ILO Convention No. 182 *Concerning the Prohibition and Immediate Action for the Elimination of the Worst Forms of Child Labor*;

    (c) identification and movement of goods produced by forced labor;

    (d) combatting forced labor and human trafficking, including on fishing vessels;

    (e) addressing violence against workers, including for trade union activity;

    (f) occupational safety and health, including the prevention of occupational injuries and illnesses;

(g)   institutional capacity of labor administrative and judicial bodies;

(h)   labor inspectorates and inspection systems, including methods and training to improve the level and efficiency of labor law enforcement, strengthen labor inspection systems, and help ensure compliance with labor laws;

(i)   remuneration systems and mechanisms for compliance with labor laws pertaining to hours of work, minimum wages and overtime, and employment conditions;

(j)   addressing gender-related issues in the field of labor and employment, including:

  (i)   elimination of discrimination on the basis of sex in respect of employment, occupation, and wages,

  (ii)   developing analytical and enforcement tools related to equal pay for equal work or work of equal value,

  (iii)   promotion of labor practices that integrate and retain women in the job market, and building the capacity and skills of women workers, including on workplace challenges and in collective bargaining,

  (iv)   consideration of gender issues related to occupational safety and health and other workplace practices, including advancement of child care, nursing mothers, and related policies and programs, and in the prevention of occupational injuries and illnesses, and

  (v)   prevention of gender-based workplace violence and harassment;

(k)   promotion of productivity, innovation, competitiveness, training and human capital development in workplaces, particularly in respect to SMEs;

(l)   addressing the opportunities of a diverse workforce, including:

  (i)   promotion of equality and elimination of employment discrimination in the areas of age, disability, race, ethnicity, religion, sexual orientation, gender identity, and other characteristics not related to merit or the requirements of employment, and

  (ii)   promotion of equality, elimination of employment discrimination, and protection of migrant workers and other vulnerable workers, including low-waged, casual, or temporary workers;

(m)   collection and use of labor statistics, indicators, methods, and procedures, including on the basis of sex;

(n)   social protection issues, including workers' compensation in case of occupational injury or illness, pension systems, and employment assistance schemes;

(o)   labor relations, including forms of cooperation and dispute resolution to improve labor relations among workers, employers, and governments;

(p)   apprenticeship programs;

(q)   social dialogue, including tripartite consultation and partnership;

(r)   with respect to labor relations in multi-national enterprises, promoting information sharing and dialogue related to conditions of employment by enterprises operating in two or more Parties with representative worker organizations in each of the cooperating Parties; and

(s)   other areas as the Parties may decide.

6.   The Parties may establish cooperative arrangements with the ILO or other international and regional organizations to draw on their expertise and resources to further the purposes of this Chapter.

Article 23.13:   Cooperative Labor Dialogue

1.   A Party may request dialogue with another Party on any matter arising under this Chapter at any time by delivering a written request to the contact point that the other Party has designated under Article 23.15 (Contact Points).

2.   The requesting Party shall include information that is specific and sufficient to enable the receiving Party to respond, including identification of the matter at issue, an indication of the basis of the request under this Chapter and, when relevant, how trade or investment between the Parties is affected.

3.   Unless the requesting and receiving Parties (the dialoguing Parties) decide otherwise, dialogue must commence within 30 days of a Party's receipt of a request for dialogue. The dialoguing Parties shall engage in dialogue in good faith. As part of the dialogue, the dialoguing Parties shall provide a means for receiving and considering the views of interested persons on the matter.

4.   Dialogue may be held in person or by any technological means available to the dialoguing Parties.

5.   The dialoguing Parties shall address all the issues raised in the request. If the dialoguing Parties resolve the matter, they shall document the outcome, including, if appropriate, specific steps and timelines that they have decided upon. The dialoguing Parties shall make the outcome available to the public, unless they decide otherwise.

6.   In developing an outcome pursuant to paragraph 5, the dialoguing Parties should consider all available options and may jointly decide on a course of action they consider appropriate, including:

(a) the development and implementation of an action plan in a form that they find satisfactory, which may include specific and verifiable steps, such as on labor inspection, investigation, or compliance action, and appropriate timeframes;

(b) the independent verification of compliance or implementation by individuals or entities, such as the ILO, chosen by the dialoguing Parties; and

(c) appropriate incentives, such as cooperative programs and capacity building, to encourage or assist the dialoguing Parties to identify and address labor matters.

Article 23.14: Labor Council

1. The Parties hereby establish a Labor Council composed of senior governmental representatives at the ministerial or other level from trade and labor ministries, as designated by each Party.

2. The Labor Council shall meet within one year of the date of entry into force of this Agreement and thereafter every two years, unless the Parties decide otherwise.

3. The Labor Council may consider any matter within the scope of this Chapter and perform other functions as the Parties may decide.

4. In conducting its activities, including meetings, the Labor Council shall provide a means for receiving and considering the views of interested persons on matters related to this Chapter. If practicable, meetings will include a public session or other means for Council members to meet with the public to discuss matters relating to the implementation of this Chapter.

5. During the fifth year after the date of entry into force of this Agreement, or as otherwise decided by the Parties, the Labor Council shall review the operation and effectiveness of this Chapter and thereafter may undertake subsequent reviews as decided by the Parties.

6. Labor Council decisions and reports shall be made by consensus and be made publicly available, unless the Council decides otherwise.

7. The Labor Council shall issue a joint summary report or statement on its work at the end of each Council meeting.

Article 23.15: Contact Points

1. Each Party shall designate, within 60 days of the date of entry into force of this Agreement, an office or official within its labor ministry or equivalent entity as a contact point to address matters related to this Chapter. Each Party shall notify the other Parties in writing promptly in the event of a change to its contact point.

2. The contact points shall:

(a) facilitate regular communication and coordination between the Parties, including responding to requests for information and providing sufficient information to enable a full examination of matters related to this Chapter;

(b)   assist the Labor Council;

(c)   report to the Labor Council, as appropriate;

(d)   act as a channel for communication with the public in their respective territories; and

(e)   work together, including with other appropriate agencies of their governments, to develop and implement cooperative activities, guided by the priorities of the Labor Council, areas of cooperation identified in Article 23.12.5 (Cooperation), and the needs of the Parties.

3.   Contact points may communicate and coordinate activities in person or through electronic or other means of communication.

4.   Each Party's contact point, in carrying out its responsibilities under this Chapter, shall regularly consult and coordinate with its trade ministry.

Article 23.16:   Public Engagement

Each Party shall establish or maintain, and consult with, a national labor consultative or advisory body or similar mechanism, for members of its public, including representatives of its labor and business organizations, to provide views on matters regarding this Chapter.

Article 23.17:   Labor Consultations

1.   The Parties shall make every effort through cooperation and dialogue to arrive at a mutually satisfactory resolution of any matter arising under this Chapter.

2.   A Party (the requesting Party) may request labor consultations with another Party (the responding Party) regarding any matter arising under this Chapter by delivering a written request to the responding Party's contact point. The requesting Party shall include information that is specific and sufficient to enable the responding Party to respond, including identification of the matter at issue and an indication of the legal basis of the request under this Chapter.

3.   A third Party that considers it has a substantial interest in the matter may participate in the labor consultations by notifying the other Parties (the consulting Parties) in writing through their respective contact points, no later than seven days after the date of delivery of the request for labor consultations. The third Party shall include in its notice an explanation of its substantial interest in the matter.

4.   Unless the consulting Parties decide otherwise, they shall enter into labor consultations no later than 30 days after the date of delivery of the request.

5.   The consulting Parties shall make every effort to arrive at a mutually satisfactory resolution of the matter through labor consultations, which

may include appropriate cooperative activities. The consulting Parties may request advice from independent experts chosen by the consulting Parties to assist them.

6. *Ministerial Labor Consultations*: If the consulting Parties have failed to resolve the matter, a consulting Party may request that the relevant Ministers or their designees of the consulting Parties convene to consider the matter at issue by delivering a written request to the other consulting Party through its contact point. The Ministers of the consulting Parties shall convene promptly after the date of receipt of the request, and shall seek to resolve the matter, including, if appropriate, by consulting independent experts chosen by the consulting Parties to assist them, and having recourse to procedures such as good offices, conciliation, or mediation.

7. If the consulting Parties are able to resolve the matter, they shall document the outcome, including, if appropriate, specific steps and timelines decided upon. The consulting Parties shall make the outcome available to the other Party and to the public, unless they decide otherwise.

8. If the consulting Parties fail to resolve the matter within 30 days after the date of receipt of a request for Labor consultations under paragraph 2, or any other period as the consulting Parties may agree, the requesting Party may request a meeting of the Commission pursuant to Article 31.5 (Commission, Good Offices, Conciliation, and Mediation) and thereafter request the establishment of a panel under Article 31.6 (Establishment of a Panel).

9. Labor consultations shall be confidential and without prejudice to the rights of a Party in another proceeding.

10. Labor consultations pursuant to this Article may be held in person or by any technological means available to the consulting Parties. If the labor consultations are held in person, they must be held in the capital of the Party to which the request for labor consultations was made, unless the consulting Parties decide otherwise.

11. In labor consultations under this Article, a consulting Party may request another consulting Party to make available personnel of its government agencies or other regulatory bodies who have expertise in the matter at issue.

12. No Party shall have recourse to dispute settlement under Chapter 31 (Dispute Settlement) for a matter arising under this Chapter without first seeking to resolve the matter in accordance with this Article.

13. A Party may have recourse to labor consultations under this Article without prejudice to the commencement or continuation of Cooperative Labor Dialogue under Article 23.13 (Cooperative Labor Dialogue).

ANNEX 23-A WORKER REPRESENTATION IN COLLECTIVE BARGAINING IN MEXICO

1. Mexico shall adopt and maintain the measures set out in paragraph 2, which are necessary for the effective recognition of the right to collective bargaining, given that the Mexican government incoming in December 2018 has confirmed that each of these provisions is within the scope of the mandate provided to the government by the people of Mexico in the elections.

2. Mexico shall:

    (a) Provide in its labor laws the right of workers to engage in concerted activities for collective bargaining or protection and to organize, form, and join the union of their choice, and prohibit, in its labor laws, employer domination or interference in union activities, discrimination, or coercion against workers for union activity or support, and refusal to bargain collectively with the duly recognized union.

    (b) Establish and maintain independent and impartial bodies to register union elections and resolve disputes relating to collective bargaining agreements and the recognition of unions, through legislation establishing:

        (i)   an independent entity for conciliation and registration of unions and collective bargaining agreements, and

        (ii) independent Labor Courts for the adjudication of labor disputes.

The legislation shall provide for the independent entity for conciliation and registration to have the authority to issue appropriate sanctions against those who violate its orders. The legislation also shall provide that all decisions of the independent entity are subject to appeal to independent courts, and that officials of the independent entity who delay, obstruct, or influence the outcome of any registration process in favor or against a party involved, will be subject to sanctions under Article 48 of the Federal Labor Law (*Ley Federal del Trabajo*) and Articles 49, 52, 57, 58, 61, 62 and other applicable provisions of the General Law of Administrative Responsibilities (*Ley General de Responsabilidades Administrativas*).

    (c) Provide in its labor laws, through legislation in accordance with Mexico's Constitution (*Constitución Política de los Estados Unidos Mexicanos*), for an effective system to verify that elections of union leaders are carried out through a personal, free, and secret vote of union members.

    (d) Provide in its labor laws that union representation challenges are carried out by the Labor Courts through a secret ballot vote, and are not subject to delays due to procedural challenges or objections, including by establishing clear time limits and procedures, consistent with Mexico's obligations under Article 23.10.3(c) and Article 23.10.10(c) (Public Awareness and Procedural Guarantees).

(e)   Adopt legislation in accordance with Mexico's Constitution (*Constitución Política de los Estados Unidos Mexicanos*), requiring:

     (i)   verification by the independent entity that collective bargaining agreements meet legal requirements related to worker support in order for them to be registered and take legal effect; and

     (ii)   for the registration of an initial collective bargaining agreement, majority support, through exercise of a personal, free, and secret vote of workers covered by the agreement and effective verification by the independent entity, through, as justified under the circumstances, documentary evidence (physical or electronic), direct consultations with workers, or on-site inspections that:

         (A)   the worksite is operational,

         (B)   a copy of the collective bargaining agreement was made readily accessible to individual workers prior to the vote, and

         (C)   a majority of workers covered by the agreement demonstrated support for the agreement through a personal, free, and secret vote.

(f)   Adopt legislation in accordance with Mexico's Constitution (*Constitución Política de los Estados Unidos Mexicanos*), which provides that, in future revisions to address salary and work conditions, all existing collective bargaining agreements shall include a requirement for majority support, through the exercise of personal, free, and secret vote of the workers covered by those collective bargaining agreements.

The legislation shall also provide that all existing collective bargaining agreements shall be revised at least once during the four years after the legislation goes into effect. The legislation shall not imply the termination of any existing collective bargaining agreements as a consequence of the expiration of the term indicated in this paragraph, as long as a majority of the workers covered by the collective bargaining agreement demonstrate support for such agreement through a personal, free, and secret vote.

The legislation shall also provide that the revisions must be deposited with the independent entity. In order to deposit the future revisions, the independent entity shall effectively verify, through, as justified under the circumstances, documentary evidence (physical or electronic), direct consultation with workers, or on-site inspections that:

     (i)   a copy of the revised collective bargaining agreement was made readily accessible to the workers covered by the collective bargaining agreement prior to the vote, and

> (ii) a majority of workers covered by the revised agreement demonstrated support for that agreement through a personal, free, and secret vote.

(g) Provide in its labor laws:

> (i) that each collective bargaining agreement negotiated by a union and a union's governing documents are made available in a readily accessible form to all workers covered by the collective bargaining agreement, through enforcement of Mexico's General Law on Transparency and Access to Public Information (*Ley General de Transparencia y Acceso a la Información Pública*), and

> (ii) for the establishment of a centralized website that provides public access to all collective bargaining agreements in force and that is operated by an independent entity that is in charge of the registration of collective bargaining agreements.

3. It is the expectation of the Parties that Mexico shall adopt legislation described above before January 1, 2019. It is further understood that entry into force of this Agreement may be delayed until such legislation becomes effective.

CHAPTER 24   ENVIRONMENT

Article 24.1:   Definitions

For the purposes of this Chapter:

Environmental law means a statute or regulation of a Party, or provision thereof, including any that implements the Party's obligations under a multilateral environmental agreement, the primary purpose of which is the protection of the environment, or the prevention of a danger to human life or health, through:

(a) the prevention, abatement, or control of the release, discharge, or emission of pollutants or environmental contaminants;

(b) the control of environmentally hazardous or toxic chemicals, substances, materials, or wastes, and the dissemination of information related thereto; or

(c) the protection or conservation of wild flora or fauna,[1] including endangered species, their habitat, and specially protected natural areas,[2]

but does not include a statute or regulation, or provision thereof, directly related to worker safety or health, nor any statute or regulation, or provision

---

[1]   The Parties recognize that "protection or conservation" may include the protection or conservation of biological diversity.

[2]   For the purposes of this Chapter, the term "specially protected natural areas" means those areas as defined by the Party in its law.

thereof, the primary purpose of which is managing the subsistence or aboriginal harvesting of natural resources; and

Statute or regulation means:

(a) for Canada, an Act of the Parliament of Canada or regulation made under an Act of the Parliament of Canada that is enforceable by action of the central level of government;

(b) for Mexico, an Act of Congress or regulation promulgated pursuant to an Act of Congress that is enforceable by action of the federal level of government; and

(c) for the United States, an Act of Congress or regulation promulgated pursuant to an Act of Congress that is enforceable by action of the central level of government.

Article 24.2:   Scope and Objectives

1. The Parties recognize that a healthy environment is an integral element of sustainable development and recognize the contribution that trade makes to sustainable development.

2. The objectives of this Chapter are to promote mutually supportive trade and environmental policies and practices; promote high levels of environmental protection and effective enforcement of environmental laws; and enhance the capacities of the Parties to address trade-related environmental issues, including through cooperation, in the furtherance of sustainable development.

3. Taking account of their respective national priorities and circumstances, the Parties recognize that enhanced cooperation to protect and conserve the environment and the sustainable use and management of their natural resources brings benefits that can contribute to sustainable development, strengthen their environmental governance, support implementation of international environmental agreements to which they are a party, and complement the objectives of this Agreement.

4. The Parties recognize that the environment plays an important role in the economic, social, and cultural well-being of indigenous peoples and local communities, and acknowledge the importance of engaging with these groups in the long-term conservation of the environment.

5. The Parties further recognize that it is inappropriate to establish or use their environmental laws or other measures in a manner which would constitute a disguised restriction on trade or investment between the Parties.

Article 24.3:   Levels of Protection

1. The Parties recognize the sovereign right of each Party to establish its own levels of domestic environmental protection and its own environmental priorities, and to establish, adopt, or modify its environmental laws and policies accordingly.

2.   Each Party shall strive to ensure that its environmental laws and policies provide for, and encourage, high levels of environmental protection, and shall strive to continue to improve its respective levels of environmental protection.

Article 24.4:   Enforcement of Environmental Laws

1.   No Party shall fail to effectively enforce its environmental laws through a sustained or recurring course of action or inaction[3] in a manner affecting trade or investment between the Parties,[4] after the date of entry into force of this Agreement.

2.   The Parties recognize that each Party retains the right to exercise discretion and to make decisions regarding: (a) investigatory, prosecutorial, regulatory, and compliance matters; and (b) the allocation of environmental enforcement resources with respect to other environmental laws determined to have higher priorities. Accordingly, the Parties understand that with respect to the enforcement of environmental laws a Party is in compliance with paragraph 1 if a course of action or inaction reflects a reasonable exercise of that discretion, or results from a *bona fide* decision regarding the allocation of those resources in accordance with priorities for enforcement of its environmental laws.

3.   Without prejudice to Article 24.3.1 (Levels of Protection), the Parties recognize that it is inappropriate to encourage trade or investment by weakening or reducing the protection afforded in their respective environmental laws. Accordingly, a Party shall not waive or otherwise derogate from, or offer to waive or otherwise derogate from, its environmental laws in a manner that weakens or reduces the protection afforded in those laws in order to encourage trade or investment between the Parties.

4.   Nothing in this Chapter shall be construed to empower a Party's authorities to undertake environmental law enforcement activities in the territory of another Party.

Article 24.5:   Public Information and Participation

1.   Each Party shall promote public awareness of its environmental laws and policies, including enforcement and compliance procedures, by ensuring that relevant information is available to the public.

---

[3]   For greater certainty, a "sustained or recurring course of action or inaction" is "sustained" if the course of action or inaction is consistent or ongoing, and is "recurring" if the course of action or inaction occurs periodically or repeatedly and when the occurrences are related or the same in nature. A course of action or inaction does not include an isolated instance or case.

[4]   For greater certainty, a "course of action or inaction" is "in a manner affecting trade or investment between the Parties" if the course involves: (i) a person or industry that produces a good or supplies a service traded between the Parties or has an investment in the territory of the Party that has failed to comply with this obligation; or (ii) a person or industry that produces a good or supplies a service that competes in the territory of a Party with a good or a service of another Party.

2.   Each Party shall provide for the receipt and consideration of written questions or comments from persons of that Party regarding its implementation of this Chapter. Each Party shall respond in a timely manner to these questions or comments in writing and in accordance with domestic procedures, and make the questions or comments and the responses available to the public, for example by posting on an appropriate public website.

3.   Each Party shall make use of existing, or establish new, consultative mechanisms, for example national advisory committees, to seek views on matters related to the implementation of this Chapter. These mechanisms may include persons with relevant experience, as appropriate, including experience in business, natural resource conservation and management, or other environmental matters.

Article 24.6:   Procedural Matters

1.   Each Party shall ensure that an interested person may request that the Party's competent authorities investigate alleged violations of its environmental laws, and that the competent authorities give those requests due consideration, in accordance with its law.

2.   Each Party shall ensure that persons with a recognized interest under its law in a particular matter have appropriate access to administrative, quasi-judicial, or judicial proceedings for the enforcement of the Party's environmental laws, and the right to seek appropriate remedies or sanctions for violations of those laws.

3.   Each Party shall ensure that administrative, quasi-judicial, or judicial proceedings for the enforcement of the Party's environmental laws are available under its law and that those proceedings are fair, equitable, transparent, and comply with due process of law, including the opportunity for parties to the proceedings to support or defend their respective positions. The Parties recognize that these proceedings should not be unnecessarily complicated nor entail unreasonable fees or time limits.

4.   Each Party shall provide that any hearings in these proceedings are conducted by impartial and independent persons who do not have an interest in the outcome of the matter. Hearings in these proceedings shall be open to the public, except when the administration of justice otherwise requires, and in accordance with its applicable law.

5.   Each Party shall provide that final decisions on the merits of the case in these proceedings are:

   (a)   in writing and if appropriate state the reasons on which the decisions are based;

   (b)   made available without undue delay to the parties to the proceedings and, in accordance with its law, to the public; and

   (c)   based on information or evidence presented by the parties or other sources, in accordance with its law.

6. Each Party shall also provide, as appropriate, that parties to these proceedings have the right, in accordance with its law, to seek review and, if warranted, correction or redetermination, of final decisions in such proceedings.

7. Each Party shall provide appropriate sanctions or remedies for violations of its environmental laws and shall ensure that it takes account of relevant factors when establishing sanctions or remedies, which may include the nature and gravity of the violation, damage to the environment, and any economic benefit derived by the violator.

Article 24.7: Environmental Impact Assessment

1. Each Party shall maintain appropriate procedures for assessing the environmental impacts of proposed projects that are subject to an action by that Party's central level of government that may cause significant effects on the environment with a view to avoiding, minimizing, or mitigating adverse effects.

2. Each Party shall ensure that such procedures provide for the disclosure of information to the public and, in accordance with its law, allow for public participation.

Article 24.8: Multilateral Environmental Agreements

1. The Parties recognize the important role that multilateral environmental agreements can play in protecting the environment and as a response of the international community to global or regional environmental problems.

2. Each Party affirms its commitment to implement the multilateral environmental agreements to which it is a party.

3. The Parties commit to consult and cooperate as appropriate with respect to environmental issues of mutual interest, in particular trade-related issues, pertaining to relevant multilateral environmental agreements. This includes exchanging information on the implementation of multilateral environmental agreements to which a Party is party; ongoing negotiations of new multilateral environmental agreements; and, each Party's respective views on becoming a party to additional multilateral environmental agreements.

Article 24.9: Protection of the Ozone Layer

1. The Parties recognize that emissions of certain substances can significantly deplete and otherwise modify the ozone layer in a manner that is likely to result in adverse effects on human health and the

environment. Accordingly, each Party shall take measures to control the production and consumption of, and trade in, such substances.[5],[6],[7]

2.   The Parties also recognize the importance of public participation and consultation, in accordance with their respective law or policy, in the development and implementation of measures concerning the protection of the ozone layer. Each Party shall make publicly available appropriate information about its programs and activities, including cooperative programs that are related to ozone layer protection.

3.   Consistent with Article 24.25 (Environmental Cooperation), the Parties shall cooperate to address matters of mutual interest related to ozone-depleting substances. Cooperation may include, exchanging information and experiences in areas related to:

(a)   environmentally friendly alternatives to ozone-depleting substances;

(b)   refrigerant management practices, policies and programs;

(c)   methodologies for stratospheric ozone measurements; and

(d)   combatting illegal trade in ozone-depleting substances.

---

[5]   For greater certainty, this provision pertains to ozone-depleting substances controlled by the *Montreal Protocol on Substances that Deplete the Ozone Layer*, done at Montreal, September 16, 1987 (Montreal Protocol), and any existing and future amendments to the Montreal Protocol to which the Parties are parties.

[6]   A Party shall be deemed in compliance with this provision if it maintains the measure or measures listed in Annex 24-A implementing its obligations under the Montreal Protocol or adopts any subsequent measure or measures that provide an equivalent or higher level of environmental protection as the measure or measures listed.

[7]   If compliance with this provision is not established pursuant to footnote 6, to establish a violation of this provision, a Party must demonstrate that the other Party has failed to take measures to control the production and consumption of, and trade in, certain substances that can significantly deplete and otherwise modify the ozone layer in a manner that is likely to result in adverse effects on human health and the environment, in a manner affecting trade or investment between the Parties. For greater certainty, a failure is "in a manner affecting trade or investment between the Parties" if it involves: (i) a person or industry that produces a good or supplies a service traded between the Parties or has an investment in the territory of the Party that has failed to comply with this obligation; or (ii) a person or industry that produces a good or supplies a service that competes in the territory of a Party with a good or a service of another Party.

Article 24.10: Protection of the Marine Environment from Ship Pollution

1. The Parties recognize the importance of protecting and preserving the marine environment. To that end, each Party shall take measures to prevent the pollution of the marine environment from ships.[8],[9],[10]

2. The Parties also recognize the importance of public participation and consultation, in accordance with their respective law or policy, in the development and implementation of measures to prevent the pollution of the marine environment from ships. Each Party shall make publicly available appropriate information about its programs and activities, including cooperative programs, that are related to the prevention of pollution of the marine environment from ships.

3. Consistent with Article 24.25 (Environmental Cooperation), the Parties shall cooperate to address matters of mutual interest with respect to pollution of the marine environment from ships. Areas of cooperation may include:

    (a) accidental pollution from ships;

    (b) pollution from routine operations of ships;

    (c) deliberate pollution from ships;

    (d) development of technologies to minimise ship-generated waste;

    (e) emissions from ships;

    (f) adequacy of port waste reception facilities;

    (g) increased protection in special geographic areas; and

---

[8] For greater certainty, this provision pertains to pollution regulated by the *International Convention for the Prevention of Pollution from Ships*, done at London, November 2, 1973, as modified by the *Protocol of 1978 relating to the International Convention for the Prevention of Pollution from Ships*, done at London, February 17, 1978, and the *Protocol of 1997 to Amend the International Convention for the Prevention of Pollution from Ships, 1973 as Modified by the Protocol of 1978 relating thereto*, done at London, September 26, 1997 (MARPOL Convention), and any existing and future amendments to the MARPOL Convention, to which the Parties are parties.

[9] A Party shall be deemed in compliance with this provision if it maintains the measure or measures listed in Annex 24-B implementing its obligations under MARPOL Convention, or adopts any subsequent measure or measures that provide an equivalent or higher level of environmental protection as the measure or measures listed.

[10] If compliance with this provision is not established pursuant to footnote 9, to establish a violation of this provision, a Party must demonstrate that the other Party has failed to take measures to prevent the pollution of the marine environment from ships in a manner affecting trade or investment between the Parties. For greater certainty, a failure is "in a manner affecting trade or investment between the Parties" if it involves: (i) a person or industry that produces a good or supplies a service traded between the Parties or has an investment in the territory of the Party that has failed to comply with this obligation; or (ii) a person or industry that produces a good or supplies a service that competes in the territory of a Party with a good or a service of another Party.

(h)   enforcement measures including notifications to flag States and, as appropriate, by port States.

Article 24.11:   Air Quality

1.   The Parties recognize that air pollution is a serious threat to public health, ecosystem integrity, and sustainable development and contributes to other environmental problems; and note that reducing certain air pollutants can provide multiple benefits.

2.   Noting that air pollution can travel long distances and impact each Party's ability to achieve its air quality objectives, the Parties recognize the importance of reducing both domestic and transboundary air pollution, and that cooperation can be beneficial in achieving these objectives.

3.   The Parties further recognize the importance of public participation and transparency in the development and implementation of measures to prevent air pollution and in ensuring access to air quality data. Accordingly, each Party shall make air quality data and information about its associated programs and activities publicly available in accordance with Article 32.7 (Disclosure of Information), and shall seek to ensure these data and information are easily accessible and understandable to the public.

4.   The Parties recognize the value of harmonizing air quality monitoring methodologies.

5.   The Parties recognize the importance of international agreements and other efforts to improve air quality and control air pollutants, including those that have the potential for long-range transport.

6.   Recognizing that the Parties have made significant progress to address air pollution in other fora, and consistent with Article 24.25 (Environmental Cooperation), the Parties shall cooperate to address matters of mutual interest with respect to air quality. Cooperation may include exchanging information and experiences in areas related to:

(a)   ambient air quality planning;

(b)   modeling and monitoring, including spatial distribution of main sources and their emissions;

(c)   measurement and inventory methodologies for air quality and emissions' measurements; and reduction, control, and prevention technologies and practices.

Article 24.12:   Marine Litter

1.   The Parties recognize the importance of taking action to prevent and reduce marine litter, including plastic litter and microplastics, in order to preserve human health and marine and coastal ecosystems, prevent the loss of biodiversity, and mitigate marine litter's costs and impacts.

2.   Recognizing the global nature of the challenge of marine litter, each Party shall take measures to prevent and reduce marine litter.

3. Recognizing that the Parties are taking action to address marine litter in other fora, consistent with Article 24.25 (Environmental Cooperation), the Parties shall cooperate to address matters of mutual interest with respect to combatting marine litter, such as addressing land and sea-based pollution, promoting waste management infrastructure, and advancing efforts related to abandoned, lost, or otherwise discarded fishing gear.

Article 24.13: Corporate Social Responsibility and Responsible Business Conduct

1. The Parties recognize the importance of promoting corporate social responsibility and responsible business conduct.

2. Each Party shall encourage enterprises organized or constituted under its laws, or operating in its territory, to adopt and implement voluntary best practices of corporate social responsibility that are related to the environment, such as those in internationally recognized standards and guidelines that have been endorsed or are supported by that Party, to strengthen coherence between economic and environmental objectives.

Article 24.14: Voluntary Mechanisms to Enhance Environmental Performance

1. The Parties recognize that flexible, voluntary mechanisms, for example, voluntary auditing and reporting, market-based mechanisms, voluntary sharing of information and expertise, and public-private partnerships, can contribute to the achievement and maintenance of high levels of environmental protection and complement domestic regulatory measures. The Parties also recognize that those mechanisms should be designed in a manner that maximizes their environmental benefits and avoids the creation of unnecessary barriers to trade.

2. Therefore, in accordance with its laws, regulations, or policies and to the extent it considers appropriate, each Party shall encourage:

    (a) the use of flexible, voluntary mechanisms to protect the environment and natural resources, such as through the conservation and sustainable use of those resources, in its territory; and

    (b) its relevant authorities, private sector, non-governmental organizations, and other interested persons involved in the development of criteria used to evaluate environmental performance, with respect to these voluntary mechanisms, to continue to develop and improve such criteria.

3. Further, if private sector entities or non-governmental organizations develop voluntary mechanisms for the promotion of products based on their environmental qualities, each Party should encourage those entities and organizations to develop voluntary mechanisms that, among other things:

    (a) are truthful, are not misleading, and take into account relevant scientific and technical information;

(b)   are based on relevant international standards, recommendations, guidelines, or best practices, as appropriate;

(c)   promote competition and innovation; and

(d)   do not treat a product less favorably on the basis of origin.

Article 24.15:   Trade and Biodiversity

1.   The Parties recognize the importance of conservation and sustainable use of biological diversity, as well as the ecosystem services it provides, and their key role in achieving sustainable development.

2.   Accordingly, each Party shall promote and encourage the conservation and sustainable use of biological diversity, in accordance with its law or policy. The Parties recognize the importance of respecting, preserving, and maintaining knowledge and practices of indigenous peoples and local communities embodying traditional lifestyles that contribute to the conservation and sustainable use of biological diversity.

3.   The Parties recognize the importance of facilitating access to genetic resources within their respective national jurisdictions, consistent with each Party's international obligations. The Parties further recognize that some Parties may require, through national measures, prior informed consent to access such genetic resources in accordance with national measures and, if access is granted, the establishment of mutually agreed terms, including with respect to sharing of benefits from the use of such genetic resources, between users and providers.

4.   The Parties also recognize the importance of public participation and consultation, in accordance with their respective law or policy, in the development and implementation of measures concerning the conservation and sustainable use of biological diversity. Each Party shall make publicly available information about its programs and activities, including cooperative programs, related to the conservation and sustainable use of biological diversity.

5.   Consistent with Article 24.25 (Environmental Cooperation), the Parties shall cooperate to address matters of mutual interest. Cooperation may include exchanging information and experiences in areas related to:

(a)   the conservation and sustainable use of biological diversity;

(b)   mainstreaming conservation and sustainable use of biological diversity across relevant sectors;

(c)   the protection and maintenance of ecosystems and ecosystem services; and

(d)   access to genetic resources and the sharing of benefits arising from their utilization.

Article 24.16:   Invasive Alien Species

1.   The Parties recognize that the movement of terrestrial and aquatic invasive alien species across borders through trade-related pathways

can adversely affect the environment, economic activities and development, and human health. The Parties also recognize that the prevention, detection, control and, when possible, eradication, of invasive alien species are critical strategies for managing those adverse impacts.

2.   Accordingly, the Environment Committee established under Article 24.26.2 (Environment Committee and Contact Points) shall coordinate with the Committee on Sanitary and Phytosanitary Measures established under Article 9.17 (Committee on Sanitary and Phytosanitary Measures) to identify cooperative opportunities to share information and management experiences on the movement, prevention, detection, control, and eradication of invasive alien species, with a view to enhancing efforts to assess and address the risks and adverse impacts of invasive alien species.

Article 24.17:   Marine Wild Capture Fisheries[11]

1.   The Parties acknowledge their role as major consumers, producers, and traders of fisheries products and the importance of the marine fisheries sectors to their development and to the livelihoods of fishing communities, including those engaged in artisanal, small scale, and indigenous fisheries. The Parties also recognize the need for individual and collective action within international fora to address the urgent resource problems resulting from overfishing and unsustainable utilization of fisheries resources.

2.   Accordingly, the Parties recognize the importance of taking measures aimed at the conservation and the sustainable management of fisheries and the contribution of those measures to providing environmental, economic and social opportunities for present and future generations. The Parties also recognize the importance of promoting and facilitating trade in sustainably managed and legally harvested fish and fish products, while ensuring that trade in these products is not subject to unnecessary or unjustifiable barriers to trade, given the negative effect that such barriers can have on the well-being of their communities who depend upon the fishing industry for their livelihood.

3.   If an importing Party is considering adopting trade restrictive measures for fish or fish products in order to protect or conserve fish or other marine species, the Parties recognize the importance that these measures be:[12]

(a)   based on the best scientific evidence available, as applicable, that establish a connection between the products affected by the measure and the species being protected or conserved;

---

[11]   For greater certainty, Article 24.17 (Marine Wild Capture Fisheries), Article 24.18 (Sustainable Fisheries Management), Article 24.19 (Conservation of Marine Species), Article 24.20 (Fisheries Subsidies), and Article 24.21 (Illegal, Unreported, and Unregulated (IUU) Fishing) do not apply with respect to aquaculture.

[12]   For greater certainty, this paragraph is without prejudice to any rights or obligations of the Parties relating to the adoption or application of trade restrictive measures for fish and fish products.

(b)   tailored to the conservation objective; and

(c)   implemented after the importing Party has:

    (i)   consulted with the exporting Party, in an effort to resolve the issue cooperatively; and

    (ii)   provided a reasonable opportunity for the exporting Party to take appropriate measures to address the issue.

4.   The Parties shall cooperate with, and, if appropriate, in, Regional Fisheries Management Organizations (RFMOs) and Regional Fisheries Management Arrangements (RFMAs), in which the Parties are members, observers, or cooperating non-contracting parties, with the aim of achieving good governance, including by advocating for science-based decisions and compliance with those decisions in these organizations and arrangements.

Article 24.18:   Sustainable Fisheries Management

1.   In furtherance of the objectives of conservation and sustainable management, each Party shall seek to operate a fisheries management system that regulates marine wild capture fishing and that is designed to:

(a)   prevent overfishing and overcapacity through appropriate measures, such as limited entry, time, area, and other restrictions, and the setting and enforcement of catch or effort limits;

(b)   reduce bycatch of non-target species and juveniles, including through the regulation of, and implementation of measures associated with, fishing gear and methods that result in bycatch and the regulation of fishing in areas where bycatch is likely to occur;

(c)   promote the recovery of overfished stocks for all marine fisheries in which that Party's persons conduct fishing activities; and

(d)   protect marine habitat by cooperating, as appropriate, to prevent or mitigate significant adverse impacts from fishing.

2.   Further, each Party shall adopt or maintain measures:

(a)   to prevent the use of poisons and explosives for the purpose of commercial fish harvesting; and

(b)   designed to prohibit the practice of shark finning.

3.   Each Party shall base its fisheries management system on the best scientific evidence available and on internationally recognized best practices for fisheries management and conservation as reflected in the

relevant provisions of international instruments aimed at ensuring the sustainable use and conservation of marine species.[13]

Article 24.19: Conservation of Marine Species

1. Each Party shall promote the long-term conservation of sharks, sea turtles, seabirds, and marine mammals through the implementation and effective enforcement of conservation and management measures. Such measures shall include:

    (a) studies and assessments of the impact of fisheries operations on non-target species and their marine habitats, including through collection of species-specific data for non-target species and estimates of their bycatch, as appropriate;

    (b) gear-specific studies and data collection on impacts on non-target species and on the efficacy of management measures to reduce those adverse impacts, as appropriate;

    (c) measures to avoid, mitigate, or reduce bycatch of non-target species in fisheries, including appropriate measures pertaining to the use of bycatch mitigation devices, modified gear, or other techniques to reduce the impact of fishing operations on these species; and

    (d) cooperation on national and regional bycatch reduction measures, such as measures applicable to commercial fisheries pertaining to transboundary stocks of non-target species.

2. Each Party shall prohibit the killing of great whales[14] for commercial purposes unless authorized in a multilateral treaty to which the Party is a party.[15]

---

[13] These instruments include, as they may apply, the *United Nations Convention on Law of the Sea* (UNCLOS), done at Montego Bay, December 10, 1982; the *United Nations Agreement for the Implementation of the Provisions of the United Nations Convention on the Law of the Sea of December 1982 relating to the Conservation and Management of Straddling Fish Stocks and Highly Migratory Fish Stocks*, done at New York, December 4, 1995 (UN Fish Stocks Agreement); the *FAO Code of Conduct for Responsible Fisheries*; the *1993 FAO Agreement to Promote Compliance with International Conservation and Management Measures by Fishing Vessels on the High Seas* (Compliance Agreement), done at Rome, November 24, 1993; the *2001 FAO International Plan of Action to Prevent, Deter, and Eliminate Illegal, Unreported, and Unregulated Fishing* (IUU IPOA), adopted at Rome, February 23, 2001; and the *2009 Agreement on Port State Measures to Prevent, Deter, and Eliminate IUU Fishing* (Port State Measures Agreement), done at Rome, November 22, 2009.

[14] Great whales are the following 16 species: *Balaena mysticetus, Eubalaena glacialis, Eubalaena japonica, Eubalaena australis, Eschrichtius robustus, Balaenoptera musculus, Balaenoptera physalus, Balaenoptera borealis, Balaenoptera edeni, Balaenoptera acutorostrata, Balaenoptera bonaerensis, Balaenoptera omurai, Megaptera novaeangliae, Caperea marginata, Physeter macrocephalus,* and *Hyperoodon ampullatus.*

[15] For greater certainty, the Parties understand that paragraph 2 does not apply to whaling by indigenous peoples in accordance with a Party's law, including for Canada the legal obligations recognized and affirmed by section 35 of the *Constitution*

Article 24.20:   Fisheries Subsidies

(a)   The Parties recognize that the implementation of a fisheries management system that is designed to prevent overfishing and overcapacity and to promote the recovery of overfished stocks must include the control, reduction, and eventual elimination of all subsidies that contribute to overfishing and overcapacity. To that end, no Party shall grant or maintain any of the following subsidies[16] within the meaning of Article 1.1 of the SCM Agreement that are specific within the meaning of Article 2 of the SCM Agreement: subsidies provided to a fishing vessel[17] or operator[18] while listed for IUU fishing[19] by the flag State, the subsidizing Party, or a relevant RFMO or RFMA in accordance with the rules and procedures of that organization or arrangement and in conformity with international law; and

(b)   subsidies for fishing[20] that negatively affect[21] fish stocks that are in an overfished[22] condition.

2.   Subsidy programs that are established by a Party before the date of entry into force of this Agreement and are subsidies referred to in paragraph 1(b) shall be brought into conformity with paragraph 1 as soon as possible and no later than three years after the date of entry into force of this Agreement.

3.   In relation to subsidies that are not prohibited by paragraph 1, and taking into consideration a Party's social and developmental priorities,

---

Act, 1982 or those set out in self-government agreements between a central or regional level of government and indigenous peoples.

[16]   For the purposes of this Article, a subsidy shall be attributable to the Party granting or maintaining it, regardless of the flag of the vessel involved or the application of rules of origin to the fish involved.

[17]   The term "fishing vessel" refers to any vessel, ship, or other type of boat used for, equipped to be used for, or intended to be used for fishing or fishing related activities.

[18]   The term "operator" means the owner of the vessel, or any person onboard, who is in charge of or directs or controls the vessel at the time of the IUU infraction. For greater certainty, the prohibition on the provision of subsidies to operators engaged in IUU fishing applies only to subsidies for fishing or fishing related activities.

[19]   "Illegal, unreported, and unregulated fishing" is to be understood to have the same meaning as paragraph 3 of the IUU IPOA.

[20]   For the purposes of this Article, "fishing" means searching for, attracting, locating, catching, taking, or harvesting fish, or any activity which can reasonably be expected to result in the attracting, locating, catching, taking, or harvesting of fish.

[21]   The negative effect of such subsidies shall be determined based on the best scientific evidence available.

[22]   For the purposes of this Article, a fish stock is overfished if the stock is at such a low level that mortality from fishing needs to be restricted to allow the stock to rebuild to a level that produces maximum sustainable yield or alternative reference points based on the best scientific evidence available. Fish stocks that are recognized as overfished by the national jurisdiction where the fishing is taking place or by a relevant RFMO or RFMA shall also be considered overfished for the purposes of this Article.

each Party shall make best efforts to refrain from introducing new, or extending or enhancing existing, subsidies within the meaning of Article 1.1 of the SCM Agreement, to the extent they are specific within the meaning of Article 2 of the SCM Agreement, that contribute to overfishing or overcapacity.

4.   With a view to achieving the objective of eliminating subsidies that contribute to overfishing and overcapacity, the Parties shall review the disciplines in paragraph 1 at regular meetings of the Environment Committee.

5.   Each Party shall notify the other Parties, within one year of the date of entry into force of this Agreement and every two years thereafter, of any subsidy within the meaning of Article 1.1 of the SCM Agreement that is specific within the meaning of Article 2 of the SCM Agreement, that the Party grants or maintains to persons engaged in fishing or fishing related activities.

6.   These notifications shall cover subsidies provided within the previous two-year period and shall include the information required under Article 25.3 of the SCM Agreement and, to the extent possible, the following information:[23]

(a)   program name;

(b)   legal authority for the program;

(c)   catch data by species in the fishery for which the subsidy is provided;

(d)   status, whether overfished, fully fished, or underfished, of the fish stocks in the fishery for which the subsidy is provided;

(e)   fleet capacity in the fishery for which the subsidy is provided;

(f)   conservation and management measures in place for the relevant fish stock; and

(g)   total imports and exports per species.

7.   Each Party shall also provide, to the extent possible, information in relation to other subsidies that the Party grants or maintains to persons engaged in fishing or fishing related activities that are not covered by paragraph 1, in particular fuel subsidies.

8.   A Party may request additional information from the notifying Party regarding the notifications provided under paragraphs 5 and 6. The notifying Party shall respond to that request as quickly as possible and in a comprehensive manner.

9.   Each Party shall notify the other Parties on an annual basis of any list of vessels and operators identified as having engaged in IUU fishing.

---

[23]   Sharing information and data on existing fisheries subsidy programs does not prejudge their legal status, effects, or nature under the GATT 1994 or the SCM Agreement and is intended to complement WTO data reporting requirements.

10. The Parties shall work in the WTO towards strengthening international rules on the provision of subsidies to the fisheries sector and enhancing transparency of fisheries subsidies.

Article 24.21:   Illegal, Unreported, and Unregulated (IUU) Fishing

1. The Parties recognize the importance of concerted international action to address IUU fishing as reflected in regional and international instruments[24] and shall endeavor to improve cooperation internationally in this regard, including with and through competent international organizations.

2. In support of international efforts to combat IUU fishing and to help deter trade in products from IUU fishing, each Party shall:

   (a) implement port state measures, including through actions consistent with the Port State Measures Agreement;[25]

   (b) support monitoring, control, surveillance, compliance, and enforcement schemes, including by adopting, maintaining, reviewing, or revising, as appropriate, measures to:

      (i) deter vessels flying its flag and, to the extent provided for in each Party's law, its nationals, from engaging in IUU fishing; and

      (ii) address the transshipment at sea of fish caught through IUU fishing or fish products derived from IUU fishing.

   (c) maintain a vessel documentation scheme and promote the use of International Maritime Organization numbers, or comparable unique vessel identifiers, as appropriate, for vessels operating outside of its national jurisdiction, in order to enhance transparency of fleets and traceability of fishing vessels;

   (d) strive to act consistently with relevant conservation and management measures adopted by RFMOs or RFMAs of which it is not a party so as not to undermine those measures;

   (e) endeavor not to undermine catch or trade documentation schemes operated by RFMOs or RFMAs;

   (f) develop and maintain publicly available and easily accessible registry data of fishing vessels flying its flag; promote efforts by non-Parties to develop and maintain publicly available and easily accessible registry data of such vessels flying its flag; and support efforts to complete a Global Record of

---

[24] Regional and international instruments include, among others, and as they may apply, the IUU IPOA, the *2005 Rome Declaration on IUU Fishing*, adopted at Rome, March 12, 2005, the Port State Measures Agreement, as well as instruments established and adopted by RFMOs and RFMAs, as appropriate, that have the competence to establish conservation and management measures.

[25] For greater certainty, this paragraph is without prejudice to a Party's status under the 2009 Port State Measures Agreement.

Fishing Vessels, Refrigerated Transport Vessels, and Supply Vessels; and

(g)   cooperate with other Parties through the exchange of information and best practices to combat trade in products derived from IUU fishing.

3.   Consistent with Article 28.9 (Transparent Development of Regulations), a Party shall, to the extent possible, provide the other Parties the opportunity to comment on proposed measures that are designed to prevent trade in fisheries products derived from IUU fishing.

Article 24.22:   Conservation and Trade

1.   The Parties affirm the importance of combatting the illegal take[26] of, and illegal trade in, wild fauna and flora, and acknowledge that this trade undermines efforts to conserve and sustainably manage those natural resources, has social consequences, distorts legal trade in wild fauna and flora, and reduces the economic and environmental value of these natural resources.

2.   Accordingly, each Party shall adopt, maintain, and implement laws, regulations and any other measures to fulfil its obligations under the *Convention on International Trade in Endangered Species of Wild Fauna and Flora* (CITES) done at Washington, D.C., March 3, 1973.[27],[28],[29]

3.   The Parties commit to promote conservation and to combat the illegal take of, and illegal trade in, wild fauna and flora. To that end, the Parties shall:

(a)   exchange information and experiences on issues of mutual interest related to combatting the illegal take of, and illegal trade in, wild fauna and flora, including combatting illegal logging and associated illegal trade, and promoting the legal trade in associated products;

---

[26]   For the purposes of this Article, the term "take" means captured, killed, or collected and with respect to a plant, also means harvested, cut, logged or removed.

[27]   For the purposes of this Article, a Party's CITES obligations include existing and future amendments to which the Parties are parties and any existing and future reservations or exemptions applicable to the Party. This paragraph only applies if all the Parties are parties to CITES.

[28]   To establish a violation of this paragraph, a Party must demonstrate that the other Party has failed to adopt, maintain, or implement laws, regulations, or other measures to fulfil its obligations under CITES in a manner affecting trade or investment between the Parties. For greater certainty, a failure is "in a manner affecting trade or investment between the Parties" if it involves: (i) a person or industry that produces a good or supplies a service traded between the Parties or has an investment in the territory of the Party that has failed to comply with this obligation; or (ii) a person or industry that produces a good or supplies a service that competes in the territory of a Party with a good or a service of another Party.

[29]   If a Party considers that another Party is failing to comply with its obligations under this paragraph, it shall endeavor, in the first instance, to address the matter through a consultative or other procedure under CITES.

(b)   undertake, as appropriate, joint activities on conservation issues of mutual interest, including through relevant regional and international fora; and

(c)   endeavor to implement, as appropriate, CITES resolutions that aim to protect and conserve species whose survival is threatened by international trade.

4.   Each Party further commits to:

(a)   take appropriate measures to protect and conserve wild fauna and flora that it has identified to be at risk within its territory, including measures to conserve the ecological integrity of specially protected natural areas, for example grasslands and wetlands;

(b)   maintain or strengthen government capacity and institutional frameworks to promote the conservation of wild fauna and flora, and endeavor to enhance public participation and transparency in these institutional frameworks; and

(c)   endeavor to develop and strengthen cooperation and consultation with interested non-governmental entities and other stakeholders in order to enhance implementation of measures to combat the illegal take of, and illegal trade in, wild fauna and flora.

5.   In a further effort to address the illegal take of, and illegal trade in, wild fauna and flora, including parts and products thereof, each Party shall take measures to combat, and cooperate to prevent, the trade of wild fauna and flora that, based on credible evidence,[30] were taken or traded in violation of that Party's law or another applicable law,[31] the primary purpose of which is to conserve, protect, or manage wild fauna or flora. These measures shall include sanctions, penalties, or other effective measures, including administrative measures, that can act as a deterrent to such trade. In addition, each Party shall endeavor to take measures to combat the trade of wild fauna and flora transhipped through its territory that, based on credible evidence, were illegally taken or traded.

6.   The Parties recognize that each Party retains the right to exercise administrative, investigatory, and enforcement discretion in its implementation of paragraph 5, including by taking into account in relation to each situation the strength of the available evidence and the seriousness of the suspected violation. In addition, the Parties recognize that in implementing paragraph 5, each Party retains the right to make

---

[30]   For greater certainty, for the purposes of this paragraph, each Party retains the right to determine what constitutes "credible evidence".

[31]   For greater certainty, "another applicable law" means a law of the jurisdiction where the take or trade occurred and is only relevant to the question of whether the wild fauna and flora has been taken or traded in violation of that law.

decisions regarding the allocation of administrative, investigatory, and enforcement resources.

7.   Further, each Party shall:

   (a)   take measures to enhance the effectiveness of inspections of shipments containing wild fauna and flora, including parts and products thereof, at ports of entry, such as improving targeting; and

   (b)   treat intentional transnational trafficking of wildlife protected under its laws,[32] as a serious crime as defined in the *United Nations Convention on Transnational Organized Crime*.[33]

8.   In order to promote the widest measure of law enforcement cooperation and information sharing between the Parties to combat the illegal take of, and illegal trade in, wild fauna and flora, the Parties shall endeavor to identify opportunities, consistent with their respective law and in accordance with applicable international agreements, to enhance law enforcement cooperation and information sharing, for example by enhancing participation in law enforcement networks, and, as appropriate, establishing new networks with the objective of developing a strong and effective worldwide network.

Article 24.23:   Sustainable Forest Management and Trade

1.   The Parties acknowledge their role as major consumers, producers, and traders of forest products and the importance of a healthy forest sector to provide livelihoods and job opportunities, including for indigenous peoples.

2.   The Parties acknowledge the importance of:

   (a)   the conservation and sustainable management of forests for providing environmental economic, and social benefits for present and future generations;

   (b)   the critical role of forests in providing numerous ecosystem services, including carbon storage, maintaining water quantity and quality, stabilizing soils, and providing habitat for wild fauna and flora; and

   (c)   combatting illegal logging and associated trade.

3.   The Parties recognize that forest products, when sourced from sustainably managed forests, contribute to fulfilling global

---

[32]   For greater certainty, the term "wildlife" is understood to include all species of wild fauna and flora, including animals, timber, and marine species, and their related parts and products. Further, for purposes of this Article, the term "protected" means a CITES-listed species or a species that is listed under a Party's law as endangered, as threatened, or as being at risk within its territory.

[33]   The term "serious crime" is to be understood to have the same meaning as paragraph 2(b) of the *United Nations Convention on Transnational Organized Crime*, done at New York, on November 15, 2000.

environmental objectives, including sustainable development, conservation and sustainable use of resources, and green growth.

4.   Accordingly, each Party commits to:

(a)   maintain or strengthen government capacity and institutional frameworks to promote sustainable forest management; and

(b)   promote trade in legally harvested forest products.

5.   The Parties shall exchange information and cooperate, as appropriate, on initiatives to promote sustainable forest management, including initiatives designed to combat illegal logging and associated trade.

Article 24.24:   Environmental Goods and Services

1.   The Parties recognize the importance of trade and investment in environmental goods and services, including clean technologies, as a means of improving environmental and economic performance, contributing to green growth and jobs, and encouraging sustainable development, while addressing global environmental challenges.

2.   Accordingly, the Parties shall strive to facilitate and promote trade and investment in environmental goods and services.

3.   The Environment Committee shall consider issues identified by a Party related to trade in environmental goods and services, including issues identified as potential non-tariff barriers to that trade. The Parties shall endeavor to address any potential barriers to trade in environmental goods and services that may be identified by a Party, including by working through the Environment Committee and in conjunction with other relevant committees established under this Agreement, as appropriate.

4.   The Parties shall cooperate in international fora on ways to further facilitate and liberalize global trade in environmental goods and services, and may develop cooperative projects on environmental goods and services to address current and future global environmental challenges.

Article 24.25:   Environmental Cooperation

1.   The Parties recognize the importance of cooperation as a mechanism to implement this Chapter, to enhance its benefits, and to strengthen the Parties' joint and individual capacities to protect the environment, and to promote sustainable development as they strengthen their trade and investment relations.

2.   The Parties are committed to expanding their cooperative relationship on environmental matters, recognizing it will help them achieve their shared environmental goals and objectives, including the development and improvement of environmental protection, practices, and technologies.

3.   The Parties are committed to undertaking cooperative environmental activities pursuant to the Agreement on Environmental Cooperation

among the Governments of Canada, the United Mexican States, and the United States of America (ECA) signed by the Parties, including activities related to implementation of this Chapter. Activities that the Parties undertake pursuant to the Environmental Cooperation Agreement will be coordinated and reviewed by the Commission for Environmental Cooperation as provided for in the ECA.[34]

Article 24.26:   Environment Committee and Contact Points

1.   Each Party shall designate and notify a contact point from its relevant authorities within 90 days of the date of entry into force of this Agreement, in order to facilitate communication between the Parties in the implementation of this Chapter. Each Party shall promptly notify, in writing, the other Parties in the event of any change of its contact point.

2.   The Parties establish an Environment Committee composed of senior government representatives, or their designees, of the relevant trade and environment central level of government authorities of each Party responsible for the implementation of this Chapter.

3.   The purpose of the Environment Committee is to oversee the implementation of this Chapter, and its functions are to:

   (a)   provide a forum to discuss and review the implementation of this Chapter;

   (b)   periodically inform the Commission and the Council for the Commission for Environmental Cooperation (Council) established under Article 3 (Council Structures and Procedures) of the Environmental Cooperation Agreement regarding the implementation of this Chapter;

   (c)   consider and endeavor to resolve matters referred to it under Article 24.30 (Senior Representative Consultations);

   (d)   provide input, as appropriate, for consideration by the Council, relating to submissions on enforcement matters under this Chapter.

   (e)   coordinate with other committees established under this Agreement as appropriate; and

   (f)   perform any other functions as the Parties may decide.

4.   The Environment Committee shall meet within one year of the date of entry into force of this Agreement. Thereafter, the Environment Committee shall meet every two years unless the Environment Committee agrees otherwise. The Chair of the Environment Committee and the venue of its meetings shall rotate among each of the Parties in English alphabetical order, unless the Environment Committee decides otherwise.

---

[34]   The Parties established the Commission for Environmental Cooperation (CEC) under Part Three of the North American Agreement on Environmental Cooperation (NAAEC).

5.   All decisions and reports of the Environment Committee shall be made by consensus, unless the Committee decides otherwise or unless otherwise provided in this Chapter.

6.   All decisions and reports of the Environment Committee shall be made available to the public, unless the Environment Committee decides otherwise.

7.   During the fifth year after the date of entry into force of this Agreement, the Environment Committee shall:

(a)   review the implementation and operation of this Chapter;

(b)   report its findings, which may include recommendations, to the Council and the Commission; and

(c)   undertake subsequent reviews at intervals to be decided by the Committee.

8.   The Environment Committee shall provide for public input on matters relevant to the Committee's work, as appropriate, and shall hold a public session at each meeting.

9.   The Parties recognize the importance of resource efficiency in the implementation of this Chapter and the desirability of using new technologies to facilitate communication and interaction between the Parties and with the public.

Article 24.27:   Submissions on Enforcement Matters

1.   Any person of a Party may file a submission asserting that a Party is failing to effectively enforce its environmental laws. Such submissions shall be filed with the Secretariat of the Commission for Environmental Cooperation (CEC Secretariat).

2.   The CEC Secretariat may consider a submission under this Article if it finds that the submission:

(a)   is in writing in English, French, or Spanish;

(b)   clearly identifies the person making the submission;

(c)   provides sufficient information to allow for the review of the submission including any documentary evidence on which the submission may be based and identification of the environmental law of which the failure to enforce is asserted;

(d)   appears to be aimed at promoting enforcement rather than at harassing industry; and

(e)   indicates whether the matter has been communicated in writing to the relevant authorities of the Party and the Party's response, if any.

3.   If the CEC Secretariat determines that a submission meets the criteria set out in paragraph 2, it shall determine within 30 days of receipt of the submission whether the submission merits requesting a response

from the Party. In deciding whether to request a response, the CEC Secretariat shall be guided by whether:

(a)   the submission alleges harm to the person making the submission;

(b)   the submission, alone or in combination with other submissions, raises matters about which further study would advance the goals of this Chapter;

(c)   private remedies available under the Party's law have been pursued; and

(d)   the submission is not drawn exclusively from mass media reports.

If the CEC Secretariat makes such a request, it shall forward to the Party a copy of the submission and any supporting information provided with the submission.

4.   The Party shall inform the CEC Secretariat within 60 days of delivery of the request:

(a)   whether the matter at issue is the subject of a pending judicial or administrative proceeding, in which case the CEC Secretariat shall proceed no further; and

(b)   of any other information the Party wishes to provide, such as:

(i)   information regarding the enforcement of the environmental law at issue, including any actions taken in connection with the matter in question;

(ii)   whether the matter was previously the subject of a judicial or administrative proceeding; and

(iii)   whether private remedies in connection with the matter are available to the person making the submission and whether they have been pursued.

Article 24.28:   Factual Records and Related Cooperation

1.   If the CEC Secretariat considers that the submission, in light of any response provided by the Party, warrants developing a factual record, it shall so inform the Council and the Environment Committee within 60 days of receiving the Party's response and provide its reasons.

2.   The CEC Secretariat shall prepare a factual record if at least two members of the Council instruct it to do so.

3.   The preparation of a factual record by the CEC Secretariat pursuant to this Article shall be without prejudice to any further steps that may be taken with respect to any submission.

4.   In preparing a factual record, the CEC Secretariat shall consider any information provided by a Party and may consider any relevant technical, scientific, or other information:

(a)   that is publicly available;

(b)   submitted by interested persons;

(c)   submitted by national advisory or consultative committees referred to in Article 24.5 (Public Information and Participation);

(d)   submitted by the Joint Public Advisory Committee (JPAC) referred to in Article 2.2 (Commission for Environmental Cooperation) of the E CA;

(e)   developed by independent experts; or

(f)   developed under the ECA.

5.   The CEC Secretariat shall submit a draft factual record to the Council within 120 days of the Council's instruction to prepare a factual record under paragraph 2. Any Party may provide comments to the CEC Secretariat on the accuracy of the draft within 30 days of the submission of the draft factual record. The CEC Secretariat shall incorporate those comments in the final factual record and promptly submit it to the Council.

6.   The CEC Secretariat shall make the final factual record publicly available, normally within 30 days following its submission, unless at least two members of the Council instruct it not to do so.

7.   The Environment Committee shall consider the final factual record in light of the objectives of this Chapter and the ECA and may provide recommendations to the Council on whether the matter raised in the factual record could benefit from cooperative activities.

8.   The Parties shall provide updates to the Council and the Environment Committee on final factual records, as appropriate.

Article 24.29:   Environment Consultations

1.   The Parties shall at all times endeavor to agree on the interpretation and application of this Chapter, and shall make every effort through dialogue, consultation, exchange of information, and, if appropriate, cooperation to address any matter that might affect the operation of this Chapter.

2.   A Party (the requesting Party) may request consultations with any other Party (the responding Party) regarding any matter arising under this Chapter by notifying the responding Party's contact point in writing. The requesting Party shall include information that is specific and sufficient to enable the responding Party to respond, including identification of the matter at issue and an indication of the legal basis for the request. The requesting Party shall deliver its request for consultations to the third Party through their respective contact points.

3.   A third Party that considers it has a substantial interest in the matter, may participate in the consultations by notifying the contact points of the requesting and responding Parties in writing no later than seven days after the date of delivery of the request for consultations. The third

Party shall include in its notice an explanation of its substantial interest in the matter.

4. Unless the requesting and the responding Parties (the consulting Parties) agree otherwise, the consulting Parties shall enter into consultations promptly, and no later than 30 days after the date of receipt by the responding Party of the request.

5. The consulting Parties shall make every effort to arrive at a mutually satisfactory resolution to the matter which may include appropriate cooperative activities. The consulting Parties may seek advice or assistance from any person or body they deem appropriate in order to examine the matter.

Article 24.30:   Senior Representative Consultations

1. If the consulting Parties fail to resolve the matter under Article 24.29 (Environment Consultations), a consulting Party may request that the Environment Committee representatives from the consulting Parties convene to consider the matter by notifying the contact point of the other consulting Party or Parties in writing. At the same time, the consulting Party making the request shall deliver the request to the contact points of any other Party.

2. The Environment Committee representatives from the consulting Parties shall promptly convene following the delivery of the request, and shall seek to resolve the matter including, if appropriate, by gathering relevant scientific and technical information from governmental or non-governmental experts. Environment Committee representatives from any other Party that considers it has a substantial interest in the matter may participate in the consultations.

Article 24.31:   Ministerial Consultations

1. If the consulting Parties fail to resolve the matter under Article 24.30 (Senior Representative Consultations), a consulting Party may refer the matter to the relevant Ministers of the consulting Parties who shall seek to resolve the matter.

2. Consultations pursuant to Article 24.29 (Environment Consultations), Article 24.30 (Senior Representative Consultations), and this Article may be held in person or by any technological means available as agreed by the consulting Parties. If in person, consultations shall be held in the capital of the responding Party, unless the consulting Parties agree otherwise.

3. Consultations shall be confidential and without prejudice to the rights of any Party in any future proceedings.

Article 24.32:   Dispute Resolution

1. If the consulting Parties fail to resolve the matter under Article 24.29 (Environment Consultations), Article 24.30 (Senior Representative Consultations), and Article 24.31 (Ministerial Consultations) within 30 days after the date of receipt of a request under Article 24.29.2 (Environment Consultations), or any other period as the consulting

Parties may decide, the requesting Party may request a meeting of the Commission pursuant to Article 31.5 (Commission, Good Offices, Conciliation, and Mediation) and thereafter request the establishment of a panel under Article 31.6 (Establishment of a Panel).

2. Notwithstanding Article 31.15 (Role of Experts), in a dispute arising under Article 24.22 (Conservation and Trade) a panel convened under Article 31.6 (Establishment of a Panel) shall:

(a) seek technical advice or assistance, if appropriate, from an entity authorised under CITES to address the particular matter, and provide the consulting Parties with an opportunity to comment on any such technical advice or assistance received; and

(b) provide due consideration to any interpretive guidance received pursuant to subparagraph (a) on the matter to the extent appropriate in light of its nature and status in making its findings and determinations under Article 31.17 (Panel Report).

ANNEX 24-A

For Canada, the *Ozone-depleting Substances and Halocarbon Alternatives Regulations, of the Canadian Environmental Protection Act, 1999* (CEPA).

For Mexico, the General Law on Ecological Equilibrium and Environmental Protection (*Ley General del Equilibrio Ecológico y la Protección al Ambiente—LGEEPA*), under Title IV Environmental Protection, Chapter I and II regarding federal enforcement of atmospheric provisions.

For the United States, 42 U.S.C. §§ 7671–7671q (*Stratospheric Ozone Protection*).

ANNEX 24-B

For Canada, the *Canada Shipping Act, 2001* and its related regulations.

For Mexico, Article 132 of the *General Law on Ecological Equilibrium and Environmental Protection* (*Ley General del Equilibrio Ecológico y la Protección al Ambiente—LGEEPA*).

For the United States, the *Act to Prevent Pollution from Ships*, 33 U.S.C. §§ 1901–1915.

CHAPTER 25   SMALL AND MEDIUM-SIZED ENTERPRISES

Article 25.1:   General Principles

1. The Parties, recognizing the fundamental role of SMEs in maintaining dynamism and enhancing competitiveness of their respective economies, shall foster close cooperation between SMEs of the Parties and cooperate in promoting jobs and growth in SMEs.

2. The Parties recognize the integral role of the private sector in the SME cooperation to be implemented under this Chapter.

Article 25.2: Cooperation to Increase Trade and Investment Opportunities for SMEs

With a view to more robust cooperation between the Parties to enhance commercial opportunities for SMEs, and among other efforts, in the context of Memoranda of Understanding that exist between Parties on SME cooperation, each Party shall seek to increase trade and investment opportunities, and in particular shall:

(a) promote cooperation between the Parties' small business support infrastructure, including dedicated SME centers, incubators and accelerators, export assistance centers, and other centers as appropriate, to create an international network for sharing best practices, exchanging market research, and promoting SME participation in international trade, as well as business growth in local markets;

(b) strengthen its collaboration with the other Parties on activities to promote SMEs owned by under-represented groups, including women, indigenous peoples, youth and minorities, as well as start-ups, agricultural and rural SMEs, and promote partnership among these SMEs and their participation in international trade;

(c) enhance its cooperation with the other Parties to exchange information and best practices in areas including improving SME access to capital and credit, SME participation in covered government procurement opportunities, and helping SMEs adapt to changing market conditions; and

(d) encourage participation in platforms, such as web-based, for business entrepreneurs and counselors to share information and best practices to help SMEs link with international suppliers, buyers, and other potential business partners.

Article 25.3: Information Sharing

1. Each Party shall establish or maintain its own free, publicly accessible website containing information regarding this Agreement, including:

(a) the text of this Agreement;

(b) a summary of this Agreement; and

(c) information designed for SMEs that contains:

    (i) a description of the provisions in this Agreement that the Party considers to be relevant to SMEs; and

    (ii) any additional information that would be useful for SMEs interested in benefitting from the opportunities provided by this Agreement.

2. Each Party shall include in its website links or information through automated electronic transfer to:

(a) the equivalent websites of the other Parties; and

(b)   the websites of its own government agencies and other appropriate entities that provide information the Party considers useful to any person interested in trading, investing, or doing business in that Party's territory.

3.   The information described in paragraph 2(b) may include:

(a)   customs regulations, procedures, or enquiry points;

(b)   regulations or procedures concerning intellectual property rights;

(c)   technical regulations, standards, or conformity assessment procedures;

(d)   sanitary or phytosanitary measures relating to importation or exportation;

(e)   foreign investment regulations;

(f)   business registration procedures;

(g)   trade promotion programs;

(h)   competitiveness programs;

(i)   SME financing programs;

(j)   employment regulations;

(k)   taxation information;

(l)   information related to the temporary entry of business persons, as set out in Article 16.5 (Provision of Information); and

(m)   government procurement opportunities within the scope of Article 13.2 (Scope).

4.   Each Party shall regularly review the information and links on the website referred to in paragraphs 1 and 2 to ensure the information and links are up-to-date and accurate.

5.   To the extent possible, each Party shall make the information in this Article available in English. If this information is available in another authentic language of this Agreement, the Party shall endeavor to make this information available, as appropriate.

Article 25.4:   Committee on SME Issues

1.   The Parties hereby establish the Committee on SME Issues (SME Committee), comprising government representatives of each Party.

2.   The SME Committee shall:

(a)   identify ways to assist SMEs in the Parties' territories to take advantage of the commercial opportunities resulting from this Agreement and to strengthen SME competitiveness;

(b) identify and recommend ways for further cooperation between the Parties to develop and enhance partnerships between SMEs of the Parties;

(c) exchange and discuss each Party's experiences and best practices in supporting and assisting SME exporters with respect to, among other things, training programs, trade education, trade finance, trade missions, trade facilitation, digital trade, identifying commercial partners in the territories of the Parties, and establishing good business credentials;

(d) develop and promote seminars, workshops, webinars, or other activities to inform SMEs of the benefits available to them under this Agreement;

(e) explore opportunities to facilitate each Party's work in developing and enhancing SME export counseling, assistance, and training programs;

(f) recommend additional information that a Party may include on the website referred to in Article 25.3 (Information Sharing);

(g) review and coordinate its work program with the work of other committees, working groups, and other subsidiary bodies established under this Agreement, as well as of other relevant international bodies, to avoid duplication of work programs and to identify appropriate opportunities for cooperation to improve the ability of SMEs to engage in trade and investment opportunities resulting from this Agreement;

(h) collaborate with and encourage committees, working groups and other subsidiary bodies established under this Agreement to consider SME-related commitments and activities into their work;

(i) review the implementation and operation of this Chapter and SME-related provisions within this Agreement and report findings and make recommendations to the Commission that can be included in future work and SME assistance programs as appropriate;

(j) facilitate the development of programs to assist SMEs to participate and integrate effectively into the Parties' regional and global supply chains;

(k) promote the participation of SMEs in digital trade in order to take advantage of the opportunities resulting from this Agreement and rapidly access new markets;

(l) facilitate the exchange of information on entrepreneurship education programs for youth and under-represented groups to promote the entrepreneurial environment in the territories of the Parties;

(m) submit on an annual basis, unless the Parties decide otherwise, a report of its activities and make appropriate recommendations to the Commission; and

(n) consider any other matter pertaining to SMEs as the SME Committee may decide, including issues raised by SMEs regarding their ability to benefit from this Agreement.

3. The SME Committee shall convene within one year after the date of entry into force of this Agreement and thereafter meet annually, unless the Parties decide otherwise.

4. The SME Committee may seek to collaborate with appropriate experts and international donor organizations in carrying out its programs and activities.

Article 25.5:   SME Dialogue

1. The SME Committee shall convene a Trilateral SME Dialogue (the "SME Dialogue"). The SME Dialogue may include private sector, employees, non-government organizations, academic experts, SMEs owned by diverse and under-represented groups, and other stakeholders from each Party.

2. The SME Committee shall convene the SME Dialogue annually, unless it decides otherwise.

3. SME Dialogue participants may provide views to the Committee on any matter within the scope of this Agreement and on the implementation and further modernization of this Agreement.

4. SME Dialogue participants may provide relevant technical, scientific, or other information to the Committee.

Article 25.6:   Obligations in the Agreement that Benefit SMEs

The Parties recognize that in addition to the provisions in this Chapter, there are provisions in other Chapters of this Agreement that seek to enhance cooperation among the Parties on SME issues or that otherwise may be of particular benefit to SMEs. These include:

(a) Origin Procedures: Article 5.18 (Committee on Rules of Origin and Origin Procedures);

(b) Government Procurement: Article 13.17 (Ensuring Integrity in Procurement Practices); Article 13.20 (Facilitation of Participation by SMEs), and Article 13.21 (Committee on Government Procurement);

(c) Cross-Border Trade in Services: Article 15.10 (Small and Medium-Sized Enterprises);

(d) Digital Trade: Article 19.17 (Interactive Computer Services); Article 19.18 (Open Government Data);

(e) Intellectual Property: Article 20.B.3 (Committee on Intellectual Property Rights);

(f)   Labor: Article 23.12 (Cooperation);

(g)   Environment: Article 24.17 (Marine Wild Capture Fisheries);

(h)   Competitiveness: Article 26.1 (North American Competitiveness Committee);

(i)   Anticorruption: Article 27.5 (Participation of Private Sector and Society); and

(j)   Good Regulatory Practices: Article 28.4 (Internal Consultation, Coordination, and Review), Article 28.11 (Regulatory Impact Assessment), and Article 28.13 (Retrospective Review).

Article 25.7:   Non-Application of Dispute Settlement

No Party shall have recourse to dispute settlement under Chapter 31 (Dispute Settlement) for any matter arising under this Chapter.

CHAPTER 26   COMPETITIVENESS

Article 26.1:   North American Competitiveness Committee

1.   Recognizing their unique economic and commercial ties, close proximity, and extensive trade flows across their borders, the Parties affirm their shared interest in strengthening regional economic growth, prosperity, and competitiveness.

2.   With a view to promoting further economic integration among the Parties and enhancing the competitiveness of North American exports, the Parties hereby establish a North American Competitiveness Committee (Competitiveness Committee), composed of government representatives of each Party.

* * *

Article 26.3:   Non-Application of Dispute Settlement

No Party shall have recourse to dispute settlement under Chapter 31 (Dispute Settlement) for a matter arising under this Chapter.

CHAPTER 27   ANTICORRUPTION

Article 27.1   Definitions

For the purposes of this Chapter:

Act or refrain from acting in relation to the performance of official duties includes any use of the public official's position, whether or not within the official's authorized competence;

Foreign public official means an individual holding a legislative, executive, administrative or judicial office of a foreign country, at any level of government, whether appointed or elected, permanent or temporary, paid or unpaid, and irrespective of that person's seniority; and an individual exercising a public function for a foreign country, at any level of government, including for a public agency or public enterprise;

IACAC means the existing *Inter-American Convention Against Corruption*, done at Caracas, Venezuela, on March 29, 1996;

OECD Convention means the existing *Convention on Combating Bribery of Foreign Public Officials in International Business Transactions*, done at Paris, France, on December 17, 1997;

Official of a public international organization means an international civil servant or an individual authorized by a public international organization to act on its behalf;

Public enterprise means an enterprise over which a government or governments may, directly or indirectly, exercise a dominant influence;[1]

Public official means an individual:

    (a)   holding a legislative, executive, administrative, or judicial office of a Party, whether appointed or elected, permanent or temporary, paid or unpaid, and irrespective of that person's seniority;

    (b)   who performs a public function for a Party, including for a public agency or public enterprise, or provides a public service, as defined under that Party's law and as applied in the pertinent area of that Party's law; or

    (c)   defined as a public official under a Party's law; and

UNCAC means the existing *United Nations Convention against Corruption*, done at New York, United States, on October 31, 2003.

Article 27.2:   Scope

1.   This Chapter applies to measures to prevent and combat bribery and corruption relating to any matter covered by this Agreement.[2]

2.   The Parties affirm their resolve to prevent and combat bribery and corruption in international trade and investment. Recognizing the need to build integrity within both the public and private sectors and that each sector has complementary responsibilities in this regard, the Parties affirm their adherence to the OECD Convention, with its Annex; the IACAC; and the UNCAC.

3.   The Parties reiterate their support for the principles contained in documents developed by APEC and G-20 anticorruption fora aimed at preventing and combating corruption and endorsed by leaders or relevant ministers, including the *G20 High Level Principles on Organizing against Corruption*; *G20 High Level Principles on*

---

[1]   Dominant influence for purposes of this definition shall be deemed to exist, *inter alia*, if the government or governments hold the majority of the enterprise's subscribed capital, control the majority of votes attaching to shares issued by the enterprise, or can appoint a majority of the members of the enterprise's administrative or managerial body or supervisory board.

[2]   For the United States, this Chapter does not apply to conduct outside the jurisdiction of federal criminal law and, to the extent that an obligation involves preventive measures, shall apply only to those measures covered by federal law governing federal, state, and local officials.

Corruption and Growth; G20 Guiding Principles on Enforcement of the Foreign Bribery Offence (2013); G20 Guiding Principles to Combat Solicitation; G20 High Level Principles on the Liability of Legal Persons for Corruption; APEC Conduct Principles for Public Officials; and the *APEC Principles on the Prevention of Bribery and Enforcement of Anti-Bribery Laws.*

4.   The Parties also reiterate their support for, and encourage awareness among their private sectors of, available anticorruption compliance guidance including the *APEC Code of Conduct for Business: Business Integrity and Transparency Principles for the Private Sector; APEC General Elements of Effective Voluntary Corporate Compliance Programs;* and *G20 High Level Principles on Private Sector Transparency and Integrity.*

5.   The Parties recognize that the description of offenses adopted or maintained in accordance with this Chapter, and of the applicable legal defenses or legal principles controlling the lawfulness of conduct, is reserved to each Party's law, and that those offenses shall be prosecuted and punished in accordance with each Party's law.

Article 27.3:   Measures to Combat Corruption

1.   Each Party shall adopt or maintain legislative and other measures as may be necessary to establish as criminal offenses under its law, in matters that affect international trade or investment, when committed intentionally, by a person subject to its jurisdiction:

   (a)   the promise, offering, or giving to a public official, directly or indirectly, of an undue advantage for the official or another person or entity, in order that the official act or refrain from acting in relation to the performance of or the exercise of their official duties;

   (b)   the solicitation or acceptance by a public official, directly or indirectly, of an undue advantage for the official or another person or entity, in order that the official act or refrain from acting in relation to the performance of or the exercise of their official duties;

   (c)   the promise, offering, or giving to a foreign public official or an official of a public international organization, directly or indirectly, of an undue advantage for the official or another person or entity, in order that the official act or refrain from acting in relation to the performance of or the exercise of their official duties, in order to obtain or retain business or other undue advantage in relation to the conduct of international business; and

   (d)   the aiding or abetting, or conspiracy in the commission of any of the offenses described in subparagraphs (a) through (c).

2.   Each Party shall adopt or maintain legislative and other measures as may be necessary to establish as a criminal offense under its law, in matters that affect international trade or investment, when committed

intentionally, by a person subject to its jurisdiction, the embezzlement, misappropriation or another diversion[3] by a public official for their benefit or for the benefit of another person or entity, of property, public or private funds or securities, or any other thing of value entrusted to the public official by virtue of their position.

3. Each Party shall make the commission of an offense described in paragraph 1, 2, or 6 liable to sanctions that take into account the gravity of that offense.

4. Each Party shall adopt or maintain measures as may be necessary, consistent with its legal principles, to establish the liability of legal persons for offenses described in paragraph 1 or 6.

5. Each Party shall disallow the tax deductibility of bribes and, if appropriate, other expenses considered illegal by the Party incurred in furtherance of that conduct.

6. In order to prevent corruption, each Party shall adopt or maintain measures as may be necessary in accordance with its laws and regulations, regarding the maintenance of books and records, financial statement disclosures, and accounting and auditing standards, to prohibit the following acts carried out for the purpose of committing the offenses described in paragraph 1:

    (a) the establishment of off-the-books accounts;

    (b) the making of off-the-books or inadequately identified transactions;

    (c) the recording of non-existent expenditure;

    (d) the entry of liabilities with incorrect identification of their objects;

    (e) the use of false documents; and

    (f) the intentional destruction of bookkeeping documents earlier than foreseen by the law.[4]

7. Each Party shall adopt or maintain measures considered appropriate by the Party to protect against unjustified treatment a person who, in good faith and on reasonable grounds, reports to the competent authorities facts concerning offenses described in paragraph 1, 2, or 6.[5]

8. The Parties recognize the harmful effects of facilitation payments. Each Party shall, in accordance with its laws and regulations:

---

[3] For Canada, "diversion" means embezzlement or misappropriation that constitute the criminal offenses of theft or fraud under Canadian law.

[4] For the United States, this paragraph applies only to issuers that have a class of securities registered pursuant to 15 U.S.C. 78l or that are otherwise required to file reports pursuant to 15 U.S.C. 78o (d).

[5] For Mexico and the United States, this paragraph applies only at the central level of government. For Canada, this paragraph applies to measures within the scope of the *Public Servants Disclosure Protection Act*, S.C. 2005, c.46, as amended.

(a)   encourage enterprises to prohibit or discourage the use of facilitation payments; and

(b)   take steps to raise awareness among its public officials of its bribery laws, with a view to stopping the solicitation and the acceptance of facilitation payments.[6]

Article 27.4:   Promoting Integrity among Public Officials[7]

1.   To fight corruption in matters that affect trade and investment, each Party should promote, among other things, integrity, honesty and responsibility among its public officials. To this end, each Party shall, in accordance with the fundamental principles of its legal system, adopt or maintain:

(a)   measures to provide adequate procedures for the selection and training of individuals for public positions considered by the Party to be especially vulnerable to corruption;

(b)   measures to promote transparency in the behavior of public officials in the exercise of public functions;

(c)   appropriate policies and procedures to identify and manage actual or potential conflicts of interest of public officials;

(d)   measures that require senior public officials, and other public officials as considered appropriate by the Party, to make declarations to appropriate authorities regarding, among other things, their outside activities, employment, investments, assets, and substantial gifts or benefits from which a conflict of interest may result with respect to their functions as public officials; and

(e)   measures to facilitate reporting by public officials of any facts concerning offenses described in Article 27.3.1, 27.3.2, or 27.3.6 (Measures to Combat Corruption) to appropriate authorities, if those facts come to their notice in the performance of their functions.

2.   Each Party shall adopt or maintain codes or standards of conduct for the correct, honorable and proper performance of public functions, and measures providing for disciplinary or other measures, if warranted, against a public official who violates the codes or standards established in accordance with this paragraph.

3.   Each Party shall, to the extent consistent with the fundamental principles of its legal system, establish procedures through which a public official accused of an offense described in Article 27.3.1 (Measures to Combat Corruption) may, as considered appropriate by that Party, be removed, suspended, or reassigned by the appropriate

---

[6]   For Canada, this subparagraph applies to measures within the scope of the *Public Servants Disclosure Protection Act*, S.C. 2005, c.46, as amended.

[7]   For Mexico and the United States, this article applies only at the central level of government. For Canada, this article applies to measures within the scope of the *Public Servants Disclosure Protection Act*, S.C. 2005, c.46, as amended.

authority, bearing in mind respect for the principle of the presumption of innocence.

4. Each Party shall, in accordance with the fundamental principles of its legal system and without prejudice to judicial independence, adopt or maintain measures to strengthen integrity, and to prevent opportunities for corruption, among members of the judiciary in matters that affect international trade or investment. These measures may include rules with respect to the conduct of members of the judiciary.

Article 27.5: Participation of Private Sector and Society

1. Each Party shall take appropriate measures, within its means and in accordance with fundamental principles of its legal system, to promote the active participation of individuals and groups outside the public sector, such as enterprises, civil society, non-governmental organizations, and community-based organizations, in preventing and combatting corruption in matters affecting international trade or investment, and to raise public awareness regarding the existence, causes, and gravity of corruption, and the threat posed by it. To this end, a Party may, for example:

   (a) undertake public information activities and public education programs that contribute to non-tolerance of corruption;

   (b) adopt or maintain measures to encourage professional associations and other non-governmental organizations, if appropriate, in their efforts to encourage and assist enterprises, in particular SMEs, in developing internal controls, ethics and compliance programs or measures for preventing and detecting bribery and corruption in international trade and investment;

   (c) adopt or maintain measures to encourage company management to make statements in their annual reports or otherwise publicly disclose their internal controls, ethics and compliance programs or measures, including those that contribute to preventing and detecting bribery and corruption in international trade and investment; or

   (d) adopt or maintain measures that respect, promote, and protect the freedom to seek, receive, publish, and disseminate information concerning corruption.

2. Each Party shall endeavor to encourage private enterprises, taking into account their structure and size, to:

   (a) adopt or maintain sufficient internal auditing controls to assist in preventing and detecting offenses described in Article 27.3.1 or 27.3.6 (Measures to Combat Corruption); and

(b)   ensure that their accounts and required financial statements are subject to appropriate auditing and certification procedures.

3.   Each Party shall take appropriate measures to ensure that its relevant anticorruption bodies are known to the public and shall provide access to those bodies, if appropriate, for the reporting, including anonymously, of an incident that may be considered to constitute an offense described in Article 27.3.1 (Measures to Combat Corruption).

4.   The Parties recognize the benefits of internal compliance programs in enterprises to combat corruption. In this regard, each Party shall encourage enterprises, taking into account their size, legal structure, and the sectors in which they operate, to establish compliance programs for the purpose of preventing and detecting offenses described in Article 27.3.1 or 27.3.6 (Measures to Combat Corruption).

Article 27.6:   Application and Enforcement of Anticorruption Laws

1.   In accordance with the fundamental principles of its legal system, no Party shall fail to effectively enforce its laws or other measures adopted or maintained to comply with Article 27.3 (Measures to Combat Corruption) through a sustained or recurring course of action or inaction, after the date of entry into force of this Agreement as an encouragement for trade and investment.[8]

2.   In accordance with the fundamental principles of its legal system, each Party retains the right for its law enforcement, prosecutorial, and judicial authorities to exercise their discretion with respect to the enforcement of its anticorruption laws. Each Party retains the right to take bona fide decisions with regard to the allocation of its resources.

3.   The Parties affirm their commitments under applicable international agreements or arrangements to cooperate with each other, consistent with their respective legal and administrative systems, to enhance the effectiveness of law enforcement actions to combat the offenses described in Article 27.3 (Measures to Combat Corruption).

Article 27.7:   Relation to Other Agreements

Nothing in this Agreement affects the rights and obligations of the Parties under the IACAC; the OECD Convention; the UNCAC; or the *United Nations Convention against Transnational Organized Crime*, done at New York on November 15, 2000.

Article 27.8:   Dispute Settlement

1.   Chapter 31 (Dispute Settlement), as modified by this Article, applies to disputes relating to a matter arising under this Chapter.

2.   A Party may only have recourse to the procedures set out in this Article and Chapter 31 (Dispute Settlement) if it considers that a measure of

---

[8]   For greater certainty, the Parties recognize that individual cases or specific discretionary decisions related to the enforcement of anticorruption laws are subject to each Party's laws and legal procedures.

another Party is inconsistent with an obligation under this Chapter, or that another Party has otherwise failed to carry out an obligation under this Chapter, in a manner affecting trade or investment between Parties.

3.   No Party shall have recourse to dispute settlement under this Article or Chapter 31 (Dispute Settlement) for a matter arising under Article 27.6 (Application and Enforcement of Anticorruption Laws) or Article 27.9 (Cooperation).

4.   Further to Article 31.4 (Consultations), each Consulting Party shall ensure that consultations include personnel of the consulting Party's government authorities with responsibility for the anticorruption issue under dispute.

5.   Further to Article 31.5 (Commission, Good Offices, Conciliation, and Mediation), any discussion held by the Free Trade Commission shall, to the extent practicable, include participation by a Minister responsible for the anticorruption issue under dispute, or their designee.

6.   Further to Article 31.8 (Roster and Qualifications of Panelists), the panel shall have expertise in the area of anticorruption under dispute.

Article 27.9:   Cooperation

1.   The Parties recognize the importance of cooperation, coordination, and exchange of information between their respective anticorruption law enforcement agencies in order to foster effective measures to prevent, detect, and deter bribery and corruption.

2.   The Parties shall endeavor to strengthen cooperation and coordination among their respective anticorruption law enforcement agencies.

3.   Recognizing that the Parties can benefit by sharing their diverse experience and best practices in developing, implementing, and enforcing their anticorruption laws and policies, the Parties' anticorruption law enforcement agencies shall consider undertaking technical cooperation activities, including training programs, as decided by the Parties.

4.   The Parties acknowledge the importance of cooperation and coordination internationally, including the OECD Working Group on Bribery in International Business Transactions, the UNCAC Conference of the State Parties and the Mechanism for Follow-Up on the Implementation of the IACAC, as well as their support to the APEC Anti-Corruption and Transparency Working Group and the G20 Anti-Corruption Working Group.

CHAPTER 28   GOOD REGULATORY PRACTICES

Article 28.1:   Definitions

For the purposes of this Chapter:

Regulation means a measure of general application adopted, issued, or maintained by a regulatory authority with which compliance is mandatory, except as set forth in Annex 28-A (Additional Provisions Concerning the Scope of "Regulations" and "Regulatory Authorities");

Regulatory authority means an administrative authority or agency at the Party's central level of government that develops, proposes or adopts a regulation, and does not include legislatures or courts; and

Regulatory cooperation means an effort between two or more Parties to prevent, reduce, or eliminate unnecessary regulatory differences to facilitate trade and promote economic growth, while maintaining or enhancing standards of public health and safety and environmental protection.

Article 28.2:   Subject Matter and General Provisions

1.   The Parties recognize that implementation of government-wide practices to promote regulatory quality through greater transparency, objective analysis, accountability, and predictability can facilitate international trade, investment, and economic growth, while contributing to each Party's ability to achieve its public policy objectives (including health, safety, and environmental goals) at the level of protection it considers appropriate. The application of good regulatory practices can support the development of compatible regulatory approaches among the Parties, and reduce or eliminate unnecessarily burdensome, duplicative, or divergent regulatory requirements. Good regulatory practices also are fundamental to effective regulatory cooperation.

2.   Accordingly, this Chapter sets out specific obligations with respect to good regulatory practices, including practices relating to the planning, design, issuance, implementation, and review of the Parties' respective regulations.

3.   For greater certainty, this Chapter does not prevent a Party from:

   (a)   pursuing its public policy objectives (including health, safety and environmental goals) at the level it considers to be appropriate;

   (b)   determining the appropriate method of implementing its obligations in this Chapter within the framework of its own legal system and institutions; or

   (c)   adopting good regulatory practices that supplement those that are set out in this Chapter.

Article 28.3:   Central Regulatory Coordinating Body

Recognizing that institutional arrangements are particular to each Party's system of governance, the Parties note the important role of their respective central regulatory coordinating bodies in promoting good regulatory practices; performing key advisory, coordination, and review functions to improve the quality of regulations; and developing improvements to their regulatory system. The Parties intend to maintain their respective central regulatory coordinating bodies, within their respective mandates and consistent with their law.

Article 28.4:   Internal Consultation, Coordination, and Review

1.   The Parties recognize that internal processes or mechanisms providing for consultation, coordination, and review among domestic authorities in the development of regulations can increase regulatory compatibility among the Parties and facilitate trade. Accordingly, each Party shall adopt or maintain those processes or mechanisms to pursue, among others, the following objectives:

(a)   promoting government-wide adherence to good regulatory practices, including those set forth in this Chapter;

(b)   identifying and developing improvements to government-wide regulatory processes;

(c)   identifying potential overlap or duplication between proposed and existing regulations, and preventing the creation of inconsistent requirements across domestic authorities;

(d)   supporting compliance with international trade and investment obligations, including, as appropriate, the consideration of international standards, guides, and recommendations;

(e)   promoting consideration of regulatory impacts, including burdens on small enterprises[1] of information collection and implementation; and

(f)   encouraging regulatory approaches that avoid unnecessary restrictions on competition in the marketplace.

2.   Each Party shall make publicly available a description of the processes or mechanisms referred to in paragraph 1.

Article 28.5:   Information Quality

1.   Each Party recognizes the need for regulations to be based upon information that is reliable and of high quality. To that end, each Party should adopt or maintain publicly available guidance or mechanisms that encourage its regulatory authorities when developing a regulation to:

(a)   seek the best, reasonably obtainable information, including scientific, technical, economic, or other information relevant to the regulation it is developing;

(b)   rely on information that is appropriate for the context in which it is used; and

(c)   identify sources of information in a transparent manner, as well as any significant assumptions and limitations.

2.   If a regulatory authority systematically collects information from members of the public through identical questions in a survey for use

---

[1]   For greater certainty and for the purposes of this Chapter, for Mexico "small enterprises" also include medium enterprises.

in developing a regulation, each Party shall provide that the authority should:

(a) use sound statistical methodologies before drawing generalized conclusions concerning the impact of the regulation on the population affected by the regulation; and

(b) avoid unnecessary duplication and otherwise minimize unnecessary burdens on those being surveyed.

Article 28.6: Early Planning

Each Party shall publish annually a list of regulations that it reasonably expects within the following 12 months to adopt or propose to adopt. Each regulation identified in the list should be accompanied by:

(a) a concise description of the planned regulation;

(b) a point of contact for a knowledgeable individual in the regulatory authority responsible for the regulation; and

(c) an indication, if known, of sectors to be affected and whether there is any expected significant effect on international trade or investment.

Entries in the list should also include, to the extent available, time tables for subsequent actions, including those providing opportunities for public comment under Article 28.9 (Transparent Development of Regulations).

Article 28.7: Dedicated Website

1. Each Party shall maintain a single, free, publicly available website that, to the extent practicable, contains all information that it is required to publish pursuant to Article 28.9 (Transparent Development of Regulations).

2. A Party may comply with paragraph 1 by making publicly available information on, and providing for the submission of comments through, more than one website, provided the information can be accessed, and submissions can be made, from a single web portal that links to other websites.

Article 28.8: Use of Plain Language

Each Party should provide that proposed and final regulations are written using plain language to ensure that those regulations are clear, concise, and easy for the public to understand, recognizing that some regulations address technical issues and that relevant expertise may be required to understand or apply them.

Article 28.9: Transparent Development of Regulations

1. During the period described in paragraph 2, when a regulatory authority is developing a regulation, the Party shall, under normal circumstances,[2] publish:

---

[2] For the purposes of paragraphs 1 and 4, "normal circumstances" do not include, for example, situations when publication in accordance with those paragraphs

(a)   the text of the regulation along with its regulatory impact assessment, if any;

(b)   an explanation of the regulation, including its objectives, how the regulation achieves those objectives, the rationale for the material features of the regulation, and any major alternatives being considered;

(c)   an explanation of the data, other information, and analyses the regulatory authority relied upon to support the regulation; and

(d)   the name and contact information of an individual official from the regulatory authority who may be contacted concerning questions regarding the regulation.

At the same time the Party publishes the information listed in subparagraphs (a) through (d), the Party shall also make publicly available data, other information, and scientific and technical analyses it relied upon in support of the regulation, including any risk assessment.

2.   With respect to the items required to be published under paragraph 1, each Party shall publish them before the regulatory authority finalizes its work on the regulation[3] and at a time that will enable the regulatory authority to take into account the comments received and, as appropriate, make revisions to the text of the regulation published under subparagraph 1(a).

3.   After the items identified in paragraph 1 have been published, the Party shall ensure that any interested person, regardless of domicile, has an opportunity, on terms no less favorable than those afforded to a person of the Party, to submit written comments on the items identified in paragraph 1 for consideration by the relevant regulatory authority of the Party. Each Party shall allow interested persons to submit any comments and other inputs electronically and may also allow written submissions by mail to a published address or through another technology.

4.   If a Party expects a draft regulation to have a significant impact on trade, the Party should normally provide a time period to submit written comments and other input on the items published in accordance with paragraph 1 that is:

---

would render the regulation ineffective in addressing the particular harm to the public interest that the regulation aims to address; if urgent problems (for example, of safety, health, or environmental protection) arise or threaten to arise for a Party; or if the regulation has no substantive impact upon members of the public, including persons of another Party.

[3]   For Canada, a regulatory authority "finalizes its work" on a regulation when a final regulation is published in Canada Gazette, Part II. For Mexico, a regulatory authority "finalizes its work" on a regulation when the final act of general application is issued and published in the Official Gazette. For the United States, a regulatory authority "finalizes its work" on a regulation when a final rule is signed and published in the Federal Register.

(a)   not less than 60 days from the date the items identified in paragraph 1 are published; or

(b)   a longer time period as is appropriate due to the nature and complexity of the regulation, in order to provide interested persons adequate opportunity to understand how the regulation may affect their interests and to develop informed responses.

5.   With respect to draft regulations not covered under paragraph 4, a Party shall endeavor, under normal circumstances, to provide a time period to submit written comments and other input on the information published in accordance with paragraph 1 that is not less than four weeks from the date the items identified in paragraph 1 are published.

6.   In addition, the Party shall consider reasonable requests to extend the comment time period under paragraph 4 or 5 to submit written comments or other input on a draft regulation.

7.   Each Party shall endeavor to promptly make publicly available any written comments it receives, except to the extent necessary to protect confidential information or withhold personal identifying information or inappropriate content. If it is impracticable to publish all the comments on the website provided for in Article 28.7 (Dedicated Website), the regulatory authority of a Party shall endeavor to publish those comments on its own website.

8.   Before finalizing its work on a regulation, a regulatory authority of a Party shall evaluate any information provided in written comments received during the comment period.

9.   When a regulatory authority of a Party finalizes its work on a regulation, the Party shall promptly publish the text of the regulation, any final impact assessment, and other items as set out in Article 28.12 (Final Publication).

10.   The Parties are encouraged to publish government-generated items identified in this Article in a format that can be read and digitally processed through word searches and data mining by a computer or other technology.

Article 28.10:   Expert Advisory Groups

1.   The Parties recognize that their respective regulatory authorities may seek expert advice and recommendations with respect to the preparation or implementation of regulations from groups or bodies that include non-governmental persons. The Parties also recognize that obtaining those advice and recommendations should be a complement to, rather than a substitute for, the procedures for seeking public comment pursuant to Article 28.9.3 (Transparent Development of Regulations).

2.   For the purposes of this Article, an expert group or body means a group or body:

(a)   established by a Party;

(b)   the membership of which includes persons who are not employees or contractors of the Party; and

(c)   the function of which includes providing advice or recommendations, including of a scientific or technical nature, to a regulatory authority of the Party with respect to the preparation or implementation of regulations.

This Article does not apply to a group or body that is established to enhance intergovernmental coordination, or to provide advice related to international affairs, including national security.[4]

3.   Each Party shall encourage its regulatory authorities to ensure that the membership of any expert group or body includes a range and diversity of views and interests, as appropriate to the particular context.

4.   Recognizing the importance of keeping the public informed with respect to the purpose, membership, and activities of expert groups and bodies, and that those expert groups or bodies can provide an important additional perspective or expertise on matters affecting government operations, each Party shall encourage its regulatory authorities to provide public notice of:

(a)   the name of any expert group or body it creates or uses, and the names of the members of the group or body and their affiliations;

(b)   the mandate and functions of the expert group or body;

(c)   information about upcoming meetings; and

(d)   a summary of the outcome of any meeting of an expert group or body.

5.   Each Party shall endeavor, as appropriate, to make publicly available any documentation made available to or prepared for or by the expert group or body, and recognizes the importance of providing a means for interested persons to provide inputs to the expert groups or bodies.

Article 28.11:   Regulatory Impact Assessment

1.   The Parties recognize that regulatory impact assessment is a tool to assist regulatory authorities in assessing the need for and potential impacts of regulations they are preparing. Each Party should encourage the use of regulatory impact assessments in appropriate circumstances when developing proposed regulations that have anticipated costs or impacts exceeding certain thresholds established by the Party.

2.   Each Party shall maintain procedures that promote the consideration of the following when conducting a regulatory impact assessment:

---

[4]   For greater certainty, this Article does not apply to Mexico's National Standardization Advisory Committees (*Comité Consultivo Nacional de Normalización*), established under article 62 of the Federal Law on Metrology and Standardization.

(a) the need for a proposed regulation, including a description of the nature and significance of the problem the regulation is intended to address;

(b) feasible and appropriate regulatory and non-regulatory alternatives that would address the need identified in subparagraph (a), including the alternative of not regulating;

(c) benefits and costs of the selected and other feasible alternatives, including the relevant impacts (such as economic, social, environmental, public health, and safety effects) as well as risks and distributional effects over time, recognizing that some costs and benefits are difficult to quantify or monetize; and

(d) the grounds for concluding that the selected alternative is preferable.

3. Each Party should consider whether a proposed regulation may have significant adverse economic effects on a substantial number of small enterprises. If so, the Party should consider potential steps to minimize those adverse economic impacts, while allowing the Party to fulfill its objectives.

Article 28.12: Final Publication

1. When a regulatory authority of a Party finalizes its work on a regulation, the Party shall promptly publish, in a final regulatory impact assessment or other document:

(a) the date by which compliance is required;

(b) an explanation of how the regulation achieves the Party's objectives, the rationale for the material features of the regulation (to the extent different than the explanation provided for in Article 28.9 (Transparent Development of Regulations)), and the nature of and reasons for any significant revisions made since making the regulation available for public comment;

(c) the regulatory authority's views on any substantive issues raised in timely submitted comments;

(d) major alternatives, if any, that the regulatory authority considered in developing the regulation and reasons supporting the alternative that it selected; and

(e) the relationship between the regulation and the key evidence, data, and other information the regulatory authority considered in finalizing its work on the regulation.

2. Each Party shall ensure that all regulations in effect are published on a free, publicly available website.

Article 28.13:   Retrospective Review

1. Each Party shall adopt or maintain procedures or mechanisms to conduct retrospective reviews of its regulations in order to determine whether modification or repeal is appropriate. Retrospective reviews may be initiated, for example, pursuant to a Party's law, on a regulatory authority's own initiative, or in response to a suggestion submitted pursuant to Article 28.14 (Suggestions for Improvement).

2. When conducting a retrospective review, each Party should consider, as appropriate:

    (a) the effectiveness of the regulation in meeting its initial stated objectives, for example by examining its actual social or economic impacts;

    (b) any circumstances that have changed since the development of the regulation, including availability of new information;

    (c) new opportunities to eliminate unnecessary regulatory burdens;

    (d) ways to address unnecessary regulatory differences that may adversely affect trade among the Parties, including through the activities listed in Article 28.17.3 (Encouragement of Regulatory Compatibility and Cooperation); and

    (e) any relevant views expressed by members of the public.

3. Each Party shall include among the procedures or mechanisms adopted pursuant to paragraph 1 provisions addressing impacts on small enterprises.

4. Each Party is encouraged to publish, to the extent available, any official plans and results of retrospective reviews.

Article 28.14:   Suggestions for Improvement

Each Party shall provide the opportunity for any interested person to submit to any regulatory authority of the Party written suggestions for the issuance, modification, or repeal of a regulation. The basis for those suggestions may include, for example, that, in the view of the interested person, the regulation has become ineffective at protecting health, welfare, or safety, has become more burdensome than necessary to achieve its objective (for example with respect to its impact on trade), fails to take into account changed circumstances (such as fundamental changes in technology, or relevant scientific and technical developments), or relies on incorrect or outdated information.

Article 28.15:   Information About Regulatory Processes

1. Each Party shall publish online a description of the processes and mechanisms employed by its regulatory authorities to prepare, evaluate, or review regulations. The description shall identify the applicable guidelines, rules, or procedures, including those regarding opportunities for the public to provide input.

2.   Each Party shall also publish online:

(a)   a description of the functions and organization of each of its regulatory authorities, including the appropriate offices through which persons can obtain information, make submissions or requests, or obtain decisions;

(b)   any procedural requirements or forms promulgated or utilized by any of its regulatory authorities;

(c)   the legal authority for verification, inspection, and compliance activities by its regulatory authorities;

(d)   information concerning the judicial or administrative procedures available to challenge regulations; and

(e)   any fees charged by a regulatory authority to a person of a Party for services rendered in connection with the implementation of a regulation, including for licensing, inspections, audits, and other administrative actions required under the Party's law to import, export, sell, market, or use a good.

Article 28.16:   Annual Report

Each Party shall prepare and make freely and publicly available online, on an annual basis, a report setting forth:

(a)   to the extent feasible, an estimate regarding the annual costs and benefits of economically significant regulations, as established by the Party, issued in that period by its regulatory authorities, on an aggregate or individual basis; and

(b)   any changes, or any proposals to make changes, to its regulatory system.

* * *

Article 28.20:   Application of Dispute Settlement

1.   Recognizing that a mutually acceptable solution can often be found outside recourse to dispute settlement, a Party shall exercise its judgement as to whether recourse to dispute settlement under Chapter 31 (Dispute Settlement) would be fruitful.

2.   Chapter 31 (Dispute Settlement) shall apply with respect to a responding Party as of one year after the date of entry into force of this Agreement for that Party.

3.   No Party shall have recourse to dispute settlement under Chapter 31 (Dispute Settlement) for a matter arising under this Chapter except to address a sustained or recurring course of action or inaction that is inconsistent with a provision of this Chapter.

ANNEX 28-A ADDITIONAL PROVISIONS CONCERNING THE SCOPE OF "REGULATIONS" AND "REGULATORY AUTHORITIES"

1. The following measures are not regulations for the purposes of this Chapter:

    (a) for all Parties: general statements of policy or guidance that do not prescribe legally enforceable requirements;

    (b) for Canada:

        (i) a measure concerning:

            (A) a military, foreign affairs, or national security function of the Government of Canada,

            (B) public sector management, personnel, pensions, public property, loans, grants, benefits, or contracts,

            (C) departmental organization, procedure, or practice,

            (D) taxation, financial services or anti-money laundering measures, or

            (E) federal, provincial, territorial relations and agreements and relations with Aboriginal Peoples, or

        (ii) a measure that does not constitute a regulation under the *Statutory Instruments Act*;

    (c) for Mexico: a measure concerning:

        (i) taxation, specifically those related with contributions and their accessories,

        (ii) public servants responsibilities,

        (iii) agrarian and labor justice,

        (iv) financial services or anti-money laundering measures,

        (v) public prosecutor's office executing its constitutional functions, or

        (vi) navy and defense; and

    (d) for the United States: a measure concerning:

        (i) a military or foreign affairs function of the United States,

        (ii) agency management, personnel, public property, loans, grants, benefits, or contracts,

        (iii) agency organization, procedure, or practice, or

        (iv) financial services or anti-money laundering measures.

2. The following entities are not a regulatory authorities for the purposes of this Chapter:

    (a)   for Canada: the Governor in Council; and

    (b)   for the United States: the President.

CHAPTER 29   PUBLICATION AND ADMINISTRATION

Section A: Publication and Administration

Article 29.1:   Definitions

For the purposes of this Chapter:

Administrative ruling of general application means an administrative ruling or interpretation[1] that applies to all persons and fact situations that fall generally within the ambit of that administrative ruling or interpretation and that establishes a norm of conduct, but does not include:

    (a)   a determination or ruling made in an administrative or quasi-judicial proceeding that applies to a particular person, good, or service of another Party in a specific case; or

    (b)   a ruling that adjudicates with respect to a particular act or practice.

Article 29.2:   Publication

1.   Each Party shall ensure that its laws, regulations, procedures, and administrative rulings of general application with respect to any matter covered by this Agreement are promptly published or otherwise made available in a manner that enables interested persons and the other Parties to become acquainted with them. To the extent possible, each Party shall make these measures available online.

2.   Each Party shall, to the extent possible:

    (a)   publish in advance a measure referred to in paragraph 1 that it proposes to adopt; and

    (b)   provide interested persons and the other Parties a reasonable opportunity to comment on a proposed measure referred to in subparagraph (a).

3.   Each Party shall ensure that its laws and regulations of general application at the central level of government are published on a free, publicly accessible website that is capable of performing searches for these laws and regulations by citation or through a word search, and shall ensure that this website is kept updated. Annex 29-A sets out each Party's websites.

Article 29.3:   Administrative Proceedings

With a view to administering all measures of general application with respect to any matter covered by this Agreement in a consistent, impartial, and reasonable manner, each Party shall ensure in its administrative

---

[1]   For greater certainty, an interpretation or ruling that is not binding is not an administrative ruling of general application.

proceedings[2] applying measures referred to in Article 29.2.1 (Publication) to a particular person, good, or service of another Party in specific cases that:

(a) a person of another Party that is directly affected by a proceeding is provided, whenever possible and, in accordance with domestic procedures, with reasonable notice of the initiation of a proceeding, including a description of the nature of the proceeding, a statement of the legal authority under which the proceeding is initiated and a general description of the issue in question;

(b) a person of another Party that is directly affected by a proceeding is afforded a reasonable opportunity to present facts and arguments in support of that person's position prior to any final administrative action, when time, the nature of the proceeding, and the public interest permit; and

(c) the procedures are in accordance with its law.

Article 29.4:   Review and Appeal

1. Each Party shall establish or maintain judicial, quasi-judicial, or administrative tribunals or procedures for the purpose of the prompt review and, if warranted, correction of a final administrative action with respect to any matter covered by this Agreement. These tribunals shall be impartial and independent of the office or authority entrusted with administrative enforcement and shall not have any substantial interest in the outcome of the matter.

2. Each Party shall ensure that, with respect to the tribunals or procedures referred to in paragraph 1, the parties to a proceeding are provided with the right to:

(a) a reasonable opportunity to support or defend their respective positions; and

(b) a decision based on the evidence and submissions of record or, if required by its law, the record compiled by the relevant authority.

3. Each Party shall ensure, subject to appeal or further review as provided for in its law, that the decision referred to in paragraph 2(b) be implemented by, and govern the practice of, the office or authority with respect to the administrative action at issue.

---

[2] For greater certainty, administrative proceedings subject to this Article do not include proceedings that result in advisory opinions or decisions that are not legally binding.

Section B: Transparency and Procedural Fairness for Pharmaceutical Products and Medical Devices³

Article 29.5:   Definitions

For the purposes of this Section:

National health care authority means, with respect to a Party listed in Annex 29-B (Party-Specific Definitions), the relevant entity or entities specified therein, and with respect to any other Party, an entity that is part of or has been established by a Party's central level of government to operate a national health care program; and

National health care program means a health care program in which a national health care authority makes the determinations or recommendations regarding the listing of pharmaceutical products or medical devices for reimbursement, or regarding the setting of the amount of that reimbursement.

Article 29.6:   Principles

The Parties are committed to facilitating high-quality health care and continued improvements in public health for their nationals, including patients and the public. In pursuing these objectives, the Parties acknowledge the importance of the following principles:

(a)   the importance of protecting and promoting public health and the important role played by pharmaceutical products and medical devices[4] in delivering high-quality health care;

(b)   the importance of research and development, including innovation associated with research and development, related to pharmaceutical products and medical devices;

(c)   the need to promote timely and affordable access to pharmaceutical products and medical devices, through transparent, impartial, expeditious, and accountable procedures, without prejudice to a Party's right to apply appropriate standards of quality, safety, and efficacy; and

the need to recognize the value of pharmaceutical products and medical devices through the operation of competitive markets or by adopting or maintaining procedures that appropriately value the objectively demonstrated therapeutic significance of a pharmaceutical product or medical device.

---

[3]   For greater certainty, the Parties confirm that the purpose of this Section is to ensure transparency and procedural fairness of relevant aspects of the Parties' applicable systems relating to pharmaceutical products and medical devices, without prejudice to the obligations in this Chapter, and not to modify a Party's system of health care in any other respects or a Party's rights to determine health expenditure priorities.

[4]   For the purposes of this Section, each Party shall define the scope of the products subject to its laws and regulations for pharmaceutical products and medical devices in its territory, and make that information publicly available.

Article 29.7:   Procedural Fairness

To the extent that a Party's national health care authority operates or maintains procedures for listing new pharmaceutical products or medical devices for reimbursement purposes, or setting the amount of that reimbursement, under a national health care program operated by the national health care authority,[5],[6] that Party shall:

> ensure that consideration of all formal and duly formulated proposals for such listing of pharmaceutical products or medical devices for reimbursement is completed within a specified period of time;[7]

(a)   disclose procedural rules, methodologies, principles, and guidelines used to assess such proposals;

(b)   afford applicants[8] and, if appropriate, the public, timely opportunities to provide comments at relevant points in the decision-making process;

(c)   provide applicants with written information sufficient to comprehend the basis for recommendations or determinations regarding the listing of new pharmaceutical products or medical devices for reimbursement by its national health care authority;

(d)   make available:

(i)   an independent review process, or

an internal review process, such as by the same expert or group of experts that made the recommendation or determination, provided that procedures that appropriately value the objectively demonstrated therapeutic significance of a pharmaceutical product or medical device.

the review process includes, at a minimum, a substantive reconsideration of the application,[9] and

---

[5]   This Section does not apply to government procurement of pharmaceutical products and medical devices. If a public entity providing health care services engages in government procurement for pharmaceutical products or medical devices, formulary development and management with respect to that activity by the national health care authority shall be considered an aspect of such government procurement.

[6]   This Section does not apply to procedures undertaken for the purpose of post-market subsidization of pharmaceutical products or medical devices procured by public health care entities if the pharmaceutical products or medical devices eligible for consideration are based on the products or devices that are procured by public health care entities.

[7]   In those cases in which a Party's national health care authority is unable to complete consideration of a proposal within a specified period of time, the Party shall disclose the reason for the delay to the applicant and shall provide for another specified period of time for completing consideration of the proposal.

[8]   For greater certainty, each Party may define the persons or entities that qualify as an "applicant" under its laws, regulations, and procedures.

[9]   For greater certainty, the review process described in subparagraph (e)(i) may include a review process as described in subparagraph (e)(ii) other than one by the same expert or group of experts.

that may be invoked at the request of an applicant directly affected by a recommendation or determination by a Party's national health care authority not to list a pharmaceutical product or a medical device for reimbursement;[10] and

> (e) provide written information to the public regarding recommendations or determinations, while protecting information considered to be confidential under the Party's law.

Article 29.8:   Dissemination of Information to Health Professionals and Consumers

As is permitted to be disseminated under the Party's laws, regulations, and procedures, each Party shall permit a pharmaceutical product manufacturer to disseminate to health professionals and consumers through the manufacturer's website registered in the territory of the Party, and on other websites registered in the territory of the Party linked to that site, truthful and not misleading information regarding its pharmaceutical products that are approved for marketing in the Party's territory. A Party may require that the information include a balance of risks and benefits and encompass all indications for which the Party's competent regulatory authorities have approved the marketing of the pharmaceutical product.

Article 29.9:   Consultations

1.   To facilitate dialogue and mutual understanding of issues relating to this Section, each Party shall give sympathetic consideration to and shall afford adequate opportunity for consultations regarding a written request by another Party to consult on any matter related to this Section. The consultations shall take place within three months of the delivery of the request, except in exceptional circumstances or unless the consulting Parties decide otherwise.[11]

2.   Consultations shall involve officials responsible for the oversight of the national health care authority or officials from each Party responsible for national health care programs and other appropriate government officials.

Article 29.10:   Non-Application of Dispute Settlement

No Party shall have recourse to dispute settlement under Chapter 31 (Dispute Settlement) for any matter arising under this Section.

---

[10]   For greater certainty, subparagraph (e) does not require a Party to provide more than a single review for a request regarding a specific proposal or to review, in conjunction with the request, other proposals or the assessment related to those other proposals. Further, a Party may elect to provide the review specified in subparagraph (e) either with respect to a draft final recommendation or determination, or with respect to a final recommendation or determination.

[11]   Nothing in this paragraph shall be construed as requiring a Party to review or change a decision regarding a specific application.

ANNEX 29-A PUBLICATION OF LAWS AND REGULATIONS OF GENERAL APPLICATION

For the purpose of Article 29.2.3 (Publication), laws and regulations of general application of each Party are published in the following websites:

(a) For Canada: http://laws.justice.gc.ca/eng/ See also: http://www.gazette.gc.ca/accueil-home-eng.html;

(b) For Mexico: www.diputados.gob.mx/LeyesBiblio/index.htm See also: www.dof.gob.mx; and

(c) For the United States: https://www.govinfo.gov/help/whats-available See also: http://uscode.house.gov/ (laws) https://www.ecfr.gov/cgi-bin/text-idx?tpl=®index.tpl (regulations)

ANNEX 29-B PARTY-SPECIFIC DEFINITIONS

Further to the definition of national health care authority in Article 29.5 (Definitions), national health care authority means:

(a) For Canada, the Federal Drug Benefits Committee. For greater certainty, Canada does not currently operate a national health care program within the scope of this Annex.

(b) For the United States, the Centers for Medicare & Medicaid Services (CMS), with respect to CMS's role in making Medicare national coverage determinations.

CHAPTER 30 ADMINISTRATIVE AND INSTITUTIONAL PROVISIONS

Article 30.1:   Establishment of the Free Trade Commission

The Parties hereby establish a Free Trade Commission (Commission), composed of government representatives of each Party at the level of Ministers or their designees.

Article 30.2:   Functions of the Commission

1.   The Commission shall:

(a) consider matters relating to the implementation or operation of this Agreement;

(b) consider proposals to amend or modify this Agreement;

(c) supervise the work of committees, working groups, and other subsidiary bodies established under this Agreement;

(d) consider ways to further enhance trade and investment between the Parties;

(e) adopt and update the Rules of Procedure and Code of Conduct applicable to dispute settlement proceedings; and

(f) review the roster established under Article 31.8 (Roster and Qualifications of Panelists) every three years and, when appropriate, constitute a new roster.

2.   The Commission may:

    (a)   establish, refer matters to, or consider matters raised by, an *ad hoc* or standing committee, working group, or other subsidiary body;

    (b)   merge or dissolve a committee, working group, or other subsidiary body established under this Agreement in order to improve the functioning of this Agreement;

    (c)   consider and adopt, subject to completion of applicable legal procedures by each Party, a modification to this Agreement of:

        (i)   the Schedules to Annex 2-B (Tariff Commitments), by accelerating tariff elimination or improving market access conditions,

        (ii)   the adjustments to the Tariff Preferential Levels established in Chapter 6 (Textile and Apparel Goods),

        (iii)   the rules of origin established in Annex 4-B (Product-Specific Rules of Origin),

        (iv)   the minimum data requirements for the certification of origin,

        (v)   any provision as may be required to conform with any change to the Harmonized System, or

        (vi)   the lists of entities, covered goods and services, and thresholds contained in the Schedules to Chapter 13 (Government Procurement);

    (d)   develop arrangements for implementing this Agreement;

    (e)   seek to resolve differences or disputes that may arise regarding the interpretation or application of this Agreement;

    (f)   issue interpretations of the provisions of this Agreement;[1]

    (g)   seek the advice of non-governmental persons or groups;

    (h)   modify any Uniform Regulations agreed jointly by the Parties under Article 5.16 (Uniform Regulations), subject to completion of applicable legal procedures by each Party; and

    (i)   take any other action as the Parties may decide.

3.   For the purposes of an action with respect to a provision that applies only as between two Parties, including the interpretation, amendment, or modification of that provision, the Commission shall be composed of,

---

[1]   For greater certainty, interpretations issued by the Commission are binding for tribunals and panels established under Chapter 14 (Investment) and Chapter 31 (Dispute Settlement).

and decisions taken by, the Commission representatives of those Parties.

Article 30.3:   Decision-Making

The Commission and subsidiary bodies established under this Agreement shall take decisions by consensus, except as otherwise provided in this Agreement, as otherwise decided by the Parties, or as provided for in Article 30.2.3 (Functions of the Commission). Unless otherwise provided in this Agreement, the Commission or a subsidiary body shall be deemed to have taken a decision by consensus if all Parties are present at a meeting when a decision is taken and no Party present at the meeting when a decision is taken objects to the proposed decision.

Article 30.4:   Rules of Procedure of the Commission and Subsidiary Bodies

1. The Commission shall meet within one year of the date of entry into force of this Agreement and thereafter as the Parties may decide, including as necessary to fulfil its functions under Article 30.2 (Functions of the Commission). Meetings of the Commission shall be chaired successively by each Party.

2. The Party chairing a meeting of the Commission shall provide any necessary administrative support for the meeting.

3. Unless otherwise provided in this Agreement, the Commission and a subsidiary body established under this Agreement shall carry out its work through whatever means are appropriate, which may include electronic mail or videoconferencing.

4. The Commission and a subsidiary body established under this Agreement may establish rules of procedures for the conduct of its work.

Article 30.5:   Agreement Coordinator and Contact Points

1. Each Party shall designate an Agreement Coordinator to facilitate communications between the Parties on any matter covered by this Agreement, as well as other contact points as required by this Agreement.

2. Unless otherwise provided in this Agreement, each Party shall notify the other Parties in writing of its Agreement Coordinator and any other contact point provided for in this Agreement no later than 60 days after the date of entry into force of this Agreement.

3. Each Party shall promptly notify the other Parties, in writing, of any changes to its Agreement Coordinator or any other contact point.

4. On the request of another Party, the Agreement Coordinator shall identify the office or official responsible for a matter and assist, as necessary, in facilitating communication with the requesting Party.

Article 30.6:   The Secretariat

1. The Commission shall establish and oversee a Secretariat comprising national Sections.

2.   Each Party shall:

(a)   establish and maintain a permanent office of its Section and be responsible for its operation and costs;

(b)   designate an individual to serve as Secretary for its Section, who shall be responsible for its administration and management; and

(c)   notify the other Parties of the contact information for its Section's office.

3.   The Secretariat shall:

(a)   provide assistance to the Commission;

(b)   provide administrative assistance to:

(i)   panels and committees established under Section D of Chapter 10 (Review and Dispute Settlement in Antidumping and Countervailing Duty Matters), and

(ii)   panels established under Chapter 31 (Dispute Settlement);

(c)   be responsible for the payment of remuneration to and expenses of panelists, assistants, and experts involved in dispute settlement proceedings under Chapter 31 (Dispute Settlement); and

(d)   as the Commission may direct:

(i)   support the work of other committees and groups established under this Agreement, and

(ii)   otherwise facilitate the operation of this Agreement.

CHAPTER 31   DISPUTE SETTLEMENT

Section A: Dispute Settlement

Article 31.1:   Cooperation

The Parties shall at all times endeavor to agree on the interpretation and application of this Agreement, and shall make every attempt through cooperation and consultations to arrive at a mutually satisfactory resolution of a matter that might affect its operation or application.

Article 31.2:   Scope

1.   Unless otherwise provided for in this Agreement, the dispute settlement provisions of this Chapter apply:

(a)   with respect to the avoidance or settlement of disputes between the Parties regarding the interpretation or application of this Agreement;

(b)   when a Party considers that an actual or proposed measure of another Party is or would be inconsistent with an obligation of this Agreement or that another Party has otherwise failed to carry out an obligation of this Agreement; or

(c)   when a Party considers that a benefit it could reasonably have expected to accrue to it under Chapter 2 (National Treatment and Market Access for Goods), Chapter 3 (Agriculture), Chapter 4 (Rules of Origin), Chapter 5 (Origin Procedures), Chapter 6 (Textile and Apparel Goods), Chapter 7 (Customs Administration and Trade Facilitation), Chapter 9 (Sanitary and Phytosanitary Measures), Chapter 11 (Technical Barriers to Trade), Chapter 13 (Government Procurement), Chapter 15 (Cross-Border Trade in Services), or Chapter 20 (Intellectual Property Rights), is being nullified or impaired as a result of the application of a measure of another Party that is not inconsistent with this Agreement.

Article 31.3:   Choice of Forum

1.   If a dispute regarding a matter arises under this Agreement and under another international trade agreement to which the disputing Parties are party, including the WTO Agreement, the complaining Party may select the forum in which to settle the dispute.

2.   Once a complaining Party has requested the establishment of, or referred a matter to, a panel under this Chapter or a panel or tribunal under an agreement referred to in paragraph 1, the forum selected shall be used to the exclusion of other fora.

Article 31.4:   Consultations

1.   A Party may request consultations with another Party with respect to a matter described in Article 31.2 (Scope).

2.   The Party making the request for consultations shall do so in writing, and shall set out the reasons for the request, including identification of the specific measure or other matter at issue and an indication of the legal basis for the complaint.

3.   The requesting Party shall deliver the request concurrently to the other Parties through their respective Sections of the Secretariat, including a copy to its Section.

4.   A third Party that considers it has a substantial interest in the matter may participate in the consultations by notifying the other Parties in writing through their respective Sections of the Secretariat, including a copy to its Section, no later than seven days after the date of delivery of the request for consultations. The Party shall include in its notice an explanation of its substantial interest in the matter.

5.   Unless the consulting Parties decide otherwise, they shall enter into consultations no later than:

(a) 15 days after the date of delivery of the request for a matter concerning perishable goods;[1] or

(b) 30 days after the date of delivery of the request for all other matters.

6. The consulting Parties shall make every attempt to arrive at a mutually satisfactory resolution of a matter through consultations under this Article or other consultative provisions of this Agreement. To this end:

(a) each consulting Party shall provide sufficient information to enable a full examination of how the actual or proposed measure or other matter at issue might affect the operation or application of this Agreement;

(b) a Party that participates in the consultations shall treat the information exchanged in the course of consultations that is designated as confidential on the same basis as the Party providing the information; and

(c) the consulting Parties shall seek to avoid a resolution that adversely affects the interests of another Party under this Agreement.

7. Consultations may be held in person or by a technological means available to the consulting Parties. If the consultations are held in person, they shall be held in the capital of the Party to which the request for consultations was made, unless the consulting Parties decide otherwise.

8. In consultations under this Article, a consulting Party may request that another consulting Party make available personnel of its government agencies or other regulatory bodies who have expertise in the matter at issue.

9. Consultations shall be confidential and without prejudice to the rights of a Party in another proceeding.

Article 31.5: Commission, Good Offices, Conciliation, and Mediation

1. If the consulting Parties fail to resolve a matter pursuant to Article 31.4 (Consultations) within:

(a) 30 days of delivery of the request for consultations;

(b) 45 days of delivery of the request if another Party has subsequently requested or has participated in consultations regarding the same matter;

(c) 15 days of delivery of the request for consultations in a matter regarding perishable goods; or

(d) another period as they may decide,

a consulting Party may request in writing a meeting of the Commission.

---

[1] For the purposes of this Chapter, perishable goods means perishable agricultural and fish goods classified in HS Chapters 1 through 24.

2.   The requesting Party shall state in the request the measure or other matter complained of and indicate the provisions of this Agreement that it considers relevant, and shall deliver the request to the other Parties and to its Section of the Secretariat.

3.   Unless it decides otherwise, the Commission[2] shall convene within 10 days of delivery of the request and shall endeavor to resolve the dispute.

4.   The Commission may:

(a)   call on technical advisers or create working groups or expert groups as it deems necessary;

(b)   have recourse to good offices, conciliation, mediation, or other dispute resolution procedures; or

(c)   make recommendations,

as may assist the consulting Parties to reach a mutually satisfactory resolution of the dispute.

5.   Unless it decides otherwise, the Commission shall consolidate two or more proceedings before it pursuant to this Article regarding the same measure. The Commission may consolidate two or more proceedings regarding other matters before it pursuant to this Article that it determines are appropriate to be considered jointly.

6.   Parties may decide at any time to voluntarily undertake an alternative method of dispute resolution, such as good offices, conciliation, or mediation.

7.   Proceedings that involve good offices, conciliation, or mediation shall be confidential and without prejudice to the rights of the Parties in another proceeding.

8.   Parties participating in proceedings under this Article may suspend or terminate those proceedings.

9.   If the disputing Parties decide, good offices, conciliation, or mediation may continue while a dispute proceeds for resolution before a panel established under Article 31.6 (Establishment of a Panel).

Article 31.6:   Establishment of a Panel

1.   If the Commission has convened pursuant to Article 31.5 (Commission, Good Offices, Conciliation, and Mediation), and the matter has not been resolved within:

(a)   30 days thereafter;

(b)   30 days after the Commission has convened in respect of the matter most recently referred to it, if proceedings have been consolidated pursuant to Article 31.5.5 (Commission, Good Offices, Conciliation, and Mediation); or

---

[2]   For the purposes of this Article, the Commission shall be composed of, and decisions taken by the Commission representatives of the consulting Parties.

(c)   another period as the consulting Parties may decide,

a consulting Party may request the establishment of a panel by means of a written notice delivered to the responding Party through its Section of the Secretariat.

2.   The complaining Party shall circulate the written notice concurrently to the other Parties through their respective Sections of the Secretariat.

3.   The complaining Party shall include in the request to establish a panel an identification of the measure or other matter at issue and a brief summary of the legal basis of the complaint sufficient to present the issue clearly.

4.   On delivery of the request, the Commission shall establish a panel.

5.   A third Party that considers it has a substantial interest in the matter is entitled to join as a complaining Party on delivery of written notice of its intention to participate to the disputing Parties through their respective Sections of the Secretariat, including a copy to its Section. The third Party shall deliver the notice no later than seven days after the date of delivery of a request by a Party for the establishment of a panel.

6.   Unless the disputing Parties decide otherwise, the panel shall be established and perform its functions in a manner consistent with this Chapter and the Rules of Procedure.

7.   If a panel has been established regarding a matter and another Party requests the establishment of a panel regarding the same matter, a single panel should be established to examine those complaints whenever feasible.

Article 31.7:   Terms of Reference

1.   Unless the disputing Parties decide otherwise no later than 20 days after the date of delivery of the request for the establishment of a panel, the terms of reference shall be to:

(a)   examine, in the light of the relevant provisions of this Agreement, the matter referred to in the request for the establishment of a panel under Article 31.6 (Establishment of a Panel); and

(b)   make findings and determinations, and any jointly requested recommendations, together with its reasons therefor, as provided for in Article 31.17 (Panel Report).

2.   If, in its request for the establishment of a panel, a complaining Party claims that a measure nullifies or impairs a benefit within the meaning of Article 31.2 (Scope), the terms of reference shall so indicate.

3.   If a disputing Party wishes the panel to make findings as to the degree of adverse trade effects on a Party of a measure found not to conform with an obligation of this Agreement or to have caused nullification or impairment in the sense of Article 31.2(c) (Scope), the terms of reference shall so indicate.

Article 31.8:   Roster and Qualifications of Panelists

1. The Parties shall establish by the date of entry into force of this Agreement and maintain a roster of up to 30 individuals who are willing to serve as panelists. The roster shall be appointed by consensus and remain in effect for a minimum of three years or until the Parties constitute a new roster. Members of the roster may be reappointed.

2. Each roster member and panelist shall:

   (a) have expertise or experience in international law, international trade, other matters covered by this Agreement, or the resolution of disputes arising under international trade agreements;

   (b) be selected on the basis of objectivity, reliability, and sound judgment;

   (c) be independent of, and not be affiliated with or take instructions from, a Party; and

   (d) comply with the Code of Conduct established by the Commission.

3. For a dispute arising under Chapter 23 (Labor) and Chapter 24 (Environment), each disputing Party shall select a panelist in accordance with the following requirements, in addition to those set out in paragraph 1:

   (a) in a dispute arising under Chapter 23 (Labor), panelists other than the chair shall have expertise or experience in labor law or practice; and

   (b) in a dispute arising under Chapter 24 (Environment), panelists other than the chair shall have expertise or experience in environmental law or practice.

4. In disputes regarding specialized areas of law not set out in paragraph 3, the disputing Parties should select panelists to ensure that the necessary expertise is available on the panel.

5. An individual shall not serve as a panelist in the same dispute in which the individual has participated pursuant to Articles 31.4 (Consultations) or Article 31.5 (Commission, Good Offices, Conciliation, and Mediation).

Article 31.9:   Panel Composition

1. If there are two disputing Parties, the following procedures shall apply:

   (a) The panel shall comprise five members.

   (b) The disputing Parties shall endeavor to decide on the chair of the panel within 15 days of the delivery of the request for the establishment of the panel. If the disputing Parties are unable to decide on the chair within this period, the disputing Party chosen by lot shall select within five days as chair an individual who is not a citizen of that Party.

(c)   Within 15 days of selection of the chair, each disputing Party shall select two panelists who are citizens of the other disputing Party.

(d)   If a disputing Party fails to select its panelists within that period, those panelists shall be selected by lot from among the roster members who are citizens of the other disputing Party.

2.   If there are more than two disputing Parties, the following procedures apply:

(a)   The panel shall comprise five members.

(b)   The disputing Parties shall endeavor to decide on the chair of the panel within 15 days of the delivery of the request for the establishment of the panel and, if the disputing Parties are unable to decide on the chair within this period, the Party or Parties on the side of the dispute chosen by lot shall select within 10 days a chair who is not a citizen of that Party or those Parties.

(c)   Within 15 days of selection of the chair, the responding Party shall select two panelists, one of whom is a citizen of a complaining Party, and the other of whom is a citizen of another complaining Party and the complaining Parties shall select two panelists who are citizens of the responding Party.

(d)   If a disputing Party fails to select a panelist within that period, that panelist shall be selected by lot in accordance with the citizenship criteria of subparagraph (c).

3.   A panelist shall normally be selected from the roster. A disputing Party may exercise a peremptory challenge against an individual not on the roster who is proposed as a panelist by a disputing Party within 15 days after the individual has been proposed, unless no qualified and available individual on the roster possesses necessary specialized expertise, including as required by Article 31.8.3 (Roster and Qualifications of Panelists), in which case a disputing Party may not exercise a peremptory challenge but may raise concerns that the panelist does not meet the requirements of Article 31.8.2 (Roster and Qualifications of Panelists).

4.   If a disputing Party believes that a panelist is in violation of the Code of Conduct, the disputing Parties shall consult and if they concur the panelist shall be removed and a new panelist shall be selected in accordance with this Article.

Article 31.10:   Replacement of Panelists

1.   If a panelist resigns, is removed, or becomes unable to serve, the time frames applicable to that panel's proceeding shall be suspended until a replacement is appointed and shall be extended by the amount of time that the work was suspended.

2.   If a panelist resigns, is removed, or becomes unable to serve on the panel, a replacement panelist shall be appointed within 15 days in accordance with the same method used to select the panelist in accordance with Article 31.9 (Panel Composition).

3.   If a disputing Party believes that a panelist is in violation of the Code of Conduct, the disputing Parties shall consult. If they concur on removing the panelist, they shall be removed and a new panelist shall be selected in accordance with this Article.

Article 31.11:   Rules of Procedure for Panels

The Rules of Procedure, established under this Agreement in accordance with Article 30.2 (Functions of the Commission), shall ensure that:

(a)   disputing Parties have the right to at least one hearing before the panel at which each may present views orally;

(b)   subject to subparagraph (f), a hearing before the panel shall be open to the public, unless the disputing Parties decide otherwise;

(c)   each disputing Party has an opportunity to provide an initial and a rebuttal written submission;

(d)   subject to subparagraph (f), each disputing Party's written submissions, written version of an oral statement, and written response to a request or question from the panel, if any, are public as soon as possible after the documents are filed;

(e)   the panel shall consider requests from non-governmental entities located in the territory of a disputing Party to provide written views regarding the dispute that may assist the panel in evaluating the submissions and arguments of the disputing Parties;

(f)   confidential information is protected;

(g)   written submissions and oral arguments shall be made in one of the languages of the Parties, unless the disputing Parties decide otherwise; and

(h)   unless the disputing Parties decide otherwise, hearings shall be held in the capital of the responding Party.

Article 31.12:   Electronic Document Filing

The disputing Parties shall file all documents relating to a dispute, including written submissions, written versions of oral statements, and written responses to panel questions, by electronic means through their respective Sections of the Secretariat.

Article 31.13:   Function of Panels

1.   A panel's function is to make an objective assessment of the matter before it and to present a report that contains:

(a) findings of fact;

(b) determinations as to whether:

   (i)   the measure at issue is inconsistent with obligations in this Agreement,

   (ii) a Party has otherwise failed to carry out its obligations in this Agreement,

   (iii) the measure at issue is causing nullification or impairment within the meaning of Article 31.2 (Scope), or

   (iv) any other determination requested in the terms of reference;

(c) recommendations, if the disputing Parties have jointly requested them, for the resolution of the dispute; and

(d) the reasons for the findings and determinations.

2. The findings, determinations and recommendations of the panel shall not add to or diminish the rights and obligations of the Parties under this Agreement.

3. Unless the disputing Parties decide otherwise, the panel shall perform its functions and conduct its proceeding in a manner consistent with this Chapter and the Rules of Procedure.

4. The panel shall interpret this Agreement in accordance with customary rules of interpretation of public international law, as reflected in Articles 31 and 32 of the *Vienna Convention on the Law of Treaties*, done at Vienna on May 23, 1969.

5. A panel shall take its decision by consensus, except that, if a panel is unable to reach consensus, it may take its decision by majority vote.

6. The panel shall base its report on the relevant provisions of this Agreement, the submissions and arguments of the disputing Parties, and on any information or advice put before it under Article 31.15 (Role of Experts).

7. The panel shall draft its reports without the presence of any Party.

8. Panelists may present separate views on matters not unanimously agreed and shall not disclose the identity of which panelists are associated with majority or minority views.

Article 31.14:   Third Party Participation

A Party that is not a disputing Party shall, on delivery of a written notice to the disputing Parties through their respective Sections of the Secretariat, including a copy to its Section, be entitled to attend any hearing, to make written and oral submissions to the panel, and to receive written submissions of the disputing Parties. The Party shall provide written notice no later than 10 days after the date of delivery of the request for the establishment of the panel under Article 31.6 (Establishment of a Panel).

Article 31.15: Role of Experts

At the request of a disputing Party, or on its own initiative, a panel may seek information or technical advice from a person or body that it deems appropriate, provided that the disputing Parties agree and subject to any terms and conditions decided on by the disputing Parties. The disputing Parties shall have an opportunity to comment on information or advice obtained under this Article.

Article 31.16: Suspension or Termination of Proceedings

1. The panel may suspend its work at any time at the request of the complaining Party, for a period not to exceed 12 consecutive months. The panel shall suspend its work at any time if the disputing Parties request it to do so. In the event of a suspension, the time frames set out in this Chapter and in the Rules of Procedure shall be extended by the amount of time that the work was suspended. If the work of the panel is suspended for more than 12 consecutive months, the panel proceedings shall lapse unless the disputing Parties decide otherwise.

2. The panel shall terminate its proceedings if the disputing Parties request it to do so.

Article 31.17: Panel Report

1. The panel shall present an initial report to the disputing Parties no later than 150 days after the date of the appointment of the last panelist. In cases of urgency related to perishable goods, the panel shall endeavour to present an initial report to the disputing Parties no later than 120 days after the date of the appointment of the last panelist.

2. In exceptional cases, if the panel considers that it cannot release its initial report within the time period specified in paragraph 1, it shall inform the disputing Parties in writing of the reasons for the delay together with an estimate of when it will issue its report. A delay shall not exceed an additional period of 30 days unless the disputing Parties decide otherwise.

3. A disputing Party may submit written comments to the panel on its initial report no later than 15 days after the presentation of the initial report or within another period as the disputing Parties may decide.

4. After considering those comments, the panel, on its own initiative or on the request of a disputing Party, may:

   (a) request the views of a Party;

   (b) reconsider its report; or

   (c) make a further examination that it considers appropriate.

5. The panel shall present a final report including any separate opinions on matters not unanimously agreed to the disputing Parties no later than 30 days after presentation of the initial report, unless the disputing Parties decide otherwise.

6.   After taking any steps to protect confidential information, and no later than 15 days after the presentation of the final report, the disputing Parties shall make the final report available to the public.

Article 31.18:   Implementation of Final Report

1.   Within 45 days from receipt of a final report that contains findings that:

   (a)   the measure at issue is inconsistent with a Party's obligations in this Agreement;

   (b)   a Party has otherwise failed to carry out its obligations in this Agreement; or

   (c)   the measure at issue is causing nullification or impairment within the meaning of Article 31.2 (Scope),

the disputing Parties shall endeavor to agree on the resolution of the dispute.

2.   Resolution of the dispute can comprise elimination of the non-conformity or the nullification or impairment, if possible, the provision of mutually acceptable compensation, or another remedy the disputing Parties may agree.

Article 31.19:   Non-Implementation—Suspension of Benefits

1.   If the disputing Parties are unable to agree on a resolution to the dispute under Article 31.18 (Implementation of Final Report) within 45 days from receipt of the final report, the complaining Party may suspend the application to the responding Party of benefits of equivalent effect to the non-conformity or the nullification or impairment until the disputing Parties agree on a resolution to the dispute.

2.   In considering what benefits to suspend pursuant to paragraph 1:

   (a)   a complaining Party should first seek to suspend benefits in the same sector as that affected by the measure or other matter that was the subject of the dispute; and

   (b)   a complaining Party that considers it is not practicable or effective to suspend benefits in the same sector, may suspend benefits in other sectors unless otherwise provided for elsewhere in this Agreement.

3.   If the responding Party considers that:

   (a)   the level of benefits proposed to be suspended is manifestly excessive; or

   (b)   it has eliminated the non-conformity or the nullification or impairment that the panel has determined to exist,

it may request that the panel be reconvened to consider the matter. The responding Party shall deliver its request in writing to the complaining Party. The panel shall reconvene as soon as possible after the date of delivery of the request and shall present its determination to the disputing Parties no later than 90 days after it reconvenes to review a request under subparagraph (a) or (b), or 120 days after it reconvenes for a request under both subparagraphs (a) and (b). If the panel considers that the level of benefits the complaining Party proposes to suspend is manifestly excessive, it shall provide its views as to the level of benefits it considers to be of equivalent effect.

4. If the panel's views are that the responding Party has not eliminated the non-conformity or the nullification or impairment, the complaining Party may suspend benefits up to the level the panel has determined under paragraph 3.

Section B: Domestic Proceedings and Private Commercial Dispute Settlement

Article 31.20: Referrals of Matters from Judicial or Administrative Proceedings

1. If an issue of interpretation or application of this Agreement arises in a domestic judicial or administrative proceeding of a Party that a Party considers would merit its intervention, or if a court or administrative body solicits the views of a Party, that Party shall notify the other Parties and its Section of the Secretariat. The Commission shall endeavor to agree on an appropriate response as expeditiously as possible.

2. The Party in whose territory the court or administrative body is located shall submit an agreed interpretation of the Commission to the court or administrative body in accordance with the rules of that forum.

3. If the Commission is unable to agree, a Party may submit its own views to the court or administrative body in accordance with the rules of that forum.

Article 31.21: Private Rights

No Party shall provide for a right of action under its law against another Party on the ground that a measure of that other Party is inconsistent with this Agreement.

Article 31.22: Alternative Dispute Resolution

1. Each Party shall, to the extent possible, encourage, facilitate, and promote through education, the use of arbitration, mediation, online dispute resolution and other procedures for the prevention and resolution of international commercial disputes between private parties in the free trade area.

2. To this end, each Party shall provide appropriate procedures to ensure observance of agreements to arbitrate and for the recognition and enforcement of arbitral awards and settlement agreements in those disputes, and to facilitate and encourage mediation procedures.

3. A Party shall be deemed to be in compliance with paragraph 2 if it is a party to and is in compliance with the *Convention on the Recognition and Enforcement of Foreign Arbitral Awards*, done at New York on June 10 1958, or the *Inter-American Convention on International Commercial Arbitration*, done at Panama on January 30, 1975.

4. The Commission shall establish and maintain an Advisory Committee on Private Commercial Disputes comprising persons with expertise or experience in the resolution of private international commercial disputes. The Committee shall, to the extent possible, encourage, facilitate, and promote through education, the use of arbitration, mediation, online dispute resolution and other procedures for the prevention and resolution of international commercial disputes between private parties in the free trade area. The Committee shall report and provide recommendations to the Commission on general issues respecting the availability, use, and effectiveness of arbitration, mediation, online dispute settlement resolution, and other dispute resolution procedures for the prevention and resolution of those disputes in the free trade area.

CHAPTER 32   EXCEPTIONS AND GENERAL PROVISIONS

Section A: Exceptions

Article 32.1:   General Exceptions

1. For the purposes of Chapter 2 (National Treatment and Market Access for Goods), Chapter 3 (Agriculture), Chapter 4 (Rules of Origin), Chapter 5 (Origin Procedures), Chapter 6 (Textile and Apparel Goods), Chapter 7 (Customs Administration and Trade Facilitation), Chapter 9 (Sanitary and Phytosanitary Measures), Chapter 11 (Technical Barriers to Trade), Chapter 12 (Sectoral Annexes), and Chapter 22 (State-Owned Enterprises and Designated Monopolies), Article XX of the GATT 1994 and its interpretative notes are incorporated into and made part of this Agreement, *mutatis mutandis.*[1]

2. For the purposes of Chapter 15 (Cross-Border Trade in Services), Chapter 16 (Temporary Entry for Business Persons), Chapter 18 (Telecommunications), Chapter 19 (Digital Trade),[2] and Chapter 22 (State-Owned Enterprises and Designated Monopolies), paragraphs (a), (b), and (c) of Article XIV of GATS are incorporated into and made part of this Agreement, *mutatis mutandis.*[3]

---

[1]   For the purposes of Chapter 22 (State-Owned Enterprises and Designated Monopolies), Article XX of the GATT 1994 and its interpretative notes are incorporated into and made part of this Agreement, *mutatis mutandis,* only with respect to measures of a Party (including the implementation of measures through the activities of a state-owned enterprise or a designated monopoly) affecting the purchase, production, or sale of goods, or affecting activities the end result of which is the production of goods.

[2]   This paragraph is without prejudice to whether a Party considers a digital product to be a good or service.

[3]   For the purposes of Chapter 22 (State-Owned Enterprises and Designated Monopolies), Article XIV of the GATS 1994 (including its footnotes) is incorporated into and made part of this Agreement, *mutatis mutandis,* only with respect to measures of a Party (including the implementation of measures through the activities of a state-owned enterprise or a designated monopoly) affecting the purchase or supply of services, or affecting activities the end result of which is the supply of services.

3.   The Parties understand that the measures referred to in Article XX(b) of the GATT 1994 and GATS Article XIV(b) include environmental measures necessary to protect human, animal, or plant life or health, and that Article XX(g) of the GATT 1994 applies to measures relating to the conservation of living and non-living exhaustible natural resources.

Nothing in this Agreement shall be construed to prevent a Party from taking action, including maintaining or increasing a customs duty, that is authorized by the Dispute Settlement Body of the WTO or is taken as a result of a decision by a dispute settlement panel under a free trade agreement to which the Party taking action and the Party against which the action is taken are party.

Article 32.2:   Essential Security

1.   Nothing in this Agreement shall be construed to:

   (a)   require a Party to furnish or allow access to information the disclosure of which it determines to be contrary to its essential security interests; or

   (b)   preclude a Party from applying measures that it considers necessary for the fulfilment of its obligations with respect to the maintenance or restoration of international peace or security, or the protection of its own essential security interests.

Article 32.3:   Taxation Measures

1.   For the purposes of this Article:

   Designated authorities means:

   (a)   for Canada, the Assistant Deputy Minister for Tax Policy, Department of Finance;

   (b)   for Mexico, the Deputy Minister of Revenue of the Ministry of Finance and Public Credit (*Subsecretario de Ingresos*); and

   (c)   for the United States, the Assistant Secretary of the Treasury (Tax Policy), or any successor of these designated authorities as notified in writing to the other Parties;

Tax convention means a convention for the avoidance of double taxation or other international taxation agreement or arrangement; and

Taxes and taxation measures include excise duties, but do not include:

   (a)   a "customs duty" as defined in Article 1.4 (General Definitions); or

   (b)   the measures listed in subparagraphs (b), (c), and (d) of that definition.

2.   Except as provided in this Article, this Agreement does not apply to a taxation measure.

3. This Agreement does not affect the rights and obligations of a Party under a tax convention. In the event of any inconsistency between this Agreement and a tax convention, that convention prevails to the extent of the inconsistency.

4. In the case of a tax convention between two or more Parties, if an issue arises as to whether an inconsistency exists between this Agreement and the tax convention, the issue shall be referred to the designated authorities of the Parties in question. The designated authorities of those Parties shall have six months from the date of referral of the issue to make a determination as to the existence and extent of any inconsistency. If those designated authorities agree, the period may be extended up to 12 months from the date of referral of the issue. No procedures concerning the measure giving rise to the issue may be initiated under Chapter 31 (Dispute Settlement) or, as between the United States and Mexico, Annex 14-D (Mexico-United States Investment Disputes), or Annex 14-E (Mexico-United States Investment Disputes Related to Covered Government Contracts) until the expiry of the six month period, or any other period as may have been agreed by the designated authorities. A panel or tribunal established to consider a dispute related to a taxation measure shall accept as binding a determination of the designated authorities of the Parties in question made under this paragraph.

5. Notwithstanding paragraph 3:

    (a) Article 2.3 (National Treatment) and other provisions of this Agreement that are necessary to give effect to that Article apply to taxation measures to the same extent as does Article III of the GATT 1994, including its interpretative notes; and

    (b) Article 2.13 (Export Duties, Taxes, or other Charges) applies to taxation measures.

6. Subject to paragraph 3:

    (a) Article 15.3 (National Treatment) and Article 17.3 (National Treatment) apply to a taxation measure on income, on capital gains, or on the taxable capital of corporations that relate to the purchase or consumption of particular services, except that this subparagraph does not prevent a Party from conditioning the receipt or continued receipt of an advantage that relates to the purchase or consumption of particular services on requirements to provide the service in its territory;

    (b) Article 14.4 (National Treatment), Article 14.5 (Most-Favored-Nation Treatment), Article 15.3 (National Treatment), Article 15.4 (Most-Favoured-Nation Treatment), Article 17.3 (National Treatment), Article 17.4 (Most-Favoured-Nation Treatment), and Article 19.4 (Non-Discriminatory Treatment of Digital Products) apply to a taxation measure, other than a taxation measure on income, on capital gains, on the taxable capital of corporations, or taxes on estates, inheritances, gifts, and generation-skipping transfers; and

(c)   Article 19.4 (Non-Discriminatory Treatment of Digital Products) apply to a taxation measure on income, on capital gains, or on the taxable capital of corporations that relate to the purchase or consumption of particular digital products, except that this subparagraph does not prevent a Party from conditioning the receipt or continued receipt of an advantage relating to the purchase or consumption of particular digital products on requirements to provide the digital product in its territory, but nothing in the Articles referred to in subparagraphs (a), (b), and (c) apply to:

(d)   a most-favored-nation obligation with respect to an advantage accorded by a Party pursuant to a tax convention;

(e)   a non-conforming provision of a taxation measure in existence as of the date of entry into force of NAFTA 1994;

(f)   the continuation or prompt renewal of a non-conforming provision of a taxation measure in existence as of the date of entry into force of NAFTA 1994;

(g)   an amendment to a non-conforming provision of a taxation measure in existence as of the date of entry into force of NAFTA 1994 to the extent that the amendment does not decrease its conformity, at the time of the amendment, with any of those Articles;

(h)   the adoption or enforcement of a new taxation measure aimed at ensuring the equitable or effective imposition or collection of taxes, including a taxation measure that differentiates between persons based on their place of residence for tax purposes, provided that the taxation measure does not arbitrarily discriminate between persons, goods, or services of the Parties;[4]

(i)   a provision that conditions the receipt or continued receipt of an advantage relating to the contributions to, or income of, a pension trust, pension plan, or other arrangement to provide pension, or similar benefits, on a requirement that the Party maintain continuous jurisdiction, regulation, or supervision over that trust, plan, fund, or other arrangement; or

(j)   an excise duty on insurance premiums to the extent that the excise duty would, if levied by another Party, be covered by subparagraphs (e), (f), or (g).

---

[4]   The Parties understand that this subparagraph must be interpreted by reference to the footnote to Article XIV(d) of GATS as if the Article was not restricted to services or direct taxes.

7.   Subject to paragraph 3, and without prejudice to the rights and obligations of the Parties under paragraph 5, Article 14.10.2 (Performance Requirements), Article 14.10.3, and Article 14.10.4 apply to a taxation measure.

8.   Article 14.8 (Expropriation and Compensation) applies to a taxation measure. However, as between the United States and Mexico, no investor may invoke Article 14.8 (Expropriation and Compensation) as the basis for a claim if it has been determined pursuant to this paragraph that the measure is not an expropriation. An investor of the United States or Mexico that seeks to invoke Article 14.8 (Expropriation and Compensation) with respect to a taxation measure must first refer to the designated authorities of the Party of the investor and the respondent Party, at the time that it gives its notice of intent under Article 14.D.3 (Submission of a Claim to Arbitration), the issue of whether that taxation measure is not an expropriation. If the designated authorities do not agree to consider the issue or, having agreed to consider it, fail to agree that the measure is not an expropriation within a period of six months of the referral, the investor of the United States or Mexico may submit its claim to arbitration under, as applicable, Annex 14.D.3 (Submission of a Claim to Arbitration) or paragraph 2 of Annex 14-E (Mexico-United States Investment Disputes Related to Covered Government Contracts).

Article 32.4:   Temporary Safeguards Measures

1.   For the purposes of this Article:

foreign direct investment means a type of investment by an investor of a Party in the territory of another Party, through which the investor exercises ownership or control over, or a significant degree of influence on the management of, an enterprise or other direct investment, and tends to be undertaken in order to establish a lasting relationship; for example, ownership of at least 10 percent of the voting power of an enterprise over a period of at least 12 months generally would be considered a foreign direct investment.

2.   This Agreement does not prevent a Party from adopting or maintaining a restrictive measure with regard to payments or transfers for current account transactions in the event of serious balance of payments and external financial difficulties or threats thereof.

3.   This Agreement does not prevent a Party from adopting or maintaining a restrictive measure with regard to payments or transfers relating to the movements of capital:

(a)   in the event of serious balance of payments and external financial difficulties or threats thereof; or

(b)   if, in exceptional circumstances, payments or transfers relating to capital movements cause or threaten to cause serious difficulties for macroeconomic management.

4. A measure adopted or maintained under paragraph 1 or 2 must:

    (a) not be inconsistent with Article 14.4 (National Treatment), Article 14.5 (Most-Favoured-Nation Treatment), Article 15.3 (National Treatment), Article 15.4 (Most-Favoured-Nation Treatment), Article 17.3 (National Treatment), and Article 17.4 (Most-Favoured-Nation Treatment);[5]

    (b) be consistent with the Articles of Agreement of the IMF;

    (c) avoid unnecessary damage to the commercial, economic, and financial interests of another Party;

    (d) not exceed those necessary to deal with the circumstances described in paragraph 1 or 2;

    (e) be temporary and be phased out progressively as the situations specified in paragraph 1 or 2 improve, and shall not exceed 12 months in duration; however, in exceptional circumstances, a Party may extend that measure for one additional period of one year, by notifying the other Parties in writing within 30 days of the extension;

    (f) not be inconsistent with Article 14.8 (Expropriation and Compensation);[6]

    (g) in the case of restrictions on capital outflows, not interfere with investors' ability to earn a market rate of return in the territory of the restricting Party on assets invested in the territory of the restricting Party by an investor of a Party that are restricted from being transferred out of the territory of the restricting Party; and

    (h) not be used to avoid necessary macroeconomic adjustment.

5. As soon as practicable after a Party imposes a measure under paragraph 1, the Party shall:

    (a) submit any current account exchange restrictions to the IMF for review and approval under Article VIII of the Articles of Agreement of the IMF;

consistent with its obligations under the Articles of Agreement of the IMF, enter into good faith consultations with the IMF on economic adjustment measures necessary to remove the restrictions in 3(a); and

    (b) adopt or maintain economic policies consistent with those consultations.

---

[5]   Without prejudice to the general interpretation of the Articles listed in this sub-paragraph, the fact that a measure a Party adopts or maintains pursuant to paragraph 1 or 2 differentiates between investors on the basis of residency does not necessarily mean that the measure is inconsistent with those Articles.

[6]   For greater certainty, a measure referred to in paragraph 1 or 2 may be non-discriminatory regulatory actions by a Party that is designed and applied to protect legitimate public welfare objectives as referred to in Annex 14-B.3(b) (Expropriation).

6. Measures referred to in paragraphs 1 and 2 shall not apply to payments or transfers relating to foreign direct investment.

7. A Party shall endeavor to provide that a measure it adopts or maintains under paragraph 1 or 2 be price-based, and if that measure is not price-based, the Party shall explain the rationale for using quantitative restrictions when it notifies the other Parties of the measure.

8. In the case of trade in goods, Article XII of GATT 1994 and the *Understanding on the Balance-of-Payments Provisions of the GATT 1994*, set out in Annex 1A to the WTO Agreement, are incorporated into and made part of this Agreement, *mutatis mutandis.* Any measure it adopts or maintains under this paragraph shall not impair the relative benefits accorded to another Party under this Agreement as compared to the treatment of a non-Party.

9. A Party adopting or maintaining a measure under paragraph 1, 2, or 6 shall:

    (a) notify, in writing, the other Parties of the measure, including any changes in it, along with the rationale for their imposition, within 30 days of its adoption;

    (b) present, as soon as possible, either a time schedule or the conditions necessary for their removal;

    (c) promptly publish the measure; and

    (d) promptly commence consultations with the other Parties in order to review the measure.

        (i) In the case of capital movements, promptly respond to any other Party that requests consultations in relation to the measure, provided that such consultations are not otherwise taking place outside of this Agreement.

        (ii) In the case of current account restrictions, if consultations in relation to the measure are not taking place under the framework of the WTO Agreement, a Party, if requested, shall promptly commence consultations with any interested Party.

Article 32.5: Indigenous Peoples Rights

Provided that such measures are not used as a means of arbitrary or unjustified discrimination against persons of the other Parties or as a disguised restriction on trade in goods, services, and investment, this Agreement does not preclude a Party from adopting or maintaining a measure it deems necessary to fulfill its legal obligations to indigenous peoples.[7]

---

[7] For greater certainty, for Canada the legal obligations include those recognized and affirmed by section 35 of the *Constitution Act 1982* or those set out in self-government agreements between a central or regional level of government and indigenous peoples.

Article 32.6:   Cultural Industries

1.   For the purposes of this Article, "cultural industry" means a person engaged in the following activities:

   (a)   the publication, distribution, or sale of books, magazines, periodicals, or newspapers in print or machine readable form but not including the sole activity of printing or typesetting any of the foregoing;

   (b)   the production, distribution, sale, or exhibition of film or video recordings;

   (c)   the production, distribution, sale, or exhibition of audio or video music recordings;

   (d)   the publication, distribution, or sale of music in print or machine readable form; or

   (e)   radiocommunications in which the transmissions are intended for direct reception by the general public, and all radio, television and cable broadcasting undertakings and all satellite programming and broadcast network services.

2.   This Agreement does not apply to a measure adopted or maintained by Canada with respect to a cultural industry, except as specifically provided in Article 2.4 (Treatment of Customs Duties) or Annex 15-D (Programming Services).

3.   With respect to Canadian goods, services, and content, the United States and Mexico may adopt or maintain a measure that, were it adopted or maintained by Canada, would have been inconsistent with this Agreement but for paragraph 2.

4.   Notwithstanding any other provision of this Agreement, a Party may take a measure of equivalent commercial effect in response to an action by another Party that would have been inconsistent with this Agreement but for paragraph 2 or 3.

5.   Notwithstanding Article 31.3 (Choice of Forum):

   (a)   dispute regarding a measure taken under paragraph 4 shall be settled exclusively under this Agreement unless a Party seeking to establish a panel under Article 31.6 (Establishment of a Panel) has been unable to do so within 90 days of the date of delivery of the request for consultations under Article 31.4 (Consultations); and

   (b)   a panel established under Article 31.6 (Establishment of a Panel) with respect to that challenge shall have jurisdiction and may make findings only with respect to:

      (i)   whether an action to which another Party responds is a measure adopted or maintained with respect to a cultural industry for purposes of this Article, and

(ii)   whether the responsive action of a Party is of "equivalent commercial effect" to the relevant action of the other Party.

Section B: General Provisions Article 32.7: Disclosure of Information

This Agreement does not require a Party to furnish or allow access to information, the disclosure of which would be contrary to its law or would impede law enforcement, or otherwise be contrary to the public interest, or which would prejudice the legitimate commercial interests of particular enterprises, public or private.

Article 32.8:   Personal Information Protection[8]

1.   For the purposes of this Article:

Personal information means information, including data, about an identified or identifiable natural person.

Each Party shall adopt or maintain a legal framework that provides for the protection of personal information.[9] In the development of this legal framework, each Party should take into account principles and guidelines of relevant international bodies, such as the *APEC Privacy Framework* and the *OECD Recommendation of the Council concerning Guidelines governing the Protection of Privacy and Transborder Flows of Personal Data (2013)*.

2.   The Parties recognize that, pursuant to paragraph 2 key principles include: limitation on collection; choice; data quality; purpose specification; use limitation; security safeguards; transparency; individual participation; and accountability.

3.   Each Party shall endeavor to adopt non-discriminatory practices in protecting natural persons from personal information protection violations occurring within its jurisdiction.

4.   Each Party shall publish information on the personal information protections it provides, including how:

(a)   individuals can pursue a remedy; and

(b)   an enterprise can comply with legal requirements.

5.   Recognizing that the Parties may take different legal approaches to protecting personal information, each Party should encourage the development of mechanisms to promote compatibility between these different regimes. The Parties shall endeavor to exchange information

---

[8]   This Article does not apply to information held or processed by or on behalf of a Party, or measures related to that information, including measures related to its collection.

[9]   For greater certainty, a Party may comply with the obligation in this paragraph by adopting or maintaining measures such as a comprehensive privacy, personal information, or personal data protection law, sector-specific laws covering privacy, or laws that provide for the enforcement of voluntary undertakings by enterprises relating to privacy.

on the mechanisms applied in their jurisdictions and explore ways to extend these or other suitable arrangements to promote compatibility between them. The Parties recognize that the *APEC Cross-Border Privacy Rules* system is a valid mechanism to facilitate cross-border information transfers while protecting personal information.

6. The Parties shall endeavor to foster cooperation between appropriate government agencies regarding investigations on matters involving personal information protection and encourage the development of mechanisms to assist users to submit cross-border complaints regarding protection of personal information.

Article 32.9:   Access to Information

Each Party shall maintain a legal framework that allows a natural person in its territory to obtain access to records held by the central level of government, subject to reasonable terms and limitations specified in the Party's law, provided that the terms and limitations applying to natural persons of another Party in the Party's territory are no less favorable than those applying to natural persons of the Party, or of another country, in the Party's territory.[10]

Article 32.10:   Non-Market Country FTA

1. For the purposes of this Article:

Non-market country is a country:

 (a) that on the date of signature of this Agreement, a Party has determined to be a non-market economy for purposes of its trade remedy laws; and

 (b) with which no Party has signed a free trade agreement.

2. At least 3 months prior to commencing negotiations, a Party shall inform the other Parties of its intention to commence free trade agreement negotiations with a non-market country.

3. Upon request of another Party, a Party intending to commence free trade negotiations with a non-market country shall provide as much information as possible regarding the objectives for those negotiations.

4. As early as possible, and no later than 30 days before the date of signature, a Party intending to sign a free trade agreement with a non-market country shall provide the other Parties with an opportunity to review the full text of the agreement, including any annexes and side instruments, in order for the Parties to be able to review the agreement and assess its potential impact on this Agreement. If the Party involved requests that the text be treated as confidential, the other Parties shall maintain the confidentiality of the text.

5. Entry by a Party into a free trade agreement with a non-market country will allow the other Parties to terminate this Agreement on six months'

---

[10]   For the United States, this provision applies to "agencies," as defined at 5 U.S.C. 551(1).

notice and replace this Agreement with an agreement as between them (bilateral agreement).

6. The bilateral agreement shall be comprised of all the provisions of this Agreement, except those provisions that the relevant Parties agree are not applicable as between them.

7. The relevant Parties shall utilize the six months' notice period to review this Agreement and determine whether any amendments should be made in order to ensure the proper operation of the bilateral agreement.

8. The bilateral agreement enters into force 60 days after the date on which the last party to the bilateral agreement has notified the other party that it has completed its applicable legal procedures.

Article 32.11: Specific Provision on Cross-Border Trade in Services, Investment, and State-Owned Enterprises and Designated Monopolies for Mexico

With respect to the obligations in Chapter 14 (Investment), Chapter 15 (Cross-Border Trade in Services), and Chapter 22 (State-Owned Enterprises and Designated Monopolies), Mexico reserves the right to adopt or maintain a measure with respect to a sector or sub-sector for which Mexico has not taken a specific reservation in its Schedules to Annexes I, II, and IV of this Agreement, only to the extent consistent with the least restrictive measures that Mexico may adopt or maintain under the terms of applicable reservations and exceptions to parallel obligations in other trade and investment agreements that Mexico has ratified prior to entry into force of this Agreement, including the WTO Agreement, without regard to whether those other agreements have entered into force.

Article 32.12: Exclusion from Dispute Settlement

A decision by Canada following a review under the *Investment Canada Act*, R.S.C. 1985, c.28 (1st Supp.), with respect to whether or not to permit an investment that is subject to review, shall not be subject to the dispute settlement provisions of Chapter 31 (Dispute Settlement).

CHAPTER 33 MACROECONOMIC POLICIES AND EXCHANGE RATE MATTERS

Article 33.1:   Definitions

For the purposes of this Chapter:

Article IV Staff Report means the report prepared by a staff team of the International Monetary Fund (IMF) for consideration by the Executive Board of the IMF in the context of a country's adherence to Article IV, Section 3(b), of the IMF Articles of Agreement;

Competitive devaluation means an action undertaken by an exchange rate authority of a Party for the purpose of preventing effective balance of payments adjustment or gaining an unfair competitive advantage in trade over another Party;

Currency Composition of Official Foreign Exchange Reserves (COFER) database means the IMF database based on voluntary and confidential participation by IMF member countries, which distinguishes monetary authorities' claims on non-residents denominated in U.S. dollars, euros, pounds sterling, Japanese yen, Swiss francs, and other currencies on a quarterly basis starting in 2005;

Exchange rate means the price of one currency in terms of another currency;

Exchange rate assessment means the IMF staff's evaluation of a country's exchange rate as presented to the IMF Executive Board as part of a Party's Article IV consultation or as published in the annual External Sector Report, consistent with recommendation 4 in the *IMF 2011 Triennial Surveillance Review—Overview Paper*, prepared on August 29, 2011;

Executive Board discussion means the discussion by the IMF Executive Board of the Party's Article IV Staff Report leading to the conclusion of the Article IV consultation, as defined in Paragraph 27 in Part III Section A of the *Modernizing the Legal Framework for Surveillance—An Integrated Surveillance Decision*, Revised Proposed Decisions, prepared on July 17, 2012;

Exports means all goods that subtract from the stock of material resources of a country by leaving its economic territory (*International Merchandise Trade Statistics: Concepts and Definitions* 2010, Chapter I, section A 1.2 of the United Nations);

Foreign exchange means the official currency of another Party or a non-Party;

Foreign exchange market means a market, wherever located, in which participants can purchase or sell foreign exchange;

Foreign exchange reserves means claims of an exchange rate authority or monetary authority on nonresidents in the form of foreign banknotes, bank deposits, treasury bills, short- and long-term government securities, and other claims usable in the event of balance of payments need, as defined in the *IMF's Balance of Payments and International Investment Position Manual*, Sixth Edition (BPM6), paragraphs 6.86–6.92;

Forward foreign exchange contract means a commitment to transact, at a designated future date and agreed-upon exchange rate, in a specified amount of specified foreign exchange (paragraph *FD 28, Financial Derivatives, A supplement to the Fifth Edition (1993)* of the *IMF's Balance of Payments and International Investment Position Manual*);

Forward positions means predetermined short-term net drains on foreign currency assets in the form of forwards, futures, and swaps, as defined in Item II.2 of the Reserves Data Template in the *IMF International Reserves and Foreign Currency Liquidity: Guidelines for a Data Template* (2013);

Imports means all goods that add to the stock of material resources of a country by entering its economic territory (*International Merchandise Trade Statistics: Concepts and Definitions* 2010, Chapter I, section A 1.2 of the United Nations);

Intervention means the purchase or sale, or the purchase or sale of a forward position, under the direction of an exchange rate authority, of foreign exchange reserves involving the currency of the intervening Party and at least one other currency;

Portfolio capital flows means cross-border transactions and positions involving debt or equity securities, other than those included in direct investment or reserve assets, as defined in the *IMF's Balance of Payments and International Investment Position Manual*, Sixth Edition (BPM6), paragraphs 6.54–6.57;

Principal representative of a Party means a senior official of the exchange rate or fiscal or monetary authority of a Party;[1] and

Spot foreign exchange market means the foreign exchange market in which participants transact for immediate delivery.

Article 33.2:   General Provisions

1.   The Parties affirm that market-determined exchange rates are fundamental for smooth macroeconomic adjustment and promote strong, sustainable, and balanced growth.

2.   The Parties recognize the importance of macroeconomic stability in the region to the success of this Agreement and that strong economic fundamentals and sound policies are essential to macroeconomic stability, and contribute to strong and sustainable growth and investment.

3.   The Parties share the objective of pursuing policies that strengthen underlying economic fundamentals, foster growth and transparency, and avoid unsustainable external imbalances.

Article 33.3:   Scope

This Chapter does not apply with respect to the regulatory or supervisory activities or monetary and related credit policy and related conduct of an exchange rate or fiscal or monetary authority of a Party.[2]

Article 33.4:   Exchange Rate Practices

1.   Each Party confirms that it is bound under the IMF Articles of Agreement to avoid manipulating exchange rates or the international monetary system in order to prevent effective balance of payments adjustment or to gain an unfair competitive advantage.

2.   Each Party should:

(a)   achieve and maintain a market-determined exchange rate regime;

(b)   refrain from competitive devaluation, including through intervention in the foreign exchange market; and

---

[1]   For greater certainty, the principal representatives of Mexico include a senior officer of the Ministry of Finance and Public Credit and a senior officer of the Central Bank.

[2]   For greater certainty, the term "exchange rate or fiscal or monetary authority of a Party" includes a central bank of a Party.

(c)   strengthen underlying economic fundamentals, which reinforces the conditions for macroeconomic and exchange rate stability.

3.   Each Party should inform promptly another Party and discuss if needed when an intervention has been carried out by the Party with respect to the currency of that other Party.

Article 33.5:   Transparency and Reporting

1.   Each Party shall disclose publicly:

(a)   monthly foreign exchange reserves data and forward positions according to the IMF's Data Template on International Reserves and Foreign Currency Liquidity, no later than 30 days after the end of each month;

(b)   monthly interventions in spot and forward foreign exchange markets, no later than seven days after the end of each month;

(c)   quarterly balance of payments portfolio capital flows, no later than 90 days after the end of each quarter; and

(d)   quarterly exports and imports, no later than 90 days after the end of each quarter.

2.   Each Party shall consent to the public disclosure by the IMF of:

(a)   each IMF Article IV Staff Report on the country of the Party, including the exchange rate assessment, within four weeks of the IMF Executive Board discussion; and

(b)   confirmation of the Party's participation in the IMF COFER database.

3.   If the IMF does not disclose publicly any items listed in paragraph (2) with respect to a Party, that Party shall request that the IMF disclose publicly those items.

Article 33.6:   Macroeconomic Committee

1.   The Parties hereby establish a Macroeconomic Committee composed of principal representatives of each Party. Article 30.2.2(b) (Functions of the Commission) does not apply to the Macroeconomic Committee.

2.   The Macroeconomic Committee shall monitor the implementation of this Chapter and its further elaboration.

3.   The Macroeconomic Committee shall meet within one year after the date of entry into force of this Agreement, and at least annually thereafter, unless the Parties decide otherwise.

4.   The Macroeconomic Committee shall, at each annual meeting, consider:

(a)   the macroeconomic and exchange rate policies of each Party, and their consequences on diverse macroeconomic variables, including domestic demand, external demand, and the current account balance;

(b) issues, challenges, or efforts to strengthen capacity with respect to transparency or reporting; and

(c) undertaking other activities as the Macroeconomic Committee may decide.

5. At each annual meeting, or as necessary, the Macroeconomic Committee may consider whether any provisions of this Chapter, except Article 33.3 (Scope), should be amended to reflect changes in monetary policy and the financial markets or should be interpreted. A decision by consensus of the Macroeconomic Committee that a provision of this Chapter should be amended shall be deemed to be a decision by consensus of the Commission to amend the provision. Amendments shall enter into force as provided for in Article 34.3 (Amendments). An interpretation issued pursuant to a decision by consensus of the Macroeconomic Committee shall be deemed to be an interpretation issued pursuant to a decision by consensus of the Commission.

6. The Commission shall not take any decision to amend or interpret a provision of this Chapter except as provided in paragraph 5.

Article 33.7: Principal Representative Consultations

1. A principal representative of a Party may request expedited bilateral consultations with a principal representative of another Party with respect to policies or measures of another Party that the principal representative of the requesting Party considers associated with competitive devaluation, the targeting of exchange rates for competitive purposes, fulfillment of the transparency and reporting commitments in Article 33.5 (Transparency and Reporting), or any other issue that the principal representative of the Party may wish to raise with respect to Articles 33.4 (Exchange Rate Practices) or 33.5 (Transparency and Reporting). A Party engaged in bilateral consultations may invite the Party not engaged in those consultations to participate and provide input.

2. If a principal representative of a Party requests bilateral consultations, the principal representatives (or their designees) of the consulting Parties shall meet within 30 days of the request to arrive at a mutually satisfactory resolution of the matter within 60 days of their initial meeting.

3. If a principal representative of a Party requests bilateral consultations with respect to another Party's fulfillment of the transparency and reporting commitments in Article 33.5 (Transparency and Reporting), whether circumstances disrupted the practical ability of the other Party to disclose publicly the items listed in that Article shall be taken into account in the consultations, with the objective of arriving at a mutually satisfactory resolution of the matter.

4. If there is failure to arrive at a mutually satisfactory resolution in any consultations under this Article, the consulting Parties may request that the IMF, consistent with its mandate:

    (a)   undertake rigorous surveillance of the macroeconomic and exchange rate policies and data transparency and reporting policies of the requested Party; or

    (b)   initiate formal consultations and provide input, as appropriate.

Article 33.8:   Dispute Settlement

1.   A Party may have recourse to dispute settlement under Chapter 31 (Dispute Settlement), as modified by this Article, only with respect to a claim that a Party has failed to carry out an obligation under Article 33.5 (Transparency and Reporting) in a recurring or persistent manner and has not remediated that failure during consultations under Article 33.7 (Principal Representative Consultations).[3]

2.   When selecting panelists to compose a panel under Article 31.9 (Panel Composition), each disputing Party shall select panelists so that each panelist:

    (a)   has served as a senior official of an exchange rate or fiscal or monetary authority of a Party or the International Monetary Fund; and

    (b)   meets the qualifications set out in paragraphs (2)(b) through (2)(d) of Article 31.8 (Roster and Qualification of Panelists).

3.   A panel established under Article 31.6 (Establishment of a Panel) to make a determination as to whether a Party has failed to carry out an obligation under Article 33.5 (Transparency and Reporting) in a recurring or persistent manner and has not remediated that failure during consultations under Article 33.7 (Principal Representative Consultations) and a panel reconvened to make a determination on the proposed suspension of benefits, in accordance with Article 31.19 (Non-Implementation—Suspension of Benefits), may seek the views of the IMF in accordance with Article 31.15 (Role of Experts).

4.   When a panel's determination is that a Party has failed to carry out an obligation under Article 33.5 (Transparency and Reporting) in a recurring or persistent manner, and has not remediated that failure during consultations under Article 33.7 (Principal Representative Consultations), the complaining Party may not suspend benefits that are in excess of benefits equivalent to the effect of that failure. In suspending benefits under Article 31.19 (Non-Implementation—Suspension of Benefits), the complaining Party may take into account only the failure to carry out an obligation under Article 33.5 (Transparency and Reporting) and not any other action or alleged failure by the responding Party.

---

[3]   For greater certainty, this Article does not provide a basis for any matter arising under any other provision of this Agreement, including Article 31.2(c) (Scope).

CHAPTER 34   FINAL PROVISIONS

Article 34.1:   Transitional Provision from NAFTA 1994

1. The Parties recognize the importance of a smooth transition from NAFTA 1994 to this Agreement.

2. Issues under consideration, including documents or other work under development, by the Commission or a subsidiary body of NAFTA 1994 may be continued under any equivalent body in this Agreement, subject to any decision by the Parties on whether and in what manner that continuation is to occur.

3. Membership of the Committee established under Article 2022 of NAFTA 1994 may be maintained for the Committee under Article 31.22.4 (Alternative Dispute Resolution).

4. Chapter Nineteen of NAFTA 1994 shall continue to apply to binational panel reviews related to final determinations published by a Party before the entry into force of this Agreement.

5. With respect to the matters set out in paragraph 4, the Secretariat established under Article 30.6 of this Agreement shall perform the functions assigned to the NAFTA 1994 Secretariat under Chapter Nineteen of the NAFTA 1994 and under, for Chapter Nineteen, the domestic implementation procedures adopted by the Parties in connection therewith, until the binational panel has rendered a decision and a Notice of Completion of Panel Review has been issued by the Secretariat pursuant to the Rules of Procedure for Article 1904 Binational Panel Reviews.

6. With respect to claims for preferential tariff treatment made under NAFTA 1994, the Parties shall make appropriate arrangements to grant these claims in accordance with NAFTA 1994 after entry into force of this Agreement. The provisions of Chapter Five of NAFTA 1994 will continue to apply through those arrangements, but only to goods for which preferential tariff treatment was claimed in accordance with NAFTA 1994, and will remain applicable for the period provided for in Article 505 (Records) of that Agreement.

Article 34.2:   Annexes, Appendices, and Footnotes

The annexes, appendices, and footnotes to this Agreement constitute an integral part of this Agreement.

Article 34.3:   Amendments

1. The Parties may agree, in writing, to amend this Agreement.

2. An amendment shall enter into force 60 days after the date on which the last Party has provided written notice to the other Parties of the approval of the amendment in accordance with its applicable legal procedures, or such other date as the Parties may agree.

Article 34.4:   Amendment of the WTO Agreement

In the event of an amendment of the WTO Agreement that amends a provision that the Parties have incorporated into this Agreement, the Parties shall, unless otherwise provided in this Agreement, consult on whether to amend this Agreement.

Article 34.5:   Entry into Force

This Agreement enters into force in accordance with paragraph 2 of the Protocol Replacing the North American Free Trade Agreement with the Agreement between the United States of America, the United Mexican States, and Canada.

Article 34.6:   Withdrawal

A Party may withdraw from this Agreement by providing written notice of withdrawal to the other Parties. A withdrawal shall take effect six months after a Party provides written notice to the other Parties. If a Party withdraws, this Agreement shall remain in force for the remaining Parties.

Article 34.7:   Review and Term Extension

1.   This Agreement shall terminate 16 years after the date of its entry into force, unless each Party confirms it wishes to continue this Agreement for a new 16-year term, in accordance with the procedures set forth in paragraphs 2 through 6.

2.   On the sixth anniversary of the entry into force of this Agreement, the Commission shall meet to conduct a "joint review" of the operation of this Agreement, review any recommendations for action submitted by a Party, and decide on any appropriate actions. Each Party may provide recommendations for the Commission to take action at least one month before the Commission's joint review meeting takes place.

3.   As part of the Commission's joint review, each Party shall confirm, in writing, through its head of government, if it wishes to extend the term of this Agreement for another 16-year period. If each Party confirms its desire to extend this Agreement, the term of this Agreement shall be automatically extended for another 16 years and the Commission shall conduct a joint review and consider extension of this Agreement term no later than at the end of the next six-year period.

4.   If, as part of a six-year review, a Party does not confirm its wish to extend the term of this Agreement for another 16-year period, the Commission shall meet to conduct a joint review every year for the remainder of the term of this Agreement. If one or more Parties did not confirm their desire to extend this Agreement for another 16-year term at the conclusion of a given joint review, at any time between the conclusion of that review and expiry of this Agreement, the Parties may automatically extend the term of this Agreement for another 16 years by confirming in writing, through their respective head of government, their wish to extend this Agreement for another 16-year period.

5.   At any point when the Parties decide to extend the term of this Agreement for another 16-year period, the Commission shall conduct

joint reviews every six years thereafter, and the Parties shall have the ability to extend this Agreement after each joint review pursuant to the procedures set forth in paragraphs 3 and 4.

6.   At any point in which the Parties do not all confirm their wish to extend the term of this Agreement, paragraph 4 shall apply.

Article 34.8:   Authentic Texts

The English, French, and Spanish texts of this Agreement are equally authentic, unless provided elsewhere in this Agreement.

END

Table of Cases

Index

References are to Sections